Contemporary Issues in Crime and Criminal Justice:

Essays in Honor of Gilbert Geis

❖

HENRY N. PONTELL
University of California, Irvine

DAVID SHICHOR
California State University, San Bernardino

Prentice
Hall

Upper Saddle River, New Jersey 07458

Library of Congress Cataloging-in-Publication Data

Contemporary issues in crime and criminal justice: essays in honor of Gilbert Geis/
[edited by] Henry N. Pontell, David Shichor.
    p. cm.
  Includes bibliographical reference.
  ISBN 0-13-087585-6 (alk. paper)
  1. Crime. 2. Criminal justice, Administration of. I. Geis, Gilbert. II. Pontell, Henry N.,
1950– III. Shichor, David.
  HV6028 .C58 2000
  364—dc21   00-040652

Publisher: Dave Garza
Senior Acquisitions Editor: Kim Davies
Assistant Editor: Marion Gottlieb
Managing Editor: Mary Carnis
Production Management: Clarinda Publication Services
Production Editor: Mark Spann
Interior Design: Clarinda Publication Services
Production Liaison: Adele M. Kupchik
Director of Manufacturing and Production: Bruce Johnson
Manufacturing Buyers: Ed O'Doughtery/Cathleen Petersen
Creative Director: Marianne Frasco
Cover Design Coordinator: Miguel Ortiz
Formatting: The Clarinda Company
Electronic Art Creation: The Clarinda Company
Editorial Assistant: Lisa Schwartz
Marketing Manager: Chris Ruel
Marketing Assistant: Joe Toohey
Marketing Coordinator: Adam Kloza
Printer/Binder: R.R. Donnelley and Sons, Inc.
Copy Editor: Mark Spann
Proofreader: Mark Spann
Cover Design: Maureen Eide
Cover Illustration: Boris Lyubner, SIS/Images.Com
Cover Printer: Phoenix Color Corp.

Contributors' works are printed with permission.

Prentice-Hall International (UK) Limited, *London*
Prentice-Hall of Australia Pty. Limited, *Sydney*
Prentice-Hall Canada Inc., *Toronto*
Prentice-Hall Hispanoamericana, S.A., *Mexico*
Prentice-Hall of India Private Limited, *New Delhi*
Prentice-Hall of Japan, Inc., *Tokyo*
Prentice-Hall Singapore Pte. Ltd.
Editora Prentice-Hall do Brasil. Ltda., *Rio de Janeiro*

10 9 8 7 6 5 4 3 2 1
ISBN 0-13-087585-6

Contents

———————————————— ❖ ————————————————

FOREWORD   ix

PREFACE   xiii

ABOUT THE CONTRIBUTING AUTHORS   xxi

I.   INTRODUCTION
Geis, Sutherland, and White-Collar Crime   1
By Robert F. Meier

II.   THEORY AND METHOD IN CRIMINOLOGICAL RESEARCH
Conceptualizing Organizational Crime in a World of
    Plural Cultures   17
By John Braithwaite

The Relationship Between Research Results and Public
    Policy   33
By Arnold Binder and Virginia Binder

Sensational Cases, Flawed Theories   45
By Diane Vaughan

III. **WHITE-COLLAR CRIME AND CORPORATE CRIME**

Control Fraud and Control Freaks   67
By William K. Black

Victims of Investment Fraud   81
By David Shichor, Dale Sechrest, and Jeffrey Doocy

Penny Wise: Accounting for Fraud in the Penny-Stock Industry   97
By Sean Patrick Griffin and Alan A. Block

Life Course Theory and White-Collar Crime   121
By Michael L. Benson and Kent R. Kerley

The System of Corporate Crime Control   137
By Peter Grabosky

IV. **CASE STUDIES OF WHITE COLLAR CRIME**

Fertile Frontiers in Medical Fraud: A Case Study of Egg and Embryo Theft   155
By Mary Dodge

The Archer Daniels Midland Antitrust Case of 1996: A Case Study   175
By Sally S. Simpson and Nicole Leeper Piquero

The Westray Mine Disaster: Media Coverage of a Corporate Crime in Canada   195
By Colin Goff

V. **STUDIES IN SOCIAL CONTROL**

Technology, Risk Analysis, and the Challenge of Social Control   213
By James F. Short, Jr.

Law Enforcement, Intercepting Communications and the Right to Privacy: The Impact of New Technologies   231
By Duncan Chappell

"Green Managers Don't Cry": Criminal Environmental Law and Corporate Strategy   253
By Joseph F. DiMento and Gabrio Forti

The Virtuous Prison: Toward A Restorative Rehabilitation 265
By Francis T. Cullen, Jody Sundt, and John Wozniak

Women in Policing: A Tale of Cultural Conformity 287
By Deborah Parsons and Paul Jesilow

VI. **INTERNATIONAL AND COMPARATIVE STUDIES**
Cross-National Comparative Studies in Criminology 307
By David P. Farrington

**The Role of Fraud in the Japanese Financial Crisis:
   A Comparative Study 321**
By Henry N. Pontell, Stephen M. Rosoff, and Jason Lam

**Trans-National White-Collar Crime: Some Explorations of
   Victimization Impact 341**
By Michael Levi

**Comparative Criminology: Purposes, Methods and Research
   Findings 359**
By Hans Joachim Schneider

VII. **VARIOUS FORMS OF CRIME**
**When Crime is not a Crime: Economic Transformations and the
   Evolution in Bankruptcy Law 377**
By Susan Will and Kitty Calavita

Youth Gangs, Crime, and Public Policy 393
By C. Ronald Huff

**Searching a Dwelling: Deterrence and the Undeterred
   Residential Burglar 407**
By Richard Wright

Foreword

Joseph T. Wells

---❖---

I knew Gilbert Geis before we were formally introduced by the late Donald R. Cressey in 1986. However, like so many others, I had met him only through his writings. But thanks to Don's retirement party, that was about to change.

There were at least a hundred people in the hotel ballroom that night. It was hard to get Don's attention—what with the crowd around him. Yet, I knew Gil Geis was there, and I was anxious to meet this man who had already exerted significant influence on my thinking about important sociological issues. And having already read *On White-Collar Crime,* I learned that since his childhood, Gil had kept track of every single book he has read. I found that fact particularly fascinating and wondered why I never thought of doing the same thing.

My persistence that evening with Don Cressey finally paid off. When the crowd around Don momentarily subsided, I waded in. "Don," I said, "I really want to meet Gil Geis." Cressey smiled and motioned over my shoulder. "Well, you won't have to wait long," Don said. "He is right behind you."

I thrust my hand in Gil's, introduced myself, and proceeded to fawn over him like he was a rock star. It was clear that Gil didn't have a clue who I was. He was nonetheless extremely gracious to the stranger in front of him.

At the time Gil and I met, Don Cressey and I had known each other for several years. As a matter of fact, it was Don who introduced me to Gil's early work, which I devoured hungrily. Unlike both Don and Gil, I had no formal training in criminology. But I did have a background that fit nicely with academics—for nearly ten years, I was an FBI agent specializing in the investigation and prosecution of white-collar crime, and had almost two hundred convictions under my belt.

After leaving the FBI, I established an investigative and consulting practice dealing with fraud detection, prevention, and education. I had sought out Don Cressey early in that career. He was able to educate me in a much larger sociological context and, in turn, claimed it was fascinating for him to hear the experiences of someone who had worked in the trenches. In short, it was a perfect merger between academics and the "real world." That merger was not destined to last, as Don passed away suddenly in July, 1987. Not only did I lose my friend; I also lost his wise counsel.

But on the eve of Don's retirement party, neither he nor Gil nor I could have possibly fathomed that—nearly fifteen years later—I would be the chief executive officer of the largest anti-fraud association in the world, or that Gil Geis would be its president.

Like so many other events in life, what has occurred between Gil and me was destined to happen. The evening we met, I found out that he owned a condominium in Austin, Texas—where I also lived. Gil had purchased the property to be near his stepson, Ted, who teaches at the University of Texas. Naturally, I encouraged the eminent Dr. Geis to visit my offices on one of his trips. I was thrilled when he called. It became tradition for us to lunch at Katz's deli, a short walk from my office. There, stuffing our faces with kosher pickles and big, juicy Reuben sandwiches, we would philosophize.

I was—by this time—in the midst of establishing a new professional organization; the Association of Certified Fraud Examiners. Its purpose was to recognize and educate that specialized cadre of individuals who concentrate exclusively on the detection and deterrence of fraud and white-collar crime. Typical CFEs include corporate and government fraud investigators, internal auditors responsible for antifraud matters, and public accountants who specialize in white-collar crime.

As with any profession, one of the first tasks was to codify a common body of knowledge. We decided that the certified fraud examiner would need expertise in four areas: fraud investigation techniques, legal elements of fraud, fraudulent financial schemes, and criminology. It was further agreed that the common body of knowledge would be set forth in the soon-to-be-created *Fraud Examiners Manual.*

Gil wrote the entire criminology section of the *Fraud Examiners Manual* in less than six months. It was an amazing feat for anyone to condense the fundamentals of criminology into a mere 400 pages. It was made possible only by the fact that he knew much of the material from memory. Since then, Gil has co-authored three separate editions of the *Fraud Examiners Manual,* which have been used to educate literally tens of thousands of antifraud practitioners. Indeed, since 1988, when the Association of Certified Fraud Examiners was organized, its membership has grown to 25,000 in over 70 countries.

In 1992, when our rolls were less than 5,000, I asked Gil to serve as president of the association. He has been a significant influence in the 500 percent growth of the organization since that time. Don't get me wrong—Gil doesn't run things. That's my job. But he tells me how. And no one could have done it better.

I have only one regret about my association with Gil; that I didn't meet him sooner. It would have been a particular honor to sit in his classroom hours on end, learning from one of the true masters. However, that was not meant to be. Instead, I have forged a tremendous friendship with Gil over the years that will continue to last, regardless of any professional collaborations. I find Dr. Geis immensely stimulating. At the time in life when most men would be looking back on their accomplishments, Gil is anxiously looking forward to the next challenge. With his quick wit and razor-sharp mind, he can both educate and entertain— often in the same sentence. But so it is with this man, the preeminent Dr. Gil Geis. There is simply no one like him.

August, 1999

Preface

This volume was assembled in honor of the preeminent criminologist and scholar, Gilbert Geis, on the occasion of his seventy-fifth birthday. Although this is a significant milestone in his life and certainly a cause for celebration, Gil deserves to be honored for many other reasons as well. First, and perhaps foremost, he is one of the most outstanding teachers and colleagues one could ever imagine. To those who know him, as well as to many who have simply met him, the combination of Gil's great warmth, caring, humor, intellect, breadth of interests, and energy mark him as one of the truly unique persons in the academic world today. As a prolific writer on a variety of topics related to law, crime, and criminal justice, his record of productivity over the past six decades, to use an analogy from his favorite sport, is similar in stature to the benchmarks set by Joe DiMaggio, Nolan Ryan, Hank Aaron, Cal Ripken, and Mark McGwire. That is, it is extremely difficult to imagine anyone ever surpassing his academic publication record. At last count, he has written or edited 21 books, 192 articles, 104 book chapters, and 30 monographs and has edited a number of special issues of journals. The incredible number of Gil's scholarly publications is matched only by the fact that it is first-rate work, written in a rich and engaging manner that appeals to scholars, practitioners, and students alike.

Gil's academic career began in 1952 in the sociology department at the University of Oklahoma, Norman. Before that, he served as a radioman in the U.S. Navy during the war years (1942–45), and as a reporter for the *Times* in Hartford, Connecticut (1946) and the *Daily Home News* in New Brunswick, New Jersey (1947–48). He earned his Ph.D. (1953) in sociology at the University of Wisconsin, Madison after receiving his M.S. (1949) at Brigham Young University and his B.A. (1947) at Colgate University. He also spent a year (1948) at the University of Stockholm in Sweden.

Gil left Oklahoma as an assistant professor in 1957, and took a position at California State University, Los Angeles, where he was promoted to associate professor in 1960 and then professor in 1963. During the 1969–70 school year, he was a visiting professor in the School of Criminal Justice at the State University of New York, Albany. In 1971 he served as a visiting professor in the Program in Social Ecology at the University of California, Irvine. The program's founder, Arnold Binder, a mathematical psychologist, convinced him to join the faculty the following year. Gil remained at Irvine and became professor emeritus in 1987, with brief stints as a visiting fellow in the Institute of Criminology at Cambridge University (1976–77), a visiting professor in the law school at the University of Sydney (1979), a distinguished visiting professor in the College of Human Development at Pennsylvania State University (1981), and a distinguished visiting professor in the John Jay School of Criminal Justice of the City University of New York (1996).

He has also been the recipient of numerous awards throughout his career as a criminologist. Among them are outstanding professor awards at California State University (1968, 1971), the Distinguished Faculty Lectureship Award at UC, Irvine (1980), the Paul Tappan Award for outstanding contributions to criminology from the Western Society of Criminology (1980), the Edwin H. Sutherland Award for outstanding contributions to theory and research in criminology from the American Society of Criminology (1985), and the Donald R. Cressey Award for excellence in fraud detection and deterrence from the National Association of Certified Fraud Examiners (1992). He has been a principal investigator or director of thirteen grants, including projects funded by the National Institute of Mental Health, the Ford Foundation, the U.S. Department of Justice, and the Federal Bureau of Prisons.

Throughout his career, Gil has also been a model citizen of his profession, serving on numerous committees and boards. He has been an associate editor or editorial board member of sixteen academic journals, and has served as a member of advisory groups and executive committees for national and international organizations and publishers, including acting as advisor to the President's Committee on Narcotic and Drug Abuse (1963–64). In 1975 he was elected president of the American Society of Criminology. Since 1992 he has served as the president of the Association of Certified Fraud Examiners.

For all of his academic success and commitment over the years, the capstone of Gil's career has to be his publication record. His writings have thus far spanned six decades and have covered an incredible range of topics, including education, race relations, Scandinavian issues, the death penalty, film censorship, prisons, biographies, probation, courts, legal rights, drugs, juvenile justice and delinquency, prostitution, crime and crime victims, policing, community corrections, rehabilitation, organized crime, prisoner rights, evaluations, rape, homicide, victimless crimes, ethical issues in law, violence, social problems, good samaritans, compensation, restitution, deterrence, witch trials, criminal justice issues, research methods, and, of course, white-collar crime. It is this last area for which he has become most well known, beginning with the publication of his classic piece, *The Heavy Electrical Equipment Antitrust Case of 1961,* in the book, *Criminal Behavior Systems: A Typology,* edited by Marshall Clinard and Richard Quinney. Ironically perhaps, this seminal work appeared as a chapter in a textbook rather than in a leading journal, and is responsible for resurrecting interest in the topic of white-collar crime, which was introduced by Edwin Sutherland decades earlier but by and large ignored by criminologists and others. The piece helped spawn a new generation of criminologists, whose primary research agenda was the study of white-collar and corporate crime. The importance of Gil's professional contribution in this regard cannot be overstated.

Since the writing of that pathbreaking piece, Gil's work in white-collar crime has been prolific and varied. It includes research on the deterrence of corporate crime, consumer fraud laws, victimization, the psychology of white-collar offenders, corporate violence, punishment issues, white-collar crime seriousness, medical fraud, legal and regulatory issues, fraud examination, organizational deviance, as well as a number of general pieces on white-collar crime.

While Gil's name is most frequently related to the study of white-collar crime, it is hard to find any major subject area in criminology, or for that matter any minor area of the discipline, in which he hasn't published. In an era of increasing emphasis on expertise confined to narrow fields of study, when, as some critics claim, scholars tend "to learn and know more and more, about less and less," Gil is a true exception. His credo is "to learn and know more and more, about more and more." Those who know him can attest to his keen interest, encyclopedic knowledge, analytical skills, and fascinating writing style dealing not only with criminological topics but a wide array of other subjects as well. Perhaps the most fitting characterization of his professional writings is that he is what is commonly called a "Renaissance man," although he would probably prefer the label, "Renaissance person."

Gil is not only one of the most prolific criminologists in the world today, but also a great teacher, mentor, and colleague. Anyone who has ever asked him to read and comment on a draft can testify to his promptness, meticulous editing (with loads of red ink), and helpful comments that invariably enhance the quality and clarity of the manuscript. He has helped many students and junior colleagues with his support, advice, encouragement, and active participation in the completion of their work. He has done so in spite of his own, always more than full, agenda, which is characterized by a meticulously kept list of works he has to complete. Those who have ever collaborated with Gil on any book, article, or other project find him to be well prepared, prompt (somewhat compulsive), and usually taking upon himself more than his fair share of the work. All these are done with a wonderful sense of humor amid entertaining conversations. His numerous co-authored publications are an excellent testimony to his ability and readiness to work constructively with others.

Gil can be a sharp critic as well. While he is urbane (almost always), he is not shy in his readiness to voice his opinions, even if they may ruffle some feathers. He is not an iconoclast for the sake of being one, but he is always ready to get into the fray and has more than once criticized some of the works of well-known social scientists.

As is suitable for a volume honoring Gilbert Geis, the pieces in this book cover a broad terrain, although many of them, naturally, are related to the topic of white-collar crime.

Blomberg and Cohen, in their introduction to the collection of essays honoring Sheldon Messinger on the occasion of his retirement, maintained that there are two main categories of festschrifts:

> At the one extreme, there is the self-indulgently personal: reminiscences and tributes that place the person being honored at the center of the stage, obsessively tracking down his or her every lifetime contribution. At the other extreme, there is the ascetically intellectual: detached scholarship that virtually ignores any personal references and seems only obliquely related to the biographical record of the person honored (Blomberg & Cohen, 1995, p. 3).

In the case of this volume the contributors were, in one way or another, connected with Gil professionally. They were asked to write a chapter on the basis of the second category; that is, following the principle of detached scholarship. However, because of Gil's extensive contributions to contemporary criminology, his works and ideas resurface in many of the chapters in this volume. Thus, we witness a certain degree of blending of the two categories; detached scholarship on the one hand, with an oblique focus on the professional contributions of Gil, on the other.

As noted above, the pieces in this volume cover many subject areas, in keeping with Gil's eclectic approach to research. Our organization of the chapters resulted from the topics the authors chose to write about, and the section headings we selected reflect a broad array of ideas. In a fitting introduction to this volume, Robert Meier compares the works of Edwin Sutherland and Gilbert Geis on the topic of white-collar crime. He notes that Gil has done more than any other scholar to bring white-collar crime into the limelight since Sutherland's pioneering work on the subject. This is followed by a selection of pieces related to theory and method in criminological research. In the first chapter, John Braithwaite discusses the ambiguities currently present in the study of organizational crime, and offers insights into how we might better go about operationalizing it in future research. Following this, Arnold and Virginia Binder examine the relationship between criminological research and public policy and, using a number of examples from the literature, caution that researchers must "not confuse what is good for society with what is good for their own careers." In the third piece in this section, Diane Vaughan uses experience gained from her study of the fatal launch of the Space Shuttle *Challenger* in 1986 to examine the problems inherent in studying "sensational cases," and warns of the danger of over-generalizing from such instances while paying too little attention to what made them different in the first place.

The next section contains pieces related to the study of white-collar and corporate crime. In the first piece, using examples drawn from the savings and loan crisis of the 1980s, William Black elaborates on the concept of "control fraud," and how it occurs both in nations ("kleptocracies") and firms. Following this, the chapter by David Shichor, Dale Sechrest, and Jeffrey Doocy examines the nature of victimization of consumers who were taken by a large telemarketing scam in California. The third chapter, authored by Sean Patrick Griffin and Alan Block, provides a criminological analysis of fraud in the penny stock industry. In the next chapter in this section, Michael Benson and Kent Kerley analyze sentencing data in order to understand the relationship between life course theory and white-collar crime. In the final chapter, Peter Grabosky analyzes issues related to corporate crime control, and provides a conceptual framework for future research.

The next set of chapters involves case studies of white-collar crime. In the first piece, Mary Dodge analyzes the nature of medical fraud at the once-famous Center for Reproductive Health, a fertility clinic at the University of California–Irvine that made international headlines when it was discovered, among other illegalities, that patient eggs and embryos had been misused by doctors. In the next piece, Sally Simpson and Nicole Leeper Piquero document the price-fixing conspiracy involving Archer Daniels Midland Company and examine individual and organizational characteristics related to the conspiracy, the techniques employed, and the various responses to the offense. In the third chapter, which examines the Westray Mine explosion in Canada, Colin Goff analyzes how and what the media reports when it provides coverage of a violent corporate act.

The following section entails studies of social control. The first piece, by James Short, examines the special problems created for social control by advances in science and technology, and offers general principles to deal with them. In the following chapter, Duncan Chappell examines the impact of certain new technologies on the ability of law enforcement agencies to intercept communications, and considers the balancing of investigative needs with the protection of personal privacy. Next, Joseph DiMento and Gabrio Forti examine issues related to the use of criminal sanctions in pollution control efforts, and the viability of "green management" in shielding companies from legal liability. Following this, Francis Cullen, Jody Sundt, and John Wozniak discuss issues related to running more humane and effective correctional institutions by providing "restorative rehabilitation" in what they term "virtuous prisons." In the final chapter in this section, Deborah Parsons and Paul Jesilow discuss the history of women in policing, and how the conflict between the crime fighting and service roles of the police have undermined most efforts to integrate women into the occupation.

The next section contains international and comparative studies. In the first chapter, David Farrington reviews his own cross-national comparisons of risk factors for delinquency, criminal career features, and rates of crime and punishment in different countries, and argues that additional comparisons in the future will serve to better inform criminological theories. In the second piece, Henry Pontell, Stephen Rosoff, and Jason Lam draw comparisons between forms of fraud present in the savings-and-loan debacle in the United States, and crimes found at the heart of the Japanese banking crisis, arguing that the Asian financial meltdown had less to do with a "currency crisis" or "falling real estate values" than it did with major problems in financial institutions and their regulation. In the next chapter, Michael Levi discusses victimization issues related to transnational white-collar crime, including how seriously it is viewed by various constituencies, and the methodological issues that need to be recognized in future inquiries. The final chapter in this section, by Hans Joachim Schneider, examines a number of topics related to the purposes, methods, and research findings of comparative criminology.

The final section of the volume relates to various forms of crime. The first selection, by Susan Will and Kitty Calavita, examines the relationship between economic transformation and the evolution of bankruptcy law and analyzes how bankruptcy, once considered a severe criminal act, has now become an investor's device and management tool. In the second chapter, C. Ronald Huff uses primary data to analyze the criminal activities engaged in by gangs, and develops public policy recommendations from the results of his study. In the concluding chapter, Richard Wright uses interview data to examine the mindset of residential burglars in order to understand the decision-making dynamics involved in such criminal activity, and what might best deter it.

When this festschrift was planned, it was a hard task to decide whom to ask to contribute, because Gil has so many close colleagues and students, not only in the United States, but all over the world. The pool of potential contributors was so large, that even if a modest number of them participated, it would have been impossible to include them all in one volume. We contacted those whom we knew had a close relationship with Gil, but there is no doubt that we also missed others who would have qualified on such grounds. This was certainly not intentional, and could be "blamed" on Gil's huge professional network. Nonetheless, the editors take full responsibility for any omissions and oversights, and apologize to any persons who would have liked to contribute to this volume. To those and all others, we simply ask that you join us in celebrating Gil's accomplishments by using this book. It is notable that all those who were asked to participate in the project agreed enthusiastically and with two or three exceptions, due to some unforeseen personal reasons, they delivered highly valuable original chapters.

We thank all the contributors to this volume for their support, especially given the rather short deadline under which they were forced to work. We also thank them for keeping this project a secret from Gil. The development of this volume took place without any knowledge on his part, as we felt that his surprise in seeing it would be an extra reward for both Gil and the contributors. For many of us, this was a taxing effort, as we interact with Gil on a regular basis. For one of the editors, this meant fraudulently representing his current work on many occasions, and keeping files labeled "Project Good Guy," in case Gil happened to be in the office while they were being used. The file label was designated by our Department Manager at the University of California–Irvine, Judy Omiya, without whose assistance this volume would not have been possible. For years Judy has dedicated herself to matters of our department, and she welcomed the chance to show her great fondness for Gil by providing superb assistance on this project. Judy kept all files in meticulous order, followed up with authors, and prepared the final manuscript for submission to the publisher. We greatly appreciate her efforts, as well as those of Teri Denman and Marilyn Wahlert, who helped with secretarial matters relating to this volume over the past year.

We also thank Neil Marquardt, Senior Editor at Prentice Hall, for his support and encouragement. After a brief discussion, Neil (in his infinite wisdom) was convinced that this would be an excellent project, and the authors greatly appreciate his confidence in their ability to make this book a first-rate contribution to the field. Upon Neil's departure, our new editor, Kim Davies, and her assistant, Lisa Schwartz, have provided us with equal support. We also thank the staff at Prentice Hall, especially Marion Gottlieb and Susan Kegler, for their excellent assistance in bringing this volume to publication in a timely fashion.

We hope that this collection of essays is suitable recognition of Gil's contribution to our field. In the spirit of his devotion to his students, the proceeds of this book will go into a scholarship fund established at the University of California–Irvine, in the name of Gilbert Geis.

Henry Pontell and David Shichor
August, 1999

REFERENCES

Blomberg, T. G., and Cohen, S. 1995. Editorial introduction: Punishment and social control. In Blomberg, T. G., and Cohen, S. eds. *Punishment and Social Control: Essays in Honor of Sheldon L. Messinger.* New York: Aldine De Gruyter.

About the Contributing Authors

--- ❖ ---

Michael L. Benson is associate professor of sociology at the University of Tennessee. He has published numerous articles on white-collar crime as well as a book, *Combating Corporate Crime: Local Prosecutors at Work,* with Francis T. Cullen. He is currently conducting research on violence against women with funding from the National Institute of Justice.

Arnold Binder is currently a professor in the Department of Criminology, Law and Society in the School of Social Ecology, University of California–Irvine. He has published extensively in the following areas: juvenile delinquency, police use of deadly force, and the design and analysis of research. And, as will be noted by those who read the article which he jointly wrote, he can be a harsh critic of inadequate research used for ego-advancement.

Virginia Binder is a professor of psychology at California State University–Long Beach. Her areas of specialization are law and psychology, and ethics and professional issues in psychology.

William K. Black is an assistant professor at the LBJ School of Public Affairs at the University of Texas at Austin, specializing in organizational crime, public finance, banking crises, and management. He has an A.B. in Economics and a J.D. from the University of Michigan, and a Ph.D. in Criminology, Law and Society from the University of California–Irvine. He served for a decade in various senior regulatory positions dealing with the savings and loan debacle.

Alan A. Block has a Ph.D. from UCLA in history. He is a professor in the Administration of Justice, professor of Jewish Studies, and the Director of the

Jewish Studies Program at The Pennsylvania State University. His areas of specialization are organized crime, human rights, and the criminology of national intelligence services. His most recent publications are "A History of Organized Crime," a "Biography of Frank Costello," and a "Biography of Jack 'Legs' Diamond," in *Violence in America: An Encyclopedia,* Simon & Schuster (1999), and "Bad Business: A Commentary on the Criminology of Organized Crime," in Tom Farer (ed.), *Transnational Organized Crime in the Americas,* Routledge (1999).

John Braithwaite is a professor in the Research School of Social Sciences, Australian National University, Canberra. Gil Geis has been his U.S. mentor since he held a Fulbright Postdoctoral Fellowship at the University of California–Irvine in 1979. Organizational crime has been a longstanding research interest. His primary current interests are restorative justice and the globalization of business regulation.

Kitty Calavita is professor of criminology, law and society at the University of California–Irvine. She is the author (with Henry Pontell and Robert Tillman) of *Big Money Crime: Fraud and Politics in the Savings and Loan Crisis* (University of California Press, 1997). She has also published extensively in the area of immigration policymaking and state theory. She is currently working on an historical analysis of the front-line enforcement of the Chinese Exclusion Laws from 1882–1910. In 2000–2001 she will serve as president of the Law and Society Association.

Duncan Chappell is a Deputy President of the Federal Administrative Appeals Tribunal in Sydney, Australia. A former Director of the Australian Institute of Criminology, he has held senior academic posts in Australia, Canada, and the United States, and has been a consultant to governments and international bodies, including the United Nations and the British Commonwealth.

Francis T. Cullen is distinguished research professor of criminal justice and sociology at the University of Cincinnati. He has recently co-authored *Combating Corporate Crime: Local Prosecutors at Work, Criminological Theory: Past to Present,* and *Offender Rehabilitation: Effective Correctional Intervention.* His current research interests include the measurement of sexual victimization, the impact of social support on crime, and the principles of effective correctional rehabilitation programs.

Joseph DiMento, Ph.D., J.D. is professor of criminology, law and society, and urban and regional planning at the University of California–Irvine. He has worked in the field of environmental law since its beginnings in 1970. He is the author of several books and numerous journal articles including treatments of crime and environmental law. These include *Environmental Law and American Business: Dilemmas of Compliance* (1986) and a co-authored chapter with Professor Geis on corporate criminal liability. He has taught at the University of Florida Law School and the University of Michigan. He served on the Science Advisory Board of the United States Environmental Protection Agency and was a Special Assistant in the Natural Resources Division of the United States Department of Justice.

Jeffrey H. Doocy is a fraud investigator for the California Department of Corporations specializing in major white-collar fraud investigations, 1985–1993. He received his M.A. in Criminological Studies at Sheffield University, England (1975), and has done graduate work at Cambridge University, England, and the University of Southern California (Public Administration). He has published in the areas of escrow fraud and telemarketing boiler room scams. He is a member of the California Association of Fraud Investigators.

Mary Dodge is an assistant professor of criminal justice at the Graduate School of Public Affairs, University of Colorado–Denver. She received an M.A. in clinical psychology and a B.A. in psychology at the University of Colorado–Colorado Springs, and received her Ph.D. in criminology, law and society at the University of California–Irvine in 1997. Her specialties include medical fraud, fraud in assisted reproductive technology, biomedical ethics and reproductive rights, the judicial process, and jury decision-making.

David P. Farrington is professor of psychological criminology at the Institute of Criminology, Cambridge University. He has served as President of the American Society of Criminology and President of the European Association of Psychology and Law, and Joint Editor of the Cambridge Criminology Series. He has been Acting Director of the Cambridge Institute of Criminology, President of the British Society of Criminology, Vice-Chair of the U.S. National Academy of Sciences Panel on Violence, a member of the U.S. National Academy of Sciences Committee on Law and Justice, and a member of the National Parole Board for England and Wales. He received the Sellin-Glueck Award of the American Society of Criminology for international study of delinquency and crime. In addition, Farrington has published over 240 papers on criminological and psychological topics, 21 books and monographs, one of which (*Understanding and Controlling Crime,* 1986) won the prize for distinguished scholarship of the American Sociological Association Criminology Section.

Gabrio Forti is a professor of criminal law and criminology at the Catholic University of Milan. Professor Forti received his degrees at Liceo Ginnasio A. Manzoni and Catholic University of Milan. Editor of *White-Collar Crime: The Uncut Version* by E.H. Sutherland (Giuffre editore, Milano, 1987), he has published books on criminal negligence and corruption, as well as several essays on organized crime, economic crime, bribery, and the criminal law of the European Union. His books include *Colpa ed Evento Nel Diritto Penale* (Giuffre editore, Milano 1990), and *La Corruzione del Pubblico Amministratore* (Milan, 1992). Recently, he completed a commentary on "public order crimes" of the Italian Criminal Code: G. Forti, "Dei delitti contro l'ordine pubblico," in *Commentario*

Breve al Codice Penale (edited by A. Crespi, F. Stella, and G. Zuccala), 3rd edition (CEDAM editore). He is currently publishing a textbook focusing on the relationship and prospects for cooperation between criminal law and criminology.

Colin Goff is an associate professor of sociology at the University of Winnipeg. He received his Ph.D. in social ecology at the University of California–Irvine in 1982. He is co-author (with Gilbert Geis) of the Introduction to Sutherland's *White-Collar Crime: The Uncut Version.* His research interests include deviance, white-collar crime, and corporate crime.

Peter Grabosky, B.A. (Colby), M.A. and Ph.D. (Northwestern), is Director of Research at the Australian Institute of Criminology. He has written widely on white-collar crime and regulatory enforcement, including *Of Manners Gentle: Enforcement Strategies of Australian Business Regulatory Agencies* (with John Braithwaite), and *Crime in the Digital Age: Controlling Telecommunications and Cyberspace Illegalities* (with Russell G. Smith). In July of 1998, he was elected President of the Australian and New Zealand Society of Criminology.

Sean Patrick Griffin is a Ph.D. candidate in the Administration of Justice at The Pennsylvania State University. A former police officer, he has worked on several state and federal research grants regarding community policing and domestic violence. His dissertation examines the social and political history of Philadelphia's "Black Mafia." His research interests include organized crime, public policy, international traffic in narcotics, law enforcement and related issues, domestic violence, and qualitative, archival, and historical research methods.

C. Ronald Huff is Dean of the School of Social Ecology and professor in the Department of Criminology, Law and Society at the University of California–Irvine. He has also taught at Ohio State University, Purdue University, and the University of Hawaii. The most recent of his ten books include *Youth Violence: Prevention, Intervention, and Social Policy; Gangs in America;* and *Convicted but Innocent: Wrongful Conviction and Public Policy.* He recently completed a National Institute of Justice–funded study of the criminal behavior of gang members and has served as a consultant on gangs, youth violence, and public policy to the U.S. Senate Judiciary Committee, the F.B.I. National Academy, the U.S. Department of Justice, and numerous other agencies and organizations throughout the Nation. Dr. Huff's honors include the Paul Tappan Award from the Western Society of Criminology, and the Herbert Bloch Award from the American Society of Criminology. In 2000–2001 he will serve as president of the American Society of Criminology.

Paul Jesilow is associate professor of criminology, law and society at the University of California–Irvine. He is the co-author of numerous articles and books including *Prescription for Profit: How Doctors Defraud Medicaid; Doing Justice in the People's Court: Sentencing by Municipal Court Judges,* and *Myths That*

Cause Crime, which was selected by the Academy of Criminal Justice Sciences as Outstanding Book of the Year. His current research focuses on community policing.

Kent R. Kerley is a Ph.D. candidate in sociology at the University of Tennessee. His areas of specialization include community policing, white-collar crime, and life course theory.

Jason Lam received his B.A. with honors in criminology, law and society at the University of California–Irvine. He is currently a law student at Boalt Hall School of Law, University of California–Berkeley.

Michael Levi is professor of criminology and has taught at Cardiff University since 1975. His major contributions have been in the fields of white-collar crime, organized crime, money-laundering, and violent crime. In addition to many articles in books and scholarly and professional journals, his books include *The Phantom Capitalists* (Grower 1981); *Regulating Fraud: White-Collar Crime and the Criminal Process* (Routledge 1988); *The Investigation, Prosecution, and Trial of Serious Fraud* (Royal Commission on Criminal Justice Research Study No. 14, London: HMSO, 1993); in collaboration with Michael Gold, *Money Laundering in the UK: An Appraisal of Suspicion-Based Reporting* (Police Foundation 1994); in collaboration with Jack Blum, Tom Naylor, and Phil Williams, *Financial Havens: Banking Secrecy and Money-Laundering* (U.N. 1998). His most recent book, with Andy Pithouse, *White-Collar Crime and Its Victims,* (on the impact of fraud on individual and institutional victims and responses to it), was published by Oxford University Press in December, 1999.

Robert F. Meier is professor and chair of the Department of Criminal Justice at the University of Nebraska–Omaha. He has held previous positions at Iowa State University, Washington State University, and the University of California–Irvine. He is the author or editor of 15 books, original and revised editions, and over 50 articles in professional journals. His scholarly interests include general processes of deviance and social control with a special interest in crime and crime-control policy. He has conducted research on a number of criminological topics, including theories of crime and victimization, forms of crime, including white-collar crime, victimless crime, and rape, as well as the topics of deterrence and legal processes. His most recent books include *Victimless Crimes? Prostitution, Drugs, Homosexuality, and Abortion* (with Gilbert Geis, 1997), *Sociology of Deviant Behavior,* 10th edition (with Marshall B. Clinard, 1998), and *The Process and Structure of Crime: Criminal Events and Crime Analysis* (with Leslie Kennedy and Vincent Sacco, forthcoming).

Deborah Parsons is an assistant professor at California State University–San Bernardino. Her Ph.D. is in Social Ecology from the University of California–Irvine. She is a former police officer and continues to be a reserve officer. Dr.

Parsons current research and writings focus on policing, particularly community policing and gender issues.

Nicole Leeper Piquero is a doctoral student in the Department of Criminology and Criminal Justice at the University of Maryland. Her research interests include corporate and white-collar crime, policing, and evaluation. Specifically, she has examined the sentencing practices of organizational defendants sentenced under the Federal Sentencing Guidelines as well as the micro-macro link in corporate crime etiology.

Henry N. Pontell is professor and chair of the Department of Criminology, Law and Society, in the School of Social Ecology at the University of California–Irvine. He has written extensively on the topics of deviance and social control, white-collar and corporate crime, punishment and deterrence, crime seriousness, jail overcrowding and litigation, criminal justice system capacity, medical fraud, and the role of crime in the savings and loan debacle. He is a past president and fellow of the Western Society of Criminology. His books include: *A Capacity to Punish: The Ecology of Crime and Punishment; Social Deviance; Prescription for Profit: How Doctors Defraud Medicaid; Profit Without Honor: White Collar Crime and the Looting of America;* and *Big Money Crime: Fraud and Politics in the Savings and Loan Crisis.* His current work includes research on international financial fraud, and new books on social deviance, and contemporary legal debates in America.

Stephen M. Rosoff is associate professor of sociology and director of the graduate criminology program at the University of Houston, Clear Lake. He received his Ph.D. in social ecology from the University of California–Irvine. He has written extensively on white-collar crime and professional deviance, particularly in the areas of medical fraud and computer crime. He is co-author of *Profit Without Honor: White-Collar Crime and the Looting of America,* and of the forthcoming book, *Making Corrections: A Crisis of Capacity in American Criminal Justice.*

Dale K. Sechrest is a professor in the Criminal Justice Department, California State University–San Bernardino. He received his Ph.D. in criminology from the University of California–Berkeley in 1974. He implemented a national program of correctional standards and accredition with the American Correctional Association (1975–84). He has published research on methadone maintenance and drug courts. He was a research associate at the Center for Criminal Justice, Harvard Law School (1973–75), and directed several research projects for the American Justice Institute (1971–73). Publications include articles on privatization in corrections, drug programs, diversion, and community corrections; and books on jail management and liability, three strikes laws, and the careers of correctional officers.

Hans Joachim Schneider is a professor of criminology, criminal law and legal psychology at the University of Westphalia in Münster, Germany. He has published more than 20 books and 400 articles in thirteen languages. A recipient of an honorary doctorate from the University of Lodz-Poland, he has been a visiting professor in various universities of Europe, North and South America, Asia, and Australia; and served as a consulting expert of the Council of Europe and the United Nations. Professor Schneider also received the Hermann Mannheim Award of the International Center of Comparative Criminology in 1998. At present, he is a guest professor at the University of Leipzig, and at the Federal Police Academy, Munster, Germany.

David Shichor is professor emeritus of criminal justice, California State University–San Bernardino. He received his Ph.D. in sociology from the University of Southern California, and taught at the Tel Aviv University, Israel prior to his arrival at CSUSB. He has written, co-authored, and co-edited several books and published numerous articles and book chapters on various topics, including juvenile delinquency, victimization, white-collar crime, corrections, and privatization in criminal justice. He is currently working on several projects on privatization, restorative justice, fraud victimization, and the mental health of jail inmates.

James F. Short, Jr. is professor emeritus of sociology at Washington State University. He has written widely in areas of sociology, criminology, and risk analysis. His latest book is *Poverty, Ethnicity, and Violent Crime* (Westview, 1997). A former Editor of the *American Sociological Review,* and Associate Editor of the *Annual Review of Sociology,* he has served as President of the Pacific and American Sociological Associations and the American Society of Criminology. He is a Fellow of the American Society of Criminology and a recipient of ASC's Edwin H. Sutherland Award. He has been a Fellow at the Center for Advanced Study in the Behavioral Sciences (Stanford), the Institute of Criminology at Cambridge University, the Rockefeller Center in Bellagio, and the Centre for Socio-Legal Studies at Oxford University. He has been the recipient of NIMH and Guggenheim Fellowships, the Bruce Smith Award from the Academy of Criminal Justice Sciences, and the Paul W. Tappan Award from the Western Society of Criminology.

Sally S. Simpson is associate professor and graduate director in the Department of Criminology and Criminal Justice at the University of Maryland. She has a longstanding interest in corporate crime, beginning with her doctoral dissertation, which explored the economic sources of antitrust offending. Her more recent interests lie in corporate crime control—specifically evaluating models of criminalization and cooperation. Excerpts of the work have most recently been published in the *Kobe University Law Review* (1998) and will appear in a book with Cambridge University Press. She was the recipient of the 1999 American Society of Criminology's Herbert Bloch Award.

Jody L. Sundt is an assistant professor in the Center for the Study of Crime, Delinquency, and Corrections at Southern Illinois University at Carbondale. She has published in the areas of correctional policy, public attitudes toward crime control, and religion in prison. Her current research focuses on the work experiences of correctional employees.

Diane Vaughan is professor of sociology at the University of California–Santa Barbara. She received her Ph.D. from Ohio State University. Her research focus has been on the dark side of organizations: how things go wrong in socially-organized settings. She has pursued this agenda in *Controlling Unlawful Organizational Behavior* (Chicago, 1983), *Uncoupling* (Oxford, 1986), and *The Challenger Launch Decision* (Chicago, 1996). Currently, she is writing *Theorizing: Analogy, Cases, and Comparative Social Organization,* doing field work for a study of air traffic control, and working on a general theory of the normalization of deviance.

Joseph T. Wells is founder and chairman of the Association of Certified Fraud Examiners, a 25,000 member professional organization headquartered in Austin, Texas. He is the author of scores of articles and training programs on fraud, most recently: *The Fraud Examiners Manual* (1st, 2nd, and 3rd editions), *Fraud Examination: A Guide to Investigative and Audit Procedures; Occupational Fraud and Abuse;* and *The Accountant's Handbook of Fraud and Commercial Crime.*

Susan Will is an assistant professor of sociology at John Jay College of Criminal Justice. She received her Ph.D. from the University of California–Irvine. Her areas of research include white-collar crime, sociology of law, and social control. She co-authored "Risky Business Revisited: White-Collar Crime and the Orange County Bankruptcy" with Henry Pontell and Richard Cheung.

John F. Wozniak is an associate professor of sociology and chair of the Department of Sociology and Anthropology at Western Illinois University. He has co-authored articles on correctional policies, public attitudes toward crime, functions and social supports of police, elderly offenders, and correctional policies. His current research interests include recent developments in criminological theories and policies, an assessment of common themes in white-collar textbooks of the 1900s, the rise of peacemaking criminology, and the application of C. Wright Mills' theory toward the study of crime.

Richard Wright is professor of criminology and criminal justice at the University of Missouri, St. Louis. His most recent book, co-authored with Scott Decker, is *Armed Robbers in Action: Stickups and Street Culture* (Boston: Northeastern University Press).

I

INTRODUCTION

Geis, Sutherland, and White-Collar Crime

Robert F. Meier

❖

Edwin Sutherland and Gilbert Geis share a strong mutual interest in white-collar crime. Each of these criminologists has made important contributions to the theory and research of white-collar crime at different times. My purpose here is to compare the contributions of each of these scholars to our understanding of white-collar crime. In so doing, I hope to elucidate the important contributions made by Gilbert Geis to this topic.

The thesis of this paper can be stated simply: the promise in the pioneering work of Edwin Sutherland on white-collar crime has been fulfilled more in the works of Geis than in the works of any other scholar. That promise was vast, and there was much work to be done at the time of Sutherland's death in 1950 in spite of his vigorous labor. While Sutherland's mark was strong, one could argue that Sutherland left the study of white-collar crime in disarray, without a definitional rudder and sufficient empirical work to power the field beyond his initial foray. While Sutherland staked the initial claim, Geis exploited it to the point where it became a major area of study and public policy. We will see that early ventures into the study of white-collar crime immediately after Sutherland's death were tentative and not especially helpful in refining and building the concept. It would be nearly two decades after Sutherland's death that the area of white-collar crime would come into its own, and the principal reason for that is the ongoing contributions of Gilbert Geis. This paper examines both biography and intellectual approaches to discern the unique contributions of Sutherland and Geis in understanding white-collar crime.

1

SUTHERLAND AND THE IRONY OF WHITE-COLLAR CRIME

It is now fifty years since Edwin Sutherland died, and with him criminology's total preoccupation with conventional, or street, crime. But Sutherland's contribution to modern understanding of white-collar crime has not been entirely clear. While he pioneered the subject matter, his legacy is marked by a lack of consensus by scholars both about the meaning of the term *white-collar crime* and the general approach that best generates the kind of theoretical and empirical understanding criminologists require. Sutherland was the leading figure in American criminology throughout most of the twentieth century, but that appellation is more likely due to his championing his theory of differential association, rather than his work on white-collar crime.

In contrast with the cosmopolitan nature of white-collar crime, Sutherland's biography is decidedly rural. He was born in 1883 in Gibbon, Nebraska and spent almost all of his time to age 21 in Grand Island, Nebraska (population at the time was about 6,000). He graduated in 1904 with a class of seventy others from Grand Island College, where his father was president. He then taught at Sioux Falls (South Dakota) College for two years before enrolling as a graduate student in sociology at the University of Chicago, where he stayed until 1908. From 1909 to 1911 he returned and taught at Grand Island College, finally returning to Chicago to finish his Ph.D. in 1913. Sutherland's family was strongly religious, and his educational experiences, except for those at Chicago, were all at religious schools (Grand Island and Sioux Falls Colleges were Baptist institutions).

Sutherland's first teaching position after his Ph.D. was at William Jewel College in Liberty, Missouri, another Baptist school. He remained there until 1919 when he began something of a cook's tour of Midwestern universities: 1919-1926 at the University of Illinois (where his interest in criminology became systematized), 1926-1929 at the University of Minnesota, 1930-1935 at the University of Chicago, and from 1935 until his death in 1950 at the University of Indiana.

Sutherland's influential criminology textbook was first published while he was at the University of Illinois, and his theory of differential association first made its tentative appearance in an edition while he was at the University of Chicago. Sutherland had taught a criminology course every year from 1913 to 1921 but, he reports, "My organized work in criminology began in 1921 when E.C. Hayes, head of the department of Sociology at the University of Illinois, asked me to write a text on criminology for the Lippincott series" (Sutherland, 1973, 13). Sutherland was unable to draw from his dissertation research for his criminological contributions. Sutherland's dissertation, titled "Unemployment and Public Employment Agencies," dealt with labor problems in the city of Chicago.

Sutherland's relatively provincial upbringing paralleled that of many of the sociologists at the University of Chicago. The faculty of the "Chicago School" stressed local issues and problems, and their reach seldom stretched beyond the city limits of Chicago. Sutherland was no hick, but he was the product of a rela-

tively sheltered existence. Sutherland's early life centered around Grand Island, but even his mature years never found him far—socially and intellectually—from those Midwestern roots.

Sutherland's work with Chic Conwell (a student in one of his classes), his jarring exposure to big city life in Chicago, and his fondness for applying differential association to all forms of crime each suggests the work of someone with first-hand knowledge of crime. But there is no record of Sutherland having had personal experience with crime. Sutherland adopted more of an insider position on his subject matter, but the closest he would come to real-life crime would be an encounter with an occasional wayward student or the library, not from personal experience. He resorted frequently to documenting crime by means of anecdotes, one being a pedestrian recital of the small-time shenanigans of a college student who worked weekends as a shoe salesman–a story according to Donald Cressey that was based on "Sutherland's personal experiences" (Geis and Goff, 1983, 178). The anecdote is indeed dull, and Sutherland may in fact have exaggerated it for illustrative purposes. Throughout his career, Sutherland adopted a social psychological perspective that focused on offenders. Sutherland was not a reductionist, but his starting point was always individual criminals, their offenses, and the learning experiences they had to bring them to their crimes.

GEIS AND THE EXTENSION OF SUTHERLAND

Gilbert Geis was born in 1925 in New York City. His parents divorced when Geis was five years old, and he was raised by his mother and grandmother in a two-family house in Brooklyn. His grandmother, who helped support the family with the sale of bootleg liquor during the Depression, died when he was thirteen. His mother was a secretary for a company in Manhattan. After graduation from high school, Geis attended New York University for one year before joining the U.S. Navy for the Second World War. He returned in 1945 to go to school, at Colgate University and the College of the Holy Cross. He attended the University of Stockholm after graduating from Colgate, but financial demands forced his return to the United States after eight months. Finding that Brigham Young University didn't charge tuition, he traveled to Utah for his master's degree in 1949, after which he entered the doctoral program in sociology at the University of Wisconsin. Geis was interested in Scandinavian area studies, and neither of his advisors, Svend Reimer and Hans Gerth, had the slightest interest in crime. His dissertation, based on field research in Norway, dealt with the operation of the municipally owned movie theaters in Oslo and the reaction of Norwegian audiences to American films. He describes his education as "ecumenical" in the sense that the schools he attended had student bodies that were predominately Protestant, Catholic, Jewish, or Mormon, but there is little hint of religious persuasion in Geis's writings.

Along the way, Geis worked for a newspaper and did considerable writing in college to help make ends meet. He would write for popular periodicals to help make ends meet, often writing different versions of the same article to suit different audiences (for example, "You and Your Cat" became "You and Your Dog" or "You and Your Parakeet," depending on the magazine.) For a time, he commuted on university buses to Madison from temporary student housing nearly an hour from campus. It was here he met fellow student Frank Remington, who would later become a well-known professor of criminal law at the University of Wisconsin.

Like Sutherland, Geis developed his interest in crime and criminology after he left graduate school. In fact, Geis reports that he never had a course in criminology. Nevertheless, his first position was as an instructor at the University of Oklahoma in 1952, where he taught race relations and criminology. Geis's interest in race relations led to a collaboration with an anthropologist on the migration patterns of African-Americans. His only notable criminological work during this time was a pulp fiction novel that involved a rape on a college campus. One of the major characters was a criminology professor.

After five years, Geis secured a position at California State University at Los Angeles, where he stayed for 13 years before taking a professorship at the University of California at Irvine in 1970. Undoubtedly his time in California was the most productive of his professional life, and the range of topics on which he has written is impressive: juvenile delinquency, victimization, organized crime, confidence swindling, criminal justice policy, bystander intervention, prostitution, drugs, crime theory, victimless crimes—and of course white-collar crime.

Geis's work has always reflected a combination of cosmopolitan orientation with the kind of basic values and approaches found in Sutherland's work. Sutherland, as noted earlier, was more influenced by a social psychological approach to crime and was more interested in the behavior of specific individuals. Although differential association can be said to be operating at both a structural and individual level, it was clearly the individual level that interested Sutherland. Through out his academic career, Geis too has focused on individual criminals, even when addressing the topic of corporate crime. But Geis is less awed by the white-collar criminals he studied than was Sutherland. To Sutherland, white-collar criminals were people with whom he could not relate; they came from different backgrounds, had different interests, and lived different lifestyles. Geis's work displays more appreciation of the social contexts of white-collar criminals, although he shares Sutherland's high degree of disapproval of their crimes.

THE USE OF IRONY

Sutherland's interest in white-collar crime stems in part from an appreciation of the subject's irony. The respectability of the white-collar criminal is what both attracts and repels Sutherland to this topic. Clearly, it is ironic that the most "respectable"—in terms of social position and reputation—are at the same time the most criminal—in terms of the dramatic consequences to society of white-collar crime. But there is another irony in white-collar crime, because explaining white-collar crime poses special challenges. Virtually all other theories of crime are explanations of early crime, or delinquency. But the white-collar criminal is, almost by definition, a law-abiding child, adolescent, and early adult. It is this respectability that permits the eventual white-collar criminal to be placed in positions where white-collar crime can take place. Corporate officers do not have histories of earlier crime or they wouldn't have been able to occupy the corporate boardroom. They are the successes of the American dream, those to whom nature or deity has provided the ambition and means to succeed in the American marketplace. Yet, in terms of the damage to society, they are the most dangerous criminals. In this sense, Sutherland (and Merton—the other major theoretical figure of the first half of the twentieth century) was talking not about the idealized notion of "getting ahead" in America (the lure to immigrants), but of the tragic consequences of the freedom and choice in this country. The criminals theorized by Merton and Sutherland want it both ways: they yearn for the rewards of society but they are unwilling or unable to achieve them conventionally. They are trapped by the desires of the society in which they live and the lack of conventional opportunity afforded them by that same society. What is a conventional opportunity to one is an unconventional opportunity to another. Criminals are fated by their socialization to want something they cannot have legally. Their only choice is to follow their desires illegally.

One of the most important motivations for Sutherland in his study of white-collar crime was to extend his theory of differential association. Sutherland's commitment to differential association was well known by the 1940s. The theory appeared in his textbook, *Criminology* (later *Principles of Criminology*). The first edition of the book appeared in 1924 and did not contain a theory of criminal behavior. The book was one of the first criminology texts and contained a summary of virtually all of the criminological literature at the time, something that cannot now be done. It offered Sutherland a platform on which to proclaim the superiority of environmental over genetic influences on behavior and undoubtedly increased Sutherland's visibility professionally as he proudly carried forth the relatively new sociological flag into intellectual battle. The text went through two editions by the time Henry McKay complemented Sutherland on his theory of crime. Not knowing what theory McKay was referring to, Sutherland (1973, 15) found the passage McKay referenced and read that crime was the result of culture conflict in particular city areas. McKay, of course, was pleased that Sutherland was sensitive to the notion of "natural areas," of which Shaw and McKay had made much, but Sutherland appears to have been naive in understanding that his statement was vaguely theoretical, let alone a theory of crime. In any case, by the next edition in 1939, differential association makes its tentative appearance as a formal theory only of "systematic" crime, not all crime, a designation that would be dropped in later editions. The importance of the theory for Sutherland is reflected in its position in the 1939 edition: it was the whole of Chapter 1.[1] The next (1947) edition contains the theory as we know it today: nine propositions directed toward explaining all criminality.

Sutherland's commitment to differential association is well known, and his fervor led him to consider the theory, at least by 1947, to have general applicability to all forms of crime. The topic of white-collar crime permitted him to demonstrate that applicability. His effort at theoretical hegemony, however, was coupled with another desire, one derived from his conservative, rural background: moralizing.

GEIS, SUTHERLAND, AND THE DEVELOPMENT OF WHITE-COLLAR CRIME

Sutherland came to the field of white-collar crime from a strong interest in conventional criminality. And for most of his work on street crime, he studied the behavior of individual criminals. Some of those criminals, such as those reflected in his data on corporate crime, acted in concert with others, while other criminals acted alone. But Sutherland never strayed far from the integrity of his subject matter within the following context.

Crime is an act defined as illegal by law. Sutherland never wavered from his strong belief that white-collar crime was technically, and in all other ways, crime. The simple idea that white-collar crime is indeed crime led to one of the most well-known debates in criminology, the Sutherland-Tappan debates. Criminologist Paul Tappan, a legally trained sociologist, took exception to Sutherland's contention that white-collar crimes were criminal acts. They were, Tappan argued, after all not in most cases handled by the police, criminal prosecutors, or criminal courts, but in administrative courts with different procedures, legal rulings, and sanctions. White-collar crime was not criminal in either a technical or social sense, Tappan implied, and to argue that it was would merely promote a political agenda.

Tappan's legal training undoubtedly shaped a narrower, more technical view, and his position was hardly outrageous. There can be a substantial difference between the formulation and enforcement of criminal codes and the formulation and enforcement of other state-defined rules. But Tappan's restricted view of crime assumes that the differences between white-collar crime and conventional crime are not related to the power and influence of the offenders, important characteristics of white-collar crime.

Geis, too, regards white-collar crime as real crime. White-collar crime is not a legal sleight-of-hand. Like Sutherland, Geis has understood well that in many cases the criminal law was not the initial point of reference because white-collar crimes were often found in the violations of administrative law. Yet, the violations of the rules of state agencies were backed by state sanctions, just as in street crime where the offender breaks the rules (criminal law) of state agencies (legislatures) that are backed by state sanctions (e.g., imprisonment). In fact, aside from incarceration, the sanctions of most white-collar crimes are virtually identical to the sanctions of criminal laws.

Criminals are those who violate the law. This principle follows from the first. It mattered little to Sutherland that white-collar criminals were violating something other than criminal law; they were violating *some* law, and that law was backed by state-sanctioned penalties; so conceived, criminals are individuals who break the law, regardless of whether contained in the criminal code or some other body of state regulations.

Geis, too, regards white-collar criminals as real criminals, both in the technically legal and in a social sense. He notes that white-collar offenders violate real law with demonstrable legal intent. They are aware that what they are doing is wrong and they attempt to avoid legal punishment. In all these things, white-collar criminals are like conventional criminals. Where white-collar criminals differ from other criminals is the lack of shame they often display. As one of Geis's electrical equipment conspirators claimed, what he had done was illegal but not criminal. Geis regards such verbiage as "smoke-and-mirrors" and dismisses them as self-serving statements designed more to protect the offender's self-concept than to describe reality.

Corporate crime is merely the actions of individual offenders. Although Sutherland's major study concerned the violations of corporations, he maintained that the activity was merely the actions of individual offenders. In this sense, Sutherland's major work, which dealt with corporate crime, was a study in white-collar crime, as the title states explicitly.

Geis's major single work on white-collar crime may be an investigation into a corporate price-fixing case: the heavy electrical equipment conspiracy. This case was a large-scale example of corporate crime, but, like Sutherland, Geis draws our attention not to the aggregate dynamics of the case, but to the individuals and their personal actions in support of the conspiracy. There is nothing abstract about this case; it is filled with concrete illegal acts by specific individuals. The conspirators develop a code to hide their actions. For example, the terms *Christmas card list* stood for the names of attendees at meetings where prices were fixed, and *choir practice* for the meetings themselves. The conspirators used only public phones and met only at trade shows so that their association didn't look unusual. Nevertheless, when the Tennessee Valley Authority, one of the largest and most frequent consumers of the large electrical turbines of these companies, noticed irregularities, the case was broken.

After the legal dust settled, there had been four grand juries that issued twenty indictments on forty-five persons and twenty-nine corporations. These actions resulted in fines of two million dollars, and seven of the conspirators were convicted. As with many cases of white-collar crime, however, Geis notes that those who were incarcerated received jail terms of thirty days or less with up to five days off for good behavior. Victims of the conspiracy also sued two of the largest corporations, Westinghouse and General Electric, in civil court. General Electric paid out $160 million by 1964, a goodly amount even for a huge corporation, but Geis notes wryly that most of this was tax deductible! Even for a large corporate price-fixing case, the action is not with corporations as entities, but with the individuals in the corporations.

The Use of Case Studies. Sutherland and Geis generally adopted a "ground up" approach in studying crime. One of the reasons to examine white-collar crime from the basis of the offender is not merely that individual criminals are the basic unit of analysis for both Sutherland and Geis, but also because each of these scholars believe that the awareness of biographic and situational experiences of offenders is critical for understanding the nature of the crime and the circumstances that brought the offender to the crime. Sutherland's motivation for doing this may have been tempered heavily by his fundamental allegiance to his theory of crime, a theory that stresses an understanding of the learning experiences of offenders through time.

Sutherland's biography of a professional thief and Geis's account of the electrical equipment conspiracy are the most obvious examples of this grounded approach, but there are others as well. Geis's more recent work on physician fraud is rife with individual cases on physician wrongdoing drawn from newspaper accounts, interviews with doctors, and official case files from state and federal agencies.

Corporate Versus White-Collar Crime

These elements of common ground between Sutherland and Geis are best illustrated in one issue: the nature of corporate crime and its relation to white-collar crime. The legal dimension of this issue is whether corporations, as distinct entities, may be held liable for corporate acts, while the social dimension is whether corporate crime is merely the actions of individuals within the corporation.

The legal issue has been largely settled in American law. For over a century, the criminal sanction has been an appropriate federal mechanism in response to corporate misconduct. The idea that corporations would be held criminally responsible actually extends back to seventeenth-century English common law (Brickey, 1995, 9), but it was not until the Sherman Antitrust Act of 1890 that this idea was expressed in American law. The Sherman Act brought a combination of civil and criminal sanctions against corporate misconduct. Even so, the issue of the use and extent of criminal sanctions against corporations has been visited by the U.S. Supreme Court on several occasions in view of the fact that the financial impact of criminal fines on corporations could be borne ultimately by innocent stockholders. Closure has not yet been reached on a number of issues, including the extent to which corporations can be held criminally responsible for the conduct of their employees, the nature and extent of criminal penalties, and the objective those sanctions are attempting to achieve.

While federal law has continually considered corporations criminally liable, state laws developed slowly in this regard, and state statutes are uneven and sometimes inconsistent with federal law. One attempt to impose uniformity in criminal law, the American Law Institute's *Model Penal Code*, last revised in 1985, provided one basis for state statutes. Section 2.07 of that Code stipulates that a corporation may be convicted of a crime if:

> The offense is a violation or the offense is defined by a statute other than the Code in which a legislative purpose to impose liability on corporations plainly appears and the conduct is performed by an agent of the corporation acting in behalf of the corporation within the scope of his office or employment.

The Code further stipulates that such crimes may be acts of omission or commission and may be violations of criminal law or regulatory rules. It also stipulates, however, that corporations may defend themselves if by a preponderance of evidence (the usual civil, not criminal, standard) the corporation can prove it attempted through "due diligence" to prevent the crime. The distance between managerial supervision of "due diligence" and the actions of individual employees who are working without corporate approval represents an important stumbling block in prosecuting these crimes.

The notion of criminal liability is closely tied to that of individual guilt. One should not be convicted for something one did not intend to do. If so, how can corporations be prosecuted and punished for something they did not do if they did not authorize the employee's actions? Corporate crimes should not be the actions of employees acting alone or with personal motives. Corporate crimes must in some sense reflect corporate policy or, at least, show that the corporation benefited from a crime it did not reasonably prevent. In other words, courts should be satisfied that the acts of individual employees represent acts of the corporation, and that the actor who commits the crime acted within the scope of his or her authority and on behalf of the corporation. Present federal law does not require that the actor be highly placed in the corporation or that corporate management performed an active role in the crime.

Sutherland and Geis have approached the issue of whether white-collar crime refers only to individual offenders or aggregates of them in a similar manner. As suggested earlier, Sutherland's major work dealt with the violations of corporations, but his attention never strayed far from the individual offenders within those corporations. His effort to apply differential association was focused on individual white-collar criminals, not the corporations as a whole. Geis too has been very grounded in his attention on individual white-collar criminals. A recent exchange with Braithwaite and Fisse reduces to the question of whether it is better to consider corporations themselves as offenders or whether the real offenders are the employees of the corporations. Braithwaite and Fisse argue that corporations in the modern world are real entities, legally and socially. Corporations act with unified purpose, and at times those acts are illegal. Geis (1995) rejects this position as needlessly abstract, preferring instead to merely regard corporate violations as the actions of individual offenders. It is, after all, he argues, not Amoco or General Motors who violate laws, but specific corporate employees who may be acting on behalf of the corporation. Whether their intent is self- or corporate-gain, these offenders are in the most real of worlds the individuals who violate the law.

Defining the Field

If there is one persistent issue in the field of white-collar crime, it is its definition. More scholars have weighed in on this topic than perhaps any other, and there is relatively little to show for this fervent attention.

Sutherland evidently was not much interested in a definition of white-collar crime, either because he thought it wasn't necessary (perhaps because his theory would explain all crime anyway, regardless of precise definition) or because he himself was confused about it.[2] His research prior to the publication of his white-collar crime book dealt with the behavior of individual criminals, while his study of the seventy largest corporations in the United States—his major research effort on the topic—involved aggregate data. Perhaps Sutherland didn't sense a contradiction here. After all, one could argue that corporate behavior is merely the behavior of the individuals in the corporation, although it is virtually conventional wisdom in criminology today that white-collar crime and corporate crime involve important behavioral and contextual differences that preclude that kind of conceptual reductionism (see Tonry and Reiss, 1993).

It should also be recognized that Sutherland's path-breaking work was possible in part because of his not narrowing his inquiry to fit some particular definition of white-collar crime. Had Sutherland addressed the definitional issue in 1949 as some scholars have today, the field might look even more parochial and confusing than it presently does. Without a restricting definition to clutter his way, Sutherland was free to span both individual and collective levels of behavior and to identify illegal acts regardless of which body of law defined the acts as illegal.

Sutherland began his interest in and study of "violations of law by businessmen" in the late 1920s (Sutherland, 1973, 78). His work was sporadic and was presented initially in his presidential address before the American Sociological Association. Even in his initial scholarly foray, however, Sutherland didn't dwell on definitional issues, although he did indicate that "white-collar crimes in business and the professions consist principally of the violation of delegated or implied trust...." (Sutherland, 1940, 3). This definition was largely ignored in the empirical work on white-collar crime that followed shortly after the publication of Suther-land's book. Clinard's (1952) study of the violations of the Office of Price Admin-istration during World War II, and Hartung's (1950) study of violations in the wholesale meat packing industry addressed, in turn, the two levels at which white-collar crime can be said to operate—the individual and corporate. Clinard's offend-ers were individuals, while Hartung's were businesses, exactly like those found in Sutherland's own research. Clinard (1952, 227) notes that white-collar crime refers to "violations of the law committed primarily by groups such as businessmen, pro-fessional men, and politicians in connection with their occupations…," after which he cites virtually all of Sutherland's publications on the subject.

Subsequent work would divide precisely along this individual-aggregate dimension with work by Cressey (1953) on embezzlement (individual) and Geis (1967) on price-fixing on the heavy electrical equipment industry (collective). But the individual-aggregate dimension has been difficult to maintain in some instances because, again, one could always argue, as Geis did, that although Westinghouse and General Electric were the major companies involved, the price-fixers were individuals (see also Geis, 1995).

Geis has never been quick to enter the definitional debate. Like Sutherland, Geis may regard white-collar crime as either so obvious not to require much expli-cation, or more likely as so hopelessly muddled, it is better left alone. "The task of defining white-collar crime," he wrote, "is in many ways wearisome, perhaps best left to those with a predilection for medieval theological debates" (Geis, 1982, 152). And, in an earlier statement, Geis's (1974, 256) frustration was even more acute: "The semantic waters have been so muddied by Sutherland that today it seems wisest to move upstream rather than to attempt a purification project."

While one solution is to ignore the definitional issue, the other is to abandon the term altogether. But Geis rejects the idea of discarding the term *white-collar crime* because he thinks it is still useful, he maintains, in galvanizing public opin-ion: "However metaphorical and imprecise, the term white-collar crime conjures up a real set of ills, and is particularly satisfactory in solidifying an emotional and intellectual concern about such ills" (Geis, 1982, 152). Rather than change the term, and in the absence of an agreed-upon definition of white-collar crime, Geis advo-cates the development of taxonomies based on the content of law, the degree of harm, characteristics of offenders, modus operandi, and types and nature of victims.

There is much to commend such a strategy. Even a national conference in 1996, sponsored by the National White Collar Crime Research Center (NWC-CRC), failed to produce an unambiguous definition. Speaking of "deviance" and "elites," conferees hammered out a relatively short definition, but there are prob-lems with it. Definitions are neither right nor wrong, but more or less useful, and if researchers and theorists find the NWCCRC definition useful, so be it. But two facts remain: there has never been a completely satisfactory definition of white-collar crime, and the field has prospered enormously without one.

EXTENDING SUTHERLAND

It is tempting—but ultimately unfruitful—to speculate where Sutherland's attention would have turned in his study of white-collar crime. Perhaps to more work refining his study of the largest corporations, perhaps to studies of particular types of white-collar crime, or perhaps to more direct applications of differential association to white-collar crime. Sutherland's death left a vacuum created by a talented criminologist who had been concerned about white-collar crime for perhaps 20 years. The then "new breed" of scholars whose work followed Sutherland (Clinard, Cressey, Hartung) simply had been at it for a short time and failed to show the breadth of interest reflected in Sutherland's work. Perhaps for these reasons, this work failed to create continued interest in white-collar crime.

By the time Geis began to write about white-collar crime, the field was languishing. No one was paying systematic attention to it, and there were no prospects for Sutherland's work being anything other than an initial foray without follow-up. Geis's work changed that by resuscitating a topic that was virtually comatose. Geis provided a neglected historical and intellectual context to our understanding of white-collar crime and did so without the dual burden of developing the field *and* a general theory of crime at the same time. These, in fact, are important intellectual legacies, and without them it is doubtful that white-collar crime would have become the popular topic it is now.

Theoretical Ecumenism

Sutherland was closely associated with a powerful theory of crime. Differential association was intended to be a general theory applicable to all crime, and the topic of white-collar crime afforded Sutherland an opportunity to show the power of the theory in a difficult test. As noted earlier, the area of white-collar crime is a particularly tricky test for theory because most criminological theory—virtually all theory at the time Sutherland was writing—was predicated on the notion that the task of theory was to show how people *become* criminal from a state of non-criminal innocence. Virtually by definition, white-collar criminals have little or no background in crime and few if any associations with conventional criminals. Their criminality comes later in the life cycle, so any theory of white-collar crime must necessarily "kick in" when these individuals are otherwise law-abiding adults. It was intellectually courageous for Sutherland to attack such a special type of crime with theoretical armament developed from conventional crime.

There are at least two major perspectives on crime causation, one that emphasizes larger social, economic, and political forces (a structural approach), and one that focuses on people and the worlds they perceive and experience (a social psychological approach). Each of these perspectives has proved useful and they dominate different traditions in criminology and the study of white-collar crime. Geis and Sutherland favor a social psychological approach but they part company from one another in thinking that conventional and white-collar crimes are explainable within the same theoretical framework. While Sutherland maintained that a single theory was able to explain white-collar crime as well as conventional crime, a viewpoint held by several more modern criminologists (e.g., Gottfredson and Hirschi, 1990; Wilson and Hernnstein, 1985), Geis has maintained that white-collar crime is a distinctive form of criminality, that the white-collar offenders are qualitatively different from conventional criminals, and that, as a result, different theoretical approaches may be required. It is also possible that efforts to control white-collar crime may be quite different from those used in restraining conventional criminality, although Geis has consistently advocated the use of the criminal sanction in the control of white-collar criminals.

Geis has largely eschewed allegiance to the lure of a grand theory of crime, including white-collar crime, and his approach may more aptly be considered an example of theoretical agnosticism. His approach to white-collar crime is not atheoretical, but it does not show the commitment to a particular theoretical perspective like that of Sutherland. Geis's writings are probably more accurately descriptive rather than theoretical, although his work does show awareness of various theoretical perspectives. The tendency toward description runs in two directions. First, Geis has written a number of "overview" papers that place white-collar crime in legal, historical, and social context. These papers are aimed at affirming the illegal quality of the acts, the serious consequences or harms from white-collar crimes, and the necessity to strengthen control efforts over this type of offending. Second, Geis has adopted a particularistic approach to his empirical work on white-collar crime. This approach relies heavily on the use of case studies of specific offenses or groups of offenses, such as the heavy electrical equipment conspiracy and physician fraud in California. The use of case studies and an examination of collections of case accounts may not lend itself to theory testing.

As a result, Geis does not tackle white-collar crime through the lenses of a particular theoretical agenda and, in fact, his specific theoretical approach may appear sometimes obscure. Much of his writings read as though they were written by an informed observer describing what he sees and little more. Such an approach may reflect his methodological allegiance to the muckrakers at the turn of the century, who were appalled at the negative consequences of power. But Geis's apparent theoretical eclectism doesn't get in the way of his research. Geis always is sensitive to the context in which the crimes occur and the larger picture of societal reaction and enforcement.

Historical and Intellectual Context

Throughout Geis's work, the theme of context is recurrent. Although trained as a sociologist, Geis draws from multidisciplinary sources and insights to create his vision and understanding of white-collar crime. These sources are varied and reflect, among other things, Geis's academic appointment in a multidisciplinary department since 1970, his keen appreciation for the nuances and insights found in literary sources, and a profound respect for the larger forces of culture, economics, politics, and history. It is difficult to identify the importance of context as an explicit theme in Geis's work, but he continually seeks to remind us that crime is ultimately related to place, time, and history. We make small excursions into understanding crime through empirical work, but most of that work is unrelated to other work and stands on its own.

Geis has never advocated doing scholarly work on the topic of white-collar crime; instead, he has suggested that *different types* of white-collar crime be studied individually so that common elements among types can be identified. He has attempted to do just this with his early work on economic white-collar crime and his later work on professional white-collar crime.

In his work on physician fraud, Geis and his colleagues (Jesilow, Pontell and Geis, 1993) attack a problem in white-collar crime that is especially troublesome. People in business are oriented toward the profit motive, and their illegal actions might be intuitively understandable given this self-serving orientation. People in the professions, however, are supposed to be oriented toward the needs of their clients, not self-interest. While we might not be surprised if a member of some occupation took advantage of consumers and we might even expect it from some occupations, professionals are supposed to be working for the greater good, for the needs and desires of their patients, students, and clients. They are supposed to have their main allegiance to the professional standards of law, medicine, education, pharmacy, or whatever professional group to which they belong. It is this other-orientation that reserves for professionals high status and income, as well as a high degree of occupational autonomy where professionals are evaluated by other professionals in the same profession rather than some outside agency.

The wayward physicians share important characteristics with other white-collar criminals. They are powerful, of high status, and seldom questioned, and their acts can have serious physical, financial, and social impacts. There is little doubt that physicians can and do violate the law, and these violations are screened by a cloak of respectability. In professionalism there is all sorts of room for mischief. Professionals may not be properly socialized about appropriate responses when faced with economic pressures. They may abuse their professional autonomy and are usually protected from public scrutiny by their social status. Furthermore, peer review may not be the best way to control professional miscreants if the controllers are themselves likely to be violators.

Geis understood that white-collar crime lacked the public outrage reserved for street crime. Like Sutherland, Geis has generally advocated the use of criminal sanctions where possible to control this behavior, but without public support or pressure it has seemed unlikely that individual white-collar criminals would face more than monetary sanctions, except in a few instances. Recent surveys show that the public increasingly believes white-collar crime is both serious and wrong. However, this shift in public attitudes has yet to translate into direct legislative attention; there has been no "getting tough" approach to white-collar crime found with street crime in the 1980s and 1990s. Yet, the populist beliefs that propelled Sutherland and to which Geis subscribes may yet yield criminal dividends in the future.

Geis's interest in types of white-collar crime, and even his seemingly separate work on witch trials (Geis and Bunn, 1997), reflects his keen eye for details and the importance of building a more general understanding from the actions of specific cases. Clearly, the stuff of criminology resides largely in the actions of specific individuals and the consequences of those actions on society and the legal system. It is a Sutherland legacy, to be sure, but it is a case that required the kind of sustained attention only given it by Geis.

CONCLUSION

White-collar crime is a popular topic. At present, there are college courses, textbooks, research monographs, research grants, a coterie of scholars who identify with the topic, and a public that has been more greatly informed by all of this work. Gilbert Geis is an important reason for all of this. Geis extended Sutherland's realism without pushing a theoretical agenda. He has striven to maintain the integrity of the subject of white-collar crime: illegal acts by individual criminals with discernible victims. While it is clear that there would be no study of white-collar crime without Sutherland's initial work, it should be equally clear that the field of white-collar crime would not have progressed to its present lofty state without the work of Gilbert Geis.

N O T E S

1. When Donald Cressey took over the book for the 1955 edition, he placed the theory of differential association, more modestly, as Chapter 4.

2. The definition Sutherland employs in his book is prefaced by the word *approximately,* an indication that he strove for a more broad conception of white-collar crime rather than a more narrow definition. There is another interpretation, certainly, of why Sutherland used the word *approximately:* Edwin Lemert (1972, 43–44) once asked Sutherland what he meant by the term *white-collar crime.* Sutherland replied that he was not exactly sure.

3. Clinard's research grew out of his work with the Office of Price Administration in Washington, D.C. from 1942 to 1945 where he was Chief of the Analysis and Reports Branch in the Enforcement Department. Hartung's article was a revision of his Ph.D. dissertation completed the previous year at the University of Michigan, perhaps the first doctoral dissertation on white-collar crime.

REFERENCES

Brickey, Kathleen F. 1995. *Corporate and White-Collar Crime: Cases and Materials.* 2nd ed. Boston: Little Brown.

Clinard, Marshall B. 1952. *The Black Market: A Study of White Collar Crime.* New York: Rinehart & Company.

Cressey, Donald R. 1953. *Other People's Money.* New York: Free Press.

Geis, Gilbert. 1967. "The Heavy Electrical Equipment Antitrust Cases of 1961." Pp. 139–150 in *Criminal Behavior Systems,* eds. Marshall B. Clinard and Richard Quinney. New York: Holt, Rinehart & Winston.

Geis, Gilbert. 1974. "Avocational Crime." Pp. 273–298 in *Handbook of Criminology,* ed. Daniel Glaser, Chicago: Rand McNally.

Geis, Gilbert, and Colin Goff. 1983. "Introduction" in *White Collar Crime: The Uncut Version,* ed. Edwin H. Sutherland, New Haven, CT: Yale University Press.

Geis, Gilbert, Robert F. Meier, and Lawrence S. Salinger, eds. 1995. *White-Collar Crime: Classic and Contemporary Views.* New York: Free Press.

Geis, Gilbert. 1995. "A Review, Rebuttal, and Reconciliation of Cressey and Braithwaite and Fisse on Criminological Theory and Corporate Crime." Pp. 399–428 in *The Legacy of Anomie Theory,* Freda Adler and William S. Laufer, eds., New Brunswick, NJ: Transaction.

Geis, Gilbert, and Ivan Bunn. 1997. *A Trial of Witches: A Seventeenth-Century Witchcraft Prosecution.* London: Routledge.

Gottfredson, Michael, and Travis Hirschi. 1990. *A General Theory of Crime.* Stanford, CT: Stanford University Press.

Hartung, Frank E. 1950. "White-Collar Offenses in the Wholesale Meat Industry in Detroit." *American Journal of Sociology,* 56: 25–35.

Jesilow, Paul, Henry Pontell, and Gilbert Geis. 1993. *Prescription for Profit: How Doctors Defraud Medicaid.* Berkeley: University of California Press.

Lemert, Edwin M. 1972. *Human Deviance, Social Problems, and Social Control,* 2nd ed. Upper Saddle River, NJ: Prentice-Hall.

Sutherland, Edwin H. 1940. "White-Collar Criminality." *American Sociological Review,* 5: 1–12.

Sutherland, Edwin. 1949. *White Collar Crime.* New York: Dryden.

Sutherland, Edwin H. 1973. *On Analyzing Crime.* Chicago: University of Chicago Press.

Tonry, Michael, and Albert J. Reiss, Jr., eds. 1993. *Beyond the Law: Crime in Complex Organizations.* Chicago: University of Chicago Press.

Wilson, James Q., and Richard Hernnstein. 1985. *Crime and Human Nature.*

II

THEORY AND METHOD IN CRIMINOLOGICAL RESEARCH

Conceptualizing Organizational Crime in a World of Plural Cultures

John Braithwaite

BEYOND WHITE COLLAR CRIME

Edwin Sutherland (1983) invented the term *white-collar crime,* changing not only the English language but criminology in a profound way. No longer was it possible for criminologists to present data based on police records to show that one neighborhood, one socioeconomic group, had a higher crime rate than another without the question being asked: "How would this result change if we took account of white-collar crime?" How could poverty be a cause of crime when business elites commit so much fraud? Sutherland rescued criminology from the conceptual confusion that arose from its systematic neglect of crimes of the powerful. It took the vigilance of Gilbert Geis (1982, 1984), the only scholar who consistently engaged with Sutherland's project through the '60s, '70s, '80s and '90s, to rescue criminology from Sutherland's own confusions and from constantly lapsing back to the study only of crimes of the powerless. But how should we conceptualize this perennially neglected terrain?

Should we talk of white collar crime or organizational crime or corporate crime? Or, instead of crime, should we talk of law-breaking (Reiss and Biderman, 1980), or deviance (Ermann and Lundman,1987), or violation of trust (Shapiro, 1990), or misconduct (Vaughan, 1988), or transgression (Michalowski and Kramer, 1987)? None of these definitional positions is necessarily an obstacle to good scholarship. What is an appropriate definition depends on one's purposes. If one is concerned about transnational corporations playing an international law-evasion game, then a definition of corporate "transgression" based on violations of United Nations codes may be appropriate. If one is concerned about a widely disapproved form of conduct, such as lying, which is not and should not be criminalized, then why not study "misconduct" or "violation of trust"?

So long as descriptions of the conduct are clear and rich, scholars can then confine inference to relevant data and ignore data not relevant to particular theoretical and policy projects.

Clearly for purposes of positive social science scholars require sharp definition of what counts as crime or deviance. In so much of this work large numbers of cases are ground through quantitative analysis in a way that renders impossible clear and detailed description of each case. Definitional clarity is our only assurance of sensible interpretation of what the data are about; it is vital for allowing replication. Quantitative data collected under neat definitional rubrics are valuable, but they are certainly not the only kind of valuable data. Aubert (1952, 266) has been the most influential advocate of ambiguous rather than neat definition:

> For purposes of theoretical analysis, it is of prime importance to develop and apply concepts which preserve and emphasize the ambiguous nature of white-collar crimes and not to "solve" the problem by classifying them as either "crimes" or "not crimes". Their controversial nature is exactly what makes them so interesting from a sociological point of view and what gives us a clue to important norm conflicts, clashing group interests, and maybe incipient social change.

From a policy analytic as well as from a sociological point of view, there may be virtue in problematizing whose law, whose ethics, and whose justice system we are interested in. This is especially so for those of us who think that effective social control is not so much about how the state enforces its law but about the nature of the interplay between government regulation and self-regulation, about whether public justice systems enfeeble or empower private justice systems.

PROBLEMATIZING THE ORGANIZATION

Just as with crime and deviance, there can be virtue in not being clear, in problematizing, just what the organization is that engages in the misconduct. When a Lockheed executive hands over a large sum of money to Adnan Khashoggi for him to use in paying off arms buyers, the choice of who is the criminal initiator of the bribe is not a simple one between the individual executive who hands over the money and the Lockheed corporation. It may be a subunit of the organization, say a division, seeking to advance its subunit interests in a way that is both against the interests of the organization as a whole and disapproved by top management of the organization. Sometimes when individual executives make corrupt payments to a politician, their behavior may manifest less about their membership of the corporation and more about their membership of a political organization that supports this politician. Sometimes when individual corporate executives resist a crime that is in the interests of the corporation, their resistance says more about their membership of a church or professional organization than about their roles as executives of their corporation.

To return to Lockheed, is the corporation that pays the bribe the better choice for the criminal or is the better choice an organization that extorts the bribe? Or is the real criminal the middle man who exaggerates the extortionate demands of the potential purchaser in order to line his own pockets? What if Mrs. Khashoggi was correct in her allegations that her husband made payoffs to Lockheed executives to get them to pay bribes to foreign governments through him (*Los Angeles Times*, 4 April, 1980)? So there is a case for blurring rather than sharpening definitions of responsible organizations, for analyzing offending in organizational contexts as social action by constellations of individuals, each one of whom has different bundles of organizational affiliations (Reiss, 1985).

PROBLEMATIZING THE STATE

The simplifying assumption that the corporation is a unitary actor for certain analytic purposes is worrying enough. But at least General Electric does have a board of directors as an ultimate authority to issue what can reasonably be described as decisions of the corporation. Not so with the state. By design the state has three relatively autonomous branches—the legislature, the executive, and the judiciary. In addition, in the regulatory arena, there are independent regulatory commissions that are not really independent, but that at least are relatively autonomous of the three branches of government.

For some analytic purposes it is useful to view the state as a unitary actor, even for some purposes to construe the state as having a unitary interest such as maximizing tax collections or winning wars. But it is more useful to view the state as an arena, a battleground where bureaucracies and factions of bureaucracies with very different conceptions of their interests and of the national interest contest the policy game.

Further, for many analytic purposes it is a mistake to theorize the state's justice system independently of private justice systems (Moore, 1978). Regulatory scholars would do well to contemplate the version of legal pluralism described in the work of Fitzpatrick (1983, 1984) and Henry (1983, 1985, 1987) as "integral plurality." This is a dialectical formulation (see also Galanter, 1981; Abel, 1982), recognizing that in any society there are many and diffuse forms of power generating their own forms of private justice. State justice systems and private justice systems are to some extent mutually constitutive. Thus, when the state seeks to regulate an aspect of private productive activity for the first time, it will typically look to "best practice" in the industry for guidance. The state law will often codify the practices that are sanctioned as acceptable and unacceptable within the private justice systems of "responsible" companies. Obversely, much private regulation is put in place to stave off state regulation, and therefore reflects the form of state law. These are just some of the ways that state law both coopts and is coopted by private justice forms.

It follows from such a version of legal pluralism that at every level there is virtue in ambiguating the definition of what is going on. Over the past decade my colleagues and I have observed hundreds of nursing home inspectors as they do their jobs. When we observe the inspector in dialogue with the director of nursing, we can view the inspector as an agent of the state enforcing state law, and the director of nursing as an agent of the corporation with the job of protecting its interests. But often we observe the two conspiring together against both the state law and the economic interests of the corporation. As they so conspire, they refer to "maintaining high nursing standards" and "the interests of the patient." We cannot analyze what is happening as the inspector being captured by the corporation or the director of nursing being captured by the state. Better to shift the definitions of the affiliations of these actors from the state and the corporation to their shared affiliation with the nursing profession. Best to shift attention somewhat from the state justice system to the private justice system of the nursing profession as a semiautonomous field (Moore, 1978).

THE CASE FOR DEFINITION
BASED ON THE LAW IN THE BOOKS

Having conceded that work under a variety of definitional frameworks can be of value, having argued that research that works with neatly sharpened definitions can be less important than work that problematizes, let us now consider how to operationalize the key construct when we do try to expand our knowledge via traditional positive social science methods.

In the context of positive social science, there is a special attraction of definitions based on the law in the books because of their superior capacity for consistent operationalization. Hard cases at the boundaries of definition are many because for some sharp operators it is a conscious strategy to play the game in the grey areas rather than in the black or the white. If we adopt the law in the books as definitional of crime, then we have recourse to the massive intellectual effort that has been devoted by the courts to developing more or less consistent ways of deciding hard cases. On the other hand, the scholar who attempts to count deviance or misconduct is on her own in grappling with the monumental problems of classifying the hard cases.

SUTHERLAND'S MESSY LEGACY

How then should we approach the problems of operationalizing organizational crime for quantitative work? Edwin Sutherland achieved two great things for criminology by inventing white-collar crime. He began a process of correcting systematic class bias in criminology, a discipline that had focused almost exclusively on the crimes of the powerless. Second, Sutherland forced a rejection of almost all criminological theory that had preceded him by pointing out that it flew in the face of the facts of the widespread nature of white-collar crime. But we must balance against these achievements the definitional mess Sutherland left in his wake. No scholar has operationalized Sutherland's definition to good effect. The definition was: White-collar crime is "crime committed by a person of respectability in the course of his occupation" (Sutherland, 1983, 7). The concept of respectability defies precision in use (Geis, 1984). Moreover, the requirement that a crime cannot be white collar unless perpetrated by a person of "high social status" is an unfortunate mixing of definition and explanation (Reiss and Biderman, 1980), especially when Sutherland used the widespread nature of white-collar crime to refute class-based theories of criminality.

The concept of organizational crime excludes that part of white-collar crime often defined as "occupational crime" (Clinard and Quinney, 1973), for example, embezzlement, Medicare fraud. But it also excludes crimes against organizations by poor individuals—social security fraud, credit card fraud. This gets us out of the most vexed definitional issue: should we adopt an offense-based definition of white-collar crime that can be operationalized in a way that results in most white-collar criminals having blue collars?

The most influential definition of organizational crime has been Schrager and Short's (1978): "Organizational crimes are illegal acts of omission or commission of an individual or a group of individuals in a legitimate formal organization in accordance with the operative goals of the organization, which have a serious physical or economic impact on employees, consumers or the general public." This is an unnecessarily complex definition. Why are the impacts limited to employees, consumers, or the general public? What about the environment or domestic animals (as in an animal welfare violations)? Why require "serious physical or economic impact" at all? Are unsuccessful attempts or conspiracies to be excluded? Are bribes that actually have beneficial economic consequences to be excluded? The phrase "In accordance with the operative goals of the organization" raises the question of the exclusion of crimes perpetrated in accordance with the operative goals of a subunit (the Australian subsidiary) but in defiance of the goals of the whole organization. Moreover, the definition needlessly locks us into a goal paradigm of organizational action.

All this argues for adaptation of the Schrager and Short (1978) definition to simplify operationalization problems by handing them over to the law and the courts. If the courts say it is an organizational crime for a pharmaceutical company to implant electrodes into the brain of a conscious monkey, then we count it as an organizational crime. So a simpler definition would be something like: "Organizational crime is crime perpetrated by formal organizations or by individuals acting on behalf of organizations." This definition makes no assumption that the crime is for gain (contrast Reiss and Biderman, 1980), this being viewed as a matter of explanation rather than definition. Moreover, it does not exclude organizational crimes that do physical harm to persons, as do definitions that restrict the scope to economic crime (e.g., Edelhertz, 1970; Leigh, 1980).

In his operationalization of white-collar crime Sutherland was content to consider illegal behavior as white-collar crime if it were punishable, even if not punished, and if the potential penalties provided for infringement were civil rather than criminal (Sutherland, 1983, 51). Tappan (1947) led a tradition insisting on proof beyond reasonable doubt in a criminal court before anything could be called a crime (see also Burgess, 1950; Orland, 1980).

Few today would refrain from taking Sutherland's side against the strong form of Tappan's (1947, 101) position that "adjudicated offenders represent the closest possible approximation to those who have in fact violated the law, carefully selected by sieving of the due process of law." For many purposes, data on arrests, crimes reported to the police, and self-reports on victim survey reports are accepted in mainstream criminology today as superior to data on convictions. The reasons criminologists pursue the "dark figure" of crime are all the more profound with white-collar crime, where offenses tend to be more difficult to detect and prove, and where the invisibility of offenses is enhanced by the reality that many victims of offenses such as price fixing and carcinogenic emissions to the environment are not aware that they have been harmed.

Tappan's position is untenable also because criminology must be concerned with the social forces implicated in the state selectively invoking the criminal label in some cases rather than others. In particular it must be concerned with why law enforcement in action is biased in favor of organizational actors in a way that the law in the books is not.

KEEPING THE PROBLEMATICS OF CRIME IN PERSPECTIVE

This essay opened with a plea for problematizing crime, deviance, and organizations and a plea for tolerance, for drawing strength from a chaos of competing definitional constructions. But I do not take this plea for problematics so far as agreeing with those who say that what is compliance with the law is such a situational social construction as to be beyond the grasp of positive social science.

It is possible for scholars who do adopt this position to accept the considerable consensus that most criminal laws should be criminal laws as revealed in the public opinion survey literature (Grabosky et al., 1987). But then they may say the following: "We might all agree that rape and environmental pollution offenses are terrible crimes in the abstract, but when people are confronted with concrete allegations there can be profound disagreement over what is rape and what is seduction, what is an environmental crime and what is an accident." It is of course true that what is a crime is socially defined through processes of situationally negotiating meanings from subjective interpretations of social action. Yet just as there is a tendency of positive quantitative criminology to underproblematize crime, there is a tendency of interpretive criminology to overproblematize it. The latter tendency arises from a methodological predilection to focus on the interpretive work of the offender.

What is a crime will always be contested by those accused of being criminals. Scholars who study the way offenders contest the social reality of crime risk a dangerous kind of political partisanship. One can study the perceptions of convicted rapists that what happened was seduction rather than rape, that the victim gave him the come on (Taylor, 1972), that she was his wife who had always liked such treatment before, and one can conclude from the persistent repetitions of such accounts that the crime is so ambiguous and contested as to be an ephemeral category of analysis. One can study the perceptions of business executives and their legal advisers that breaches of environmental or occupational health and safety laws of which they are convicted are not really crimes, and conclude that the law is inherently tentative rather than fixed and certain in these areas. Yet we should not forget that we are talking to actors who have an interest in rendering the law ambiguous. We could equally talk to feminists or victims about rape, trade unions about occupational health and safety offenses, environmental groups about pollution, to prosecutors or regulatory agencies. These constituencies might just as actively struggle to project clarity into the law as accused offenders struggle to project ambiguity.

It is an enormously valuable type of scholarship to study the struggle between those with an interest in clarifying and those with an interest in muddying the criminal–noncriminal distinction. My first concern is that we do not get carried away with the interpretive work being done on one side of that struggle in a way that leads us to misperceive the criminal law as nothing but shifting sand. Rather, the product of that interpretive struggle is a core area of uncontroversially criminal conduct with a fringe of shifting sand of varying widths, depending on the domain of law—wide with tax law, narrow with weights and measures offenses.

To get at that uncontroversial core of the criminal law, one might do better than to tap the perceptions of either rapists on the defensive or feminists on the offensive. One might be more interested in the interpretive work of actors who are in a kind of Rawlsian original position—who do not bring a history of personal interest to their interpretive work, which inclines them to want particular cases to be either ambiguous or clear. Where do we find such people and how do we study them? This line of thought might lead us to a remarkable discovery—the judge and jury! Moreover, the interpretive work that matters is that which constitutes the content of the law in practical institutional contexts, which are the arenas where law is made.

There is, then, a contradiction in studying the views of those with an interest in problematizing the law to study the problematics of legal definition. Interestingly, when we put offenders in more of an "original position" by asking them about how they interpret the delinquencies of their children rather than their own crimes, all the evidence is that they disapprove of delinquency in a similar way to law-abiding parents, rather than excuse it as problematic (e.g., West, 1982, 49).

The study of how offenders problematize the criminal law is valuable for a number of reasons. It helps illuminate how conflict over the content of the law unfolds; it engenders an appreciative stance toward the offender; and it sensitizes us to the possibility that crime is a more problematic category than we might otherwise concede. All I am saying is that on this last score, we should be wary of the partisanship of taking the offender's perception of the problematic nature of the law as definitive. The most valuable contribution of this style of research is not in the way it can undermine the possibility of explanatory criminological theory, but in the way it can contribute toward it.

Most of us refrain from crime most of the time because to seize the criminal opportunity is unthinkable to us—we would not consider beginning to calculate the costs and benefits of committing murder, rape, or a Love Canal disaster. Studying the views of criminals on how the law seems so problematic to them is one route to understanding why a particular crime was thinkable to them in a way it is not to others. Far from defeating the mission of explanatory theory building, interpretive sociology should be one of the most important tools of the theory builder's trade.

In suggesting that we rely essentially on the definitional work of legislatures and the interpretive work of judges and juries in deciding what is organizational crime, I am certainly not advocating a return to Tappan. Rather, what I would have us do is use the law-making of legislatures and the interpretive work of judges and juries to locate that consensual core area of the criminal law, which is not shifting sand. Then one can begin to face the challenge of operationalizing white-collar crime in a way that will generate a cumulative body of positive social science data that can be used to build theories of organizational crime.

TIGHTENING UP SUTHERLAND

This might imply a limited parting of company with Sutherland's view that "A combination of two abstract criteria is generally regarded by legal scholars as necessary to define crime; namely, legal description of an act as socially injurious and legal provision of penalty for the act" (Sutherland, 1945, 133). Sutherland's definition excludes torts for which the law provides only for remedy by compensation, but it includes civil breaches of the law for which punitive damages are provided and civil offenses for which noncriminal penalties can be applied. This may be an insufficiently cautious approach to ensuring that the definition is confined within the core area of consensus. On the other hand, one suspects that the community is insensitive to lawyers' distinctions between criminal and civil penalties because, as Sutherland pointed out, the differences tend to be unprincipled and arbitrary. Under the Australian Trade Practices Act, antitrust offenses need only be proved on the balance of probabilities and are sanctioned by "pecuniary penalties," while consumer protection offenses in the same act must be proved beyond reasonable doubt and are punished by criminal fines. Yet the maximum "pecuniary penalties" provided for the former are ten times the maximum criminal fines provided for the latter! Little wonder then that Australian journalists invariably report antitrust cases as "prosecutions," which result in "fines" for those "convicted." But the suspicion that the community views civil penalties imposed on organizational law breakers as in the same moral category as criminal fines is only a suspicion. Until systematic empirical work is done to show that this is the case, we are probably best to reject Sutherland's advice and limit the definition of organizational crime to criminal violations.

OPERATIONALIZATION BY CIVIL ADJUDICATION

Does this mean that research that measures rates of organizational crime by counting impositions of civil penalties should be ignored? Certainly not. So long as the civil penalty proceedings relate to forms of conduct that could have been prosecuted criminally, civil penalties data are in fact comparatively good. They are superior to arrests, police reports, self-reports, or victim survey results in the sense that there has at least been a formal adjudication that found the law was violated, if only adjudication to a balance of probabilities standard. In the American legal system most civil penalty proceedings against business are for forms of conduct for which, if the prosecution could only prove criminal intent beyond reasonable doubt, they could proceed criminally. Moreover, in areas such as occupational health and safety and environmental protection, American civil penalty proceedings are generally for forms of conduct that are dealt with as strict liability criminal offenses in British Commonwealth countries. So there is an international comparability dimension to the debate.

To adopt the view that civil adjudications of guilt should not be taken as evidence of crime is to constrain criminology with class-biased methods. This is so because a characteristic of the mobilization of law is that power is exercised such that ruling-class crimes are diverted to civil adjudication much more than working-class crimes.

This, however, does not justify counting either civilly adjudicated or voluntary recalls of dangerous products in operationalizing white-collar crime. Even a governmentally mandated recall by no means implies that the law was breached, and the action taken is remedial rather than punitive. Such administrative actions are therefore not even a satisfactory way of operationalizing Sutherland's definition. The inclusion of this particular form of administrative action was a weakness of the classic Clinard and Yeager (1980) study.

OPERATIONALIZATION BY QUALITATIVE METHODS

For many purposes, it will be preferable for the organizational crime researcher to attempt to get closer to the reality of the level of crime by relying on self-reports such as the data on bribery revealed by the Securities and Exchange Commission's voluntary disclosure program of the 1970s (U.S. Senate, 1976; Herlihy and Levine, 1976). Self-reports of white-collar crime can also be obtained by unstructured interview research (e.g., Braithwaite, 1985). Then there is the possibility of observational studies of offending or of enforcement directed at offending (e.g., Hawkins, 1984).

It is unfair to criticize a researcher for analyzing the Ford Pinto case as if it has some relevance to our understanding of organizational crime because Ford was acquitted of homicide. It is possible for scholars who have worked on the Pinto case to have the view that the jury was right to acquit Ford in the particular case that was brought to trial (because of particular circumstances of that case) but that if another instance of an exploding gas tank had been tried the result would have been different. I know scholars of the case who, rightly or wrongly, have this view. The Ford Pinto case is a troubling one precisely because this view may be wrong (Lee and Ermann, 1999). The point is that we cannot expect researchers who have that view about why their case study is of organizational crime to come clean and openly argue for it in print. I have had enough threats of lawsuits from large corporations to come counsel them against this. All they need do is describe the facts as they found them and leave it to others to make the judgment whether the findings constitute a contribution to our knowledge about organizational crime.

To some extent we simply must tolerate this state of affairs if we are to rectify the class bias of empirical criminology. In deciding to tolerate some definitional inexplicitness with respect to white-collar crime, we should also be mindful of tolerance of it in mainstream criminology. We would not necessarily disapprove of a qualitative gang researcher reporting how an observed delinquent act unfolded even though the actor was subsequently acquitted on certain charges relating to the behavior.

Some readers will think this much ado about nothing. What one ought to do is simply study social control—analyze cases of social disapproval being mobilized in the community in different ways such as by media moralizing, regulation, or criminalization. One does the research because one is interested in understanding the different ways that social control is mobilized, why it is mobilized in some cases and not others, why it is patterned the way it is, and what the consequences of these different modalities of control are. There is of course a great deal to be said for doing research for these reasons. However, there is also something to be said for generating data that will inform theories of crime. If it is theories of crime that we want rather than theories of social control or of the mobilization of law, then we must study phenomena that fit the definition of crime. If we want our scholarship to make a contribution toward the control of crime, then we are also required to generate data that fit the definition of crime. To the extent that it is the latter purposes we wish to serve with our research, then the very great difficulties of definition and operationalization discussed in this article cannot be ducked.

The greatest intellectual dishonesty is to side-step the question of what is crime by orienting one's work as a study of social control or of the sociology of law, and then drawing inferences from the work concerning the explanation of crime or suggesting from it causal propositions about the effects of certain policies on organizational crime.

GETTING ON WITH THE JOB

When we do qualitative work, the important thing is that our description be thick, fair, eliciting the contrary social constructions of what happened embraced by different actors. Then we can be true to the aspiration set by Aubert for our scholarship. Equally, by doing this we best serve explanatory social science. The positive social scientist can then go to our data and make her own judgment: "Yes, I am persuaded that this should count as a case of crime" for purposes of refuting a particular theory. Or perhaps, "No, this does not satisfy the requirements of a definition of organizational crime, but it does satisfy the requirements of a definition of organizational 'transgression,'" and can be used with other cases to refute a theory about organizational transgression.

We have advanced a number of grounds for tolerance of definitional chaos in our field and for work that problematizes definitional orthodoxy. These include the need to be open to multiple moralities, the need for an appreciative stance toward the offender, to understand the politics of conflict over different conceptions of wrongdoing and the role of the power over definition in it, and the need to understand how definitions change historically and cross-culturally.

For the purposes of explanatory theory, I have argued a preference for violations of the criminal law as the foundation for defining organizational crime as the key dependent variable. The statute books and case law supply the most passably coherent and consensually accepted definition in contemporary democracies. Until it can be shown empirically that civil penalty impositions are in the same moral category, sharing in the community consensus over the seriousness of organizational crime, it is best to reject Sutherland's position that only a legal description of an act as socially injurious and legal provision of penalty for the act are needed to regard conduct as crime.

Apart from this, we might take Sutherland's side against Tappan, operationalizing crime as behavior that is criminally punishable but not necessarily criminally punished. This renders permissible the operationalization of organizational crime by civil adjudication, self-report, and observational methods. Despite the difficulties, greater attention must be directed to ensuring a correspondence between the behaviors analyzed by these methods and that which is criminally punishable.

FROM CONCEPT TO THEORY

So far I have not stated a fundamental reason for advocating this dialectic within our research community between work that problematizes definitions and work within a positive tradition where definitions are sharpened by conformity to law. The reason is that we can see fertile theoretical and policy advances down both tracks, and even more fertile possibilities if both paths are pursued to the point where they constructively intersect.

Sutherland's project of a unified theory of crime that can account for both common crime and white-collar crime continues to be the most exciting one in criminology. Some bold contributions have been made to this enterprise (e.g., Cohen and Machalek, 1988; Gottfredson and Hirschi, 1987). Elsewhere I have argued at length that much conventional criminological theory can be adapted to the explanation of organizational crime (Braithwaite, 1989a,b). In our enthusiasm for debunking theories that ignore the widespread nature of organizational crime, we have mostly failed to take seriously the challenge of building theories that do.

My own preference is for theory that construes processes of shaming as central to understanding variation in rates of both common and organizational crime. In *Crime, Shame and Reintegration* I argue that shaming can be counterproductive, making crime problems worse. The key to why some societies have higher crime rates than others lies in the way different cultures go about the social process of disapproving wrongdoing. When disapproval is communicated within a cultural context of respect for the offender, as opposed to stigmatization of the offender, shaming can be an extraordinarily powerful, efficient, and just form of social control.

If this is a fertile field to plough, it implies attraction to the criminal law as the basis of definition. This is because violation of the criminal law is uniquely designed to be shameful or stigmatic, and for most people in most cultures it is to some degree so perceived. When actors know that a particular way of behaving is a crime, the choice to engage in that form of conduct takes on a very different meaning to them from other behavioral choices. If shaming is crucial to understanding variations in misconduct, then violation of the criminal law is likely to be the best definitional foundation on which we can build.

The role of the state in conferring the shameful status of crime on certain forms of misconduct is crucial. But at the same time it is clear that the most potent forms of shaming are not those undertaken by the state, but those of intimates. Thus following this theoretical path implies both an interest in crime as defined by the state and pursuit of the problematics of how wrongdoing is socially constructed in informal processes of social control.

My position here is not so different from that of Habermas (1986) when he complains of legalization supplanting communicative action with legal norms. Habermas argues for a shift in the way we view law, from law as regulator toward law as "institution," with laws functioning as "external constitutions." Rather than enforcing norms, the law sets down procedural guidelines for informal settlements that facilitate communicative action. Niklas Luhmann (1986), like Habermas, is concerned about an overproduction of positive law, about attempts to impose the rationality of the legal subsystem on other subsystems in the society. A crisis of the contemporary regulatory state occurs because the legal subsystem is unresponsive to the patterns of life in the other subsystems it tries to regulate.

The solution according to Luhmann and Teubner (1983) is relexion, an approach where each subsystem internally restricts itself, thereby enabling integration with other subsystems. For the control of organizational crime, reflexive law means the legal system empowering and enabling self-regulation. Close American resonances with this Continental tradition are Nonet and Selznick's (1978) responsive law and Sigler and Murphy's (1988) Interactive Corporate Compliance (see also Frank and Lombness, 1988). So is the cooperative regulation tradition that one sees in the work of Schlotz (1984a, 1984b), Bardach and Kagan (1982), and in different ways in the work of the Oxford regulation scholars (Hawkins, 1984; Baldwin and Hawkins, 1984) and the work of our Australian group on the interaction between government regulation and self-regulation. (Fisse and Braithwaite, 1988, 1993; Braithwaite, Grabosky, and Fisse, 1986; Fisse and French, 1985; Ayres and Braithwaite, 1992; Gunningham and Grabosky, 1998). This all means taking self-regulation and business ethics seriously as the crucial mediators of regulatory effectiveness rather than as subjects to be sneering and cynical about.

There are in fact a disparate array of emerging scholarly traditions that converge on the need to view law as constitution rather than medium, on the need for flexibility, discretion, and exploration of ambiguity. Joel Handler (1988) has masterfully depicted how this convergence can arise from the attack on formalism and liberal legalism that one can discern in business regulatory scholarship, the new scholarship on the regulation of dependent people, alternative dispute resolution, feminist jurisprudence, Critical Legal Studies, Continental reflexive law, and modern/postmodern communitarian moral philosophy. The emerging theoretical currents are exciting and challenging.

I have not had space to say anything of analytical value about them here except this. Reaping their rewards requires an openness to ambiguity in the way we define our terms. I concur with Donald Levine (1985) that one of the problems of Western social science has been The Flight from Ambiguity. We would do well to reverse the tendency in positive social science discourse to root out metaphor, irony, and analogy. In the natural sciences as well as the social sciences progress can be hastened by valuing language for "being vivid and evocative more than for its denotational precision." (Levine, 1985, 1).

> Darwinian theory will not resolve to a single significance nor yield a single pattern. It is essentially multivalent. It renounces a Descartian clarity, or univocality. Darwin's methods of argument and the generative metaphors of The Origin lead ... into profusion and extension. The unused, or uncontrolled, elements in metaphors such as "the struggle for existence" take on a life of their own. They surpass their status in the text and generate further ideas and ideologies. They include "more than the maker of them at the time knew." (Beer, 1983, 9).

At the same time I have argued, like Levine, that the appreciation of ambiguity has its limits: "it must be linked to a willingness and an ability to press toward disambiguation at appropriate moments" (Levine, 1985, 219). The form of disambiguation I have advocated is operationalization of organizational crime according to the law in the books, and the appropriate contexts suggested for disambiguation are those where we seek to build and test explanatory theories of crime.

REFERENCES

Abel, Richard 1982. *The Politics of Informal Justice.* Vol. I. New York: Academic Press.

Ayres, Ian, and John Braithwaite. 1992. *Responsive Regulation: Transcending the Deregulation Debate.* Oxford: Oxford University Press.

Aubert, Vilhelm. 1952. "White-Collar Crime and Social Structure." *American Journal of Sociology* 58:263-71.

Baldwin, Robert, and Keith Hawkins. 1984. "Discretionary Justice: Davis Reconsidered." *Public Law* 1984:570-99.

Bardach, Eugene, and Robert A. Kagan. 1982. *Going By the Book: The Problem of Regulatory Unreasonableness.* Philadelphia: Temple University Press.

Beer, Gillian. 1983. *Darwin's Plots.* London: Routledge and Kegan Paul.

Braithwaite, John. 1985 "Corporate Crime Research: Why two Interviewers are Needed." *Sociology* 19:136-8.

Braithwaite, John. 1989a. *Crime, Shame and Reintegration.* Sydney: Cambridge University Press.

Braithwaite, John 1989b. "Criminological Theory and Organizational Crime." *Justice Quarterly* 6:333-358.

Braithwaite, John, Peter Grabosky, and Brent Fisse. 1986. Occupational Health and Safety Enforcement Guidelines: Report to the Victorian Department of Labour. Melbourne.

Burgess, E.W. 1950. "Comment." *American Journal of Sociology* 56:34.

Clinard, Marshall, and Richard Quinney. 1973. *Criminal Behavior Systems: A Typology.* New York: Holt, Rinehart & Winston.

Clinard, Marshall, and Peter Yeager. 1980. *Corporate Crime.* New York: Free Press.

Cohen, Lawrence E., and Richard Machalek. 1988. "A General Theory of Expropriative Crime: An Evolutionary Ecological Approach." *American Journal of Sociology* 94:465-501.

Edelhertz, Herbert. 1970. *The Nature, Impact and Prosecution of White Collar Crime.* Washington, D.C.: National Institute of Law Enforcement and Criminal Justice.

Ermann, M. David, and Richard J. Lundman. 1987. *Corporate and Governmental Deviance.* 3rd ed. New York: Oxford University Press.

Fisse, Brent, and Peter French. 1985. "Corporate Responses to Errant Behaviour: Time's Arrow, Law's Target," in *Corrigible Corporations and Unruly Law.* eds. B. Fisse and P. French. San Antonio: Trinity University Press.

Fisse, Brent, and John Braithwaite. 1983. *The Impact of Publicity on Corporate Offenders.* Albany: State University of New York Press.

Fisse, Brent, and John Braithwaite. 1988. "Accountability and the Control of Corporate Crime: Making the Buck Stop," in *Understanding Crime and Criminal Justice.* eds. Mark Findlay and Russell Hogg. Sydney: Law Book Company.

Fisse, Brent, and John Braithwaite. 1993. *Corporations, Crime and Accountability.* Cambridge: Cambridge University Press.

Fitzpatrick, Peter. 1983. "Law, Plurality and Underdevelopment" in *Legality, Ideology and the State.* ed. D. Sugarman. London: Academic Press.

Fitzpatrick, Peter. 1984. "Law and Societies." *Osgood Hall Law Journal* 22:115-128.

Frank, Nancy, and Michael Lombness. 1988. *Controlling Corporate Illegality: The Regulatory Justice System.* Cincinnati: Anderson.

Galanter, Mark. 1981. "Justice in Many Rooms: Courts, Private Ordering and Indigenous Law." *Journal of Legal Pluralism* 19:1-47.

Geis, Gilbert. 1982. *On White-Collar Crime.* Lexington, Mass: Lexington Books.

Geis, Gilbert 1984. "White-collar and Corporate Crime," in *Major Forms of Crime* ed. R.F. Meier, Beverly Hills: Sage.

Gottfredson, Michael, and Travis Hirschi. 1987. "The Causes of White Collar Crime." Paper to Annual Meeting of American Society of Criminology, Montreal.

Grabosky, Peter N, John Braithwaite, and Paul R. Wilson. 1987. "The Myth of Community Tolerance Toward White-Collar Crime." *Australian and New Zealand Journal of Criminology* 20:33-44.

Gunningham, Neil, and Peter Grabosky. 1998. *Smart Regulation: Designing Environmental Policy.* Oxford: Clarendon Press.

Habermas, Jurgen. 1986. "Law as Medium and Law as Institution," in *Dilemmas of Law in the Welfare State.* ed. G. Teubner. Berlin: Walter de Gruyter.

Handler, Joel 1988. "Dependent People, the State, and the Modern/Postmodern Search for the Dialogic Community." *UCLA Law Review* 35:999-1113.

Hawkins, Keith. 1984. *Environment and Enforcement: Regulation and the Social Definition of Pollution.* Oxford: Clarendon.

Henry, Stuart. 1983. *Private Justice: Toward Integrated Theorising in the Sociology of Law.* London: Routledge and Kegan Paul.

Henry, Stuart. 1985. "Community Justice, Capitalist Society, and Human Agency: The Dialectics of Collective Law in the Cooperative." *Law and Society Review* 19:303-27.

Henry, Stuart. 1987. "Private Justice and the Policing of Labor: The Dialectics of Industrial Discipline." In *Private Policing.* eds. C. D. Shearing and P.C. Stenning. Beverly Hills: Sage.

Herlihy, Edward D., and Theodore A. Levine. 1976. "Corporate Crisis: The Overseas Payment Problem," *Law and Policy in International Business* 8:552.

Lee, Matthew T., and M. David Ermann. 1999. "Pinto 'Madness' as a Flawed Landmark Narrative: An Organizational and Network Analysis." *Social Problems* 46:30-47.

Leigh, Leonard. 1980. *Economic Crime in Europe.* London: Macmillan.

Levine, Donald. 1985. *The Flight from Ambiguity: Essays in Social and Cultural Theory.* Chicago: University of Chicago Press.

Luhmann, Niklas. 1986. "The Self-reproduction of Law and its Limits." In *Dilemmas of Law in the Welfare State.* ed. G. Teubner. Berlin: Walter de Gruyter.

Michalowski, Raymond J., and Ronald C. Kramer 1987. "The Space Between Laws: The Problem of Corporate Crime in a Transnational Context," *Social Problems* 34:34-53.

Moore, Sally Falk. 1978. *Law as Process: An Anthropological Approach.* London: Routledge and Kegan Paul.

Nonet, Philippe, and Philip Selznick. 1978. *Law and Society in Transition: Toward Responsive Law.* Harper: New York.

Orland, Leonard. 1980. "Reflections on Corporate Crime: 'Law in Search of Theory and Scholarship'." *American Criminal Law Review* 17:501-20.

Reiss, Albert J. 1984. "The Control of Organizational Life." In *Perspectives in Criminal Law.* eds. A.N. Doob and E.L. Greenspan. Aurora: Canada Law Book.

Reiss, Albert J., and A. Biderman. 1980. *Data Sources on White-Collar Law Breaking.* Washington D.C.: U.S. Govt. Printing Office.

Scholtz, John T. 1984a "Deterrence, Cooperation and the Ecology of Regulatory Enforcement." *Law and Society Review* 18:179-224.

Scholtz, John T. 1984b. "Voluntary Compliance and Regulatory Policy." *Law and Policy* 6:385-404.

Schrager, Laura S., and James F. Short. 1978. "Toward a Sociology of Organizational Crime." *Social Problems* 25:406-19.

Shapiro, Susan. 1987. "The Social Control of Impersonal Trust." *American Journal of Sociology* 93:623-58.

Sigler, Jay A., and Joseph E. Murphy. 1988. *Interactive Corporate Compliance: An Alternative to Regulatory Compulsion.* New York: Quorum Books.

Sutherland, Edwin H. 1945. "Is 'White-Collar Crime' Crime?" *American Sociological Review* 10:132-39.

Sutherland, Edwin H. 1983. *White Collar Crime: The Uncut Version.* New Haven: Yale University Press.

Tappan, Paul W. 1947. "Who Is the Criminal?" *American Sociological Review* 12:96-102.

Taylor, Laurie. 1972. "The Significance and Interpretation of Replies to Motivational Questions: The Case of Sex Offenders." *Sociology* 6:23-39.

Teubner, Gunter. "Substantive and Reflexive Elements in Modern Law." *Law and Society Review* 17:239-85.

U.S. Senate 1976. Report of the Securities and Exchange Commission on Questionable and Illegal Corporate Payments and Practices: Hearings of Banking, Housing and Urban Affairs Committee, 94th Cong., 2nd Sess.

Vaughan, Diane 1988. "Organizational Misconduct: A Method for Theory Elaboration." Paper to American Society of Criminology Meeting, Chicago.

West, Donald J. 1982. *Delinquency: Its Roots, Careers and Prospects.* London: Heinemann.

The Relationship Between Research Results and Public Policy

Arnold Binder
Virginia L. Binder

❖

GOALS OF RESEARCH

Rosenberg (1988) has presented two ways of conceiving the goal of social science: improving prediction or increasing intelligibility. The latter does provide an epistemological basis for many branches of the social sciences, such as anthropology and urban sociology. But prediction is central for social scientists (Rosenberg 1988, 197, 198) "interested in knowledge that can be applied to informing social. . .policy, that can be used to predict the consequences of planning or its absence."

Not only is it likely that most criminologists would subscribe to the goal of improving prediction generally, but the use of their research results for purposes of recommending policy directions has been a focus from the earliest days. Indeed, as Petersilia (1991, 2) has pointed out in her Presidential Address before the American Society of Criminology [ASC], the formation of criminology as a field of study and the foundation of the ASC were "strongly grounded in practical concerns of the criminal justice system." Moreover, she argues in her concluding statement (1991, 14); "[Criminology] is defined by a major social phenomenon—crime—and the system and agencies established to address that phenomenon," and that, consequently, criminologists should be policy-directed in their research. Similarly, two years later, Blumstein (1993, 1) argued in his Presidential Address to the same body that "an important mission of the ASC and its members involves the generation of knowledge that is useful in dealing with

33

crime and the operation of the criminal justice system. . .and then helping public officials to use that knowledge intelligently and effectively. . ."

DISSEMINATION OF RESEARCH KNOWLEDGE

There is a substantial body of well-established factual knowledge in criminology. No rational person would, for example, doubt that males in the age range 15 to 24 commit serious crimes at a considerably higher rate than people in other comparable age and gender brackets, that the expense of incarceration increases with age, or that the arrest rate for drug offenses has been higher for nonwhites than for whites. One can feel safe in using such information to guide policy makers, as, for example, to a strategy of crime control that does not lead to a policy of filling prison cells with old people (see Skolnick, 1995). On the other hand, the theoretical structures in criminology are wobbly and there is new information generated regularly, as reported in the many avenues of publication used by criminologists and by noncriminologists doing research in crime-related areas. There is, moreover, an obvious interaction between theory and information generation in that new information is obtained in the context of awareness of, or even testing of, a poorly anchored theory, and the scientific method involves repeated investigations to confirm findings and to strengthen theoretical positions.

The process of scientific advancement flows more or less as follows: a novel result is found, the investigator publishes the relevant study, then other investigators replicate the study under identical or similar conditions. Given the accepted role of criminologists to influence public policy, as discussed above, where in the process of accumulating new knowledge is it appropriate to use that knowledge to guide or influence policy-makers in appropriate directions?

Suppose, to illustrate, a well-controlled experiment were conducted and it was found that juveniles who were immediately taken into custody ("arrested") for minor assaultive or violent behavior were proportionately less likely to repeat the behavior than juveniles who were counseled and released to parents. Would you recommend, on the basis of the results of the experiment, that police departments arrest youngsters who show minor assaultive or violent behavior, even if the behavior is as minor as smashing a teacup at the foot of the victim? Surely you would not.

EMPIRICAL RESULTS, SALESMANSHIP, AND PUBLIC POLICY

Yet, Sherman and Berk (1984) did indeed conduct that sort of experiment in Minneapolis, reported the results in the literature, and simultaneously conducted a campaign urging police departments throughout the country to adopt a policy of presumptive arrest in cases of domestic violence/assault. An essential difference between the general opposition one would expect in the case of arresting youths for minor violence and the general advocacy of Sherman and Beck (and the widespread acceptance of that advocacy) was one of political correctness. With the forceful support of women's advocacy groups and general societal feelings about the matter, it was easier to recommend arresting spousal abusers, no matter how minor, as Sherman and Berk did on the basis of one flimsy study, than to recommend the arrest of youths similarly. For a picture of just how flimsy the study and its conclusions were, see Binder and Meeker (1988), Binder and Meeker (1992), and Binder and Meeker (1993).

Indeed, later research did not confirm the general findings of Sherman and Berk, but there was of course not a parallel campaign to urge police departments to halt the arrest practices (e.g., see Pate and Hamilton, 1992). Note, too, the following conclusion from an article published eight years after the initial report in which one of the original investigators was a participant (Berk et al. 1992, 706):

> What then are the policy implications [of subsequent research based on the Sherman and Berk results]? First, there is some evidence that arrest works better for some suspects than others. However, the case is hardly overwhelming, and its meaning unclear. Therefore, we believe that there are no direct policy implications except for the general warning that a particular arrest will not necessarily lead to a beneficial outcome.

Nevertheless, as a result of the publication of the initial results and the conspicuous dissemination, many men were subjected to arrest with unknown general consequences for them, their mates, and, perhaps, their families. Here is the summary phrasing following a very critical evaluation of the Minneapolis experiment by Binder and Meeker (1988, 356):

> Although the Minneapolis study represents a reasonable first effort to determine the effects of various police responses in domestic violence situations, the results are far too inconclusive to justify the impact it has had on police departments across the nation. Clearly there is little justification for statements [in the propaganda pamphlet prepared by Sherman and Berk for the Police Foundation] such as the following, "and on the basis of this study alone, police should probably employ arrest in most cases of minor domestic violence."

Here is another example of strong advocacy that the results of a single study be used for wide-range implementation. Haney, Banks, and Zimbardo (1973)—the psychological researchers behind the highly controversial Stanford Prison Experiment—arranged for a slide-show, allowed television coverage, and provided Senate testimony about their results. Though the study was prematurely discontinued because of the negative effects on the "normal" college student participants, the researchers believed such dramatic effects provided even stronger evidence for their premise that prison behavior results from the demands of the situation rather than the personalities of the guards or prisoners. In defense of the study, which was challenged on both methodological and ethical grounds, Zimbardo (1973) noted as positive outcomes the wide media coverage, including features on national television, in *Life* magazine and the *New York Times Magazine*, an invitation to appear before a Senate subcommittee, and numerous public speaking engagements. He points out with obvious pleasure that he has provided supporting evidence for a class action lawsuit against the New York State Department of Corrections and for legal action to prevent the construction of a large prison complex in California, and that he served as a consultant for a project designed to reform the juvenile delinquency facilities in Louisiana. All of this resulted from a dramatic, but incomplete single study that could not be replicated because of the ethical issues involved. Surprisingly, in a review of the impact of the study and the status of the field 25 years later, Haney and Zimbardo (1998) argue that their study had insufficient impact and recommend broad policy changes based on the results.

The following is *still another* example of active leap from research to recommended policy on the basis of a single, and utterly inadequate, compilation of data. This was an evaluation of state and local programs aimed at crime prevention that was "congressionally mandated." In addition to being a report to Congress, there was a "Target Audience" designated as consisting of "Federal, State and local policymakers; criminal and juvenile justice professionals, practitioners, and researchers; educators, and leaders of community organizations promoting prevention of crime, juvenile delinquency, and drug abuse" (Sherman et al. 1998, 1, 2). Clearly the investigators expected substantial impact on a wide basis because of the supposed importance of their analyses. The reporters (1998, 3), immodestly (and inaccurately), argue that "all conclusions reported in this Research in Brief reflect the state of scientific knowledge as of late 1996 when the initial review was concluded." The search for relevant evidence was based overwhelmingly on (1998, 4) "evaluations that had been published in scientific journals. . .several reviews of such studies. . .[and] some unpublished evaluations." There was emphasis on the "mainstream outlets in criminology."

Notice the anomaly in two contrasting quotes from the report (Sherman et al. 1998, 12):

- The central conclusion of the report is that the current development of scientific evidence is inadequate to the task of policymaking. Many more impact evaluations using stronger scientific methods are needed before even minimally valid conclusions can be reached about the impact on crime of programs costing billions each year.
- More than 20,000 copies of the full report have been downloaded from the Internet, with governors, State legislatures, congressional committees, and several other nations requesting briefings on the results in the first year after the full report was submitted to Congress. The United Kingdom has relied heavily on this report in drafting its new strategy for reducing crime.

In short, the reviewers admit to the inadequacy of data in a survey, but are delighted that its results are being used widely by policymakers. As an additional source of doubt, certain important evaluations of criminological interventions, using sound research designs, have appeared in books prior to 1996 outside of the criminology/criminal justice area, and there is no evidence that they were used in the evaluative process of Sherman et al. despite their argument that the report reflects "the state of scientific knowledge as of late 1996." Examples are the important contribution in juvenile diversion by Davidson et al. (1990); the findings of the promising research of Henggeler and colleagues (1992, 1993), reported in psychological journals, using a multisystemic treatment approach with serious juvenile offenders; and a review of the literature by Mulvey, Arthur, and Reppuci (1993) on the prevention and treatment of juvenile delinquency in another major clinical psychology journal.

Finally, The Rahway State Prison Juvenile Awareness Project (often referred to as "Scared Straight"), though originated and publicized by practitioners in conjunction with prisoners, provides a dramatic example of the willingness of those working in the field to adopt an appealing program and the difficulties encountered trying to derail the implementation of such a widely adopted program. Practitioners were captivated with the ease, efficiency, and modest cost of cutting delinquency by exposing juveniles to encounters with "lifers" in prison along with the harshness of the prison environment. Revelation of the lack of evidence for the initial successes claimed by the organizers of the program, as well as follow-up research showing that exposure to prison experiences may actually increase the rate of delinquent activities and have a negative and demeaning impact on the young visitors (Lundman, 1984), made little impact as programs were still being initiated several years after the follow-up findings appeared.

And, just as the support of the women's movement unquestionably added to the ease of disseminating the results of the Sherman and Beck research, Heeren and Shichor (1984) believe that both the public concern with the increasing crime rate and the eagerness for a "get tough" model in dealing with crime fostered the enthusiasm of many to adopt a quick fix by copying the "Scared Straight" approach.

Clearly, in each of the above examples there was a leap based on the results of very early work, often with a very active advocacy on the part of the investigators and occasionally with most unfortunate results. Wellford (1997, 3) summarized the state of affairs nicely as follows:

> . . .we should be concerned about the fact that we have far more impact on public policy than we deserve. Someone produces a modestly adequate piece of research demonstrating that some type of program has some kind of positive effect on some kind of crime in some place for some limited time, and suddenly the program is adopted as a national model. . . Later on . . .we conduct some evaluation research and demonstrate that the program has very modest, if any, consequences and yet the program continues to be used.

Similarly, Petersilia (1987, 107) has acknowledged that "Practitioners have been known to act on very preliminary and unproved conclusions, with unfortunate results" while emphasizing the responsibility of researchers to be responsible in pointing out the limitations of their findings.

CONCEPTUAL FRAMEWORK

Given the premature, in our opinion even irresponsible, use of research results to influence public policy, what is the valid, responsible, relationship between the two? There is an important relevant message in the arguments of Rossi (1987). His summary of the results of program evaluations over the years, most particularly in the area of crime and criminal justice, led to the critical conclusion (1987, 18): "few large-scale social programs have been found to be even minimally effective. There have been even fewer programs found to be spectacularly effective." That conclusion was expressed in two laws, stating, first, any assessment of the impact of a social program can be expected to show no effect or zero impact, and, second, the more sophisticated the evaluative approach, the more likely is a finding of no effect or zero impact. The persistent findings of failure among social programs result, principally, from inaccurate or insufficient understanding of the nature of the problem and from faults in the theoretical bases linking problem and appropriate programs.

Essential to a responsible move from empirical findings to implementation of or change in policy, he argues, is the thorough development of relevant theory that forms the core, the underpinnings of policies and proposed program. In his words (1987, 18), "Effective social policies and programs cannot be designed consistently until it is thoroughly understood how changes in policies and programs can affect the social problems in question." The need is particularly striking in the realm of crime and criminals where (1987, 13), "The knowledge base for developing effective crime policies and programs simply does not exist."

But, policy revision and implementation are ongoing processes that cannot always wait for decades of research and theory that reflects thorough understanding. As Rich (1981, 40) has indicated by way of illustration, "Decision makers in Washington [where a research proposal was being considered] operate under radically different time constraints than social scientists do; they need to have answers quickly."

While systematic study, as recommended by Merton in 1949, of the factors in social research that facilitate or impede its use for policy decisions has never been fully developed, there is enough information to specify guiding principles. The results of the study of Weiss and Bucuvalas (1980) are helpful in achieving that end. They determined the criteria used by high-level decision makers for using or rejecting research results on the basis of their readings of and reactions to actual research reports. Key criteria were the quality of the study, conformity with prior expectations, and utility for implementation.

Clearly, we think that there are important contributions that social science, particularly criminology, can make in decisions regarding public policy, but we see clear limitations. Using the framework presented by Weiss and Cohen (1993, 210), we are in a mid-position between "cynics" who have grave doubts about the value of social research in policy formation, and the "idealists" who (1993, 210) "see substantial distinctive value in the ideas and evidence produced by social science research." Indeed, we are close to the midposition articulated by Lindblom (1990) and Weiss and Cohen (1993); in their arguments, social science and social scientists make their contributions by supplementing or amplifying the preexisting information and knowledge of policy makers. According to Weiss and Cohen, social science supplementation has its effects in the policy area by summarizing social conditions, social phenomena, and the effects of changing conditions; by modifying preexisting knowledge on the basis of new concepts or different modes of analysis; or by presenting evidence that directly or indirectly challenges general understandings.

It would seem appropriate at this point to introduce a structure emphasized by Pelz (1978). He adopted concepts presented earlier by Caplan, Morrison, and Stambaugh (1975), by Knorr (1977), and by Rich (1981—but an earlier dissertation was available to Pelz) in distinguishing between "hard" and "soft" scientific knowledge and among "instrumental," "conceptual," and "symbolic" uses of that knowledge. Hard knowledge is based primarily on the direct results of experimentation, while soft knowledge includes broad understandings of phenomena, general principles, and conceptual structures. Instrumental use of knowledge refers to a direct knowledge of specific research results in deciding among policy alternatives, conceptual use refers to awareness or understanding of a frame of reference based on social knowledge in such decisions, and symbolic use refers to the use of social knowledge to legitimate a predetermined policy decision.

While it is worth keeping these distinctions in mind to appreciate the many facets of the relevant relationships, the distinctions among categories are far from clear. Even the distinction between conceptual and symbolic is blurred. In Pelz's (1978, 352) words, "If information serves to confirm the decision maker's *own judgement* of the situation, we have conceptual use. If the evidence helps him to justify his position to *someone else*, such as a legislative committee or a public group, the use is symbolic."

Using the preceding structures and recommendations, the following are examples of what we consider model ways for the use of research results in public policy.

Hirschi (1995) considers the results of studies of many varieties for a theoretical perspective emphasizing the relationship between inadequate child-rearing practices and juvenile delinquency. Even where there are such adverse conditions as divorce, poverty, or perturbations in the neighborhood, he emphasizes (1995, 127): "[f]amilies can rise above their circumstances and save their children from crime and delinquency." The policy implications are concentration on "parent-management training" and, by various paths, strengthening "weak families," even where the weakness results from the presence of only a teenage mother. His position, too, leads to keeping the police and social service systems away from involvement in family policy.

Sampson (1995), on the other hand, has focused on research and its policy implications at the community level. He presents a "social ecological model of crime" that is anchored by the work in Chicago, starting in the early 1920s, of Shaw and McKay (1972). That anchoring, as enhanced by research over subsequent years, established that the degree of violent behavior in a community is related to residential instability, especially in the context of poverty; the more dense the housing and population are in an area, the higher the rate of violent crime; and communities with more family disruption are likely to have higher levels of criminal violence. The empirical evidence used to establish those (and related concepts) is incorporated in a theory that points to "changing places, not people." That theory, too, enables deductions regarding the negative effects of existing policy on the amount of crime—as, for example, municipal policies that encourage ecological concentration by race and poverty.

Over the last 30 years, Gerald R. Patterson and numerous collaborators at the Oregon Social Learning Center (e.g., see Forgatch and Patterson, 1998; Bank et al, 1991) have developed a model of delinquency that focuses on family and social factors that contribute to delinquency, the means of predicting which children are more likely to misbehave, a treatment method that can be applied in the home and in schools, and systematic evaluation of the effectiveness of the treatments, including follow-up. Where necessary, predictions and treatments are refined as additional data are collected. Policy implications stress the importance of the family unit in coping with aggressive behavior.

One may ask at this point: What is the initial difference between the use of the research results of Sherman et al. (1998) and the research analyses of people such as Hirshi, Sampson, and the Patterson group for policy discussions. We look quite unfavorably on the first but favorably on the latter three, and yet both seem to be based on literature reviews. Sherman and his coworkers, in short, covered virtually the entire field of criminology/criminal justice in their review, and made recommendations for policy ranging in areas that include visits by nurses for infants, vocational training for male ex-offenders, organization in schools, gun buyback, individual counseling in schools, neighborhood watch programs, arrests of minors for minor offenses, and so on. In a few of the areas, the investigators did have relevant expertise, but mostly they did not. On the other hand, Hirshi, Sampson, and Patterson have decades of experience in the narrow areas they covered; they understood thoroughly the implications of empirical results in the context, and developed their policy recommendations on that understanding. To repeat the words of Rossi (1987, 18): "Effective social policies and programs cannot be designed consistently until it is thoroughly understood how changes in policies and programs can affect the social problems in question." On the other hand,

Sherman et al. (1998, 1) presented "major conclusions. . .to Congress. . .based on a systematic review of more than 500 scientific evaluations of crime prevention practices," and admitted that they omitted reports (1998, 4) "outside the mainstream outlets in criminology."

RECOMMENDATIONS FOR THE USE OF RESEARCH IN POLICY FORMULATION/RECISION

Using those principles and guidelines, the following are our recommendations for the use of the results of criminological research in policy formation from the perspective of the criminologist:

1. The research base must of course be solid, which implies quality of design, thorough peer review, and replication. If a study produces findings that are markedly contrary to accepted practice or available knowledge, this applies even more forcefully. The importance of such features to policy decision-making was demonstrated by Weiss and Bucuvalas (1980). As one would expect from a supplementation perspective, moreover, Weiss and Bucuvalas (1980, 308) argue: "[Decision-makers] invoke a criterion derived from their direct involvement in the substantive area, and they assess the extent to which research outcomes agree with their firsthand experience and professional judgment."

2. The sampling of units in the various studies forming the research base must be such to allow generalizing to the populations affected by the policy decisions in question. To illustrate a gross violation of this principle, in the Sherman and Berk (1984a) experiment, there was a 59% prior arrest rate among male suspects and a 60% unemployment rate for victims and suspects, yet there was the general recommendation for the police to arrest (1984a, 355) "in most cases of minor domestic violence."

3. There should be a means of estimating the potential harmful effects that may result from policy influenced by social research. If arrests do decrease immediate moderate spousal abuse, do they, in the longer run, have more devastating effects on families? (See the relevant discussions in Binder and Meeker, 1988.) One, by way of this line of thinking, must be very cautious in applying the results of a narrowly designed experiment in policy decision making. An experiment aimed at answering a specified theoretical question will almost certainly have no focus on potential "side effects." Pharmaceutical research without such features would be ludicrous.

4. The research should provide clear direction for policy-makers "either for immediate action or for considering alternative approaches to problems" (Weiss and Bucuvalas 1980, 311). In other words, the research should

show where and how to make changes, or redirect thinking on current philosophy or guiding principles of operation.

5. Social scientists should never be open, persistent advocates of their research products in the sense described by Binder and Meeker (1988, 1992, 1993). Perhaps the most blatant example of that process, bordering on high-pressure sales, occurs in the efforts of Sherman and Berk, in the report from the Police Foundation (1984b) mailed to police departments throughout the country. That was followed by a press release and many other efforts at influencing media coverage. In the words of Sherman and another colleague (Sherman and Cohn, 1989) the research was "actively promoted" and there was an attempt to "orchestrate the release of the experimental results for maximum press coverage" (1989, 120).

Some of the key issues noted by Sechrest and Bootzin (1996) in discussing how research literature may bear on public policy are difficulties in the generalizability of findings and the problem of overadvocacy on the part of policy consultants. Since few initial positive findings hold up in replication by others, researchers should obviously make clear the limitations of their findings and not confuse what is good for society with what is good for their own careers. It seems that this conservative approach is more often found in reports to the scientific community than in information released to and/or publicized by the media, whether intentional or not.

REFERENCES

Bank, Lew, J. Hicks Marlow, John B. Reid, and Gerald R. Patterson. 1991. "A Comparative Evaluation of Parent-Training Interventions for Families of Chronic Delinquents." *Journal of Abnormal Child Psychology* 19:15–33.

Berk, Richard D., Alec Campbell, Ruth Klap, and Bruce Western. 1992. "The Deterrent Effect of Arrest in Incidents of Domestic Violence: A Bayesian Analysis of Four Field Experiments." *American Sociological Review* 57:698–708.

Binder, Arnold, and James W. Meeker. 1988. "Experiments as Reforms." *Journal of Criminal Justice* 16:347–58.

Binder, Arnold, and James W. Meeker. 1992. "Arrest as a Method to Control Spouse Abuse." Pp. 129–40 in *Domestic Violence. The Changing Criminal Justice Response*, ed. by E.S. Buzawa and C.G. Buzawa. Westport, CT: Arburn House.

Binder, Arnold, and James W. Meeker. 1993. "On the Policy Implications of the Domestic Violence Experiment Replications." *American Sociological Review* 58:886–88.

Blumstein, Alfred. 1993. "Making Rationality Relevant-The American Society of Criminology 1992 Presidential Address." *Criminology* 31:1–16.

Caplan, Nathan, Andrea Morrison, and Russell J. Stambaugh. 1975. *The Use of Social Science Knowledge in Policy Decisions at the National Level: A Report to Respondents*. Ann Arbor, MI: Institute for Social Research, The University of Michigan.

Davidson, William S. II, Robin Redner, Richard L. Amdur, and Christina M. Mitchell. 1990. *Alternative Treatment for Troubled Youth.* New York: Plenum Press.

Forgatch, Marion S., and Gerald R. Patterson. 1998. "Behavioral Family Therapy." Pp. 85–107 in *Case Studies in Couple and Family Therapy: Systemic and Cognitive Perspectives*, ed. by Frank M. Dattilio. New York: Guilford Press.

Haney, Craig, Curtis W. Banks, and Phillip G. Zimbardo. 1973. "Interpersonal Dynamics in a Simulated Prison." *International Journal of Criminology and Penology* 1:69–97.

Haney, Craig, and Phillip G. Zimbardo. 1998. "The Past and Future of U.S. Prison Policy: Twenty-five Years after the Stanford Prison Experiment." *American Psychologist* 53:709–727.

Heeren, John, and David Shichor. 1984. "Mass Media and Delinquency Prevention: The Case of 'Scared Straight.'" *Deviant Behavior* 5:375–386.

Henggeler, Scott W., Gary Melton, and Linda A. Smith. 1992. "Family Preservation Using Multisystemic Therapy: An Effective Alternative to Incarcerating Serious Juvenile Offenders." *Journal of Consulting and Clinical Psychology* 60:953–961.

Henggeler, Scott W., Gary Melton, Linda A. Smith, Sonja K. Schoenwald, and Jerome H. Hanley. 1993. "Family Preservation Using Multisystemic Treatment: Long-term Follow-up to a Clinical Trial with Serious Juvenile Offenders." *Journal of Child and Family Studies* 2:283–293.

Hirschi, Travis. 1995. "The Family." Pp. 121–140 in *Crime,* ed. James Q. Wilson and Joan Petersilia. San Francisco: ICS Press.

Knorr, Karen D. 1977. "Policymakers' Use of Social Science Knowledge: Symbolic or Instrumental?" Pp. 165–82 in *Using Social Research in Public Policy Making*, ed. Carol H. Weiss. Lexington, MA: Heath.

Lindblom, Charles E. 1990. *Inquiry and Change*. New Haven, CT: Yale University Press.

Lundman, Richard J. 1984. *Prevention and Control of Juvenile Delinquency*. New York: Oxford University Press.

Merton, Robert K. 1949. "The Role of Applied Social Science in the Formation of Policy: A Research Memorandum." *Philosophy of Science* 16:161–81.

Mulvey, Edward P., Michael W. Arthur, and N. Dickon Reppucci. 1993. "The Prevention and Treatment of Juvenile Delinquency: A Review of the Research." *Clinical Psychology Review* 13:133–157.

Pate, Anthony M., and Edwin E. Hamilton. 1992. "Formal and Informal Deterrents to Domestic Violence: The Dade County Spouse Assault Experiment." *American Sociological Review* 57:691–97.

Pelz, Donald C. 1978. "Some Expanded Perspectives on Use of Social Science in Public Policy." Pp. 346–57 in *Major Social Issues. A Multidisciplinary View*, ed. J. J. Milton Yinger and Stephen J. Cutler. New York: The Free Press.

Petersilia, Joan. 1987. *The Influence of Criminal Justice Research*. Santa Monica, CA: The Rand Corporation.

Petersilia, Joan. 1991. "Policy Relevance and the Future of Criminology—The American Society of Criminology 1990 Presidential Address." *Criminology* 31:1–16.

Rich, Robert F. 1981. *Social Science Information and Public Policy Making*. San Francisco: Jossey-Bass Publishers.

Rossi, Peter H. 1987. "The Iron Law of Evaluation and Other Metallic Rules." Pp. 3–20 in *Research in Social Problems and Public Policy*, ed. Joann L. Miller and Michael Lewis. Greenwich, CT: JAI Press.

Rosenberg, Alexander. 1988. *Philosophy and Social Science.* Boulder, CO: Westview Press.

Sampson, Robert J. 1995. "The Community." Pp. 193–216 in *Crime,* ed. James O. Wilson and Joan Petersilia. San Francisco: ICS Press.

Sechrest, Lee B., and Richard R. Bootzin. 1996. "Psychology and Inferences about Public Policy." *Psychology, Public Policy, and Law* 2:377–392.

Shaw, Clifford R., and Henry D. McKay. 1972. *Juvenile Delinquency and Urban Areas*, rev. ed. Chicago: University of Chicago Press.

Sherman, Lawrence W., and Richard A. Berk. 1984a. "The Specific Deterrent Effects of Arrest for Domestic Assault." American Sociological Review 49:261–72.

Sherman, Lawrence W., and Richard A. Berk. 1984b. "The Minneapolis Domestic Violence Experiment." Policy Foundation Reports, No. 1. Washington, DC: Police Foundation.

Sherman, Lawrence W., and Ellen G. Cohn. 1989. *Police Policy on Domestic Violence, 1985: A National Survey.* Crime Control Reports No. 1. Washington, DC: Crime Control Institute.

Sherman, Lawrence, Denise C. Gottfredson, Doris L. MacKenzie, John Eik, Peter Reuter, and Shawn D. Bushway. 1998. *Preventing Crime: What Works, What Doesn't, What's Promising.* Washington, DC: National Institute of Justice, Research in Brief.

Skolnick, Jerome H. 1995. "What Not to Do about Crime—The American Society of Criminology 1994 Presidential Address." *Criminology* 33: 1–15.

Weiss, Carol H., and Michael J. Bucuvalas. 1980. "Truth Tests and Utility Tests: Decision Makers' Frames of Reference for Social Science Research." *American Sociological Review* 45:302–13.

Weiss, Janet A., and David K. Cohen. 1993. *An Heretical Heir of the Enlightenment. Politics, Policy, and Science in the Work of Charles E. Lindblom.* Boulder, CO: Westview Press.

Wellford, Charles F. 1997. "Controlling Crime and Achieving Justice—The American Society of Criminology 1996 Presidential Address." *Criminology* 35: 1–11.

Zimbardo, Phillip G. 1973. "On the Ethics of Intervention in Human Psychological Research: With Special Reference to the Stanford Prison Experiment." *Cognition* 2: 243–256.

Sensational Cases, Flawed Theories[1]

Diane Vaughan

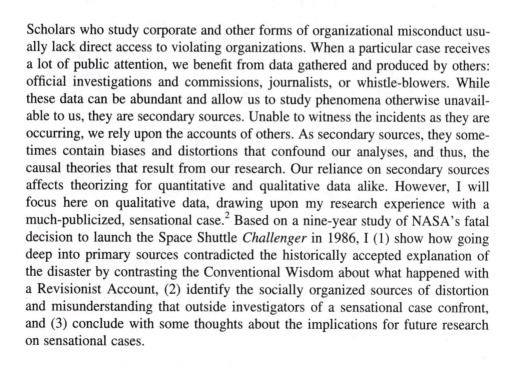

Scholars who study corporate and other forms of organizational misconduct usually lack direct access to violating organizations. When a particular case receives a lot of public attention, we benefit from data gathered and produced by others: official investigations and commissions, journalists, or whistle-blowers. While these data can be abundant and allow us to study phenomena otherwise unavailable to us, they are secondary sources. Unable to witness the incidents as they are occurring, we rely upon the accounts of others. As secondary sources, they sometimes contain biases and distortions that confound our analyses, and thus, the causal theories that result from our research. Our reliance on secondary sources affects theorizing for quantitative and qualitative data alike. However, I will focus here on qualitative data, drawing upon my research experience with a much-publicized, sensational case.[2] Based on a nine-year study of NASA's fatal decision to launch the Space Shuttle *Challenger* in 1986, I (1) show how going deep into primary sources contradicted the historically accepted explanation of the disaster by contrasting the Conventional Wisdom about what happened with a Revisionist Account, (2) identify the socially organized sources of distortion and misunderstanding that outside investigators of a sensational case confront, and (3) conclude with some thoughts about the implications for future research on sensational cases.

THE RESEARCH: STARTING ASSUMPTIONS, CONTRADICTIONS, AND SURPRISE

When the *Challenger* disaster occurred on January 28, 1986, then-President Reagan appointed a Presidential Commission to investigate the cause of the tragedy. At that time, I was looking for a case of organizational misconduct that involved a large organization (but not a corporation) for a three-case project I had begun.[3] The public hearings of the Presidential Commission appointed to investigate the accident and the media began revealing to the public NASA history and what had transpired during the launch decision. The case appeared to meet all qualifications for organizational misconduct, as I was defining it:

> Violations of laws, rules, or administrative regulations by an individual or group of individuals in an organization who, in their organizational role, act or fail to act in ways that further the attainment of organization goals.

The accident seemed to me to be an example of organizational misconduct because of the presence of the three factors most commonly associated with organizational misconduct: competitive pressures and resource scarcity; organizational characteristics—structure, processes, and transactions—that create opportunities for misconduct; and regulatory failure. These three structural factors, in combination, affect individual choice, encouraging individual decisions to violate rules and engage in harmful, violative acts in the interest of organization goals.[4]

From the Commission's televised hearings and media accounts, I learned that on the eve of the disastrous launch, NASA managers were warned against launching by engineers at Morton Thiokol, Inc., the manufacturer of the solid rocket booster, the technical cause of the accident, yet NASA went against this recommendation, proceeding with launch. I also learned that on that night NASA managers at Marshall Space Flight Center had violated rules about passing information about the engineers' complaints about the booster problem up the hierarchy to their superiors. Moreover, the Commission discovered a history of decision making from 1977 to 1985 in which NASA continued to fly the shuttle with known flaws in the joint of the solid rocket booster. During these early years, other rules were violated: industry rules about the design and requirements for use of the O-rings. In addition to these rule violations, televised and published accounts verified that the space agency was under extraordinary economic strain, which resulted in production pressure to launch shuttles in keeping with an extremely tight launch schedule. The capstone was regulatory failure. So inadequate was safety regulation at NASA that the Commission called it "The Silent Safety System."

I began collecting published media accounts and tracking the revelations of the Presidential Commission investigation as news was breaking. In June of 1986, Volume I of the Presidential Commission Report was published. The Commission concluded that the technical cause of the accident was the failure of a rubber-like O-ring that lay in a joint of the left solid rocket booster. But they also implicated NASA management and indicated that "decision making was flawed" at the space agency. The extensive documentation of flawed decision making, rule violations, and production pressures at NASA created what became the historically accepted explanation of the tragedy: NASA managers, experiencing production pressure in a year when many important launches were planned that were essential to the future of the space program, ignored the advice of contractor engineers and went forward with the launch, violating rules about reporting problems up the hierarchy in the process. The historically accepted explanation was a form of rational choice theory, wherein managers weighed the costs and benefits of their actions. Thus the incident conformed to traditional explanations of elite and white-collar deviance in sociology: the amorally calculating manager model.[5]

This model is a consequentialist model that locates the cause of organizational misconduct in the utilitarian calculations of individuals, precluding any other influences upon individual choice. In contrast, my interest was in examining the social context: how organization, environment, and regulatory failure might have impinged on the decisions of these managers. Volume I contained over 230 pages of analysis, documents, reproductions of memoranda and letters, and quotes from the Commission's hearings testimony, along with extensive detail about how both the organization and the technology operated. This volume, I decided, would be the basis for my analysis, along with the now-extensive files I had created from newspapers, journals, and magazines. But as I began analyzing Volume I, I learned that some of my most basic assumptions about the technology were wrong: for example, according to engineers, the shuttle did not explode. There was a structural break-up and a fireball, but no explosion. More serious were challenges to my hypothesis about what went on in the organization, discovered when I went beyond Volume I into the other four volumes of the Commission report, published months later in the summer of 1986.[6] For this to be an example of misconduct, I needed to verify the connection between production pressures, organization goals, and the rule violations by Marshall managers: the macro-micro connection. I chose to examine what appeared to be the most egregious of the reported violations the Commission uncovered: (1) Marshall Solid Rocket Booster Project Manager Lawrence B. Mulloy's sequence of six waivers of the booster joints' Criticality 1 status, which allowed six flights to proceed without altering the design after that Criticality 1 status was imposed, and (2) this same manager's waiver of a launch constraint, which allowed the vehicle to continue flight after the launch constraint was imposed. These waivers appeared to be the surreptitious acts of a manager under extreme launch pressure.

In order to examine these rule violations closely and consider them within the social context of decision making, I concentrated on Volumes IV and V of the Commission Report. These volumes contained the full transcription of testimony at the Commission's hearings and appendices containing copies of rules about launch decision making. Now 13 months into the project, I discovered that the Commission had made a mistake. Mulloy's waivers were absolutely *in keeping with NASA rules, not violations of them.* The Commission had misunderstood NASA procedures. Both in the televised hearings (and so also in the hearing transcripts) and in Volume I, the Commission used the word waiver as a verb: e.g., Mulloy waived the Criticality 1 status. But I discovered that in NASA language, "waiver" is a noun. A waiver is a mechanism for giving Criticality 1 items an extra review. Hundreds of items on the shuttle were Criticality 1 (the orbiter wings, for example, which had no back-up in case of failure, and thus were Criticality 1—if a wing failed, crew, mission, and vehicle were lost). When the contractor engineering analysis determines, through tests, calculations, and adjustments to the technical component that it is safe to fly, an item with Criticality 1 status can fly. So a project manager then must issue a waiver so that launch can proceed. Each of Mulloy's waivers were the consequence of the extra reviews by Thiokol engineers, who recommended proceeding with launch for every mission prior to the *Challenger* mission. Moreover, these waivers were always recorded; not the secretive surreptitious acts I believed, based on the Commission's hearings and Report. Waivers were routine at NASA—a safety procedure, a precautionary measure, not a rule violation.

This discovery altered the course of my project. Obviously, the Presidential Commission had not fully understood aspects of NASA culture, and therefore had mistakenly interpreted waivers as rule violations when they were not. Now, I questioned other reported rule violations, and so shifted my attention from the eve-of-launch to the history of decision making. Were these other "alleged" rule violations true rule violations? And how had the competitive environment, organization characteristics, and regulatory failure affected NASA decisions on the eve-of-launch *and* in the past? Thus the research became an historical ethnography. I turned from my original focus on the eve-of-launch to include a reconstructed chronology of the past from archival data and interviews. I turned to original archival data collected by the Presidential Commission, stored at the National Archives. These data had not been examined by other investigators. They included over 200,000 pages of original documents and 9,000 pages of interview transcripts. A team of government investigators working for the Commission conducted interviews with 160 NASA and contractor employees. They interviewed them on two topics: the eve-of-launch teleconference and the history of the solid rocket booster problems at NASA. For most of the 160 people, the National Archive files contain two lengthy transcripts. Of the 160, only forty percent testified before the Presidential Commission, so these transcripts were a very important source of information. In addition, I relied extensively on the three-volume Report of the House Committee on Science and Technology, published in October 1986. Contradicting many of the findings of the Commission, this Report was published later, by which time the media had gone on to other sensational stories, so the historically accepted explanation of the *Challenger* disaster remained intact. Finally, I also conducted lengthy personal interviews.

These primary sources of data showed how the official investigation and media accounts had distorted history. I discovered many more contradictions to the historically accepted explanation of the launch decision produced by the Presidential Commission hearings, Volume I, and the media accounts in the year the disaster occurred. Here are some (but by no means all) of the contradictions that I found. First, I list the Commission-generated, media-mediated conventional interpretation (the Conventional Wisdom) of events at NASA, then my discoveries (the Revisionist Account).

THE CONVENTIONAL WISDOM (CW)
VERSUS THE REVISIONIST ACCOUNT (RA)

- CW: Commissioner Feynman's famous television demonstration of O-ring response to cold when a piece of a ring was dipped in ice water revealed to NASA managers and engineers and the Presidential Commission the technical cause of the accident.

  RA: All engineers and managers knew that when rubber gets cold, it gets hard. The eve-of-launch teleconference had centered on this issue, so when the disaster occurred, the people doing the hands-on engineering immediately assumed that the cold had affected the O-rings. Feynman enlightened the Commission, but not the teleconference participants, and not people at NASA associated with the Solid Rocket Booster Project. Also, his demonstration missed the complexity of the engineering problem on the eve-of-launch. It involved not only O-ring resiliency in cold temperatures but also joint dynamics under enormous ignition pressures and timing in milliseconds.

- CW: Thiokol engineers had convincing engineering analysis on eve-of-launch and strong argument against launching.

  RA: All teleconference participants, including Thiokol engineers, agreed that the engineering argument was weak and not convincing. They posed a correlation between O-ring damage and cold temperature, but had data in their presentation that contradicted their no-launch position. Only one Thiokol engineer (Arnie Thompson) believed they had a good engineering analysis.

- CW: Marshall managers suppressed information about problems, violating NASA reporting rules. Thus individual secrecy contributed to the disaster.

  RA: Marshall managers followed all rules about reporting problems. Structural secrecy, not individual secrecy, contributed to the disaster: Hierarchy, division of labor, specialization, and segmentation that typify complex organizations divided information and knowledge, blocking understanding about the technology for people not directly working on the boosters.

- CW: NASA had to get *Challenger* off the pad that morning because of production pressure, the Teacher in Space mission, and President Reagan's State of the Union message, scheduled for that night.

  RA: For every launch date, NASA establishes two launch windows. Temperature in the afternoon was going to be in the 40s or 50s; if Marshall managers truly believed it was risky, they could have delayed until afternoon without jeopardizing the goals of the space agency.

- CW: Cold O-rings, eroded by hot gases, didn't do their job. Erosion caused the disaster.

  RA: The O-rings were the cause of the technical failure, but contingency also had an effect. If the O-rings had failed, they would have failed in first 600 milliseconds after ignition, resulting in a launch pad disaster. The O-rings were eroded by hot ignition gases, as Thiokol engineers had predicted, but joints held. Fifty-three seconds into the launch, however, an unpredicted and unprecedented wind shear shook the shuttle violently, dislodging the charred material that was sealing the booster joint, allowing hot gases to penetrate first the booster and then the external tank. If there had been no wind, the astronauts might have lived.

- CW: Marshall managers violated safety rules on eve-of-launch, failing to report information about the teleconference up the hierarchy to superiors.

  RA: Marshall managers followed every reporting rule, doing exactly as they and other shuttle project managers were required to do and had done in the past.

- CW: Marshall managers were risk-takers, acting amorally, throughout the history of shuttle program, putting production pressures and deadlines ahead of safety.

  RA: Marshall Space Flight Center had a reputation with Thiokol and among the other NASA space centers as extremely conservative—in fact, they were criticized as *too* conservative; Marshall personnel had the nickname of "dinosaurs." Ironically, in the history of decision making, the positions of Thiokol and Marshall were often the reverse of what they were on the eve-of-launch: the Marshall managers involved in the *Challenger* teleconference often argued against Thiokol engineers recommendations to launch, delaying launch for safety reasons.

- CW: The eve-of-launch teleconference was initiated by Thiokol engineers, concerned about cold.

  RA: Marshall manager Larry Wear called Thiokol in Utah to see if Thiokol engineers had any concerns about the cold. If he had not called, the teleconference would not have happened because Thiokol engineers in Utah were unaware of temperature at the launch site at the Cape, and Thiokol officials who were at the Cape (including Thiokol Project Manager Al McDonald), when asked, told the launch director that they did not see any problems with the cold and the booster.

- CW: Thiokol engineers were unanimously opposed to launching *Challenger*.

   RA: Thiokol engineers were divided: some were in favor of launch, some were opposed.

- CW: Memos written by engineers at both Marshall and Thiokol were objecting to the solid rocket booster design as early as 1978, but managers didn't listen, overriding engineering opinion.

   RA: Every management decision to fly prior to 1986 was based on Thiokol engineers' analysis about risk acceptability and recommendations to launch. The same engineers that objected on the eve-of-launch believed it was safe to fly, based on engineering analysis, during those years, and so recommended to their management. Memos surfacing after the disaster, authored by unhappy engineers, became part of the collective memory. But memos were taken out of the stream of actions in which they were created. What was omitted from the public record was that as problems occurred, the same engineers fixed them, finding the design acceptable.

- CW: On the eve-of-launch, Thiokol engineers believed there would be a catastrophe.

   RA: One engineer, Thiokol's Robert Ebeling, said afterward he thought there would be a catastrophe, but he said nothing during the teleconference. None of the other engineers, including Roger Boisjoly, the engineer who most vigorously protested against the launch, foresaw catastrophe. They were very concerned. They foresaw problems and expected more erosion, but none believed a disaster would occur. Boisjoly, exiting the teleconference and angry about the outcome, stopped by a colleague's office, telling him that when the boosters were disassembled after the mission returned he should document the damage well because they would have a new data point enabling them to gain more insight about cold-temperature effects on O-rings.

- CW: After the disaster, Head of Astronaut Office John W. Young criticized NASA to the media, stating that the shuttle contained so many risky parts that astronauts on previous missions were lucky to be alive.

   RA: Young, as Head of Astronaut Office, was part of NASA's launch decision chain, participating at the top of the Flight Readiness Review, the formal prelaunch decision making procedure. He heard all the engineering analyses for all technical components of the shuttle prior to each launch. He, along with the rest of top NASA administrators, had consistently given the final okay for all launches.

The Conventional Wisdom provided the basis for amoral calculation as the historically accepted explanation of this event. The Commission's televised hearings and Volume I of the Commission's final report were the basis for many, if not most, public definitions of the situation. Receiving near-universal praise for what was the most extensive and expensive public investigation to date, the Commission successfully identified many problems at NASA that contributed to the tragic loss of the *Challenger* crew. In Volume I, however, we repeatedly read that "NASA" did this or "NASA" did that—a language that simultaneously blames everyone and no one, obscuring who in the huge bureaucracy was actually doing what. Top administrators making policy, middle managers, and the engineers at the bottom of the launch decision chain who were doing the risk assessments were indistinguishable. The Commission's report did not officially blame any specific individuals. But their questioning of NASA managers in the televised hearings, the erroneous finding that NASA middle managers violated rules in both the history of decision making and on the eve-of-launch, and the Commission report conclusion that the "decision making was flawed" focused public attention in one place. The public drama created the impression that NASA middle managers alone were responsible for the tragedy. This impression was reflected in a comment one FBI agent jokingly uttered to Marshall Solid Rocket Booster Project Manager Lawrence Mulloy as he left the hearings following testimony one day, "After they get you for this, Mulloy, they're going to get you for Jimmy Hoffa."[7]

Other aspects of the Commission investigation added to the public imagery of managerial wrong-doing. For example, the Commission's inability to fully grasp NASA reporting rules resulted in many posttragedy accounts that had Marshall Solid Rocket Booster Project Manager Mulloy suppressing information when he presented the engineering assessments to top NASA administrators. But a late-breaking video recording of Mulloy briefing top administrators prior to STS 51-E (the flight following the January 1985 cold weather launch) showed a full oral review of the O-ring problem that was consistent, both in form and content, with guidelines for NASA Level I reporting requirements.[8] The existence of this video was not known to the NASA or Commission investigations at the time of the hearings.[9] Therefore, neither Mulloy's full briefing nor the video of it were acknowledged in Volume I of the Presidential Commission's report. Because the video was discovered after Volume I had gone to press (it was published months before the other volumes), it was mentioned and transcribed only in Volume II, which contains nine appendices of technical reports of densely-packed detail in small print.[10] Had this video surfaced during the Commission hearings and its existence and transcription been reported in Volume I—or a press conference been called when it turned up—the historical record about managerial wrong-doing and "who knew what when" at NASA might have been different.

Another important distortion resulted from the selection of witnesses to testify. For the televised hearings, nearly eighty witnesses were called. Working engineers were underrepresented. Seven were asked, all of whom were opposed to the launch. But fifteen working engineers participated in the teleconference. The National Archives interview transcripts show that not all engineers who participated in the teleconference agreed with the position that Boisjoly and Thompson represented so vigorously. The engineers who differed did not testify, so these diverse views never became part of posttragedy accounts. Furthermore, since the emphasis of the questioning was on the launch decision, the fact that the same working engineers who opposed the *Challenger* launch were responsible for the official risk assessments and recommendations for all booster launch decisions in the preceding years also got lost.

NASA managers were certainly implicated and responsible for their actions. But for the average citizen, the focus on managerial wrongdoing deflected attention from these other significant aspects of this historic incident. The Commission's report, and the other posttragedy accounts that were based upon it, misled the public about the causes of the accident. It prevented them from understanding that the conditions that caused the disaster were not eliminated, so another disaster could happen. The causes of the accident went beyond the actions of individuals to the environment, the NASA organization, and the developmental nature of the shuttle technology.

1. **The Environment.** By focusing on amorally calculating managers, public attention was diverted from elite networks: top NASA administrators, Congress, and the administration who made decisions that politicized the space program, created economic strain and production pressures, and put the teacher, Christa McAuliffe, on the shuttle. Their responsibility for the disaster and its consequences never became the center of public attention. Today, the agency remains politicized, economically dependent upon Congress, and underfunded. It continues to try to relieve economic strain by managing impressions in order to curry favor with the public and Congress, as the recent John Glenn mission attests.

2. **The Risky Technology.** Although both the Presidential Commission and the House Committee on Science and Technology stressed that shuttle technology was still developmental and therefore extremely risky, the emphasis on amoral calculating managers left the public unaware of the unprecedented character of the technology, its developmental character, and the sheer difficulty that engineers encounter in assessing risk for this ambiguous, uncertain technology. The public assumes high-risk technology is based on science, and therefore exact diagnosis is possible. But the

shuttle is a large-scale technical system that cannot be fully tested on the ground. Engineers do calculations, ground tests, and lab tests, but they cannot predict or test for the forces of the environment the vehicle will experience in space.

3. **The NASA/Contractor Organization.** Traditionally, when things go wrong in organizations, individuals are blamed: operator error, amorally calculating managers, incompetence, failure to abide by rules, etc. However, organizations, while a great asset that allows us many modern efficiencies, have their dark side.[11] They are comprised of structures, processes, transaction systems, and institutional logics that affect the cognition, meaning, and action of individual employees. These characteristics are common to all organizations, producing harmful outcomes, even when personnel are well trained, well-intentioned, have adequate resources, and do all the correct things.

Scholars are only too familiar with what Scott Sagan calls "the politics of blame."[12] In the historically accepted explanation of the tragedy, a failed booster technology, a flawed decision-making structure, and amorally calculating managers were the culprits. Leaving managers twisting in the wind was the best of all possible outcomes for NASA because the cure was easy: fire and retire responsible managers, fix the decision-making structure and the technology, and go on. The program could not survive public awareness that the technology was as risky as it really was/is because that awareness would have jeopardized the myth of routine and economical space flight that secured the space agency's future. And it definitely was not in the interest of the space agency or the White House to have top administrators implicated. The focus on managers effectively kept the public from wondering who put Christa McAuliffe on the shuttle in the first place.

THE SOCIALLY ORGANIZED SOURCES OF DISTORTION AND OUTSIDER MISUNDERSTANDING

Public understanding of this historic event developed, not from immediate experience, but from accounts created by the official investigations, media, and other posttragedy analysts. The *Challenger* disaster generated an enormous amount of archival information as well as much conflicting public discourse, making possible analysis of a complex technical case not possible otherwise. But this advantage had an accompanying disadvantage. Dorothy Smith reminds us:

> Our knowledge of contemporary society is to a large extent mediated to us by documents of various kinds. Very little of our knowledge of people, events, social relations and powers arises directly from our own experience. Factual elements in documentary form, whether as news, data, information or the like, stand in for an actuality which is not directly accessible. Socially organized practices of reporting and recording work upon what actually happens or

has happened to create a reality in documentary form, and though they are decisive to its character, their practices are not visible in it.[13]

The historically accepted explanation of the *Challenger* disaster developed from the documentary accounts produced by many. The account of the Presidential Commission was definitively influential in the production of all others. The Commission findings were extensive and complex, covering every possible point of inquiry. But as the major initial source of public information, it was also the major initial source of public misunderstanding. The Commission's findings were distorted by three factors: Retrospection and hindsight, autonomy and interdependence between the Commission and the NASA/contractor system, and documentary accounts and the reduction of information. These three factors are common sources of outsider misunderstanding when organizations do bad things. Although this discussion focuses on the Commission, it logically extends to the media. And to us, as scholars who tend to use media and official investigation sources as starting points for research.

Retrospection and Hindsight

Starbuck and Milliken point out that when observers who know the results of organizational actions try to make sense of them, they tend to see two kinds of analytic sequences.[14] Starting from the bad result and seeking to explain it, observers seek the incorrect actions, the flawed analyses, and the inaccurate perceptions that led to the result. Nearly all explanations of crisis, disaster, or organization failure single out how managers "failed to spot major environmental threats or opportunities, failed to heed well-founded warnings, assessed risks improperly, or adhered to outdated goals and beliefs."[15] In contrast, analyses of success celebrate accurate managerial vision, wise risk-taking, well-conceived goals, and diligent, intelligent persistence, despite scarce resources and other obstacles. These two analytic sequences lead to a selective focus that oversimplifies what happened. First, they focus attention on individual decision makers, putting managerial perceptions as the cause of all organizational outcomes. Second, they neglect the importance and complexity of organizations as a locus of individual decision making. Third, they obliterate the complexity and ambiguity of the task environments that people once faced. Paying attention to all these factors, Turner, in *Man-made Disasters*, notes the tendency for a problem that was ill-structured in an organization to become a well-structured problem after a disaster, as people look back and reinterpret information preexisting the disaster, ignored or minimized at the time, that afterward takes on new significance as signals of danger.[16]

The Commission followed the pattern of which Starbuck, Milliken, and Turner warned: Starting from the bad result and seeking to explain it, the Commission and its investigators sought out the incorrect actions, the flawed analyses, and the inaccurate perceptions that led to the result. Selective attention to information that seemed to explain the harmful outcome led the Commission to ignore the fact that NASA had frequently exercised caution, delaying many launches for safety reasons. In hindsight, the solid rocket booster joint problem became a well-structured problem for the Commission, as the tragedy made salient, and selectively focused attention on the NASA decisions that seemed to lead inexorably to it. The Commission saw damage to the O-rings as a coherent trajectory of strong signals of potential danger, but for managers and engineers working on the problem, signals were mixed, weak, and routine as the problem unfolded chronologically. Retrospection led the Commission to call teleconference engineers who protested the launch to testify, omitting the testimony of those who were in favor of it. Furthermore, retrospection led the Commission to extract actions from their historical and organizational context in a stream of actions, the sequence of events and structures of which they were a part. Engineering memos complaining about the boosters became central to the documentary account, whereas the correction of booster design inadequacies and participation in launch recommendations by those same engineers never became part of the documentary record. Robbed of social and cultural context that gave them meaning, many NASA actions became hard to understand, controversial, and, in some cases, incriminating. The result was a systematic distortion of history that obscured the meaning of the events and actions as it existed and changed for the participants in the situation at the time the events and actions occurred.

Interorganizational Regulatory Relations: Autonomy and Interdependence

Outside investigators have a structural relationship with the organizations they investigate that can be a source of distortion and outsider misunderstanding. Elsewhere, I have written about how autonomy and interdependence affect regulatory relationships.[17] The Commission was acting in its capacity as a presidentially appointed regulatory body mandated to investigate and identify the cause of the disaster. Autonomy and interdependence affect all regulatory relationships and are consequences of interorganizational relations between the regulator and the regulated organization. The problem of autonomy grows out of the physical separateness of regulated and regulator. When situated external to the regulated organization, regulators have trouble penetrating organizational boundaries, which creates difficulty for the monitoring, discovery, and investigative stages of regulation. External regulators are restricted to information gathered after the fact and have trouble understanding the culture, language, and technology of regulated organizations. Interdependence refers to the fact that, despite being separate, autonomous bodies, regulator and regulated can be bound together by resource exchange or common interests, so that their past, present, and future are linked: they rise and fall together. Interdependence affects the blame-placing and sanctioning part of the process, frequently resulting in compromised sanctions. The work of regulatory bodies is always affected (to greater or lesser extent) by both autonomy and interdependence, despite the intensity and resources devoted to a particular regulatory effort.

As a regulator situated external to NASA, the Commission's investigation clearly was affected by both autonomy and interdependence. With a mandate to publish a report within 180 days, the Commission was faced with an enormous task. Although many Commission members were affiliated with the aerospace community, and two, Sally Ride and Neil Armstrong, were astronauts, none were familiar with solid rocket booster technology, nor were they familiar with NASA rules and procedures for hazard assessments or launch decisions. Also, NASA engineering culture and the language were tremendous obstacles for the investigators. In many sections of the hearings testimony, NASA and Thiokol managers and engineers clearly were working very hard to explain both the technology and the decision-making procedures to stymied Commission members. This problem was exacerbated because the Commission was faced with a deadline and an overwhelming amount of original documents, so relied on two strategies that selectively reduced and sorted the information on which they based their analysis.

First, they created a small organization, with an Executive Director and large staff to help them gather information. Their organization was hierarchical, and included a team of government investigators for interviewing plus special Task Forces, led by Commission members, to investigate the technical aspects of the accident. This team divided up the work, reporting to the Commission members. In striking parallel with what happened at NASA regarding the solid rocket boosters, the investigation was affected by structural secrecy and the successive reduction of information. Because of the division of labor, no one person had all the information. The team members collectively discussed (but selectively) what each member had found, then forwarded information they believed was important to the Commission. They omitted much, reducing the complexity of the event in the process (e.g., it was the team of government investigators who recommended which engineers were to be called to testify). Second, all documents, interviews, and testimony were computerized, so Commission members could scan the data base to look for, say, a specific engineering memo or action. Although this gave them speedy access to information, it also was selective, extracting actions from the chronological context.

The problem of interdependence is obvious in the selection of people to be on the Commission. Having Commission members who were outsiders qualified to conduct an accident investigation involving aerospace technology was essential to having a thorough investigation that would be publicly credible *and* provide the skills necessary to diagnose what happened. However, these same decision criteria meant that Commission members also all had a vested interest in

NASA's continued well-being. The appointment of William Rogers was propitious in the same doubled-edged sort of way. As a lawyer and in his former capacity as Attorney General of the United States, Rogers had been involved in the Warren Commission investigation and others. In terms of carrying out a rigorous investigation, his experience was an advantage. For example, it was Rogers who decided that the hearings should be televised and that all information collected by the Commission should be made accessible to the public at the National Archives. This decision was made out of his concern about the conspiracy theories that continued to circulate about the Kennedy assassination, which he believed was due to the fact that the government investigation was closed and all documents were sealed.

However, in view of the fact that he was a Republican appointed by the White House and what we know about interdependence and the effect of common interests on regulation, we necessarily must conclude that his willingness to get to the bottom of things at NASA may have been jeopardized by a political agenda. It is clear, however, that Commission members were not of one mind, nor did they share a common worldview that was affected by links to the White House. Sally Ride, for one, was outraged by what happened; the astronauts who died were part of her NASA family. And Richard Feynman went his own way throughout the investigation, paying little attention to Rogers.[18] Regardless of the idiosyncratic positions and views of the individuals, autonomy and interdependence are structural characteristics that have systematic effects on social control, and they were factors here.

Documentary Accounts and the Reduction of Information

The third and final socially organized source of distortion and outsider misunderstanding was how the Commission's findings were disseminated and used by others. At the same time that documentary accounts were proliferating, expanding what was known about certain aspects of the accident, a successive and systematic reduction of information was in progress. The televised hearings and the summary Volume I represented only a small portion of the findings contained in Volumes II through V. And those volumes were further reduced from the several hundred thousand pages of data the Commission gathered. The media, working from the televised hearings and Volume I, seized on some of the discoveries, covering them extensively, while ignoring others. Not that this was intentional. Each posttragedy account reconstructed the *Challenger* accident or some aspect of it for other audiences. Each analyst was faced with the same problems the Commission faced: overwhelming detail about technical issues, NASA organization structure and procedures, and organizational and human history. Each published account had to be abbreviated because, first and obviously, the full account could never be known. Second, limits on the time available to gather, understand, and absorb information, on the time and space available in which to tell the story, and on the audience's ability to wade through the details made it imperative that each analyst shorten and simplify.

So facts were presented, individual actions were described, but of necessity excised from the stream of actions that gave them their essential meaning. This shrinking of information from the original documentary sources and the excising of action from historic context also was true of the Presidential Commission's report, which was a systematic, thorough, detailed attempt to construct an historic chronology that took into account both the organization and its context. The House Committee on Science and Technology investigation report was not published until October 1986. Advantaged by the data collected by the Commission and beginning with a review of the Commission report, the House Committee went on to write a report that contradicted some of the Commission's main conclusions, among them the finding of rule violations by middle managers. But the House Committee report, coming later, never received the same media attention. From the published and televised accounts, the public—overwhelmed with information—reduced it even more. Unable to retain all the information, they latched on to something that explained for them the unexplainable and went on. The image of amorally calculating managers, production pressures, and a controversial eve-of-launch teleconference at NASA was a consistent image that dominated the documentary accounts. Consequently, many people, at the time vicariously witnessing the event through the televised hearings and the media, believed wrongdoing by middle management was behind the launch decision.

SENSATIONAL CASES: CAUTIONARY TALES FOR SCHOLARLY INQUIRY

The *Challenger* disaster qualifies as a sensational case, not simply because the media made it one, but because it was experienced as one by the millions who witnessed it. It was an historic event and national tragedy that became embedded in the collective memory. But my research-based explanation of it was far from sensational. The cause of the *Challenger* disaster was not amorally calculating managers. Neither was it organizational misconduct (as traditionally defined) because no rules were violated. No evil individuals were behind what happened at the space agency. It was, as Merton has so famously written, "the unintended consequences of purposive social action."[19] The causes of the tragedy lay in the generic structures and processes of organizations and their institutional environments. This finding does not deny the importance of individual actions (or individual responsibility, for people always must be held accountable for their acts), but shifts attention to the situated character of individual choice.[20] Nor does it deny that something bad happened with serious implications for other cases of organizational misconduct—even those where amoral calculation is a factor.

At NASA, the environment of the organization, organization structures, processes, transaction systems, and institutional logics normalized signals of danger, thus blinding people to the harmful consequences of their acts. The result was that Marshall and Thiokol managers and engineers alike repeatedly made official decisions in which incidents of technical deviation from performance expectations for the boosters were redefined as normal and acceptable for space flight. Moreover, as missions accumulated, they accepted more and more technical deviation—including the new condition of cold temperature that officially became an acceptable risk on the eve of the *Challenger* launch. It is important to note that the normalization of deviance is not a cognitive construct. It is an institutional and organizational construct, for these factors can neutralize actions, directing behavior toward organization goals even when individuals themselves object to a particular line of action. Neither the harmful outcome nor the normalization of deviance that led to it are banal, but it can truly be said that the organizational environment, institutional logics, organization structures, processes, and transaction systems that were the origins of the disaster were banal.

The *Challenger* disaster is not an isolated example of the discrepancy between an historically accepted explanation of a sensational case and what research based on primary sources produces. Lee and Ermann's recent reanalysis of the Ford Pinto case reveals the complexity behind the amoral calculator explanation that has stood as the historically accepted explanation of that incident.[21] One by one, Lee and Ermann dismantle the blocks of the Conventional Wisdom and replace them with their Revisionist Account, based on interviews with former Ford employees and their analysis of trial transcripts and original documents, classified for years after the case was officially settled. They, too, undertook an organizational analysis, finding that the explanation of this sensational case was not sensational: No amoral calculators were found. They conclude, ". . .a consciously cynical decision did not produce an unsafe fuel tank design. . . There was no 'decision' to market an unsafe product, and there was no 'decision' to market a safe one."[22] Like the *Challenger* case, generic organization structures and processes, not amoral calculation, intersected to produce an unintended consequence. The decision(s) to launch and continue launching a flawed Pinto on the market, they conclude, was the outcome of "institutionally embedded unreflective action" produced by organizational subunits embedded in a larger network of organizational relations.[23]

These two cases may not be representative: Scholars who dig deep into primary sources to research other cases publicly identified as examples of amoral calculation may verify the historically accepted explanation. The affirmation or refutation of amoral calculation as a causal explanation notwithstanding, these cases are cautionary tales with implications for future research. We, too, are vulnerable to the sources of distortions and outside misunderstanding: Retrospection and hindsight, autonomy and interdependence, and documentary accounts and the reduction of information. But for scholars, sensational cases raise additional concerns.

1. We must maintain a critical stance about the media and official inquiries. In research on corporate and organizational misconduct, we sometimes tend to see the media as our colleagues because, in keeping with our critical stance toward the power elite, journalists tantalize us with exposés that attack the powerful. Scholars educated in the wake of Watergate and the heyday of Ralph Nader may also rejoice when commissions produce findings that take the side of the less powerful, as when the Presidential Commission blamed NASA managers and supported working engineers. In our enthusiasm for the bounty of information sensational cases produce, we must remind ourselves of what sociological research tells us about the social construction of news[24] and how official inquiries produce knowledge for public consumption.[25] Nichols has written extensively on both these topics.[26] Acknowledging the substantial literature examining how moral entrepreneurs construct social problems and media participation in these transformations, he notes the comparative neglect of official inquiries by scholars:

> Interpretive work on public issues is often accomplished through official inquiries that combine documentary researches and interrogation of witnesses. Such investigations generate texts (especially transcripts, interim and final reports) in which inquisitors claim both to articulate authoritative versions of events, and to provide authoritative guidance on policy options. Within official inquiries, public hearings with live witnesses are routinely held, sometimes in an open-ended series that facilitates continual redefinition of central problems. When controversial issues are probed, the products of hearing are often disseminated in mass media, thereby affecting how large external audiences define situations. Although these processes are of interest to symbolic interactionists, official inquiries have so far received relatively little attention.[27]

Maintaining a critical stance toward the media and official investigations also extends to avoiding a rush to judgment in the opposite extreme: In explaining why their inquiries produce the kind of accounts that they do, we should hesitate before assuming cause. How they construct accounts is an empirical question. Official investigations and media are themselves organizations with goals and interests. Rather than attributing their accounts to amoral calculation or conspiracy, we might find that the realities they construct are explained by a complex mix of factors: (1) both the media and official investigations possess generic organizational structures and processes that often produce unanticipated consequences—recall that the autonomy and interdependence that affected the Presidential Commission investigating the *Challenger* tragedy are generic problems of social control;[28] (2) both may be influenced by the near-universal American cultural belief in individualism, which creates a general societal tendency toward reductionistic explanations when bad things happen, thus neglecting the social forces that affect individual action;[29] (3) they may lack sensitivity to and skill at identifying aspects of organizations as they might bear on the actions of employees and participants; (4) both the media and official inquiries are political actors, comprised of individual participants with a variety of interests and dependencies that each tries to preserve. These produce internal conflicts that may be played out in different ways, depending on the investigation; (5) both operate on deadlines, which circumscribe the time available for the investigative task and thus the thoroughness of their analysis.

2. Available data give a distinctive shape to any causal analysis. Although sensational cases present us with abundant data, it is important to remain sensitive to the limitations of that data. Often, research on sensational cases of corporate and organizational misconduct is retrospective and dependent upon secondary sources. Both retrospection and secondary sources have effects on the theories of cause produced in our own accounts. This caveat may seem prosaic and even unnecessary, but sometimes we operate on taken-for-granted assumptions without questioning them. Since much of sociological research is retrospective, we tend to take that for granted, perhaps losing sight of it as a possible problem; also, the determination a primary source and a secondary source can become confused; at least in my experience it did. I spent quite a long time with Volume I of the Presidential Commission, treating it as a primary source—and compared with the hearings and the information pouring from the media in the first six months after the tragedy, it was. However, I spent several months analyzing it before I realized it was a secondary source: a summary volume of a five-volume Commission report. As a summary, it distilled a much broader, deeper data base consisting of voices not heard and documents not presented that told a more complex story.

Both my *Challenger* research and Lee and Ermann's analysis of the Ford Pinto case benefited from available data. We had access to primary sources: personal interviews, transcripts of interviews conducted by official investigators, and extensive original documents produced by the respective organizations in years before the incidents. Our analyses of these two sensational cases was different from those of scholars who had published research on these same cases before us because we not only had structural data but also had microlevel data on decision making. The extensiveness and quality of the decision making data in these two case studies showed more complex explanations for three reasons. First, the data to which we had access circumvented the problem of retrospection: In both case studies, it permitted a reconstruction of events as they were occurring within the organization at the time those events were taking place. Second, the available data allowed us to focus on the organization as a key unit of analysis, examining internal structures and processes as they intersected with external networks and the institutional domain. Third, in both cases available data allowed macro-micro connections to be made, joining social structural conditions with individual actions and choices.

3. One advantage of a sensational case is that it is sensational. Consequently, it produces huge amounts of information, otherwise unavailable to us. Passas' work on the BCCI scandal, Zey's on Michael Milken, and Calavita et al. on the savings and loan crisis are three recent others that immediately come to mind.[30] At the same time that we are inundated with information from the media and official inquiries that engage in the production of knowledge about these incidents, the

sensational case also can give us access to original data, created at the time. In fact, we may have more access to original documents with the sensational case than with one that does not receive so much attention, leading to a more complete analysis because the modern organization, unlike the "street criminal," produces a documentary record that allows us to reconstruct the past. The benefits are great. However, these advantages—the sensational aspect of the case and the extensive data available—combine to produce very particular problems for research.

The first problem is that many sensational cases may develop what Nichols calls a "landmark narrative": an historically accepted explanation that, despite variations on the theme, is a shared, overarching definition of the situation that is commonly held.[31] Gamson, in *Talking Politics*, shows how media frames become cultural understandings that shape the beliefs and actions of individuals.[32] These landmark narratives influence our decision to investigate a particular case. We read the secondary sources and develop an understanding that shapes the theoretical perspective and assumptions that we bring to our analysis. Our data—and data sources—are always biased. Typically, in research, we control for these biases by conservative methods, such as analytic induction and primary data sources, that force us to consider alternative possibilities and hypotheses, intentionally seeking out information and sources that will challenge our assumptions. The second problem with the sensational case—and one that compounds the problem of the landmark narrative—is that the data from documents are often vast and unwieldy. Not only does this require new methods of data management and analysis, but these data will produce information that both supports and contradicts the historically accepted explanation. A landmark narrative develops from information that *surfaces* and becomes publicly acknowledged as part of the historically accepted explanation. That supporting information surfaces because it is more readily accessible and understood. Initially, we tend to support our starting hypotheses because we begin with the information that is readily accessible and understood. But as we dig deeper and deeper into what begins to feel like a bottomless pit of data, we may begin to discover information that contradicts the assumptions based on the historically accepted explanation.

In the *Challenger* case, I experienced these discoveries as mistakes in my own understanding, based on common sense assumptions about the case I initially developed as the media and the presidential investigation repeatedly affirmed circumstances surrounding the event that seemed to typify it as an example of organizational misconduct.[33] My discovery of facts that contradicted my starting assumptions went on throughout the research project. The research took nine years both because the sensational case produced data that were abundant and because it had an historically accepted explanation: I continued to discover mistaken assumptions that forced me to continually reconceptualize the analysis and keep on digging. Committed to the principles of analogical theorizing and analytic induction, I persisted, pursuing discrepant bits of information for many years. But nine years devoted to one project is not an option for many, without tenure and under pressure to publish. The person who takes on a sensational case needs to be aware of and weigh the costs and benefits.

4. Finally, the sensational case is, of course, a case study. This quality brings up yet one final cautionary tale. Shapiro once wrote, "Trying to develop general theory from a sensational case is like trying to teach Introductory Sociology from readings in the *National Enquirer*."[34] What she was pointing out was the tendency to generalize from a case study, without paying attention to what is different about it. Sensational cases are indeed different, which is why they become publicly identified as sensational in the first place. Many are unique because of the amount of harm done, the drama inherent in the harmful act, the duration of the pattern of offensive behavior, the size, public character, or success of the organization, or the distinctive position, public reputation, or number of the individuals who commit the harmful act. Scholarly inquiry into sensational cases of organizational misconduct must not only pay attention to how and why they are different, but also be balanced by inquiry into the nonsensational: the small organization, the routine and undramatic offense with extensive harm, the outcome with limited harm, the offenses of marginal or failing organizations—all those that the media and official investigations ignore.[35]

NOTES

1. An earlier version of this paper was presented at the Annual Meetings of the American Society of Criminology, Boston MA, November 16–19, 1995.

2. Diane Vaughan. *The Challenger Launch Decision: Risky Technology, Culture, and Deviance at NASA.* Chicago: University of Chicago Press, 1996.

3. The project was about analogical theorizing: building general theory across case studies of similar events, phenomena, or activities that occur in different social settings. In my first case, I had developed a theory of organizational misconduct, and was planning a book that compared three examples of misconduct in organizational forms of varying size and complexity. I had chosen and was working on two cases: police misconduct and violence and abuse in the family, and wanted a third that was a complex organization. For detail, see Diane Vaughan, "Theory Elaboration: The Heuristics of Case Analysis," in Charles Ragin and Howard S. Becker, *What is a Case? Explorations into the Foundations of Social Inquiry.* New York: Cambridge University Press, 1992; Diane Vaughan, "The Macro/Micro Connection in "White Collar Crime Theory," in Kip Schlegel and David Weisburd (eds.), *White Collar Crime Reconsidered.* Boston: Northeastern University Press, 1992; Diane Vaughan, *Theorizing: Analogy, Cases, and Comparative Social Organization* (in preparation).

4. These three factors act in combination to produce organizational misconduct. Their ability to do so is discussed in detail in Chapters 3, 4, and 5 of Diane Vaughan, *Controlling Unlawful Organizational Behavior.* Chicago: University of Chicago Press, 1983.

5. Robert A. Kagan and John T. Scholz, "The Criminology of the Corporation and Regulatory Enforcement Strategies." In *Enforcing Regulation*, ed. Keith Hawkins and John M. Thomas. Boston: Kluwer-Nijhoff, 1984.

6. Presidential Commission on the Space Shuttle *Challenger* Accident, *Report to the President by the Presidential Commission on the Space Shuttle Challenger Accident.* 5 volumes. Washington D.C.: Government Printing Office, 1986.

7. Lawrence B. Mulloy, telephone interview by author, 19 March 1993.

8. Lawrence B. Mulloy, Level I Flight Readiness Review, 51-E, 21 February 1985, Reel .098, Motion Picture and Video Library, National Archives, Washington, D.C.

9. For explanation, see House Committee, *Investigation: Hearings*, Vol. I, 410–412.

10. For acknowledgment of the video and a transcript, see Presidential Commission, *Report*, Vol. II, H2, H42.

11. Diane Vaughan, "The Dark Side of Organizations: Mistake, Misconduct, and Disaster." *Annual Review of Sociology* 25 (1999): 271–305.

12. Scott Sagan, *The Limits of Safety*. Princeton: Princeton University Press, 1993.

13. Dorothy E. Smith. "The Social Construction of Documentary Reality," *Sociological Inquiry* 44 (1974): 257–267.

14. William H. Starbuck and Frances J. Milliken, "Executives' Perceptual Filters: What They Notice and How They Make Sense," in *The Executive Effect*, ed. Donald Hambrick (Greenwich CT: JAI Press, 1988).

15. Ibid., 38.

16. Barry Turner, *Man-Made Disasters* (London: Wykeham, 1978); Barry Turner, "The Organizational and Interorganizational Development of Disasters," *Administrative Science Quarterly* 21 (1976): 383, 392–93. Perrow found that in the accident at the nuclear power plant at Three Mile Island, warning signals before the accident were seen as "background noise;" only in retrospect did they become signals of danger to insiders. Charles Perrow, "The President's Commission and the Normal Accident," in *The Accident at Three Mile Island: The Human Dimensions*, eds. David Sills, Charles Wolf, and Vivian Shelanski (Boulder: Westview Press, 1981).

17. Diane Vaughan, *Controlling Unlawful Organizational Behavior*. Chicago: University of Chicago Press, 1983, Chapter 6; "Autonomy, Interdependence, and Social Control: NASA and the Space Shuttle Challenger," *Administrative Science Quarterly* 35 (June 1990): 225–257; *The Challenger Launch Decision: Risky Technology, Culture, and Deviance at NASA*. University of Chicago, 1996, Chapter 8.

18. Richard P. Feynman, *What Do You Care What Other People Think? Further Adventures of a Curious Character*. New York: Norton, 1988.

19. Robert K. Merton, "The Unanticipated Consequences of Social Action." *American Sociological Review* 1 (1936): 894–904.

20. Diane Vaughan, "Rational Choice, Situated Action, and the Social Control of Organizations." *Law & Society Review* 32 (1998): 23–61.

21. Matthew T. Lee and M. David Ermann, "Pinto 'Madness' as a Flawed Landmark Narrative: An Organizational and Network Analysis." *Social Problems* 46 (1999): 30-47.

22. Ibid.: 43.

23. Ibid., 43.

24. Malcomb Spector and John Kitsuse, *Constructing Social Problems* Menlo Park, CA: Cummings, 1977; Gaye Tuchman, *Making News*. New York: The Free Press, 1978; Herbert Gans, *Deciding What's News*. New York: Pantheon, 1979; Victoria Swiggert and Ron Farrell, "Corporate Homicide: Definitional Processes in the Creation of Deviance," *Law & Society Review* 15 (1980): 161–182; Michael Schudson, "Why the News is the Way it Is," *Raritan* 2 (Winter 1983): 109–125; Noam Chomsky and Edward Herman, *Manufacturing Consent: The Political Economy of the Mass Media* New York: Pantheon, 1988; James Curran and Michael Gurevitch, eds., *Mass Media and Society*. London: Edward Arnold, 1992. William A. Gamson, *Talking Politics*. New York: Cambridge University Press, 1992.

25. See, e.g., Anthony Platt, ed., *The Politics of Riot Commissions.* New York: Macmillan, 1971; Michael Lipsky, "Social Scientists and the Riot Commission," *Annals of the American Academy of Political and Social Sciences* 394 (1971): 72–83; Mirra Komarovsky, ed., *Sociology and Public Policy: The Case of Presidential Commissions.* New York: Elsevier, 1975; William L. F. Felstiner, Richard L. Abel, and Austin Sarat, "The Emergence and Transformation of Disputes: Naming, Blaming, Claiming. . .", *Law & Society Review* 15 (1980–81): 631–654; Charles Perrow, "The President's Commission and the Normal Accident." In David Sills, V.B. Shelanski, and C.P. Wolf, eds., *Accident at Three Mile Island.* Boulder CO: Westview, 1982: 173-184. Jacqueline Choiniere, "The Grange Commission: Why Nurses are Scapegoats." *Resources for Feminist Research* 14 (1985–86): 11–23.

26. Lawrence Nichols, "Reconceptualizing Social Accounts: An Agenda for Theory Building and Empirical Research." In *Current Perspectives in Social Theory.* Greenwich CT: JAI Press, 10 (1990): 113–144; Lawrence T. Nichols, "Discovering Hutton: Expression Gaming and Congressional Definitions of Deviance." In *Studies in Symbolic Interaction.* Greenwich CT: JAI Press, 11 (1990): 309–337; Lawrence T. Nichols, "'Whistleblower' or 'Renegade': Definitional Contests in an Official Inquiry." Unpublished manuscript, 1991; Lawrence T. Nichols, "Bank of Boston as Landmark Narrative," *Social Problems* 1991.

27. Lawrence T. Nichols, "'Whistleblower' or 'Renegade': Definitional Contests in an Official Inquiry." Unpublished manuscript, 1991: 1.

28. For insights about structures and processes relevant to Commissions, see Paul F. Lazarsfeld and Martin Jaeckel, "The Uses of Sociology by Presidential Commissions." In Mirra Komarovsky, ed., *Sociology and Public Policy: The Case of Presidential Commissions.* New York: Elsevier, 1975: 117–143, and Robert K. Merton, "Social Knowledge and Public Policy: Sociological Perspectives on Four Presidential Commissions." In Mirra Komarovsky, ibid.: 153–178.

29. In the disaster literature, this cultural belief is demonstrated when official inquiries consistently define cause as "operator error." See e.g., Charles Perrow's account of the President's Commission that investigated the accident at Three Mile Island. Charles Perrow, "The President's Commission and the Normal Accident." In *Accident at Three Mile Island*, eds. David Sills, V.B. Shelanski, and C. P. Wolf. Boulder CO: Westview, 1982: 173–184; Lee Clarke and James F. Short, Jr., eds., *Organizations, Uncertainties, and Risk.* Boulder CO: Westview, 1992; Scott Sagan, *The Limits of Safety.* Princeton: Princeton University Press, 1993; Diane Vaughan, *The Challenger Launch Decision*, op. cit.

30. Nicos Passas, "I Cheat, Therefore I Exist: The BCCI Scandal in Context," in *Emerging Global Business Ethics*, W. Hoffman, S. Kamm, R.E. Frederick, and E. Petry (eds.). New York: Quorum Books; Mary Zey, *Banking on Fraud.* New York: Aldine, 1993; Kitty Calavita, Henry Pontell, and Robert Tillman, *Big Money Crime.* Berkeley: University of California Press, 1997.

31. Lawrence T. Nichols, "Bank of Boston as Landmark Narrative," op. cit.

32. William A. Gamson, *Talking Politics.* New York: Cambridge University Press, 1992.

33. See Vaughan, *The Challenger Launch Decision*, Chapter 2.

34. Susan Shapiro, "The New Moral Entrepreneurs: Corporate Crime Crusaders." *Contemporary Sociology* 12 (1983): 304–5.

35. See, e.g., Hugh Barlow, "From Fiddle Factors to Networks of Collusion," *Criminology, Law, and Social Change* 29 (1993): 319–337; Sections of Chapters 2, 8, and 9 in Stephen M. Rosoff, Henry N. Pontell, and Robert Tillman, *Profit Without Honor: White-Collar Crime and the Looting of America.* Upper Saddle River NJ: Prentice-Hall, 1998; Sections of Chapters 4, 5, and 6 of Gary S. Green, *Occupational Crime.* 2nd. ed. Chicago: Nelson Hall, 1997.

III

WHITE-COLLAR CRIME AND CORPORATE CRIME

Control Fraud and Control Freaks

William K. Black

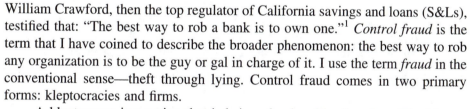

William Crawford, then the top regulator of California savings and loans (S&Ls), testified that: "The best way to rob a bank is to own one."[1] *Control fraud* is the term that I have coined to describe the broader phenomenon: the best way to rob any organization is to be the guy or gal in charge of it. I use the term *fraud* in the conventional sense—theft through lying. Control fraud comes in two primary forms: kleptocracies and firms.

A kleptocracy is a nation that is being plundered by its rulers. The biggest thieves in the world, probably throughout the history of the "civilized" world, have been kleptocrats.[2] The most costly thefts from firms are perpetrated by those who control them.[3]

The two variants of control fraud share four important traits: exploiting control increases the "take" from fraud, the need to maintain control causes the leaders to act like "control freaks" over their citizens and employees, their ability to control their firms and nations makes it extremely difficult to prosecute their frauds, and the combination of these elements ruins the firms and nations that are being looted. The harm caused dwarfs the (huge) gains from control fraud.

Kleptocracies and control frauds against firms, however, have some significant differences. Most of these differences make kleptocracies far worse than control fraud against a firm. The first difference is scale; a kleptocrat devastates a nation, whereas a control fraud hurts a firm's creditors and wipes out its shareholders. The "collateral damage" from kleptocracy is also far greater. People lose their freedom, even their lives, to kleptocratic control freaks, and the nation's economy may be ruined. Kleptocrats, however, have greater occupational risks—coups, assassinations, and revolutions. Another major difference is that no one finds it bizarre that a national leader would loot his or her country. We may find it appalling that the head of a church or a charity would defraud the organization, but we know from bitter experience that such frauds are a real risk. However, many folks consider the idea that a chief executive officer (CEO), especially one who owned 100 percent of the firm's stock, would loot his own company preposterous. Why destroy something you own? This final difference adds greatly to the difficulty of preventing control fraud against firms.

The focus of this article is on how and why control frauds create a firm culture supporting fraud, as well as efforts to restrain regulators and prosecutors. The dynamics of control fraud favor CEOs who are successful control freaks. Being a control freak, however, intensifies the already destructive effects of cultivating a culture of fraud among the senior managers. The result is larger losses to the firm's creditors. The effort to control the regulators can expand the collateral damage to the country of control fraud by corrupting politicians and regulators. This article addresses control frauds against for-profit firms, not kleptocracies.

The next section explains why control frauds can be uniquely destructive, why the concept is not preposterous even if the CEO owns all the firm's stock, and why waves of control fraud can occur, as they did during the savings and loan debacle. I then turn to an explanation of why creating a culture supporting control fraud is vital for the CEO and how that culture is created by control freaks. I conclude with a brief discussion of why the efforts to extend such control beyond the firm to protect against regulators and prosecutors can lead to scandal.

CONTROL FRAUD 101

There are three fundamental reasons why control fraud can be so devastating. First, large firms have massive assets, so the potential "take" from fraud can be large. Worse, the losses from fraud generally vastly exceed the gains to the fraudulent. Firms generally understand that fraud by employees is one of the biggest threats to their survival and adopt a panoply of protective devices, called "internal controls," to protect against the threat. Common controls include internal auditors, and limits and division of authority, e.g., limits on a vice president's authority to write checks on the firm's account without the approval of a senior VP. The internal controls, however, are like a home burglar alarm—the homeowner has the code to turn it off, and the CEO of a firm can "turn off" the internal controls.

Second, control fraud greatly reduces the risk of detection and prosecution. It uses means to "milk" the firm (discussed below) that look on their face to be legitimate and cause the firm to *appear* to be highly profitable, and it brings in outside experts to "bless" the fraudulent transactions in ways that can deflect blame from the CEO. Control frauds can be notoriously complex, making prosecution very difficult even if the fraud is detected.[4]

Third, control fraud poses special risks because many people don't believe it exists. It does seem irrational for a person who owns all the stock of a firm to destroy it through fraud. Why kill your own golden goose? In addition to common sense, there's finance theory, which teaches that when a substantial part of a CEO's wealth is invested in stock of the firm the CEO has the best possible incentive.[5] In his book about Donald Dixon, *after* Dixon's multiple felony convictions related to his role as CEO of Vernon Savings (known, not too affectionately as "Vermin Savings" by its federal regulators), James O'Shea concluded:

> To a man, Dixon and his fellow entrepreneurs probably didn't set out to destroy and plunder the savings and loans they had acquired. *That wouldn't have made any sense.* Keeping the thrifts alive was the only way they could keep their pockets full. They were simply agents of avarice who operated on the financial margin and got carried away.[6] (Emphasis added)

What O'Shea missed in his analysis turns out to be a point that is on the cutting edge of white-collar crime theory. As theory has developed, we have come to understand how a firm can be used as a "weapon." For example, it is expensive to dispose of hazardous wastes properly. Firms spring up that offer to dispose of such waste much more cheaply—they do so by dumping it illegally. We also know that the firm can be a "victim." Employee theft of merchandise and embezzlement are two common crimes.[7] In control frauds, the firm serves as *both* a weapon and a victim. The firm is used to defraud creditors (and other shareholders if they exist), and the firm's resources are converted to the use of the CEO/owner.[8]

O'Shea has ignored the role of the firm as a weapon to defraud a firm's *creditors*. A corporation is owned by its shareholders, and the firm receives cash when it sells it stock. However, shareholders normally provide only a minority of the firm's funds. Much of the money comes from creditors, i.e., people who *loan* money to the firm. The firm's debts to creditors are called "liabilities." There is a simple formula: Assets − Liabilities = Capital. "Capital" represents the interests of the shareholders. If it is negative, then the firm is insolvent, and if it closes the shareholders get *nothing* in bankruptcy. Equally important, however, is the fact that the shareholders do not lose anything more whether the firm ends up being insolvent by one dollar or by one billion dollars. (This is what "limited liability" means—the shareholders are *not personally* liable for the debts of the firm.) Conversely, if a healthy firm does exceptionally well, the gains go *entirely* to the shareholders, the creditors do not get paid anything extra. Think of the combination as a coin toss: heads, the controlling shareholder wins; tails, the creditors lose.

These facts create an incentive to engage in control fraud where either the controlling shareholder has little of his own funds invested in the firm's stock or the owner/CEO realizes that the firm is failing.[9] This incentive is strongest where a host of factors come together, but the central factor is the ability to overstate the value of assets.[10] It's pretty hard to overstate the value of assets that have a clear market value. If a friend tried to get you to pay twenty dollars for a tube of toothpaste, claiming it was unique, you would refuse to buy it. But the market value of some assets is very unclear, for example, a huge, unique, real estate project that will take three years to build. The value of such assets is determined by a type of expert known as an appraiser. The firm engaged in control fraud *chooses* the appraiser and the outside accounting firm that audits its financial statements. During the S&L debacle, it turned out to be easy to obtain grotesquely inflated appraisals and secure "clean" audit opinions from the nation's top accounting firms.[11] All of this is made worse by what economists call "asymmetrical information"—the CEO is likely to know more about the true (which is to say *insolvent*) nature of the firm than will outsiders like the firm's creditors and regulators.

So, a control fraud occurs when a firm is failing or already insolvent. The owner/CEO inflates the value of firm assets. Inflating the value of the firm's assets produces four benefits to the fraud, each arising from the formula: Assets - Liabilities = Capital. By inflating assets the CEO inflates capital. First, it makes the firm appear healthy, staving off pressure from creditors and regulators. Second, it makes it appear insane that the owner/CEO could be involved in control fraud, because it really does not make any sense for him or her to loot a highly profitable firm. Third, it provides a means and a justification for converting firm assets to the owner's personal benefits by making increased stock dividends, salaries, bonuses, and perks appear appropriate. Fourth, the fraud is likely to raise the value of the firm's stock, which benefits the controlling owner.

With this background, we can now understand what O'Shea missed. (The irony is that O'Shea did note all these factors in his book, but missed the implications.) Did Dixon invest substantial amounts of his own funds to acquire Vernon Savings? No. He borrowed the money from the prior owner and from a felon.[12] Was Vernon Savings insolvent at the time Dixon bought it? Yes, and it became ever more insolvent under Dixon.[13] Did Dixon inflate the value of Vernon Savings' assets? Yes, massively.[14] Did Dixon loot Vernon Savings? Yes, and he did so from the outset.[15] Dixon's control fraud was criminal, but it was not nonsensical.

The S&L debacle also exemplifies how waves of control fraud can be produced in a particular time and industry. The national commission appointed to study the causes of the debacle concluded:

> The typical large failure was a stockholder-owned, state-chartered institution in Texas or California where regulation and supervision were most lax. . . The failed institution typically had experienced a change of control and was tightly held, dominated by an individual with substantial conflicts of interest. . . In the typical large failure, every accounting trick available was used to make the institution look profitable, safe, and solvent. Evidence of fraud was invariably present as was the ability of the operators to "milk" the organization through high dividends and salaries, bonuses, perks and other means.[16]

Waves of control fraud occur when firms in a particular industry are failing in large numbers and the industry provides a far superior environment for control fraud relative to other industries. The widespread failures mean that both opportunistic and reactive control fraud are likely to be maximized. Opportunistic control fraud refers to folks like Don Dixon who are looking for opportunities to engage in fraud and seek out the best environment to do so.[17] As the national commission on the S&L debacle found, the vast bulk of the worst failures involved new entrants to the industry. The mass insolvency of the S&L industry provided fantastic opportunities to Dixon and his ilk: they could acquire an S&L for practically nothing, the regulators could not close many failed S&Ls because of lack of resources, and deregulation and desupervision provided superior means to obtain total domination of the firm, inflate asset values, and loot the firm.

Reactive control fraud refers to the incentive of owner/CEOs who already own failing or insolvent firms. In better times, running profitable firms, any incentives they had to engage in fraud were outweighed by the risks of prosecution and the gains from running a legitimate, profitable firm. Once their S&Ls became insolvent, however, the balance tipped for a few of these CEOs, and they committed control fraud.[18]

CREATING A CRIMINAL CULTURE

There is a real separation between firms used as a weapon and firms used as a victim in terms of creating a criminal culture at the firm. A classic example of the firm as a weapon is price fixing. Two or more competitors get together secretly (because price fixing violates the antitrust laws, which carry both criminal and civil penalties) and agree to raise their prices. This is one version of what economists call a cartel, and the conventional economic wisdom is that such cartels almost always fail quickly—not because of the antitrust laws, but because the rivals have a profit incentive to secretly cheat on the deal by cutting price slightly and selling far more goods.[19] Some cartels, however, have defied this conventional wisdom and lasted for over a decade until they were detected by prosecutors. Gilbert Geis' now-classic study of the heavy electrical equipment cartel demonstrated the key to its stability—the creation of a criminal culture in which new employees were socialized by more senior mentors into their role as servants of the price-fixing conspiracy.[20] Of course, no one, least of all a white-collar businessman, wants to think of himself as a felon, so a major aspect of the socialization was to help the employees rationalize the conspiracy as normal and desirable.

It is vastly more difficult to create a criminal culture when the firm is to serve as the victim, not the weapon, of fraud. Consider the problems facing a VP who wants to defraud his firm. He has to worry about internal controls designed to stop such fraud. Sometimes, because he knows how the controls work, he can spot a flaw and exploit it, but often the amounts he can take through such a window of opportunity are small, and he will usually have to create false documents that may be detected in the future. The most infamous example, Nick Leeson, who caused well over a billion dollars in losses and destroyed his firm, Barings Bank, the oldest investment banking firm in England, appears to have personally netted only small amounts through his fraud.[21] It would be far better to enlist other employees, particularly those running the internal controls, in his conspiracy. Sometimes that works, but the enlistment process is inherently risky; if the person rejects the conspiracy the VP may lose his job, be prosecuted, and have any hope of a future career destroyed.

Control frauds avoid most of these difficulties, which is why a fraudulent CEO poses not simply a somewhat greater risk to the firm than a fraudulent senior VP, but a massively greater risk. Such control frauds come in two primary forms: organized crime and seemingly legitimate business. The classic organized crime control fraud is known as a "bust-out."[22] The mob takes over a formerly legitimate business through some form of extortion. It proceeds to defraud the firm's creditors. For example, the bar buys large quantities of liquor on credit. The mob resells the liquor, burns down the bar for the insurance proceeds, and walks away. The people who commit a bust-out obviously know that they are crooks, and creating a mob culture is not the focus of this article.

A control fraud of a seemingly legitimate business also needs to create a special firm culture, but one in which the officers and employees need not believe that they are involved in crime. This calls for more subtle skills by the CEO. The really clever control frauds do not require the employees and officers to commit clear crimes, prevent them from gaining direct knowledge of the CEO's fraud, and convince them that the CEO/owner is a hero and the regulators and prosecutors the villains.

There are two fundamental ways in which the CEO can loot his seemingly legitimate firm, though in each case the ultimate victims are the creditors (and other shareholders). The first, least-subtle means is through conflict-of-interest schemes in which firm assets are converted to his private use through transactions with entities he controls. In the case of a bank, the CEO would cause the bank to make a loan to a real estate development firm in which he had a (hidden) interest. The real estate development firm would then default on the loan. Conflict-of-interest schemes are efficient fraud devices, i.e., a high percentage of firm assets can be converted to the CEO's personal use, but they are riskier devices because proving criminal intent is relatively easy once the conflict is discovered.

The more subtle means is for the CEO to cause the bank to make a *really* bad loan to an *unrelated* real estate developer. At first blush, this appears a nutty idea, but it is actually a stroke of genius as a fraud device. When accounting principles and practices get sufficiently perverted, it makes (fraudulent) sense to lend money to the worst borrowers you can find—*knowing* that they will default on their loans. Awful borrowers provide two big benefits to a subtle control fraud. They are willing to *agree* to pay higher interest rates than other borrowers, which produces greater *accounting* income to the bank, and they are willing to do reciprocal favors for the CEO/owner that are crucial to the longevity of the control fraud.[23]

The reasons awful borrowers are willing to promise to pay extremely high interest rates to banks engaged in control fraud are easy to understand. They have no alternative—honest and competent bankers won't lend them money. They also don't have anything to lose because the bank requires no downpayment and provides the money to "pay" the interest payments. They typically have no *personal* liability for the debts because they borrow through shell corporations. Having no intention of ever repaying either the principal or interest on the loan from their own resources, the borrowers have no downside financial risk. S&Ls engaged in control fraud frequently gave the borrowers an upfront "profit" payment. Further, many of these borrowers found ways to divert loan proceeds that were supposed to cover construction expenses to their personal benefit. So, it was a guaranteed "win" from the standpoint of the debtor.

Of course, making bad loans presents a serious problem to a control fraud down the line. Defaults are inevitable, which should require the lender to recognize large losses and perhaps lead the regulators to take over the bank or S&L. Here is where the bad borrowers provided unique services to aid the control fraud. The cruder scheme was for the lender to simply refinance the bad loan, i.e., send "good money after bad," to prevent the default. The better scheme was known in the trade as "trash for cash." The lender would loan enough funds (the "cash") to a bad borrower not only to build his favored project but also to purchase the real estate projects that were collateral on the earlier loans to other bad borrowers who had already defaulted (the "trash"). This would not only prevent the default but also create new accounting "profits."[24]

Either variant of control fraud against a seemingly legitimate lender requires the lender to adopt a policy of making a large volume of awful loans. This fact has several important implications. First, the firm will die, and it will die ugly, causing massive losses to the creditors unless the fraud is stopped very early. Vernon Savings, for example, had a *96 percent default rate* on its loans once the regulators stopped the "cash for trash" scam.[25] It will be hard to stop the fraud early because the firm will report that it is highly profitable and that loan defaults are rare. Second, if a wave of such frauds occur they can act like a financial tsunami, ruining regional economies (such as Texas in the mid-to-late 1980s) by causing a massive glut of office space that leads to a collapse of rental rates.[26] Third, one can see why such control frauds required the CEO/owners to be control freaks that shaped and perverted firm culture. I now turn to that point.

TRADITIONAL BANKING AND SAVINGS AND LOAN CULTURE

What do you think of when you think of the culture of a bank or S&L? Probably stuffy, conservative suits for the bankers, and polyester plaid or people like Jimmy Stewart in *It's A Wonderful Life* for the S&L. What do you think about when it comes to their approach toward lending? Ads on cable television by competitors parody it all the time—banks are slow to lend and require all kinds of paperwork and analysis, and then loan committee meetings before approving even small loans to individuals. Consider the challenge this posed to those engaged in control fraud. It seems like the worst possible starting point. You want to adopt a policy of making terrible loans, but the people working for you have been brought up to view making bad loans as sinful.

CREATING A FRAUD-FRIENDLY CULTURE

The scary part is that perverting this traditional banking culture proved to be an easily resolved problem for control frauds. If control frauds can overcome so readily a hostile culture, it is scary to think what they'll be able to achieve in industries with more fertile soils. Control frauds warped banking culture by acting like control freaks who dominated all aspects of the firm's culture. The most notorious example, Charles Keating of Lincoln Savings and Loan, created a culture that has been compared to the movie *The Stepford Wives*, in which employees and officers wanted to "be like" Charlie.[27] We can examine Keating's methods as a way of developing a better understanding of how firm culture can be shaped.

The most obvious key is leadership—the CEO always has a strong hand in shaping firm culture. This is one of the key advantages to control fraud. Like a kleptocrat, Keating used a combination of carrot and stick. He influenced most people the old fashioned way—he bought them! Keating paid individuals, mostly from relatively undistinguished backgrounds, huge salaries. Secretaries in his inner circle earned over $50,000 as long ago as 1984.[28] Keating could also be ruthless in firing people—the best way to get fired was to ask difficult questions.

Keating also used the cliches about S&L culture to change Lincoln Savings culture. His people would be identified as *rejecting* traditional S&L culture. Indeed, Keating was famous for deriding traditional S&L managers as dinosaurs. The image he sold to his people was that of the anti-S&L ethos. If S&Ls abhor risk, we will embrace it. If S&Ls love to document their deals, analyze them fully, and meet in committees before making loans, we will do none of those things. If S&Ls love to make home mortgage loans, we will stop making home loans.[29]

Keating's fundamental message to his troops was one of *superiority*. They were smarter, braver, and *more moral* than their *enemies*—the last term is important, as Keating made his people believe that anyone with a contrary view (particularly regulators) was an enemy. Superiority is a message we all like to hear from our boss; it isn't a hard sell.

The combination of believing that one is superior and that those who criticize you are enemies creates a culture that aids control fraud. If you know that you are a genius (because your boss tells you so, and pays you accordingly), then it follows that your boss is probably a genius. It also means that you can, and should, ignore criticism from regulators. It also means that really stupid practices, such as making loans to people who obviously aren't creditworthy, or allowing Michael Milken of Drexel *carte blanche* to buy and sell any junk bond for you without your review or approval, must be brilliant practices.[30] Indeed, if your enemies, the regulators, attack such practices, it follows that the practices must be good. In short, the culture creates an unshakable faith in the CEO.

Keating nurtured this faith through a series of steps. One of the other great advantages of control fraud is the ability to do all the hiring of officers. Keating tended to hire young people with no S&L experience and give them very high salaries and impressive titles—but little substantive responsibility. Keating was able to keep from trying the faith of his charges because of equally clever strategy. The type of huge real estate loans (all of them multimillion dollar deals) that Lincoln Savings made allowed Keating to personally direct every loan deal. The failure to document, analyze, and discuss the proposed deals prevented seeds of doubt from being planted among the faithful. Normal review would have disclosed how bad the loans were to his staff. Similarly, if Milken's junk bond deals (supposedly on Lincoln's behalf, but frequently to benefit Milken) had been subject to scrutiny by Keating's staff, awkward facts would have been revealed.

The other key was the old cliche: "nothing succeeds like success." Lincoln Savings (like the other control frauds) *reported* that it was highly profitable, indeed, it reported at times that it was the *most* profitable S&L in

America. (It was, of course, deeply insolvent and losing money due to the control fraud. It ended up costing the taxpayers *$3 billion—the most expensive S&L failure in history*.)[31] Think what it would have been like to be a young officer at Lincoln Savings: everyone around you told you what a genius Keating was, and how stupid the regulators were who claimed he was mismanaging the S&L. Then the latest financial information came in and you were told that you were working at the best, most profitable S&L in America. Who would you believe?

It is also critical that, unlike a senior officer, a CEO can create a culture aiding control fraud without ever overtly enlisting another in his or her fraud. Keating's means of shaping firm culture actually allowed him to picture himself as occupying the moral high ground. His enemies were the immoral ones. Keating's background helped him exploit this aspect of the firm culture. Keating's prior claim to media fame was as a vociferous opponent of pornography. He used Lincoln Saving's funds to make large charitable donations to Mother Teresa, and made much of his personal association with her. He described the regional regulators, based in San Francisco, as part of a homosexual/propornography conspiracy against him. No one who worked at Lincoln Savings had to rationalize being a crook. They were told that they were literally on the side of the angels fighting the figurative demons.[32]

While Keating was most extravagant and careful in his creation of a firm culture, he was typical among S&L control frauds in seeing the need, and finding the means, to very quickly change the culture of what had been a very traditional S&L. Others used different methods. One of the reasons Don Dixon's Vernon Savings became known as "Vermin" was his liberal use of prostitutes to make friends and influence people. Vernon Savings had been a very conservative shop with a religious board of directors prior to Dixon's acquisition. He arranged a trip for the directors to California, provided them with prostitutes, and never had another problem with his (thoroughly compromised) board! He also provided prostitutes to Texas' top state S&L regulator.[33] The means vary, but the goal does not. Control frauds are fully capable of using the stick to develop firm culture, but carrots generally work better. The top fraudsters want to be loved by their staffs. It doesn't simply help them commit fraud, it feels good.

COLLATERAL DAMAGE FROM CONTROL FREAKS

Those who engage in control fraud don't suddenly become control freaks because it is useful to their frauds. They have controlling personalities before they become CEO. When they are faced by external efforts to stop their frauds, they are likely to try to control these external forces, not simply counter them. Their ability to do so, of course, is more limited than their ability to dominate and pervert firm culture; however, a further advantage of control fraud is that it allows means to attack, delay, and even control external forces. Again, the contrast between fraud against the firm by a CEO and senior VP is striking. If the senior VP defrauds the firm, the firm may ally itself with the regulators and prosecutors to attack the officer. When the CEO is the criminal, all the firm's resources may be brought to bear to blunt the external threat. The firm's public relations staff can arrange news stories attacking the regulators, the firm's lawyers can bring suit against the government, copious experts can be hired by the firm to justify the CEO's actions, and the firm's lobbyists can attempt to get the legislative or executive branches to come to the aid of the CEO.

The S&L debacle demonstrated how these efforts at external control can create "collateral damage" (military jargon made famous most recently in the bombing of Serbia for damage to unintended targets) well beyond the firm that is being defrauded. Once more, Keating is the best-known example, but such efforts were common by other control frauds.[34] Keating was quite remarkable because he showed an ability to influence so substantially so many key branches of government. The result was a national political scandal that became known as the "Keating Five" affair (because of the five U.S. senators involved). A scandal that Keating had only peripheral involvement in, led primarily by Texas control frauds, helped cause the resignation in disgrace of Speaker of the House James Wright.[35]

Money has been described as "the mothers' milk of politics," and control frauds have lots of money. Indeed, one of the reasons Keating's staff was so grossly overpaid was that they were expected to make large political contributions to politicians of Keating's choosing. In addition, Keating caused Lincoln Savings to make extremely large "soft money" contributions to groups controlled by two of the senators that would eventually become part of the Keating Five. Keating also hired top lobbyists, public relations specialists, and experts (most notably Alan Greenspan, currently Chairman of the Federal Reserve) to aid his effort to block the federal regulators through congressional or executive branch intervention. Ultimately, Keating was able to get a *majority* of the U.S. House of Representatives to cosponsor a resolution calling on the regulators to back off, to convince five U.S. senators to meet privately with the regulators for the same purpose, and to get President Reagan to appoint a member of Keating's choosing to the three-member board that ran the S&L regulatory agency. That member's first material act was, after secret, grossly improper work with Keating's legal staff, to propose a subtle change in the regulations to immunize Lincoln's massive violation. His actions were detected, and he resigned in disgrace. What is less well-known is that Keating came very close to securing the appointment of *two* members of the regulatory agency, which would have given him majority control of the agency. With Keating in de facto control of the agency, the S&L debacle (estimated to cost $150 to 175 billion[36]) could have grown so large as to do far more than regional economic damage.[37]

Control fraud will kill the firm. Obviously, the fraudulent CEO/owner has the incentive to lengthen the time that he can defraud the firm and reduce the dangers of prosecution. He has the ability, because he controls the firm, and the mindset to seek to control external forces. If he succeeds, he will cause severe injury to the creditors and create a political scandal once the failure occurs. But, even if he does not succeed in controlling the regulators, his attempts may still cause a scandal that further lowers the trust of the people in their political system. Control fraud can cause injuries that go well beyond the economic.

NOTES

1. Quoted in U.S. Congress, House Committee on Governmental Operations 1988: 34.

2. Diamond, Jared M. 1997. *Guns, Germs, and Steel: The Fates of Human Society*. New York: W.W. Norton & Co.

3. Rosoff, Stephen M., Henry N. Pontell, and Robert H. Tillman, 1998. "Fiduciary Fraud: Crime in the Banking, Insurance, and Pension Fund Industries," in *Profit Without Honor*. Upper Saddle River, New Jersey: Prentice Hall, 190–225; National Commission on Financial Institution Reform, Recovery and Enforcement. 1993. *Origins and Cause of the S&L Debacle: A Blueprint for Reform*. A Report to the President and Congress of the United States. Washington, D.C.: Government Printing Office, July.

4. Calavita, Kitty, Henry N. Pontell, and Robert H. Tillman. 1997. *Big Money Crime*. Berkeley, California: University of California.

5. Easterbrook, Frank H., and Daniel R. Fischel. 1991. *The Economic Structure of Corporate Law*. Cambridge, MA: Harvard University Press.

6. O'Shea, James. 1991. *The Daisy Chain*. New York: Pocket Books, p. 279.

7. Rosoff, Stephen M., Henry N. Pontell, and Robert H. Tillman. 1998. *Profit Without Honor*. Upper Saddle River, New Jersey: Prentice Hall.

8. Calavita, Kitty, Henry N. Pontell, and Robert H. Tillman. 1997. *Big Money Crime*. Berkeley, California: University of California.

9. The same factors can also produce an incentive to engage in excessive risk. If the owner/CEO causes the firm to invest in ultra high-risk activities, there is a chance that the gamble will succeed and produce exceptional profits that he will capture. Should the gamble fail, the (huge) losses will be borne by the creditors, not the owner/CEO. The perverse incentive to engage in fraud or excessive risk is termed *moral hazard* by economists. Black, William K., Kitty Calavita, and Henry N. Pontell. "The Savings and Loan Debacle of the 1980s: White-Collar Crime or Risky Business?" *Law and Policy* 17 (1995): 23–55.

10. Akerlof, George A., and Paul M. Romer. "Looting: The Economic Underworld of Bankruptcy for Profit." Edited by William C. Brainard and George L. Perry. *Brookings Papers on Economic Activity* 2 (993): 1–73.

11. National Commission on Financial Institution Reform, Recovery and Enforcement. 1993. *Origins and Cause of the S&L Debacle: A blueprint for Reform*. A Report to the President and Congress of the United States. Washington, D.C.: Government Printing Office, July.

12. O'Shea, James. 1991. *The Daisy Chain*. New York: Pocket Books.

13. Ibid.

14. Ibid.

15. Ibid.

16. National Commission on Financial Institution Reform, Recovery and Enforcement. 1993. *Origins and Cause of the S&L Debacle: A Blueprint for Reform*. A Report to the President and Congress of the United States. Washington, D.C.: Government Printing Office, July: pp. 2-3.

17. Black, William K. 1998. *The Best Way to Rob a Bank is to Own One* (Unpublished dissertation).

18. Ibid.

19. Browning, Edgar K., and Mark A. Zupan. 1999. *Microeconomic Theory & Applications*. 6th ed. Reading, Mass.: Addison-Wesley.

20. Geis, Gilbert. 1967. "White Collar Crime: The Heavy Electrical Equipment Antitrust Cases of 1961," in *Criminal Behavior Systems: A Typology*, ed. M. Clinard and Q. Richard. New York: Holt, Rinehart & Wilson.

21. The internal control flaws that Leeson exploited were so severe as to amount to a shocking disregard by the firm of the basics of internal control. "Report of the Board of Banking Supervision Inquiry into the circumstances of the Collapse of Barings." 1995. Return to an Order of the Honourable The House of Commons dated 18 July 1995. London: HMSO.

22. Pizzo, Stephen, Mary Fricker, and Paul Muolo. 1991. *Inside Job*. New York: HarperPerrennial.

23. Black, William K., Kitty Calavita, and Henry N. Pontell. "The Savings and Loan Debacle of the 1980s: White-Collar Crime or Risky Business?" *Law and Policy* 17 (1995): 23–55.

24. Ibid.

25. O'Shea, James. 1991. *The Daisy Chain*. New York: Pocket Books.

26. Akerlof, George A., and Paul M. Romer. "Looting: The Economic Underworld of Bankruptcy for Profit." Edited by William C. Brainard and George L. Perry. *Brookings Papers on Economic Activity* 2 (993): 1-73.

27. Binstein, Michael, and Charles Bowden. 1993. *Trust Me*. New York: Random House.

28. Ibid.

29. Ibid.

30. Milken and Drexel would later plead guilty to multiple felonies. Drexel failed as a result of liabilities arising from these crimes. Stewart, James B. 1991. *Den of Thieves*. New York: Random House. For a vigorous defense of Milken, see: Fischel, Daniel. 1995. *Payback: The Conspiracy to destroy Michael Milken and His Financial Revolution*. Stewart was a *Wall Street Journal* reporter; Fischel is a law professor at the University of Chicago and was formerly an outside expert for Milken, Drexel, and Lincoln Savings.

31. Calavita, Kitty, Henry N. Pontell, and Robert H. Tillman. 1997. *Big Money Crime*. Berkeley, California: University of California.

32. Binstein, Michael, and Charles Bowden. 1993. *Trust Me*. New York: Random House.

33. O'Shea, James. 1991. *The Daisy Chain*. NY: Pocket Books. pp. 67-68.

34. Calavita, Kitty, Henry N. Pontell, and Robert H. Tillman. 1997. *Big Money Crime*, Berkeley, California: University of California.

35. Jackson, Brooks. 1988. *Honest Graft*. New York: Alfred A. Knopf. Mayer, Martin. 1990. *The Greatest-Ever Bank Robbery*. New York: Charles Scribner's Sons. For a different perspective, much more favorable to Speaker Wright, see: Barry, John M. *The Ambition and the Power*. New York: Penguin.

36. National Commission on Financial Institution Reform, Recovery and Enforcement. 1993. *Origins and Cause of the S&L Debacle: A Blueprint for Reform*. A Report to the President and Congress of the United States. Washington, D.C.: Government Printing Office, July.

37. Black, William K. 1998. *The Best Way to Rob a Bank is to Own One*. (Unpublished dissertation; University of California, Irvine).

Victims of Investment Fraud

David Shichor,
Dale K. Sechrest,
and
Jeffrey Doocy

There is a growing volume of literature that focuses on various kinds of white-collar crimes, including corporate crime. There are some who refer to most white-collar crimes as business crimes, because they are committed in the course of otherwise legitimate business activities, usually for material gain. Often, the business organization involved in illegal activities is in a financially pressed situation. On the other hand, professional literature dealing with organizations established for illegal business practices is sparse. Illegal activities conducted through these entities cannot always be characterized as white-collar crimes or business crimes, according to the traditional definitions, because in these cases illegal behavior is not incidental to legitimate, everyday business activities. Due to the similarities, the distinction between white-collar crime and fraud victimizations are often blurred; thus, for this paper the terms are used interchangeably. Many boiler-room type of telemarketing operations are involved in fraudulent activities, although not all of them necessarily promote scams (Stevenson, 1998). A notable exception to the paucity of empirical research on fraud victimization is the study conducted by Titus, Heinzelmann, and Boyle (1995), on the victims of personal fraud, which they define as "involving the deliberate intent to deceive with promises

* Note: The authors are indebted to Gil Geis, who is an active participant in the larger, ongoing project that has led to the development of this chapter. The conclusions reached are those of the authors and do not represent the positions or opinions of the California Department of Corporations.

of goods, services, or other financial benefits that in fact do not exist or that were never intended to be provided" (p. 54).

The growth of telemarketing as a tool of modern marketing strategy for legitimate, as well as for illegitimate, businesses may make the operation of fraudulent schemes and scams harder to recognize. It is easier for smooth-talking boiler-room salespersons to find prospective victims off-guard and victimize them through the phone when they do not have to establish a face-to-face relationship with them.

The telemarketing scheme that this paper focuses on was devised to get potential investors involved in bogus investments. It belongs to the category of offenses that Moore (1980, 32) calls "sting and swindles," which are described as "stealing by deception by individuals (or 'rings') who have no continuing institutional position and whose major purpose from the onset is to bilk people of their money." Edelhertz (1983) calls these schemes "white-collar crime as business." In offenses that fit into this category "the provision of goods, services, or property is only an excuse to grasp monies that bear no recognizable relationship to what is provided" (p. 116). He specifically mentions the "sale of worthless desert land or investment securities. . . based on fraudulent descriptions" (p.117). Investments and "fiduciary" frauds typically target individual victims.

Edelhertz pointed to several problem areas in the control of white-collar crimes. One of them has a special relevance for our research, namely, the problem of "reconciling the need to protect the public with deregulation policies" (p. 120). The sociopolitical atmosphere of the 1980s, with the business-friendly Reagan administration promoting a free-market system and deregulation, have facilitated the reinvigoration of the caveat emptor approach to business, resulting in an increase in various kinds of white-collar crime and fraud. This trend reached its crescendo in the national savings and loan debacle (Pontell and Calavita, 1993).

Since our interest is in learning about the victims of fraud and their victimization, Edelhertz's analysis of the elements of fraudulent operations is useful. He finds five elements present in a fraud:

(a) Intent to commit a wrongful act. . .
(b) Disguise of purpose or intent.
(c) Reliance by perpetrator on ignorance or carelessness of the victim.
(d) Acquiescence by victim in what he believes to be the true nature and content of the transaction.
(e) Concealment of crime by
    1. Preventing the victim from realizing that he has been victimized, or
    2. Relying on the fact that only a small percentage of victims will react to what has happened, and making provisions for restitution to or other handling of the disgruntled victim, or
    3. Creation of a deceptive paper, organizational, or transactional facade to disguise the true nature of what has occurred (Edelhertz, 1970, 12).

The last point is emphasized by Wheeler and Rothman (1982), who note the importance of organizations in white-collar crimes, because organizations are viewed by the public as more substantial than individuals and, therefore, prospective victims are more likely to trust them. This was seen in the fraudulent operations on which our research focuses. In this study the two major perpetrators of the fraud created between 150 and 200 partnerships to conduct their investment scheme (Goldman, 1995).

THE EFFECTS OF FRAUD ON VICTIMS

The above elements of fraud victimization may have profound effects on the victims. They often reinforce the victims' perception that they acted "foolishly" and may cause them to be deeply embarrassed. Also, victims of fraud easily can be blamed for their own victimization. Often they are not seen as bona fide victims by the public, by the officials, and even by the various victim services. An "ideal victim," according to Christie (1986, 18–19), is "a person or a category of individuals who—when hit by crime—are most readily given the complete and legitimate status of being a victim." He further indicates that the ideal victim has put a reasonable effort into self-protection. In the case of investment fraud, on which this study focuses, it is hard to claim that the victims have made sufficient efforts for self-protection. Many of them were defrauded because they were not vigilant enough to find out about the risks involved in investing with telemarketers unknown to them, and even more so, often they were driven by greed rather than by prudence and concern for financial safety (Schlegel and Weisburd, 1992). Walsh and Schram (1980, 42–43) draw an interesting parallel between victims of fraud and the victims of rape regarding their "innocence":

> . . . the victim might be presumed to have cooperated in order for the crime to occur, the statutory proofs required to sustain the charge will hinge on a showing of the blamelessness of the victim's conduct. The victim cannot logically suggest that cooperation was not forthcoming, since the fact of cooperation is already presumed.

Some people may become "chronic victims"; in other words, they may be victimized repeatedly by fraud. Blum (1972, 238) found three characteristics that describe this kind of victim: one, that they were "always looking for a deal"; second, some of them could not resist the aggressive sales techniques; and third, they had an unrealistic belief in other people. The plight of these victims can be neutralized by claiming that the first type of victims were "greedy," and in the case of the other two types of victims that they had not learned from their experiences while they should have done so.

There are some additional reasons that victims of white-collar crimes in general, and victims of investment fraud in particular, are viewed and related to differently than victims of "street crimes." The limited concern shown fraud victims is undoubtedly a reflection of the more lenient official and public attitude toward white-collar and fraud-related crimes and their perpetrators than toward street crimes and street criminals. Generally, investment fraud victims are seen as economically well-to-do people; therefore they do not seem to need as much sympathy because they can take their losses with relative ease. The professional interest in these victims is limited also among victimologists (Shichor, 1998), a fact that can be seen in the contents of victimology textbooks. For example, Karmen, in his introduction (1996, p. 10) states that his widely used textbook "focuses almost entirely on victims of street crimes." Similarly, other recently published victimology textbooks either do not deal with fraud victims or deal with them very briefly in just a few pages (see Doerner and Lab, 1995; Kennedy and Sacco, 1998; Meadows, 1998; Wallace, 1998). This neglect stems, at least partially, from the "paternalistic" approach of many social scientists who try to be helpful and supportive of weak, poor, and vulnerable victims. This is true for "liberal" and various shades of "left-oriented" victimologists, who look at victimization as the outcome of the culture of violence rooted in the core of the capitalist social structure. Consequently, they consider victims as pawns in the hands of conservatives, who use them to initiate strict laws and policies against street crimes and street criminals (Elias, 1993; Phipps, 1986).

According to this view, the most vulnerable individuals for victimization by street crimes are the poor and disenfranchised elements of society. This approach toward victims and victimization is not unique to the American scene but can be found in other industrial societies as well (see Mawby and Walklate, 1994). On the policy level, victim compensation and victim assistance programs that are usually operated or supported by government agencies and by nonprofit organizations concentrate on street crime victims (Roberts, 1990). This policy is based on the observation that:

> Victimization studies have shown that the impact of crime is uneven. It falls disproportionately on the poorer and more vulnerable section of the population and serves to compound the growing economic and social inequalities which have risen dramatically over the past decade (Matthews and Young, 1992, p. 2).

Conservatives also jumped on the bandwagon of violent victimization. In the 1980s, President Reagan appointed a task force to address the problems of victims of violent crime. Similarly, a Victims' Bill of Rights was enacted by several states. These measures, which focused on the problems of victims of violent crimes, not only were prompted by the genuine concern for the plight of these victims but also often disguised attempts to increase the severity of punishment for street criminals and the limitations of their legal rights. These policies were further supported by business interest groups that could cash in on the fear of crime generated by the media and by politicians who kept the crime issue on the front burner for their own political advantage. As for business, whole industries thrived on crime-related products and services and the profits derived from them. These included personal and home security products (alarms, detection systems, guns, etc.), private security services, insurance, counseling services, and various industries connected with different forms of crime control and corrections (see Lilly and Knepper, 1993). Women and other social activist groups who usually fought for liberal causes also joined this trend in their efforts to bring attention to violent crimes that are primarily directed against females, such as sex crimes, domestic violence, and child abuse.

VICTIM EXPERIENCES

All these developments diverted interest from white-collar and fraud-related crimes and consequently from the victims of such crimes. Since the 1970s the main source of information on victims and victimization became the National Crime Survey (NCS), which is now called the National Crime Victimization Survey (NCVS). These surveys collect a large amount of data, but do not contain information on white-collar and fraud victimization and victims. For practical reasons, at present the collected aggregate data serve as the basis of most victimological analysis and literature, and further add to the neglect of white-collar and fraud victimization.

In most cases, when white-collar and/or financial fraud victims are mentioned this topic is considered only as a side issue. One would expect more interest in and concern with these victims in the aftermath of the Wall Street securities scandals and the savings and loan debacle of the 1980s, in which many middle-class people lost their life savings. This lack of concern has a symbolic importance because it reinforces the caveat emptor mentality that is pervasive in the business world and conveys to the public, and especially to potential offenders, the message that fraud victims are not "real" victims. However, individual victims of these offenses, in spite of the fact that they are seen as well-to-do, greedy, and sophisticated investors who are taking calculated risks and who know about the business world, are not necessarily such. Shapiro (1984, 34), in her research on securities violations, found that among the victims there were only a few who could be considered wealthy and/or sophisticated investors. She came to the conclusion that the majority of them demonstrated "considerable naivete and gullibility-investing."

In another study focusing on the collapse of a small Southern loan company because of fraud by its management, Shover, et al. (1994) found that the majority of victims were of modest means and seeking safe investments. This kind of victimization may have long-term effects on elderly victims. The authors cite the case of an 82-year-old widow who could not sleep for months because the fear that she would lose her home. These kinds of fears were expressed by several victims of the large-scale investment fraud perpetrated during the 1980s (Shichor, et al., 1996) on which this chapter is focusing. Similarly, in the widely publicized Lincoln Savings and Loan case, many retirees were duped into unsafe investments and lost their life savings (see Calavita and Pontell, 1990).

Victims of fraud, in certain aspects, may have more negative experiences than victims of street crimes. It is common for the victims of all crimes to ask the penetrating question: "why me?" or "what did I do wrong?" That is, what was the reason for being "targeted" to become the victim? This question reflects a degree of self-blaming. Fraud and most white-collar crimes involve deceit. Victims are often tricked into participating in their own deception. Generally, these crimes involve breach of the victim's trust (Shapiro, 1990). Victims tend to ask themselves the disturbing question: "how could I be so stupid to fall for this scheme?" Thus, apart from the financial effects, this type of victimization impacts their self-concept and self-esteem, which in many cases may be even more devastating for the victim than their material loss. Therefore, victimization by fraud tends to cause not only financial harm but psychological damage as well (Levi, 1992). It can even affect husband-and-wife relationships (Sechrest, et al. 1998). The cumulative effect of material and psychological problems on the victims is expressed vividly by a victim of the investment fraud that is the focus of the current study:

> I did not know there was a scheme or a scam until I went into "bankruptcy" or whatever. I almost had a nervous breakdown. I have practically no income. I'm almost 71 years old and I borrowed from equity on my house. I owe almost $75,000. The first mortgage was just paid off after 30 years. It has totally caused a major loss of self-esteem and realization of victimization. I considered suicide. I am losing my home. (quoted in Shichor, et al., 1996, 105).

Victim embarrassment, coupled with the lack of compensation, results in a gross under-reporting of these kinds of offenses (Tomlin, 1982). Victim compensation programs by state agencies do not cover financial victimization, and restitution from the offenders is usually not forthcoming (Granelli, 1992). Recovery of some losses must be pursued through civil procedures that are often too lengthy and may become expensive. If corporations are involved in questionable practices, individual victims may have a hard time being compensated because of the superior legal services that big companies can afford. There is also a neglect and differential handling of these crimes by the media which, in turn, contribute to the neglect of fraud victims (Chermak, 1995).

JUSTICE SYSTEM RESPONSE

Victims of fraud have problems also with the justice system. As mentioned earlier, in many respects they are treated much like rape victims in that it is often presumed that they have cooperated with the alleged offenders. In this sense they have to prove that they are blameless (Walsh and Schram, 1980). Victims of investment fraud often feel that the system is not there to protect them and to punish the offender, and this appears to be more likely in the case of fraud. A victim of a consumer fraud expressed this opinion: "the court should be there to protect the innocent. I have come to the conclusion that our system is set up specifically to protect the criminal" (Jesilow, et al. 1992, 166). Similarly, Shover, et al. (1994) found that many victims of bank fraud that they have interviewed were more upset with the ways the authorities handled their case than with the perpetrators of the fraud. It is sometimes hard to accept, but victims should be aware that they deal with the "criminal justice system" and not with a "victim justice system."

Victims often feel defenseless, and many believe that the authorities should better control and regulate the telemarketing business; however, legal and constitutional issues (e.g., the First Amendment) are involved in the regulation of this industry. These legal complexities are exploited by slick and skillful operators. While the victims are still licking their wounds, impostors such as the "two Daves," the main operators of the investment scam that we are dealing with, not only remained unpunished more than seven years after their operation was closed by state investigators, but there are reports that at least one of them is still involved in fraudulent schemes.

VICTIMS OF THE "TWO DAVES" FRAUD

The current study focuses, as noted, on the victims of a large-scale investment fraud that was perpetrated by the "two Daves," David Bryant and David Knight, during the 1980s until 1991, when their operation was closed down by the investigators of the California Department of Corporations. The two perpetrators set up companies that were selling phony investment schemes, mostly gas and oil leases through telemarketing. They basically ran large-scale boiler-room operations. While the headquarters of the 150 to 200 partnerships operated by the "two Daves" were in southern California, they were selling their "investments" nationwide. The number of victims of these operations is estimated to be between 7,000 and 8,000, although some estimates put the number around 12,000. The amount of money involved exceeded $160 million and may have been well over $200 million (Goldman, 1995).

The data for this study were based on two sources. One, the demographic and personal information available on 8,516 identifiable victims of these investment schemes in the files of the California Department of Corporations. This database deals with the victims of twenty-four of the above mentioned "companies" for the period of 1984 to 1992. These companies were operating under names that projected a certain level of credibility, such as "Remington Securities, Inc." (25 percent of the victims), "Broker's Investment Corporation" (14 percent), "Ellman & Howe Securities" (11 percent), and "Brighton Industries, Inc." (8 percent). The second source of information is based on the data that were collected through a questionnaire mailed to a random sample of the victims. From the 281 questionnaires sent, 152 (54.1 percent) completed questionnaires were returned, a figure considered to be a relatively high return rate.

Data Analysis

The analysis of 8,489 cases in which information was available indicated that among the victims-investors, 4,106 (48.4 percent) were males only, 1,194 (14.1) percent were females only, and in 2,837 (33.4 percent) of the cases couples were listed as investors. As mentioned, the scope of the investment fraud was nation-wide, but the majority of the victims (55.8 percent) were from California, which is not surprising considering that the "two Daves" headquarters was in southern California; thus the scam operations were run from this state, possibly because of the size of the population and the relative affluence of the region: 10.1 percent of the victims were from Illinois, 8.1 percent from Minnesota, 6.9 percent from Ohio, and 5.0 percent from Colorado. The reasons for this distribution are not clear. It may be that the Daves had professional and personal connections in the above states, or there were other factors that made these states attractive for their scam operations or in other ways facilitated them, such as the favorable legal environment.

The amount of investment by the victims varied a great deal. The smallest amount was $500 by two investors (apparently that was the minimum sum that could be invested in a partnership), the largest amount was $550,000 by one investor. About one third, 2,803 (32.9 percent) invested less than $10,000; 40.6 percent invested between 10 and 20,000; 21.4 percent between 20 and 40,000, and the remaining 5.1 percent invested more than $40,000. The most-frequently invested amount (the mode) was $10,000 by 2,905 victims, a bit over one third of the total (34.1 percent). The median amount of investment was $9,687. Only about one quarter, 2,257 (26.5 percent) put $20,000 or more into these partnerships. The amount invested varied by gender. Males tended to invest higher amounts, 5.9 percent of them more than $40,000; 4.7 percent of the females invested more than $40,000; and 3.9 percent of the couples invested more than $40,000.

As mentioned, a questionnaire was sent to 281 randomly selected victims in January, 1994. This figure was roughly 3 percent of the known victims. Out of these, 152 questionnaires that could be used for analysis were returned. This 53.9 percent return was considered adequate for analysis.

The responses to this survey reveal additional information about the identity of the victims, the ways they were recruited to participate in these schemes, their attitudes and perceptions toward their victimizers and their victimization, and the ways the authorities handled their case.

The perception of investors as an affluent group seemed erroneous. In dollars based on 1990 values, over half the investors (59.1 percent) had a yearly family income of less than $60,000; 15 percent had even less than $30,000. Only 17.3 percent had more than $90,000 annual income. About one third, 34.4 percent, lived in metropolitan areas, 37.1 percent in cities having more than 50,000 population, 19.9 percent in small towns, and 6.6 percent in rural areas. Thus the large majority, more than 70 percent, came from urban environments where usually people are exposed to various investment opportunities and supposedly more informed about them.

The overwhelming majority of the respondents (97.3 percent) listed "promises of gain" as the most-often mentioned promise made by telemarketers at the first call. Another often mentioned selling point was tax breaks; 86.8 percent reported this factor, which was probably more important among respondents in the higher income brackets. The mentioning of possible risk factors by the agents was reported by 88.2 percent of the respondents, and this high figure shows that the agents were aware of the legal responsibilities of investment marketing and wanted to be sure that they fulfilled them, at least formally. It was not mentioned how they talked about these risks, although it is likely that they mostly played down the possibility of losing money in their sales pitch.

After receiving three to four initial calls, almost all the victims reported that there were later calls to them from the agents; in fact, more than two-thirds (66.7 percent) of the victims reported that they received six or more calls. About half the investors reported receiving additional material concerning their "investment" after the receipt of the prospectus, which is legally required to be sent by all companies that seek investments from the general public.

The majority of the victims (59.6 percent) reported that they discussed the investment with someone else before making their final decision. However, there was a major difference between males and females in this regard. While among the males only 56.2 percent reported doing so, 80 percent of females discussed their investment decision. Most of the participants (64.4 percent) discussed the issue with only one person. The most-often mentioned person with whom they discussed the investment was their spouse (32.8 percent) followed closely by discussion with an expert (30.3 percent). In spite of the relatively high percent of discussion with "experts" (the qualification of the experts was not detailed, i.e., whether they were gas and oil, financial, or other experts) the victims got involved in this fraudulent investment.

Interestingly, the great majority of respondents (82.3 percent) reported that initially they had reservations about investing in the above partnerships. There was a clear difference in this respect between males and females—86.6 percent of the male victims reported such reservations, compared with only 55.5 percent of the females. The obvious question is: what convinced these individuals to invest in spite of the high level of reservations reported? The first and most important reason by far was the "agent's persuasiveness"; 72.4 percent indicated this factor. Two other factors mentioned as second and third in importance were the attractiveness of the "prospectus," and the "advice of others." These answers highlight the importance of the verbal skills and the manipulative ability of individual agents, which was probably enhanced by the instructions and "pep talks" of the boiler-room operators themselves. Stevenson (1998, 92) emphasizes the importance of middle-class verbal skills among boiler room pitchmen and the repetitious learning of the pitches. The salesmen have to learn "how to open a pitch, mastering the close and comeback techniques, practicing voice control, and taking charge of a telephone conversation." Also, the presentation of the scheme as a legitimate, "dignified," and successful operation illustrated by a well-written and nicely illustrated prospectus was important. Almost all the victims expressed their suspicion that many details were falsely represented to them. According to the respondents, the most-often mentioned (38.3 percent) misrepresentation was the claim of a "high return" on the investment; "low risk" as another misrepresentation was mentioned by 14.3 percent, and being a "reliable and legitimate company" was mentioned by 13.5 percent of the respondents.

The distribution of amounts invested by the sample of survey participants was somewhat different from the distribution for the total population of victims discussed earlier. There was a slightly higher percent of small investments ($10,000 or less); 37.1 percent in the sample vs. 32.9 percent in the total population, but there was a greater difference in the major investments ($100,000 or more); 9.8 percent among the sample vs. 1.0 percent in the total victim population. Many investors in the survey invested more than once with the "Daves." About 60 percent invested more than three times, and about 30 percent six times or more. This pattern may have been influenced by the fact that the perpetrators tried to manipulate the victims through the familiar way of providing some returns at the beginning in order to gain their victims' confidence and encourage them to continue to pour money into their schemes. An indication of this practice is the fact that more than half of the respondents (55.4 percent) reported that they received some return on their investment, most of them up to $1,000, although thirteen of them received more than $5,000. Regarding the relationship between the sum invested and the extent of the return, the greater the amount invested, the more likely the subject was to report some return. However, of 69 subjects who reported the amount of cash returned, 82 percent got back less than $5,000, and most (45%) got less than $1,000 on investments of up to $50,000. Larger investments yielded slightly greater returns.

A further review of the pattern of reinvestment indicated that females were more likely to reinvest (60 percent), than males (50.9 percent). The participants also were asked whether they had any previous experience with similar investments. About one-third of them (34.7 percent) answered in the affirmative. The next question to those who were previously involved in similar investments asked about the outcome of their experiences. Seventeen percent reported that the previous experience turned out "very well," 43.4 percent thought that it was "OK," and 39.6 percent reported that it turned out "poorly." Interestingly, the relatively high percent of respondents who had a negative experience with their previous investments were ready to try it again. It would be instructive to know how many of these respondents were finally deterred from investing again in similar investments.

When the victims' reactions to their loss in these fraudulent investments were solicited in the survey, the largest group (39.2 percent) expressed anger and dismay; 23.1 percent reported similar sentiments, but presented their feelings more mildly, stating that they were disappointed, shocked, and could not believe that this would happen to them. A smaller proportion, 10.9 percent, were philosophical about their loss, showing an acceptance of the fact. One respondent even looked at this outcome with a stoic view as a part of the risk one takes when he/she invests; another 5.9 percent expressed helplessness and sadness rather than anger; and, finally, a small number (five, 2.9 percent) showed some "active" response by stating that they will never again be involved in such a scheme. One respondent even demanded legal action against the perpetrators; sadly, it was reported that one victim apparently died because of effects of his loss in this fraud.

A few questions were asked concerning the actual actions taken as a reaction to the fraud. It turned out that most of the victims did not do much about the current situation concerning the case. There was an attempt to take some action in this case through an organization that had been established for purposes of recovering the losses; 37.8 percent of the victims belonged to this organization, while 62.2 percent did not join. Among the fifty-seven individual victims who did join, the majority (forty-five, 78.9 percent) reported that they are active or very active in this organization. When the respondents were asked to evaluate the activities of this organization, more than 40 percent did not answer. Among those who did rate the activities of this organization, about half had a positive view and the other half expressed various degrees of dissatisfaction. Obviously, this evaluation was dependent on the expectations that individuals had concerning the possibility of certain actions that would lead to the recovery of at least some of their investments.

Similar considerations were taken into account when questions were asked regarding the actions of the authorities in this case. The first question posed focused on the respondents satisfaction or dissatisfaction with the authorities' handling of the case. The overwhelming majority of respondents, 69.5 percent, as expected, were not satisfied, versus only 16 percent who reported that they were satisfied with the authorities' actions in this case; 13.7 percent reported that they didn't know anything about the authorities' response to this apparently fraudulent scheme. This may indicate that the respondents in this last group were uninformed about what was happening with this case and/or it may be a further indication of the authorities' failure to keep the victims informed about the status of their investigation. It is worthwhile to mention that there were some differences in the answers of males and females. While among males 17.4 percent were satisfied with the authorities' handling of the case, only one (6.3 percent) female expressed the same view. While we do not have any direct answer for this discrepancy, we may speculate about some reasons, e.g., males may have more investing experience and are more familiar with the "relaxed" attitudes of the authorities in protecting the public from victimization by fraud.

Following this line of questioning, the respondents were asked their opinion about what actions should be taken in this case. Roughly one third of the victims surveyed did not answer this question, either because they did not know what to suggest or because they considered this as a "lost case." Among those who did relate to this question, 32.7 percent claimed that they don't know what action should be taken. These two groups ("no answer" and "don't know") accounted for 53.6 percent of the total number of respondents. The fact that the majority of victims didn't know or didn't suggest any actions regarding this large-scale fraud may indicate the prevalence of an anomic state of mind among the victims. It was a situation which they did not expect, were not familiar with, and didn't know how to relate to. Among those who suggested some actions, the majority wanted a more aggressive stand to be taken against the perpetrators, so that they will be punished, and some suggested that the case should be settled (it was not completely clear what was meant by this suggestion).

Finally, the respondents' recommendations for future preventive actions to avoid similar kinds of victimization by fraud of other potential investors were solicited. This was an open-ended question, therefore, a wide variety of suggestions were offered, which were not easily summarized. The suggestions can be divided into two major categories: (1) actions by government agencies; (2) actions by potential individual investors.

The suggested actions by government may be subdivided into legislative actions and actions by control agencies. Legislative actions include stricter laws and regulations for the investment industry (licensing, bonding); outlawing solicitation; prohibiting dealings that are unregulated by the SEC; establishing a government office that can advise on these investments; dissemination of more public information, and printing warnings on advertising literature. These suggestions were given by 45.9 percent of the respondents. Actions by the control agencies include punishing fraudsters to deter them from defrauding victims; reporting to the police (with the assumption that some action will be taken); and to monitor boiler room operations. These control agencies' activities were recommended by 13.9 percent of the survey participants.

The various recommendations for individual investors implied that there is a personal responsibility either not to get involved in these investment schemes at all ("hang up the phone," "invest only with known companies," "avoid limited partnerships," etc.), or to be careful and to conduct personal investigations making sure that the investments are legitimate, to "be skeptical" of investment offers, and/or to make sure that the investor can afford the investment and the potential loss of money ("don't invest if can't afford it"). These recommendations for the potential investors were made by 40.2 percent of the respondents.

DISCUSSION AND CONCLUSIONS

One of the recurring themes in the analysis of white-collar and fraud-related crimes is that the victims of these crimes tend to be neglected in comparison to the victims of the so-called "street crimes," in spite of an increase in studies dealing with these victims. It is not an isolated occurrence that the "two Daves" were not seriously punished for their large-scale fraud, which victimized thousands of would-be investors, and that their victims were not able to recover even a fragment of their losses.

Our research is not unique with respect to this outcome. The case of one of the better-known investment frauds, the Home-Stake oil scam (McClintick, 1977), which started in the 1950s and continued into the early 1970s, showed many similarities to the current case, but there were some differences as well. Probably the major difference was that among the Home-Stake investors there were a number of celebrities, well-known lawyers, politicians, businessmen, and business executives. Quite a few of them invested six-figure sums in the project. The main purpose of the investment was to create tax shelters. This case also demonstrated that the regulatory and the criminal justice systems did not pay enough attention to early warnings about fraudulent activities by the perpetrators, and that they were not seriously punished when the case was handled by the criminal justice system. The main figures were placed on probation and had to pay relatively modest fines, and the victims lost their investments. It was interesting to learn that even rich, seasoned, and influential investors can be duped and are not immune to becoming victims of fraud.

In many cases, even if the Federal Trade Commission (FTC) is successful in putting the fraudulent operations out of business through the courts, the regulators and the criminal investigators fail to collect what they win in court and to distribute it to the victims (Leeds, 1999, p. A6). A recent article the *Los Angeles Times* reported that "con artists who have made Southern California the nation's fraud capital operate in a world where crime pays—so long as they make the cash disappear." Often the scam operators transfer the money that they made to offshore financial havens, find legal loopholes to use the bankruptcy laws for protection, or simply spend it. The end result is the same, and the victims do not get restitution. The authorities are not successful, and often are not very interested in following these cases. They do not seem to be a high priority for the criminal justice system, while many victims are forced into serious financial hardships because of the scams.

This situation obviously raises hostile feelings and negative attitudes among the victims toward the regulators and against the entire criminal justice system. These feelings and attitudes are sometimes as strong or even stronger than the animosity against the perpetrators themselves, because of the recognition that the very same system that should enforce the laws does not provide protection for victims who abide by the same laws. These feelings are exacerbated by the fact that many street criminals go to prison for relatively minor crimes (such as some of the three-strikes sentences in California), and these offenders often get away with large sums of money and then return to "business as usual" before too long. A fact that clearly adds insult to injury.

REFERENCES

Blum, R. H. 1972. *Deceivers and Deceived*. Springfield, IL: Charles C. Thomas.

Calavita, K., and H. N. Pontell. 1990. "Heads I win, tails you lose: Deregulation, crime and crisis in the Savings and Loan industry." *Crime and Delinquency* 36 (3): 309–341.

Chermak, S. M. 1985. *Victims in the News: Crime in the American News Media*. Boulder, CO: Westview.

Christie, N. 1986. "The ideal victim." In Fattah, E. A., ed. *From Crime Policy to Victims Policy*. New York: St. Martin's Press.

Doerner, W. G., and S. P. Lab. 1995. *Victimology*. Cincinnati, OH: Anderson.

Edelhertz, H. 1983. "White-collar and professional crime: The Challenge for the 1980s." *American Behavioral Scientist* 27 (1): 109–128.

Edelhertz, H. 1970. *The Nature, Impact and Prosecution of White-Collar Crime*. Washington, D.C.: U.S. Department of Justice, Law Enforcement Assistance Administration.

Elias, R. 1993. *Victims Still: The Political Manipulation of Crime Victims.* Newbury Park, CA: Sage.

Goldman, S. 1995. "The Two Daves." *California Lawyer*, February, 44–49.

Granelli, J. S. 1992. "Getting their Day in Court." *Los Angeles Times*, A1 (March 1).

Jesilow, P., E. Klempner, and V. Chiao. 1992. "Reporting consumer and major fraud: A survey of complaints." In Schlegel, K., and D. Weisburd, eds. *White-Collar Crime Reconsidered.* Boston, MA: Northeastern University Press.

Karmen, A. 1996. Crime Victims: *An Introduction to Victimology*, 3rd ed. Belmont, CA: Wadsworth.

Kennedy, L. W., and V. F. Sacco. 1998. *Crime Victims in Context.* Los Angeles: Roxbury.

Leeds, J. 1999. "For Nation's Scam Artists Crime Does Pay." *Los Angeles Times*, pp. A1, A6 (April 20).

Levi, M. 1992. "White-Collar Crime Victimization." In Schlegel, K., and D. Weisburd, eds. *White-Collar Crime Reconsidered.* Boston, MA: Northeastern University Press.

Lilly, J. R., and P. Knepper. 1993. "The Corrections-Commercial Complex." *Crime and Delinquency* 39(2):150–166.

Matthews, R., and J. Young. 1992. "Reflections on Realism." In Young, J., and R. Matthews, eds. *Rethinking Criminology: The Realist Debate.* London: Sage.

Mawby, R. I., and S. Walklate. 1994. *Critical Victimology.* London: Sage.

McClintick, D. 1977. *Stealing from the Rich: The Home-Stake Oil Swindle.* New York: M. Evans and Company.

Meadows, R. J. 1998. *Understanding Violence and Victimization.* Upper Saddle River, NJ: Prentice-Hall.

Moore, M. H. 1980. "Notes Toward a National Strategy to Deal with White-collar Crime." In Edelhertz, H., and C. Rogovin, eds. *A National Strategy for Containing White-Collar Crime.* Lexington, MA: D.C. Heath.

Phipps, A. 1986. "Radical Criminology and Criminal Victimization: Proposals For the Development of Theory and Intervention." In Matthews, R., and J. Young, eds. *Confronting Crime.* London: Sage.

Pontell, H. N., and K. Calavita. 1993. "White-collar Crime in the Savings and Loan Scandal." *Annals of the Academy of Political and Social Science* 525:31–45.

Roberts, A. R. 1990. *Helping Crime Victims.* Newbury Park, CA: Sage.

Schlegel, K., and D. Weisburd, eds. (1992). *White-Collar Crime Reconsidered.* Boston: Northeastern University Press.

Sechrest, D. K., D. Shichor, J. H. Doocy, and G. Geis. 1998. "A Research Note: Women's Response to a Telemarketing Scam." *Women & Criminal Justice* 10 (1):75–89.

Shapiro, S. P. 1990. "Collaring the Crime, not the Criminal: Reconsidering the Concept of White-collar Crime." *American Sociological Review*, 5:346–365.

Shapiro, S. P. 1994. *Wayward Capitalists.* New Haven, CT: Yale University Press.

Shichor, D. 1998. "Victimology and the Victims of White-collar Crime." In Schwindt, H.D., E. Kube, and H. H. Kuhne, eds. *Festschrift fur Hans Joachim Schneider.* Berlin: Walter de Gruyter.

Shichor, D., J. H. Doocy, and G. Geis. 1996. "Anger, Disappointment and Disgust: Reactions of Victims of a Telephone Investment Scam." In Sumner, C., M. Israel, M. O'Connell, and

R. Sarre, eds. *International Victimology: Selected Papers from the 8th International Symposium*. Canberra, Australia: Australian Institute of Criminology.

Shover, N., G. L. Fox, and M. Mills. 1994. "Long-term Consequences of Victimization by White-Collar Crime." *Justice Quarterly* 11:75–98.

Stevenson, R. J. 1998. *The Boiler Room and Other Telephone Sales Scams*. Urbana, IL: University of Illinois.

Titus, R.M., F. Heinzelmann, and J.M. Boyle. 1995. "Victimization of Persons by Fraud". *Crime and Delinquency* 41(1):54–72.

Tomlin, J. W. 1982. "Victims of White-collar Crimes." In Schneider, H. J., ed. *The Victim in International Perspective*. Berlin: Walter de Gruyter.

Wallace, H. 1998. *Victimology: Legal, Psychological, and Social Perspectives*. Boston: Allyn and Bacon.

Walsh, M. E., and D. D. Schram. 1980. "The Victim of White-collar Crime: Accuser or Accused?" In Geis, G., and E. Stotlend, eds. *White-Collar Crime: Theory and Research*. Beverly Hills, CA: Sage.

Wheeler, S., and M. L. Rothman. 1982. "The Organization as Weapon in White-Collar Crime." *Michigan Law Review* 80 (7):1403–1426.

Penny Wise
Accounting for Fraud
in the Penny-Stock Industry

Sean Patrick Griffin
and
Alan A. Block

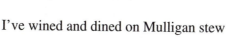

I've wined and dined on Mulligan stew
and never wished for turkey.
As I hitched and hiked and grifted too
From Maine to Albuquerque.

"The Lady is a Tramp"
Rodgers and Hart

U.S. Representative Markey: "Is there any legitimate market for penny stocks in the United States?"

Fraudster Lorenzo Formato: "I don't believe so. I don't think so."

Trading in penny stocks in the United States is to a large extent a racketeering enterprise, probably without peer in the realm of the securities industry.[1] As we shall demonstrate, the primary purpose of the major penny-stock firms is "to provide a vehicle for the perpetration of illegal activity for personal gain." Their "crimes are premeditated, organized, continuous, and facilitated by the participation of public officials."[2] According to Kitty Calavita and Henry N. Pontell, this means penny-stock companies are organized criminal enterprises.

Unfortunately, the underworld of penny stocks has rarely been looked at by criminologists.[3] Probably the best known theoretical statements on the subject are the following: "small penny stock firms may find themselves more likely to be classified as violators because they cannot 'authoritatively reinterpret (within limits) what the rules mean';" and the contention that "regulatory compliance is a fluid process that involves negotiated interpretations of both rules and facts."[4] We will show, however, that constant and consistent fraudulent practices are the norm in the penny-stock world since its creation, and are the primary reasons why penny-stock traders may be more likely classified as violators. This has nothing to do with other types of securities firms, which may or may not be consistent rule breakers. Selling stock in bogus firms cannot be successfully negotiated no matter how artfully presented. In the world of penny stocks regulatory compliance is anathema pure and simple.

The most sustained theoretical discussion about fraud, although not focused on penny-stock crimes in particular nor the securities markets in general, was sparked by Michael Gottfredson's and Travis Hirschi's claims about white-collar crime.[5] As is well known by now, Gottfredson and Hirschi concluded that fraud, embezzlement, and forgery are rare events within the general schema of crimes, and that their origins lie almost completely in the realm of individual psychology—a lack of "self control" on the part of the violator. Furthermore, they opine that

> Ordinary occupations require people to be in a particular place at a particular time. They also require educational persistence, willingness and ability to defer to the interests of others, and attention to conventional appearance. These occupational requirements tend to be inconsistent with the traits comprising criminality. White-collar occupations therefore tend to demand characteristics inconsistent with high levels of criminality. In other words, selection processes inherent in the high end of the occupational structure tend to recruit people with relatively low propensity to crime.[6]

Their approach discounts actual criminogenic business environments, including related political structures, as well as the past criminal practices in a variety of industries in which highly organized white-collar crimes have been and continue to be normal and routine events.[7] Additionally, by only relying upon data from the FBI's Uniform Crime Reports on cases of fraud, embezzlement, and forgery,[8] Gottfredson and Hirschi miss the far more fruitful data on securities fraud found in the arena of civil law.[9] The National Association of Securities Dealers (NASD), as well as the Securities and Exchange Commission (SEC), *may* "refer cases involving evidence of criminal activity for further investigation and possible indictment," but they are far more likely to seek civil remedies.[10] Edwin Sutherland's reasoning approximately half a century ago is still applicable:

> Persons who violate laws regarding restraint of trade, advertising, pure food and drugs, and similar business practices are not arrested by uniformed policemen, are not tried in criminal courts, and are not committed to prisons; their illegal behavior receives the attention of administrative commissions and of courts operating under civil or equity jurisdiction. For this reason such violations of law are not included in the criminal statistics nor are individual cases brought to the attention of scholars who write the theories of criminal behavior. The

sample of criminal behavior on which the theories are founded is biased as to socioeconomic status, since it excludes these business and professional men. The bias is quite as certain as it would be if the scholars selected only red-haired criminals for study and reached the conclusion that redness of hair was the cause of crime.[11]

ON THE WORLD OF PENNY STOCKS

> *"A financial market is where sheep are protected from wolves by other wolves."*[12]

Contemporary penny-stock traders have been compared by Robert L. Frick and Mary Lynne Vellinga to the "people who sold swampland in Florida as prime real estate."[13] Both the Florida wheelers and dealers of the 1920s and the penny-stock traders of the past thirty years or so used "lies and price manipulations to bilk people out of hundreds of million of dollars." Frick and Vellinga conclude the penny-stock market has never really been "what it's supposed to be: a conduit through which money from small investors travels to legitimate young companies in need of venture financing."[14]

What is a Penny Stock and Where Did it Come From?

In the United States the historical lineage of penny-stock dealers goes back to the nineteenth century gold and silver mines of the American west, in particular to the Colorado gold rush in the 1880s.[15] Prospectors had little capital and turned to selling shares to finance their ventures. Those unable to lure more substantial investments sold shares for as little as a penny. Penny-stock mining frauds operated in other countries as well. For instance, in 1888 a Welsh gold-mining firm swindled investors after a phony ore test in "the presence of certain notable personages."[16]

On the heels of the nineteenth century miners came the oil and gas promoters. Oil, like precious metals, made people more than a little money crazy, and by 1918 towns like Fort Worth, Texas, were home to motley armies of "lease sharks, grafters and grabbers, operators, speculators, and gamblers."[17] In the western mecca of Los Angeles, the Department of Justice figured that stock swindlers hawking oil securities of one kind or another, many for little more than $1, were making about $100,000 a week in 1923.[18]

Up until the stock market crash in 1929 and the subsequent Depression, stock swindling in general was an American pastime, and there was nothing fundamentally different about penny-stock frauds than other security swindles. Legislation enacted in the Depression, particularly the Securities Act of 1933, which created the Securities and Exchange Commission (SEC), was intended to restore a measure of public confidence in securities trading. And it did, though historians Roger and Diana Olien conclude the SEC was unable to deter "small-time confidence men," because of its preference for "the promotion of disclosure more than the punishment of fraud."[19] In the same vein, they remark that the SEC functions like a "regulatory black hole" when it comes to "pink sheet" firms. Pink sheets, of course, refer to a weekly list of firms trading in over-the-counter stocks along with their price quotes on securities. The list, which is printed on pink paper, is published by the National Quotation Bureau, a private firm headquartered in Jersey City, New Jersey.

In general, penny stocks are considered those securities not listed on a recognized exchange; hence they are traded over-the-counter, and information about them is only available on the pink sheets. In 1989 it was estimated that around 13,000 stocks, ranging in price from a penny to $3, were traded through the pink sheets.[20] There is some quibbling over this definition, however, because thousands of over-the-counter securities are listed on NASDAQ, which stands for the National Association of Securities Dealers Automated Quotation System. This computerized listing is provided to broker-dealers, enabling them to enter price quotations if they choose to become market makers. A market maker is a broker-dealer that regularly buys and sells a particular security.[21] Some analysts and regulators prefer not to call those stocks which are NASDAQ-listed, penny stocks, no matter what their price may be. Others are not quite so picky.

This issue has to do only with the degree of regulatory control over the market. For example, to get onto NASDAQ a company is required to have a minimum of several millions in assets and just slightly less in shareholders' equity.[22] Perhaps more importantly, for a stock to be listed on NASDAQ it must have at least two market makers. The reason for this should be obvious: a single market maker can with ease and virtual impunity illegally manipulate a security's price. Pink-sheet firms and the stocks they trade are only required to be registered with the SEC.

These regulatory differences are often less than they seem, for NASDAQ's listing requirements do not have to be maintained. A listed firm's assets can plummet five-eighths and retain its NASDAQ standing, and a stock is not "delisted" when its market makers shrinks to but one.[23] When it comes to determined, organized-crime–driven securities fraud, a NASDAQ listing probably does not have the deterrent value its supporters claim. Nevertheless, NASDAQ securities average nine market makers per security, thus promoting competitiveness, while the pink sheet stocks typically have only one. Though penny-stock criminals work both pink sheet stocks and firms and NASDAQ ones, it is clear why the former is thought by a proportion of analysts and examiners to represent the true bottom feeders of the securities world and accounts for the squabble over just what a penny stock is.[24]

The Issue Of Trust

Several keen-sighted observers, Susan Shapiro pre-eminently, have commented that stock swindlers "manipulate trust,"[25] which seems the equivalent of never giving a "sucker an even break." This problem is not exclusive to stock swindlers, of course. In fact, all types of commerce are and have been caught in the "information-trust" dilemma. That is why private firms were established whose job has been to verify commercial goods for importers. The world's largest, the Societe Generale de Surveillance (SGS) which began in the nineteenth century, is headquartered in Geneva, Switzerland, operates in over 140 countries through 1,170 offices, and employs more than 30,000 people.[26] The only reason SGS exists is because buyers and sellers cannot trust one another— SGS ensures "goods delivered are what the customer ordered and that they are delivered to the proper recipient and invoiced at a fair price."[27] But, one might wonder, what guarantees the agent's fidelity? The answer is nothing but the need to be trusted to stay in business. One would think, however, that is exactly what importers and exporters would have demanded of one another instead of turning to a supposedly disinterested and competent third party. If the third party dissembles, the principals are back to square one. Given the interests at stake in these affairs, imagine the shudder that went through firms when SGS president, Robert Burgess, Jr. was found floating in New York's East River in the spring of 1990. He had been shot in the head.[28]

On the issue of third parties, there is a commercial and philosophical conundrum with no end in sight, as Eeuwke Faber recently asserted in a study of the Dutch marine insurance industry.[29] In the world of securities, there are several third parties, including private associations of securities dealers at the state and national level, state government regulators, and the SEC, whose work is based on creating sufficient rules to compel broker-dealers to give true disclosure, thereby creating trust between sellers and buyers of securities. Underlying this is the concept of the "rational investor." That is, there simply cannot be a rational investor without honest and full disclosure, though no one guarantees the rational investor will be successful and no one knows whether the informed investor is more likely to succeed than the intuitive investor. What the SEC does is to try and reduce the risks of what is always essentially a gamble.[30] They want to make sure the casino is as honest as possible. The pink-sheet hustles are akin to floating crap games, and their overseers stand in the tradition of the "grifters," long- and short-term con artists.

Moreover, the initial battle lines between regulators and fraudulent penny-stock dealers are drawn over the quality and quantity of information, not whether the game is fixed. When it has been determined that the information was spotty, typically after laborious procedures, the penalties have been excessively mild. "Wrist slapping" has never discouraged serious criminal entrepreneurs, which is why Marshall Zolp, "a multiple violator of securities laws," was nevertheless able to successfully convince millions of dreamers to invest in a "self-cooling beverage can," and why another perennial violator grossed $300 million selling securities in a flimflam called GoldCor, which promised to convert "black Costa Rican beach sand into gold" using a "secret black box."[31] The grifters of the penny-stock world are correct in their belief that there are millions of fools hot to make a fortune, and all that separates them from the loot are some pettifogging rules and regulations. When things become more serious they have the wisdom to use "house" lawyers whose specialty is stretching cases out for years using all sorts of cunning legal artifices and influential political associates. During these legal marathons the fraudsters continue to plunder guileless investors. Oftentimes the regulators feel that they are themselves trapped inside the numbing *Bleak House* of law.

Continuity and Change

The history of penny stocks after World War II reveals several boom times, such as the early 1950s when the Atomic Energy Commission announced that it would buy all the uranium anyone could find. There was a rush of activity in Utah for uranium and plutonium stocks. Most proved utterly worthless, and some were actually traded over the counter of a Salt Lake City coffee shop.[32] After the uranium surge the next high times for penny stocks were in the years 1959–1962, 1967–1971, and 1979–1983. In these periods penny stocks were mostly a regional curiosity emanating from the mining and energy mania that primarily racked the Denver plateau and eastern Idaho.[33] Denver, Salt Lake City, and Spokane, Washington, were the chief hubs. But beginning in 1983, at around the tag end of the last regional surge, the penny-stock industry underwent a dramatic shift. It broke out of its primarily intermountain home and its fundamental relationship with "hot issues" such as uranium and oil shale to become national. The North American Securities Administrators Association (NASAA) in a 1989 report to Congress noted the change in the size and scope of the penny-stock market and attributed it to a change in the methodology of the fraudsters. NASAA claimed the criminals' emphasis shifted "from the primary market of initial public offerings (IPOs) to the secondary or 'after' market." This "sea-change," as NASAA characterized it, was done through the much greater use of what are called "'blank check' blind pools."[34]

In the old days, often referred to as the "chicken or feathers cycle,"[35] a penny-stock criminal firm made its money through an initial public offering of some phony and/or overvalued security. Over the course of time, stock swindlers refined the idea and began conning investors to give them money for investments in unspecified companies. They were asking for what came to be known as a "blank check." A "blank check," when combined with what is called a "blind pool," was simply more of the same. The "blind pool" typically stands for a sham corporation that has been created to "merge with other closely-held public companies in order to bypass federal and state securities regulation, gain immediate access to the secondary market and serve as a vehicle for market manipulation."[36] Canadian commentator Diane Francis describes "blind pools" as "venture capital outfits" that raise money without needing to tell the investors there was a "specific plan" in mind for use of their money.[37]

The secondary market became the arena for making really big money. It works like this: a public offering for the stock of a sham company, which is merging with another usually unspecified firm already registered with the SEC, is made. Investors are not informed that the bulk of the shares are owned by the swindler's firm. (This practice is known as "scalping" and is a violation of the Investment Advisors Act of 1940.[38]) The price is then driven up, made all the easier when the crooked firm is the sole market maker. At some predetermined peak, the swindlers sell their shares in this new firm, the product of the merger, in what is called the secondary market. For the insiders to hit the peak and get out, the investing public cannot be allowed to sell their shares. The criminal firm simply refuses to execute sell orders on behalf of its clients. The firm's sales representatives, who do the scripted telephoning to hook the unwary, are ordered to either hang up when a client calls who wants to sell, or not to answer the phone during "selling" times.

"Blank checks" and "blind pools" rely on the most important technical innovation the criminal stock firm has—the telephone, which by the 1980s evolved to include 800 numbers, call waiting, call screening, and the availability of specialized phone lists, and was hooked into fax machines and computers. The stock swindlers' basic tool has become better and better. Their methods reveal the kinship between the penny-stock racket and the classic swindler's "boiler-room" operation[39]—high pressure promotion by telephone of a phony commodity by people who usually haven't the foggiest idea about what it is they are promoting.

An example of this can be seen in the activities of Lorenzo Formato, who was a high school dropout working as an auto mechanic when he decided to emulate a friend with an expensive car. His friend was a stock swindler. Formato started out on the telephone with Mayflower Securities, the progenitor of some of the most important penny-stock criminals in U.S. history. He had the "gift of gab," and a prodigious work ethic. He worked the phones sometimes 100 hours a week; he also created his own highly persuasive "cold pitch." Though completely ignorant of the brokerage business, he had more clients than anyone else at Mayflower within six months. He didn't know what stocks were, but he did know that selling them could make him a lot of money. He sold and sold, "never knowing," he stated, "whether or not the stock was any good, whether or not the company had any profits, whether or not the company even existed."[40] Formato was a boiler-room phenomenon.

The contemporary penny-stock boiler room depends upon a large work force of telephone solicitors who are deliberately chosen for their lack of experience in, and knowledge of, the securities industry. Many, in fact, quickly leave once they realize they are part of a criminal enterprise. Some, of course, "choose not to see."[41] They are run by high-octane managers whose sole responsibility is to keep their sales representatives relentlessly on task, snaring unsophisticated people and talking them into giving them money for nothing but a "dream," as

Formato stated.[42] It is the relentless pressure by the managers on the callers-solic-itors, and theirs, in turn, on the unsophisticated credulous public that is at the heart of the penny-stock swindle.

THE HOUSE OF FRAUD: ROBERT E. BRENNAN

> *"Bob Brennan was, in my opinion, one of the smartest men that ever entered the over-the-counter brokers' industry as far as being able to manipulate stocks and manipulate people."[43]*

In the late twentieth century no one better exemplifies the issues we have been discussing than Robert E. Brennan, a baron in the world of penny-stock fraud and related financial crime. No one has garnered more money, official scrutiny, and subsequent bad publicity than Brennan. His activities have been the subject of critical commentary in *The New York Times*, *The Philadelphia Inquirer*, *The Washington Post*, the *Newark Star Ledger*, the *Bergen County Record*, and in *Barron's*, *Business Week* and *Forbes*, whose reporter Richard L. Stern once suggested that Brennan's brokerage firm "is to reputable brokerage houses what a street vendor is to Nieman Marcus."[44] His response to bad publicity was to wage a media war of his own, defying the content of thousands of words of sharp criticism and defending his activities. A look at his career, however cursory it must be at this stage of the research, also reveals the many frustrations of third-party regulators, although eventually a measure of success would be theirs.

The Early Years

Brennan received a degree in accounting at Seton Hall University in East Orange, New Jersey, and two years later was recruited into the penny-stock firm of Mayflower Securities by Eugene Mulvihill, the owner and president, and himself a legend in the underworld of financial crime.[45] Brennan's path may have been eased by his father, who was also a Mayflower man. He began work at Mayflower in 1969 when he was 24 years old. He was an extremely self-pos-sessed and skillful salesman. His first brush with regulators took place in 1971, an action based on Brennan's fraudulent trading after only six months at Mayflower. He was suspended for 30 days by the New Jersey Bureau of Securi-ties for unethical trading of mutual funds.[46] Around that time, Brennan replaced Mulvihill as Mayflower's president. Two years later the New Jersey regulators again suspended him for 30 days for unethical trading.[47]

Mayflower hit the skids in the spring of 1974 but was temporarily rescued that May with a quarter-million-dollar loan from Harold Derber (Hyman Tushverderber), a fraudster and drug smuggler born in the Soviet Union who had become a British subject.[48] The grateful Brennan has commented that Derber's loan saved his "economic life."[49] He has denied allegations that his firm was washing Derber's drug profits, which were estimated by federal authorities at around $15 million.[50] Also in 1974, Derber was arrested on drug charges. He had three tons of marijuana on his Florida property, but the charges were dropped because of an illegal search warrant. However, police intelligence sources stated Derber was "one of the largest traffickers in marijuana in the United States."[51] Derber was most closely associated with another Brennan partner, Rehavan (Ray) Adiel, who was at one time Israel's military attache to Panama. Derber and Adiel's relationship went back to at least the early 1960s.[52]

The year 1974 was a tumultuous one for Brennan and his associates. In addition to the bailout of Mayflower by Derber, and Derber's arrest, the SEC filed two charges against Brennan and Mayflower for stock manipulation and fraud. The result was a negotiated settlement and a fifteen-day suspension of Mayflower's trading activities. However, before the suspension took effect, Brennan created a new penny-stock company called First Jersey Securities. On the day Mayflower was officially suspended, November 8, 1974, Brennan opened First Jersey, which he owned and controlled completely.[53] There was not a great deal of difference between Mayflower and First Jersey: 40 of the 100 sales representatives from Mayflower, all of its officers, and its clients' accounts were transferred to First Jersey. It was Mayflower for all intents and purposes.[54] The skirmishes with regulators continued, of course. Within just a few months of First Jersey's opening, the head trader and Brennan's brother-in-law, Anthony Nadino, was charged by the SEC with market manipulations.[55] In July 1976, the vice president of First Jersey, Robert Gary Berkson, was found guilty of stock fraud.[56]

While this investigation was in progress, Harold Derber was murdered, shot in the back as he exited his Porsche on a Miami street.[57] Ray Adiel's first reaction was to rush to Panama to secure $10 million Derber had on deposit there in the Banque de Paris. Derber's killing took place on the night before his scheduled testimony before the SEC concerning "his dealings with First Jersey,"[58] leading experienced investigators to conclude the murder likely deterred some First Jersey employees from cooperating with the government.[59] Subsequent investigations of First Jersey revealed a sweet deal between Derber, Brennan, and Brennan's father, Henry, made in March 1975. It was a penny-stock deal, and it netted Derber $131,746 in six weeks. Brennan's father pocketed $68,000.[60] There is a postscript to the Derber drug saga. Ten months after his murder, Derber's freighter, the *Night Train*, was seized in The Bahamas carrying fifty-four tons of Colombian marijuana, then the largest marijuana seizure in history.[61]

Regulatory Attacks

In 1979, First Jersey's Rochester manager, Jamie C. Spangler, Jr., was indicted for conspiracy to defraud.[62] That same year, the SEC filed an administrative proceeding against First Jersey that was ultimately joined by a 1983 SEC complaint, both of which were settled in November 1984 when First Jersey was permanently barred from "further violations of securities law."[63] First Jersey paid no attention to the ban. However, something consequential had taken place. Tacked onto the settlement was a provision giving the SEC the right to place a "consultant" into First Jersey to watch over and report back on its sales practices. The SEC appointed Benjamin L. Lubin as First Jersey's consultant on January 28, 1985. Lubin filed two reports: the first on June 15, 1985; the second and final one on October 1, 1986. Lubin made twenty-five recommendations dealing with upgrading First Jersey's sales procedures.[64]

Prior to Lubin's final report, Brennan had decided to restructure his operation, figuring out a way to undercut whatever Lubin finally recommended. That summer he stepped down as First Jersey's Chairman and CEO, installing Fredric Rittereiser (a former New York City cop) as Chairman and John E. Dell as CEO. He then covered his political side "by hiring an impressive array of former public sector talent." Chris Welles of *Business Week* listed the talent: W. H. Dumont, the former U.S. Attorney in Newark; John J. Degnan, the former New Jersey Attorney General, and Richard J. Hughes, a former New Jersey Governor. They joined up with several retired officials from the SEC and NASD who had investigated Brennan in the past.[65] It should also be noted that in addition to his ability to secure powerful political supporters, Brennan had also corrupted several individuals inside the regulatory bodies. Whoever they were, they filched important documents concerning First Jersey. For instance, in December of 1980, a large filing cabinet filled with First Jersey material "disappeared from a locked hearing room at the SEC's New York regional headquarters." Five years later, around 20,000 crucial pages of First Jersey papers mysteriously departed the New York headquarters of NASD. This occurred soon after NASD had reactivated a 1979 complaint. In the winter of 1985, computer disks from First Jersey vanished from the SEC's regional office in Arlington, Virginia.[66]

Brennan was still not secure. There were other charges brought to bear on his operation.[67] For instance, in October 1985, the SEC filed what would turn out to be the most important complaint ever against First Jersey and Robert Brennan. It charged "excessive markups on sales" of securities of Sovereign Chemical and Petroleum Products, Rampart Inc., and Quasar Microsystems.[68] And in 1986, the NASD "accepted an offer of settlement in a proceeding against Brennan, First Jersey and Nadino" for exorbitant markups dealing with the warrants of a company named Transnet.[69] Brennan and Nadino were fined $25,000 each and suspended for ten days from associating with any NASD dealer. First Jersey was fined $300,000.[70] While First Jersey's retail sales operations ended in December 1986, there were still cases wending their way through the sometimes glacial legal system, including the latently crucial SEC one, that would not come to trial for nine years.[71] One class action suit brought by former clients claiming they lost considerable sums in "fraudulent stock actions," was settled in 1987, with First Jersey paying $10 million.[72]

Brennan's Accomplishments

Through 1986, Brennan had been able to take First Jersey to almost unprecedented heights for a penny-stock firm. In a dozen years, he and his closest associates controlled somewhere between 40 and 60 percent of the nation's entire over-the-counter market. In 1986, the work force under his control stood as the fifteenth largest securities sales force in the nation;[73] his customers numbered over 350,000; the annual revenue take was over $200 million.[74] Less than ten years before, Brennan's firm had garnered only $4 million in revenues.[75] And then came the fundamental change in the penny-stock world, when the development of "blank check blind pools" forever changed the earning potential. In 1981 his take was $35 million.[76] Five years later, the revenues had grown by more than 660 percent. In 1984 his advertising budget for First Jersey was $19 million. That placed him third among all brokerage firms. The top spender was Shearson Lehman at $22 million. Merrill Lynch came in second, nosing out Brennan by only $1 million.[77] This gargantuan budget was unparalleled for a penny-stock firm, considering that all such firms represented only five percent of all SEC brokerage firms.[78] In the autumn of 1985, one of the stocks that Brennan manipulated had more shareholders than CBS or Motorola.[79] First Jersey had amassed almost one-half-billion dollars in revenues in just twelve years.[80]

The Middle Years: Maneuvering to Hold Off the Regulators

Brennan's new path, initially marked in the summer of 1986, led him to Sherwood Capital Group, Incorporated, which "sort of" bought First Jersey's thirty-six retail offices in December 1986. Sherwood was a small over-the-counter firm with only six offices, headed by a longtime friend of Rittereiser's, Raymond Meselsohn.[81] Sherwood was anxious to amalgamate and had tried to merge the month prior to the First Jersey deal with another major fraudulent New Jersey penny-stock firm, Rooney, Pace.[82] The agreement between Sherwood and First Jersey called for Meselsohn to step aside as Chairman, to be replaced by Rittereiser.[83]

The Sherwood gambit did not last very long. The regulators were on it too quickly, and that prompted Brennan and his associates to another action. In 1988, they split Sherwood into two parts, placing twelve offices with F. N. Wolf & Co., which was born on May 11 of that year, and fourteen with Hibbard Brown and Company, created on May 20. Eleven of the twelve F. N. Wolf regional vice presidents were from First Jersey.[84] In September 1991, another piece of the Brennan puzzle was put in place. This was the acquisition of L.C. Wegard & Co. Brennan's front-man in this was Leonard B. Greer, who had long handled the First Jersey account at Paine Webber.[85]

As the boss of L. C. Wegard, Greer received $2 million in loans from Brennan's non-profit Dehere Foundation, ostensibly established to honor a Seton Hall basketball player and to stop gun violence—its charter said nothing about stopping fraud—and $500,000 from yet another Brennan company, this one called Austin Bernet. Bernet also channeled a $5 million loan to Hibbard Brown in 1992. Other contributions to Greer were done through buy-back penny-stock deals.[86]

As of June 1993, 29 of the 31 offices selling for F. N. Wolf, Hibbard Brown, and L. C. Wegard were managed by veterans from First Jersey. The year before F. N. Wolf hired John Dell, known as Brennan's right-hand man in the days of First Jersey, as a multimillion-dollar-a-year securities analyst.[87] Hibbard Brown's head trader was none other than Brennan's brother-in-law, Anthony Nadino, first charged with stock manipulation in 1976, as noted earlier. He was not able to stay out of trouble. In July 1993, the NASD filed charges against Hibbard Brown for fraudulent behavior. The firm and its sole owner, Richard P. Brown (a Brennan front), were ordered to pay $8.7 million in restitution to its customers. The NASD also barred Brown and Nadino from future association with any NASD member. Both men were fined $150,000.[88] Faced with too much pressure, both F. N. Wolf and Hibbard Brown, in the space of six weeks, filed for bankruptcy. The game, of course, was not nearly over. Emerging to take their place was J. W. Charles Securities located in Boca Raton, Florida,[89] one of the centers for penny-stock firms—known by *afficionados* as "Maggot Mile." All of F. N. Wolf's managers, as well as selected personnel from Hibbard Brown, joined the Charles work force, which was already populated by former workers from the flamboyantly fraudulent penny-stock firm, Blinder-Robinson & Co. (aka Blind 'Em and Rob 'Em), which started out in Englewood, Colorado.[90]

The Later Years: Taking Stock

A look at which Brennan-influenced firms are left is revealing: J. W. Charles is one, and Dickinson & Co., based in Des Moines, Iowa, is another. Dickinson deserves a closer look. The chairman of Dickinson is Marshall Swartwood, who bought the firm in 1990 and populated it with sharpers from F. N. Wolf and J. W. Gant, yet another crooked penny-stock firm.[91] Swartwood's most interesting associate and friend was Eugene Mulvihill,[92] mentioned earlier as the founder of the *virus* called Mayflower Securities. Swartwood had also been the market maker for at least six of Brennan's 112 companies. Clearly, Swartwood was part of the inner circle.[93]

Swartwood also worked for a Mulvihill company called Great American, which had bought New Jersey property formerly owned by Playboy Enterprises.[94] Playboy purchased the property at New Jersey's Great Gorge in anticipation of statewide legal casino gambling. It didn't happen, and Mulvihill stepped in as a resort developer. Another member of the Great American team was Brennan. Great American did not do very well, and when the situation became dire, the company helped itself to around $30 million from a trust fund established by the esteemed Averill Harriman in 1984 for his children.[95] The trustees were Clark Clifford, former Secretary of Defense and by 1984 a major BCCI co-conspirator, Harriman's widow Pamela, the stepmother of the Harriman children, and William Rich III.[96] The administrator was Paul Warnake, the former head of the Arms Control and Disarmament Agency and chief U.S. negotiator with the Soviets over nuclear weapons for many years.[97] It seems that it was primarily Rich who placed the trust in jeopardy through his deals with Mulvihill, which began in 1988.[98] The following year Rich began investing Harriman funds in a Great American project that worked out quite well, earning the trust $2 million in six months. Unfortunately, that was quickly followed by a second investment in another Great American project that ended up draining the trust of millions. The Harriman children, who achieved their majority decades ago, are suing. Trustee Clark Clifford, it should be noted, who fronted for BCCI, the secret owner of First American Bank,[99] lent $5.5 million of First American's money to Great American. Luckily for him, the money was repaid when Japanese investors came on the scene.[100]

The web of significant relations that are a hallmark of Brennan's career, are exceedingly complex, and often appear in unexpected places. It should not be surprising, therefore, to learn that Brennan moved significant amounts of money, somewhere between $20 and $30 million, into trusts in a foreign sanctuary.[101] His choice was Gibraltar. He set up two trusts, named Seton and Benedictine, in January 1993, in anticipation of the trial from the SEC case filed so many years ago. The trial did not start until June, 1994, and when Brennan finally testified he was declared a hostile witness. This likely prompted him to set up his third Gibraltar trust, Cardinal. (These were not the only trusts Brennan hastily established. The known others are REB, KAB, and Christopher [named for his children], Family Investment, and PAB [at the time his wife's initials]).[102] The trustees of Cardinal, Benedictine, and Seton are Dennis Gaito, his accountant for many years,[103] and Ronald J. Riccio, his close friend, attorney, and business partner, who also happened to be the Dean of the Seton Hall Law School.[104] And therein lies another important grid of Brennan's power.

Brennan himself was a long-term member of Seton Hall's Board of Regents. In addition to Dean Riccio,[105] other Brennan friends and associates holding positions at the university include the former Chancellor John J. Petillo, Peter W. Rodino, Jr., who held an endowed Chair at the Law School and was a multiterm Congressman from New Jersey who came to fame during the Nixon impeachment hearing;[106] and Stephen A. Stripp, U.S. Bankruptcy Judge in Trenton, N.J., who was an adjunct professor at the law school. This grid came to life during the series of trials stemming from the SEC charges filed in 1985.

The case was finally tried in the summer of 1994, nine years after the initial filing, and decided one year later. Brennan and First Jersey were hammered. The judgment against them, handed down in Federal Court, was $78 million, which the SEC is still (as of June 1999) trying to figure out how to collect.[107] The collection difficulty stems from Brennan's and First Jersey's bankruptcy declarations filed a few months after the 1995 decision, (Stripp was the judge until he wisely recused himself after his relationship with Brennan became common knowledge[108]) and from Brennan and First Jersey's appeal of the SEC sanction. That appeal was heard in the spring of 1996 and decided in the waning days of that year. In each instance, Brennan's Seton Hall connections labored in his vineyard. Dean Riccio was First Jersey's lead attorney in the appeal case which, nevertheless, ended up with another defeat.

Brennan also faced two quite serious bankruptcy suits, which were finally settled in 1998. The first was filed in 1993 by investors, the second by the New Jersey State Bureau of Securities in 1995 following Brennan's bankruptcy declaration made to insulate him from the $78 million judgment mentioned above. On the very day he filed his declaration, August 7, 1995, Brennan gave his attorneys (including Riccio) 200,001 shares of Brennan's International Thoroughbred Breeders, Inc. (ITB), which they turned around and sold for $600,000 and then returned $150,000 to Brennan.[109] In 1998, U. S. Bankruptcy Judge Kathryn C. Ferguson approved a settlement on both cases, which ordered Brennan to cough up $55 million to be divided among swindled investors. However, he has not been heard to cough from his new Juno Beach, Florida, residence.[110]

With Brennan, there is never an end to either fraud or litigation. Back in August 1995 the New Jersey authorities charged him with a civil racketeering suit for $150 million. This too wended its way through the greatly fatigued system. Given how much he already owes, and the unlikelihood of his ever paying full value for his past sins, his recent (June 28, 1999) $100 million settlement of this action, which had reached the astronomical sum of $1.2 billion thanks to RICO's triple damages, is unlikely to leave anyone feeling satisfied.[111] He remains the master of financial disaster, the "Johnny Appleseed of massive penny-stock fraud."[112]

FRAUD TRIUMPHANT: CONCLUSION

> *"The honest trading of securities is the 'soul' of a successful capitalist economy."*[113]

> *"They are buying a dream when they buy a penny stock. The dream of course turns out to be a nightmare."*[114]

Penny-stock crime is flourishing; the boiler room is not vanishing; and the Internet is providing new technology for securities swindlers.[115] Congressional efforts to stem the criminal tide have not been successful. In 1990, Congress passed The

Securities Law Enforcement Remedies and Penny Stock Reform Act, mandating a quotation system for the trading of penny stocks. The NASD then instituted the Over The Counter Bulletin Board (OTCBB), "the first electronic quotation system for securities not listed on NASDAQ or a national stock exchange including penny stocks and other thinly traded securities."[116] However, this merely provided one more layer of false legitimacy that mesmerized prospective penny-stock customers.

In 1997, Mary L. Schapiro, President of NASD Regulation, noted the dilemma: "Another factor that we believe contributes to the increasing fraud in this area is a perception by the public, frequently fostered by dishonest brokers, that the OTCBB is akin to a highly regulated market such as The Nasdaq Stock Market." She declared—"It is not."[117]

In a NASAA survey of customer complaints in 1997 the rise was 34 percent, and it included familiar issues such as brokers refusing to sell investor's stock, unauthorized trading, and "churning" accounts to fraudulently increase commissions. The SEC reported customer complaints concerning "cold calls" rose almost 60 percent between 1995 and 1997. During the latter year the SEC, in a routine examination of seventy penny-stock firms, detected serious problems in two thirds of them. Thus the SEC found a surge in penny stock fraud— "SEC officials estimate investors lose hundreds of millions of dollars a year to fraudulent practices in the sale of small, thinly traded stocks."[118] While some analysts believe the volume of customer complaints really reflect the rise in transactions, NASAA holds that complaint figures are more significant because "a burgeoning stock market with high returns generally means investors are content and refrain from logging complaints."[119] Other state regulators assert the customer complaint figure underestimates the problem because many investors do not realize when they have been bamboozled and many also do not know where to lodge complaints.

Neal Sullivan, the executive director of NASAA, reported in the winter of 1998 about "systemic boiler-room practices at entire firms."[120] And in the spring of 1999, NASAA President Peter Hildreth said "[T]oday we have an ideal climate for fraud. Millions of new investors, many of whom expect unrealistically high returns, are looking for places to put their money. At the same time, we're living through an Internet-driven technology revolution that is a boom to investors and con artists alike."[121]

There are, naturally enough, several theoretical channels one could sail through in the broiling penny-stock ocean. We prefer to be guided by Edwin Sutherland once again. In his classic 1949 study Sutherland noted that financial criminals benefitted from a "relatively unorganized resentment of the public toward white-collar crimes."[122] This may well account for a 1995 SEC study that found two thirds of the brokers who had been the subject of official investigations for violating securities laws were still employed in the securities industry.[123]

This also may account for those penny-stock frauds that run on for decades. The Brennan cases show a history of approximately thirty years. And the cases of sophisticated penny-stock organized crime keep rolling on. Thus, on June 9, 1998, eight management-level stock brokers were indicted for work performed at L. C. Wegard, the firm discussed earlier as one more example of the Brennan empire.[124] This long-term continuity is further buttressed by looking at the companies whose shares were being flogged by the L. C. Wegard syndicate. One of them was Brennan's company ITB, founded in 1980. Additionally, the underwriter for the ITB deal was the criminal penny-stock company Rooney, Pace, whose own history bears a resemblance to that of First Jersey.

In 1983, Randolph Pace, one of the owners of Rooney, Pace, was censured by the SEC because one of his brokers was engaged in fraud; in 1986, Pace was suspended for three months for fraudulent statements; in 1987, he was suspended for nine months for market manipulation; and, in 1988, the firm Rooney, Pace, was expelled from the securities industry. At some point, however, Pace took control (perhaps secretly) of yet another penny-stock firm called Sterling Foster and Company. On November 9, 1998, he was indicted on "charges of masterminding a $100 million fraud," using Sterling Foster.[125] Charged with Pace was Alan Novich, a lawyer and a dentist. Adam Lieberman, the president "and nominal 100% shareholder of Sterling Foster," was named a co-conspirator but not a defendant, as were several others, including Michael Krasnoff and Michael Lulkin.[126] After the NASD suspended Pace, he and Lieberman entered into a "secret unlawful agreement, to form Sterling Foster." Pace provided his partner with capital, arranged for him to "obtain a securities clearing agreement for Sterling Foster with Bear Stearns Securities Corp.," worked out Lieberman's compensation package, and arranged to secretly "receive Sterling Foster's net profits."[127] Working out of office space on Lexington Avenue in Manhattan, the conspirators concocted and utilized a series of companies to carry out the scheme (KAM Group, Inc., Dune Holdings, Bigelow Ventures, Inc., Carico, Inc., M.D. Funding, and Special Equities, Inc.[128]) and then sold shares or arranged "bridge financing" for the following: Lasergate Systems, Inc., Florida, Advanced Voice Technologies, Inc., Delaware, Com/Tech Communication Technologies, New York, Embryo Development, Delaware, Applewoods, Inc., Delaware, and ML Direct, Inc., Delaware.[129]

One of Pace's most important actions in constructing the Sterling Foster criminal enterprise was getting the securities clearing agreement with the well-known firm Bear Stearns Securities Corp. We wonder, naturally enough, how he did it, particularly after his firm had been booted out of the securities industry several years before. Others, such as *Forbes* magazine, also wondered,[130] for it was activities such as these that kicked off an investigation in 1998 by the SEC's Market-Regulation Division, headed by Richard Lindsey. The SEC wanted to determine whether Bear Stearns purposely "ignored signs of fraudulent activity at the small firms for which it clears transactions."[131] Somewhat surprisingly, in March 1999, Lindsey resigned his post to join the firm he was so busy investigating—Bear Stearns. Even more dismaying, it turned out that SEC Chairman Arthur Levitt had called Bear Stearns' CEO in January 1999, on Lindsey's behalf. Bear Stearns promptly created a new position for Lindsey, who became a senior managing director at Bear Stearns Securities Corporation, "the company's clearing division that processes trades for brokerage firms."[132] We may never know whether or not Lindsey used his investigation to leverage a high-paying job from Bear Stearns, nor what precisely motivated Chairman Levitt to lend his weight to Lindsey's quest. Nonetheless, we do know this cannot have helped the SEC investigation into corrupt cronyism.

Brennan and his crowd seem like some tireless engines fueled by an endless supply of high-octane avarice. In 1998, yet another member of the Brennan "funny money" squirearchy turned up in a complicated series of deals. The founder and Chairman of Greenwood Racing, Robert W. Green, a Brennan associate who had bought Philadelphia Park from Brennan's ITB in 1990, was trying to acquire Freehold Raceway—a central New Jersey track—owned by ITB supposedly now *sans* Brennan. Green of course knew whether Brennan had a backdoor relationship with ITB, because he himself was a shareholder in the firm. The New Jersey deal finally fell through in 1999, when it was discovered that Green had helped Brennan move money out of the United States at the very time Brennan strategically claimed he was bankrupt and thus couldn't pay on the $78 million judgment to defrauded investors. Here's how they did it. Brennan sent approximately $11 million through an aptly named company, Pirates Associates, to a quite small British firm, UK Food Products, owned by Green. That firm then lent some portion of the money to PAB Aviation, in which Brennan had an, as yet, unidentified interest. (As mentioned earlier, PAB were the initials of Brennan's wife's name as well as the name of a trust he established in 1993.[133]) Additionally, UK Food assigned PAB's mortgage to Pirates Associates. It was a tidy conspiracy partially unraveled by Regina Barrett, an SEC accountant, immeasurably helped by Brennan's former wife.[134]

There is no end to the criminal machinations in the penny-stock industry, and the paucity of enforcement—always too little and often too late for the millions of victims of serious fraud. This is serious business run by folks who have shown educational persistence, the ability to keep regular business hours, who pay attention to conventional appearance, but are not known for their deference to the interests of others. They are known for their ability to work closely with members of state, federal, and educational elites, however. They thus display at the very least three quarters of the traits that are supposedly inconsistent with criminality. Nevertheless, penny-stock fraud is a white-collar occupation whose selection processes tend to recruit people with a relatively high propensity for crime. Indeed, many of the well-dressed and well-educated brokers who cut their eye teeth with Mayflower, First Jersey, Hibbard Brown, F. N. Wolf, L. C. Wegard, and the multitude of other penny-stock firms from the Brennan past, are no doubt exceptionally busy right now cold-calling suckers from their offices in South Florida, or routing them through the Internet to a fool's dream.

NOTES

1. We wish to thank Stu Allen for his extraordinary assistance and wise counsel, and Keith Traynor for sharing his expertise and knowledge. We presented an early version of this paper at the 5th Liverpool Conference on Fraud in 1996, and a later one at the 1998 American Society of Criminology conference in Washington, D.C.

2. Kitty Calavita and Henry N. Pontell, "Savings and Loan Fraud as Organized Crime," *Criminology*, November 1993, p. 529.

3. Although the penny-stock world has been missed, criminologists have spent a fair amount of time and effort on other types of financial crimes. Among the most compelling are Michael Levi, *The Phantom Capitalists: The Organization and Control of Long-Firm Fraud* (London: Heinemann, 1981); Kitty Calavita, Henry N. Pontell, and Robert H. Tillman, *Big Money Crime: Fraud and Politics in the Savings and Loan Crisis* (Berkeley: University of California Press, 1997); Stephen Pizzo, Mary Fricker, and Paul Muolo, *Inside Job: The Looting of America's Savings & Loans* (New York: Harper Perennial, 1991); Elizabeth Luessenhop and Martin Mayer, *Risky Business: An Insider's Account of the Disaster at Lloyd's of London* (New York: Scribner, 1995), Mary Zey, *Banking on Fraud: Drexel, Junk Bonds and Buyouts* (New York: Aldine de Gruyter, 1993); Frank Partnoy, *F.I.A.S.C.O.: Blood in the Water on Wall Street* (New York: W. W. Norton & Co., 1997).

4. Nancy Reichman, "Moving Backstage: Uncovering the Role of Compliance Practices in Shaping Regulatory Policy," in Kip Schlegel and David Weisburd, eds., *White-Collar Crime Reconsidered* (Boston: Northeastern University Press, 1992), pp. 256–57. Reichman here is quoting from Stewart Clegg's 1989 study *Frameworks of Power*.

5. See Travis Hirschi and Michael R. Gottfredson, "Causes of White-Collar Crime," *Criminology*, 1987, vol. 25, no. 4, pp. 949–974; Darrell Steffensmeier, "On the Causes of 'White-Collar' Crime: An Assessment of Hirschi and Gottfredson's Claims," *Criminology*, 1989, vol. 27, no. 2, pp. 345–358; Travis Hirschi and Michael Gottfredson, "The Significance of White-Collar Crime for a General Theory of Crime," *Criminology*, 1989, vol. 27, no. 2, pp. 359–371; Michael Gottfredson and Travis Hirschi, *A General Theory of Crime* (Stanford, California: Stanford University Press, 1990); Gary E. Reed and Peter Cleary Yeager, "Organizational Offending and Neoclassical Criminology: Challenging the Reach of a General Theory of Crime," *Criminology*, 1996, vol. 34, no. 3, pp. 357–382; Carey Herbert, Gary S. Green and Victor Larragoite, "Clarifying the Reach of *A General Theory of Crime* for Organizational Offending: A Comment on Reed and Yeager," *Criminology*, 1998, vol. 36, no. 4, pp. 867–884; and finally, Peter Cleary Yeager and Gary E. Reed, "Of Corporate Persons and Straw Men: A Reply to Herbert, Green and Larragoite," *Criminology*, vol. 36, no. 4, pp. 885–898.

6. Gottfredson and Hirschi, *A General Theory of Crime*, p. 191.

7. See Stephen M. Rosoff, Henry N. Pontell, and Robert Tillman, *Profit Without Honor: White-Collar Crime and the Looting of America* (New Jersey: Prentice Hall, 1998). Also Robert J. Stevenson, *The Boiler Room and Other Telephone Sales Scams* (Urbana and Chicago: University of Illinois Press, 1998) in which he states "the reason that more is known about the petty thefts conducted by college students (typically shoplifting) than about the social structures that

produce systemic fraud is due to a curious lack of sociological interest in how businesses work in the planet's premier business culture," p. 214.

8. On this issue Steffensmeier in "On the Causes of 'White-Collar' Crime: An Assessment of Hirschi and Gottfredson's Claims," states "the UCR offense categories of fraud, forgery, and embezzlement are *not* appropriate indicators of white-collar or occupational crime because the typical arrestee in these categories committed a nonoccupational crime", p. 346.

9. See Marshall B. Clinard, Peter C. Yeager, Jeanne Brissettte, David Petrashek, and Elizabeth Harries, *Illegal Corporate Behavior* (Washington, D. C.: National Institute of Law Enforcement and Criminal Justice, Department of Justice, 1979).

10. National Association of Securities Dealers, Inc., *Securities Regulation in the United States*, 3rd ed., Washington, D. C., 1996, p. 42. Also see Rosoff, Pontell, and Tillman, Chapter 5, pp. 190–225.

11. Edwin H. Sutherland, *White Collar Crime* (New Haven: Yale University Press, 1983, the uncut version), pp. 6–7.

12. Joseph N. DiStefano, "Seeking the sense in the behavior of the investing public," *Philadelphia Inquirer* (March 21, 1999) p. E1. DiStefano was quoting MIT Professor Stephen A. Ross, who is known as a "behavioral agnostic."

13. Robert L. Frick and Mary Lynne Vellinga, *Keys to Risks and Reward of Penny Stocks* (New York: Barron's, 1990), p. 7.

14. Ibid.

15. North American Securities Administrators Association, *The NASAA Report on Fraud and Abuse in the Penny Stock Industry*, submitted to the Subcommittee on Telecommunications and Finance, Committee on Energy and Commerce, U.S. House of Representatives, September 1989, p. 23.

16. Kenneth Gooding, "Lured to ruin by fool's gold," *Financial Times* (April 19/April 20 1997), p. 1.

17. Roger M. Olien and Diana Davids Olien, *Easy Money: Oil Promoters and Investors in the Jazz Age* (Chapel Hill: The University of North Carolina Press, 1990), p. 74.

18. Jules Tygiel, *The Great Los Angeles Swindle: Oil, Stocks, and Scandal During the Roaring Twenties* (New York: Oxford University Press, 1994), p. 36.

19. Olien and Olien, p. 172.

20. U.S. House of Representatives, Committee on Energy and Commerce, Subcommittee on Telecommunications and Finance, *Hearings: Penny Stock Market Fraud*, "Statement of John C. Baldwin, President, North American Securities Administrators Association," August 21 and September 7, 1989, Serial No. 101-80, p. 125.

21. David Ratner, *Securities Regulation In a Nutshell* (St. Paul, Minnesota: West Publishing, 1978), p. 153.

22. Frick and Vellinga, p. 13.

23. Ibid., p. 14.

24. North American Securities Administrators Association, p. 36.

25. See, for example, Susan P. Shapiro's, *Wayward Capitalists: Target of the Securities and Exchange Commission* (New Haven: Yale University Press, 1984), which is organized around the principle of trust, its violation and manipulation by crooks, and the SEC as the guarantor of trust, and her "Collaring the Crime, Not the Criminal: Reconsidering the Concept of White-Collar Crime," *American Sociological Review*, vol 55, no. 3, June 1990, pp. 346–365.

26. Ian Rodger, "FT Exporter," *The Financial Times* (May 5, 1994), p. XXIX.

27. Ibid.

28. "Export Firm's President Is Found in East River," *The New York Times* (March 28, 1990), p. B6.

29. Eeuwke Faber, "Shipping and Scuttling: Criminogenesis in Marine Insurance," *Crime, Law And Social Change: An International Journal* vol. 28, no. 2, spring 1997, pp. 111–135.

30. Martin Mayer in his *Stealing the Market: How the Giant Brokerage Firms, with the Help from the SEC, Stole the Stock Market from Investors* (New York: Basic Books, 1992) states on page 5 that "[S]tock markets are by their nature somewhat 'inefficient'—that is, the prices of the securities traded in these markets may be susceptible to movements that do not reflect the success or failure of the companies that issued the shares and the industries of which they are a part."

31. U.S. House of Representatives, *Hearings: Penny Stock Fraud*, p. 123.

32. North American Securities Administrators Association, p. 2.

33. Canada, of course, was always surging with penny-stock mining firms. In fact, the Securities and Exchange Commission placed the following Canadian penny-stock mining firms on its "Foreign Restricted List," on April 13, 1967: Bayonne Mine, Ltd.; Ironco Mining & Smelting Company, Ltd.; Kenilworth Mines, Ltd., Mack Lake Mining Corporation, Ltd.; Norart Minerals Limited; St. Stephen Nickel Mines, Ltd; and Victoria Algoma Mineral Company, Ltd. This was over 50 percent of the Canadian firms placed on the list. The data can be found in the SEC's release No. 4861.

34. North American Securities Administrators Association, p. 12.

35. Ibid., p. 11.

36. Ibid., p. 12.

37. Diane Francis, *Bre-X: The Inside Story* (Toronto: Key Porter Books), 1997, p. 54.

38. Ratner, p. 154.

39. See Stephenson.

40. U.S. House of Representatives, *Hearings: Penny Stock Fraud*, p. 103.

41. See U.S. House of Representatives, Committee on Energy and Commerce, Subcommittee on Oversight and Investigations, *A Staff Report: Securities Activities of First Jersey Securities, Inc., and Robert Brennan, Owner and Former Chairman* (Washington, D.C.: Government Printing Office, December 1987), p. 42.

42. U.S. House of Representatives, *Hearings: Penny Stock Fraud*, p. 103.

43. Ibid.

44. Richard L. Stern and Laura Saunders, "Doesn't Anyone Remember?," *Forbes*, August 1, 1983, p. 31.

45. U.S. House of Representatives, *A Staff Report*, p. 1.

46. Ibid.

47. Ibid., p. 2.

48. Ibid.

49. North American Securities Administrators Association, p. 57.

50. "Newspaper says First Jersey not making money for customers," *United Press International* (April 13, 1986).

51. See *Business Week* (August 25, 1986), p. 13.

52. See United States District Court Southern District of Florida, Miami Division, Talco Capital Corporation, Plaintiff, *v.* Canaveral International Corps and Bimini Run, Ltd., Defendants, January 23, 1964, Civ. No. 63–125. 225 F. Supp. 1007. And, Court of Appeals of Washington, Division Two, Sparkman and McLean Company, Plaintiff, v. Harold Derber et. al., Defendants, A. M. Schwitalla, Appelant, Balanced Investments Corporation et. al., Respondents, No. 213–40668–2, February 25, 1971.

53. U.S. House of Representatives, *A Staff Report*, p. 2.

54. Ibid.

55. United States District Court for the Southern District of New York, Securities and Exchange Commission, Plaintiffs, *v.* First Jersey Securities, Inc., and Robert E. Brennan, Defendants, 85 Civ. 8585 (RO), 890 F. Supp. 1185, June 1995.

56. John F. Berry, "First Jersey Inc.: A Bullish Broker of Inflated Stock," *Washington Post* (May 20, 1979), p. A1.

57. Matthew Purdy, "Brennan's Paper Empire," *Philadelphia Inquirer* (April 13, 1986), p. 2. Also see, "Newspaper says First Jersey not making money for customers," *United Press International BC* (April 13, 1986). There are no page numbers for the business cycle (BC) of the wire service.

58. Ibid.

59. Authors' interview with former SEC investigator, March 20, 1997.

60. U.S. House of Representatives, *A Staff Report*, p. 43. Oddly enough, Brennan's father had become a Catholic priest two years earlier, in 1973, and joined the Order of the Servants of the Sick. Richard L. Stern and Laura Rohmann, "Come Grow With Us," *Forbes* (March 1, 1982), p. 44.

61. William R. Amlong and Patrick Riordan, "Witness Murdered," *Miami Herald* (April 18, 1978), p. 1.

62. Berry, "First Jersey Inc."

63. U.S. House of Representatives, *A Staff Report*, p. 4.

64. Ibid., pp. 2–3.

65. Chris Welles, "What's Behind Bob Brennan's Sudden Exit at First Jersey," *Business Week* (August 18, 1986), p. 88.

66. Ibid.

67. SEC v. First Jersey.

68. Ibid.

69. Ibid.

70. James Sterngold, "First Jersey Securities Selling Retail Branches," *New York Times* (December 24, 1986), p. D1.

71. See, United States District Court for the Southern District of New York.

72. Ibid.

73. United Press International, December 23, 1986.

74. U.S. House of Representatives, *Hearings: Penny Stock Fraud*, p. 158.

75. Stern and Rohmann, p. 31.

76. Ibid.

77. Richard L. Stern, "The Golden Boy," *Forbes* (July 16, 1984), p. 109.

78. U.S. House of Representatives, *Hearings: Penny Stock Fraud*, p. 1.

79. Gary Weiss, "The Sad Saga of a Penny-Stock Company," *Business Week* (May 15, 1989), p. 124.

80. U.S. House of Representatives, *Staff Report: First Jersey*, p. 41.

81. Chris Welles, "Trying Not To Be A Second First Jersey," *Business Week* (January 12, 1987), p. 44.

82. "Rooney Pace gets capital" *Crain's New York Business* (November 3, 1986), p. 28. Also see "SEC Censures Rooney, Pace," *New York Times* (November 15, 1986), p. 49; and Richard L. Stern, "Incompetence Inc.," *Forbes* (December 1, 1986), p. 38, and Stern and Michael Fritz, "Where were the cops," *Forbes* (April 6, 1987), p. 60; and Stern and Matthew Schifrin, "Crime wave—'Robbing a bank's no crime compared to owning one!' *Bertolt Brecht*," *Forbes* (June 29, 1987), p. 67.

83. Peter Elsworth, "Rittereiser to the rescue at First Jersey Securities," *Reuters Business Cycle* (August 31, 1986).

84. Marilee Loboda Braue, "Brennan's wide web of brokerage links," *Bergen Record* (August 21, 1994), p. B1.

85. The SEC put L. C. Wegard out of business in 1995. See, "Ex-Brokers at Wegard Indicted," *Pittsburgh Post-Gazette* (November 14, 1997), p. E1.

86. SEC *v.* First Jersey.

87. Braue, p. B1.

88. Jeff Brown, "NASD Ousts NY Broker," *Philadelphia Inquirer* (July 19, 1994), p. C1.

89. Rick Eyerdam, "Boca brokerage buying 'penny' firm," *South Florida Business Journal* (December 17, 1993), p. 1.

90. Blinder-Robinson was like a mirror image to the multifarious Brennan operations. Meyer Blinder, President of Blinder-Robinson, in 1987 took down $7.4 million in salary, which was more than the combined 1987 salaries and bonuses of the CEOs from Merrill Lynch, Shearson Lehman Hutton, and First Boston. From 1979 through 1989, Blinder-Robinson had been the principal of over 35 regulatory actions in 29 states. This is in addition to numerous SEC and NASD proceedings. See the North American Securities Administrators Association, pp. 12–18. Also see Matthew Schifrin, "Blinder, Robinson—Blind 'em and rob 'em," *Forbes* (April 20, 1987), p. 33. Schifrin details the relationships among First Jersey Securities, Rooney Pace, and Blinder Robinson; and Florida Comptroller Gerald Lewis, Administrative Proceeding, *In the Matter of: Blinder-Robinson & Co., Inc., et. al.,* No. 1097–S–5/89, May 17, 1989.

91. Amy Feldman and Neil Weinberg, "Call me Dickinson," *Forbes* (January 30, 1995), p. 47.

92. Ibid.

93. Dale Kasler, "Forbes tars Dickinson: D.M. brokerage fights brutal magazine article," *Des Moines Register* (January 19, 1995), p. S8.

94. See United States Bankruptcy Court for the District of New Jersey, In the Matter of: Princeton-New York Investors, Inc. and Seasons Resorts, Inc., Debtors. Robert P. Gibbons, Trustee in Bankruptcy, Plaintiff *v.* First Fidelity Bank, N. A., AHC, Inc., Eugene Mulvihill, et. al., and Great American Recreation, Inc., Defendants. Chapter 11, Case Nos., 94-25534, 94-25535, ADV., NO. 95-2826, April 25, 1996.

95. James Ahearn, "A Vernon Real Estate Deal that Cost a Fortune," *Bergen County Record* (September 28, 1994), p. B6.

96. Matthew Schifrin, "Amiable Dunces," *Forbes* (January 2, 1995), p. 43.

97. Christopher Ogden, *Life of the Party: The Biography of Pamela Digby Churchill Hayward Harriman* (New York: Warner Books, 1995), p. 471.

98. Ibid., p. 475.

99. Peter Truell and Larry Gurwin, *False Profits: The Inside Story of BCCI, the World's Most Corrupt Financial Empire* (Boston: Houghton Mifflin Co., 1992), pp. 50, 51, 54-55, 75, 108, 128, 325.

100. David Hage, "Sliding down a very slippery ski slope," *U. S. News and World Report* (November 21, 1994), pp. 78, 82.

101. Matthew Futterman, "As Brennan's assets unravel, another ton of bricks awake," *Philadelphia Inquirer* (March 2, 1997), p. D 12. The following material is from this source unless otherwise cited.

102. We briefly discuss PAB in the conclusion.

103. Gaito's accounting firm—Mortenson and Associates, P. C.—was also involved in "transactions in which Brennan transferred $16,750,000 to Swiss bank accounts." See, United States Bankruptcy Court for the District of New Jersey, in re: Robert E. Brennan, Debtor. In re: First Jersey Securities, Inc., Debtor. Case No. 95-35502, Chapter 11, Case No. 95-35503, Chapter 11, filed September 29, 1995.

104. Riccio is the sole trustee of Brennan's Family Investment Trust. See Securities and Exchange Commission, Proxy Statement, Primedex Health Systems, Inc., May 9, 1994, p. 3.

105. Ronald J. Riccio, "A Message from the Dean," Seton Hall University, School of Law, at www.shu.edu:8080/law/viewbook/deansletter.html. In this missive, Dean Riccio ironically said: "Here at Seton Hall our goal is to provide a rigorous but sensitive legal education while at the same time impressing upon our students not only the importance of service to others but also the enormous ethical and moral responsibilities which will be theirs as lawyers."

106. Proxy Statement, Primedex Health Systems, Inc., pp. 2, 3. Brennan owned 10,300,000 shares of Primedex; Rodino 25,000, Riccio 4,051,875, and Petillo 13,300,000. Also see Securities and Exchange Commission, Primedex Health Systems Inc., Form 10-K, , SEC File Number 000-19019, Filed April 3, 1996, in which the following is disclosed: "Primedex, the Company's former principal stockholder, Robert E. Brennan. . ., F. N. Wolf & Co., Inc., ('AFNW'), the underwriter of the Company's December 1992 and June 1993 public offerings, FNW's parent company, Wolf Financial Group, Inc ('WFG'), John E. Dell, Hibbard Brown & Company, Inc., ('HIBBARD'), a broker-dealer and its president, Richard P. Brown and another publicly owned corporation, Site-Based Media, Inc. ('SITE')" were charged in a civil complaint with violations of the "federal securities laws and the Racketeer Influenced Corrupt Organizations ('RICO') Act."

107. Associated Press, "Judge Oks Brennan—Investors Accord," June 9, 1998.

108. See the discussion about Stripp in Matthew J. Dowling, "Brennan faces $150 million suit in fraud charges," *Setonian* (October 5, 1995), at www.shu.edu/depts/setonian/1995-96/oct05/bren1.html.

109. John T. Ward, "Court Slams Payment To Lawyers From Bankrupt New Jersey Penny-Stock Fraud," *The Star-Ledger* (Newark) (June 15, 1999).

110. Ibid.

111. Jeffrey Gold, "Brennan Settles on Lifetime NJ Ban," *Associated Press* (June 28, 1999); also see Gold's "Penny-stock tycoon settles state charges," *Associated Press* (June 25, 1999).

112. "Brennan, First Jersey fined $71 million," *The Atlanta Journal and Constitution* (June 21, 1995), p. 3E; the quote—"the Johnny Appleseed of massive penny-stock fraud"—was by SEC lawyer Thomas Newkirk.

113. Rosoff, et. al., p. 143.

114. Penny Stock Market Fraud, p. 103.

115. Robert A. Rankin, "Internet Fraud Is on the Rise," *Philadelphia Inquirer* (June 1, 1999), D. 1. Also see Marcy Gordon's, "Yellow flag raised on stock trades via Internet," *Associated Press* (January 28, 1999), and "SEC levels charges of online fraud," *Associated Press* (February 26, 1999), and "Internet Gives New Forms for Fraud," *Associated Press* (March 22, 1999) at http://search.washingtonpost.com/wp-srv/WAPO/19990322/V000266-032299-idx.html. Also see Trinity Hartman, "Regulators fall behind as investment frauds soar on Internet," *The Philadelphia Inquirer* (March 25, 1999), D. 2.

116. National Association of Securities Dealers, Inc., p. 31.

117. Mary L. Schapiro, "Keynote Address at the District 7 Compliance Seminar," Atlanta, Georgia, September 25, 1997, at www.nasd.com/pp1_12.html.

118. NASD, p. 31.

119. Ibid.

120. Neal Roland, "Complaints by investors proliferate," *Philadelphia Inquirer* (February 14, 1998), p. B1.

121. NASAA president Peter Hildreth quoted in Marcy Gordon's, "Investing in insurance for terminally ill is ripe for scam," *Associated Press* (May 25, 1999).

122. Edwin H. Sutherland, p. 59.

123. U.S. Securities and Exchange Commission, Division of Market Regulation, "The Large Firm Project," 1995.

124. "Brokers Charged in Fraud," *New York Times* (July 9, 1998), p. B8. These indictments followed similar charges against eight L. C. Wegard brokers filed on November 13, 1997.

125. Frances A. McMorris, "Former Owner of Rooney Pace Indicted in Fraud," *Wall Street Journal* (November 10, 1998), p. B12.

126. United States District Court, Southern District of New York, United States of America *v.* Randolph Pace and Alan Novich, *Indictment*, sent to the authors by one of the investigators.

127. Ibid., p. 8.

128. Ibid., pp. 2–3.

129. Ibid., pp. 9–12.

130. Gretchen Morgenson, "Wall Street sleaze: why did prestigious Bear, Stearns get cozy with so many discredited bucket shops," *Forbes* (February 24, 1997), pp. 114–119.

131. Marcy Gordon, "Levitt's help in getting Wall St. job for regulator is questioned," *Philadelphia Inquirer* (May 20, 1999).

132. Ibid.

133. Futterman, p. D 12.

134. See Frank Fitzpatrick's "Owner appears close to decision on Freehold-Garden State deal," *Philadelphia Inquirer* (October 21, 1998); "Two offers weighed for N. J. tracks," *Philadelphia Inquirer* (October 22, 1998), "Philadelphia Park owner can take over tracks, with condition," *Philadelphia Inquirer* (December 22, 1998), and "Transfer of funds altered the deal for N. J. tracks," *Philadelphia Inquirer* (January 15, 1999).

Life Course Theory and White-Collar Crime

Michael L. Benson
and
Kent R. Kerley

The past two decades have witnessed an explosion of research on developmental and life course theories of crime (for recent reviews, see Loeber and Stouthamer-Loeber, 1996; Farrington, 1994). As is often the case with theoretical developments in criminology, the rise of these new approaches has had little impact on the study of white-collar crime. White-collar crime researchers have not applied life course concepts to their area of study. Likewise, life course criminologists have ignored the implications of white-collar crime for the life course approach.

The lack of communication between these two areas is regrettable for several reasons. With respect to white-collar crime, it means that the area is isolated from developments in mainstream criminology. White-collar crime researchers generally fail to employ conceptual tools from the life course approach that may help them derive a deeper understanding of white-collar criminal behavior. Some of these tools may help researchers make more creative use of recent findings on white-collar offenders, or they may suggest new avenues for investigation. For example, recent studies indicate that most of the people convicted of violating what are typically considered white-collar crime statutes are not powerful upper-class business executives, but rather middle class, or even lower-middle class, small-scale entrepreneurs and employees (Weisburd, et al. 1991; Croall, 1989; Daly, 1989). Contrary to popular belief a substantial number of white-collar offenders have criminal records (Benson and Moore, 1992; Weisburd, 1990). These findings call into question the stereotypical image of the white-collar offender as a person who comes from the most privileged sectors of society and who is the polar opposite of the ordinary "street criminal." At least some white-collar criminals appear to be more like street criminals than previously envisioned, and life course concepts may be usefully applied to them.

Just as white-collar crime researchers have ignored the life course, life course investigators have ignored white-collar crime. They have yet to deal with the finding that most people convicted of white-collar crimes are notably older than those convicted of street crimes (Benson and Moore, 1992; Weisburd, et al. 1991). Indeed, the typical white-collar offender commits his or her first offense at an age when most street criminals have aged out of crime. This pattern raises troubling questions for life course theories of continuity and change in criminal careers (Moffitt, 1997; Sampson and Laub, 1993). Originally conceived to account for crime trajectories among individuals who begin their careers as children or young adolescents, these theories are silent regarding those who begin much later.

The primary goal of this chapter is to explore both theoretically and empirically how the life course approach might be applied to white-collar offenders. We begin by briefly reviewing life course theory and some of the major findings with respect to crime. Next, using data from a study of sentencing patterns in federal courts, we investigate the lives of a large sample of persons convicted in federal court. The two principal objectives of the empirical analyses are (1) to compare the social trajectories and criminal careers of those convicted of white-collar offenses versus those convicted of common street offenses and (2) to interpret the findings from the perspective of life course theory. We conclude by offering some observations on the implications of white-collar crime for life course theory as well as the implications of life course theory for our understanding of white-collar crime.

THE LIFE COURSE PERSPECTIVE

The life course perspective is a broad, multidisciplinary intellectual movement. It encompasses ideas and empirical observations from a variety of disciplines, including history, demography, biology, developmental psychology, and sociology. As an emerging paradigm, it is not an explicit theory of anything, but rather a new way of thinking about and studying human lives and development (Elder, 1996).

In its simplest sense, the life course may be defined as "the duration of a person's existence" (Riley, 1986). The duration of a person's existence, however, does not simply consist of a continuous flux of undifferentiated time and experience. Rather, our lives are composed of a sequence of phases that are socially constructed and that are recognized by individuals and society as being different from each other. The different phases typically are separated from one another by normatively defined transitions that tend to be ordered in the sense that certain events are expected to be followed by other events most of the time (Mayer and Muller, 1986).

Elder (1985) defines the life course as the interconnected trajectories of a person as he or she ages through life. A trajectory is a sequence of linked states within a conceptually defined range of behavior or experience. It is a career or pathway over the life span. Transitions are always embedded in trajectories, and the states that make up a trajectory are always linked to one another by transitions (Elder, 1996). Life course theorists conceive of trajectories in three different domains of human behavior and functioning—biological, psychological, and social. Trajectories in different domains are intimately connected and have reciprocal effects on each other.

According to the life course perspective, aging and developmental change must be viewed as a continuous process that occurs throughout life. Development is not limited to children and adolescents. Rather, aging and development are processes that adults experience as well. They occur continuously and are influenced by social and historical conditions and changes (Elder, 1996).

With respect to crime, a distinctive feature of the life course approach is that it treats crime as both a dependent and an independent variable. Involvement in crime at one life stage has consequences for trajectories in other domains at other stages in life (Hagan and Palloni, 1988; Hagan, 1997; Hagan, 1993). For example, early involvement in delinquency and crime often leads to later problems for individuals in their occupational trajectories (Hagan, 1993).

Life course researchers have demonstrated that there is both stability and change in offending behavior over time (Farrington, 1994; Sampson and Laub, 1993; Nagin and Farrington, 1992). The degree of stability versus change depends in great measure on whether one is looking forward or backward. Looking backward from the vantage point of an adult criminal one is virtually certain to see a history of juvenile delinquency and early childhood conduct problems. Indeed, based on studies of adult criminals, some have concluded that early childhood conduct problems are a necessary cause for the development of adult criminality. To explain this continuity in crime, life course theorists have proposed various types of latent traits (Caspi, et al., 1994; Nagin and Farrington, 1992; Gottfredson and Hirschi, 1990). Latent traits are unobservable individual personality, cognitive, or temperament traits that remain stable over time and that cause crime throughout the life course.

Although early childhood conduct problems are a strong predictor of delinquency and adult criminality (Farrington, 1994), they are by no means a perfect one. Prospective studies, those that look forward from childhood on, indicate that continuity is rarely certain. Most children who display conduct problems early in life do *not* go on to become serious juvenile delinquents, and most juvenile delinquents do *not* become adult career criminals. Prospective longitudinal studies indicate that anywhere from 57 to 70 percent of children who have conduct problems early in life do not exhibit similar problems later in life (Loeber and Dishion, 1983).

A significant contribution of the life course approach has been the identification of different trajectories in crime. Moffitt (1997) proposes a theory in which there are two types of offenders who follow distinctly different crime trajectories. Life course–persistent offenders display conduct problems as young children, become involved in serious delinquency before they are teenagers, and continue to offend at high rates into adulthood. Adolescence-limited offenders follow a different trajectory. They do not begin to offend until the early teenage years and usually desist as they enter adulthood. Some investigators suggest there may be a third trajectory called low level chronics. These offenders start early and offend for long periods of time but at lower rates than life course–persistent offenders (Nagin, et al., 1995).

Because the life course approach is rooted in the idea that early trajectories are important, investigators have focused on family factors as correlates and predictors of crime and delinquency (Loeber and Stouthamer-Loeber, 1986). What happens in the home when children are young plays a significant role in determining initial trajectories into crime. Children whose parents reject them or who fail to supervise and be involved with them are more likely to perform poorly in school, develop conduct problems, and become juvenile delinquents than children who have better relations with their parents (Loeber and Stouthamer-Loeber, 1986). The home life of children who go on to become adult criminals is typically characterized by neglect and harsh or erratic discipline by parents (Sampson and Laub, 1993; West and Farrington, 1973). Additionally, the early home life of delinquents and adult criminals is often characterized by poverty. They are born into large families that live in substandard housing in the worst areas of town. Not surprisingly, children raised in large, poor families are at greater risk of developing conduct problems and delinquency than their more well-off counterparts (Farrington, 1994).

THE LIFE COURSE AND WHITE-COLLAR OFFENDERS

It is widely assumed that white-collar criminals come from different social backgrounds than typical street criminals. The distribution of social characteristics is expected to vary significantly between those who commit white-collar crimes and those who commit street crimes. The former are thought to have higher social status on average than the latter. Since white-collar crimes often involve an occupational position, it is assumed that white-collar criminals have better employment histories and are better off financially than common criminals. In sum, the life course trajectories of white-collar criminals are expected to differ from those of common criminals along almost all relevant dimensions, such as occupational stability, educational achievement, family background, and of course, criminality.

Unfortunately, most of what we know about the social and criminal backgrounds of white-collar offenders comes from case studies of offenders or offenses selected because the high social status of the offenders or the egregious nature of the offense made them especially noteworthy (Simon and Etizen, 1990; Cullen, et al., 1987; Geis, 1977). The few studies that have investigated large samples of individuals convicted of white-collar offenses indicate that the case study approach paints a misleading picture. The vast majority of those who violate white-collar statutes are middle-class individuals who have committed relatively banal offenses (Weisburd, et al., 1991; Croall, 1989; Daly, 1989) and often have prior criminal records (Benson and Moore, 1992; Weisburd, et al., 1990).[1]

Although recent research has modified our image of the typical white-collar offender, it certainly does not indicate that white-collar and common criminals are the same. White-collar offenders may not all come from the privileged sectors of society but neither do they share social space with common criminals. Based on their analysis of persons convicted in federal court, Weisburd, et al. (1991, p. 73) conclude that

> whatever else may be true of the distinction between white-collar and common criminals, the two are definitely drawn from distinctively different sectors of the American population. While there is substantial diversity in the types of people that are found in white-collar crime, even the lowest end of our offender hierarchy is easily distinguished from offenders in common-crime categories. . . [White-collar offenders] appear to represent the very broad middle of society.

Weisburd and colleagues show that, as adults, those who commit white-collar and common offenses come from different sectors of the population. The question remains unanswered, though, as to how they come to occupy these different sectors. How do the life courses of white-collar and common offenders differ? How early do they begin to diverge? Equally important, what happens in the life course of the typical white-collar offender that causes an older, previously law-abiding middle class individual to break the law? To address these questions, we turn now to our data.

DATA AND METHODS

In this study, we reanalyze data collected as part of a project on sentencing patterns in federal district courts.[2] The sampling frame for the original study consisted of defendants sentenced in eight federal district courts between 1973 and 1978. The eight districts were selected to represent variation in regional location and size.[3]

Although the term *white-collar crime* is now over 50 years old, its definition nevertheless continues to provoke significant controversy. Disagreement arises mainly over whether the term should be defined according to offense- or offender-based criteria (Shapiro, 1990; Coleman, 1989; Steffensmeier, 1989; Edelhertz, 1970). In this paper, an offense-based definition is used. This approach has been used in a number of well-regarded studies on white-collar crime (Weisburd, et al., 1990; Benson and Walker, 1988; Wheeler, et al., 1982; Hagan, et al.,

1980). The offenses designated as white-collar are bank embezzlement, bribery, false claims and statements, income tax violations, mail fraud, and postal embezzlement. The cases involve 2,643 individuals sentenced for these six white-collar crimes and 2,512 individuals sentenced for four common crimes (bank robbery, homicide, narcotics offenses and postal forgery).[4] We refer to these ten offenses as the selection offenses, as these were the offenses that made the individuals eligible for inclusion in the original study and that we used initially to classify offenders as either white-collar or common.

Data were gathered primarily from presentence investigation reports (PSIs). PSIs are prepared by probation officers to give judges a well-rounded picture of convicted defendants. For each offender, data are available on a variety of personal characteristics, including family background, occupational history, marital status, physical and mental health status, residential location, financial status, and criminal record. The most recent 120 PSI reports per offense from each of the five largest districts and the most recent forty PSI reports per offense from the three smaller districts were selected for the sample.[5]

RESULTS

Before we examine patterns in the life courses of the individuals in this study, it is useful to consider the demographic characteristics of the sample at the time of their conviction for the selection offense. Table 1 shows that the common criminals are younger and more likely to be non-whites than the white-collar criminals. Except for bank embezzlement, a substantial majority of offenders in all of the selection offense categories are male.

TABLE 1   Demographic Characteristics of White-Collar and Common Offenders

Type of Offender	Mean Age	% Male	% White
White-Collar	41	77.6	73.9
Bank embezzlement	31	52.3	75.4
Bribery	47	87.1	75.8
False claims	39	68.8	53.8
Income tax	49	91.4	89.1
Mail fraud	38	83.8	77.4
Postal embezzlement	34	89.5	65.0
Common	30	84.2	49.0
Forgery	31	75.3	49.2
Homicide	29	80.9	15.1
Narcotics	31	86.5	78.3
Robbery	28	93.4	46.3

Family Background

Life course researchers have devoted considerable attention to the effects of family background and early childhood socialization on later criminality. Early childhood socialization experiences are considered crucial either for preventing or for failing to prevent later deviance and criminality. However, there has been "no significant effort to link white-collar crime to family background or abnormalities in early socialization" (Coleman, 1987).

In an effort to fill this gap in the literature, we investigate the family backgrounds of the white-collar and common offenders. Four measures of family background are available in the data set. These measures index whether the defendant "was raised in a family environment," "had family members with a criminal record," "was an abused, neglected or abandoned child," and whether the defendant's "parents or guardians had difficulty providing the necessities of life." For each of these measures, we report the percentage experiencing the disadvantaged condition.

As Table 2 shows, the vast majority of white-collar and common criminals begin life in some type of family environment. Less than 10 percent, and in most cases less than 5 percent, of those in the white-collar and common crime offense categories were not raised in a family environment. But white-collar and common offenders are raised in different kinds of families. Only about 6 percent of white-collar offenders had family members with a criminal record, compared to nearly

TABLE 2   Family Background Characteristics of White-Collar and Common Offenders

Type of Offender	% Not Raised in a Family Environment	% With at Least One Criminal Family Member	% Abused, Neglected or Abandoned as a Child	% With Parents having Difficulty Providing the Necessities of Life
White-Collar	5.8	6.0	6.1	15.0
Bank embezzlement	3.3	4.1	5.4	10.7
Bribery	9.0	2.1	2.3	18.8
False claims	3.4	7.8	4.8	20.5
Income tax	3.8	5.1	6.9	12.3
Mail fraud	10.0	10.8	11.1	12.5
Postal embezzlement	4.9	9.1	8.7	13.3
Common	4.2	19.3	18.5	25.4
Forgery	6.3	19.4	18.6	26.3
Homicide	4.2	18.1	20.3	28.5
Narcotics	2.0	14.2	12.7	19.7
Robbery	4.2	25.3	23.0	28.3

20 percent for common offenders. Also, except for mail fraud, the percentage of white-collar offenders abused, neglected, or abandoned during childhood is less than 10 percent. In contrast, nearly one quarter of the bank robbers and one fifth of the forgers were mistreated in some fashion as children.

Finally, white-collar offenders are much less likely to be raised in poverty than common offenders. Only 15 percent of the white-collar offenders were raised by parents who had difficulty providing necessities, while more than one quarter of the common offenders came from disadvantaged backgrounds. For homicide and bank robbery offenders, the percentage is nearly 30 percent. The family background of the typical narcotics offender, however, looks more like that of a white-collar rather than a common offender. White-collar and common offenders begin life in different places.

Experiences in School

The statistical gap between white-collar and common offenders widens in school. Indeed, by the time they are in school the two groups can be clearly distinguished. Two measures in the data set rate the defendant's "overall academic performance in school" and "overall social adjustment in school." As Table 3 shows, taken together about half of all common offenders had below average or poor academic performance and social adjustment in school, while only a quarter of white-collar offenders had the same problems. By the time they are in school those convicted of bank robbery, forgery, or homicide already appear to be following trajectories slanting toward trouble and difficulty. Approximately 60

TABLE 3   School Background Characteristics of White-Collar and Common Offenders

Type of Offender	% With Below-Average or Poor Academic Performance	% With Below-Average or Poor Social Adjustment in School
White-Collar	25.9	22.3
Bank embezzlement	17.7	13.1
Bribery	24.7	25.0
False claims	31.0	26.6
Income tax	19.5	16.3
Mail fraud	37.8	32.6
Postal embezzlement	27.1	18.8
Common	52.1	45.1
Forgery	56.8	47.9
Homicide	48.7	45.0
Narcotics	39.9	25.2
Robbery	61.7	60.1

percent of all bank robbers and forgers and nearly half of all murderers had below- average or poor academic performance in school, and a similar proportion had trouble adjusting socially in school. In contrast, the percentage of white-collar offenders with below-average academic performance or social adjustment in school is much smaller, ranging between 13 percent (bank embezzlement) and 38 percent (mail fraud).

Trajectories in Adult Life

The divergence in trajectories between white-collar and common offenders becomes more pronounced in adulthood. Table 4 presents a statistical portrait of the social characteristics of offenders at the time of conviction. Like Weisburd, et al. (1991), we find that white-collar and common criminals occupy distinctly different positions and have achieved different statuses in the social hierarchy. Compared with common offenders, white-collar offenders are two to three times more likely to be married, have a college degree, be steadily employed, be home owners, have a steady residence, and have financial assets over $10,000 (see Table 4). Narcotics offenders are an exception to these general patterns, as they appear to occupy a middle ground between the white-collar offenders and the other common crime offenders.

In addition to the differences in adult life positions, adult life activities also appear to differ between white-collar and common offenders. As a group, white-collar offenders are considerably more involved in their communities than common offenders (see Table 5). About 19 percent of the white-collar offenders were involved in social or other community groups, compared to 5 percent for common offenders. White-collar offenders are over three times more likely to be involved in church or other religious activities than common offenders, 11.9 percent to 3.4 percent, respectively. They are also twice as likely to attend church regularly, 31.1 percent to 16 percent, respectively. Finally, the friends of white-collar offenders appear to be more upstanding or law-abiding than those of common offenders. Only 9 percent of the white-collar offenders were judged to have friends likely to promote criminal behavior, compared with 40.3 percent of the common offenders (see Table 5).

Although white-collar offenders lead more conventional lives than common offenders, they could not be described as highly integrated into community life. Nor can they be considered upper class. Over 80 percent of white-collar offenders are *not* involved in community groups. Nearly 90 percent are *not* involved in church-related activities, and about 70 percent do *not* attend church regularly. Additionally, only about two thirds of white-collar offenders had steady employment and steady residences at the time of their conviction. Taken together, these results indicate that many white-collar offenders are not the pillars of the community frequently portrayed in popular works on white-collar crime. Rather, they appear to be rather ordinary people leading middle-class lives.

TABLE 4 Adult Life Characteristics of White-Collar and Common Offenders

Type of Offender	% Married	% With College Degree	% With Steady Employment	% Homeowners	% With Residential Stability	% With Assets > $10,000
White-Collar						
Bank embezzlement	61.9	17.0	65.8	50.3	63.5	35.3
Bribery	54.2	9.4	64.9	41.7	55.2	13.5
False claims	72.2	23.3	76.1	63.2	72.6	58.4
Income tax	49.5	18.0	53.8	40.0	55.9	28.3
Mail fraud	76.0	23.1	81.2	70.5	77.2	60.4
Postal embezzlement	54.9	13.6	46.5	31.3	49.7	19.0
Common	62.9	1.4	73.4	48.5	65.2	11.1
Forgery	28.2	3.3	24.1	11.8	38.5	4.5
Homicide	26.8	1.5	20.7	9.5	32.9	2.7
Narcotics	23.9	0.6	25.6	9.7	50.6	1.4
Robbery	35.0	9.7	36.8	21.4	40.3	11.8
	26.2	1.0	13.6	6.0	33.1	1.7

TABLE 5   Adult Life Activities of White-Collar and Common Offenders

Type of Offender	% Involved in Social or Community Groups	% Involved in Church or Religious Activities	% Who Attend Church Regularly	% With Friends Likely to Promote Criminal Behavior
White-Collar	18.8	11.9	31.1	9.0
Bank embezzlement	17.5	13.4	34.2	7.2
Bribery	26.4	16.5	34.9	2.0
False claims	15.0	9.4	31.6	6.6
Income tax	23.9	11.6	31.2	9.1
Mail fraud	10.9	8.9	26.0	21.8
Postal embezzlement	14.7	8.4	22.0	8.4
Common	4.8	3.4	16.0	40.3
Forgery	4.7	3.5	16.4	28.4
Homicide	4.6	5.7	19.0	19.1
Narcotics	5.6	2.1	17.3	62.5
Robbery	4.2	2.7	12.2	46.9

Onset of Offending and Trajectories in Crime

The term *white-collar career criminal* seems like an oxymoron. The white-collar criminal is generally assumed to be a "one-shot" offender, whose first encounter with the criminal justice system is his or her last (Weisburd, et al., 1990). To make a career out of crime involves a commitment to deviance and nonconformity, which is assumed to be the antithesis of the white-collar offender's lifestyle.

In this section, we explore the prior criminal records of offenders in the sample. Table 6 shows the average number of prior arrests for white-collar and common offense categories. Not surprisingly, the average number of prior arrests is generally lower in the white-collar offense categories (1.65) compared with the common offense categories (5.90). However, there is considerable variation within the white-collar offense categories. The average number of prior arrests ranges from a low of 0.50 in the bank embezzlement category to a high of 3.65 in the mail fraud category. Eight out of ten common offenders had one or more prior arrests before their selection offense, compared with four out of ten white-collar offenders. Although common offenders are more than twice as likely to have prior arrests, a sizeable number of white-collar offenders are not strangers to the criminal justice system. About 12 percent of the white-collar offenders had four or more prior arrests and may be properly classified as career criminals.

Finally, we explore potential differences between white-collar and common offenders with regard to age at onset into crime. As seen in Table 7, for both

TABLE 6   Prior Arrests for White-Collar and Common Offenders

Type of Offender	Mean	SD
White-Collar	1.65	3.61
Bank embezzlement	.50	1.73
Bribery	.62	2.00
False claims	2.28	4.00
Income tax	1.69	3.17
Mail fraud	3.65	5.52
Postal embezzlement	.85	1.94
Common	5.90	6.62
Forgery	6.34	6.48
Homicide	7.02	9.00
Narcotics	3.52	4.42
Robbery	6.93	5.75

TABLE 7   Average Age at Onset of Offenders with Prior Arrests and First-Time Offenders for White-Collar and Common Crimes[1]

Type of Offender	Median Age at Onset for Prior Arrests	Median Age at Onset for First-time Offenders
White-Collar	24 (970)	40 (1571)
Bank embezzlement	21 (87)	28 (404)
Bribery	30 (108)	49 (374)
False claims	24 (229)	38.5 (236)
Income tax	29 (218)	49 (302)
Mail fraud	22 (282)	36 (159)
Postal embezzlement	20.5 (46)	33 (96)
Common	19 (1986)	26 (451)
Forgery	19 (537)	25 (119)
Homicide	18 (392)	26.5 (76)
Narcotics	20 (477)	28.5 (178)
Robbery	18 (583)	23 (78)

[1] Numbers are listed in parentheses under age.

first-time and multiple offenders the average age at onset into criminal activity is much higher for white-collar than for common offenders. For offenders with prior records, the average age at first offense is 24 for white-collar offenders compared with 19 for common offenders. For offenders whose first offense was the selection offense, the average age for white-collar offenders is 40 years, compared with 26 years for common offenders. Over 60 percent of white-collar offenders truly are "late starters."

THINKING ABOUT WHITE-COLLAR CRIME AND THE LIFE COURSE

Like Weisburd, et al. (1991), we find that the individuals who violate what are typically considered white-collar crime statutes come more from the middle rather than the upper social classes. The theoretical significance of these offenders should not be ignored. Although they are not powerful business executives or government officials, neither are they marginalized lower-class outsiders. Their trajectories in crime do not fit either the life course–persistent or adolescence-limited pattern identified by Moffitt (1997). On the other hand, neither do they resemble the powerful corporate executives popularized by Sutherland (1949) and others. So, where do they fit into criminological theory and how may life course theory be applied to them?

Most white-collar offenders do not follow the conventional trajectories identified by life course theory. Their official offending careers start relatively late in life, when they are more or less securely ensconced in the middle class. In the various domains of adult life, such as family and occupation, they appear to be following conventional trajectories. One searches in vain for early precursors or early hints of trouble in the life history of the typical white-collar offender. For most of these individuals, their offenses appear to come out of nowhere. Their crimes do not appear to be part of longstanding patterns of antisocial conduct, nor do they appear to be deeply rooted in a troubled social background. With respect to the life course approach, these findings suggest that latent traits are not appropriate for explaining white-collar crime. White-collar crime appears to be more a function of adult life experiences as opposed to a latent personality trait or a disturbed social background.

Regarding crime during adulthood, life course researchers have focused on identifying factors that distinguish those who stop offending from those who persist. Persistence in offending is thought to be caused by a latent trait and by the narrowing of legitimate opportunities that follows extensive involvement in crime. To explain desistence from offending, Sampson and Laub (1993) have proposed an age-graded theory of informal social controls. According to this theory, transitions that increase informal social control in adulthood, such as getting married or finding a good job, lead to desistence from crime. Because onset into offending in adulthood is assumed to be very rare, it has been ignored by life course researchers. However, as the data presented in this paper demonstrate, most white-collar offenders do not begin to offend until they are well into adulthood. From the perspective of life course theory, how can this pattern of late starting be understood?

One possible approach is to focus on events in trajectories in other domains of adult life that may trigger involvement in white-collar crime. For example, two important domains of adult life are family and occupation. Some research suggests that at least some white-collar offenders are responding to dire family circumstances when they decide to become involved in white-collar crime (Daly, 1989; Benson, 1985). Other research suggests that changes in motivational stressors arising out of one's occupational position may underlie onset into white-collar crime. For example, a sudden downturn in business revenues may force a small businessperson to resort to unlawful means to keep the business afloat (Benson, 1985). From the perspective of life course theory, the key point is to analyze the causes of white-collar crime in the context of trajectories in other domains of life.

Another potential application of the life course approach to white-collar crime involves thinking of crime as a social event in the life course (Hagan and Palloni, 1988). That is, rather than focusing exclusively on white-collar crime as a dependent variable, we should examine not only its causes but also its short- and long-term consequences. Hagan (1993) argues that involvement in delinquency as an adolescent has different consequences depending on the individual's neighborhood and class standing. For lower-class boys raised in disorganized neighborhoods, acquiring a delinquent criminal record narrows future occupational opportunities, but this is less true for middle-class boys from stable neighborhoods. Some research suggests that collateral consequences of conviction for a white-collar crime also are not uniform. They may be strongly influenced by class standing or occupational position (Benson, 1989; Benson, 1984). By thinking about white-collar crime as a social event that has consequences for the life course as well as causes, we may better illuminate the role of social class and social power in shaping societal reactions to crime. We may also better integrate the study of white-collar crime with important theoretical trends in mainstream criminology and sociology.

ENDNOTES

1. The idea that not all white-collar offenders come from the privileged sectors of society is not entirely new. Many of the embezzlers studied by Cressey in the early 1950s held what can only be described as menial occupational positions, such as gas station attendant (Cressey, 1953).

2. The data used in this study were made available by the Inter-University Consortium for Political and Social Research. Data for Sentencing in Eight United States District Courts, 1973–1978 were originally collected by Brian Forst and William Rhodes. Neither the collectors of the original data nor the Consortium bear any responsibility for the analyses and interpretations presented here.

3. The jurisdictions were New Jersey, Eastern New York, Connecticut, Northern Ohio, Middle Florida, Western Oklahoma, Northern New Mexico, and Northern California.

4. Following Wheeler, et al. (1982), we designated postal forgery as a common crime offense primarily because it is a nonviolent, financially oriented property offense that is unlikely to be

committed by offenders of white-collar social status. In the federal judiciary, most cases of postal forgery involve individuals who have stolen government issued checks for welfare or social security benefits from mail boxes. Whether the defendant is charged with the crime of postal theft or postal forgery depends mainly on whether he or she is caught at the time of the theft or while trying to cash the stolen check by forging the recipient's endorsement.

5. Because of the relative scarcity of PSI reports for false claims, bribery, and mail fraud, about 500 cases were selected nationwide for each of these crimes. We deleted cases where the defendant was a corporation.

REFERENCES

Benson, Michael L. 1984. "The Fall From Grace: Loss of Occupational Status Among Convicted White-Collar Offenders." *Criminology* 22(4):573–93.

_____. 1985. "Denying the Guilty Mind: Accounting for Involvement in a White-Collar Crime." *Criminology* 23(4):583–609.

_____. 1989. "The Influence of Class Position on the Formal and Informal Sanctioning of White-Collar Offenders." *Sociology Quarterly* 30(3):465–80.

Benson, Michael L., and Esteban Walker. 1988. "Sentencing the White-Collar Offender." *American Sociological Review* 53:294–302.

Benson, Michael L., and Elizabeth Moore. 1992. "Are White-Collar and Common Offenders the Same: An Empirical and Theoretical Critique of a Recently Proposed General Theory of Crime." *Journal of Research in Crime and Delinquency* 29(3):251–72.

Caspi, Avshalom, Terrie E. Moffitt, Phil A. Silva, Magda Stouthamer-Loeber, Robert F. Krueger, and Pamela S. Schmutte. 1994. "Are Some People Crime-Prone? Replications of the Personality-Crime Relationship Across Countries, Genders, Races, and Methods." *Criminology* 32(2):163–94.

Coleman, James W. 1987. "Toward An Integrated Theory of White-Collar Crime." *American Journal of Sociology* 93(2):406–39.

_____. 1989. *The Criminal Elite*. New York: St. Martin's Press.

Cressey, Donald. 1953. *Other People's Money*. New York: The Free Press.

Croall, Hazel. 1989. "Who Is the White-Collar Criminal." *British Journal of Criminology* 29(2):157–74.

Cullen, Francis T., William J. Maakestad, and Gray Cavendar. 1987. *Corporate Crime Under Attack*. Cincinnati, OH: Anderson.

Daly, Kathleen. 1989. "Gender and Varieties of White-Collar Crime." *Criminology* 27(4):769–94.

Edelhertz, Herbert. 1970. *The Nature, Impact and Prosecution of White-Collar Crime*. Washington, D. C.: U. S. Department of Justice.

Elder, Glen H. Jr. 1985. "Perspectives on the Life Course." Pp. 23–49 in *Life Course Dynamics: Trajectories and Transitions, 1968–1980*, ed. by Glen H. Elder. Ithaca, NY: Cornell University Press.

_____. 1996. "Human Lives in Changing Societies: Life Course and Developmental Insights." Pp. 31–62 in Developmental Science, ed. by Robert B. Cairns, Glen H. Elder, and E. J. Costello. New York: Cambridge.

Farrington, David P. 1994. "Human Development and Criminal Careers." Pp. 511–84 in *Oxford Handbook of Criminology*, ed. by Mike Maguire, Rod Morgan, and Robert Reiner. New York: Oxford University Press.

Geis, Gilbert. 1977. "The Heavy Electrical Equipment Antitrust Cases of 1961." Pp. 117–32 in *White-Collar Crime*. Rev. ed., ed. by Gilbert Geis and Robert Meier. New York: MacMillan.

Gottfredson, Michael R., and Travis Hirschi. 1990. *A General Theory of Crime*. Stanford, CA: Stanford University Press.

Hagan, John. 1993. "The Social Embeddedness of Crime and Unemployment." *Criminology* 31(4):465–92.

_____. 1997. "Crime and Capitalization: Toward a Developmental Theory of Street Crime in America." Pp. 287–308 in *Developmental Theories of Crime and Delinquency*, Ed. Terence P. Thornberry. New Brunswick, NJ: Transaction Publishers.

Hagan, John, Ilene H. Nagel-Bernstein, and Celesta Albonetti. 1980. "The Differential Sentencing of White-Collar Offenders in Ten Federal District Courts." *American Sociological Review* 45:802–20.

Hagan, John, and Alberto Palloni. 1988. "Crimes As Social Events in the Life Course: Reconceiving a Criminological Controversy." *Criminology* 26(1):87–100.

Loeber, Rolf and T. Dishion. 1983. "Early Predictors of Male Delinquency: A Review." *Psychological Bulletin* 94(1):68–99.

Loeber, Rolf, and Magda Stouthamer-Loeber. 1986. "Family Factors As Correlates and Predictors of Juvenile Conduct Problems and Delinquency." Pp. 29–149 in *Crime and Justice: An Annual Review of Research*, vol. 7, edited by Michael Tonry and Norval Morris. Chicago: University of Chicago Press.

_____. 1996. "The Development of Offending." *Criminal Justice and Behavior* 23(1):12–24.

Mayer, Karl U., and Walter Muller. 1986. "The State and the Structure of the Life Course." Pp. 217–45 in *Human Development and the Life Course: Multidisciplinary Perspectives*, ed. Aage B. Sorensen, Franz E. Weinert, and Lonnie R. Sherrod. Hillsdale, NJ: Lawrence Erlbaum Associates.

Moffitt, Terrie E. 1997. "Adolescence-Limited and Life course -Persistent Offending: A Complementary Pair of Developmental Theories." Pp. 11–54 in *Developmental Theories of Crime and Delinquency*, ed. Terence P. Thornberry. New Brunswick: Transaction Publishers.

Nagin, Daniel S., and David P. Farrington. 1992. "The Stability of Criminal Potential Form Childhood to Adulthood." *Criminology* 30(2):235–60.

Nagin, Daniel S., David P. Farrington, and Terrie E. Moffitt. 1995. "Life Course Trajectories of Different Types of Offenders." *Criminology* 33(1):111–39.

Riley, Matilda W. 1986. "Overview and Highlights of a Sociological Perspective." Pp. 153–75 in *Human Development and the Life Course: Multidisciplinary Perspectives*, ed. Aage B. Sorensen, Franz E. Weinert, and Lonnie R. Sherrod. Hillsdale, NJ: Lawrence Earlbaum Associates.

Sampson, Robert J. and John H. Laub. 1993. *Crime in the Making: Pathways and Turning Points Through Life*. Cambridge, MA: Harvard University Press.

Shapiro, Susan P. 1990. "Collaring the Crime, Not the Criminal: Reconsidering 'White-Collar Crime'". *American Sociological Review* 55(3):346–65.

Simon, David R., and Stanley D. Etizen, eds. 1990. *Elite Deviance*. 3rd ed. Boston: Allyn & Bacon.

Sutherland, Edwin. 1949. *White-Collar Crime*. New York: Dryden.

Steffensmeier, Darrell. 1989. "On the Causes of 'White-Collar' Crime." *Criminology* 27(2):345–58.

Weisburd, David, Ellen F. Chayet, and Elin J. Waring. 1990. "White-Collar Crime and Criminal Careers: Some Preliminary Findings." *Crime & Delinquency* 36(3):342–55.

_____. Stanton Wheeler, Elin Waring, and N. Bode. 1991. *Crimes of the Middle Classes: White-Collar Offenders in the Federal Courts*. New Haven: Yale University Press.

West, Donald J, and David P. Farrington. 1973. *Who Becomes Delinquent?* London: Heinemann.

Wheeler, Stanton, David Weisburd, and Nancy Bode. 1982. "Sentencing the White-Collar Offender: Rhetoric and Reality." *American Sociological Review* 47(5):641–59.

The System
of Corporate
Crime Control

Peter Grabosky

Criminologists for quite some time have recognized that the criminal justice system is a very imperfect instrument of social control. They remind us that there are other, more effective, institutions of social control within society, such as the family, the educational system, and the church, which constitute the first line of defense against crime. Indeed, the problem of crime, and the role of the criminal justice system, is likely to intensify when the influence of these other, more fundamental, social institutions weaken. As Donald Black (1976) so elegantly put it, law varies inversely with other forms of social control.

Corporate crime deserves equal treatment. Much contemporary discourse about corporate illegality tends to dwell upon the magnitude of harm that it imposes and on the official sanctioning (or lack thereof) of corporate offenders. While not dismissing the importance, indeed, the necessity, of the state responding to corporate crime as *crime*, this essay calls for a more-expansive conception of corporate crime control, which would harness a wider variety of institutions and influences. Just as the effective control of conventional street crime requires something more than increased risk of arrest, conviction, and imprisonment, so too does the control of corporate crime require a more-comprehensive approach, based on a wider array of institutions.

The urgency of this more-expansive view of corporate crime control is reinforced by the fundamental changes that began to occur in Western democracies about two decades ago with the Thatcher/Reagan ascendancies. Since that time, pressures on governments to reduce public expenditures and to foster a climate favorable to business have become dominant facts of political life. They are destined to remain so, well into the twenty-first century, as global markets and competitive pressures militate against direct governmental intervention in business activities. In this sense, the high-water mark of command and control regulation by government agencies would appear to have passed. Somewhat ironically, in parallel to these trends, one sees increasing demands upon and expectations of government to provide a cleaner environment, a safer workplace, and a fair marketplace.

Although governments today may be less inclined directly to intervene in the affairs of business, they appear quite willing to coopt nongovernmental actors in furtherance of regulatory objectives. Alternatively, they may create circumstances in which market forces, or the natural inclinations of nongovernmental institutions, perform quasiregulatory functions. What we may be witnessing is not so much an abdication of government responsibility for the control of corporate crime, but rather a transformation of corporate social control. Ironically, what we are experiencing could well entail less government regulation resulting in more control over business.

The remainder of this essay will discuss some of the basic elements of a wider conception of corporate crime control. To continue the analogy with street crime, we seek to identify nongovernmental institutions which are in a position to contribute to the prevention of corporate crime. In so doing, we must bear in mind that no one institution, governmental or private, will provide an ironclad bulwark against corporate illegality. Rather, it is a combination of complementary institutions and instruments which will provide the best solution. The latter half of the essay will offer one way of looking at such combinations.

REQUIRED THIRD-PARTY VIGILANCE AND DISCLOSURE

The idea that regulatory compliance can only be monitored by public servants has become an antiquated notion. Governments increasingly require third-party participation in the regulatory process. This mandatory participation tends to involve a required degree of vigilance, and the disclosure of regulatory violations coming to the attention of the third party. Perhaps the most direct of these is what might be termed conscription (Grabosky, 1995a). Governments may simply command third parties to assist with one or more processes of compliance. Cash transaction reporting requirements have become increasingly common in western democracies over the past quarter century. In essence, these mandate that banks and other institutions defined as "cash dealers" systematically report transactions in excess of a certain amount, and other transactions that might appear suspect, to regulatory authorities. These requirements render more difficult the task of concealing ill-gotten gains, or of concealing legitimate income from taxation authorities.

In some regulatory domains, governments may require regulated entities to subject themselves to independent scrutiny and compliance certification by third parties. A common, if not always effective, example is that of financial auditing. Critics might argue that financial scandals such as the savings and loan collapses of the 1980s occurred *despite* the safeguards of auditing. But consider the indecent liberties that might be taken if companies were not obliged to submit to such independent scrutiny.

Examples may be drawn from other areas; required environmental audits and impact assessments are becoming part of the regulatory landscape in many jurisdictions. Mandatory independent certification of compliance with occupational health and safety standards is also likely to become more common. The National Performance Review chaired by U.S. Vice President Gore recommended that occupational health and safety inspections be performed by private inspection companies, or by nonmanagement employees (Gore, 1993, 34).

The pivotal role played by professional advisors in the prevention and control of white collar and corporate crime is widely recognized (Grabosky, 1990; Tomasic, 1991). Such professional roles may be encouraged by special accreditation or other considerations accorded their practitioners by regulatory authorities. One example are tax advisers who are formally accredited by taxation authorities (Klepper, Mazur, and Nagin, 1991; Tomasic and Pentony, 1991). Professions may be created and invested with legitimacy by the state in order to facilitate just such a role (Gilb, 1966; Halliday and Carruthers, 1990). Kraakman (1986) uses the term *gatekeepers* to refer to private parties who are in a position to disrupt misconduct by withholding their cooperation from a wrongdoer.

Beyond audit and inspection requirements, corporations may be required by governments to comply with standards developed in the private sector (Cheit, 1990). In addition, regulatory authorities can make it obligatory that companies hold liability insurance as a condition of doing business. Conditions of a private insurance contract may equal or exceed government licensing conditions in terms of stringency, and surveillance on the part of the insurer may surpass that of government (Ferreira, 1982; Heimer, 1985; Shapiro, 1987, 209; Katzman, 1988; Osborne and Gaebler, 1992, 223). To the extent that "regulation by insurance" achieves or surpasses public compliance goals, regulatory authorities are free to focus their limited resources on targets less amenable to alternative control mechanisms, or those posing a greater risk of noncompliance.

VOLUNTARY PUBLIC INTEREST ACTIVITY

Public interest organizations have a long history of contribution to corporate crime control. From the initial identification of harmful corporate activity, through continued vigilance of corporate conduct, representatives of the public interest have been instrumental in setting policy agendas. Indeed, many regulatory agencies owe if not their origins, their continued existence to the persistence of interest groups. The work of Ralph Nader and his colleagues, initially in the field of motor vehicle safety, then across the range of corporate harms, was preceded by health, labor, and conservation organizations a century ago.

Public interest organizations vary widely in the specificity of their focus, their strategy, and their tactics. From nuclear safety, to consumer protection, to the preservation of endangered species, to workplace health and safety, they include both the global and the local. They may play an adversarial role vis-a-vis industries, individual companies, or government agencies, or may engage in constructive engagement with public and/or private sector institutions.

By conferring public status on organized interest groups, governments provide an orderly forum for interest articulation, which can enhance communication and minimize conflict. By presenting information to deliberative forums, interest groups can contribute to balanced, objective decision making. In so doing they may provide data, interpretation, or a perspective that might not, in the ordinary course of events, be drawn to the attention of decision makers. This can enhance the range of policy alternatives available to government. Moreover, government agencies often lack the foresight or the resources to invest in strategic intelligence, the collection of information bearing upon likely developments in a given policy environment. Nongovernment organizations can serve to monitor the performance of regulatory agencies and regulated entities, and to inform public forums of compliance problems and regulatory inadequacies (Ayres and Braithwaite, 1992; Cohen and Rogers, 1992).

PRIVATE REGULATORY ENFORCEMENT

Private enforcement can serve as a useful complement to enforcement by public regulatory authorities, particularly under circumstances where government agencies may be subject to political or fiscal constraint.

There are two basic avenues by which governments can enlist the resources of private interests to enforce compliance. The first entails the creation of certain specified rights, conferring them upon private parties, and leaving it up to those private parties to enforce. Many systems of patent, trademark, and copyright rely on such private enforcement. Companies and securities regulators also encourage private actions on the part of aggrieved parties (Coffee, 1986). Successful private litigation may result in damage awards that exceed civil or criminal penalties available to the state (Galanter and Luban, 1993), and the deterrent effect posed by many potential private enforcers should not be underestimated.

A second avenue of private enforcement entails empowering third parties to undertake enforcement actions on behalf of the state. The principle is by no means a modern one. A fourteenth-century English statute specified that 25 percent of fines imposed on stallholders engaged in trade after the close of a fair be paid to citizens intervening on behalf of the King (5 Edw III, ch.5 (1331); Boyer and Meidinger, 1985, 948).[1]

Private enforcement in the public interest is alive and well in many jurisdictions, most notably the United States, where a number of federal environmental laws contain provisions for private enforcement. In addition, the False Claims Act (31 USC 3729-3733) enables citizens who become aware of frauds perpetrated against the federal government to bring civil actions against the perpetrator. The Act was originally introduced during the Civil War to combat unscrupulous conduct by contractors to the Union Army. Since its reincarnation in 1986, the False Claims Act has served as the basis for numerous citizen suits, most of which have been brought by employees alleging fraud on the part of defense contractors and healthcare providers.[2] The government itself has the discretion to join the action, or it may remain at arm's length if it so chooses. In the event the action succeeds, up to 25 percent of the damages may be awarded to the citizen-plaintiff, with the majority going to the United States Treasury.

In Britain, the generally available right of private prosecution has been exercised in the public interest by third parties. Each year, the Royal Society for the Prevention of Cruelty to Animals investigates tens of thousands of complaints and successfully prosecutes about 2,000 cases (Harlow and Rawlings, 1992).

SELF-REGULATORY INITIATIVES

The concept of self-regulation is a broad one, and may embrace activity ranging from the voluntaristic and spontaneous on the one hand, to a regimen of self control that is essentially coerced on the other. In general, enforced self-regulation entails the requirement that the regulatee develop its own compliance program, which is then subject to approval by regulatory authorities (Bardach and Kagan, 1982, 223–240; Braithwaite, 1982; Ayres and Braithwaite, 1992, Ch. 4). Ayres and Braithwaite observe that this can result in a tailor-made compliance program superior to that which might be designed and mandated by government authority.

Quality control can be extended to include all aspects of a company's operations, including health, safety, and environmental performance. Increasingly, companies are embracing principles of total quality management, based on a commitment to excellence rather than any requirements imposed from without.

Some self-regulatory initiatives lie in between the polar extremes of spontaneity and coercion. These tend to be driven by the specter of government intrusion, or perhaps by a significant adverse event that can threaten the industry's public image. In those industries there is a degree of "shared fate," where the reputation of all players can be tainted by the misconduct of just one. Following the

Three Mile Island incident, members of the U.S. nuclear power industry joined to establish one of the most rigorous regimes of self-regulation yet seen (Rees, 1994). The informal social controls exerted by one's peers may preclude the necessity of state intervention.

REGULATORY ENDOWMENTS

In some instances, governments may become aware that certain regulatory functions are already being performed or could be performed by private parties. In such cases, governments may be content to rely upon this activity as the primary regulatory mechanism, using public resources as a backup.

Standards developed in the private sector are often accepted and given official status by public agencies. Among the more familiar are the electrical safety standards developed by Underwriters Laboratories (Cheit, 1990) and a variety of standards developed by supranational institutions such as the International Standards Organization (ISO). In some regulatory systems, the task of developing rules is delegated to private interests. The U.S. Securities and Exchange Commission has delegated considerable rule-making function to professional self-regulatory organizations (Shapiro, 1987, 214; Ayres and Braithwaite, 1992, 104). The National Association of Securities Dealers (NASD) may impose fines and suspensions upon individuals and firms for violations of securities laws and NASD rules. Actions may be appealed to the SEC and subsequently to U.S. Federal Courts (Hyatt, 1993). Galanter (1981) refers to such arrangements as "regulatory endowments."

INDUCEMENTS FOR COMPLIANCE

Governments may offer incentives directly to targets of regulation to induce compliance, or to engage in a desired course of conduct (Grabosky, 1995b). Regulatory authorities may offer incentives for self-regulatory investments or for the engagement of professional services that would foster compliance. Port authorities in Rotterdam offer quicker turnaround and reduced fees for those ships with exemplary environmental performance. Many nations' tax systems provide that costs incurred in furtherance of regulatory compliance are tax deductible. Inducements of this kind are likely to be perceived as more legitimate than are commands. For this reason, they are likely to be more effective.

In various regulatory regimes, companies that have an approved compliance program in place, or that subject themselves to a regular compliance audit by an independent assessor, may qualify for license fee rebates, or may be subject to less scrutiny by regulatory authorities.[3]

FOSTERING MARKET FORCES

A seventh means of enlisting private energies in furtherance of regulatory objectives is to create conditions that permit the constructive operation of market forces. These may entail a backdrop of statutory requirement or may occur more or less spontaneously.

Market forces and institutions perform a number of functions in furtherance of corporate crime prevention. Markets are important educational media. Public consciousness of issues relating to the environment, health, and safety can be significantly raised by exposure to market discourse. Institutions wishing to portray themselves as socially responsible often do so through markets. The very task of choosing between market alternatives provides an opportunity for comparing products on a number of dimensions relating to compliance. Ordinary citizens who may be largely ignorant of issues relating to health or the environment may acquire new information in their role as consumers. Growing consumer demand for environmentally preferable products inspires the generation of information relating to the product and its relation to the environment. New generations of consumers are in turn educated.

One manifestation of relatively spontaneous market forces is the exercise of purchasing power by large retailers in furtherance of environmental protection. Large organizations increasingly like to present themselves as virtuous corporate citizens, and environmentally friendly. Companies such as Boots the Chemist and Sainsbury's in the United Kingdom, Wal-Mart in the United States, and the Body Shop internationally, place demands upon their suppliers or prospective suppliers that may include minimal packaging or chemical input and the use of recycled or recyclable materials. In so doing, these large-scale buyers send powerful signals to the market—signals that governments may be unable or unwilling to send. As one observer put it, "When McDonald's says 'Jump', 500 suppliers ask 'How high?'"(Earle, 1996)

In contrast to the market's rewarding a virtuous company for good corporate citizenship, consumers may be in a position to punish corporate wrongdoing. The boycott, or concerted avoidance of certain purchases, may be mobilized against products or producers engaged in illegal or otherwise undesirable activity. Current campaigns against apparel manufactured in countries lacking fair labor practices are but one example. No manufacturer of consumer products likes to be portrayed as the employer of sweated labor in some Third World dictatorship.

Companies affect each other's behavior. Purchasers influence suppliers; in industry, the interchange between buyers and suppliers generates incentives to innovate (Porter 1990, 590). Suppliers' practices can bear upon a retailer's public image, and buyers are increasingly sensitive to the risk of being tainted by a supplier's questionable environmental image. To this end, buyers are tending increasingly to scrutinize products from a "cradle to grave" perspective, noting considerations such as energy efficiency in manufacture, minimization and responsible disposal of waste, economical use of materials in packaging, and recyclability of product. Anticipated purchasing power may also influence product design. Large buyers are able to dictate content and packaging requirements to an extent that governments would find difficult, if not impossible.

The emergence of collaborative relationships between private corporate actors may become an important means of fostering compliance. Canaan and Reichman (1993) refer to "regulatory communities"—networks and partnerships in which participants foster technology transfer and engage in other forms of joint venture in furtherance of environmental objectives, beyond the purview of governments. Spontaneously occurring alternatives to regulation have also developed among financial institutions, with regard to the organization of arrangements for interbank credit card operations such as Visa and Mastercard (Oedel, 1993).

Markets are also arenas of surveillance (Dandeker, 1990, 64). In addition to the surveillance normally exercised in the market by competitors, the scrutiny accorded compliance behavior by banks, insurers, and institutional investors can be formidable (Vogel, 1986).

Entire industries have developed to assist businesses in remaining on the good side of the law. Many can justifiably claim that they can both save their clients money, and keep them out of trouble. Shapiro (1987, 205) refers to "private social control entrepreneurs for hire." This is perhaps nowhere more evident than in the environmental services industry, where consultants are able to assist clients in reducing raw materials and energy consumption, and in reducing emissions and waste. Not only do they help client companies achieve a better bottom line, they can contribute to a positive corporate image, which may in turn be valuable in its own right.

By marketing their services these consultants not only help generate demand, they perform an educative function. Indeed, recognizing the inevitability of trends toward increased environmental awareness, some have become environmental advocates in their own right (Deloitte Touche Tohmatsu, 1993). Industry associations urge best practice environmental management (Australian Manufacturing Council, 1993). Prominent businesspeople publicly pronounce that good environmental management is not only intrinsically worthy but also profitable (Schmidheiny, 1992). This activity is quite independent of any government direction.

One of the virtues of market-based orderings is that they tend to be perceived as noncoercive, or in any event, as less coercive than government commands. Thus market signals, no matter how dictatorial they may be in reality, create less resentment than government direction (Osborne and Gaebler, 1992, 290).

The Role of the State

To be sure, many of the above quasi-regulatory activities owe their very existence to government regulatory initiatives in the first place. Although stimulated and bolstered by the existence of command and control regulation, these institutions and forces take on a life of their own, potentially eclipsing the influence of the state.

In between the extremes of rigid command and control on the one hand, and laissez-faire deference to market forces on the other, governments may play a facilitative role, creating the conditions within which private regulatory orderings may flourish. Governments, after all, are significant consumers in their own right, and can use their own purchasing power to send strong market signals. By providing a legal framework that will permit orderly private redress, and by facilitating the involvement of nonstate actors, governments may foster quasiregulation by third parties, while conserving their own limited resources for deployment where they can do the most good.

For there will always be those cases where less formal systems of social control will fail. They are likely to be least effective against corporate offenders who are small (and who may therefore be lacking in compliance capacity), incompetent, and not situated in a market context where they are vulnerable to consumer pressure.

A CONCEPTUAL FRAMEWORK FOR THE ANALYSIS OF CORPORATE CRIME CONTROL

Perhaps the most important work on the regulatory process published during the 1990s was Ayres and Braithwaite's *Responsive Regulation: Transcending the Deregulation Debate* (Ayres and Braithwaite, 1992).

The book's subtitle refers to what had become a sterile, ideologically based debate between advocates of strict regulatory control by a strong state on the one hand, and those calling for the abdication of the state in favor of market forces on the other. As they, and others (e.g., Shearing, 1993) have observed, regulatory space is more diverse and complex than the simplistic "either-or" model would have us believe.

The Ayres and Braithwaite analysis advocated wider participation in the regulatory process, to include not only government agencies and regulated entities but also third parties representing public interests (Public Interest Groups, or PIGs). The concept of regulatory tripartism, embracing the possibility of constructive collaboration between the three main institutional forms, is already manifest in a variety of settings, such as tripartite regimes for the regulation of occupational health and safety, and at a more general level, corporatist governance (Grabosky and

Braithwaite, 1986, 66; Streeck and Schmitter, 1985; Schmitter and Lembruch, 1979).

Ayres and Braithwaite used a simple, but elegant graphical depiction—the pyramid—to represent the circumstances of interaction between regulator and regulatee. Based on ideas developed in Braithwaite's earlier work on the regulation of coal mine safety (Braithwaite, 1985), the pyramid represents the range of sanctions available to a regulatory agency to encourage compliance, and to respond to noncompliance when this occurs.

The two-dimensional pyramid depicted in the figure below represents the range of instruments available to the state. In the ideal regulatory context, the regulatee does the right thing without any threat or inducement from government. Compliance flows naturally from self-regulatory systems that are already in place. To the extent that departures from compliance come to the attention of regulatory authorities, however, they are met with state response, which has the capacity to escalate or deescalate, depending on the subsequent comportment of the regulatee. The responsiveness of the state to compliance or noncompliance on the part of the regulatee is the essence of Ayres and Braithwaite's title.

The location of state action in vertical space on the Ayres/Braithwaite pyramid represents coerciveness—the severity of regulatory response. At the base of the pyramid, praise or some form of material inducement for good citizenship serves to encourage compliance.

According to Ayres and Braithwaite, state response should be commensurate with the offender's transgression. Simple persuasion and the provision of information are mobilized in the face of initial minor transgressions. Persistent noncompliance is met with escalating severity of response, through warning letters, civil penalties, criminal penalties, and ultimately, license suspension and revocation, the latter representing what might be described as corporate capital punishment. As severity of regulatory response escalates, successive instruments

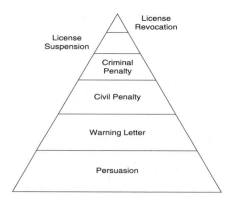

of increasing coerciveness are represented by increasing proximity to the apex of the pyramid. The triangular shape of the pyramid, that is, the relative width of its base and sharpness of its apex, implies that most regulatory interventions are relatively benign, and coercive instruments are mobilized only when lesser interventions prove insufficient to secure compliance.

The concept of a pyramid depicting a range of regulatory instruments is a compelling one, as it illustrates the basis for much greater regulatory flexibility than would accompany the existence of but a single deterrence option. One can readily envisage how a regulatory posture tailored to a particular context of noncompliance, and adaptable to improvements or deterioration in compliance performance, can be superior in terms of both justice and efficiency to a single standardized response. The latter situation contains a substantial risk of underregulation, on the one hand, or of regulatory overkill on the other.

Despite its elegance and usefulness as a heuristic, the Ayres-Braithwaite pyramid suffers from oversimplification. It reflects state regulatory action and state regulatory action alone, and thereby fails to represent the activity of both regulated entities and third parties. Indeed, one of the significant contributions of Ayres and Braithwaite's book is the support they give to the concept of regulatory tripartism and the constructive role they envisage for nongovernmental actors, particularly public interest groups, in the regulatory process. Ayres and Braithwaite themselves recognize that there is much more to the regulatory process than the activities of governments.

For example, *public interest groups* engage in education and persuasion of a recalcitrant corporate actor, often in a manner more convincing than do state agents. Should this not suffice to improve corporate compliance, interests groups can engage in public denunciation, often quite strident.

Consumer campaigns in favor of "dolphin-friendly" tuna or clothing made in nonexploitative settings can reward socially responsible business and punish the unconcerned. When the consumer is a national organization with massive buying power, the impact can be that much greater.

Banks may refuse to lend to a prospective borrower with a poor record of health, safety or environmental performance; *insurers* may refuse to insure them against loss.

Industry associations can withdraw accreditation or certification from a member who does not conform to required performance standards. In industries such as organic agriculture or meat export, certification may give a producer a competitive edge. Indeed, where certification is a *sine qua non* of access to a market, denial of such certification by an industry self-regulatory regime may inflict a form of corporate capital punishment.

Moreover, the pyramid fails to represent the interactive nature of regulatory life—the fact that many regulatory components are not unilateral phenomena, but rather hybrid instruments or institutions, combining elements of state, regulated entity, and third-party activity. These various instruments in turn, may impact upon each other, enhancing or lessening the influence of a given component or set of components (Grabosky, 1994). We noted above how the spectre of state intervention can inspire strong self-regulatory initiatives, and how the state may require a corporate actor to engage the services of a rigorous gatekeeper.

Even when these regulatory elements are institutionally independent, they may exert significant influences upon each other, which in turn may have important consequences for compliance on the part of regulated entities. For example, the shadow of liability law, shaped within a legal system sustained by the state, may move insurers to require the implementation of rigorous internal control systems as a condition of writing pollution liability insurance. Intriguingly, private institutions of the insurance industry may be in a position to exercise more coercive power over a company than could a state regulatory agency.

Ayres and Braithwaite, in their chapter on tripartism, demonstrate how an active public interest sector can energize state regulatory authorities and thereby reduce the likelihood of capture by the private sector. Third parties can also bring influence directly to bear upon companies, by mobilizing adverse publicity in the aftermath of a significant violation or by dealing in a constructive manner with the firm, beyond the regulatory gaze of government. For example, the Environmental Defense Fund assisted McDonald's Corporation to develop a plan for the purchase of products made from recycled materials for use in the latter's restaurants (Grabosky, 1994).

TOWARD A THREE-DIMENSIONAL PYRAMID

One can build upon the work of Ayres and Braithwaite by adding another dimension to their pyramid. The model presented here goes beyond the depiction of instruments available to state regulatory authorities, to incorporate the other institutions that make up a regulatory system—regulated entities themselves and their industry associations—and third parties, both public interest institutions and commercial actors.

To depict this wider conception of a regulatory system we shall use a graphic representation of a tetrahedron, depicted from three perspectives in Figure 2. This object has a triangular base and three triangular faces, with the apex at point (X). Figure 2a depicts the object from a perspective directly above the apex. The unshaded face in Figure 2a (A-B-X) represents the state regulatory apparatus; it is, in fact, the Ayres/Braithwaite pyramid. The face marked with horizontal lines (A-C-X) represents the target of regulation, whether individual firm or industry association. The third, partially shaded face (B-C-X) represents third parties, including not only public interest actors, but also commercial third parties such as institutions of finance and insurance.

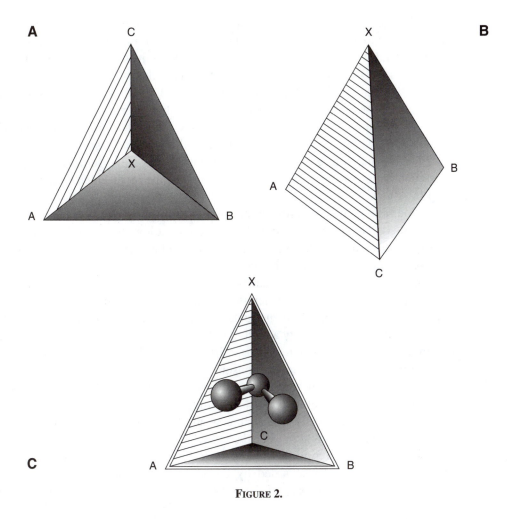

FIGURE 2.

Figure 2b depicts the object from an elevated viewpoint facing the C-X edge—that is, the edge that forms the intersection of regulated industry and third party. Figure 2c portrays the inside of the space as if one were looking directly through the side representing the state regulatory apparatus.

The vertical dimension, that is, the altitude of a point in the tetrahedron, represents coerciveness. The higher the location in the object, the more coercive the regulatory instrument. One should bear in mind that the dimensions of the tetrahedron represent theoretical limits; the fact that the state possesses the power of corporate capital punishment does not imply that it is occasionally, or ever, invoked. The actual configuration of a regulatory system "in action" can be depicted by a form, or more likely, a set of forms, located within the tetrahedron. This has been done in Figure 2c.

It is also important to note that the exercise of regulatory coercion is by no means a monopoly of the state. Each of the three main institutional actors—state, industry and third parties—have extremely coercive instruments at their disposal. In the case of the nongovernmental institutions, industry, and third parties, these in practice may exceed the coercive capacity of the state. Market forces may bring about the demise of a company in a way that regulators cannot.

For example, an industry association may suspend or expel a member. Thus disciplinary boards of medical societies and the National Association of Securities Dealers may put a member out of business. This is the self-regulatory manifestation of corporate capital punishment, and can be represented by a point at the top of A-C-X.

Massive damages in tort by an injured third party can be catastrophic to a corporate defendant. So too could foreclosure on a loan to a corporate entity by a bank or other financial institution. These too can be tantamount to corporate capital punishment, and may be represented by a point at the apex of B-C-X.

But there is more to a tetrahedron than its external surfaces. Unlike the Ayres-Braithwaite pyramid, which is two-dimensional, this is a three-dimensional space. To the extent that a given regulatory instrument combines elements of state, self-regulatory, or third-party activity, it can be depicted as a form within the tetrahedron. Theoretically, any regulatory instrument can be located within the space, depending upon its institutional sponsor (or sponsors) and its coerciveness.

For example, the power of a government agency to withdraw the license of a nuclear power generator, thereby shutting it down, is a regulatory instrument that is wielded unilaterally. As such, it would be located on the government surface of the tetrahedron, at or near the apex.

By contrast, a hybrid instrument such as a prize for the revegetation of former mine sites, jointly awarded by the government and the mining industry, would be located at the base of the tetrahedron, between government and industry faces.

The actions of a bank in requiring certification with ISO 14000 as a condition of finance would be represented by a plane located between third party and regulated industry, midway to the apex of the tetrahedron. A decision of the lending institution to cancel the loan could elevate the plane closer to the apex.

A graphic illustration is provided in Figure 2c, which depicts forms situated inside the tetrahedron. The center sphere, situated midway up the pyramid close to the intersection of target and third party faces, might represent private civil litigation.

The sphere situated to the left, near the face of the government regulatory apparatus at the intersection with the self-regulatory face, could represent a degree of self-regulation required by regulatory authorities as an alternative to prosecution.

Ayres and Braithwaite refer to governments empowering public interest groups and enlisting their participation in the regulatory process. Indeed, the first

part of this chapter described a variety of ways in which nongovernmental interests, whether citizens' groups or commercial interests, may be harnessed in furtherance of regulatory objectives (Grabosky, 1995a). As we have observed, these
may entail formal conscription, as when banks are required to report cash transactions over a certain threshold to regulatory authorities; to delegation or deference to private actors, as when societies for the protection of cruelty to animals
investigate and prosecute cases of alleged abuses of animals. The sphere to the
right of Figure 2c, located between the third party and government faces, slightly
lower on the vertical axis and close to the government face, could entail the government's provision of resources or conferring standing on public interest organizations for the purpose of engaging in civil litigation against a regulatory target.

All of these regulatory mechanisms, whether state, private, or hybrid, are
amenable to graphic presentation in three-dimensional space. Their vertical location within the tetrahedron will reflect the degree of coerciveness with which they
impact on the organizational life of the regulatee; their horizontal location will
reflect their institutional (or interinstitutional) form.

The heuristic value of our three-dimensional conceptualization of regulatory
space should be obvious. It permits a graphic representation of entire regulatory
systems, enabling one to visualize their coercive properties, as well as to visualize the mix of their constituent institutional forms. It also permits comparison of
systems in terms both of coerciveness and institutional composition.

Any location on or within the tetrahedron can be represented by precise
coordinates and is thus amenable to formal (i.e., quantitative) representation.
Although current scholarship on regulatory systems may not have attained the
sophistication in conceptualization and measurement that this would require, the
next generation of regulatory scholars may include those who might wish to
undertake more precise description or modeling of regulatory systems. This could
permit a degree of hypothesis testing and theory building that has thus far been
largely absent from the literature on regulation. Much as aeronautical engineers or
molecular biologists are able to visualize the systems with which they deal, so too
could future "regulatory systems engineers" explore alternative institutional forms.

CONCLUSION

Contemporary liberal commentary on conventional crime condemns retribu-
tivism, harsher sentences, and greater investments in police and prisons. Rather,
the governing discourse is that of crime prevention, based on the argument that
upstream social investments will obviate the need for the deployment of costly
(and arguably futile) criminal justice expenditures after the offense.

At the same time, criminologists' responses to white-collar crime tend to be
relatively vengeful and unforgiving. Their call is often for strict regulatory

regimes, accompanied by penalties for noncompliance, often draconian penalties in cases involving significant harm to the public.

This contradiction has begun to fade somewhat, in light of the growing realization that the capacity of the state to control both individual and corporate behavior indeed has its limits. The twenty-first century state will be neither omnipresent or omnipotent. For this reason, it is all the more essential that complementary institutions of corporate social control be fostered and nurtured. So it is that one sees the state seeking to coopt private institutions in furtherance of law enforcement and regulatory objectives. At the same time, one sees private institutions seeking a market niche in regulatory space. Just as a vast private security industry has grown up to complement our sworn police, so too has a corporate social control industry emerged to complement government regulatory agents. In the domain of white collar crime there would appear to be abundant opportunities for analogs of third-party policing (Buerger and Mazerolle, 1998) and community-based policing.

There will still be a role for the state in corporate crime control, but, as is the case with conventional crime, the future of corporate crime control promises to be considerably more interesting and diverse than one would have anticipated a generation ago.

ACKNOWLEDGMENT

Portions of this chapter have been adapted from an article entitled "Inside the Pyramid: Towards a Conceptual Framework for the Analysis of Regulatory Systems," *International Journal of the Sociology of Law*, 25, (3) (Sept. 1997): 195–201.

NOTES

1. The cause of action whereby citizens were empowered to sue on behalf of the state became known as Qui Tam (qui tam pro domino rege quam pro se ipso in hac parte sequitur), which may be translated as "who brings the action for the king as well as for oneself" (Caminker, 1989; Callahan and Dworkin, 1992).

2. http://www.falseclaimsact.com/history.html

3. The principle of relaxing regulatory requirements for companies with exemplary compliance records was recommended by the U.S. National Performance Review (Gore, 1993, 63).

REFERENCES

Ayres, Ian, and Braithwaite, John. 1992. *Responsive Regulation: Transcending the Deregulation Debate*. New York: Oxford University Press.

Bardach, Eugene, and Kagan, Robert. 1982. *Going By The Book: The Problem of Regulatory Unreasonableness*. Philadelphia: Temple University Press.

Black, Donald. 1976. *The Behavior of Law*. New York: Academic Press.

Boyer, Barry, and Errol Meidinger. 1985. "Privatizing Regulatory Enforcement." *Buffalo Law Review* 34: pp 833–964.

Braithwaite, John. 1982. "Enforced Self-Regulation: A New Strategy for Corporate Crime Control." *Michigan Law Review* 80:1466–1507.

Braithwaite, John. 1985. *To Publish or Persuade: Enforcement of Coal Mine Safety*. Albany, NY: State University of New York Press.

Buerger, Michael, and Mazerolle, Lorraine. 1998. "Third Party Policing: A Theoretical Analysis of an Emerging Trend." *Justice Quarterly* 15(2):301–328.

Callahan, Eletta, and Dworkin, Terry. 1992. "Do Good and Get Rich: Financial Incentives for Whistleblowing and the False Claims Act." *Villanova Law Review* 37:273–336.

Caminker, Evan. 1989. "The Constitutionality of Qui Tam Actions." *Yale Law Journal* 99:341–388.

Canaan, Penelope, and Reichman, Nancy. 1993. "Ozone Partnerships: The Construction of Regulatory Communities and the Future of Global Regulatory Power." *Law and Policy* 15(1):61–74.

Cheit, Ross. 1990. *Setting Safety Standards: Regulation in the Private and Public Sectors*. Berkeley: University of California Press.

Coffee, John. 1986. "Understanding the Plaintiff's Attorney: The Implications of Economic Theory for Private Enforcement of Law through Class and Derivative Actions." *Columbia Law Review* 86(4):669–727.

Cohen, Joshua, and Rogers, Joel. 1992. "Secondary Associations and Democratic Governance." *Politics and Society* 20(4):393–472.

Dandeker, C. 1990. *Surveillance, Power and Modernity*. New York: St. Martin's Press.

Deloitte Touche Tohmatsu. 1993. Coming Clean: Corporate Environmental Reporting-Opening up for Sustainable Development. London: Deloitte Touche Tohmatsu International.

Earle, Ralph, Jr. 1996. Personal Communication, Alliance for Environmental Innovation, Boston, November.

Ferreira, J. 1982. "Promoting Safety Through Insurance." Pp.267–288 in E. Bardach and R. Kagan, eds. *Social Regulation: Strategies for Reform*. San Francisco: Institute for Contemporary Studies.

Galanter, Marc. 1981. "Justice in Many Rooms." *Journal of Legal Pluralism* 19:1–47.

Galanter, Marc, and Luban, David. 1993. "Poetic Justice: Punitive Damages and Legal Pluralism." *American University Law Review* 42:1393–1463.

Gilb, Corinne. 1966. *Hidden Hierarchies: The Professions and Government*. New York: Harper and Row.

Gore, Albert. 1993. *From Red Tape to Results: Creating a Government that Works Better and Costs Less*. Washington, D.C.: U.S. Government Printing Office.

Grabosky, P.N. 1990. "Professional Advisors and White Collar Illegality: Towards Explaining and Excusing Professional Failure." *University of New South Wales Law Journal* 13(1):73–96.

Grabosky, P.N. 1994. "Green Markets: Environmental Regulation by the Private Sector." *Law and Policy* 16(4):420–48.

Grabosky, P.N. 1995a. "Using Non-governmental Resources to Foster Regulatory Compliance." *Governance* 8(4):527–50.

Grabosky, P.N. 1995b. "Regulation by Reward: On the Use of Incentives as Regulatory Instruments." *Law and Policy* 17(3):256–281.

Graboky, Peter, and Braithwaite, John. 1986. *Of Manners Gentle: Enforcement Strategies of Australian Business Regulatory Agencies*. Melbourne: Oxford Press.

Halliday, Terence, and Carruthers, Bruce. 1990. "The State, Professions and Legal Change: Reform of the English Insolvency Act, 1977–1986." Paper presented to the World Congress of Sociology, Madrid, August 13–17.

Harlow, Carol, and Rawlings, Richard. 1992. *Pressure Through Law*. London: Routledge.

Heimer, Carol. 1985. *Reactive Risk and Rational Action*. Berkeley: University of California Press.

Hyatt, James. 1993. "NASD Disciplines Individuals, Firms Charged with Securities Violations." *The Wall Street Journal*, 20 December, p A7A.

Katzman, Martin. 1988. "Societal Risk Management Through the Insurance Market." Pp. 21—42 in R. Hula, ed. *Market-Based Public Policy*. London: Macmillan.

Klepper, Steven, Mazur, Mark, and Nagin, Daniel. 1991. "Expert Intermediaries and Legal Compliance: The Case of Tax Preparers." *Journal of Law and Economics* 34(1):205–229.

Kraakman, Rainier. 1986. "Gatekeepers: The Anatomy of a Third-Party Enforcement Strategy." *Journal of Law, Economics and Organization* 2:53–104.

Osborne, David, and Gaebler, Ted. 1992. *Reinventing Government*. Boston: Addison-Wesley.

Porter, Michael. 1990. "The Competitive Advantage of Nations." New York: Free Press.

Rees, Joseph V. 1994. *Hostages of Each Other: The Transformation of Nuclear Safety Since Three Mile Island*. Chicago: University of Chicago Press.

Schmidheiny, Stephan. 1992. *Changing Course: A Global Business Perspective on Development and the Environment*. Cambridge, MA: MIT Press.

Schmitter, Philippe, and Lembruch, Gerhard, eds. 1979. *Trends Towards Corporatist Intermediation*. Beverly Hills, CA: Sage Publications.

Shapiro, Susan. 1987. "Policing Trust." Pp. 194–220 in C. Shearing and P. Stenning, eds. *Private Policing*. Beverly Hills: Sage Publications.

Shearing, Clifford. 1993. "A Constitutive Conception of Regulation." Pp. 67–80 in P. Grabosky and J. Braithwaite, eds. *Business Regulation and Australia's Future*. Canberra: Australian Institute of Criminology.

Streeck, Wolfgang, and Schmitter, Philippe. 1985. *Private Interest Government: Beyond Market and State*. Beverly Hills, CA: Sage Publications.

Tomasic, Roman. 1991. "Taxation Law Compliance and the Role of Professional Tax Advisers." *Australian and New Zealand Journal of Criminology* 24(3):241–257.

Tomasic, Roman, and Pentony, Brendan. 1991. "Taxation Law Compliance and the Role of Professional Tax Advisers." *Australian and New Zealand Journal of Criminology* 24(3):241–257.

Vogel, David. 1986. *National Styles of Regulation: Environmental Policy in Great Britain and the United States*. Ithaca, NY: Cornell University Press.

IV

CASE STUDIES OF WHITE-COLLAR CRIME

Fertile Frontiers in Medical Fraud: A Case Study of Egg And Embryo Theft

Mary Dodge

❖

In 1995, an array of irregularities—some minor, others undoubtedly criminal, erupted in regard to a fertility clinic at the University of California, Irvine (UCI). Ricardo Asch, Jose Balmaceda, and Sergio Stone, the three medical doctors who ran the clinic, faced allegations involving the "theft" of human eggs and embryos, the use of a non–FDA-approved drug, misconduct in scientific research, and questionable financial and insurance billing activities. The accusations, thrust into the limelight by several whistleblowers, led to a criminal conviction, a torrent of lawsuits, and the firing of key university administrators. State and federal agencies, including the Federal Bureau of Investigation (FBI), the Internal Revenue Service (IRS), the Food and Drug Administration (FDA), and the California Medical Board (CMB), joined forces to investigate the matter.

The charge that the fertility physicians at the Center for Reproductive Health (CRH) had engaged in the theft of eggs and embryos lay at the heart of the allegations and represented the most dramatic aspect of the scandal. Experts and commentators expressed their dismay, claiming that the charges were "the most devastating and disturbing actions in the history of assisted reproduction."[1] UCI Chancellor Laurel Wilkening stated, "I have never encountered such depraved behavior on the part of faculty members in my entire life."[2] The physicians appointed to the clinical investigation panel found the theft accusation to "be the most serious and troubling of all the allegations because of the profound ethical and moral questions involved in transfer of donor [o]ocytes and embryos."

The UCI fertility clinic case is notably complex. It concerns novel and often-controversial reproductive procedures. The procedures involve infertile couples who have a deep emotional commitment to the success of the intervention. They are carried out by medical practitioners who stand to make dazzling amounts of money if they can successfully implant an embryo in an impressive percentage of those who come to them for help. Success in reproductive medicine comes from a competitive struggle in a field rampant with thwarted promises and the crumbled hopes of those who seek to fulfill a major element of the American Dream—begetting a genetic offspring.

ORGANIZATIONAL EXPLANATIONS AND COVER-UPS

Initially, few realized the full extent of the egg and embryo misappropriation, partly because the university officials persistently engaged in calculated schemes to protect their reputations and avoid institutional liability. The original lawsuit filed by the university against the fertility doctors, on May 16, 1995 at the Orange County Superior Court, did not include an allegation of egg and embryo misuse. That charge had been omitted because university administrators claimed it was unsubstantiated. On May 25, in an amendment to the initial lawsuit, the university now believed that the three doctors had "transplanted patients' eggs into other patients without obtaining the donors' consent." The additional charges were added only after the local newspaper headlined the story that several clinic patients maintained that their eggs were used without consent. Wilkening, in an interview with the *Los Angeles Times*, claimed that the allegations of human egg misuse were so outrageous that she disbelieved their occurrence until the university investigation confirmed two cases early in May 1995.[3]

The assertions from university administrators that the egg theft charges were unsubstantiated in May appear to be untrue. An internal report, finished in March 1995, supported the allegation and there had been similar findings by the internal auditors as early as 1992. UCI officials, attempting to justify their position, maintained that the investigators were unable to reach a definitive conclusion to the allegations. This statement also appears to be erroneous, because University of California legal counsel had notified UC San Diego in March that the investigators "concluded that inappropriate egg transfer occurred at the UCI clinics."[4] The reluctance by UCI officials to provide a comprehensive and accurate report may have been an effort to protect patients or to rationalize their slow response. It also may have been a cover-up to conceal their aims to reach a settlement with the doctors before the charges became public. Or it may have seemed necessary to try to rebut charges that egg thefts occurred after UCI first discovered the problem and was in a position to prevent further victimization, but had failed to do so.

In June 1995, university administrators still were uncertain about the number of eggs and embryos that were used by the doctors without consent, but believed it might be six. That initial estimate proved to be way off target. On July 5, a university press release stated: "Recently received new, credible evidence raises additional concerns about the medical treatment of approximately thirty CRH patients who may have been involved in unconsented transfers of eggs or embryos."[5] In response to the rising number of cases, Arthur Caplan, director of biomedical ethics at the University of Pennsylvania, exclaimed, "It shifts this thing from what was a fairly smoky inferno to a complete, all-out twelve alarm disaster."[6]

The roster of patients alleging victimization by Asch continued to grow during the following months. By early November 1995, university officials were granting that as many as sixty patients may have been involved. This new information was first disclosed in the newspaper when a reporter obtained a handwritten list prepared by Teri Ord, the clinic's embryologist. The list detailed the "donors," the number of eggs harvested, the number of eggs donated, and the recipients, though it contained no information regarding births or whose sperm was used to fertilize the eggs. The list, according to Ord, documented all egg transfers from November 1986 through January 1994 and tracked egg transfers from 110 women to 93 recipients; 27 of the women who had been contacted by reporters claimed they had not consented to the donation of their eggs and embryos.[7]

University officials at first asserted that they were unaware that such a list existed. A few days later, Byron Beam, an attorney at the UC Office of the General Counsel in Oakland, acknowledged that he had received the list in October and had overlooked it because it was included in a "two-inch-thick" stack of documents. In response to accusations that UCI had engaged in further subterfuge, Beam wrote:

> To my horror and chagrin (since I told the Chancellor's office we did not have a purported list of egg donors and recipients), without any identifying marking, and inserted in what appeared to be unrelated series [treatment] sheets, I found several handwritten pages of what now appears to be lists of patients who had eggs donated to them outside the paid donor program.

Beam, in his letter, acknowledged his failure to promptly review the documents and apologized for putting the chancellor and the university in an embarrassing position.

University officials attempted to downplay the significance of the list, but admitted that there was a need to contact the possible victims. Wilkening stated, "Although the information in the seven-page list and in the raw data is not enough by itself to say for certain if a transfer was consented or not, we are taking the approach that all these patients deserve to be informed."[8] This was a dramatic shift in the university's position.

On November 17, 1995, Wilkening admitted that the scandal might involve more than 200 women. By late November the number of patients involved in possible illicit transfers was placed at more than 300 by university officials; a startling increase from three to more than 300 suspect cases in seven months, though university administrators were unsure if all 304 women they sought to contact were actual victims of unapproved egg transfers. A confidential document that surfaced in mid-1997 lists 435 patients who were believed to have been involved in the unconsented transfers and research.

PATIENT EXASPERATION AND VICTIMIZATION

Their awareness of missing eggs created an unprecedented level of anger and despair in many patients. Under normal circumstances the gratitude patients feel toward the fertility specialist is profound if the treatment results in a birth. If the treatment fails, however, the couple may become enraged with the physician.[9] Many CRH patients felt a different kind of emotion. Some maintained that they had been "raped on a genetic level." Elizabeth Shaw Smith expressed her outrage over Asch's alleged actions: "I feel they used me. They manipulated my body and stole my eggs and my money."[10] Kimberly DuBont, who was treated by Asch in 1990, believes that most of her eggs were used for research, although the whereabouts of six of the eggs are unknown. DuBont explained that the possibility that a child was born from her missing eggs "would be the worst of all." She stated: "It would kill me. I would feel totally empty inside. I can't imagine anything worse. All of this is as awful as it can be now. I hate to say it, but I'm learning to expect the worst."[11] Nancy Vanags expressed similar feelings after learning that eighteen of her eggs may have been implanted in at least three other women. She labeled the likelihood as deeply traumatic: "It's hell. I know no other way to describe it."[12]

Additional details involving the alleged unconsented use of eggs and embryos crystallized as approximately 100 patients filed lawsuits against the doctors and the university. The patients accused the doctors of negligence, fraud, conspiracy, battery, infliction of emotional distress, and racketeering. The doctors were said to have "intentionally or negligently sold, donated, converted, misappropriated or destroyed eggs." Lawsuits also have been filed that accuse the physicians of deliberately overstimulating women in a calculated scheme to steal their eggs.

Barbara Moore and her husband, who, at the time, were both practicing attorneys in Orange County, believe that her eggs were taken by Asch and Balmaceda and then implanted in another woman, who gave birth to a boy. Moore, who underwent treatment in 1991, says she was told by the doctors that clinic policy restricted the number of embryos transferred during a procedure to a maximum of four. She and her husband specifically decided to freeze any remaining embryos. Moore described her interaction with Asch in a written statement:

> After the GIFT procedure was performed on me, Dr. Asch of CRH told us he had harvested seven eggs, four of which were put into my fallopian tube. We were informed that the three remaining eggs were fertilized with my husband's sperm and frozen in an embryonic state for our future use.[13]

Moore suggests that Asch deliberately deceived her regarding clinic policy because patient reports and research publications show that he often transferred more than four eggs or embryos. The more serious deception involves Moore's claim that Asch lied about the number of eggs harvested: "We have been informed that fourteen eggs were harvested, not seven," she stated. "We were further informed that three of the fourteen eggs were intentionally implanted in a different woman."[14]

The alleged recipient of Moore's eggs maintains that their son was conceived with an egg donated by a family friend. Asch, however, acknowledges that Moore's eggs were used without consent. He explained that the recipient was a close personal friend of a clinic worker, who had been forced to resign in 1992 after allegations arose that she had engaged in theft and insurance fraud. In addition to implicating the clinic worker, Asch inferred that Balmaceda was responsible for the transfer.[15]

Loretta and Basilio Jorge declared that her eggs, and possibly their embryos, were taken without consent in January 1989 and implanted in another woman. They took legal action, demanding testing to determine if they are the genetic parents of twins, now seven years old, born to the other couple. The Jorges say that as the "biological parents" they are desperate to know "their children." To confirm their suspicions, the Jorges arranged to have the children they allege are theirs secretly videotaped and photographed. After seeing the child and the picture, Loretta Jorge stated: "That's the way I walked when I was a little girl. I know definitely the egg is mine. If this is [the result of implanted] embryos, definitely 100 percent I'm going to take those children. If it's (only my) eggs, I have to be more considerate."[16] The birth parents, who believe the child is a product of their own eggs, are outraged that someone dare lay claim to their children and horrified at the prospect of a custody battle. Such a case, according to John Robertson, a leading legal expert in reproductive technology, presents a new challenge because no legal precedent exists, and the situation involves "deep, intensely held values about personal identity, family and morality."[17]

The most highly publicized case involves Debbie and John Challender. The couple explained how they learned of the alleged embryo misuse:

> Last May, two reporters arrived on our doorstep with my medical records. They asked us to look at them, and I began to realize the most terrible thing—that [some of] our embryos had been given to other couples, without our permission. We were devastated.[18]

Debbie Challender held a press conference, and granted interviews to a variety of magazine publications and television talk shows. She explained her actions: "I've come forward so that this crime won't be swept under the rug. What happened to us was nothing less than theft by doctors who acted for their own profit and prestige."[19] But the Challenders also profited after selling their story for a television movie, charging for interviews, and settling their lawsuit with the university.

Challender, who had struggled with infertility for ten years, started treatment with Asch in 1991. She had forty-six eggs harvested. A successful procedure resulted in the birth of their son; the couple had requested that the extra embryos be frozen. They believe, and their medical records indicate, that at least three eggs were implanted without their consent in another woman who gave birth to twins—a boy and a girl. The birth mother also received eggs from at least four other unsuspecting donors.

The Challenders have strong feelings about the embryos. Mr. Challender says, "The embryos they stole, those were my children."[20] According to his wife: "Some tell us that it is impossible to have an emotional bond with embryos, but they don't understand."[21] The couple have expressed a desire to meet the twins and have expressed concern that the children are being raised in a nonChristian household by Jewish parents. They claim that they will not seek custody, although they have requested a DNA test to determine if they have a biological connection to the twins. Ironically, four years later, the Challenders have been accused of abandoning their frozen embryos after they failed to respond to requests for storage payment and a decision on their disposition.[22]

Patients also discovered their ova had disappeared. The exact number and whereabouts of the eggs and embryos in these cases is uncertain. For example, a Lebanese couple claim that "several" of their eight eggs, which were harvested in early 1995, are not accounted for. Christie Simons had eighteen fertilized embryos cryopreserved after a 1991 procedure, and four have "disappeared." Crispina and Mark Calvert, the couple involved in one of the first surrogate custody cases in the United States, were again in the headlines after learning that their two frozen embryos could not be located. In 1990, an embryo created from Mark's sperm and Crispina's egg was implanted in a surrogate—Asch performed the procedure. The surrogate later reneged on the contract. The Calverts made legal history a year later when the California Court of Appeal ruled that the gestational surrogate had no parental rights to the child.[23]

Among the most damaging accusations of egg theft were those by women who claimed that while undergoing routine diagnostic procedures their eggs were stolen and harvested without their knowledge. Merrill Mahon underwent fertility treatment in 1987, 1989, and 1993, and she believes that during a routine laparoscopy procedure five eggs were removed without her knowledge. Kathleen Linden asserted that eggs were removed without her knowledge in June, 1988; however, she admitted that Asch later told her he had removed the eggs to check the quality. She also says that Asch informed her that the eggs could not be used for pregnancy.[24] Pamela Kaoud knew that her eggs were being harvested, but believed they would be used only for diagnostic purposes to determine the causes of her infertility. Kaoud later discovered, she claims, that the eggs had been sold, fertilized, and implanted in another woman.[25]

Some of the lawsuits were unique. Ashley MacCarthy says that in 1989 Asch persuaded her to donate her fifteen eggs to women as an act of charity. She was unable to use them, after having invested nearly $20,000 in treatment, because of problems with her husband's sperm and their rising financial debt.[26] She now believes that her eggs were sold to other patients. MacCarthy described her experience with Asch: "Every time I came in he would pressure me. Asch would ask: 'What are you going to do with these eggs? There are many women who could use these eggs.' It was that persistent and sophisticated manipulation,"[27] she noted. A couple from Florida filed a lawsuit, although there was no evidence that their eggs or embryos were missing; when they heard the news reports they apparently decided it was the thing to do.[28]

PHYSICIAN EXPLANATIONS AND EXCUSES

Asch and Balmaceda denied that they had used eggs or embryos without consent. During the initial investigation, university administrators found this position untenable because the physicians were "unable or unwilling" to provide documentation to support their claims. One high-ranking university physician stated that Asch said he had "no idea what was going on" and seemed to act as if the situation was "too trivial to be bothered with."[29] Balmaceda denied any involvement: "I have never given eggs or embryos without previous consent from the donor to any patient ever. I insist none of the cases in which mismanagement of eggs is alleged is from the clinic I directed."[30]

In time, it became impossible to stay with the position that nothing had gone awry at the clinic. Asch and his criminal defense lawyer, Ronald Brower, admitted that there appear to be cases where there are problems. Brower explained that if the university found such cases, "we'd be pleased to help them get at the truth and deal with the problem."[31] Asch maintains that he has never knowingly used anyone's eggs or embryos without permission.[32]

When strong evidence emerged that substantiated the unconsented transfers, the doctors called them "mistakes." Balmaceda asserted that any problems were accidental: "We will not pretend we never made mistakes, but they [the patients] have access to all information we can give them, and I hope they don't lose their trust in us."[33] Asch finally admitted "mistakes," but placed the blame on UCI Medical Center and clinic staff members.

Asch in particular attributed the difficulties to inadequacies in the number and quality of the personnel provided by medical center. He said he had complained repeatedly to hospital administrators about the employees. Asch attempted to remove himself from the situation by arguing that he was not responsible for running the clinic, asserting that whatever happened there with the eggs and embryos was "because of people that were supposed to check on consent forms and did not."[34] Balmaceda, without directly implicating the staff, commented, "There is no way in hell the doctor who does the transfer knows what he's putting back unless somebody tells him."[35] Asch commented that a few eggs had been misappropriated, but placed primary responsibility for the mishaps on his assistant, Teri Ord.

Ord claimed, however, that Asch told her which eggs and embryos to use. "He would come to me and specifically tell me take Patient A's eggs and you give them to Patient B," she said.[36] CRH employees never questioned the doctors. One hospital employee said that staff members were "afraid to come forward" because they might lose their jobs. Ord, when asked why she failed to confront Asch, explained:

> You didn't ask Dr. Asch things like that. You didn't question what he did. I never questioned him. I couldn't go and accuse a good and famous doctor of something I had no proof of. He was very clearly telling me specifically what to do. It wasn't my place to question him. I didn't have any firsthand knowledge. I didn't know for sure.[37]

Ord's finger pointing has an odd side. In an early interview, when asked if she knew eggs were being used without proper consent, she stated, "It never crossed my mind."[38] Later, in her deposition, Ord noted that she suspected the misappropriation as early as 1991.[39] Perhaps the change in Ord's testimony represents an attempt to cooperate with authorities that was fueled by anger over Asch's accusations that she may have been responsible for the problems.

Asch condemned everyone, including UCI Medical Center employees, university administrators, patients, and attorneys. He blamed the press for promoting UCI's self-serving lies. In one interview with reporters he exclaimed, "I blame all of you."[40] Asch stated that there were "evil forces within employees of UCI that did forge consent forms, that did falsify information, both at the level of consent forms, medical charts, perhaps even laboratory charts, and I think that's the way it happened."[41] Asch blamed the university for being unwilling to accept responsibility for its part in the wrongdoing. He insisted that he was a target for corrupt, sloppy, and vengeful university administrators: "I feel [university officials] know the mistakes that were done, and I'm sure they know intimately their responsibility in this. . .[T]hey want to find a scapegoat in me."[42]

Asch's explanations of what had transpired also placed partial blame on the patients. In one interview, Asch said of the patients: "They never care about the embryos they have left for eight years and then it's 'my little babies.'"[43] Asch accused "unscrupulous lawyers" of manipulating patients. "They want to deteriorate my reputation, they want to hurt me, they want to humiliate me, and they have been successful in doing that."[44] Asch surmised that many of the patients who had filed lawsuits were confused, greedy, or manipulated by an attorney. In response to the patients' lawsuits, Asch stated:

> I think there are three categories of patients. One category of patients [has a] genuine complaint. People in which eggs were misappropriated without their wishes, and for those I can only tell you one thing: I will fight back against everyone, trying to defend myself and clear my name because I know I haven't done anything intentional in those cases. But I'm also going to fight back for them, try to help them to give justice to their lives as well. The second group of patients are only being fueled by opportunistic attorneys, cases in which there is no merit whatsoever. There is a third group of patients in which there is nothing at all in their cases, and they are inventing stories. They are very opportunistic, trying to jump on the bandwagon, trying to get financial benefit from all of this.[45]

MISTAKES AND MISCONCEPTIONS

These cases might have been unintentional mixups in the use of eggs and embryos. Physicians commonly acknowledge the possibility of medical mistakes. Robyn Rowland warns that "no woman can know for sure that the egg or embryo placed back inside her body was that which came from her body."[46] In a particularly dramatic event, a woman in Holland, after an in vitro fertilization (IVF) procedure, gave birth to twins—one white baby and one black baby. The couple and the hospital believe that an unclean pipette used in the procedure contained the sperm that fertilized one of her eggs.

Laboratory accidents sometimes result in the loss of eggs and embryos. John Robertson, author of *Children of Choice*, points out that embryos may be inadvertently destroyed, can become stuck in a petri dish, or may dry up.[47] Malpractice charges are avoided because couples are not informed of these mishaps, or are told that the "oocyte did not fertilize," "the zygotes did not cleave," or "your embryos were not viable."[48]

A 1995 lawsuit against a Rhode Island fertility clinic shows the potential for laboratory mishaps. Two couples claimed that their embryos were lost or misplaced. A hospital physician explained that any missing embryo would have died during routine procedures and that the death of embryos is not unusual. There may have been a legitimate accident, and the use of the term *lost* may have been a poor choice of words on the part of the attending physician.[49] The lawyer representing the couples explained, "In light of what happened in California, one of those possibilities is that the embryos went to someone else."[50]

The CRH doctors obviously were concerned about potential accidents. On social occasions, Asch talked about his patients and the embryos in storage:

> I worry about everything. I worry every day that I go to my house about frozen embryos that are in my laboratory; that there is going to be a fire and they are going to be gone one day. One day someone would come and steal them.[51]

Asch and Balmaceda, most observers maintain, were emotionally, physically, and financially vested in their patients, the use of their ovum, and the storage of their embryos. They had an estimated 5,000 embryos in their care.

Mistakes obviously happened at the UCI fertility clinics. One alleged case at CRH was explained to me as a lack of communication. A patient had agreed to donate her eggs, but Asch advised against the move until it was known whether her own procedure was successful. Asch then went to Morocco. Balmaceda was covering the surgery, which coincided with a donor cycle. He used the eggs without knowing that Asch and the patient had determined she should not donate them. In another case, a doctor had mistakenly inseminated a woman with the wrong man's sperm. The procedure did not result in a pregnancy, but the patients filed a lawsuit.

The fertility clinic had established elaborate procedures to avoid mistakes, however. Ord believed that clinic procedures made it "impossible" for mistakes to happen: "We had so many safeguards set up to make sure that we did not transfer the wrong eggs to the wrong person or the wrong embryos to the wrong person. That would have been completely impossible."[52] Asch was asked several years earlier in an interview if he worried that a mixup may occur in which a frozen embryo from one couple could mistakenly be implanted in another. "We have worried until we set up specific standards by which that is impossible. It is extremely unlikely," he explained.[53]

Consent was one area of the clinic's management that was ignored by Asch.[54] The nursing staff initiated, developed, and instituted the use of consent forms. Investigators for the university reported: "Physician notes rarely documented a discussion of choices, and no particular attention was paid to documenting a review of options or complications or risks and benefits. It was unclear whose responsibility it was to either document or determine that patients understood and consented to treatment." Asch told investigators that he never reviewed consent and was not involved in seeking them. "I didn't think that was my particular duty to be checking every single consent form. If you look at a consent form from that time, [it] doesn't even have a place for a signature from a doctor," he stated.[55]

Nonetheless, Asch had primary responsibility for discussing the donation of eggs with his patients, and patient statements indicate that he did raise the subject with some. One patient wrote:

> During all my encounters with Dr. Asch, I was treated with extreme compassion and a high regard for my wishes and moral concerns. Each time I began a course of action, I was informed of the odds of success, never given false hope or promise, and always asked to sign documentation giving authorization and indicating my wishes for unused eggs and/or embryos.[56]

Another patient recalled that Asch asked her if she would be willing to donate her eggs:

After my first unsuccessful GIFT, Asch asked me, "Would you be willing to donate? You have so many eggs." My first reaction was no and I said I would think about it. I only had one night to think about it because my surgery was the next day and I decided yes to do it. It was very hard to do and there was no incentive, it was just that I had lots. But, he asked me, he didn't just go in and take them. No manipulations.[57]

Clearly, Asch was involved in some instances in advising and acquiring consent for the use of extra eggs and embryos. In one case, Ord claimed that clinic nurses had warned her that a patient had not consented to donation before an embryo transfer, but she says that Asch told her the patient had given verbal consent.[58]

In the majority of suspect cases it is unlikely that infertile couples consented to the donations or sale of their ovum. Jane Frederick claimed that in her four years as a physician at CRH, during which she performed more than 400 procedures, she never had an infertile couple who wanted to donate eggs.[59] Balmaceda stated that although it was uncommon for infertile couples to donate since cryo-preservation had become feasible, it did occur occasionally.[60] Asch and Balmaceda noted in a 1993 journal publication that cryopreservation methods had "markedly reduced the availability of donated oocyte from women who are themselves in infertility treatment."[61] Other researchers have found that couples who do not use their frozen embryos are four times more likely to destroy extra embryos than to donate.[62]

MOTIVE AND OPPORTUNITY

What motive would Asch have to engage in activities that would jeopardize his career, lifestyle, and reputation? Clearly, financial gain may have played a primary role. Certainly, the unique and experimental aspects of reproductive medicine and the climate at the University of California campus created a unique opportunity for fraud. Like other white-collar crimes, violations in the medical field are difficult to prove; demonstrating criminal intent almost invariably is problematic.[63] The extent of fraud in reproductive medicine is unknown and probably unknowable. Kenneth Ryan, Professor Emeritus of Ob/Gyn at Harvard University, says that the problems in assisted reproductive medicine that were highlighted in the UCI scandal are not isolated incidents.[64] John Robertson, however, believes that incidents of abuse are small, but recognizes the need for regulation to protect consumers from fraud, misrepresentations, and incompetent practitioners.[65]

Fertility specialists, who practice with little oversight and accountability, are trusted to obey the law, but their autonomy creates numerous opportunities for errant activities. Accusations and rumors of "egg snatching" have been broached since the development of IVF, and issues of consent have sometimes been raised.[66] Gena Corea tells of several Massachusetts doctors who conducted an "egg hunt" over the course of a fifteen-year research project. They allegedly took hundreds of eggs from poor women receiving charity medical care and employed questionable consent procedures.[67] Landrum Shettles, a pioneer in IVF, caused an uproar in the 1950s when he commented that "nice little old ladies" frequently ask where he obtained human eggs for his experiments and he replied: "Most of them I just poached."[68] This comment, albeit spoken in jest, reflects the sometime cavalier attitudes researchers develop toward women's bodies.[69]

The most obvious (and oversimplified) explanation for the alleged egg theft is greed. The treatment of infertility is a private enterprise driven by profit. Successful fertility doctors establish financially lucrative practices. Physicians are often faced with a conflict when entrepreneurial goals overshadow the persona of a healer. Marc Rodwin, author of *Medicine, Money and Morals*, describes this conflict of interest:

> Doctors are made of the same stuff as other people, they have the usual passions, follies, virtues, and vices. Ideals may attract them—yet they must also make a living. Medicine almost inevitably involves a tension between the physicians' commitment to healing others and their economic self-interest.[70]

Charles Bosk, after observing surgeons at a large hospital, presents a more cynical viewpoint. He notes that "the doctor-patient relationship is an economic transaction in which the physician's primary motivation is to maintain a privileged and protected position for himself in the marketplace."[71]

The growth in the number of specialty clinics in reproductive medicine has created a fiercely competitive market; predictions are that a surplus of potential service providers in the United States is imminent.[72] Despite a rise in infertility, the patient population is limited because many couples lack the financial resources for treatment. This has led to cutthroat business practices. For example, one California physician explained to me that his initial attempts to recruit an associate of Asch's from Texas to help establish an IVF lab were unsuccessful. The doctor believes Asch interfered because he wanted to avoid competition in the western region.[73]

The competitive nature of the business also has led to unsavory situations. A reproductive specialist accused his major competitor of stealing his employees and patients. There have been cases in which patient lists were stolen from clinic garbage cans and payoffs were made to insiders for information. The clinic's pilfered trash included patient names, phone numbers, test results, treatment plans, and personal messages for both the clinic physicians and employees. The paranoia resulting from this case led one doctor to install surveillance cameras at his office and home.[74]

Fraudulent activity in assisted reproductive medicine can improve profits. For example, the exact number and quality of a patient's eggs or embryos are known only by the doctor and the embryologist. Consequently, any number of eggs can be removed and used without a patient's knowledge. Eggs and embryos can be sold to recipients at high prices. Using a hypothetical case as an example, a UCI physician explained that it would be legal for a doctor to pay an egg donor $1,000 and split the eggs among ten patients at $10,000 per recipient. One fertility specialist tells of a physician who implanted lesser quality or "dead" embryos in women, so that the implant would fail, and the patients would return for further expensive procedures.[75]

But it seems unlikely that money was the overriding impetus for what happened at CRH. The doctors were successful, their services were sought after. CRH reported earnings of $4.5 million from January 1992 to August 1994. The total cost of one procedure ranged from $10,000 to $15,000 and it was estimated that 500 to 700 patients a year were seen at the UCI clinic. The Saddleback clinic handled approximately 500 patients a year. On a typical day at the UCI clinic dozens of women filled the waiting room; some patients would wait eight hours to see Asch.

Success rates are a crucial element in a clinic's reputation and ability to attract patients. Success rates run the gamut. Some clinics report rates as high as 50 percent and others report no live births.[76] These rates are easily manipulated. Numerous variables must be taken into account when clinics report their successes. Clinics may fail to distinguish among chemical pregnancies, spontaneous abortions, ectopic pregnancies, and viable pregnancies that result in live births. Rates also vary according to procedure and the number of embryos implanted. The chance of a pregnancy increases with each additional embryo implanted; the odds increase from 20 percent using one embryo to 38 percent with three embryos.[77]

The Federal Trade Commission (FTC) has taken legal action against several fertility providers who were said to have misrepresented pregnancy rates. Professional groups for their part have made efforts to standardize success rate criteria.[78] The American Society for Reproductive Medicine and the Society for Assisted Reproductive Technology have a registry of clinics that voluntarily submit their success figures, and since 1990 they have tracked site-specific data. One clinic, after the UCI debacle, hired an outside audit firm to confirm the accuracy of its figures.

The Center for Reproductive Health had high success rates. Some believed the alleged misuse of eggs was related to attempts to increase these rates. Asch's success was about 3 percent higher than average—approximately 25 percent of Asch's patients became parents.[79] In a 1996 publication, Asch boasted a 47.4 percent pregnancy rate for GIFT procedures based on 97 patients seen at his clinic between January 1989 and March 1991.[80] Innuendos that any fertility clinic with high success rates must be doing something illicit are common.

Asch's personality may have contributed to his actions. Profiles of white-collar offenders show no distinctive set of personality traits, but criminologist

James Coleman notes that egocentrism, recklessness, and ambition are attributes commonly ascribed to perpetrators.[81] Ambition is a common trait among academics and is usually essential for success in the university environment. Asch's ambition appeared almost boundless. A clinic employee observed that he often talked of winning a Nobel Prize.[82] He seemingly cut corners in the competitive race for fame, and he certainly was known to have employed experimental and unorthodox practices to treat infertility.

Fertility doctors are seen as gods by many of their patients. This type of reverence may have fostered a "divine-like" self-image in Asch. Opponents of assisted reproduction often raise the argument that the practice encroaches in an area best left to God.[83] Asch himself warned that a physician must resist the temptation to "play too close to God."[84] One patient, who after twelve years of attempting to become pregnant, went through a successful GIFT procedure with Asch, declared, "I believe he works for God."[85] Another patient reportedly called for Asch and asked, "Is God there?" Alan DeCherney, a fertility specialist at the Department of Ob/Gyn at UCLA, stated, "What's distressing all of us is that these doctors apparently thought they were above the rules and able to play God."[86] Robyn Rowland warns of the danger of such veneration:

> Leaders of research in the reproductive area are deified as if they are "acting as God." The danger of this deification is that both the medical profession and the community may feel that medical teams are not accountable to the society in which they work.[87]

In many ways this explanation appears to fit the portrait of Asch that emerged after the scandal. Physicians and colleagues who knew him believe that his ego played a primary role in his legal problems.[88] In *Prescription For Profit*, a study of fraudulent billing practices, the authors connect attitudes of doctors with their acts: "Arrogance may have to do with committing fraud, an arrogance that high-handily dismisses the violation of program rules as insignificant behavior."[89]

The difficulty in explaining Asch's action is the disparity between a man who is seemingly kind, sensitive, and generous and the same person who is said to commit unconscionable acts. It is unlikely that Asch decided one day to steal some eggs. He probably drifted into deviance—a process that is hardly perceived by the actor.[90] When faced with the choice of destroying or donating extra eggs, Asch may have decided to give the eggs to women who needed them. A UCI physician speculated that if one woman had forty-eight eggs and Asch used eight in a procedure, rather than throw away the remaining forty he gave or sold them to other patients.[91] Medical records showed that the number of eggs harvested from CRH patients was high, and often ranged from twenty-five to fifty eggs.

In 1986 and 1987, CRH had no paid donor program and no facilities to freeze embryos. The majority of egg thefts were said to have occurred at the

AMI/Garden Grove clinic.[92] Ord, the embryologist, stated:

> When we started doing this in California, there was not a good freezing program. Nobody knew how to freeze embryos very well yet. It was very early on in IVF, and therefore, the chances of having a pregnancy with frozen embryos were small. . . .I assumed a lot of patients donated that way. We had a lot of egg donations.[93]

The use of others' eggs may have been spurred by an altruistic desire to help patients create babies. Fertility specialists are known to have circumvented ethical guidelines to provide what they deemed to be good quality treatment. One fertility doctor admitted that during his medical residency at Georgetown University in Washington, D.C. he used his own sperm for donations that resulted in thirty-three pregnancies, despite professional mandates limiting sperm donations to ten recipients.[94] Cecil Jacobson, a well known Virginia physician and fertility treatment pioneer, achieved national notoriety after reports that he had artificially inseminated women with his own sperm without their knowledge. Jacobson, convicted of fraud, received a five-year prison sentence. He may have fathered as many as seventy children over a span of twelve years. Jacobson claimed to have acted for the benefit of the patients: "I knew my semen was safe because I haven't slept with anyone but my wife in our thirty-five years of marriage," he said.[95]

If Asch was attempting to help patients, he could justify the alleged egg misuse as a form of generosity that would do more good than harm. Jonathan Von Berkom, a former consultant to the National Institutes of Health, commented on this temptation:

> This has always come up when you have one woman who has a disproportionate number of eggs and another woman who is very nice and very deserving and doesn't have enough eggs. "Wouldn't it be nice to give her a few?"[96]

A UCI physician supported Asch: "Was he doing good? Did he say what the hell? What's an egg or two among friends?"[97] A patient, grappling with the possibility that Asch had engaged in fraud, noted: "You could tell he was truly caring. The only thing I can think is maybe he was caring too much. He would want everyone to have a baby and wanted to make that dream come true for more people."[98] Asch, himself, questioned his possible motive and stated that if he "had" misused eggs and embryos it would have been done to make people happy.[99]

CONCLUSION

Asch traveled the road to fame and fortune with all the trappings of the American Dream. Much of the fertility clinic's work involved visionary and entrepreneurial pursuits that championed the family, education, prominence, and prosperity. Steven Messner and Richard Rosenfeld have pointed out that endeavors to succeed in a culture that glorifies competition, ambition, and money may produce a backlash, a darker side:

> There is a paradoxical quality to the American Dream. The very features that are responsible for the impressive accomplishments of American society have less desirable consequences as well. The American Dream is a double-edged sword, contributing to both the best and the worst elements of the American character and society.[100]

In this case, the dream involved doctors who came to UCI as superstars. They quickly established a successful practice, continued to bolster their academic reputations, and lived a lavish lifestyle. The doctors were under heavy pressure from patients who expected a miracle. The university expected them to do research and publish path-breaking scientific articles. It also wanted them to earn money, a great deal of it. In this context, the doctors' drive and ambition, following Messner and Rosenfeld's depiction of the American Dream, may have resulted in wrongdoing. Asch also probably believed, based on his past experience, that he could do what he did without repercussions.

Motive was linked with opportunity. Asch was allowed to act without restriction by his patients, his colleagues, and the university, all with self-serving agendas. He was encouraged to push conventional boundaries. His patients were desperate for a child. His colleagues sanctioned his behavior because they desired to establish credibility in a controversial field of medicine. The university fostered and hid his deviance in the name of income, recognition, and reputation.

NOTES

1. Michael Granberry and Rebecca Trounson, "Charges' Impact Worries Many in Fertility Field," *Los Angeles Times* 26 May 1995.

2. Julie Marquis, "UC Irvine Won't Defend Doctors in Embryo Suit," *Los Angeles Times* (August 1995).

3. Marquis, "UC Irvine Won't Defend Doctors."

4. KPMG Peat Marwick, "UCSD Audit Report," 24 January 1996.

5. UCI Press Release, 5 July 1995.

6. Kim Christensen and Peter Larsen, "30 Fertility Cases UCI Says More Couples' Eggs Mishandled," *Orange County Register* 6 July 1995.

7. Susan Kelleher, Kim Christensen, David Parrish, and Michelle Nicolosi, "UCI Scandal Doubles: Secret Handwritten List Reveals at Least 60 Fertility Victims," *Orange County Register* (4 November 1995).

8. Meghan Sweeney, "Wilkening Discusses Scandal," *New University* 20 (November) 1995.

9. Mimi Meyers, Ronny Diamond, David Kezur, Constance Scharf, Margot Weinshel, and Douglas S. Rait, "An Infertility Primer for Family Therapists: Medical, Social, and Psychological Dimensions," *Family Process* 34(1995):219–229.

10. Kelleher, et. al., "UCI Scandal Doubles."

11. Michael Granberry, "Woman Alleges Asch Sent Her Embryos to Researcher," *Orange County Register* (6 September 1995).

12. Julie Marquis and Michael Granberry, "7 Couples Sue UC, Alleging Misuse of Eggs," *Los Angeles Times* (8 August 1995).

13. "Anonymous Letter Alleges Eggs Used Without Consent," *Orange County Register* (19 May 1995).

14. Ibid.

15. Personal interview with Ricardo Asch, 14 February 1999.

16. Susan Kelleher and Kim Christensen, "Fertility Patients Fight Over Twins," *Orange County Register* (18 February 1996).

17. John A. Robertson, "The Case of the Switched Embryos," *Hastings Center Report* 25(1995): 13–19.

18. "I Was Robbed of My Embryos," *Glamour*, (January) 1996, p. 66.

19. Susan Littwin, "Fertility: Why One Mother May Never Know Her Babies," *Redbook* December 1995, p. 85.

20. Michelle Nicolosi, "Fertility: Family Speaks Out," *Orange County Register* (8 June 1995).

21. "I Was Robbed of My Embryos."

22. Personal interview with Orange County attorney, 23 April 1999.

23. *Anna J v. Mark C*, 234 Cal.App.3d 1557 (1991).

24. Ernie Slone, "Three More Former Patients File Suit," *Orange County Register* (29 January 1996).

25. Susan Kelleher, "Three More Fertility Patients Sue Physicians and University," *Orange County Register* (13 January 1996).

26. Susan Kelleher, et. al., "UCI Scandal Doubles."

27. Ibid.

28. "Former Asch Patient Sues in Egg-theft Case No. 42," *Orange County Register* (13 March 1996).

29. Personal interview with UCIMC physician, 21 June 1996.

30. Susan Kelleher and Ana Menendez, "Balmaceda Wants UCI to Pay Legal Fees," *Orange County Register* (1 June 1996).

31. Personal interview with Ronald Brower, 5 February 1996.

32. Personal interview with Ricardo Asch, 14 February 1999.

33. J.R. Moehringer, "UCI Doctor Defends Actions," *Orange County Register* (1 June 1995).

34. Ivan Sciupac, "Ricardo Asch: In His Own Words," *New University* (1 April) 1996.

35. Susan Kelleher and Kim Christensen, "Fertility Fraud: Baby Born After Doctor Took Eggs Without Consent," *Orange County Register* (19 May 1995).

36. ABC Primetime Live, "Switched Before Birth," November 1994.

37. Michael Granberry, "Ex-Asch Aide Tells of Early Suspicions of Egg Misuse," *Los Angeles Times* (29 February 1996).

38. Susan Kelleher and Ernie Slone, "Asch Called the Shots, Ex-aide Says," *Orange County Register* (29 February 1996).

39. Ibid.

40. Kim Christensen and Jim Mulvaney, "Asch Blames All on Staff, UCI," *Orange County Register* (27 February 1996).

41. Sciupac, "Ricardo Asch: In His Own Words."

42. Kim Christensen and Jim Mulvaney, "Asch Blames All."

43. ABC Primetime Live, "Switched Before Birth."

44. Ibid.

45. Ivan Sciupac, "Asch Speaks About His Role in Scandal," *New University* (8 April) 1996.

46. Robyn Rowland, "Reproductive Technologies Harm Women," in *Reproductive Technologies*, ed. by Carol Wekesser (San Diego: Greenhaven Press, 1996):37–43.

47. John A. Robertson, *Children of Choice: Freedom and the New Reproductive Technologies* (Princeton: Princeton University Press, 1994).

48. John A. Robertson, "Legal Troublespots in Assisted Reproduction," Fertility and Sterility, 65(1996):11–12.

49. Personal communication with UCI College of Medicine faculty member, 11 April 1996.

50. "Fertility Clinic is Sued Over the Loss of Embryos," *New York Times* (1 October 1995).

51. ABC Primetime Live, "Switched Before Birth."

52. Granberry, "Ex-Asch Aide."

53. ABC Primetime Live, "Switched Before Birth."

54. UCI Clinical Panel Report, 17 March 1995.

55. Sciupac, "Ricardo Asch: In His Own Words."

56. Personal communication with former CRH patient, July 1995.

57. Personal interview with former CRH patient, 22 January 1996.

58. Susan Kelleher and Ernie Slone, "Asch Aide Queried Over Actions," *Orange County Register* (1 March 1996).

59. California Legislature, Senate Select Committee on Higher Education, "A Hearing to Investigate UC Irvine's Fertility Clinic," 14 June 1995 (hereafter cited as CA Senate). Testimony of Jane Frederick.

60. CA Senate, Testimony of Jose Balmaceda.

61. Roberta Lessor, Nancyann Cervantes, Nadine O'Conner, Jose Balmaceda, and Ricardo H. Asch, "An Analysis of Social and Psychological Characteristics of Women Volunteering to Become Oocyte Donors," *Fertility and Sterility* 59(1993):65–71.

62. Catherine V. Hounshell and Ryszard J. Chekowski, "Donation of Frozen Embryos After In Vitro Fertilization is Uncommon," *Fertility and Sterility* 66(1996):837–838.

63. Paul Jesilow, Henry N. Pontell, and Gilbert Geis, *Prescription for Profit* (Berkeley: University of California Press, 1993).

64. Kenneth Ryan, "National and International Responses to the Ethical Problems of ART," Paper Presented at the UCI Ethics Conference, 12 April 1996, Irvine, CA.

65. John A. Robertson, *Children of Choice*.

66. Christine Overall, *Ethics and Human Reproduction: A Feminist Analysis* (Boston: Allen & Unwin, 1987).

67. Gena Corea, *The Mother Machine: Reproductive Technologies from Artificial Insemination to Artificial Wombs* (New York: Harper & Row, 1985).

68. Ibid.

69. Janice G. Raymond, "Reproductive Gifts and Gift Giving: The Altruistic Woman," *Hastings Center Report* 20(1990):7–11.

70. Marc A. Rodwin, *Medicine, Money and Morals* (New York: Oxford University Press, 1993).

71. Charles L. Bosk, *Forgive and Remember* (Chicago: University of Chicago Press, 1979).

72. William R. Phipps, "The Future of Infertility Services," *Fertility and Sterility* 66(1996):202–204.

73. Personal interview with physician, Fall 1996.

74. Anonymous personal interviews and fieldwork, 1996.

75. Personal interview with fertility specialist, Fall 1996.

76. Shannon Brownlee, "Regulation of Reproductive Technologies: An Overview," in *Reproductive Technologies*, ed. Wekesser, 150–157.

77. Lori B. Andrews, *New Conceptions: A Consumer's Guide to the Newest Infertility Treatments* (New York: Ballantine Books, 1985).

78. Michael A. Katz, "Federal Trade Commission Staff Concerns with Assisted Reproductive Technology Advertising," *Fertility and Sterility* 64(1995):10–12.

79. Personal communication with former SART officer, 12 April 1996.

80. V. Alam, L. Weckstein, Teri Ord, Sergio Stone, Jose P. Balmaceda, and Ricardo H. Asch, "Cumulative Pregnancy Rate From One Gamete Intrafallopian Transfer (GIFT) Cycle With Cryopreservation of Embryos: A Practical Mathematical Calculation," *Human Reproduction* 8(1993):559–562.

81. James W. Coleman, "Motivation and Opportunity: Understanding the Causes of White-Collar Crime," in *White-Collar Crime: Classic and Contemporary Views*, 3rd ed., ed. by Gilbert Geis, Robert F. Meier, and Lawrence M. Salinger (New York: Free Press, 1995):360–381.

82. CA Senate, Testimony of Marilyn Killane.

83. Ted Howard and Jeremy Rifken, *Who Should Play God?* (New York: Dell Publishing, 1977).

84. Tracy Weber and Julie Marquis, "In Quest for Miracles, Did Fertility Clinic Go Too Far?" *Los Angeles Times* (4 June 1995).

85. Barbara Kingsley, "Faith in Doctor Who Aided Birth Still Unshaken," *Orange County Register* (19 May 1995).

86. Adam Pertman, "Calif. Furor Clouds Work in Infertility," *Boston Globe* (24 June 1995).

87. Robyn Rowland, *Living Laboratories: Women and Reproductive Technologies* (Bloomington: Indiana University Press, 1992).

88. Personal interview with physician, Fall 1996.

89. Jesilow, Pontell, and Geis, *Prescription for Profit*.

90. David Matza, *Delinquency and Drift* (New York: Wiley, 1964).

91. Personal interview with UCIMC physician, Winter 1996.

92. Personal interview with UCIMC official, Winter 1996.

93. Kelleher and Slone, "Asch Called the Shots."

94. Lori B. Andrews, *New Conceptions: A Consumer's Guide to the Newest Infertility Treatments* (New York: Ballantine Books, 1985).

95. Robert F. Howe, "Fertility Doctor's Intention: Expert Says He Donated Own Sperm to Help," *Washington Post* (23 November 1991).

96. Tracy Weber and Michael Granberry, "Babies Are Bottom Line For Clinics," *Los Angeles Times* (23 May 1995).

97. Personal interview with UCIMC physician, 21 August 1996.

98. Personal interview with former CRH patient, 22 January 1996.

99. Personal interview with Ricardo Asch, 14 February 1999.

100. Steven Messner and Richard Rosenfeld, *Crime and the American Dream*, 2nd ed. (Belmont, CA: Wadsworth, 1997).

The Archer Daniels Midland Antitrust Case of 1996: A Case Study

Sally S. Simpson
and
Nicole Leeper Piquero

Since Sutherland identified white-collar crime as an area of study in 1939, scholars from diverse fields have explored the etiology and control of white-collar and corporate crime. Although still understudied relative to street crime, research has lead to important discoveries about the nature of crime (and victimization, see, e.g., Levi, 1992; Stitt and Giacopassi, 1993; Szockyj and Fox, 1996) within and by organizations (Finney and Lesieur, 1982; Clinard and Yeager, 1980; Vaughan, 1983, 1992; Coleman, 1987; Braithwaite, 1984; Simpson, Paternoster, and Piquero, 1998). Studies of specific crime types, including antitrust (Simpson, 1986, 1987; Jamieson, 1994), financial (Calavita and Pontell, 1993; Zey, 1993;), manufacturing (Cullen, Maakestad, and Cavender, 1987), and environmental (Shover, Clelland, and Lynxwiler, 1986; Yeager, 1991; Barnett, 1994) have identified characteristics of industries and firms that increase offending propensities, while crime prevention and control has been explored as a general issue (Reichman, 1992; Braithwaite and Makkai, 1994; Snider, 1995; Friedrichs, 1996) or more specifically by focusing on case prosecution (Mann, 1985; Friedrichs, 1996; Benson and Cullen, 1998;) and sentencing (Wheeler, Weisburd, and Bode, 1982; Hagan and Parker, 1985; Hagan and Palloni, 1986; Weisburd, Waring, and Wheeler, 1990; Cohen, 1991, 1992a).

Many theoretical and empirical advances have been made in the field; yet, scholars working within this genre understand how extremely complex conducting such research can be. Unlike studying "street crime" or individual criminal causes, there is a dearth of good quantitative data for empirical investigations or theory development and testing (Cohen, 1992b; Simpson, Harris, and Mattson, 1995; Friedrichs, 1996). Consequently, many, if not most, of the advances in the field are attributable to qualitative researchers using case study techniques. Perhaps the most notable example of this approach is Gilbert Geis's incisive description of the 1961 electrical industry price-fixing conspiracies.

Using published court records and various other documentation, Geis (1967, 141) was able to "test and refine" Sutherland's hunches and hypotheses about corporate offenses and offenders. Importantly, he also raised a set of questions about corporate offending and crime control that have, in many ways, shaped the corporate crime research agenda for the past 30 years. For instance:

How does the structure and culture of organizations promote corporate crime?

What are the individual, organizational, and environmental motivations for offending?

Do regulatory/criminal justice agencies and the media take business offenses seriously?

These research questions provide the basis for our study. We investigate a modern-day price-fixing scam that was operated by Archer Daniels Midland (ADM) throughout the 1990s. Using court records that describe the offense (two criminal counts) and the plea bargain along with secondary data sources, we will establish the facts of the case, describe the court proceedings, and other relevant criteria that illuminate the nature of antitrust offending, the situational context in which it occurs, and responses to it by criminal justice authorities, the media, and corporate top management.

FACTS OF THE CASE

Archer Daniels Midland (ADM), a major agricultural corporation that bills itself as the "supermarket to the world," pleaded guilty to two counts of conspiracy to restrain trade and agreed to pay unprecedented criminal fines in the amount of $100 million for antitrust violations on October 15, 1996. The guilty plea ended an almost four-year investigation by the Federal Bureau of Investigation (FBI) that began with the help of a former ADM director, Mark Whitacre.[1]

Mark Whitacre began working for ADM in October 1989 as president of the company's newly formed Biochem Products Division. Among other products in this division, lysine, an amino acid which is used as a protein additive in poultry and pork feed that ensures the proper growth of the animal, was to be the shining

star. The company invested over $150 million to ensure that they would become
the world leader in lysine (Henkoff, 1995). In order to attain world dominance,
ADM needed to focus all of their immediate attention on achieving market share
and later focus on profitability (essentially, as espoused by Whitacre, the marketing plan was to dominate the lysine products industry via predatory pricing). As
anticipated, ADM quickly attained market share. Lysine prices fell from $1.30
per pound to $.60 per pound, costing the company (and its main competitors)
millions of dollars per month (Henkoff, 1995).

After about a year of heading-up the division (which was still losing money
despite attaining a significant share of the lysine market), Whitacre was informed
by ADM officials Michael (Mick) Andreas, vice-chairman and son of chairman
Dwayne Andreas, and Jim Randall, ADM president, that he was to work more
closely with Terry Wilson, the president of the corn-processing division.
Whitacre was concerned by this pairing because Wilson was rumored throughout
the company to be involved with price-fixing. Ostensibly, the two managers were
to take the business to the next level of doing business—to focus on turning a
profit. As a first step, Whitacre and Wilson arranged to meet with Ajinomoto Co.
Inc. and Kyowa Hakko Kogyo Co., the two major Japanese competitors in the
lysine business, suggesting that the three companies form an amino acids association (Henkoff, 1995). The association was being billed as a joint effort to promote and expand the lysine business, but its real function was to serve as a cover
for the secret price-fixing meetings. As a rationale for working together, Wilson
used production capacity, usage levels, and profit figures to show the Japanese
that the customers, not the producers, were benefitting from the current situation.
He argued, "the competitor is our friend, and the customer is our enemy"
(Henkoff, 1995, 55)

The two Japanese companies, Ajinomoto Co. Inc. and Kyowa Hakko
Kogyo Co., came separately to visit ADM's plant in Decatur, Illinois toward the
end of the summer in 1992 in order to observe the capacity at which the plant was
designed to operate (250 million pounds per year). Shortly after the visit, ADM
began experiencing a contamination problem, which kept increasing their production costs. ADM officials began to suspect sabotage and extortion on the part
of one of the two Japanese companies, based upon information provided to them
from Whitacre.

Whitacre claimed that Mr. Fujiwara from Ajinomoto contacted him to inform
him that his company had placed a mole within ADM who was responsible for the
contamination problem that ADM was experiencing. Fujiwara apparently wanted
$10 million wired to a Swiss bank account in exchange for identifying the mole and
providing ADM with technology used by Ajinomoto to reduce the contamination
problem (Eichenwald, 1997). Whitacre relayed these demands to Mick Andreas,
who in turn informed ADM's CEO, Dwayne Andreas. The FBI became involved
when Dwayne Andreas called an associate at the Central Intelligence Agency

(CIA) in London, who indicated this was a matter to be handled by the FBI. According to Whitacre, Michael Andreas was extremely agitated about the FBI investigation and expressed concern that his father had not "thought about all the ramifications of this" (Henkhoff, 1995, 57).

Whitacre reports that before he was to meet with the FBI, he was coached by Mick Andreas to refrain from mentioning two things in particular. First, he was not to mention that ADM tried to buy technology from the employee at Ajinomoto; rather, he was told to tell the FBI that the employee had approached him about selling the technology. Second, Michael Andreas told Whitacre to lie about which phone he used to speak to the Ajinomoto employee. It was likely that the FBI would plan on taping all conversations made on that line in order to record conversations regarding the sabotage, and Mick didn't want the FBI tapping phones that had been used to talk to the Japanese about product pricing. Whitacre, accompanied by Mark Cheviron, head of ADM security, told the FBI exactly what he was told to say at their offices in Decatur. However, when FBI agent Brian Shepard showed up at Whitacre's house on November 3, 1992 in order to install a recorder into his phone line, Whitacre decided to tell him the truth about everything, including trying to buy the technology from Ajinomoto, the phone line, and the beginning stages of price-fixing at ADM within the lysine business.

The sabotage story became suspicious when Whitacre later claimed that Mr. Fujiwara lowered his asking price to six million dollars. The suspicion gave rise to an FBI investigation into Whitacre's sabotage claims. Consequently, Whitacre failed two polygraph tests and later admitted to FBI agent Brian Shepard on December 22, 1992, that the sabotage incident was a hoax and that Michael Andreas never agreed to buy stolen technology. Despite being the prime suspect in the extortion case, Whitacre, in an attempt to save face with the FBI, revealed that he and other ADM officials were engaged in price-fixing (Eichenwald, 1997). Shortly thereafter, Whitacre voluntarily began recording conversations and meetings at ADM for the FBI in hopes of attaining incriminating evidence for price-fixing and stealing technology from other companies both from within the lysine business as well as in other divisions throughout ADM. In exchange for cooperation with the FBI, they declined to inform ADM about the Fujiwara hoax.

As a result of the secret recordings made by Whitacre, on June 27, 1995, federal agents raided ADM headquarters in Decatur, Illinois (Henkhoff, 1995). Two days later, officials at ADM learned that Whitacre was an informant for the FBI, and on August 7, 1995, Whitacre was fired from ADM and accused of embezzling $2.5 million from the company (the total amount would later be increased to $9 million) by means of submitting phony invoices for reimbursements. Once payments were received, the money was transferred to offshore bank accounts. Whitacre claimed that the off-the-book compensations were made with full knowledge of ADM executives and often encouraged as bonuses for ADM employees. FBI agents were informed of the illegal payoffs by Whitacre, but only after he had learned that ADM was going public with the accusations.

ADM CHARGES AND SENTENCING

ADM plead guilty to two criminal felony charges of conspiracy to restrain trade, one for lysine and the other for citric acid, an organic acid that is used in a variety of foods and beverages, including soft drinks, and is also used as a preservative in prepared foods. Both charges violate Section 1 of the Sherman Act (15 U.S.C. § 1). The lysine charge stated that beginning in June 1992 and continuing through June 27, 1995, ADM and coconspirators, Ajinomoto Co, Inc., Kyowa Hakko Kogyo Co. Ltd., and Sewon America, Inc. (a Korean company), engaged in a conspiracy to suppress and eliminate competition by fixing the price and allocating the volume of sales of lysine offered to consumers worldwide. Similarly, the citric acid charge noted that beginning around January 1993 and continuing through June 27, 1995, ADM and coconspirators engaged in a conspiracy to suppress and eliminate competition by fixing the price and allocating the volume of sales of citric acid offered to consumers worldwide.

As part of the plea agreement, ADM admitted wrongdoing for the above two charges and agreed to pay a total of $100 million in criminal fines. Sentencing was determined pursuant to the Unites States Sentencing Guidelines. Both the plaintiff and the defendant agreed that for sentencing purposes, the volume of commerce affected in this case was in excess of $100 million for both the lysine and citric acid markets. ADM was required to pay criminal fines of $70 million for the lysine misconduct and $30 million for the citric acid wrongdoing within 90 days of sentencing. The criminal fine for citric acid was reportedly substantially lower because of the valuable cooperation ADM gave to the investigation (George Wells & Associates, 1996). No term of probation was ordered in either case. In addition to the two criminal fines, ADM was required to pay a total of $400 in special assessments ($200 for each case). Special assessments identify the dollar amount of mandatory special assessments ordered by the court. Court-ordered restitution was also not ordered in either case because of the restitution already paid or agreed to be paid by the defendant.

In exchange for cooperation with federal investigations, the government agreed not to bring any criminal charges, with the exclusion of federal tax laws, against any of ADM's employees or subsidiaries or affiliates except for Michael D. Andreas and Terrance S. Wilson, for offenses that were committed prior to the date of the plea agreement for the antitrust conspiracies or for any alleged misappropriations of technology. In addition, any information obtained by the government could not be used against any ADM employee or subsidiary except for prosecution of perjury, making false statements or declarations, or obstruction of justice.

In addition to the criminal penalties, ADM agreed to pay, under various civil suits and settlements, $80 million. ADM's total legal obligations related to the conspiracy are in excess of $190 million (Stewart, 1996; Antitrust Litigation Reporter, 1996).

Charges and Sentencing: Other Conspirators

Along with ADM, several other companies and individuals working within these respective companies were also charged with misconducts arising from the lysine price-fixing scandal. The Department of Justice clearly implies that the plea agreement entered into by ADM on October 15, 1996 was due to the cooperation and valuable information provided by these companies and individuals (Antitrust Report, 1996).

On August 27, 1996, three companies agreed to a plea agreement and admitted their role in the price-fixing conspiracy. Kyowa Hakko Kogyo Company and Sewon America Incorporated agreed to plead guilty, and Ajinomoto Company agreed to plead no contest. Both Kyowa Hakko Kogyo and Ajinomoto were fined the maximum amount of $10 million, while the fine for Sewon America was left to be decided by the courts. In addition to paying the criminal fines, each of the three companies agreed to hand over relevant documents to the government as well as provide witnesses to testify in the United States. Despite agreeing to the plea agreement, a snag arose for Ajinomoto when, on October 19, 1996, federal Judge Castillo refused to accept their initial plea of no contest due to mounting evidence that they destroyed relevant documents at the beginning of the investigation and insisted that the company had four weeks to change their plea to guilty or face indictment. Ajinomoto pleaded guilty on November 15, 1996 to one count of conspiracy.

In addition to the agreements made with the above three companies, individuals from each of the companies also took part in the August 27, 1996 plea agreement. Kanji Mimoto from Ajinomoto Company, Masaru Yamamoto from Kyowa Hakko Kogyo Company, and Jhom Su Kim from Sewon America Incorporated all pleaded guilty and paid fines ranging from $50,000 (for Yamamoto) to $75, 000 (for Mimoto and Kim). As part of the plea agreement, these individuals agreed to cooperate fully with the investigation.

On December 3, 1996 a federal grand jury indicted three former ADM employees, Michael Andreas, Mark Whitacre, and Terrance Wilson, along with a Japanese executive, Kazutoshi Yamada, for conspiring to violate the Sherman Antitrust Act (15 USC §1) by allegedly engaging in a three-year worldwide conspiracy to eliminate competition by fixing the price and allocating the sales volume of lysine. Also on the day of indictment, one additional company, Cheil Jadang

Limited from Seoul, Korea, also agreed to plead guilty and pay a $1.25 million fine for its part in the lysine conspiracy.

The three defendants, Andreas, Whitacre, and Wilson, appeared in court on December 20, 1996 and pleaded not guilty before U.S. District Judge Rebecca Dallmeyer. Each defendant was released on $4,500 bond. A bench warrant was issued for Kazutoshi Yamada because he was not in the country for the arraignment. The criminal trial began on July 9, 1998 and lasted until September 17, 1998, when a jury found Andreas, Whitacre, and Wilson guilty of conspiring to fix the global price and allocate the sales volume of lysine. Each defendant faced a maximum penalty of three years in prison and a fine of $350,000 or up to twice the amount gained by the crime or lost by the victims. After much litigation, a federal judge decided that the three defendants would not be charged more than $350,000 and scheduled sentencing for July 9, 1999.

While defending his role in the price-fixing scam, Whitacre was also indicted by a grand jury on January 15, 1997 on forty-five criminal counts for embezzling $9 million from ADM, money laundering, filing false income tax returns, and obstruction of justice (Walsh, 1997). He pleaded guilty to 37 counts on October 10, 1997 and was sentenced on January 13, 1998 to serve a nine-year sentence and ordered to pay $11.4 million in restitution to ADM.

ASSESSING THE CASE

Techniques of the Conspiracy

Similar to participants in other conspiracy cases (e.g., Geis, 1967), it was apparent that ADM conspirators understood that their behaviors were unlawful. Meetings were held in secret—mostly in motel rooms both within and outside of the country (Gersten, 1996). In Whitacre's case, he made incriminating telephone calls not from work (where he might be overheard), but from his home. Although there are few details about the meetings themselves, according to court documents, it was during these clandestine meetings and subsequent conversations that participants agreed to set lysine and citric acid prices at certain levels and to allocate among the corporate conspirators the volume of sales to be sold by each (*U.S. v. Archer Daniels Midland Company*, U.S. District Court, Northern District of Illinois, Eastern Division).

Noteworthy in this case is the extent to which price-fixing appeared to be standard operating procedure for ADM. Not only did rumors swirl around about Terry Wilson, but co-workers at ADM indicated to Whitacre that price-fixing was a common practice within the company. He describes his introduction to the illegal conduct (Henkoff, 1995, 53):

> It was during my first year or so at the company that I started hearing about price-fixing at ADM—in four or five other divisions. People said it was fairly common. I didn't see it, but I heard about it from people who were involved in it directly or indirectly. It wasn't an everyday topic. But it was stuff I would hear a couple of times a month. And one thing people would tell me when it came up was to beware of Terry Wilson, the president of the corn-processing division. But I didn't give it much thought. I was busy getting my business established.

Based on case indictments and Whitacre's accounts, knowledge about price-fixing permeated the company all the way to the top, including the CEO, the president, and the legal staff. In one interview, Whitacre described how surprised he was when ADM's general counsel joked about price-fixing meetings when he saw Whitacre and Wilson together (Henkoff, 1995, 61). Later he alleges that CEO Dwayne Andreas and ADM president Jim Randall both knew about the price-fixing—although neither was indicted or prosecuted in the case.

> I had Dwayne Andreas on a couple of tapes as he was being updated on the price-fixing discussion. And Jim Randall was on tapes a lot talking about ADM stealing technology. I had Randall walking in on price-fixing discussions between me and Mick Andreas and Terry Wilson (Henkoff, 1997:91).

While Andreas and Randall both denied involvement and agreed to cooperate with the government's investigation of the case, the companies' recent criminal history can be read as testimony supportive of Whitacre's accusations. In the late 1970s, ADM pleaded no contest to charges that it (along with two other firms) conspired to fix prices on contracts in the Federal Food for Peace Program. In 1982, although the case was later dismissed for lack of evidence, the company was charged with fixing corn fructose prices. Most recently, the firm settled class action suits (to the tune of $1.5 million) that claimed ADM had fixed carbon dioxide prices (Eichenwald, 1996).

Environmental, Organizational, and Individual Motivations for the Conspiracy

The ADM case is an intriguing case because it challenges some of the basic assumptions about the environmental and organizational causes of antitrust offending. For instance, it is commonly argued that antitrust offending is a consequence of firm profit-squeeze (i.e., firms offend because they are in dire economic circumstances, Geis, 1967). Yet, ADM's 1995 profit was approximately $700 million (Gersten, 1996) on revenue of $12.6 billion (Stewart, 1996). However, one cannot dismiss profit-squeeze arguments altogether, given the fact that Whitacre's division was hemorrhaging millions of dollars monthly. This was occurring after ADM invested $1.5 billion in BioProducts with the expectation that the division would generate one-third of the company's earnings by 1997 (Henkoff, Rao, and Jaynes, 1995, 67). Cost considerations appear to have influenced top management's decision to team Whitacre with Terry Wilson in order to teach him "how ADM does business" (Henkoff, 1995, 53).

The divisional structure at ADM also appears to have facilitated the price-fixing. First, ADM divisions were organized around distinct products or product groups that were headed by management teams. These units were responsible for production, distribution, and marketing. Thus divisional management was fairly autonomous (Whitacre reported directly to Mick Andreas, as did other presidents). And, even though divisional price-fixing activities did not appear to be a well-kept secret within the company, the divisional lines of authority protected those at the very top of the firm. Second, this type of corporate structure promotes competition between divisions—especially since evaluations of divisional performance are most apt to be based on quantitative and not qualitative criteria (see, e.g., Simpson and Koper, 1997). Price-fixing, therefore, may have been a strategy to secure and maintain division profit levels (relative to other divisions)—thus ensuring that the intraorganizational bottom-line evaluation was positive.

A final organizational consideration that facilitated the conspiracy is the composition of ADM's board of directors. Many have speculated that when the CEO is also chair of the board, s/he gains important access to the external environment. The CEO, as chair, can manipulate and filter information that the board receives. Moreover, boards dominated by insiders are less apt to challenge their day-to-day supervisor (Simpson and Koper, 1997; Weidenbaum, 1995). Press accounts of the case emphasized that Andreas stacked the board with ADM insiders, family, and friends. The board was conspicuously quiet about the criminal charges, even though the potential cost to shareholders—whose interests ostensibly are represented by the board—would be significant should the maximum punishment be rendered. (ADM stock slumped badly after charges were announced.) Only one board member (out of seventeen) spoke publicly about the charges. F. Ross Johnson (former CEO of RJ Nabisco) described the ADM conspirators as "scumbags" and suggested that the company appeared to have a "criminal mentality" (Henkoff, Rao, and Carvell, 1995). Institutional investors challenged Andreas to include more external board members with the assumption that ADM and Andreas will be more accountable to shareholders with a more open board of directors (and not squander profits to pay for criminal activity). James Burton, CEO of Calpers—one of the larger institutional investors in ADM—assessed the $100 million fine as ". . .real money that could have been used in many ways to improve the profitability of the company. We ask once again, what was the board doing?" (Stewart, 1996, 40).

Individual level motivations are more difficult to ascertain from the available sources. Whitacre, who is the most public participant, emerges as somewhat of a paradox. As whistle-blower and mole, he worked closely with the FBI for over two years, tape-recording conversations among ADM managers and coconspirators. Whitacre claims that he cooperated with legal authorities because price-fixing is bad business practice, he did not want to lie to FBI investigators, and he thought that he would be a hero (Henkoff, 1995; Henkoff, Rao and Jaynes, 1995). Up to this point, his motivations and experiences are similar to those of other whistle-blowers (Glazer and Glazer, 1989). Even his later suicide attempt does not deviate from the depression and anxiety reported by others in similar situations.

Ultimately, however, Whitacre was charged with price-fixing along with Mick Andreas and Terry Wilson. He stopped cooperating with the prosecution, pleaded innocent to the charges, and later filed a lawsuit against the FBI, charging:

- that on at least four occasions, an FBI agent told him to destroy price-fixing tapes that were unfavorable to the government's case.
- that his constitutional rights were violated by the FBI because agents failed to provide him with an attorney or doctor in a timely manner—even when he discussed the possibility of killing himself.
- that he was never read his Miranda rights.
- that the Justice Department ignored tapes that implicated Dwayne Andreas in the price-fixing conspiracy.

At the same time that Whitacre directed accusations against the FBI, he revealed that he suffered from bipolar disorder (i.e., manic-depression) and claimed that the disorder was triggered by his mistreatment by the FBI (Henkoff, Rao, and Gunn, 1997).

It is difficult to determine whether Whitacre is a genuine victim of organizational mistreatment (first by ADM and then by legal representatives) or whether his participation in illegal activities at ADM (including under-the-table payments to avoid taxes), fabrication of sabotage stories, and charges against the FBI reveal a grand conspirator. Certainly, there is evidence that Whitacre was a well-respected and admired manager. Colleagues at ADM and Degussa (his former employer) describe a man collegial, hard-working, and enthusiastic about his work. One reported, "I think he's an excellent manager, very people-focused. . . managers seem to piss somebody off at some time. Mark may have been an exception to that rule. Until now, of course" (Henkoff, Rao, and Jaynes, 1995, 65). Moreover, it is not unreasonable to believe that law enforcement agents are selective in their enforcement efforts. Dwayne Andreas, ADM's CEO, has powerful friends in both political parties. Between 1991 and 1996, his donations to each political party, coupled with those from the company, exceed $2.5 million (Babcock, 1996, A07). Among those noted as friends and donation recipients of

Andreas' largess include President Clinton, former senator Bob Dole, and the late President Richard Nixon and senator Hubert Humphrey. Given the facts of the case and the lack of available public information about other players besides Whitacre, one can only speculate about Whitacre's true motivations.

Response of Top Management, Media, and the Law

Geis (1967), in his review of the electrical cases, noted how differently General Electric (GE) and Westinghouse responded to their conspirators. GE took a punitive line, while Westinghouse exculpated participants. ADM appears to be more similar to Westinghouse than to GE in how it responded to the conspirators. Whitacre was fired and smeared. Terry Wilson and Mick Andreas continued in their posts until October, 1996. The former "retired" from the company, while the latter went on a temporary leave of absence. Dwayne Andreas, who continued to lead the company, apologized to shareholders for the price-fixing scandal and named three other executives to help him share CEO duties. These included James Randall (ADM president who Whitacre claims participated in the conspiracy), Charles Bayless (president of ADM's processing division), and G. Allen Andreas (a nephew of the CEO). The board awarded Mick Andreas a 15 percent raise, after which his temporary leave from the company was announced. Dwayne Andreas also was given a salary increase by the board (a slight increase to his already hefty $3 million salary, Henkoff, 1996).

The law enforcement community and the media, on the other hand, appear to have taken this case very seriously. Media coverage was fairly extensive. The story was picked up and followed by major and minor newspapers, news magazines, and trade publications. Generally, accounts were descriptive, but on occasion, they were fairly critical. For instance, the lead paragraph in an article in the *U.S. News & World Report* began,

> "Archer Daniels Midland Co. bills itself as the 'supermarket to the world.'" Very soon, possibly this week, federal prosecutors are expected to pin a far less wholesome description on the international grain-processing giant. The word they will use: felon" (Pound and Cohen, 1996, 56).

Moreover, the story did not die. The case was followed from Whitacre's exposure as a mole, through the investigation, charges, plea agreement, and subsequent individual and coconspirator indictments and sentences.

The legal community, from FBI investigators to prosecutors and judges, pursued the case doggedly. The $100 million fine levied against the firm was the largest ever in an antitrust case. The next closest fine (for $15 million) is not really in the same ballpark (Eichenwald, 1996). Two companies (Kyowa Hakko Kogyo and Ajinomoto) were prescribed the maximum fine available. The organizations not only had to face criminal charges from the U.S. government but also had to deal with the backlash of civil law suits, which caused the companies to pay out millions of more dollars, and even had to face criminal charges from the Canadian government (Willitts, 1998). Further, while it is generally easier to charge companies with wrongdoing than individuals (let alone individuals working for foreign companies), in this case the Justice Department successfully charged individual conspirators at ADM, as well as managers from Japanese and Korean companies. Thus, like Geis (1967), we find Sutherland's contentions that the legal community is afraid to antagonize business or that media fail to report corporate crime in a critical manner to be overly pessimistic. It may be that crime reporting generally is more a function of sensationalism (the magnitude of the case, who is involved, titillating or sordid details) than neglect or disregard for the seriousness of corporate crime. And, if Whitacre is correct that Dwayne Andreas and Jim Randall were players in the conspiracy but were protected from prosecution, it is clear that the legal system is imperfect. However, equally clear is the evidence that the system does not completely pander to the interests of the business class.

SUMMING UP

The case study is a useful tool to assess what is known about a phenomenon, to develop empirical generalizations from observations that may be explored by others, to inform theory, and to identify new areas of research. The ADM case substantiates what others have observed about the nature and context of antitrust offending. The culture of ADM and its multidivisional structure facilitated and supported the price-fixing conspiracy. The company as a whole, and top management in particular, placidly or actively (depending on whose account is believed) treated price-fixing as standard operating procedure ("the way ADM does business"). Indeed, evidence suggests that "the ADM way" included, in addition to price-fixing, predatory pricing, tax fraud, and industrial espionage. The corporate culture, in the words of board member Ross Johnson, had a criminal mentality.

Like Geis (1967), we believe that price-fixing at ADM was driven by cost considerations. However, we note that profits at the division level were the most salient concerns for managers, since ADM's overall financial performance was strong. This suggests that research should explore the ways in which intraorganizational pressures interact with organizational structure and strategy (e.g., new product line development) to promote illegality.

Lastly, we note that ADM lacked the kind of oversight that a diligent board would provide, and we could not ascertain from public information whether the company had an internal compliance system or not. However, the fact the legal counsel could joke about price-fixing meetings suggests that even if such a system were in place, it was not a very serious or effective one. During the past 30 years, since Geis wrote his case study, most research has focused on risk factors for corporate offending. We suggest that perhaps now the agenda could shift toward crime prevention factors—to paraphrase a recent University of Maryland Report to Congress on street crime prevention, the new agenda would explore "What Works, What Doesn't, and What's Promising in Corporate Crime Prevention."

NOTES

1. The appendix contains a description of products and players (corporate and individual) involved in the conspiracy as well as a detailed time line of events from discovery through sentencing.

REFERENCES

Antitrust Report. 1996. "Archer Daniels Midland Charged with Criminal Price-fixing of Lysine." *Federal Activity* 23(5):7.

Antitrust Litigation Reporter. 1996. "ADM Settles Civil Price-Fixing Suit for Record $100 Million". October.

Babcock, Charles R. 1996. "ADM and Its Executives Have Been Generous to Both Parties and Dole." *The Washington Post* (October 15):A07.

Barnett, Harold C. 1994. *Toxic Debts and the Superfund Dilemma*. Chapel Hill: University of North Carolina Press.

Benson, Michael L., and Francis T. Cullen. 1998. *Combating Corporate Crime: Locals Prosecutors at Work*. Boston: Northeastern University Press.

Braithwaite, John. 1984. *Corporate Crime in the Pharmaceutical Industry*. Routledge & Kegan Paul.

Braithwaite, John, Toni Makkai. 1994. "The Dialectics of Corporate Deterrence". *Journal of Research in Crime and Delinquency*, 31(4):347–373.

Calvita, Kitty, and Henry N. Pontell. 1993. "Savings and Loan Fraud as Organized Crime: Toward a Conceptual Typology of Corporate Illegality". *Criminology* 31(4):519–548.

Clinard, Marshall B., and Peter C. Yeager. 1980. *Corporate Crime*. New York: The Free Press.

Cohen, Mark A. 1991. "Corporate Crime and Punishment: A Study of Social Harm and Sentencing Practice in the Federal Courts, 1984–1987". *Boston University Law Review* 71(2):247–280.

Cohen, Mark A. 1992a. "Sentencing Guidelines and Corporate Criminal Liability in the United States". *Business and the Contemporary World*, 4(3):140–157.

Cohen, Mark A. 1992b. "Environmental Crime and Punishment: Legal/Economic Theory and Empirical Evidence on Enforcement of Federal Environmental Statutes." *The Journal of Criminal Law and Criminology*, 82(4):1054–1108.

Cohen, Mark A., and Sally S. Simpson. 1997. "The Origins of Corporate Criminality: Rational Individual and Organizational Actors." Pp. 33–51 in William S. Lofquist, Mark A. Cohen, and Gary A. Rabe, eds., *Debating Corporate Crime*. Cincinnati, OH: Anderson.

Coleman, James W. 1987. "Toward an Integrated Theory of White-Collar Crime." *American Journal of Sociology* 93:406–439.

Cullen, Francis T., William J. Maakestad, and Gary Cavender. 1987. *Corporate Crime Under Attack: The Ford Pinto Case and Beyond*. Cincinnati. OH: Anderson Publishing.

Eichenwald, Kurt. 1996. "Archer Daniels Midland Agrees to Big Fine for Price-fixing." *New York Times* (October 15).

Eichenwald, Kurt. 1997. "The Tale of the Secret Tapes." *New York Times* (November 16).

Finney, Henry C., and Henry R. Lesieur. 1982. "A Contingency Theory of Organizational Crime." Pp. 255–299 in Samuel B. Bacharach, ed. *The Sociology of Organization*, vol. 1. Greenwich, CT: JAI Press.

Friedrichs, David O. 1996. *Trusted Criminals*. Belmont, CA: Wadsworth.

George Wells & Associates. 1996. "Justice Department will Extend HFCS and Citric Acid Price-Fixing Probe." *Washington Beverage Insight* 29(23).

Geis, Gilbert. 1967. "White Collar Crime: The Heavy Electrical Equipment Antitrust Cases of 1961." Pp. 139–151 in Marshall B. Clinard and Richard Quinney, eds. *Criminal Behavior Systems: A Typology*. New York: Holt, Rinehart, & Winston, Inc.

Gersten, Alan. 1996. "Analysts: ADM Pays Fine, Keeps Rolling Short-Term Pain, Long-Term Gain Seen." *Journal of Commerce* (October 16): 1A.

Glazer, Myron P., and Petina M. Glazer. 1989. *The Whistleblowers*. New York: Basic Books.

Hagan, John, and Alberto Palloni. 1986. "Club Fed and the Sentencing of White-Collar Offenders Before and After Watergate." *Criminology* 24:603–622.

Hagan, John, and Patricia Parker. 1985. "White-Collar Crime and Punishment." *American Sociological Review* 50:302–316.

Henkoff, Ronald. 1995. "My Life as a Corporate Mole for the FBI." *Fortune* (September 4):52.

Henkoff, Ronald. 1996. "ADM Still Doesn't Get It; Price Fixing." *Fortune* (November 11):30.

Henkoff, Ronald. 1997. "I Thought I Was Going to Be a Hero." *Fortune* (February 3):87.

Henkoff, Ronald, Rajiv M. Rao, and Tim Carvell. 1995. "Checks, Lies, and Videotape." *Fortune* (October 30):109.

Henkoff, Ronald, Rajiv M. Rao, and Madeline Jaynes. 1995. "So Who is This Mark Whitacre, and Why is He Saying These Things About ADM?" *Fortune* (September 4):64.

Henkoff, Ronald, Rajiv M. Rao, and Eileen P. Gunn. 1997. "Betrayal: Together, The Feds and Mark Whitacre Won the Biggest Price-Fixing Case Ever. So Why Have They Turned on Each Other?" *Fortune* (February 3):82.

Jamieson, Katherine M. 1994. *The Organization of Corporate Crime: Dynamics of Antitrust Violations*. Thousand Oaks, CA: Sage Publications.

Levi, Michael. 1992. "White-Collar Crime Victimization." Pp. 169–192. In Kip Schlegel and David Weisburd, eds. *White-Collar Crime Reconsidered*. Boston: Northeastern University Press.

Mann, Kenneth. 1985. *Defending White-Collar Crime: A Portrait of Attorneys at Work*. New Haven, CT: Yale University Press.

Pound, Edward T., and Gary Cohen. 1996. "The Price of Price Fixing." *US News & World Report* (September 30):56.

Reichman, Nancy. 1992. Moving Backstage: Uncovering the Role of Compliance Practices in Shaping Regulatory Policy. Pp. 244–268. In Kip Schlegel and David Weisburd, eds. *White-Collar Crime Reconsidered*. Boston: Northeastern University Press.

Shover, Neal, Donald A. Clelland, and John Lynxwiler. 1986. *Enforcement of Negotiation: Constructing a Regulatory Bureaucracy*. Albany, NY: SUNY Press.

Simpson, Sally S. 1986. "The Decomposition of Antitrust: Testing a Multilevel, Longitudinal Model of Profit Squeeze." *American Sociological Review* 51:859–875.

Simpson, Sally S. 1987. "Cycles of Illegality: Antitrust Violations in Corporate America." *Social Forces* 64:943–963.

Simpson, Sally S., Anthony R. Harris, and Brian A. Mattson. 1995. "Measuring Corporate Crime." Pp. 115–140 in Michael B. Blankenship, ed. *Understanding Corporate Criminality*. New York: Garland.

Simpson, Sally S., and Christopher S. Koper. 1997. "The Changing of the Guard: Top Management Characteristics, Organizational Strain, and Antitrust Offending." *Journal of Quantitative Criminology* 13:373–404.

Simpson, Sally S., Raymond Paternoster, and Nicole Leeper Piquero. 1998. "Exploring the Micro-Macro Link in Corporate Crime Research." Pp. 35–68 in Peter Bamberger and William J. Sonnenstuhl, eds. *Research in the Sociology of Organizations, Special Volume on Deviance in and of Organizations*. Greenwich, CT: JAI Press.

Snider, Laureen. 1995. "Regulating Corporate Behavior." Pp. 177–210 in Michael B. Blankenship, ed. *Understanding Corporate Criminality*. New York: Garland.

Stewart, Janet Kidd. 1996. "ADM to Pay $100 Million Penalty; Record Fine Ends US Criminal Probe." *Chicago Sun-Times* (October 15):39.

Stitt, B. Grant, and David J. Giacopassi. 1993. "Assessing Victimization from Corporate Harms." Pp. 57–83 in Michael B. Blankenship, ed. *Understanding Corporate Criminality*. New York: Garland.

Sutherland, Edwin. 1949/1983. *White Collar Crime: The Uncut Version*. New Haven, CT: Yale University Press.

Szockyj, Elizabeth, and James G. Fox. 1996. *Corporate Victimization of Women*. Boston: Northeastern University Press.

Vaughan, Diane. 1983. *Controlling Unlawful Organizational Behavior: Social Structure and Corporate Misconduct*. Chicago: University of Chicago Press.

Vaughan, Diane. 1992. "The Macro-Micro Connection in White-Collar Crime Theory." Pp. 124–145 in Kip Schlegel and David Weisburd, eds. *White-Collar Crime Reconsidered*. Boston: Northeastern University Press.

Vaughan, Diane. 1996. *The Challenger Launch Decision*. Chicago: University of Chicago Press.

Walsh, Sharon. 1997. "Former ADM Executive Indicted; Whitacre Charged with Stealing $9 Million While FBI Informant." *The Washington Post* (January 16):E1.

Weidenbaum, M. 1995. "The Evolving Corporate Board." *Society* 32:9–16.

Weisburd, David, Elin Waring, Stanton Wheeler. 1990. "Class, Status, and the Punishment of White-Collar Criminals." *Law and Social Inquiry* 15:223–243.

Wheeler, Stanton, David Weisburd, and Nancy Bode. 1982. Sentencing the White-Collar Offender: Rhetoric and Reality. *American Sociological Review* 47:641–659.

Willitts, William J. 1998. "Ajinomoto, Sewon Fined for Price-fixing in Food Industry." *The Ottawa Citizen* (July 24):D6.

Yeager, Peter. 1991. *The Limits of Law: The Public Regulation of Private Pollution*. Cambridge University Press: Cambridge.

Zey, Mary. 1993. *Banking on Fraud*. New York: Aldine De Gruyter.

APPENDIX

Products

Citric acid	An organic acid used in a variety of foods and beverages, including soft drinks, and as a preservative in prepared foods.
HFCS	High fructose corn syrup—a sweetener used in soft drinks (i.e., Coke and Pepsi)—product with the largest dollar market (of the three products)—not charged with price-fixing and exempt from prosecution because of plea agreement assuming they comply with the investigation.
Lysine	An amino acid used as an additive in poultry and pork feed that spurs the growth of the animals; a $600 million a year industry.

Players

Individuals

Marty Allison	Head of European Marketing for ADM—Fired
Dwayne Andreas	Chairman and Chief Executive of ADM (Michael's dad)
Michael (Mick) Andreas	Vice chairman and executive vice president of ADM (Dwayne's son)
Mark Cheviron	Head of ADM security
Sidney Hulse	Head of North American Marketing for ADM—Fired
Jhom Su Kim	From Sewon America Inc—paid fine and cooperated with investigation
Kanji Mimoto	From Ajinomoto Co.—paid fine and cooperated with investigation
James (Jim) Randall	ADM president
Reinhard Richter	President of ADM's Mexican subsidiary—Fired
Brian Shepard	FBI agent—head of FBI in Decatur, IL
Mark Whitacre	Former ADM directory and FBI informant
Terrance (Terry) Wilson	President of corn-processing division at ADM
Masaru Yamamoto	From Kyowa Hakko Kogyo Co.—paid fine and cooperated with investigation

Corporations

Ajinomoto Co. Inc.	(Japan) pleaded no contest but later pleaded guilty to lysine price-fixing
Kyowa Hakko Kogyo Co.	(Japan) pleaded guilty to lysine price-fixing
Sewon America Inc.	(South Korea) pleaded guilty to lysine price-fixing
Cheil Jadang Ltd.	(Seoul) pleaded guilty to lysine price-fixing

Time Line*

1984-1989	Whitacre works at Degussa, a German chemical company.
September 1989	ADM starts in lysine business (planning and designing).
October 1989	Whitacre became president of ADM's Biochem Products Division.
February 1991	ADM lysine business is up and running.

---

*Many items on time line came from Eichenwald (1997).

1992

February 1992   Whitacre formally introduced to ADM's price-fixing practices—he
                         began working with Wilson (serving as Whitacre's mentor) [*Fortune*
                         9/14/95]

April 1992   Whitacre and Wilson fly to Tokyo Japan to meet separately with
                         executives from Ajinomoto and Kyowa—talk of forming an amino
                         acid association.

June 23, 1992   ADM, Ajinomoto and Kyowa executives meet in Mexico City,
                         Mexico; no deals were made.

Late Summer 1992   Executives and engineers from Ajinomoto and Kyowa separately
                         visit ADM plant in Decatur, Illinois.

August 1992   Dwayne Andreas hears of a supposed plot of sabotage against ADM
                         by Japanese competitors and contacts the CIA.

October 1, 1992   Meeting in Paris, France.

November 3, 1992   Whitacre and Shepard have a four-hour conversation in Shepard's
                         car in Whitacre's driveway.

November 4, 1992   Whitacre begins cooperating and informing for the FBI.

December 22, 1992   Whitacre admits to the FBI he made up the sabotage story.

1993

January 9, 1993   Whitacre signs an agreement to be an informant for the FBI.

April 15, 1993   Meeting in Chicago, Illinois.

April 28, 1993   Meeting in Chicago, Illinois.

April 30, 1993   Meeting in Decatur, Illinois.

May 1993   Meeting in Tokyo, Wilson suggests forming a trade association to
                         cover secret meetings.

June 24, 1993   Meeting in Vancouver, Canada.

October 25, 1993   M. Andreas meets with Whitacre and two senior executives of
                         Ajinomoto to agree on total lysine production for 1994 in Irvine,
                         California.

November 23, 1993   A bogus invoice for $220,000 is sent to ADM for services rendered.
                         Whitacre approves the amount and paid the company. The money
                         goes into an account belonging to Whitacre.

December 8, 1993   During a meeting in Tokyo, lysine makers agree to report monthly
                         sales figures to an executive at Ajinomoto.

1994

March 10, 1994   During a meeting in Makaha, Hawaii, lysine makers swap sales data
                         and discuss the proposed trade group.

May 3, 1994   Whitacre submits bogus invoices and contracts to pay $2.5 million
                         to a foreign account for a firm (ABP International) that is controlled
                         by Whitacre.

October 13, 1994   Meeting in Chicago, Illinois.

1995

January 18, 1995   Meeting in Atlanta, Georgia.

February 21, 1995   Whitacre authorizes payment of $3.75 million to a company with a
                         Swiss bank account. The money is wired to an account controlled
                         by Whitacre.

June 27, 1995	Federal agents raid ADM headquarters in Decatur, Illinois.
June 29, 1995	ADM learns that Whitacre was an FBI informant.
August 1995	Whitacre admitted taking millions of dollars in off-the-book payments from ADM; ADM claims he embezzled the money; Whitacre claims it was part of an offshore compensation scheme approved by top management; prosecutors claim the payments violated Whitacre's immunity agreement with the Department of Justice (DOJ).
August 7, 1995	Whitacre is fired from ADM—six weeks after ADM learned of his undercover role; ADM accused him of embezzling $9 million from the company, $2.5 million of which was stolen while he was working with the FBI.
August 9, 1995	Whitacre attempts suicide by running his car inside his garage with the door closed. Whitacre's gardener finds him and revives him.
September 21, 1995	ADM fires three other executives they also accused of theft (Hulse, Allison, and Richter).
Early October 1995	Whitacre becomes chief executive of Future Health Technologies (a startup medical biotechnology firm).

1996

July 19, 1996	Federal judge approves ADM's agreement to pay $25 million to settle several civil suits contending lysine price-fixing.
August 27, 1996	Kyowa Hakko Kogyo Co. and Sewon America, Inc. plead guilty, and Ajinomoto Co. pleads no contest to price-fixing conspiracy for lysine; Ajinomoto and Kyowa Hakko Kogyo will each pay the maximum fine of $10 million while the amount for Sewon will be determined by the court. In addition to the fines, each of the three companies agrees to hand over documents to the government and will provide witnesses to testify. Kanji Mimoto (Ajinomoto Co.), Masaru Yamamoto (Kyowa Hakko Kogyo Co.), and Jhom Su Kim (Sewon America, Inc.) plead guilty, and paid fines ranging from $50,000 (Yamamoto) to $75,000 (Mimoto and Kim) and agree to cooperate fully with the investigation.
September 1996	ADM agrees to pay $65 million to settle two lawsuits charging securities fraud and price-fixing; $35 million to settle California charges accusing conspiracy with competitors for citric acid; $30 million to a shareholder in Illinois; in both cases ADM admits NO wrongdoing.
September 21, 1996	ADM sues Whitacre for embezzlement.
October 15, 1996	DOJ announces that ADM has agreed to plead guilty ("anticompetitive conduct") and pay a $100 million fine for its action in two international conspiracies (lysine—$70 million and citric acid—$30 million) which was to be paid by January 17, 1997.
October 17, 1996	Shareholders annual meeting; D. Andreas apologizes to shareholders and offers to resign. His resignation was rejected by the directors of ADM.
October 24, 1996	M. Andreas announced he was taking a temporary leave of absence (after the directors awarded him a 15% raise and raised his father's $3 million salary); T. Wilson would be retiring for medical reasons.

October 19, 1996	Federal Judge Castillo refuses to accept a plea of no contest from Ajinomoto due to evidence that they destroyed some relevant records.
November 15, 1996	Ajinomoto Co. pleads guilty in U.S. District Court to one count of conspiring with ADM, Kyowa Hakko Kogyo Co. and Sewon Co. to price-fixing of lysine.
November 22, 1996	Whitacre files a wrongful termination suit against ADM; charging that they fired him for cooperating with DOJ and defamed him by using embezzlement for his dismissal.
December 3, 1996	Michael D. Andreas, Terrance S. Wilson, and Ajinomoto Co. Managing Director Kazutoshi Yamada are indicted by a grand jury for conspiring to violate the Sherman Antitrust Act 15 USC § 1 by allegedly engaging in a three-year worldwide conspiracy to eliminate competition by fixing the price and allocating the sales volume of the feed additive lysine in the United States and worldwide. Mark E. Whitacre is also indicted on charges of price-fixing (lysine); says he will NO longer cooperate with prosecutors and plans to plead innocent. Cheil Jedang Ltd. (Seoul) agrees to plead guilty and pay $1.25 million fine for its part in the lysine case.
December 20, 1996	M. Andreas, T. Wilson, and M. Whitacre plead not guilty before U.S. District Judge Rebecca Dallmeyer on criminal charges of conspiring to fix prices; each was released on $4,500 bond; A bench warrant was issued for the 4th defendant, Kazutoshi Yamada—he was not in the country (*Washington Post* 12/20/96).

1997

January 15, 1997	A federal grand jury indicted Mark E. Whitacre on forty-five criminal counts for embezzling $9 million form ADM, money laundering, filing false income tax returns, and attempting to obstruct justice (*Washington Post* 1/16/97).
September 25, 1997	Whitacre files for bankruptcy.
October 10, 1997	Whitacre pleads guilty to thirty-seven criminal charges of fraud, money laundering, and tax evasion.

1998

January 13, 1998	Whitacre is sentenced (for pleading guilty to stealing $9 million from ADM) to serve a nine-year sentence and ordered to pay $11.4 million in restitution to ADM.
July 9, 1998	Criminal trial starts for three former ADM executives.
September 17, 1998	Jury finds Andreas, Whitacre, and Wilson guilty of conspiring to fix the global price and allocate the sales volume of lysine. Each are facing a maximum penalty of up to three years in jail and a $350,000 fine. However, the government can seek up to twice the amount gained by the crime or lost by the victims.
September 17, 1998	Federal judge Manning refused to reverse the convictions of Andreas, Whitacre, and Wilson, citing an abundance of evidence to support the conviction [*Milwaukee Journal Sentinel* 1/1/99].

1999

January 7, 1999	Sentencing scheduled for Andreas, Whitacre, and Wilson; postponed.
June 4, 1999	Federal judge decided that Andreas, Whitacre, and Wilson could not be charged more than $350,000 a piece.
July 9, 1999	Sentencing scheduled for Andreas, Whitacre, and Wilson.

The Westray Mine Disaster: Media Coverage of a Corporate Crime in Canada

Colin Goff

❖

"Anyone who wants to dig underground here is building a graveyard, not a mine."

Robert Hoegg, a retired miner

It has been a traditional complaint directed toward the news media that they have ignored stories about corporate crimes. Instead, attention has been placed on street crimes and sensational court cases involving high-profile violent offenders. According to Wright, Cullen, and Blankenship (1985), this omission "helps to reproduce inequality by directing public attention away from the enormous costs —including violent costs—associated with the 'crimes of the powerful.'"

However, there is evidence emerging that this trend is changing. Increasing media concern with the "social movement" against white-collar and corporate crime has led the news media to pay more attention to the 'crimes of the power-ful.' In the United States, the Milken insider trading scandal on Wall Street and the Lincoln Savings and Loan fraud case have been highly profiled by the media. Similarly, in Canada, various massive fraud court cases have been detailed by the media, such as the Principal Trust affair and the "Apartment Flip" scandal in Ontario. The media reports on these and other similar cases have raised great interest among the viewing and reading audience, if only for the reason that so many members of the public have been victimized by these fraudulent activities.

However, most of the in-depth media reports about corporate crime cases have centered on the nonviolent crimes of economic fraud and price-fixing. Virtually left ignored are those cases involving corporate actions that led to deaths among their employees as well as members of the public. Another limitation of the media is their tendency to focus on the criminal acts of individuals who work for the corporation rather than provide any insight about the role of the corporation or the "internal organizational climate" (Hills, 1987, 191).

Two notable exceptions to the media's reluctance to report corporate crimes involving violent behavior exist. Swigert and Farrell (1980) analyzed the media coverage of the Ford Pinto case in which the Ford Motor Company was charged with the offense of "reckless homicide" in Illinois. The authors carefully followed the news media's reports of the case and detected a change in how the media reported the actions of Ford Motor Company over time. Initially, the difficulties associated with the Ford Pinto were portrayed as a manufacturing problem. It was not until much later, during the grand jury hearings, that the actions of the Ford executives began to be analyzed. In addition, the researchers talked about the "personalization of harm," in which there was an increasing amount of attention placed upon the victims, and the fact that the incident was increasingly seen as a criminal act by the authorities until, of course, criminal charges were laid against Ford.

Wright, Cullen, and Blankenship (forthcoming) conducted a more detailed study into a case of corporate crime when twenty-five workers were killed during a fire at the Imperial Food Products Inc. chicken processing plant in Hamlet, North Carolina. They divided the newspaper accounts of the trial into various legal categories. They created two main categories, culpability and sanction. The category of culpability included the subcategories of "cause," "harm," "intent," and "responsibility." While the newspapers detailed the harm of the fire, they gave little if any indication that the corporate violence could be seen as a crime. As the authors found, the "reports did not define the deaths as homicides, nor did they raise the possibility that the corporation or individual executives might be eligible for prosecution." The media, they discovered, acted in a reactive rather than proactive mode. "It was not until the government announced the manslaughter plea bargain that the criminality of the violence was reported. This attention, however, occurred in the third time interval, during which the coverage was the least extensive and least prominently placed in the newspapers." Wright, Cullen, and Blankenship found that the news reports focused on the breakdown of government safety regulations as the "cause" of the worker deaths.

In the following study, we report on a Canadian coal mine explosion that caused the deaths of twenty-six miners. However, we start our newspaper analysis from the actual day of the explosion rather than looking exclusively at the trial(s). It was our intention to follow media accounts from the very beginning to see if the media took a proactive rather than reactive stance as well as to determine when and how they talked about the criminality of the corporation and/or mine managers.

The corporation involved, Curragh Resources, Inc. was to appear in court on criminal negligence charges in February, 1995, while four mine managers were scheduled to appear in court to face manslaughter charges at the end of March, 1995.

THE WESTRAY MINING DISASTER

When the Westray Mine officially opened on September 11, 1991, it was the cause of much celebration in the surrounding communities of Plymouth and Stellarton, Nova Scotia. Traditionally, unemployment in the area was high (over 25 percent), and many of the younger people had to leave to other parts of Canada to find employment. Westray promised to turn things around in a significant way: fifteen to twenty years of employment at good wages were guaranteed for 200 local residents and, of course, spinoff benefits for the local economy.

On May 9, 1992, just eight months after it opened, a predawn explosion at the Westray mine killed all twenty-six men on the night shift and completely demolished the mile-deep mine. The cause of the explosion was not immediately known, but initial assessments indicated that a methane gas fire ignited a coal dust explosion. Fifteen bodies were recovered, while eleven bodies were left in the mine due to the dangerous conditions in the mine shaft following the explosion.

Critics argued that the Westray mine should never have opened. The mine site had a history of high methane gas levels and had, over the decades, been responsible for the deaths of some 290 miners. However, the mining company, Curragh Resources, informed both federal and provincial authorities it was using the most recent and sophisticated testing equipment in order to ensure the safety of the miners working underground.

Once the immediate concerns about the explosion and recovering the bodies of the twenty-six miners (eleven bodies were never recovered) killed in the explosion subsided, numerous questions were raised almost immediately about the safety conditions in the mine. The media reported many safety problems at the Westray mine during its brief eight months of operation. In the preceding twelve months before the fatal explosion, the Nova Scotia Department of Labor recorded numerous dangerous incidents and hazards, including ten cave-ins and five reports of excessive coal dust levels. They also documented the need for limestone dust to be spread in order to neutralize the explosive qualities of the dust. In the Department of Labor records, however, there is only one reference to inspectors formally requesting the mine managers to comply with provincial regulations and reduce high methane levels.

The explosion produced a number of investigations into possible wrongdoing at the mine. There was an investigation by the Department of Labor into possible violations of the provincial Occupational and Safety Act, and a criminal investigation conducted by the Royal Canadian Mounted Police (RCMP). Both led to a number of charges being laid against Curragh and the mine managers.

METHODS

Sample

In order to evaluate the coverage of the Westray mine disaster, we conducted a content analysis of four newspapers (*The Globe and Mail*, *Halifax Chronicle Herald*, *Winnipeg Free Press*, and the *Vancouver Sun*). These newspapers were selected because of their national and regional coverage. *The Globe and Mail* was selected because it is considered Canada's national newspaper and, at the same time, gives much coverage to central Canadian news, while the other three newspapers represent some of the leading newspapers in the eastern, prairie, and pacific regions of Canada, respectively. These newspapers were not randomly selected; rather, they were chosen because they represent the four main regions as well as the nation. Previous studies have also used small sample studies: for example, Swigert and Farrell (1980) used a sample size of one, Morash and Hale (1983) used five, and Wright, Cullen, and Blankenship (forthcoming) looked at ten papers.

CONTENT CATEGORIES

The content categories were selected by reviewing the literature on corporate crime as well as the previous studies in the area. The main content categories selected from this review included cause, harm, intent, responsibility, and charges. No reference is made to sanctions because a court trial has not yet taken place. Our content categories, however, had to take into consideration other aspects of the disaster. Two new categories were developed because we are studying media coverage before as well as during the trial. These two new content categories were added: (1) politics and (2) probes, that is, federal and provincial government investigations into the cause of the explosion. The lines of each story were coded by one of the authors and checked by one of the other authors. In case of a disagreement, the third author solved the disagreement.

Cause

Almost immediately following the explosion, there were questions raised about the cause of the explosion and whether the disaster could have been prevented. The initial questions explored the possibility that the actions of either the workers (or a worker) or Curragh somehow caused the explosion. As a result, the content category of "cause" was divided into two subcategories: miners and the corporation. This reflects a concern about how the cause of the explosion was portrayed in the media. Were the workers at fault, i.e., did they ignore safety rules? Did the miners formally approach the corporation and register complaints about mine safety? Did Curragh ignore the safety warnings made by the miners or government inspectors, or did they attempt to make sure that the mine was safe? Any newspaper articles that did not describe the cause of the explosion were coded "no mention of safety."

Harm

The initial concern of the media concerning harm focused on the twenty-six miners who lost their lives in the explosion. Shortly thereafter, however, attention expanded to include both the families and friends of the dead miners. The impact of the disaster of the explosion was also explored by the media, particularly as it affected the local economy. Thus this category included three types of harm: (1) direct harm, i.e., those killed in the explosion; (2) residual harm, i.e., the family and friends of the workers; and (3) community harm, i.e., the impact on the community, such as the loss of employment and economic benefits. If there was no reference to harm, the newspaper article was categorized as "no mention of harm."

Intent

This category is important because it is necessary to prove intent in order to lay criminal charges. Since we are interested in corporate crime, this category specifically focuses on the way Curragh's role in the mine disaster was perceived by the media. Two different types of intent were used: (1) "overt" intent, such as ignoring safety orders, and (2) "indirect" intent, such as safety systems not meeting proper standards. If there was no mention of intent, the article was categorized as "no mention of intent."

Responsibility

Since our analysis of the mine disaster involves the initial explosion through to the conclusion of the trials, our interest lies in evaluating how responsibility for the explosion was constructed by the media. For example, did the responsibility for the explosion change over time? In this category, "management" refers to any statement that places the blame for the deaths of the workers on the management. Second, "corporation" refers to references stating that the corporation (Curragh Resources, Ltd.) was responsible for the deaths. Third, "regulatory agencies" refers to those articles where regulatory agencies and their inspectors were held responsible for the deaths of the workers. Fourth, "general responsibility" refers to instances where no specific actor was identified. Failure to mention responsibility was categorized as "no mention."

Charges

This category involves specific mention of actual charges being laid against Curragh or the mine managers. Various investigations were conducted after the explosion to assess whether or not Curragh or the mine managers could be charged with the violation of any laws. First, "provincial safety laws" relates to references to charges related to the Nova Scotia Occupational and Safety Health laws. Second, "mining regulations" relates to instances where newspaper articles made reference to charges being laid under the Nova Scotia Mining Regulation Act. Third, "criminal law" refers to possible or actual criminal law charges. Fourth, "civil law" is concerned with the possibility of violations of the civil law. No reference to charges was classified as "no mention of charges."

Politics

The role of politics in the explosion became an issue concerning both the federal and provincial governments' role in the funding and operation of the mine. "Funding" reflects a concern about the involvement of the federal and provincial governments' funding of Westray and if it compromised their position on safety issues. Second, "involvement" refers to whether or not the two governments overlooked proper safety standards in their initial reports concerning the viability of the mining operation. Third, "special favors" assesses whether or not the governments gave any special considerations to Curragh at any time during the planning stages or during its operation. Finally, the category of "no mention" refers to instances where there was no mention of politics.

Probes

A number of official inquiries were conducted into the explosion. Some were wide ranging, such as the provincial inquiry that was set up to explore a wide range of issues related to the explosion. "Provincial inquiry" therefore refers to the official Nova Scotia government probe into the disaster. Other inquiries were started to explore the possibility that laws may have been violated and that charges should be laid against the responsible parties. "Criminal inquiry" refers to the RCMP investigation, while "regulatory agency" deals with those incidents when a provincial regulatory agency investigated the explosion. "Royal Commission" relates to any references made to the federal Royal Commission that was charged with investigating the disaster. Finally, "challenge to provincial inquiry" deals with those instances when articles made reference to any legal challenges made against the legality of the provincial government inquiry. Last, articles that do not mention any investigation were categorized as "no mention."

Editorials

Editorials refers to all opinions related to the story. This includes both editorials proper and articles written by columnists. These articles are important because they go beyond the "objective" fact-based works produced by reporters. Editorials allow the writer to make associations between various events as well as to offer personal opinion. In this category, two types of editorials are identified— (1) editorials as written by the editorial staff of each newspaper, and (2) independent opinions written by newspaper columnists. Both of these were coded according to the categories listed above.

Time Intervals

As mentioned by Wright et al. (1985), news coverage is a dynamic process that changes over time. Three distinct time intervals were identified that correspond to important aspects of the Westray disaster. The first time interval began on the first day of coverage, May 11th, 1992 and ended one week later. The second interval began on May 18th, 1992 and ended on September 12, 1992, when attention centered on the probes. The third interval began on September 13, 1992 and continued to June 30, 1994.

RESULTS

Our results differ from all other previous research efforts exploring newspaper reporting of a corporate crime. It is not possible to directly compare the total number of newspaper articles covering the Westray disaster with the other studies because they focused mainly on trials. The number of articles in our study totalled 331. As revealed in Table 1, we discovered the number of media reports for each time period increased—from 35 in the first time interval (which covered one week) to 135 in the second (which covered a sixteen-week period) and 161 (which included thirty-eight weeks) in the third. All categories increased for each time interval (see Table 1) with the exception of intent, which experienced a minimal decrease between the second and third time intervals (25 to 21 articles) and cause, which decreased from 56 to 38 articles between the same time periods.

TABLE 1   Number of Categories by Time Interval

Category	Interval 1	Interval 2	Interval 3	Total
Cause	16	56	38	100
Harm	33	81	117	212
Intent	4	25	21	50
Responsibility	5	14	22	41
Charges	2	38	108	148
Politics	9	43	46	98
Probes	10	61	91	162

Throughout all time intervals, the media featured the Westray disaster as a high-profile story. The mean page number for interval 1 was A6, and all articles were located in the first section of the four newspapers. During the second interval, Westray was given more specialized treatment through weekend features located in a wide range of newspaper sections. The mean page number for the second time interval was 6.2 for section A, 9.0 for section B, 13.2 for section D, and 74.0 for section G. No articles appeared in either sections C or F. In the third interval the mean page number for section A was 7.8, section B was 5.5, section C was 7.2, and section D was 7.3.

The mean number of lines per story (Table 2) indicates how much information was given about Westray during each time period. There was remarkable similarity in the number of lines found in each time interval. There was a total of 90.1 lines during interval 1, 91.7 lines during interval 2, and 98.4 lines in interval 3.

Harm

This category was the largest of all the categories—212 (or 64%) of the articles mentioned something to do with harm. Table 1 reveals the media focused most of their attention on this issue during interval 1, as it was mentioned in all but two of the thirty-five newspaper articles. Direct harm was the most important subcategory during interval 1, and continued to be throughout both the second and third time intervals. Residual harm figured prominently during interval 1, but its' significance decreased substantially during the following two time intervals. During time interval 2, its significance became almost nonexistent. Community harm, on the other hand, became marginally more important during the third interval, as more attention was given to the impact of the mine layoffs within the community.

Probes

This was the second-largest category, with 162 articles discussing an inquiry or investigation. The most significant section of this category dealt with the provincial government inquiry into the mine disaster. Each article that discussed this topic averaged just under thirteen lines in time interval 1, and while the number of lines decreased to 5.54 in interval 2, it increased to 9.41 lines per article in time interval 3. The provincial government inquiry was virtually the only issue discussed in intervals 1 and 2. The first mention of the provincial inquiry occurred just seven days after the explosion on May 16, when Premier Cameron announced that "(n)othing and no person with any light on this tragedy will escape the scrutiny of this tragedy." While this subcategory continued to dominant this category during the next two time intervals, the subcategories of criminal inquiry and challenges to the provincial government inquiry became almost as significant during the third time interval. A police investigation into the possibility of criminal negligence at the mine was first discussed by the media on

TABLE 2   Mean Number of Lines by Categories by Time Intervals

Category	Interval 1	Interval 2	Interval 3
Cause			
1. Miners			
a. Negligence	.62	.42	.14
b. Safety	4.30	.07	4.07
2. Corporation			
a. Negligence	3.31	5.32	7.33
b. Safety	1.55	1.60	0
3. No mention	19	79	123
Harm			
1. Direct	2.12	1.05	1.13
2. Residual	1.03	.16	.33
3. Community	0.61	.38	.85
4. No mention	1	13	3
Intent			
1. Overt	6.01	11.60	7.54
2. Indirect	3.33	1.10	1.31
3. No mention	31	110	140
Responsibility			
1. Management	0	.28	.63
2. Corporation	.35	1.08	.24
3. Regulatory Agency	.35	3.74	1.49
4. General	0	.89	1.80
5. No mention	30	108	136
Charges			
1. OSHA	0	2.47	6.72
2. MR Act	2.04	3.63	.62
3. RCMP	4.07	7.26	4.01
4. Civil	0	0	.41
5. No mention	33	97	53
Politics			
1. Funding	7.80	4.97	3.81
2. Role	1.07	1.38	9.57
3. Favors	0	1.78	.86
4. No mention	26	92	115
Probes			
1. Provincial	12.7	5.54	9.41
2. RCMP	0	.63	6.01
3. Regulatory Agency	0	.09	0
4. Royal Commission	0	.56	.45
5. Challenge	0	0	7.05
6. No mention	25	92	70

June 13. Just over three months later, on September 17, the Halifax Chronicle Herald announced the police had sufficient evidence to charge the corporation with criminal negligence, although the report noted that no criminal charges were pending against the mine managers. Two weeks later, however, it was announced that the RCMP were "investigating into the criminal responsibility of three members of the mine's management."

There was also considerable media attention to the challenges against the various inquiries by both Curragh and the mine managers. These legal arguments involved constitutional issues, as legal counsel for both corporation and the mine managers argued, successfully as it turned out, that their clients could not be tried for both regulatory and criminal cases for the same action. As a result of this successful legal argument, the regulatory charges were dropped.

Charges

The various subcategories of the "charges" category received significant amounts of attention during all time intervals. As indicated in Table 1, during the first time interval the discussion of charges for violations of both regulatory or criminal law offenses were discussed just twice. During the second time interval, this category increased substantially to a total of thirty-eight articles. Most of the attention went to the topic of criminal charges. As a result of the actual laying of charges during the third time period under both the provincial Occupational and Safety Act (OSHA) and the federal Criminal Code, these two subcategories increased to 6.72 and 4.01 articles lines per article respectively.

On October 5, 1992, the first charges were laid against Curragh. On this date the Nova Scotia Department of Labor laid fifty-two charges under OSHA against Curragh and four mine managers. Under OSHA, each charge contains the potential for a one-year jail sentence and a maximum $10,000 fine, or both. The charges alleged violations of coal dust levels in the mine, lack of adequate ventilation, alteration to methane detectors, and an apparent lack of compliance by mine managers to correct safety violations formally registered by mine inspectors. Thirty-four of these charges were dropped on December 10, 1992, as the province decided not to prejudice the RCMP criminal investigation. The remaining eighteen charges were dropped soon after in order to avoid jeopardizing the constitutional rights of anyone who faces criminal charges.

Charges of criminal negligence were first mentioned on June 13, 1992, when a newspaper report stated the RCMP were investigating "criminal negligence at the mine." During the remainder of the second time interval, discussion of charges under the Criminal Code were received in-depth coverage. The issue of criminal charges extended into the third time interval with continuing, if not sporadic, announcements of suspected criminal wrongdoing. On September 19, 1992, for example, it was reported the RCMP "allege that Curragh Resources Inc.

. . .caused the death of 15 miners." Two weeks later, on October 2, there was the first mention that the mine managers were facing criminal charges. Charges of manslaughter and criminal negligence causing death were laid on April 20, 1993, against Curragh and two mine managers, respectively.

Responsibility

Responsibility was rarely dealt with by the media, with only 41 of the 331 newspaper articles referring to this issue. Attention was directed to the actions of a provincial regulatory agency—the Nova Scotia Department of Labor—whose mandate it was to enforce safety standards. Concern was raised about the enforcement of safety legislation, and whether or not inspectors were lax in their duties. While mine inspectors formally ordered the mine managers just ten days before the explosion to clean up potentially explosive coal dust "immediately to 'prevent explosions,'" they never returned to see if their orders were carried out. Curragh had placed bags of limestone in the mine, but still had seven days left before they were in violation of the order. However, the media discovered this formal complaint, made just two weeks prior to the explosion for excessive coal dust, was the ninth since the start up of the operation. The other eight complaints were informal, and the mine managers always promised to implement a plan for diluting the coal dust. Despite these warnings, "work at the mine never stopped and documents show little evidence that those problems were adequately addressed."

Cause

The cause of the explosion throughout all three intervals was placed squarely on the mine managers' negligence about safety at the mine site. According to the media, it became apparent that the specific cause of the explosion was the mine managers' lack of concern over the high methane levels and failure to follow provincial government safety orders. During the first two time intervals, however, the media reported on Curragh's concern about safety issues. On May 11, for example, three days after the explosion, mine managers informed the media the "necessary safety precautions were taken," that the mine contained the "most modern methane detection monitors" and "the explosion occurred so quickly that nothing could be done to prevent it." Workers were portrayed as being concerned about safety in the mine, but their complaints about safety issues went unheeded by the mine managers.

Politics

While this category ranked fifth in terms of the total number of articles printed, it was given some of the greatest amount of attention in terms of the total number of lines published. In the third interval almost ten lines in each newspaper article which dealt with this issue were devoted to this issue. Each time interval saw increasing concern over the role of both the federal and provincial governments.

The immediate media concern, however, was over government funding for the mine and whether or not this led to a lack of concern over health and safety matters. The fact that Curragh received $80 million in federal loan guarantees and $12 million in provincial funding proved to be the source of much media speculation about whether both levels of government ignored health and safety issues. Curragh was also the recipient of $3.6 million from the federal government for tax purposes, with the result that they ended up with a "profit" of some $4 million from the funding they received from federal and provincial governments.

In the third time interval, the subcategory of "funding" grew dramatically. The more the media found out about the financial involvement of both governments, the more they questioned the ability of either level of government to insure proper safety conditions at the mine. Many articles expressed a concern that the investigations would not be comprehensive and would cover-up most of the important issues. For example, it was discovered the federal government ignored advice from its own mining experts. In a report prepared by the Canada Center for Mineral and Energy Technology investigating the feasibility of the mine, the investigator concluded that Westray's plan for dealing with methane seepage and ventilation "does not give one confidence."

Intent

Table 1 reveals this category was rarely discussed by the media in terms of the total number of articles, with only fifty articles mentioning this topic. However, in terms of the total number of lines per article, this category ranked among the highest. For example, overt intent never received less than six lines per article for all three time intervals. Immediately following the explosion, questions were raised about Curragh's overt intent. The focus of media attention first centered on Curragh's knowledge of the problems and their lack of action about safety in the mine. A partial list of questions about Curragh's actions included the tampering of methane monitors so they would not go off. It was later discovered that Curragh allowed workers to bring unauthorized equipment into the mine. The emphasis on overt intent suggests the media attempted to bring to light the excessive risks involved with working at the mine.

Indirect intent was a minor issue with the exception of interval 1, before the media had found the answers to many of the questions they were asking about mine safety. Once these answers were obtained, the media were quick to focus their energies upon direct intent.

Editorials

As there were only a total of twenty editorials, we decided this figure was too small to categorize them according to the three time intervals. Instead, we totalled all the lines into a cumulative figure for each subcategory. These totals and subcategories are found in Table 3.

Cause. Very little attention was given to this category. Miners' negligence received six lines, and Curragh's negligence received five lines. Most of the attention was given to the critics category, but this only received mention in fifty-five lines. Thirteen editorials did not mention cause.

Violation. This category also received very little attention in the editorials. Provincial safety laws received mention in thirty lines, while mining regulations and criminal law received only two lines each.

Harm. This category was of greater interest. Both direct and residual harm received significant attention. Direct harm was mentioned in fifty-seven lines, while residual and community harm were mentioned in seventy-three and eight lines, respectively.

Responsibility. The editorials were not concerned with the issue of responsibility. In fact, this was one of the categories that received the least amount of attention. The subcategories of management and corporation received no mention whatsoever. The category of "general" was mentioned in only eleven lines, while regulatory agencies were mentioned in five.

Intent. Closely related to the above category, this category also received minimal attention. The subcategory "overt intent" received no attention at all, while "indirect" received only fourteen lines.

Politics. This was the most frequently mentioned category, with a total of 404 lines. The editorial writers were much more concerned with searching out political wrongdoing than they were with attaching legal blame for the deaths of the twenty-six miners. "Special favors" received the most attention with 170 lines, followed closely by provincial and federal government involvement with 168 lines. Political and federal funding received sixty-six lines, and there was no mention of politics in six articles.

Probes. This category also received a significant amount of attention. However, the majority of the editorials focused on only one subcategory, the provincial

TABLE 3   Number of Editorials for all Time Intervals

Editorials	Interval 1–3
Cause	
1. Miners	
a. Negligence	6
b. Safety	0
c. No mention	9
2. Corporation	
a. Negligence	5
b. Safety	0
c. No mention	13
Harm	
1. Direct	57
2. Residual	73
3. Community	8
4. No mention	4
Intent	
1. Overt	0
2. Indirect	14
3. No mention	19
Responsibility	
1. Management	0
2. Corporation	0
3. Regulatory Agency	5
4. General	11
5. No mention	15
Charges	
1. OSHA	30
2. MR Act	2
3. RCMP	2
4. Civil	0
5. No mention	14
Politics	
1. Funding	66
2. Role	168
3. Favors	170
4. No mention	6
Probes	
1. Provincial	233
2. RCMP	38
3. Regulatory Agency	1
4. Royal Commission	0
5. Challenge	60
6. No mention	8

inquiry. There was great concern about the scope and legitimacy of the inquiry and whether or not the mandate was appropriate. There was also concern about the constitutionality of the inquiry. The subcategory "challenge" received only sixty lines.

DISCUSSION

What emerges from this analysis is a picture of how and what the media reports when it provides coverage on a violent corporate act. Similar to other studies of newspaper coverage (e.g., Swigert and Farrell; Wright et al.), our interest lies in how newspapers construct the reality of corporate violence for their readers. Our analysis differs, however, because we studied the pretrial reports of four news-papers. Newspaper coverage of such events are important because they inform us about the quality of the investigations into the particular issue, how certain key actors—such as different government agencies as well as individual politi-cians—react both officially and unofficially, and the different legal challenges to potential official actions. Pretrial coverage, then, can give us insights into a whole series of events that may have a significant impact on the actual trial.

Some observers of corporate and white-collar crime believe that much of what actually happens in the courtroom depends on the actions of officials during the pretrial investigations and discussions between prosecutors and defendants. If corporate officials are treated leniently, then much of the reason(s) may be found in the actions of the investigators before any trial begins. And, as Croall (1992) suggests, not only do the "distinctive characteristics of white collar crime strongly affect legal proceedings," but the "proceedings for different groups of offenders varies considerably." Since this is an analysis of a case in which twenty-six miners died, possibly due to criminal negligence, one would expect it to receive the type of newspaper coverage that it did. Three hundred and thirty-one newspaper articles over a fifty-five week period attests to the great interest of the media. But what did the media give their attention to?

The newspaper reports clearly reflected the immense harm that resulted from the explosion. The deaths of the 26 miners, the residual harm suffered by the families, and the harm to the community were all given constant exposure. Throughout the whole time period under analysis, there were only seventeen newspaper articles which contained no mention of harm.

The category of "cause" reveals the media consistently blamed Curragh Resources, Inc. for the explosion. The subcategory of "corporation–negligence" more than doubled in the number of lines between intervals one and three—from 3.31 lines to 7.33 lines per article, respectively. "Cause" was an issue for the media from the start of their coverage. On the first day of newspaper coverage of the explosion, the *Halifax Chronicle Herald* quoted the United Steelworkers Union representative at the mine as saying "safety procedures have been 'cir-cumvented' by the company, both out of neglect and a desire to get the mine in operation as soon as possible." Another article reported miners were "'scared to death' about working conditions at Westray but they were afraid complaints would cost them their jobs." Over the three time intervals, Curragh's concern for miner safety decreased from 1.55 lines per article when the issue was raised to none at all. During the first time interval the media also raised the issue that the miners may have inadvertently caused the explosion by violating safety regulations. A newspaper report on May 16, 1992, quoted a miner (who had quit his job at Westray) saying that numerous safety rules were constantly broken. For example, he stated miners used propane torches and smoked in the mine—activities forbidden by provincial safety regulations. These accusations soon died, and workers were thereafter viewed as being very concerned about safety.

What becomes apparent is that the media downplayed the criminal aspect of the Westray mining disaster. The legal issues of "intent" and "responsibility," as they applied to both Curragh Resources, Inc. and the mine managers at the Westray mine site, were given little exposure. These two categories, when combined, totalled ninety-one articles, seven articles less than the next smallest category, "politics," which consisted of ninety-eight articles. The category of "intent" never accounted for more than 20 percent of the total number of articles for any one time interval, while, for the category of "responsibility," that figure never exceeded 15 percent. These findings are similar to those found by Wright, et al., who discovered that the newspaper "reports did not define the deaths as homicides," or that "the corporation and individual executives might be eligible for prosecution." Instead, the media essentially played a reactive rather than a proactive role. When safety or criminal charges were laid in court, they dutifully reported the events but did not make much of an effort to detail or elaborate on such issues.

The media ignored calling the Westray mine explosion a "homicide" and rarely if ever followed up on this issue with any investigative reports. Corporate officials at Curragh Resources' head office in Toronto began to legally distance themselves from the mine managers' lack of concern about safety when it became apparent criminal charges were going to be laid. For example, on October 16, 1992 (just 10 days after the provincial Department of Labor had laid fifty-two charges under the provincial OSHA), Curragh executives released a memo indicating they "threatened" the mine managers with disciplinary actions "unless steps were taken to improve working conditions underground."

Instead, media attention focused on the categories of "harm," "charges," and "probes." These three categories, when combined, were mentioned in a total of 522 articles. All three categories experienced substantial levels of growth during both the second and third time intervals. The category of "probes" increased by thirty articles, while "harm" increased by thirty-six articles and "charges" by a total of seventy articles.

What became clear to the media was that the Westray mine managers consistently ignored safety orders handed to them by provincial safety inspectors.

Documents obtained by *The Globe and Mail* revealed that "on 9 occasions over 14 months prior to the explosion, Department of Labor officials urged Westray to improve its system of distributing limestone dust to dilute the explosive coal dust. Mine managers always agreed to institute a plan for diluting the coal dust." While the media criticized the mine managers for their lack of concern about safety, they also pointed out the number of informal orders coupled with the lack of sufficient enforcement procedures by provincial regulatory officials was clearly unacceptable. For awhile, it appeared the same trend about improper enforcement of government safety standards was appearing in the Westray mine explosion as it had in Wright, et al.'s study of the Imperial Food Products, Inc. plant. They discovered that their news reports "constructed the worker deaths as a breakdown in government safety regulation. . .and the failure of OSHA to conduct an inspection of working conditions." News reports about the Westray mine indicated it was "given a kid-glove treatment by every government department they came in contact with," and that workers safety concerns "fell on deaf ears, whether in the company or in the government." And the Minister of Labor was quoted as saying "he did not know why no charges were laid or no order was made to close the mine" when questioned some two weeks after the explosion. As the media's investigation into the enforcement of safety standards progressed, they discovered more cases of lax enforcement procedures. On July 30, 1992, it was reported by the *Halifax Chronicle Herald* that the Department of Labor took no action "after a March 28 cave-in which produced high methane levels with as much as four percent in the southwest part of the plant."

In our analysis, however, we found the newspaper coverage of the actions of the regulatory agencies were used to investigate whether or not there were any special favors accorded Westray by the provincial government. There was a strong suspicion that senior Department of Labor officials gave the Westray mine "special treatment" over safety issues. This potential connection was first reported on August 26, 1992, when an article in the *Halifax Chronicle Herald* quoted the lawyer representing the families of the dead miners as saying that the "more insidious spinoff may have been the corruption of a system in which government officials and mines personnel allowed suspicious financial deals and a deadly combination of violations of law and safety practices."

What was unique about the media coverage of the Westray mining disaster was the manner and degree to which the media went to explore the possibility of political wrongdoing. Indeed, it was in these categories that the media acted in a significant proactive manner, particularly in the editorials. A great amount of attention was placed on the role of the federal and provincial governments in allowing the mine to receive the appropriate licenses to operate in apparent unsafe conditions as well as their disregard for ensuring proper safety standards. The fact that this area was once represented in the House of Commons by the Prime Minister of Canada, as well as the then-Premier of Nova Scotia, no doubt gave the media incentive to explore the possibilities of political wrongdoing. It was the actions of the politicians and governments, and not those of Curragh, that held the attention of the media prior to the court cases. Indeed, it was the media's attention upon the actions of the politicians and government agencies that provided the main counterforce to the possibility of any shortcomings occurring in the planned public inquiry of the mine explosion. Their determination, while unrewarded in the sense of not uncovering any major examples of political wrongdoing, made the government and its various agencies wary of taking any shortcuts or sidestepping important issues. Given all the attention on the disaster, it appears they have succeeded by getting the corporation and mine managers to court.

REFERENCES

Croall, H. (1992). *White Collar Crime*. Buckingham: Open University Press.

Evans, S. S. and Lundman, R. J. (1983). "Newspaper Coverage of Corporate Price-Fixing." *Criminology* 21, (4):529–41.

Hills, S. L. (1987). *Corporate Violence: Injury and Profit for Death*. Totowa, NJ: Rowman and Littlefield.

Morash, M. and Hale, D. (1987). "Unusual Crime or Crime as Unusual?" Images of Corruption at the Interstate Commerce Commission." Pp. 129–149 in T. S. Bynum (ed.) *Organized Crime in America*. Monsey Press, NY.: CT Press.

Swigert, V. L. and Farrell, R. A. (1980). "Corporate Homicide: Definitional Processes in the Creation of Deviance." *Law and Society Review* 15, (1):161–82.

Wright, J. P., Cullen, F. T., and Blankenship, M. L. (1985). "The Social Construction of Corporate Violence: Media Coverage of the Imperial Food Products, Inc. Fire." *Crime & Delinquency* 41:20–36.

V

STUDIES IN SOCIAL CONTROL

Technology, Risk Analysis, and The Challenge of Social Control*

James F. Short, Jr.

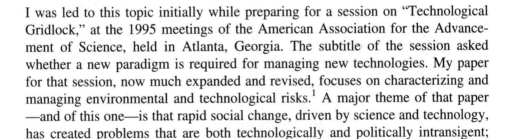

I was led to this topic initially while preparing for a session on "Technological Gridlock," at the 1995 meetings of the American Association for the Advancement of Science, held in Atlanta, Georgia. The subtitle of the session asked whether a new paradigm is required for managing new technologies. My paper for that session, now much expanded and revised, focuses on characterizing and managing environmental and technological risks.[1] A major theme of that paper —and of this one—is that rapid social change, driven by science and technology, has created problems that are both technologically and politically intransigent; thus seemingly beyond our ability to reach acceptable solutions by democratic means.

The example cited in the abstract is the failure of political, economic, and scientific institutions in the United States to reach agreement as to the best, and safest, means of disposing of the high-level nuclear waste (HLNW) that results from the generation of electric power by nuclear reactors. Disagreements concerning this problem are technical, economic, but most of all social and political. The controversy has resulted in what has become known as technological or

*An earlier version of this paper was presented at the annual meeting of the Japanese Association of Sociological Criminology, held in Yokohama, October 24, 1998. This is yet another effort on my part to join my first sociological specialty (criminology) with my second (risk analysis). See, also, Randall and Short, 1983; Short, 1984, 1999. I am grateful to Charles Tittle and Robert K. Merton for constructive comments.

managerial "gridlock," that is, the apparent inability to solve the problem by democratic political means. Similarly, protection of nuclear stockpiles against contamination, theft and/or terrorist acquisition has achieved global proportions. Although they have not as yet become "gridlocked," control of biotechnologies against criminal appropriation and other misuse poses similar threats (see Henderson, 1999).

Amidst much speculation as to how and why such problems are to be addressed, a recently issued report of a National Research Council panel offers a provocative challenge.[2] Titled *Understanding Risk: Informing Decisions in a Democratic Society*, the report modifies and elaborates the notion of risk *assessment*, traditionally the most "science-oriented" phase of risk analysis (see Stern and Fineberg, 1996). The panel advocates a change in terminology, calling for risk *characterization*, thus signifying a broader process that recognizes the necessity of making this phase of risk analysis more responsive to the people who will be affected by decisions involving risky and uncertain outcomes. If it is to be successful, the report argues, risk characterization must be considered at the very *beginning* of risk decision making and become *integral* to it. It should recognize all significant concerns and reflect both analysis and deliberation, with appropriate input from interested and affected parties, and it should be appropriate to policy decisions that are made regarding risks that are identified in the process. That is, when decisions that expose people to risks are to be made, officials of responsible governments or corporations must recognize the concerns of interested and affected parties and involve them in the analyses and deliberations through which risk-related decisions affecting policies and practices are made.

TAKING STAKEHOLDERS SERIOUSLY

Criminologists will recognize in this language the sorts of considerations that are associated with developments such as "community" and "problem-oriented" policing, community courts and corrections, concerns for the rights and the welfare of crime victims, and for those convicted of crime; that is, recognition of concerns beyond specific criminal behaviors, the apprehension, trial, and conviction of criminals, and their punishment or treatment. Such policies are based, also, on awareness of the importance of involving in law making and enforcement interested parties in addition to legislatures and law enforcement agencies, and beyond individual victims and perpetrators of crime.

The theoretical principles underlying these developments are seldom recognized. The first, stated explicitly more than 40 years ago, is that a "stake in conformity" is important in promoting law-abiding behavior by individuals, and in preventing criminal behavior, *because it motivates individuals to be law abiding* (Toby, 1957). It follows from this principle that failure to recognize and reward stakeholders weakens their motivation to endorse and abide by legal mandates. Second, because persons, groups, organizations, and communities (in addition to the perpetrators, immediate victims, and the enforcers of criminal laws) are involved both in the production of crime and as victims, interested parties (stakeholders) in law making, law breaking, and enforcement include, *by definition*, these persons, groups, organizations, and communities. In the present context, because much of the behavior, and many of the risks at issue, are subject to civil and/or administrative law, this principle applies to these bodies of law, as well. This principle, and a third of more recent vintage, is continually evolving: many risks have increased in scale (in time, space, and complexity) and in their interdependency (tighter coupling; see Perrow, 1984). Corresponding changes in the scale of risk characterization and management are required.

Large scale networks of nations, corporations, institutions, and non-governmental organizations (NGOs) increasingly influence and control activities such as law and rule-making and enforcement, and the conduct of multitudinous affairs that involve and affect large numbers of people, individually and in a variety of collective forms. Hazards such as ozone depletion, climate change, and toxic threats, rapidly changing market conditions throughout the globe, and ethnic conflicts that threaten international security spawn new international organizations that are designed to cope with many such problems. Treaties are formulated, international conferences are held, findings and goals promulgated, and social movements and social movement organizations (SMOs, an increasingly important category of NGO) emerge as interested parties and seek to have their voices heard and their concerns addressed. In the course of all of this activity laws change, new rules are developed, and criteria for determining culpability are altered. Individual and collective obligations also change, often by legal mandate, resulting in new types of law breaking and new classes of law breakers.

The NRC panel's insistence that "interested and affected parties" be represented in analyses and deliberations of risk characterization challenges traditional risk assessment and risk management theories and practices which, until recently, have focused almost exclusively on technical assessments of risks and management policies and decisions based on those assessments. By emphasizing that "all significant concerns" should be recognized, the notion of stakeholders thus is extended.

This paper extends the notion of stakeholders beyond traditional concerns of criminology and risk analysis. Stakeholders include communities, ethnic groups, corporations, nations, and NGOs. My thesis is that rapid social change, driven largely by advances in science and technology, poses unprecedented challenges for all of the social and behavioral sciences, as well as other scientific, political, economic, and social institutions. I phrase this theme more broadly than the customary concerns of criminology in order to promote participation and cooperation of all interested and affected parties in the making and enforcement of laws and rules concerning these new challenges.

Taking the notion of stakeholders seriously is important for still other theoretical reasons. Robert K. Merton noted more than half a century ago the consequences of severe disjunctures between culturally generated goals and the socially structured means of their attainment (Merton, 1938). Merton's chief focus was on strains created for those whose opportunities for success—a culturally mandated goal—were handicapped by virtue of their position in the social order (e.g., social class, racial, or ethnic status), although he was equally sensitive to anomic strains among the successful (see Merton, 1964).

Strains related to risks and uncertainties of "late modernity" are of a different order. One of the "dominant sources of dynamism of modernity," Anthony Giddens (1990) argues, is the *reflexivity* of human societies. In cultures dominated by tradition, reflexivity—defined as the uniquely human ability to continuously monitor one's own behavior and its contexts—"inserts any particular activity or experience within the continuity of past, present, and future" as these are understood by virtue of "recurrent social practices" (Giddens, 1990, 37). In contrast, the "reflexivity of modern social life consists in the fact that social practices are constantly examined and reformed in the light of incoming information about those very practices. . ." (p. 38). Although he recognizes that much variation exists in the extent to which individuals, groups, and organizations think, plan, and act on the basis of such reflection, Giddens illustrates his point by noting that "virtually everyone contemplating marriage has some idea of how family institutions have been changing, changes in the relative social position and power of men and women, alterations in sexual mores, etc.—all of which enter into processes of further change which they reflexively inform" (p. 43). Put more broadly, citizens in all late modern states not only have access to official statistics and reports from other statistics producing entities ("constitutive of state power and many other modes of social organization"); they are virtually bombarded with such information, and much more on every topic imaginable in the form of commercial advertising, media "experts," neighbors, politicians, local pundits, and other information sources.

The resulting surfeit of information is received and interpreted in a variety of contexts, often in fragmented and confusing form; hence, the seeming paradox that increased information, and access to it, results not in more certainty as to choices among possible courses of action and decision making, but in less. Information overload and inequities related to differential access to information and expertise lead, in turn, to an increase in *uncertainty*. In his discussion of this phenomenon Giddens turns the popular social construction that conflates science and certainty on its head: "In science," he observes, "*nothing* is certain, and nothing can be proved," despite the fact that "scientific endeavor provides us with the most dependable information about the world to which we can aspire. In the heart of the world of hard science, modernity floats free" (p. 39).[3]

For most people, even in the most modern of societies, the effects of modernity on everyday life are not quite as free-floating as this; nor are they with regard to many of the concerns of criminology. Life has always been uncertain, and many aspects of living are less uncertain in the past. Traditions, customs, laws, and rules continue to exert strong influences on thinking and decision-making in families and communities, and in behavior related to crime. Nevertheless, the advent of late modernity clearly has eroded many of those traditions and customs, as well as laws and rules that are designed formally to control much human behavior. Here the strain lies in the disjuncture between cultural elements (scientific and technological developments seemingly beyond common—or expert—understanding), related fears generated by risks and uncertainties, acknowledged and unacknowledged (which, in turn, may alter cultural phenomena), and the lack of clear personal and institutional means of their control.

Advances in information technology both enhance the efficiency of institutions of social control and complicate their tasks. New crimes are created (computer crime) and old crimes (e.g., fraud and "con games") assume new forms, and the boundaries of civil rights are stretched (whether, or how, to control access to pornography). Criminal networking beyond geographical and political boundaries become possible; information about criminal techniques can be disseminated on a scale hitherto impossible. The possibilities seem endless. For these types of crime the active participation and cooperation of the citizenry are especially critical.

Ulrich Beck (1992) theorizes that developments associated with late modernity profoundly change the underlying logic of society, from the "logic of wealth distribution in a society of scarcity to the logic of risk distribution in late modernity" (p. 20). Risk is "*politically reflexive*," leading to "anxiety-based solidarity" among affected populations (p. 21, emphasis in original; p. 49, et. passim). Although he acknowledges that many of the risks of the emerging "risk society" have a "boomerang effect" that victimizes all, Beck hypothesizes that fear of "invisible" hazards may serve as a motivator for collective action toward changing the status quo which denies protection.

Beck offers little evidence as to whether, or how, this may come about. Evidence is, in fact, sketchy at best. Studies in the United States find that the victims of hazards often are stigmatized, rather than sympathized with, thus perhaps displacing anxiety (see, e.g., Edelstein, forthcoming; Picou and Gill, forthcoming; Erikson, 1994). Still, field research conducted by Andrew Szasz suggests that immediate concerns over toxic wastes, combined with more general environmental concerns, have in some cases been joined with civil rights concerns to create potentially powerful social movements and social movement organizations (SMOs) with considerable political influence.[4]

ON MEASURING EFFECTS

The research literature often depicts the effects of both crime and physical hazards (natural and man-made) in monetary terms and in terms of physical injury or death rates for political units (cities, regions, nations). Important as these are, less tangible effects, e.g., on values and cultural understandings regarding "morality, equity, justice, and honor," (see Rappaport, 1996, p. 65), are ignored. The latter are likely to become even more important as risks and uncertainties assume more global dimensions. Most of the research literature on these topics has a distinctly local character, even though some types of crime (drug "epidemics," white-collar and organized crime) and some types of hazard (floods, droughts, and earthquakes) have widespread consequences that cross community and regional boundaries.[5] Portrayals of effects on daily life tend to emphasize immediate physical conditions that affect social and economic aspects of life in local communities. Increasingly, however, daily life is likely to be affected by events far removed from local communities and beyond the purview of local community control. For example, although international attention to bioterrorism has focused primarily on its use by rogue governments, local incidents such as the sarin gas attack in Tokyo, in 1995, demonstrate the potential for widespread use of biological agents for criminal purposes by private parties.

Complicating problems of control, compared to the past there is today less uncritical acceptance by citizens—individually and collectively—of tradition, in general, and of authority and agencies of control. Expertise is also subject to challenge, in part as a result of conflicting claims amidst the glut of information bearing on human problems, from the most trivial to the most serious. Science, and its handmaiden, rational choice, are not immune to such challenges. The very nature of science, in which knowledge often is incomplete and ever changing, frequently produces conflicting findings and claims, adding to confusion and weakening acceptance of scientific claims to authority. Rational thought, so vital to understanding complex problems, loses its hold on many who view with alarm the challenges posed by rapid and unpredictable social change.

There are no easy answers to such problems; nor assurance that they would be accepted if there were. But important clues emerge from recent research and theoretical and didactic explorations by social and behavioral scientists. The remainder of this paper draws upon a few of these in the search for possible solutions.

SEARCHING FOR SOLUTIONS

Governments throughout the world now struggle with complex and seemingly intransigent problems. Some of these fall clearly within the purview of criminology: international production and distribution of illegal drugs and related "money laundering," and fraud that cuts across international boundaries, control of nuclear stockpiles against possible theft and illegal sale, as well as other types of organized criminal activity and international terrorism, ethnic "cleansing" and genocide—and other behaviors that either are, or seem likely to come, within the purview of national and international law. Regrettably, a long list could be generated.

These types of crime are a far cry from the preoccupation of most criminologists with juvenile delinquency, so-called "street crime," or white-collar crime as traditionally conceptualized. Note, however, that both traditional crimes and technologically driven problems such as the disposal of high level nuclear waste and international terrorism involve very large numbers and types of individuals, organizations, and other collective entities. Indeed, the reach of some of these problems, e.g., a variety of nuclear-related issues and sustainable human ecology (Freese, 1997) are such that all inhabitants of the earth may be considered stakeholders. As knowledge regarding such issues becomes more refined and diffused, the likelihood that their control will come under the rubric of national and international law and other control mechanisms increases.

My argument is not that all the world's peoples must become one gigantic focus group! Rather, there are many ways for stakeholders to become involved in understanding and control of both criminal and other risk-related problems. In addition to the obvious connections between drug trafficking and other forms of organized crime, and street crime in local precincts, it is likely that additional behaviors will be criminalized—or will in any case come to be regulated in ways that will require stakeholder involvement if they are to be successful.

Let me illustrate by returning briefly to the nuclear waste controversy. I cannot, of course, review the controversy in detail (see, e.g., Rosa and Clark, forthcoming; Flynn, et al., 1995; Dunlap, et al., 1993; Shrader-Frechette, 1993). Suffice to say that nuclear power and its residues (high-level nuclear waste) are especially threatening because—like many other global and large-scale criminal activities—known and potential control failures threaten widespread devastation (in the case of nuclear failure, contamination and destruction extending far beyond local and national boundaries). Understanding them, and their management, therefore, are of more than local or national concern.

Disposal of high-level nuclear waste has created controversy among many segments of the United States: (1) between the State of Nevada and much of the rest of the country, while creating concern in other states through which high-level nuclear waste would pass on its way to a repository located at Yucca Mountain; (2) between power companies and the U.S. Department of Energy; (3) among and between Native American (Indian) tribes; (4) among citizen groups representing a variety of causes; and (5) among scientists. At least as important as the technical aspects of the controversy, however, is the manner in which the controversy has been handled by the United States government.

The Nuclear Waste Disposal Act of 1984 mandated exploration of the feasibility of establishing a high-level nuclear waste facility among several sites, each of which was to be scientifically evaluated as to its safety and suitability for a repository. Yucca Mountain, in Nevada, was one of those sites. As later revised in 1987, however, the law dropped consideration of other sites and specified Yucca Mountain as the only site to be evaluated. The new law stimulated a great deal of controversy among many parties, resulting in delays extending far beyond initially projected dates of completion and acceptance of HLNW.

Driven by Congressional impatience with the controversy, and the expensive and time-consuming process of implementing it, abandonment of the more scientifically sound comparative strategy was followed by proposed legislation that would weaken, rather than strengthen, democratic processes, traditional state's rights, and judicial review, as well as legally established standards and review processes designed to protect human health and safety and the environment. The nuclear industry has also behaved badly, attempting to sway public opinion in Nevada by mounting a public relations campaign that failed to convince Nevadans of the safety of a repository or of the fairness of the process leading to the selection of Yucca Mountain as the site of a repository. Scientific exploration of Yucca Mountain has raised additional questions as to its safety (see Kerr, 1999). The result of all the controversy has been increasing distrust in the federal government among Nevadans and many others, especially distrust of the U.S. Department of Energy, and increased public fears and other social conflicts.

As a case study, nuclear waste in the United States is a good example of how *not* to deal with a highly complex and serious problem. Even more to the point, however, problems such as the disposal of high-level nuclear waste and many problems of a criminal nature extend beyond national boundaries and involve very large-scale organizations.

How do we cope with such problems? Attempts to understand them have a rich, but relatively recent history, with roots in a variety of disciplines, theoretical, and empirical traditions. European and British scholarship concerning risk emphasizes the importance of social systems (see Luhmann, 1989, 1993; Beck, 1992; and Giddens, 1990), and culture (Douglas, 1985, 1986; Douglas and Wildavsky, 1982). A theme running through much risk theory in Europe is the deeply unsettling character of late modernity (Giddens) and "risk society" (Beck), noted above. Uncertainty, it is argued, combined with reflexivity, threatens ontological security (defined as confidence "in the continuity of. . .self-identity and in the constancy of the surrounding social and material environments of action"; Giddens, 1991, 92) and creates high levels of anxiety.

In contrast to European themes, risk-related scholarship in the United States has had a strong empirical cast, due in part to "political demands for social control and a cultural tendency to stress pragmatism over ideology" (Cohen, forthcoming). A substantial body of research and field experience documents a variety of approaches to the search for solutions, and suggest general principles that may enhance the success of whatever approach is taken.

SOME GENERAL PRINCIPLES

I began this essay with the premise that creation of "stakes in conformity," and recognition of stakeholders in decision-making processes, is a necessary condition for successful control of the broad class of risks under discussion here. Historically, nation states and international corporations have achieved their objectives chiefly through the exercise of economic and military power. Although these doubtless will always have a major, and in many cases a deciding, role to play, the prospect of virtually continuous warfare—economic and/or military—underlines the importance of moving beyond them. At the very least we must combine the exercise of economic and military power with policies and strategies designed to create and maintain agreed-upon policies with respect to global problems and "stakes in conformity" with them. How might this be accomplished?

Principle One

Inclusion of stakeholders in the analysis of problems, and deliberations leading to decisions, raises a variety of problems. Even identifying various categories of "interested and affected parties" is difficult and complex; determining how their interests are to be represented even more so. Although social scientists have a long history of studying such problems, only recently have they become involved in risk-related issues, and then chiefly at local, or at most state and regional levels. Arguably, however, an important reason for notable failures of past policies has been the lack of sufficient consideration of the interests of parties affected by such policies. This is clear with regard to problems such as the production, distribution, and abuse of illegal drugs and other organized criminal behavior, the generation and disposal of toxic wastes, domestic abuse, and the protection of scarce natural resources (e.g., violation of environmental laws and the killing of endangered species). The importance of the task, therefore, can hardly be exaggerated.

This principle, and the next—and means for their achievement—are closely related.

Principle Two

Although the performance of existing institutions in meeting these challenges will be critical to their successful resolution, it is very likely that new, intermediate, institutions will be necessary if adequate stakeholder representation is to be achieved. Again, this idea is neither new nor unprecedented. A host of new institutions have been created since World War II specifically to respond to worldwide problems for which existing institutions were deemed inadequate. Social scientists have addressed this trend from different perspectives. The "enlightenment" model advanced by Morris Janowitz (1971, 1976) and others—many of them his students and close colleagues (see Suttles and Zald, 1985)—argues that, while "the key institution for initiating social change" was the national polity, in practice, institution building occurred primarily as the result of interinstitutional linkages at the local level (Suttles, 1985). The model recognizes—indeed, encourages—learning by trial and error as a means of changing existing institutions and building new ones. James Coleman's focus is quite different, arguing that the weakening of traditional/primordial institutions such as the family makes the creation of new institutions necessary as a means of "rationally reconstructing" society (Coleman, 1993).

These models are not, of course, mutually exclusive, and it is likely that experimentation with a variety of approaches will be necessary. Indeed, some already are well underway. Among the most important, for present purposes, are those designed explicitly to promote participation and consensus among stakeholders (interested and affected parties) regarding issues of risks to communities and geographical regions. The NRC panel report referred to in the introduction to this essay discusses "Six Cases in Risk Analysis and Characterization" that illustrate different approaches that agencies might find useful for adaptation. The disclaimer that none of the cases was entirely successful in characterizing the risks at issue, suggests the enormous difficulty of the task. Each, suffice to say, emphasizes the importance of sharing technical analyses of risks and uncertainties with stakeholders and involving them in policy decisions and implementation.

Another example is the "Cooperative Discourse" model of achieving procedural agreement among stakeholders in communities that must choose between controversial options with regard to risks in the social policy arena—in the specific instance, the location of toxic waste disposal facilities. In such cases substantive agreement often is extremely difficult to achieve either by abstract reasoning or empirical fact-finding precisely because *stakeholders disagree about the conventional criterion of acceptability of costs and benefits, and because uncertainty is undeniable.* Agreement, in principle, that all interested and affected parties should have an equal opportunity to influence the *policy decision making process* has proved to be successful in generating consensus, even among residents of communities chosen for a clearly unwanted facility. In practice, citizen panels work together with local officials, scientists, and engineers, in an iterative process of deliberation (see Jaeger, et. al., forthcoming).

Research and field experience document a variety of approaches that have been taken in the search for solutions, and suggest general principles that may enhance the success of whatever approach is taken. All documented cases, however, deal with local, state, or regional risk analyses, far below the scale of the risks here under discussion. Nevertheless, there are encouraging signs.

Principle Three

If they are to be successful, all institutions must enjoy a large measure of legitimization. Institutional legitimacy, in turn, requires trust in the competence and the fiduciary responsibility of institutional policies and personnel. That is, the clients of institutions must trust functionaries to perform their duties competently and in the common interest, rather than in their narrow personal interests.[6]

Note that here our concern is not so much with interpersonal trust; rather it is with trust in (1) the institutions and organizations to which responsibility for control has been allocated; (2) the *fairness of procedures* for arriving at control strategies; and (3) *shared understandings as to appropriate ways of discovering and applying knowledge.* Clearly, science-based knowledge, coupled with advanced technologies, must be a primary component of any reasonable approach to problems such as those under discussion. Trust in the methods of science is, therefore, critical. Of equal importance, however, is trust in procedures so that interested and affected parties regard them as fair and just.

Although trust in science is high in much of the world, it is also suspect in some quarters even in the most advanced societies.[7] And, although science is the most obvious and necessary approach to complex global problems, solutions also require other workable ways of discovery and application. Indeed, because scientific findings often have large distributional consequences, reliance solely on science (and on scientists and science-based institutions) would be counter-productive, as many in the scientific community recognize. Distinguished physicist Harvey Brooks warns, especially, against suppression of uncertainties on the grounds that decisions based on "a wide band of uncertainty creates different winners and losers and hence is inherently political." (Brooks, 1988, p. viii.)

Another take on this issue is the importance of recognizing *the inevitability of uncertainty*. As historian David Lowenthal (forthcoming) argues, institutions with environmental decision-making responsibilities must cease their efforts to wrestle certainty from uncertainty—still another very large issue requiring social and behavioral science input from researchers, theorists, and educators.

Principle Four

A fourth principle—also involving large and difficult issues for social science inquiry—is suggested by Carol Heimer's (1985) analysis of how insurance companies insure themselves against "moral hazard," that is, hazards that are related to the character or the conduct of insured persons. Examples include carelessness (as in the case of fire) or fraud (as when insured assets are fraudulently valued for insurance purposes). In such cases, insurance companies negotiate with clients to create a "community of fate"; that is, to make fulfillment of the insurance contract contingent on responsible behavior by the insured.

Principle Five

It is important that the rule of law be maintained in efforts to control global problems. As Don Cressey once noted, in correspondence concerning a paper I had sent him,[8] insistence that the state (or other legally constituted body) *specify in advance* the behaviors that are punishable by the state is *a platform for human rights*. Sticking to the idea that there is no crime without violation of the criminal law is powerful protection against arbitrary actions by officials. It is important, therefore, that control efforts be legally sanctioned and legitimized.

Annelise Riles, trained in both law and anthropology, and a participant in the United Nations Fourth World Conference on Women, held in Beijing in 1995, discusses the importance of global conferencing in transforming international law into a force beyond "doctrine and politics" (American Bar Foundation, 1999).[9] "International law," she argues, "is increasingly becoming governance by fact, attracting participation and action, in ways that doctrine and politics have not, by allowing for measurement and comparison." Her personal experience and her research lead her to conclude that international and global conferencing promote "soft law"—"agreements that are not legally binding and do not carry sanctions" —in order that governments may debate proposals and establish international standards. The networking (among individuals, groups, and organizations with common interests) encouraged by conferencing promote social organizations that "subtly shape political commitments and what 'counts' as action" (p. 9). Riles notes, however, that conferencing is not always successful in addressing issues of interest to participants, and that it is important for "real-world" problems and issues to be addressed.

Principle Six

Nongovernmental organizations (NGOs) are likely to be critical in this process. No better example can be found than the case of genocide and war crimes (Gutman, 1999).[10] Since World War II, beginning with the Nuremberg Tribunal, a series of conventions have sought to establish in law the principle that "systematic crimes against civilians that occur inside a country but then can be tried elsewhere" ("crimes against humanity") are, in fact, criminal and subject to prosecution. Most of these activities have taken place under the auspices of the United Nations (UN). Throughout, however, NGOs have played a critical role, first in pressuring the UN to include strong language regarding human rights, later in pressuring governments to respond more forcefully to acts of genocide and other crimes carried out by governments against their people (see Korey, 1998). Gutman concludes that "left to themselves, governments may well repeat the mistakes of the past. Under pressure from a more activist public," however, they "will have to establish institutions to restore order" (Gutman, 1999, 3). NGOs may well be the vehicles through which public activism is most likely to occur.

Principle Seven

Finally, a cautionary principle: developments such as these not only tax traditional social control policies and practices, but also threaten to erode individual rights (see, especially, Marx, 1988). Although democracy is growing throughout the world, contrary to the vision of such dystopian writers as Orwell, individual liberties are nonetheless subject to increased threat, as nations, corporations, and other large-scale organizations and institutions cope with increasingly complex problems of control.

CONCLUSION

The problems here at issue are increasingly similar to those posed by "The Tragedy of the Commons," Garrett Hardin's (1968) seminal analysis of the dilemma faced by users of common resources on which many are dependent. Hardin argued that "rational" users of common-pool resources (CPRs) inevitably make demands on them that lead to their destruction. Like technologically driven social control problems, management of CPRs is increasing in scale and complexity, and faced with accelerating rates of change. Both types of problems require institutions that can create and maintain effective collective response to problems that are increasingly global in nature. Harmful behavior by individuals, corporations, dissident groups, and even nation-states requires collective action on a far larger scale than has been the case in the past. Traditional *distinctions* between individual and corporate behavior that is defined as criminal, and the behavior of nations that once was considered to be beyond the purview of other nations, are changing rapidly. Similarly, dependence on CPRs is increasingly global in nature, beyond the control of individual nations.

The assumption of collective responsibility among nations (e.g., the UN and NATO) for affairs within nations invites and extends the threat of terrorism by dissident groups beyond national boundaries. Coupled with the universal dependency of modern societies on technologies and public measures related to public health and safety, societies have become especially vulnerable to terrorism. This applies equally to CPRs.

As Hardin himself later recognized, his thesis required modification. Reexamination of CPR problems offers the hope, if not the promise, of possible relief (see Ostrom, et al., 1999). Management is the key. Experience in their management, at local, regional, national, and international levels, suggests several fundamental principles to long-term, sustainable CPR management. Consistent with the present thesis, stakeholder participation and the development of norms (laws and rules) and institutions that stakeholders view as fair and just are critical to the success of such efforts. The authors of this assessment conclude that "institutional diversity may be as important as biological diversity for our long-term survival" (Ostrom, et al., 1999, p. 278).

All of these analyses and suggestions necessarily are made in the spirit of what Heinz Eulau, referring to policy scientists, called "the self-restraint that should be their hallmark in the face of uncertainty or ignorance. . ." (1985, p. 71). The inevitability of risk, uncertainty, and ignorance is surely a call for serious scholarship and deliberation. The seriousness and the complexity of risk and uncertainty render the balance between action and self-restraint ever more difficult.

NOTES

1. Forthcoming in a volume in the JAI series, *Research in Social Problems and Public Policy* (JAI Press, 1999) edited by William Freudenburg and T.I.K. Youn.

2. The National Research Council is the "action arm" of the National Academies of Science and Engineering, and the Institute of Medicine.

3. Economic theory has, of course, devoted much effort to uncertainty for many years.

4. Theoretical and research inconsistencies in this area remind us again of the importance of "establishing the phenomenon" to be explained (see Merton, 1987).

5. Regarding crime, see, e.g., Anderson, 1990, 1998; Ianni, 1972, 1974; Meier and Short, 1982; regarding technological hazards, see Couch and Kroll-Smith, 1991.

6. Gary LaFree (1998) argues that the rise in street crime in the United States in the 1960s and early 1970s was due to a decline in the legitimacy of political, economic, and family institutions in the U.S. There is ample evidence that trust and confidence in many institutions declined in the United States during the 1960s and 1970s, and that high levels of distrust remain. Legitimacy of new institutions with such large and complex responsibilities is certain to be a serious problem.

7. The social and behavioral sciences are met with even greater skepticism than are the physical and biological sciences; but that must be the topic of another essay.

8. "Criminology: Modern Controversies" (Short, 1983).

9. Riles is a Research Fellow of the American Bar Foundation (ABF). The referenced article appears in the ABF publication, *Researching Law: An ABF Update*.

10. See Gutman and Rief, eds., 1999 (as of this writing, forthcoming).

REFERENCES

American Bar Foundation. 1999. "The Character of Information in International Conferences and Commodities Markets." *Researching Law: An ABF Update* 10(1): (Winter):1, 8–10.

Anderson, Elijah. 1998. *The Code of the Streets.* New York: Norton.

Anderson, Elijah. 1990. *Streetwise: Race, Class, and Change in an Urban Community.* Chicago: University of Chicago Press.

Beck, Ulrich. English translation by Mark Ritter. 1992. *Risk Society: Towards a New Modernity.* Newbury Park, CA: Sage.

Brooks, Harvey. 1988. "Foreword." In John D. Graham, Laura C. Green, and Marc J. Roberts. *In Search of Safety: Chemicals and Cancer Risk.* Cambridge, MA: Harvard University Press.

Cohen, Maurie, ed. forthcoming. *Risk in the Modern Age: Social Theory, Science and Environmental Decision-Making.* London: Macmillan.

Coleman, James. 1993. "The Rational Reconstruction of Society." *American Sociological Review*, 58(1):1–15.

Couch, Stephen R., and J. Stephen Kroll-Smith, eds. 1991. *Communities at Risk: Collective Responses to Technological Hazards.* New York: Peter Lang.

Douglas, Mary. 1985. *Risk Acceptability According to the Social Sciences.* New York: Russell Sage.

Douglas, Mary. 1986. *How Institutions Think.* Syracuse: Syracuse University Press.

Douglas, Mary and Aaron Wildavsky. 1982. *Risk and Culture: An Essay on the Selection of Technological and Environmental Dangers.* Berkeley: University of California Press.

Dunlap, Riley, Michael E. Kraft, Eugene A. Rosa, eds. 1993. *Public Reactions to Nuclear Waste: Citizens' Views of Repository Siting.* Durham, NC: Duke University Press.

Edelstein, Michael. forthcoming. "Outsiders just don't understand: The Need for Contextual Inquiry about Life in the Contaminated World." In M. Cohen, ed. forthcoming. *Risk in the Modern Age: Social Theory, Science and Environmental Decision-Making.* London: Macmillan.

Erikson, Kai. 1994. *A New Species of Trouble: Explorations in Disaster, Trauma, and Community.* New York: Norton.

Eulau, Heinz, and Vera McCluggage. 1985. "Proliferation and the Institutional Structure of the Congressional Committee system." In G. Suttles and M. Zald, eds., *The Challenge of Social Control: Citizenship and Institution Building in Modern Society; Essays in Honor of Morris Janowitz.* Norwood, NJ: Ablex.

Flynn, James, James Chalmers, Doug Easterling, Roger Kasperson, Howard Kunreuther, C.K. Mertz, Alvin Mushkatel, K. David Pijawki, and Paul Slovic. 1995. *One Hundred Centuries of Solitude: Redirecting America's High-Level Nuclear Waste Policy.* Boulder, CO: Westview.

Freese, Lee. 1997. *Environmental Connections, Advances in Human Ecology*, Supplement 1 (Part B). Greenwich, CT: JAI Press.

Giddens, Anthony. 1990. *The Consequences of Modernity.* Stanford, CA: Stanford University Press.

Gutman, Roy. 1999. "Bringing Genocide to Justice." *The Washington Spectator* 25(5) (March 1):1–3.

Hardin, Garrett. 1998. "Extensions of 'The tragedy of the commons,'" *Science* 280:680–682.

Hardin, Garrett. 1968. "The tragedy of the commons," *Science.* 162:1243–1244.

Heimer, Carol, and Lisa R. Staffen. 1998. *For the Sake of the Children: The Social Organization of Responsibility in the Hospital and the Home.* Chicago: University of Chicago Press.

Heimer, Carol. 1985. *Reactive Risk and Rational Action: Managing Moral Hazard in Insurance Contracts.* Berkeley: University of California Press.

Henderson, Donald A. 1999. "The Looming Threat of Bioterrorism." *Science* 283 (26 February):1279–1282.

Ianni, Francis A.J. 1974. *Black Mafia: Ethnic Succession in Organized Crime.* New York: Simon & Schuster.

Jaeger, Carlo C., Ortwin Renn, Eugene A. Rosa, and Thomas Webler. forthcoming. *Risk, Uncertainty, and Rational Action.*

Janowitz, Morris. 1976. *Social Control of the Welfare State.* New York: Elsevier.

Janowitz, Morris. 1971. *Institution Building in Urban Education.* Chicago: University of Chicago Press.

Kempton, Willett, James S. Boster, and Jennifer A. Hartley. 1995. *Environmental Values in American Culture.* Cambridge, MA: MIT Press.

Kerr, Richard A. 1999. "Yucca Mountain Panel says DOE Lacks Data." *Science* 283 (26 February):1235–36.

Korey, William. 1998. *NGOs and the Universal Declaration of Human Rights.* New York: St. Martin's Press.

LaFree, Gary. 1998. *Losing Legitimacy: Street Crime and the Decline of Social Institutions in America.* Boulder, CO: Westview.

Lowenthal, David. forthcoming. "An Historical Perspective on Risk." In Maurie Cohen, ed., *Risk in the Modern Age: Social theory, Science and Environmental Decision-Making.* London: Macmillan.

Luhmann, Niklas, English translation by John Bednarz, Jr. 1989. *Ecological Communication.* Chicago: University of Chicago Press.

Luhmann, Niklas. (English translation by Rhodes Barrett.) 1993. *Risk: A Sociological Theory.* New York: deGruyter.

Marx, Gary T. 1988. *Under Cover: Police Surveillance in America.* Berkeley, CA: University of California Press.

Meier, Robert F., and James F. Short, Jr. 1982. "The Consequences of White-collar Crime." In H. Edelhertz and T. Overcast, eds.*White-Collar Crime: An Agenda for Research.* Lexington, MA: Lexington Books.

Merton, Robert K. 1987. "Three Fragments from a Sociologist's Notebooks: Establishing the Phenomenon, Specified Ignorance, and Strategic Research Materials." *Annual Review of Sociology* 13:1–28.

Merton, Robert K. 1964. "Anomie, Anomia, and Social Interaction: Contexts of Deviant Behavior." In M. Clinard, ed. *Anomie and Deviant Behavior.* New York: Free Press.

Merton, Robert K. 1938. "Social Structure and Anomie." *American Sociological Review* 3:672–82.

Ostrom, Elinor, Joanna Burger, Christopher B. Field, Richard B. Norgaard, and David Policansky. 1999. "Revisiting the commons: Local lessons, global challenges." *Science* 284 (April): 278–282.

Perrow, Charles. 1984. *Normal Accidents: Living with High-Risk Technologies.* New York: Basic Books.

Picou, J. Stephen, and Duane Gill. forthcoming. "The Exxon Valdez Disaster as Localized Environmental Catastrophe: Dis(similarities) to the Risk Society." In M. Cohen, ed. forthcoming. *Risk in the Modern Age: Social Theory, Science and Environmental Decision-Making.* London: Macmillan.

Randall, Donna M., and James F. Short, Jr. 1983. "Women in Toxic Work Environments: A Case Study of Social Problem Development." *Social Problems* 30 (April):410–424.

Rappaport, Roy A. 1996. "Risk and the Human Environment." *Annals of the American Academy of Political and Social Science* 545 (May):64–74.

Rosa, Eugene A., and Donald L. Clark, Jr. forthcoming. "Historical Routes to Technological Gridlock: Nuclear Technology as Prototypical Vehicle." In W.R. Freudenburg and T.I.K. Youn, eds. *Institutional Failure in Environmental Management; Research in Social Problems and Public Policy* Vol. 7. Greenwich, CT: JAI Press.

Shrader-Frechette, K.S. 1993. *Burying Uncertainty: Risk and the Case Against Geological Disposal of Nuclear Waste.* Berkeley: University of California Press.

Short, James F., Jr. 1999. "Characterizing and Managing Environmental and Technological Risks: Some Requirements for a New Paradigm," in W. Freudenburg and T. Youn, eds. *Institutional Failure in Environmental Management, Research in Social Problems and Public Policy* Vol .7. Greenwich, CT: JAI Press.

Short, James F., Jr. 1984. "The Social Fabric at Risk: Toward the Social Transformation of Risk Analysis." *American Sociological Review* 49(6):711–725.

Short, James F., Jr. 1983. "Criminology: Modern Controversies." In Sanford H. Kadish, Editor-in-Chief. *Encyclopedia of Crime and Justice.* Vol. 2:556–566, New York: The Free Press.

Stern, Paul C., and Harvey V. Fineberg, eds. 1996. *Understanding Risk: Informing Decisions in a Democratic Society.* Washington, DC: National Academy Press.

Suttles, Gerald D. 1985. "A Tribute to Morris Janowitz." In G. Suttles and M. Zald, eds. *The Challenge of Social Control: Citizenship and Institution Building in Modern Society; Essays in Honor of Morris Janowitz.* Norwood, NJ: Ablex.

Suttles, Gerald D., and Mayer N. Zald, eds. 1985. *The Challenge of Social Control: Citizenship and Institution Building in Modern Society; Essays in Honor of Morris Janowitz.* Norwood, NJ: Ablex.

Szasz, Andrew. 1994. *EcoPopulism: Toxic Waste and the Movement for Environmental Justice.* Minneapolis: University of Minnesota Press.

Toby, Jackson. 1957. "Social Disorganization and a Stake in Conformity." *Journal of Criminal Law, Criminology, and Police Science* 48 (May/June):12–17.

Law Enforcement, Intercepting Communications, and the Right to Privacy

The Impact of New Technologies

Duncan Chappell

In April 1998, in a special report on wireless technologies, the respected journal *Scientific American*[1] provided a fascinating account of the new communication systems that are set to revolutionize the way in which we interact with one another around the globe. The report included a description of fleets of satellites, which it was said should soon make it possible to reach someone anywhere on the earth using nothing more than a small handset.[2]

In September 1998 this possibility became a reality as the first of these fleets, launched by the pioneering satellite telephone company Iridium, came into operation.[3] At a reported cost of US$3.4 billion, the Iridium system is based on a constellation of sixty-six low-earth orbit (LEO) satellites, which operate like a global cellular system, passing signals between them in a cell-like formation so that a user can be reached anywhere on the planet. Iridium is the first of a number of similar LEO-based networks, which are to become operational in the next five years.[4]

The services provided by Iridium include voice, data at 2.4 kilobytes per second, and paging. The design requirements of the system make it possible for the handheld unit to be usable from inside a moving vehicle, reflecting the Iridium company's marketing plan, which is said to rely heavily upon serving international business travelers. It is a complex system in which:

> . . .the satellites are designed to communicate not only with the earth stations but also with one another. To route traffic properly, each satellite must carry a set of stored routing tables from which new routing instructions are chosen every few minutes. Signals from the ground

are transmitted in bursts, or "packets," each of which includes the address of its intended destination. At the satellite the signals are demodulated so that address can be read and the packets retransmitted to their next destination.

This destination may be a hand held Iridium subscriber unit, or it may be a gateway earth station. If neither is in view, then it will be one of the four nearest satellites—the one ahead or behind the same orbital plane, or the nearest satellite in the adjacent orbital plane to the east or west. Although it complicates the design of the system, the use of these cross-links will permit global service with only a dozen gateway earth stations.[5]

The Iridium system has clearly posed some formidable technological challenges to those who have been involved in its design and implementation. This new and exciting development in the field of communications also poses formidable challenges to those concerned in the investigation of crime, and especially crime that transcends national boundaries. It must be presumed that not all of the targeted international business customers for these new satellite-based personal communication systems will be law-abiding citizens. These systems have obvious benefits for the conduct of both legitimate and illegitimate business enterprises, and a wealth of contemporary data and experience show that criminals are enthusiastic consumers of new technologies such as this, which provide their nefarious activities with a fresh competitive edge.

One competitive edge that a system such as Iridium promises to give criminals is an ability to conduct their communications in an interception-free environment. More will be said below about this issue, but here it is sufficient to highlight just one of the significant barriers that will confront the law enforcement community in gaining legal authority to intercept communications by persons subscribing to Iridium's services. Take, for example, an Australian subscriber who is believed, on reasonable grounds, to be involved in the importation from Southeast Asia of significant quantities of heroin. If an interception warrant were to be sought by an authorized law enforcement agency in Australia in regard to that subscriber, any execution of that warrant would have to involve the consent and agreement of a foreign government because the Iridium earth station gateway for Australia is located in Thailand. Current mutual assistance arrangements between Australia and Thailand do not extend to the interception of communications.[6] While this situation is known to be the subject of ongoing dialogue between governmental officials from the two countries, it will almost certainly take some time to resolve the delicate legal and political issues involved.

Quite apart from this not-insignificant barrier in Australia to the lawful interception of Iridium-linked communications, and it must be presumed in many other countries that similarly lack an Iridium gateway on their own soil, there are also unresolved technological barriers to such interception, which are too complex to outline here.[8] It will be demonstrated shortly that remedies are being sought for these technological problems, but in combination they provide a graphic illustration of the way in which the general revolution in communications is proceeding at such a pace that law enforcement interests and concerns are at best scrambling to remain in contention. As the authors of a recent study of "crime in the digital age" have remarked:

> . . .[T]he advent of digital communications, combined with global trends towards privatization and deregulation of the telecommunications industry, have posed new challenges for law enforcement. A proliferation of carriers and service providers may make it difficult to discern which one to approach for assistance in undertaking surveillance of a particular target. Moreover, telecommunications systems can be designed to be more or less accessible to interception. . .
> As if the above challenges were not formidable enough, they in turn are compounded by the increasing accessibility of encryption technology. . .
> In addition to encryption, law enforcement agencies are concerned about the development and convergence of other technologies such as digital compression, high speed data links, multiplex cables, and asynchronistic transfer mode technology. These all contribute to reducing law enforcement access to voice and data transmissions. The democratization of telecommunications technology, that is, its widespread accessibility to ordinary citizens, has begun to make many traditional law enforcement techniques obsolete.[9]

This revolution in communications has also come at a time of renewed concern about the protection of personal privacy, and of deep mistrust of government in many western democracies. Thus the balancing of legitimate law enforcement interests with those of privacy rights, such as those incorporated in Article 12 of the Universal Declaration of Human Rights,[10] or in Article 17 of the International Covenant on Civil and Political Rights,[11] has become an issue that has attracted sustained attention, analysis, and controversy around the globe.

In this paper, attention is focused mainly upon those aspects of this issue that relate to transnational crime and to the current and future needs of law enforcement to combat such crime. It is suggested that the current arrangements for intercepting communications available to most law-enforcement agencies are still locked largely within national boundaries. This situation, which already restricts the scope and effectiveness of the investigation and prosecution of transnational crime, is certain to deteriorate further if new and cooperative approaches are not put in place to deal with criminal activities that transcend national borders.

The paper has three parts. In Part 1 a brief review is made of the perceived contemporary benefits for law enforcement of retaining the power to intercept communications, and of the information available concerning the level of use of this power in a number of nations. It should be emphasized that in conducting this review, and throughout the paper, principal consideration is given to the lawful interception of communications involving voice, data, and allied transmissions through a range of telecommunication facilities. The paper does not address the broader topic of electronic surveillance, including the use of various eavesdropping devices, nor does it consider the questions associated with the secretive interception and surveillance of communications conducted in the name of national security by a wide array of intelligence agencies around the world.[12]

In Part 2, consideration is given to the present legal and regulatory framework that surrounds the interception powers provided to law enforcement, and the way in which it is sought to balance these powers with the protection of personal privacy. Reference is made, by way of example, to the legal regimes in place in a number of democratic nations, which allow the interception of communications.[13]

In Part 3, and flowing from the analysis contained in Part 2, the paper turns to the ongoing dialogue at national, regional, and international levels about how best to respond to the threat of transnational crime in this revolutionary communications environment.

PART 1: INTERCEPTION OF COMMUNICATIONS: BENEFIT, USE, AND COST ISSUES

Telephone Interception

> Hit a brick wall. . .and the trail's gone cold. Perhaps your case could do with a little help? We might just give you the breakthrough you're looking for. . .
>
> Sound too good to be true? It's not! A simple telephone call to. . . . . . . or after hours . . . . could provide you with a powerful investigative and surveillance tool which continues to have a great success rate. "Give us a call."[14]

While most law-enforcement agencies are unlikely to be as bold and proactive in their "marketing" of the benefits of telephone interception as the Australian police force that produced the brochure from which this quotation is taken, most agencies would agree that wiretapping (the term used most typically in the United States) or telephone tapping (the term adopted more frequently in European and Commonwealth countries) is a potent investigative and surveillance tool with a high rate of success. A recent and authoritative reinforcement of this view comes from another Australian source, the Royal Commission into the New South Wales Police Service, which, in its final report on corrupt practices within that agency, noted that:

> From the outset the Royal Commission had sought the power to intercept telephone conversations because:
>
> - it is a power possessed by the ICAC [Independent Commission Against Corruption] and by the [NSW Police] Service, the agencies otherwise entrusted with the responsibility to investigate police corruption. It is also a power given to the NSW Crime Commission;
>
> - it is an invaluable aid in detecting corruption, particularly that of an ongoing kind, in an environment where groups of persons suspected of corrupt practices are

aware that they are under investigation and are likely to communicate with each other to frustrate or prevent their exposure;

- it is a valuable security measure, so far as it provides an opportunity to intercept planned interference with Commission operations, or threats to the safety of witnesses and Royal Commission staff; and

- it provides the best evidence of corruption, being much more persuasive and reliable than the word of a corrupt colleague or accomplice.[15]

Notwithstanding strong representations made by the New South Wales Government and other bodies to the Federal Government, the source of constitutional power in the Australian Commonwealth to act on the matter, the Wood Royal Commission was denied a telephone interception capacity—a denial that the Royal Commission claimed seriously impaired its operational effectiveness.[16] Despite this refusal, the Federal Government in Australia has not been reluctant in recent years to expand significantly the number of law-enforcement agencies in the country permitted to have an interception capacity. Within Australia the administration of criminal justice is primarily the responsibility of the six states and two territories that make up the Federation.[17] Since the late 1970s when the present statutory and regulatory framework was established in the form of the *Telecommunications (Interception) Act* 1979 (TI Act) to control telephonic interception, the list of agencies designated as being eligible to engage in such interceptions has increased from just one (the Australian Federal Police [AFP]) to ten. Today, all but one of the state police forces possess this authority, and in addition the interception power has been extended to special investigative bodies such as the Independent Commission Against Corruption (ICAC) and the Police Integrity Commission (PIC), both situated in New South Wales.[18]

This "agency creep" as it has been termed, which has been accompanied by an extension of the range of offenses for which an interception warrant may be obtained, has attracted substantial criticism from civil liberties groups concerned about privacy protection and the extension of police power.[19] Such criticism has been fueled by the official statistics, published as part of the TI Act's accountability provisions, which suggest that the use of the interception power by Australian police is much more extensive than in some other similar Western democracies with common law traditions such as Canada,[20] the United Kingdom, and the United States. The most recent national interception statistics for Australia (from 1 July 1997 to 30 June 1998) are displayed in Table 1.[21] It will be seen that in that year, and in the two preceding years, more than 600 applications were made, and less than 2 percent of applications were rejected by the judicial officers considering the issue of warrants. Table 2 shows the categories of serious offenses for which the applications were made. Drug-related offenses clearly predominated. Finally, Table 3 displays the number of prosecutions and convictions which resulted from lawfully obtained intercept information.

TABLE 1　Australian Interception Applications
1994–1998

Agency	Application	94/95	95/96	96/97	97/98
Australian	Made	234	233	188	141
Federal Police	Refused/withdrawn	3	2	4	1
	Issued	231	231	184	190
National Crime	Made	106	105	84	98
Authority	Refused/withdrawn	1	2	6	0
	Issued	105	103	78	98
NSW Police	Made	100	102	94	140
	Refused/withdrawn	0	1	0	0
	Issued	100	101	94	140
NSW Crime	Made	90	112	117	83
Commission	Refused/withdrawn	1	0	0	0
	Issued	89	112	117	83
ICAC	Made	0	3	7	15
	Refused/withdrawn	—	0	0	0
	Issued	—	3	7	15
South Australia	Made	41	45	32	41
Police	Refused/withdrawn	0	4	0	4
	Issued	41	41	32	37
Victoria Police	Made	127	158	116	82
	Refused/withdrawn	1	2	1	0
	Issued	126	156	115	82
Western Australia	Made	N/A	N/A	N/A	34
Police	Refused/withdrawn				4
	Issued				30
TOTAL	Made	698	758	638	684
	Refused/withdrawn	6	11	11	9
	Issued	692	747	627	675

Source: Adapted from Department of the Attorney General *Telecommunication (Interception) Act* 1979. *Report for the Year Ending 30 June* 1998, Canberra, Department of the Attorney General, 1998 Chapter 4 *(Interception Report).*

These statistics seem to affirm that the interception of telecommunications by Australian law enforcement agencies does pay dividends in terms of the administration of criminal justice. Certainly this was the conclusion drawn by a recent Federal review (the Barrett Review)[22] conducted by a senior official of the Department of Finance, who found clear evidence of:

> the effectiveness of TI both as a surveillance mechanism in its own right and in enhancing the effectiveness of other surveillance methodologies. The evidence suggests that it does the latter better than any of the other surveillance methods. The Review was told by the Drug Operations Division, Eastern Division (AFP), that at least half of the successfully resolved drug operations are directly attributable to efficient TI practices. Evidence was given that in certain cases a conviction would not have been possible without evidence from TI activity.

TABLE 2   Offense Categories Australian Warrant Applications
           1994–1998

Offense	94/95	95/96	96/97	97/98
Murder	121	108	102	143
Kidnapping	3	4	9	15
Narcotics Offense	259	233	174	196
Special Investigation	69	92	7	44
Loss of Life	8	10	4	20
Serious Personal Injury	32	58	52	56
Serious Damage to Property	12	0	1	8
Trafficking in Drugs	223	194	197	174
Serious Fraud	11	27	16	11
Serious Loss of Revenue	0	18	31	16
Bribery or Corruption	—	17	37	39
Organized Crime Offense	—	—	23	26
Money Laundering Offense	—	3	4	21
Offense Against Part VIA of the Crimes Act	1	0	16	1

Source: Adapted from *Interception Report*, Chapter 4.

TABLE 3   Australian Prosecutions and Convictions
           Based on Lawful Intercepts – 1998

Offense	TOTAL	
	Prosecution	Convictions
Murder	18	14
Kidnapping	1	1
Narcotics Offense	49	29
Loss of Life	2	2
Serious Personal Injury	20	11
Serious Damage to Property	0	0
Trafficking in Drugs	217	152
Serious Fraud	2	2
Serious Loss of Revenue	13	4
Organized Crime Offense	1	1
Other Offenses	123	113
TOTAL	451	329

Source: Adapted from *Interception Report*, Chapter 4.

Security agencies also illustrated that the most reliable and highest quality intelligence is based on TI information. While the evidence is largely qualitative, it is sufficiently convincing to conclude that TI can be a very cost effective surveillance mechanism.[23]

The Barrett Review did provide some unclassified information about the operational costs and related interception capacities of Australian law-enforcement agencies. The recurrent costs of TI for these agencies in 1992-1993 was said to be above $(AUD)10.5 million, with just over 100 interception lines in operation.[24] The Barrett Review also referred to data supplied by the Victorian Police, which showed that in terms of most recurrent costs over a designated period for different methods of surveillance, TI provided the lowest-cost solution.[25] Although convinced of the current cost effectiveness of TI, the Barrett Review was less sanguine about the longer-term situation because of the then-looming changes in technology that have been referred to above.[26] More will be said about this aspect of the Barrett Review in Part 3 of this paper.

Detailed comparative data is not readily available from most other nations about the use and cost-effectiveness of TI. However, in the United States, the Administrative Office of the United States Courts does provide a very comprehensive annual report to Congress, as required under the provisions of the *Omnibus Crime Control and Safe Streets Act* of 1968, on the number and nature of federal and state applications for orders authorizing or approving the interception of wire, oral, or electronic communications.[27] The latest of these reports, for 1998, shows that in that year a total of 1329 communication interceptions were authorized nationwide.[28] When it is remembered that in approximately the same period, 1 July 1997 to 30 June 1998, the number of similar authorizations made in Australia exceeded 600, and that the population of the United States is well over ten times larger than that of Australia, it is quite apparent that the frequency of use of TI in the Antipodes far outstrips that of the United States.[29] Longer-term trends data from the United States, shown in Table 4, confirm that 1998 was not an atypical year in interception activity.

The Office of the United States Court Report for 1998 also records that nationwide in that year the average number of people whose conversations were intercepted per order was 190. On average, 1,858 conversations were intercepted per wiretap, and 19 percent of these produced incriminating evidence.[30] The average cost of each intercept order was about $(US)58,000.[31] The report observed that "federal and state prosecutions often note the importance of electronic surveillance in obtaining arrests and convictions."[32] During the year in review, 3,450 people were arrested based on electronic surveillance, and a conviction rate was obtained of 26 percent.[33]

The official publications cited so far in this paper concerning the general benefits, use, and cost of interception activities in countries such as Australia and the United States do provide both a broad measure of public accountability for the intrusions into personal privacy that these activities represent, as well as some means of assessing whether or not such intrusions are justified. It would be very naïve, however, to assume that these publications represent a complete or accurate portrayal of the true extent of interception activities, even within two nations with

TABLE 4   **Australian Prosecutions and Convictions Based on Lawful Intercepts – 1998**

Year	Federal	State	Total
1968	0	174	174
1969	33	268	301
1970	182	414	596
1971	285	531	816
1972	206	649	855
1973	130	734	864
1974	121	607	728
1975	108	593	701
1976	137	549	686
1977	77	549	626
1978	81	489	570
1979	87	466	553
1980	81	483	564
1981	106	483	589
1982	130	448	578
1983	208	440	648
1984	289	512	801
1985	243	541	784
1986	250	504	754
1987	236	437	673
1988	293	445	738
1989	310	453	763
1990	324	548	872
1991	356	500	856
1992	340	579	919
1993	450	526	976
1994	554	600	1154
1995	532	526	1058
1996	581	568	1149
1997	569	617	1186
1998	566	763	1329

Source: Adapted from *Interception Report*, Chapter 4.

robust democracies and a longstanding commitment to human rights.[34] Wiretapping, to utilize the American terminology, is an activity conducted in nearly every country in the world and is frequently abused. For example, the United States Department of State, in its annual *Country Report on Human Rights Practices*, consistently reports widespread, illegal, or uncontrolled use of wiretaps by both government and private groups in many countries.[35] The Washington, D.C.–based human rights group, Privacy International, has also reported that:

Human rights groups, reporters and political opponents are the most common targets of surveillance by government intelligence and law enforcement agencies and other non-governmental groups. In some countries, such as Honduras and Paraguay, the state owned telecommunications companies were active participants in helping the security services monitor human rights advocates. In other countries, multiple forms of surveillance are used. For example, in 1991, wiretaps and hidden microphones were found in the offices of the Mexican Human Rights Commission, More recent press reports estimated that there are 200,000 illegal wiretaps in Mexico currently in place.

These problems are not limited to developing countries. In the US, litigation conducted by the Computer Professionals for Social Responsibility under the Freedom of Information Act revealed that the FBI monitored computer networks used by political and advocacy groups. French counter-intelligence agents wiretapped the telephones of prominent journalists and opposition party leaders during the mid-1980s. There have been numerous cases in the United Kingdom which revealed that the British intelligence services monitor social activists, labor unions, and civil liberties groups.

Thus, there is an obvious need for human rights groups to be concerned with wiretapping. Governments often monitor human rights groups to discover what they know, who their sources are, and what their future activities will be. The lack of secure communications creates the threat of physical harm to many people in the human rights field.[36]

The scope of the present paper does not extend to an examination of these threats to human rights groups posed by wiretapping, but these threats do point to the need for substantial vigilance when considering any proposed extension of wire-tapping authority to accommodate the interests and concerns of law enforcement in dealing with transnational crime and, in particular, drug trafficking. Many of the countries targeted by law enforcement as the source of supply for heroin, cocaine, and other narcotic drugs are also nations that have poor human rights records. Thus reliance on wiretap information from these countries may come at a price which includes using data gathered "from the fruit of a poisoned tree," as part of the broader and ongoing surveillance of human rights groups by brutal and oppressive regimes.

PART 2: LEGAL AND REGULATORY FRAMEWORKS FOR INTERCEPTION

There are hardly any investigations today in which not at least one or even several telephone taps are put in place. It is not merely the high evidential value which plays a role. Telephone taps are to an increasing extent used as a tactical means, for example in addition to or during the surveillances and for the preparation of tactical measures. Contrary to the U.S., the legal threshold for telephone taps is lower in my country [Germany]. They have to be ordered by a judge in principle, provided that certain requirements are fulfilled. . .

Elsewhere in Europe, police reliance on wiretaps is at least as common as it is in Germany and the United States. In Italy, where many more cases are developed by wiretaps than from informants or undercover operations, one FBI attache noted that the police have "much broader wiretap authority. . . They can just call the magistrate and get an oral OK. It's very informal and quick. . .compared to the US." Much the same is true in Spain, where wiretapping was initially authorized by the 1980 "Antiterrorist Act." In Austria, Switzerland, Denmark, and the Netherlands, wiretaps are similarly considered relatively routine.[37]

This brief overview of the authority to engage in telephone tapping in a number of European nations emphasizes the diverse and seemingly lax nature of the legal and regulatory framework established to control this invasive police power, even in a region acknowledged to have achieved significant harmonization of many of its laws and associated governmental structures. Like their counterparts in many other countries, these frameworks have often been the subject of controversy and scrutiny because of their impingement on personal privacy rights. Thus both the European Commission of Human Rights and the European Court of Human Rights have considered a number of cases over the past two decades involving challenges to the validity of telephone tapping schemes in place in certain member states of the European Union (EU).[38]

France is the EU country that has been said to have "the most ambiguous legal attitude" toward telephone tapping.[39] An estimated 70,000 telephone taps were claimed to have been utilized annually in France up until the late 1980s.[40] These taps were not even considered to be illegal until 1970, when the French legislature amended the penal code to make intercepting or eavesdropping of private telephone conversations a minor offense.[41] The legislature, however, did not provide any specific authorization for telephone tapping, and the practice continued amid debate at various levels of the French judiciary about the admissibility of evidence obtained from these interceptions. In 1988 the European Commission of Human Rights criticized the then-ongoing police practice of employing telephone tapping without the authorization of a *juges d'instruction* (examining magistrate). The Commission was also critical of the failure of the French penal code to provide sufficient safeguards against telephone tapping. The Commission said that this failure was a breach of Article 8 (the right to privacy) of the European Convention on Human Rights.[42]

In 1990 the European Court of Human Rights confirmed the correctness of this view expressed by the Commission, ruling in *Huvig and Kruslin*[43] that the French law permitting the interception of telephone calls was too imprecise and in breach of Article 8 of the Convention. This condemnation resulted in the passage of new legislation permitting such interception in serious offenses.[44] The authority of a *juge d'instruction* was required before an interception warrant was issued, and any recording had to be destroyed at the end of the period of limitation on prosecutions.[45] Provided these rules were complied with, evidence obtained from an interception would be regarded as admissible evidence at trial. Further, when reaching a verdict the trial judge was only allowed to rely on evidence that had been lawfully obtained and that did not violate the rights of the defendant.[46]

Legal commentators have stressed how little uniformity still exists among European nations, and at a broader level among common law jurisdictions, in the rules relating to the use that may be made of evidence obtained by the interception of communications. In the English decision of *R v Governor of Pentonville, ex parte Chinoy*,[47] for example, the prosecution in the course of extradition proceedings sought to use a secretly taped recording of a conversation between French undercover agents and the applicant. French lawyers provided evidence to the English court that without the authority of a *juge d'instruction* these recordings were a criminal offense under French law, and a violation of Article 8 of the European Convention of Human Rights. Although the recorded conversations would have been inadmissible in a French Court, they were still held to be admissible in the English court to secure the applicant's extradition to the United States.

In another, more recent English decision, which also involved extradition proceedings, *R v Governor of Belmarsh Prison and another, ex parte Martin*,[48] the United States government sought the return of the applicant to face charges of conspiracy surrounding his alleged involvement in terrorist activities of the Irish Republican Army (IRA). The applicant was arrested and subsequently imprisoned in England pending the outcome of the extradition request. He then applied for a writ of habeas corpus, challenging his imprisonment on the ground that the evidence against him was contained in unlawful intercepted phone calls made to him in Ireland by two coconspirators in Florida. These calls had been intercepted in Florida by United States government agents. The applicant contended that the calls were inadmissible in all proceedings before the English court, having been intercepted in breach of Section 1 of the United Kingdom's *Interception of Communications Act* 1985.

Section 1 of that Act makes it an offense intentionally to intercept a communication in the course of its transmission by means of a public telecommunications system. The reach of that offense is extended by Section 10(2) of the Act, which provides:

> For the purposes of this Act a communication which is in the course of its transmission otherwise than by means of a public telecommunication system shall be deemed to be in the course of its transmission by means of such a system if its mode of transmission identifies it as a communication which—(a) is to be or has been transmitted by means of such a system; and (b) has been sent from, or is to be sent to, a country or territory outside the British Islands.

One of the arguments advanced by the applicant was that under this provision the interception of the calls in Florida was an offense if at some point that intercepted communication had passed through a public telecommunication system in the United Kingdom. To establish that such passage had occurred required proof that the intercepted communication between Florida and Ireland had taken a route through the United Kingdom, rather than one of two alternative routes used in the electronic switching of international telecommunications traffic between these two locations. The evidence revealed that the choice of routes was purely fortuitous, depending on the volume of traffic at any particular time, and it was impossible to establish which route had been taken by the intercepted calls. The applicant therefore failed on this point, although as one commentator has suggested, if the route had been established

> the extraordinary result would be that the criminality of the interception would depend on the chance selection of a route of which the potential perpetrator had neither knowledge or control.[49]

Apart from pointing to the vagaries between nations of the rules relating to the admissibility of evidence obtained from intercepted telecommunication, the decisions in *Chinoy* and *Martin* also illustrate some of the growing dilemmas for the existing legal and regulatory frameworks governing such interceptions in responding to crime that transcends the borders of one country. These frameworks were in large part developed at a time when telecommunication systems were still in a nondigital format, and when crime was viewed mainly as a problem to be addressed by individual states. This situation has changed dramatically during the past decade, as mentioned earlier in this paper, but the legal and regulatory framework required to cope with this globalization of both communications and crime has yet to be established. The situation is not, however, entirely bleak, nor without promise of innovation in designing new legal and regulatory structures that take account of these changes affecting us all so profoundly. Attention is now turned to these innovations and, in particular, to those which relate to the forging of new mutual assistance partnerships between law enforcement across a broad spectrum of countries.

PART 3: RESPONDING TO CHANGE

1. States should review their laws governing criminal offenses, jurisdiction, law enforcement powers and international cooperation, as well as their measures dealing with law enforcement training and crime prevention, to ensure that the special problems created by Transnational Organized Crime are effectively addressed.
2. With the aim of improving mutual assistance, States should, as needed, develop mutual legal assistance arrangements or treaties, and exercise flexibility in the execution of requests for mutual assistance.
3. States should, where feasible, render mutual assistance, notwithstanding the absence of dual criminality. . .
26. We emphasize the relevance and effectiveness of techniques such as electronic surveillance, undercover operations and controlled deliveries. We call upon States to review domestic arrangements for those techniques and to facilitate international cooperation in these fields, taking full account of human rights implications. We encourage States to exchange experiences of their use.
27. We emphasize the importance of giving the fullest possible protection to sensitive information received from other countries. The competent authorities of different States, should advise each other as to the requirements regarding the disclosure of

> information in the course of judicial and administrative proceedings, and discuss in advance potential difficulties arising from those requirements. A transmitting State may make conditions for the protection of sensitive information before deciding whether to transmit it. A receiving State must abide by the conditions agreed with the transmitting State.[50]

These recommendations form part of a broader set of proposals made to combat transnational organized crime by a group of senior experts meeting in Paris in April 1996 under the auspices of the Group of 8 (G8) industrialized nations. They are recommendations that reflect the concerted and ongoing effort by the G8, and the United Nations (UN)[51] to promote international agreement and action on this front. Much has also been achieved in this field by international bodies such as the Organization of Economic Cooperation and Development (OECD), the World Bank, and the Commonwealth.[52] Regional groups have also played a part, including the EU.

In Europe, in particular, significant bilateral and multilateral arrangements have been made over recent decades to respond to the recurring threat from terrorism by groups such as the IRA in the United Kingdom, the Red Brigade in Italy, and the Baader-Meinhof gang in Germany.[53] Many tactics and laws devised to suppress these groups, including the widespread use of telephone tapping and related surveillance by a range of police and intelligence agencies, have since been adapted to deal with drug trafficking and organized crime. An ongoing series of multilateral legal arrangements to promote closer coordination and cooperation among European police agencies has also resulted in this region now becoming what is probably the world's leading "best-practice" model of how to combat most forms of transnational crime.[54]

Despite this best-practice plaudit, commentators have pointed to the continuing absence from current mutual assistance arrangements within Europe of provisions to intercept telecommunications. The primary instrument currently governing mutual assistance between member States of the EU is the Council of Europe Convention on Mutual Assistance in Criminal Matters of 1959, which came into force in 1962.[55] The Convention, supplemented by an Additional Protocol, which came into force in 1982, is now applied in 30 states, including all 15 EU members. The protocol is a force in 24 states, including 13 EU members.

Neither the convention nor the protocol deal with policing and law enforcement issues, including the interception of communications. However, discussions that commenced in 1996 in the EU relating to the negotiation of a new convention for mutual criminal assistance now seem to have embraced these issues as part of a wider initiative, promoted by the Federal Bureau of Investigation (FBI) in the United States, to secure an international agreement on an interception standard for telecommunications among all interested countries. This standard or requirement would be a part of any new telecommunications development and would have to be incorporated in any new technology. The FBI's initiative, stimulated by the revolution in communications outlined earlier, has in the main attracted favorable governmental responses not only from European nations but also from countries as far afield as Australia. Thus in 1994 the Barrett Review remarked that:

> It would obviously be in Australia's interests to support strongly any initiative such as that currently being promoted by the FBI in the United States. . . If there is both European and North American acceptance of such a 'standard' this should ensure that switch and other relevant manufacturers would provide a "built in" interception capability for any *new* technology.[56]

This is not the place to provide an exhaustive account of the origin and subsequent advancement of the FBI initiative, which commenced in the early 1990s.[57] It is an initiative that has provoked fierce criticism from civil liberty groups such as the American Civil Liberties Union (ACLU), the Electronic Privacy Information Center (EPIC), and the Electronic Frontier Foundation (EFF) in the United States, who have continued to assert that the FBI has failed to substantiate the need for new and extraordinary government surveillance capabilities.[58] This criticism stalled the implementation of the initiative in any legislative form until 1994, when passage was obtained in the United States Congress of the Communications Assistance for Law Enforcement Act (CALEA).

The provisions of CALEA required telephone carriers in the United States to ensure continued government interception capabilities, despite changes in technology, by October 1998.[59] The Act was intended:

> to balance three key policies
>
> 1. to preserve a narrowly focused capability for law enforcement agencies to carry out properly authorized intercepts
> 2. to protect privacy in the face of increasingly powerful and personally revealing technologies and
> 3. to avoid impeding the development of new communication services and technologies.[60]

More than US$500 million was set aside by Congress to pay for the cost of adapting new technology to meet government interception capabilities. In addition, procedures were established for the issue by the U.S. Attorney General of a notice of future capacity of intercept requirements to the communications industry within one year of CALEA's enactment. Acting under delegated authority from the attorney general, the FBI issued such a notice in October 1995, but it was later withdrawn in the wake of widespread public criticism, and a new notice was issued in January 1997.[61] The latter notice called for a substantial increase in surveillance both of landline and wireless communications over the next 10 years with a total maximum capacity of more than 57,000 simultaneous intercepts to be conducted in the United States. This notice was rejected by industry and privacy groups alike for proposing an even greater capacity for interceptions by carriers than was currently required, at a prohibitive cost.[62] Critics suggested that among the new interception features sought by the FBI that were not subject to CALEA were packet-switching information; wireless telephone call location information; packet data content delivery information; and multiparty monitoring information.[63] These critics urged that the October 1998 deadline for compliance with CALEA's provisions should be extended to no earlier than October 2000 to permit more rigorous review of the FBI's proposals before setting industry interception capability standards.[64] An industry-wide extension has now been granted by the U.S. Federal Communications Commission until June 2000, while a closely aligned debate also continues in the United States and abroad concerning a cryptography policy for global communications.

As in the case of interception standards, the FBI has been playing a leading role in the cryptography policy debate. Cryptography—"the art or science that treats of the principles, means and methods for rendering plain text intelligible and for converting encrypted messages into intelligible form"[65]—was until recently largely the preserve of governments and their agencies, bent upon maintaining secrecy in their communications. In contemporary society that preserve has been shattered irrevocably by the development and widespread distribution of powerful encryption computer software, which has made it possible for any two people, anywhere in the world to hold a secret conversation or communication that is beyond the surveillance ability of even the most powerful code-breaking computer.

The debate over encryption has pitted computer industry and civil liberty groups against law enforcement and intelligence agencies.[66] It is a debate that is not only central to the maintenance and growth of trade and commerce, and to privacy protection, but also to the ability of law enforcement and national security bodies to understand what they are still able to intercept. On behalf of the law enforcement community, the FBI has therefore been lobbying actively to limit or prevent the use of encryption in the United States, and its export abroad. A concerted effort has been made to require manufacturers and users of encryption to lodge in escrow with independent authorities the special key needed to unlock and make intelligible encoded data. This so-called key escrow system would allow law enforcement agencies in the United States, or elsewhere, to gain access to a key to crack a code in the course of a criminal investigation.

Critics of the key escrow proposal have suggested that it poses a serious threat to privacy because there is a danger that access to keys could be abused by law enforcement agencies and others. It would also be a system that would require the United States, and other democratic countries, to share key escrow information with law enforcement agencies in nations with poor human rights records. These nations could use the keys to break codes used by dissidents to conduct their communications.[67] Computer industry officials in the United States have also claimed that existing controls on the export of powerful encryption technology abroad have already failed to prevent foreign companies supplying similar technology without any key escrow arrangements. This growing foreign role has diminished the ability of the FBI and other law-enforcement agencies to demand new safeguards or ways to decipher the communications of criminals who use encryption.[68]

The global debate on cryptography policy is far from over. Within the scope of this paper it has not been possible to do more than hint at the complexity of the issues involved in the debate, nor to do more than point to the concerns of those most affected by any policy, of whom law enforcement is just one of the interested parties. The recent review conducted of Australian cryptography policy probably summed up the situation correctly when it said:

> The wide and easy availability of cryptography will enhance the privacy of citizens, where they have control over the use to which data is being put ...It will adversely impact on the capability and investigative approach of law enforcement agencies and the security service and may, consequently, provoke some redefinition of that fundamental relationship between citizen and state. To presage the imminent end to civilization, however, which some foreign law enforcement advocates assert will ensue should their favored approach not be adopted, is neither a novel prophecy nor lends substantial assistance to the debate. . .
>
> The conundrum for government is the encryption genie is out of the bottle: a genie with the potential to enhance data security and personal and corporate privacy but also to provide a shield of invisibility for criminals and others.[69]

TOWARD THE FUTURE, AND VERY RAPIDLY

This paper commenced with a description of a new communication system whose development, let alone deployment, would no doubt have been viewed by many as a topic of science fiction only a decade ago. In cyberspace a Web year has been described as 90 days and going down.[70] Amid such revolutionary happenings the world of law enforcement is also being buffeted by unstoppable forces that may well make traditional investigative practices redundant, or largely ineffective, in an extremely short time. Nowhere are these forces more evident and influential than in the arena of communications technology. Just where these forces will lead law enforcement cooperation in its bid to respond to the threat of transnational crime is very hard to predict. When queried recently about this issue, and the presence of the Australian gateway for Iridium in Thailand, the head of an Australian law enforcement agency said this demonstrated:

> . . .that the present regimes for mutual legal assistance are fast proving inadequate even for traditional investigations, let alone those which involve the need to intercept communications or to overcome encryption of both local and international computer carried traffic. For example, the encryption key may be held in a third country and I am not yet satisfied that we have adequate regimes to enable law enforcement authorities to access that key let alone a framework in which the evidentiary problems can be overcome as one seeks to prove what the encrypted message actually said.
>
>   All of this is no doubt the basis of international conferences and a great deal of academic work but at the practical level I think we are fast running into a significant brick wall.[71]

Another senior law-enforcement official interviewed during the gathering of information for this paper told the author that he had real concerns about the future, and especially about the impact of encryption:

> I have real concerns. That might sound dramatic, but I didn't have concerns six months ago about this so it's just more and more consideration of the issues. What happens when law enforcement can't do the business of law enforcement? Can't gather evidence and the uptake in encryption into everything we do because everything we do is going to be online: shopping; watching tennis; paying bills. I mean, I do it now from home. It's all on line. So if I can't get in there and encrypt it. The other side of that is, well, technical surveillance. Law enforcement must develop it's technical surveillance. So that might be the answer. So I'm trying to give you a balanced view. There are limitations over technical surveillance. If a dog and a human being are always in the house you can't use technical surveillance. That's a reality. Now if you tell that, then every criminal will buy a dog.[72]

It seems rather unlikely that every criminal will buy a dog, or that law enforcement will be blocked entirely by a brick wall. Ways will be found to divert around the wall, and the canine threat will be countered by some ingenious device yet to be discovered. The present international conference must surely be the source of additional fruitful and authoritative ideas concerning how this diversion might be achieved. There may even be some among the participants who can also offer advice regarding how to overcome the technical surveillance problem that has been posed!

ACKNOWLEDGMENT

In preparing this paper the author has received substantial and generous research assistance and advice from many people including: John Broome, Mark Cowan, Shannon Cuthbertson, Geoffrey Dabb, Peter Ford, Adam Graycar, Keith Inman, Agnes Levine, Rick McDonell, Judy Maynard, Tonita Murray, Jennifer Norberry, Kevin O'Connor, Jan Sadler, Dianne Stafford and Maree Weicks.

    To each of these people the author wishes to express his gratitude, and also his reassurance that responsibility for the material utilized in the paper, and the views expressed, are his alone. Where reference is made to any personal comments made to the author during the course of his research, the identity of the commentator has been kept anonymous, unless permission was obtained to use their name in this paper.

NOTES

1. "Special Report: The Unwired World. An Insiders Guide to the Future Technologies of Telecommunications." *Scientific American* (1998) 278:4, 59–84.

2. JV Evans, "New Satellites for Personal Communication," note 1 above, at 60–67.

3. Current information concerning the implementation plans for the services provided by the Iridium company can be found at their Web site. These services are linked to regional sub-groupings—in the case of Australia, for example, they encompass the nations of the South Pacific.

4. See Evans, note 2 above, who suggests that while many different systems have been proposed, only five appear likely to be put in place, with Iridium leading the field. Four of the five systems are U.S. based.

5. Evans, note 2 above, at 64.

6. Personal communication with Peter Ford, First Assistant Secretary, Information and Security Law Division, Commonwealth Attorney General's Department. The mutual assistance problem on this issue is not limited to Thailand. Australia's current mutual assistance legislation cannot at present accommodate a request from a foreign country to intercept a telecommunication on Australian soil.

7. There are also difficulties in Australia sharing information obtained from a lawful intercept with other countries.

8. An excellent account of the new technologies involved in the communications revolution, and their related interception problems, is contained in U.S. Congress, Office of Technology Assessment *Electronic Surveillance in a Digital Age* OTA-BP-ITC-149, Washington DC : US Government Printing Office, July 1995 (OTA Report). For the purposes of the OTA Report electronic surveillance was considered to consist of both the interception of communications content (wiretapping) and the acquisition of call identifying information through the use of pen register devices or through taps and traces.

9. P.N. Grabosky and R.G. Smith, *Crime in the Digital Age. Controlling Telecommunications and Cyberspace Illegalities*, Sydney, Federation Press: 1994:206–207.

10. Article 12 states: "No-one shall be subjected to arbitrary interference with his privacy, family, home and correspondence, nor to attacks upon his honor and reputation. Everyone has the right to protection of the law against such interference or attacks."

11. Article 17 states: "1. No-one shall be subjected to arbitrary or unlawful interference with his privacy, family, home and correspondence, nor to attacks upon his honor or reputation. 2. Everyone has the right to protection of the law against such interference or attacks."

12. For example, a recent article in *Le Point*, a respected French news weekly, reported that France systematically eavesdrops on phone conversations in the United States and other countries through a worldwide network of electronic facilities designed to capture satellite transmissions. See J. Fitchett, "Eavesdropping by the French is Worldwide Magazine says," *International Herald Tribune*, 16 June 1998.

    It is also widely acknowledged that the United States Central Intelligence Agency, and the National Security Agency, use telephone, electronic, and satellite intercepts to obtain information on a global basis. See J. Bamford, *The Puzzle Palace*, New York, Penguin Books, 1982; A. Nadelmann, *Cops Across Borders. The Internationalization of U.S. Criminal Law Enforcement*, University Park, Pennsylvania State University Press, 1993, 299.

13. The paper's author is involved in the administration of this regime in Australia. This involvement dates from 7 February 1998, when a new procedure came into effect under an amendment to the Commonwealth's *Telecommunications (Interception) Act* 1979 (the TI Act) for the issue

of interception warrants to Australian law enforcement agencies. The amendment allowed the nomination of designated members of the Administrative Appeals Tribunal (AAT) to undertake the function, previously performed by judicial officers of the Federal Court, and the Family Court, of issuing interception warrants. The present author was one of 16 AAT members nominated from around the country to undertake this function. The AAT President, the Hon Justice Jane Mathews, a judge of the Federal Court, also appointed the author as the Tribunal's coordinator of this new function.

14. Excerpt from a current brochure issued as an aid to investigators by a telecommunications interception unit within a large Australian law enforcement agency.

15. Royal Commission to the New South Wales Police Service. *Final Report, Volume 1: Corruption.* Sydney, Government of the State of New South Wales, 1997, 21. The Royal Commission which was presided over by a judge of the New South Wales Supreme Court, the Hon. Justice JRT Wood, is usually referred to as the Wood Royal Commission.

16. See above, p. 21.

17. For contemporary descriptions of the Australian criminal justice system see, in general, D. Chappell and P.R. Wilson, eds., *The Australian Criminal Justice System: The Mid 1990's* (4th Edition), Sydney, Butterworths, 1994. In the past two decades there has also been a rapid expansion in the involvement of Federal authorities in the criminal justice arena. See D. Chappell, "A Review of Federal Law Enforcement Arrangements," in D. Chappell and P.R. Wilson, eds. *Australian Policing Contemporary Issues,* 2nd ed., Sydney, Butterworths, at 126–146.

18. The only State and Territorial jurisdictions that now lack this interception capacity are Queensland, the Australian Capital Territory (ACT), and the Northern Territory. The ACT is at present policed, under a contractual arrangement, by the AFP, which is able to make application in its own right for interception warrants.

19. See S. Bronitt, "Electronic Surveillance, Human Rights and Criminal Justice," *Australian Journal of Human Rights* (1997) 3(2):183–207.

20. See Bronitt above, p. 184, where it is noted that Australia, with a smaller population, authorizes more than twice as many interception warrants as Canada.

21. These statistics, and related tables, are contained in Department of the Attorney General *Telecommunication (Interception) Act* 1979. *Report for the year ending 30 June 1998,* Canberra, Commonwealth of Australia, 1998.

22. P.J. Barrett, *Review of the Long Term Cost Effectiveness of Telecommunications Interception,* 1 March 1994.

23. See above, p. 94.

24. See above, p. 94–95

25. The Victorian Police data showed the following costs per day (in $AUD) of different methods of surveillance: TI $570; optical (video) $1376; listening device $1630; physical surveillance $1895; location positioning (vehicle tracking) $2772. Barrett Review, note 22 above, at 91.

26. See note 22 above, p. 4.

27. Office of the United States Courts *Report of the Director of the Administrative Office of the United States Courts on Applications for Orders Authorizing or Approving the Interception of Wire, Oral or Electronic Communications for the period January 1 through December 31, 1998,* Washington D.C., Office of the United States Courts, 1999.

28. See above, p. 5. From 1997 to 1998 the total number of intercepts authorized by federal and state courts in the U.S. increased by 12 percent, reflecting sustained growth in applications concerned with the surveillance of drug-trafficking activities.

29. The present population of Australia is about 18 million people, and of the United States about 230 million.

30. See note 27 above, p. 10.

31. See above.

32. See above. Note 27 above p. 11.

33. See above.

34. For example, during the 1980s an Australian Royal Commission on drug trafficking and related issues found that widespread and unauthorized telephone tapping had been conducted by New South Wales police. See P. Grabosky, *Wayward Governance: Illegality and its Control in the Public Sector*, Canberra, Australian Institute of Criminology, 1989, p. 47.

35. The 1994 report, for instance, noted that such abuse of wiretaps occurred in seventy nations.

36. D. Banisar, *Bug Off! A Primer for Human Rights Groups on Wiretapping*, Washington DC, Privacy International, 1995, p. 1.

37. Nadelmann, note 12 above, pp. 243–246.

38. See above, pp. 195–196.

39. See above, p. 240.

40. See above.

41. See above.

42. See above.

43. (1990) ECHR, Series A, Vol 176.

44. S. Nash, "European Cooperation in telephone tapping" *New Law Journal* (1995):954–955.

45. See above. In France, time bars exist on criminal prosecutions.

46. See above.

47. (1992) 1 ALL ER 317.

48. (1995) 2 ALL ER 548.

49. See I.M. Yeats, "Extradition," *ALL ER Annual Review 1995,* pp. 277–278. The general provisions relating to the interception of telecommunications in the United Kingdom are reviewed in Halsbury, 11(1):270–280; 11(2):1165.

50. Senior Experts Group on Transnational Organized Crime P8—*Senior Experts Group Recommendations*, Paris, France, 12 April 1996

51. The UN has convened a number of meetings on this issue since an inaugural gathering, hosted by the Italian government, held in Naples in November 1995.

52. For example, *The OECD Guidelines Governing the Protection of Privacy and Transborder Flows of Personal Data* have been particularly influential in establishing international benchmarks in this area.

53. See Nadelmann, note 12 above, pp. 195–196.

54. These multilateral arrangements have included the Schenegen Agreement and the establishment of EUROPOL. See also Nadelmann, note 12 above pp. 195–196.

55. For a useful summary of the evolution of mutual assistance arrangements in the EU, see Statewatch, "EU Convention on Mutual Assistance." *Statewatch Bulletin* (1997) 7(4/5). The summary can also be found at the Statewatch Web site on http://www.poptel.org.uk/cgi-bin/dbs2/statewatch?query=telephone+tapping&mode=records&start=39028lin

56. Barrett Review, note 22 above, p. 6.

57. A description of the way in which this initiative has been exported to Europe will be found in Statewatch, "EU and FBI Launch Global Telecommunications Surveillance system," *Statewatch Bulletin* (1997) 7(1).

58. See ACLU Creed and Network. "Reply comments of the ACLU, EPIC and EFF in the matter of Communications Assistance for Law Enforcement Act." CC Docket No. 97-213, Federal Communications Commission, Washington D.C., http://www.aclo.org/congress/1g121297a.html

59. See above.

60. (1994) H.R. Rep No. 103-827, 103d Cong., 2d Sess., pt 1, at 13.

61. See ACLU, note 58 above, p. 5.

62. See above, p. 6.

63. See above, p. 10.

64. See above, p. 11. It should be noted that the FBI's initiative which led to the passage of CALEA in 1994, also resulted in further and significant comparative developments in other regions of the world. With joint EU and United States backing a memorandum of understanding (MOU) was drawn up in 1996 designed to foster a strategy to ensure global compliance with new "tappable" telecommunication requirements. Non-EU countries were invited to adopt the same requirements as those applied to the EU, and the United States, for network and service providers. By October 1996 Australia, Canada, and the United States had expressed their strong support for the requirements to the European Council, and meetings of experts from these countries, together with the EU and several other supportive nations, have continued since that time under the title of the International Law Enforcement Telecommunications Seminar (ILETS). See Statewatch, note 57 above, pp. 3–4.

65. See Gerard Walsh, *Review of Policy Relating to Encryption Technologies*, Canberra, Department of the Attorney General, 1996, Terms and Abbreviations (the Walsh Report). This report was the outcome of a study by Gerard Walsh, a former Deputy Director General of the Australian Security Intelligence Agency (ASIO). The report was listed for sale in January 1997 by the Australian Government Publishing Service but was then withdrawn from the sale list. After a successful freedom-of-information request by Electronic Frontiers Australia (EFA), an edited version of the report was released in June 1997. EFA has since obtained permission to publish this version on the Internet, and references in this paper are to that publication source.

66. There is very substantial literature on this subject area but the Walsh Report provides an excellent overview of the major issues involved. See also K. Holland, "Recent International Legal Developments in Encryption," Security, Law and Justice Branch, Attorney General's Department, Canberra, 1998.

67. See, for example, Editorial "Encryption for Privacy," *International Herald Tribune* 6 July 1998; J. Markoff, "Industry and Law Enforcers Face Off on High-Tech Prying." *International Herald Tribune*, 28 February—1 March 1998.

68. See above.

69. Walsh Report, note 65 above, paras 1.1.18—1.1.20.

70. See above, para 1.1.16.

71. Personal communication, May 1998.

72. Personal interview, August 1998.

"Green Managers Don't Cry:" Criminal Environmental Law and Corporate Strategy

Joseph F. DiMento
and
Gabrio Forti

Thirty years of environmental law have generated a flood of ideas on the best ways to enforce rules aimed at protecting natural resources and controlling pollution. Among the enforcement mechanisms, once rare in the environmental field, are criminal sanctions. Yet, while a significant trend toward employing criminal sanctions developed, mainly in the United States but also in other nations, so too did an appreciation that doing business in ways that are environmentally sensitive is good business. These parallel developments in the criminal justice system and in the private sector have created tensions in business-government relations but also have generated opportunities for new, cooperative means of reaching environmental law's aims.

This essay first summarizes the availability and use of criminal sanctions in pollution control efforts. It then defines green management and elaborates its meaning. Finally it addresses the questions: Can green management be a significant factor in shielding the firm from legal liability? Should it be?

CRIMINAL SANCTIONS AS MAINSTREAM JUSTICE SYSTEM RESPONSE

Leading Statutory Provisions

The existence of criminal provisions in environmental law is, literally speaking, not a new phenomenon. One of the first federal statutes used in actions against polluters of the nation's waters was the 1899 Rivers and Harbors Act, which provides for both criminal monetary penalties and imprisonment for violations. But modern environmental law began with the major regulatory laws of the early 1970s. Each of the leading statutes has incorporated a provision regarding criminal sanctions. Recent amendments have strengthened the earlier provisions. The Clean Air Act; The Resources Conservation and Recovery Act; Superfund, i.e., the Comprehensive Environmental Response Compensation and Liability Act (CERCLA); and The Clean Water Act have created the most important case law in this field (Gaynor and Bartman, 1999).

States also added these provisions, some focused on media-specific environmental violations, some more general, such as that in Oregon, and some very general, such as the famous "Be a Manager: Go to Jail" provision on corporate liability in the California Code (Corporate Criminal Liability Act of 1998). Fines under contemporary criminal environmental laws range from $2,500 to $50,000 per day per violation ($1 million for a corporate defendant for knowing endangerment), and up to fifteen years imprisonment.

Other countries are making this policy choice as well. The Canadian Environmental Protection Act of 1988 provides for large monetary fines and substantial imprisonment time. Germany, Italy, Spain, The Netherlands, France, Brazil, and Australia all have increased their emphasis on criminal enforcement of pollution control and natural resource protection laws (Nespor et al., 1996). Some African countries have made illegal disposal of hazardous wastes a capital offense. Asian nations—including Korea, Singapore, Thailand, Taiwan, and Japan —now also have strong criminal enforcement provisions.

Record of Use

From the time when the Environmental Crimes Unit in the United States Department of Justice was established in 1983, the trend toward use of criminal sanctions has been clear. In the early years (1983-1986) the federal government brought about forty indictments per year. By 1995, 563 criminal cases had been initiated at the federal level, 517 years of imprisonment had been imposed, and 374 years of actual confinement recorded. Criminal fines have also been significant, with almost $77 million being imposed in 1996 and $169.3 million in fiscal year 1997. With passage of the Pollution Prosecution Act of 1990 the figures climbed after Congress ordered The United States Environmental Protection Agency (EPA) to hire 200 environmental criminal investigators. Furthermore, Congress has been relatively generous in authorizing funding for environmental enforcement (Bellew and Surtz, 1997). The EPA in the last decade and a half became somewhat of a criminal justice entity; its investigators have several authorities associated with criminal enforcement including the ability to carry firearms and to make arrests.

Some Examples

There is no "typical" case. Some actions have involved punishments of giant Fortune 500 corporations for violations of very specific provisions of the major federal regulatory laws, such as the emission control requirements of the Clean Air Act. Others have targeted small, sloppily run businesses, such as battery recycling and plating companies under general criminal endangerment codes. The record includes federal actions against an aerospace company for a hazardous waste law violation which resulted in two deaths ($6.5 million fine); against a quasigovernmental transportation entity for violations of water law (a five-year suspended sentence and a fine of $2.75 million); against individual mushroom farmers who were also corporate officers for water law violations (thirty days in jail and a $50,000 fine); against cruise ship companies for illegal dumping in violation of the Act to Prevent Pollution from Ships ($250,000 fine); against sewage treatment plant owners for bypassing treatment mechanisms and dumping effluent at night at a popular surfing beach (over two years confinement for each defendant); against shipping companies for spilling hundreds of thousands of gallons of oil (a $75 million fine); against facility operators for submitting false monitoring reports to government officials; against traders in endangered species; and against smugglers of Freon, an ozone depleting substance, into the United States through Florida, Texas, and California. Similar cases are successfully brought under state law.

Available Sanctions

Available sanctions are not limited to monetary fines and prison time. Public policy and individual prosecutors have been creative in punishing. Among sanctions available in various jurisdictions under one or other criminal theory: dissolving the corporation; imposing monetary fines aimed at forcing divestiture; rescinding of government contracts, grants, and licenses; debarment from doing business with the government; restitution; community service; probation, including requirements that the violators publicize in major national newspapers the offenses, the fact of conviction, and steps planned to prevent recurrence of the offenses. Violators may be required by court order to develop a compliance program or to submit to the court a program for detection and prevention of violations, and/or detailed monitoring reports.

Liability Joint and Several, Vicarious, Corporate

With this increased vigilance under both criminal and civil law for environmental protection, naturally, has come increased business concern with legal liability. Potential liability results from several phenomena in the regulatory environment of the firm, i.e., in its relationships with government generally and the criminal justice system more specifically. The evolution of legal liability rules has included an increased focus on *toxic tort liability* under common law doctrine and related statutory law such as Superfund (CERCLA). It includes also *strict liability* or liability without fault and *joint and several liability* (holding that even for a minor contribution to an environmental problem—such as transporting a small quantity of a regulated material to a hazardous waste site—a party may be liable for the full cost of clean up if the other parties cannot be found or are without resources. The Monsanto Company, for example, was unable to convince a court that it should not be liable under Superfund law for its contributions, which it argued were small, to a waste site that contained 7000 fifty-five gallon drums of chemical waste that the facility owners had allowed to be improperly disposed. Monsanto was only one of several generators of the waste and arguably not a primary contributor. But the court said that Monsanto had the burden of disproving causation and lectured that "a million gallons of certain substances could be mixed together without significant consequences, whereas a few pints of others improperly mixed could result in disastrous consequences."[1]

The vicarious liability doctrine may impose liability on some actors for the actions of others, based solely on the relationship between the parties. The situation can arise within a firm and also across firms. The *responsible corporate officer* doctrine has been read into some major federal environmental legislation. This imposes liability on an officer regardless of participation if he or she was in a position to prevent and correct the violation. Parent corporations may someday be held liable for the criminal behavior of subsidiaries (Gaynor and Bartman, 1999). And a particular set of concerns involving liability for the firm arises from the fact that in some of the world's jurisprudence, the *corporation itself* can be liable for wrongdoing: corporate criminal liability.

Furthermore, the requirement of *mens rea*, the mental element that a prosecutor must establish in a criminal proceeding, has been very liberally interpreted in some criminal environmental cases, especially when a violation is seen as negatively affecting the public welfare. Some courts have concluded that the only knowledge required is that of doing the act, not that the act was a violation of a known regulatory prohibition.[2]

GREEN MANAGEMENT AS AN EVOLVING INNOVATIVE INDUSTRY RESPONSE

Green Management Defined

New pressures from several sources, government and public opinion being among the most forceful, have led business to consider and in many cases adopt a new form of business strategy colloquially called "green management." Without any single precise definition, green management or environmental management is a set of activities and orientations of the firm aimed at decreasing negative impacts or increasing positive impacts of its actions on the environment, even when regulatory standards will be surpassed. It is the business strategy which embraces environmental protection rather than seeing it as a threat to business success. Green management variously includes ecolabeling, ecoauditing, ecoaccounting, ecomarketing, environmental quality life cycle analysis, environment-oriented management systems, environmental compliance programs, process reforms, and environment-focused research and development. It often involves internal restructuring and alterations of relations with the outside business and government environment, aimed at using fewer natural resources and using them more efficiently and with a minimum of environmental impact. It treats as equally important economic and environmental objectives.

Definitions of "going green" must confront several complicating factors. What exactly constitutes sound behavior from an ecological perspective is one issue. For example, chlorofluorocarbons (CFCs), presently the target of an international phase-out, until recently were considered safe products. A "green product" is not always easily identifiable. Canada's giant grocery chain Loblaws said that, to be green, a product must be equal in every respect to the products already in commerce except for its impact on the environment. A more elaborate approach was used by Volvo, employing an "EPA" system. A product would be evaluated according to several indices: impact on natural resources and extraction of primary resources, use of land, and emissions into air, water, and the soil. The result of this system is an environmental load figure, which allows for comparison across different materials. Then there is the issue of talk versus action. "Flowery happy talk" is the way one federal judge described the so-called environmental strategy of one firm. Changing production processes, monitoring compliance with internal and external standards, deciding on the basis of environmental as well as economic objectives—these are the operational parts of a true green strategy.

From a regulatory perspective, green management can also have several definitions. It can mean the adoption of an environmental audit system such as that defined by the EPA: "systematic, documented, periodic and objective review by regulated entities of facility operations and practices related to meeting environmental requirements."[3] It can translate to addition of a comprehensive environmental management system: "an explicit statement of corporate policy, commitment of management and resources, training, response mechanisms, and internal discipline" (Carr and Thomas, 1997). The European Union (EMAS) and the International Standards Organization (the 14000 series) have established criteria for environmental management.

Several major companies have adopted some form of green management strategy. Among the largest are Apple Computer, Colgate-Palmolive, Nissan, Hitachi, Lufthansa, Anheuser-Busch, and Coca-Cola. Among the more famous of the small firms is Patagonia, a specialized, high-end recreational clothing company in Southern California, which has historically dedicated a percentage of its sales revenue to environmental organizations. Recently *The New York Times* described Ford Motor Company's new Chief Executive Officer, a descendant of the founder, Henry Ford, as a major figure in environmental management. The new CEO has chronicled his efforts to move the giant auto maker into a resources protection and pollution control orientation.

Examples of Strategies

To be more concrete, actions that the firm can take to be considered green are numerous. They include (1) promoting a high-level corporate executive to a role of compliance officer—he or she reports directly to the chief executive officer, works with regulatory agencies, and monitors regulatory compliance; (2) appointing environmentalists to the Board of Directors; (3) creating internal audit systems to decrease the incidence of environmental violations; (4) installing information systems that ensure that instances of noncompliance are communicated to high-level management; and (5) signing on to environmental codes of conduct such as the Ceres Principles in the United States and its cousins in Japan and Germany. (An example principle is corporate commitment to protection of whistle-blowers against retaliation.) Less formally, the firms can develop and lead the field in green-labeling campaigns; foster recycling programs that exceed government rules; and sponsor environmental education programs. Green management thus can vary from a single strategy, such as an audit, to a complete management system. In the latter case, environmental protection is a central objective, and compliance is sought not only for meeting existing governmental requirements but also to achieve self-motivated corporate environmental objectives.

Green Management's General Rationales

Green management has been advocated to meet many social objectives: improved quality of the product, a greater commitment on the part of personnel to activities of the firm, improved relations with the local community and with various interest groups, better interactions with the media, lower insurance policy costs, better relations with financial institutions, reduced exposure to business risks, overall reduction of costs, and competitive advantages domestically and in world markets. Good green compliance also may make it easier for the firm to comply with, and avoid enforcement activities under, environmental law. Harvard Business School Professor Michael Porter cites the Tobyhannan Army Depot case as an example of how innovation can help the firm, avoiding exposure to law suits. Between 1985 and 1992, improvements in the way the company undertook its sandblasting and related operations reduced its generation of hazardous waste by over 80 percent, thereby avoiding over seven million dollars in environmental liability costs, on top of the disposal costs, which were also dramatically reduced.

A corporate image can be turned around dramatically by discovering green. Dow Chemical is an example. Dow took several steps to change its former image as one synonymous with Agent Orange and with company-led attacks on what it called nit-picking ridiculous environmental regulations. It created an Environmental Advisory Council connected to senior management. The company provided incentives, including monetary bonuses, to employees who help to reach environmental goals. It introduced an environmental criterion as part of each employee's appraisal form, and it developed several practices to control emissions and dramatically limit dangerous hazardous waste disposal activities. It moved quickly to be listed among the top environmental business champions.[4] Consider the opposite public relations effect of being described (in *The New York Times*) as having "the worst environmental record of any company," as a Connecticut corporation was recently.

Green Management and Legal Liability

Some firms also look to green management as a means of insulating them from increasingly severe liability rules and from the increasingly aggressive actions of public prosecutors throughout the criminal process—from the point of seeking disclosure of sensitive documents to requesting tough penalties of the courts. Green management from this perspective should limit the need to disclose information gathered by the firm for purposes of analyzing and coming into compliance or for meeting internal environmental objectives. Green management should be the basis for legal conclusions, under both statutory and common law, that liability be circumscribed and punishment limited for the company that tries to be a good environmental citizen. Environmental management attempts should move federal enforcers to opt for administrative actions when faced with the option of proceeding civilly, criminally, or under administrative enforcement provisions. Green management should evoke sympathy in the courts for the firm subjected to liability rules that seem unfair when applied in the context of numerous "pro-environment" actions of the company. Both judges and juries should be influenced by the green behavior of the firm. Good green management should make enforcers less eager to draconianly apply severe liability doctrines. It should be a counterinfluence to forces seeking to punish top good green management for the actions of lower-level employees.

Green management may make government less interested in prosecution because roles have been established in the company and processes initiated that indicate a commitment to compliance with environmental law. From a broader perspective, green management activities may translate to a political climate opposed to mandating further rules and standards for an industry sector.

A GREEN MANAGEMENT PROTECTION?
DEFENSES, IMMUNITIES, AND PRIVILEGE

While some commentators assert that green firms should be less susceptible to prosecution and more able to defend themselves in environmental lawsuits, others take a different, or at least an additional, stance. They argue that these firms should be *differentially treated* by public prosecutors. Those companies that make protection of the environment a priority, that take good faith steps to be in compliance with the myriad pollution control regulations, and that report to the government violations they were unable to avoid and that they themselves detected, should benefit from several types of protections against prosecution and punishment. Their environmental audit and related reports should be protected against use in cases against them. Their behaviors should be counted as mitigating factors in punishments that are imposed, or they should be immune from legal actions.

The savings to the firm from a more understanding federal enforcement policy can be substantial. The GTE Corporation, faced with a $2.38 million fine for violations of emergency planning law and Clean Water Act violations, settled with EPA for about $52,000—allowed in part because the violations were identified by the company's own audit (Turner, 1998). The hope for better treatment however is not universally realized; and in fact environmental management can be used in ways that counter the firm's interests. Consider the case of the Proctor and Gamble Manufacturing Company (Carr and Thomas, 1997, 987). It was forced to pay almost $400,000 to settle a controversy involving its compliance with environmental law. The case involved installation of air pollution control equipment to reduce methanol emissions. The company received the penalty despite the fact that the violation was uncovered through Proctor and Gamble's own good-faith compliance inspection, which had been earlier approved by a local air quality management agency.

There is, however, some movement on the public side toward kinder and gentler consideration of the green firm. Some jurisdictions have created privileges for audit materials—which go well beyond attorney client and work product privileges. Prosecutors are urged or directed to offer at least some protection against criminal charges for companies that have real comprehensive audit systems, where prompt response is made to those environmental violations that are uncovered (Carr and Thomas, 1997, 99). The United States Department of Justice has created a guidance document to give federal prosecutors information on factors which should be applied in deciding on use of prosecutorial discretion in the face of environmental management efforts by firms. The document guides the decision over bringing criminal charges. Although it does not recognize an environmental audit privilege, its focus is clearly to reward environmentally progressive companies potentially subject to being charged criminally.

Similarly, EPA has used special settlement agreements to lessen penalties imposed on a company. Under its program on Supplemental Environmental Projects, in exchange for environmentally sensitive actions that a company volunteers to undertake and are not legally required, penalties imposed on violators are reduced. The agency has also extended the date of compliance for sources that achieve early reductions of hazardous air pollutant emissions. In addition, EPA concluded that for violations discovered though audits that display due diligence, prosecution will not be recommended. The agency stated that "where violations are found through voluntary environmental audits or efforts that reflect a regulated entity's due diligence, and are promptly disclosed and expeditiously corrected, EPA will not seek gravity-based (i.e., noneconomic benefit) penalties and will generally not recommend criminal prosecutions against the regulated entity" (EPA, 1995). The agency has two other prongs of its policy on treating "good actors." It will not seek criminal penalties in cases where there is no serious harm and the firm has in good faith identified, disclosed, and corrected violations; and it will not routinely require environmental audits for companies demonstrating systematic compliance.

Federal legislation has been periodically introduced that would create a privilege against disclosure of information collected for environmental self-assessment both for proceedings at the administrative level and in the courts; a good-faith voluntary audit would be inadmissible in federal courts. In the related occupational health and safety arena, proposed legislation would also exempt companies from inspections by the federal Occupational Safety and Health Administration (OSHA) if their compliance and self-regulation efforts were cer-tified by an outside firm (Kovach et al., 1997). The bill would also create a priv-ilege against having to disclose the results of a firm's safety and health audits.

Furthermore, sentencing guidelines, such as those proposed for federal pros-ecution of organizations, have incorporated mitigation factors for companies that have taken measures to comprehensively protect the environment, although the notion of imposing stricter penalties on companies that had no prior compliance programs was rejected by the U.S. Sentencing Commission (Duran, 1995).

At the state level, Oregon was the first to create an environmental audit or self-evaluation privilege. Now, about nineteen states have some form of privilege varying from immunity from penalties to a complete privilege for environmental audit materials.

The policy positions taken on these enforcement changes by environmen-talists, government officials, and business are becoming clearer. But how sound is a public policy of protections from liability for the green firm?

On the one hand, it seems eminently reasonable to experiment with some forms of protection while also monitoring the firm's response. There are several good reasons to reward the generally compliant firm acting in good faith to pro-mote environmental goals. "There is a limit beyond which it is no longer realis-tic or fundamentally fair to criminalize mere mistakes in judgment, such as in the spill reporting requirements arena, where there are frequently multiple tenable interpretations" (Carr and Thomas, 1997, 97). Secondly, the complexity of fed-eral and state environmental law makes noncompliance the rule, not the excep-tion, even for the best performing firms; thus, if good-faith self-examinations discover violations, the result should be considered a positive outcome, not the basis for liability—criminal or otherwise.[5] Also there is a risk of "overfiling" (or "topfiling") (i.e., concurrent or close-in-time federal and state enforcement action) and even of double jeopardy in light of the dual sovereignty federalism of the United States enforcement system (Kellner, 1998). Additionally, the ability of governmental enforcers to subpoena audits and self disclosures provides little incentive for the company to do a comprehensive, rigorous self-analysis. "Granting the legal privilege would prevent employers from having to reveal the results of their self-safety audits and, therefore, allow them to identify the situations, abate the hazard, and avert the possibility of receiving an OSHA fine" (Covet et al., 1997, 177). Finally, promoting environmental protection objectives may be best done when the focus is not on absolute compliance but on innovation, which can ultimately lead to more complete environmental clean up (Porter and van der Linde, 1995).

However, there is another side to the policy analysis. Proceeding slowly toward these reforms is warranted. As the Department of Justice has recently articulated, the federal government now has a very good mix of strong enforcement for wrongdoers and "leniency for good actors." There are several reasons to move cautiously. First, in practice, the application of special treatment regimes can be so complex as to be unworkable. Factors to be employed may either create excessive discretion in the individual prosecutor's office, in effect delegating without standards, or become so numerous as to be unworkable. Consider the factors under one model; in order to be eligible for favorable treatment a company must engage in regularized audit procedures; have audit integrity safeguards; undertake comprehensive evaluation of all pollution sources; provide for timely implementation of audit recommendations; have an adequate resource commitment to the audit and follow-up; incorporate environmental criteria into overall company performance evaluations; adopt control measures beyond existing law; and create and use a strong institutional policy to meet environmental requirements (Carr and Thomas, 1977, 105).

Furthermore, audits can be manipulated to cover illegal violations. As Darnell (1993) has noted, another potential weakness is that the corporate defendant may act disingenuously with audit programs. It may include large amounts of potentially damaging information about the firm's behavior with the aim of shielding that information from use later in enforcement proceedings. The privilege may jeopardize the right-to-know of citizens, which is a strong element of law and public policy in the United States and increasingly in Europe (DelSole, 1997). In fact in reaching its conclusion against recognition of a privilege for environmental audits, the EPA Final Policy states: "privilege, by definition, invites secrecy instead of the openness needed to build public trust in industry's ability to self-police." The privilege policy may also reward companies who defer remediation of problems, giving them an economic advantage over those who comply in a timely manner (Turner, 1998). Finally, there may be a serious conflict in state and federal law with regard to prosecution. The EPA has claimed that broad immunities and protections provided by some states can interfere with federal enforcement efforts.

Proponents do counter that potential abuses of more cooperative procedures can be controlled. Government can invoke exceptions to the privilege; preclude the privilege where environmental law requires that information be developed, maintained, and reported; and legislate sunset provisions, i.e., fixed dates for automatic repeal of the law unless it is shown to promote compliance effectively.

CONCLUSIONS

In some circumstances green management should be the basis for prosecutorial leniency, less corporate liability, and greater immunities. Green managers should be treated with some enforcement lenience. An appropriate criminal justice and policy response, however, needs to be based on understanding what those circumstances are. At least the following seem worthy of further consideration: The firm should have a solid record of considerable compliance most of the time, as reflected over a period of years. The firm should have evidence that it is working on even more complete systems that will avoid reported violations in the future, such as provided for under the International Standards Organization's environmental guidelines (ISO 14001). Where there have been violations, self-reporting should be prompt. The environmental management system should be one that actually influences the performance of people responsible for environmental impact. It should incorporate a collection of incentives and disincentives aimed at achieving compliance to the fullest extent possible. Finally, prosecutorial leniency should be compatible with the welfare of the communities within which the firm operates and upon which it has impacts.

Part of the challenge of determining the right balance in treatment of green managers comes from the enhanced influence of the private sector in communicating its perspectives, independently of the substance behind its assertions. One need not take the position that corporate crime has been normalized (Snider, 1997) to conclude that it is premature to move rapidly toward an environmental policy that relies heavily, if not exclusively, on the goodwill of the large enterprise organization. Managers should not fear if their environmental systems are well conceptualized, well designed, consistent with public policy goals, and actively and fully implemented. But they might have good reason to cry if "green" is no more than corporate window dressing. Managers should not be protected, immunized, or privileged when hiding real environmental violations that have serious consequences to the physical environment and to human health, in situations where there is, as Judge Posner wrote, every incentive to hire managers willing to commit crimes on the corporation's behalf.

NOTES

1. *United States v. Monsanto* 858 F.2d 160 (4th Cir. 1988), *cert. denied*, 490 U.S. 1106 (1989).

2. The courts are not unanimous on this point. See for example *United States v. Ahmad*, 101 F. 3d 386, 390 (5th Cir. 1996).

3. 60 Fed. Reg. 66,706-12 1995.

4. Faye Rice, "Who Scores Best on the Environment?" *Fortune Magazine*, July 26, 1993 @ p. 114.

5. Shweiki (1996) reports that a recent survey found that only 33% of corporations claim to be 100% in compliance with all state and federal environmental regulations.

BIBLIOGRAPHY

Bellew, Sean, and Daniel Surtz. 1997. "Criminal Enforcement of Environmental Laws: A Corporate Guide to Avoiding Liability," *Villanova Environmental Law Journal* 8:205.

Blabolil, Sandee, et al. 1997. "Environmental Crimes." (Twelfth Survey of White-Collar Crime.) *American Criminal Law Review* 34(2):491–554.

Carr, Donald A., and William L. Thomas. 1997. "Devising a Compliance Strategy Under the ISO 14000 International Environmental Management Standards." *Pace Environmental Law Review* 15:85–231.

Curran, Steve. 1995. "Environmental Crimes," (Tenth Survey of White-Collar Crime.) *American Criminal Law Review* 32(2):245–308.

Darnell, Robert W. 1993. "Environmental Criminal Enforcement and Corporate Environmental Auditing: Time for a Compromise?" *American Criminal Law Review* 31(1):123–143.

DelSole, E.P. 1997. "An Environmental Audit Privilege: What Protection Remains After EPA's Rejection of the Privilege?" *Catholic University Law Review* 46(2):325–370.

Environmental Protection Agency. 1995. EPA Final Policy Guidance Document, Incentives for Self-Policing: Discovery, Disclosure, Correction and Prevention of Violations. 60 Fed. Reg. 66706

Garland, Norman. 1996. "The Unavailability to Corporations of the Privilege Against Self-Incrimination: A Comparative Examination." *New York Law School Journal of International and Comparative Law* 16:55–77.

Gaynor, Kevin, and Thomas Bartman. 1999. "Criminal Enforcement of Environmental Laws," *Colorado Journal of International Environmental Law and Policy* 10(Winter): 39.

Geis, Gilbert, and Joseph DiMento. 1995. "Should We Prosecute Corporations and/or Individuals?" in Frank Pearce and Laureen Snider, *Corporate Crimes: Contemporary Debates.* Toronto: University of Toronto Press.

Kellner, Katherine C. 1998. "Separate but Equal: Double Jeopardy and Environmental Actions." *Environmental Law* 28(1):169–189.

Kovach, Kenneth A. et. al. "OSHA and the Politics of Reform: An Analysis of OSHA Reform Initiatives Before the 104th Congress." *Harvard Journal on Legislation* 34:169–190.

Lemkin, Jason M. 1996. "Deterring Environmental Crime Through Flexible Sentencing: A Proposal for the New Organizational Sentencing Guidelines." *California Law Review* 4(2):307–376.

Nespor, Stefano, Antonella Capria, Beniamino Caravitta, Joseph DiMento, et al., eds. *A World Survey of Environmental Law.* Milano Giuffre Editore.

Porter, Michael E., and Claas van der Linde. 1995. "Green and Competitive." *Harvard Business Review* 73:120.

Porter, Michael E. 1991. "America's Green Strategy." *Scientific American* 168 (April).

Shweiki, Opher. 1996. "Environmental Audit Privilege and Voluntary Disclosure Rule: the Importance of Federal Enactment." *American Criminal Law Review* 33(4): 1219–1249.

Snider, Laureen. 1997. "Nouvelle Donne Legislative et. Causes de la Criminalite Corporative." *Criminologie* XXX(1).

Stensvang, John-Mark. 1997/98. "The Fine Print of State Environmental Audit Privileges." *Journal of Environmental Law* 16:69.

Turner, Andrew. 1998. "Mens rea in Environmental Crime Prosecutions: Ignorantia Juris and the White Collar Criminal." *Columbia Journal of Environmental Law* 23:217.

Yeager, Peter Cleary. 1993. "Industrial Water Pollution," in Michael Tony and Albert J. Reiss, Jr. *Beyond the Law: Crime in Complex Organizations.* Chicago: University of Chicago Press.

The Virtuous Prison: Toward a Restorative Rehabilitation

Francis T. Cullen,
Jody L. Sundt,
and
John F. Wozniak

The most startling fact in corrections is the seemingly unstoppable rise in the nation's prison population. In 1970, the number of inmates in state and federal prisons on any given day did not reach 200,000; three decades later, this figure was more than six times higher, with the population in excess of 1.2 million (Gilliard, 1998; Langan, Fundis, Greenfeld, and Schneider, 1988). When offenders in jail are added, America's incarcerated population now tops 1.8 million (Gilliard, 1998). Not surprisingly, most criminologists have decried this enormous jump in imprisonment. They often note that, with the exception of Russia, the United States has the highest incarceration rate worldwide—several times higher than most advanced industrial nations (Mauer, 1994). Merely making this observation, it seems, is enough to confirm that something is amiss in our correctional policy.

The most common assertion is that the United States should not place so many of its residents behind bars. Although we largely agree with this contention, we will leave the specific merits of this claim for others to debate (compare, e.g., Bennett, DiIulio, and Walters, 1996 and Reynolds, 1997 with Clear, 1994; Currie, 1998; and Irwin and Austin, 1994). What concerns us here, however, is the concomitant tendency for criminologists to remain silent on precisely *what prisons should be like*. Because criminologists' main concern is that imprisonment should be used sparingly (i.e., only for the incorrigibly violent or for those committing truly heinous crimes), they couple their criticism of the "imprisonment binge" with a call for policy makers to create more viable "alternatives to incarceration."

Although the logic here makes sense—if too many people are locked up, alternatives to prison are essential—this kind of thinking obscures or neglects a related question: Short of releasing them, what should be done with the offenders who remain incarcerated? If at all, criminologists respond with the admonition that prisons should be "more humane." Exactly what this means is only infrequently spelled out (for exceptions, see Johnson, 1996; Toch, 1997).

Why do criminologists generally fail to draft a blueprint for the prison environment? To an extent, their scholarly interests lie outside the substantive area of institutional corrections; instead, their critique of "imprisonment" is part of a broader salvo at the conservatives' "get tough" movement on crime. We suspect, however, that something else is also involved. Since the stunning critique of institutionalization elucidated in Goffman's (1961) *Asylums* and illustrated by the Stanford prison experiment (Haney, Banks, and Zimbardo, 1973), many criminologists have embraced the view that total institutions, and correctional facilities in particular, are *inherently* inhumane. Efforts to improve prisons are thus seen as doomed and, even worse, as serving to *legitimate* the very idea that prisons are *potentially* humane. In this view, a "humane prison" is an oxymoron and a dangerous one at that. The stubborn reality is that even when prison administrators have the best of intentions, institutions will remain coercive and dehumanizing (see, e.g., Rothman, 1980).

This conceptualization of prisons is part of a more general view of *state* social control that has been nearly hegemonic in criminology over the past generation. By the early 1970s, criminologists—by all accounts a progressive group politically—had embraced the view that "nothing works" in corrections and, more generally, that virtually all attempts by the state to control crime were coercive. Scarcely a decade before, they were optimistic—sometimes cautiously, sometimes wildly—that government was an integral part of the solution to crime (President's Crime Commission on Law and Enforcement and Administration of Justice, 1968). The continuing turmoil of the 1960s and revelations of abuse of power by state officials, however, diminished this hope and resulted in a jaundiced view of the willingness and capacity of the government's "agents of social control" to improve offenders' lives (Cullen and Gilbert, 1982; Garland, 1990). Criminologists, especially those of a "critical" perspective, were prone to see virtually any intervention to control crime as a strategy of power concealed beneath a phony rhetoric voiced by naive reformers or disingenuous state officials. In subsequent years, this view became, ironically, uncritically accepted and part of the professional ideology of criminologists.

Binder and Geis (1984) capture this phenomenon in their revealing analysis of how criminologists portray juvenile diversion programs. They note that diversion might legitimately be described as an effort to spare juveniles criminal sanctions in exchange for their participation in programs that provide these youths—many at risk for future illegal conduct—with much-needed social services. These programs are run by youth and nonprofit agencies and provide "family counseling, restitutive arrangements, help with securing work, employment counseling, and intervention with schools" (p. 635). Instead, criminologists commonly portray diversion as "stigmatizing" and as "dramatizing the evil" of "kids." This labeling is carried out by "agents of social control." Positive program results are dismissed as methodologically unsound (see also, Gottfredson, 1979). Most salient, diversion is said to invidiously "widen the net of social control." Such rhetoric, argues Binder and Geis (1984, 630), should be deconstructed to illuminate its ideological purpose:

> The phrase "widening the net" is, of course, employed pejoratively, with the intent to evoke an emotional response. It conjures up visions of a mesh net that is thrown over thrashing victims, incapacitating them, as they flail about, desperately seeking to avoid captivity. The net is maneuvered by "agents of social control," another image-provoking term, this one carrying a Nazi-like connotation. Both terms are employed for purposes of propaganda rather than to enlighten.

Where does this kind of thinking lead us? Binder and Geis (1984, 636) contend that the favored policy recommendation is a preference for "no action"—for nonintervention by the criminal justice system (see also, Travis and Cullen, 1984). When taking "no action" is patently absurd (i.e., when a serious crime has been committed), then the preference is for exercising the least control possible. In this view, the goal should not be to "do good" but to "do the least harm possible" (Fogel, 1988; Gaylin, Glasser, Marcus, and Rothman, 1978). As rising prison populations over the past thirty years reveal, this minimalist approach to crime control has not proven persuasive. It also has led, as we have argued, to an absence among criminologists of systematic thinking about what prisons should be like.

We do not believe that it is responsible for criminologists to refrain from entering the ongoing conversation about what prisons are for and how they should be organized. As noted, the failure to participate in this policy discourse has not stemmed the use of imprisonment in the United States. In this context, the risk of somehow "legitimizing" prisons seems the least of our worries. Worse still, by not articulating a compelling vision for imprisonment—by merely being naysayers for thirty years—criminologists have provided the get-tough crowd with an unprecedented opportunity to redefine the purpose and nature of imprisonment. As Clear (1994) observes, the result has been a "penal harm movement" that has made the infliction of misery on inmates not something to hide but to celebrate. Further, the generic critique of prisons as inherently inhumane, while correct in the sense that all institutions are depriving, ignores the reality that not all prisons are equally depriving (DiIulio, 1987; Wright, 1994). Some facilities expose inmates to violence and inspire fear, some do not; some provide decent amenities, some do not; some provide opportunities to be productive and to change, some do not. To ignore this reality is to forfeit the opportunity to improve the quality of life for America's inmate population.

Given these considerations, we propose that it is time for criminologists—especially progressive criminologists—to speak up and articulate what prisons should be for and like. In the end, we anticipate that a cacophony of voices will be needed to clarify what a progressive approach to institutional corrections should entail. Our purpose here thus must be seen as modest and as advancing but one possible option. This caveat stated, we offer as a model for corrections *the virtuous prison*.

At its core, this approach suggests that the fundamental goal of the prison experience should be to foster "virtue" in inmates, which is usually defined as "moral goodness" or "moral excellence" (*Webster's New Universal Unabridged Dictionary*, 1979, 2042). Prisons should be considered moral institutions and corrections a moral enterprise. Inmates should be seen as having the obligation to become virtuous people and to manifest moral goodness. This statement announces that there are standards of right and wrong and that offenders must conform to them inside and outside of prisons. The notion of a virtuous prison, however, also suggests that the correctional regime should be organized to fulfill the reciprocal obligation of providing offenders with the means to become virtuous. Much like the founders of the penitentiary did when they designed detailed daily routines for inmates to follow (Rothman, 1971), careful attention should be paid to how each prison would be arranged to enhance the goal of moral regeneration. Such efforts should include using existing criminological knowledge on "what works" to change offenders.

The virtuous prison is being advanced as a *progressive* reform—as a way of humanizing imprisonment and of contributing to the commonwealth of communities. We recognize the dangers inherent in preaching morality, but we also suggest that there are dangers—already realized—in rejecting morality. A *progressive* approach is, by its very nature, value-laden, not value-free. We should not be afraid of *rediscovering the morality* that informed earlier, progressive-oriented prison reforms. We also assert that the idea of a virtuous prison has decided advantages over two other models for imprisonment: "the legal prison" and "the painful prison." These issues are explored in the pages ahead.

REDISCOVERING MORALITY

Progressive criminologists are not without the capacity for moral outrage. They (and we) are indignant about the social and economic injustices that contribute to the uneven distribution of crime in the United States. They show little sympathy for white-collar offenders and castigate corporations who wantonly exploit the environment and commit violence against workers and consumers. Even so, it is politically incorrect or, in the least, unfashionable, to speak of traditional "street" offenders and their misdeeds as "immoral." Take, for example, James Q. Wilson's (1975, 235) now-famous claim that "wicked people exist.

Nothing avails except to set them apart from innocent people." Why should this assertion—arguably correct to a degree—bother progressive criminologists (and us) so much? Why does such moral judgmentalism evoke a visceral feeling of discomfort and make us flush with anger?

In part, we suspect, the rejection of moralism as applied to individual offenders is not so much what it says but what it may unwittingly—or not so unwittingly—obfuscate. By focusing on an individual offender's moral failing, it is easy to ignore the role of the social structure and material inequity—the so-called "root causes"—in the individual's wayward life course. It also is easy to claim that we must "set apart" this individual lawbreaker without pricking our consciences about how we, as a society, may have played a role in the offender becoming "wicked."

Another consideration, however, is the evolving belief among progressives that the trumpeting of morality is not done in good faith but is merely another strategy of power. Moral claims thus are not true but are merely exercises in rhetoric that mask darker political and class-based interests. "Moral crusades" and the speeches of "moral entrepreneurs" are not to be taken at face value but are to be viewed skeptically and deconstructed. What are they really after? What's the hidden agenda?

This view of morality has had salient effects within corrections, most notably with the attack on rehabilitation in the 1970s and beyond. Because advocates often borrowed the language and logic of the medical model, offender treatment has at times been portrayed strictly as a scientific, technical task: finding and using the most scientifically appropriate treatments to change lawbreakers into law abiders. But rehabilitation is, at its core, a moral enterprise. It depends on the existence of social consensus about shared values—about what is right and what is wrong (see Allen, 1981). It is morally judgmental; it accepts a standard for moral and legal behavior and defines those not meeting this standard as in need of adjustment (see Garland, 1995).

Beginning in the late 1960s and early 1970s, progressive criminologists became uneasy about rehabilitation for these very reasons; the treatment ideal's moral claims were seen as illegitimate. Thus, once upon a time, the founders of the penitentiary and of the juvenile court were viewed as humanitarian reformers; now they were unmasked as seeking to "discipline" poor offenders so that they could be productive workers for the capitalists and as becoming "child savers" to reaffirm existing class arrangements and to provide gender-appropriate occupational opportunities (Foucault, 1977; Platt, 1969). Moral crusades thus were redefined as immoral crusades. Similarly, social workers, counselors, and all others tied to the correctional "establishment" were transformed from members of the "helping professions" into "agents of social control" who abused their power so as to control, not improve, offenders (Rothman, 1980). Benevolence thus was supposedly unmasked for what it "really" was: coercion. And offenders, as Binder and Geis (1984, 644) note, became the "underdog, who tends to be seen as a romantic force engaged in a liberating struggle with retrogressive establishment institutions." In its more extreme form, "crime" and "criminals" were reduced to social constructions—words always to be bracketed by quotes to show that there is no objective standard of morality or legality. In its milder form, criminologists simply denied that offenders were different and in need of any change—a position that subsequent research has shown to be foolish (Andrews and Bonta, 1998; Raine, 1993). Moral condemnation of offenders and their harmful behavior was not in vogue. Regardless, if there was nothing really wrong with offenders, then rehabilitation had no legitimate function: there was nothing in them to fix.

Let us hasten to say that these criticisms of rehabilitation had important kernels of truth to them, although not nearly the amount of truth that their advocates confidently imagined (Cullen and Gilbert, 1982; see also, Garland, 1990). This way of thinking, however, also had the distinct disadvantage of directing how a whole generation of criminologists understood corrections. In particular, it became "taken for granted" that prisons were inhumane and immoral places; that "nothing worked" in prisons for the betterment of offenders; and that claims by correctional workers to help offenders were a camouflage for their desire to continue to exercise unfettered discretion over powerless inmates. In this context, there was a tendency to see inmates as twice victimized—once by the social injustices that prompted them to break the law, and a second time by the correctional system that subjected them to inhumane conditions certain to drive them further into crime. The idea that offenders might have engaged in morally reprehensible conduct and that prisons should serve to morally reform them was—and, to a large extent, still is—out of sync with this line of reasoning (Newman, 1983). Discussions of a virtuous prison would have been dismissed out of hand, and those proposing such a foolish venture would have been characterized as criminologically illiterate. This may remain the case.

The difficulty for many criminologists, however, is that they were, and are, largely bereft of any positive agenda for the prison—short, again, of abolishing it or minimizing its use. As they turned away from rehabilitation, most criminologists followed the crowd and embraced the "justice model." They liked this approach because it argued that offenders, including the incarcerated, should be accorded an array of legal rights that would protect them against the power of the state to sanction them unfairly or too harshly. After all, who could be against justice? But this approach was strangely disconnected from the very criminology they practiced. The justice model is based on the legal fiction of the atomized individual offender who freely chooses to break the law and earn the right to be punished. Most criminologists, however, spent their professional lives documenting that, at most, the choice of crime is socially bounded and, in too many cases, that the odds of lawbreaking among people exposed to at-risk environments—the victims of social injustice—are astronomical. We return to the limits of a legal model shortly.

In the end, then, we propose that criminologists, especially progressive scholars, recognize the importance of talking about virtue or morality *in formulating correctional policy in prisons*. This call is not, we believe, a departure from progressive principles but a rediscovery of them. The great reforms in American corrections—for example, the penitentiary and the rehabilitative ideal that led to offender classification and treatment programs—drew their power in large part from the willingness of their advocates to speak about right and wrong and about what prisons should be about. As Zebulon Brockway (1870, 42) eloquently observed more than a century ago in Cincinnati at the National Congress on Penitentiary and Reformatory Discipline:

> It will be noticed that there is a wide difference in these two views of crime; a difference so wide that every prison system must be founded upon one or the other of them, and not by any possibility upon both; for a system, so founded, would be divided against itself, and could not stand. Just here, thorough discussion is needed, for irrevocable choice must be made. If punishment, suffering, degradation are deemed deterrent, if they are the best means to reform the criminal and prevent crime, then let prison reform go backward to the pillory, the whipping-post, the gallows, the stake; to corporal violence and extermination! But if the dawn of Christianity has reached us, if we have learned the lesson that *evil is to be overcome with good*, then let prisons and prison systems be lighted by this law of love. Let us leave, for the present, the thought of inflicting punishment upon prisoners to satisfy so-called justice, and turn toward the two grand divisions of our subject, the real objects of the system, vis.: *the protection of society by the prevention of crime and reformation of criminals.* (Emphasis in the original.)

We recognize that our views risk being discounted as naïve—as ignoring that many progressive reforms have had untoward consequences and that these reforms rarely were constructed to ruffle the feathers of the rich and powerful by calling for the redistribution of valued resources. We cannot fully debate this issue here, but we will make three brief responses. First, critics of past progressive reforms somehow assume that "things would have been better" in the absence of these reforms. Our experiences over the past thirty years, however, provide a sobering rebuttal to the view that the opposite of the traditional progressive model of individualized treatment is the dawn of a new era of humanity in corrections. Second, with appropriate reflection and caution, the mistakes of the past are not inevitably repeated. The alternative view—that all correctional reforms are doomed to corruption and failure—is a recipe for continued inaction. Third, conservatives have rushed into the correctional arena equipped with their moral interpretation of offenders and of what should be done *to*—not *for*—them. Without a competing moral vision, the odds of achieving a more humane approach to corrections are diminished.

Finally, we should take notice that our urging to rediscover morality and to create virtuous prisons are not completely "pie-in-the-sky" ideas. Later, for example, we will discuss a closely allied development: the emergence of faith-based prisons. But we can also draw attention to the growing restorative justice movement (Levrant, Cullen, Fulton, and Wozniak, 1998). This approach, which many progressives are now embracing because it is community-based and not prison-based, is at its core a moral enterprise. It is unabashed in defining the misdeeds of offenders as blameworthy and inexcusable; but it is equally unabashed in holding out the possibility that through the offender's hard work to compensate victims and to change for the better, the gift of forgiveness from victims, and the support of the community, the restoration of offenders—as well as victims and the community—is possible. Whatever its faults and potential problems (Levrant et al., 1998), restorative justice shows that correctional responses are not limited to the infliction of pain but can attempt to achieve nobler goals and real-life outcomes. This is a lesson, we trust, that might be fruitfully generalized to our understanding of prisons—a possibility we will revisit later.

THE LEGAL PRISON

The attack on rehabilitation in the 1970s fractured the consensus that corrections should be about correcting people. As the hegemony of the treatment ideal shattered, conservatives rushed in to propose an alternative approach: using prisons to inflict pain on offenders for lengthy periods of time. As noted, those on the left, including progressive-oriented criminologists, trumpeted the alternative "justice model of corrections" (see, e.g., Fogel, 1979; Fogel and Hudson, 1981; Morris, 1974).

Within prisons, the prime target of the leftists was the discretion exercised by correctional staff and by parole boards. They bristled at the idea that offenders should be "coerced" into treatment under the threat that their early release from prison depended on program participation and their being "cured." In an inhumane prison environment, staff could not be trusted to exercise their discretion fairly and with expertise. Parole boards were depicted as either political hacks or as well-meaning folks who unwittingly placed inmates in the position of have to "con" board members so as to earn their release from prison. Justice model advocates thus argued that all indeterminacy in sentencing, parole boards, and enforced therapy should be eliminated. But this approach wanted something more: the allocation to inmates of an array of legal rights that would ensure their protection against the abuses visited upon them by correctional staff and by life in an inhumane environment.

In short, whereas advocates of rehabilitation hoped to fashion therapeutic communities, those favoring the justice model wished to construct a "legal prison"—an institutional community built on the principles of restraining state power and of according inmates virtually every legal right available to them in the free society. At times, this approach was characterized as a "citizenship model of corrections." In Conrad's (1981, 17–19) words, the prison "should become a school for citizenship" in which inmates were granted the rights to personal safety, to care, to personal dignity, to work, to self-improvement, to vote, and to a future. Although based on pure speculation, Conrad and other reformers believed that once inmates were offered the opportunity to enjoy and exercise the rights of citizens, the prison would become orderly and more humane. Once citizenship was learned inside prisons, its effects might generalize and make offenders more responsible as they returned to the free society. As Conrad (1981, 19) observed:

> Justice depends on reciprocity between the state and its citizens and among citizens themselves. A man whose rights are not protected by the state has no rights. A man who has no rights cannot be expected to observe the rights of others. If justice is really therapy, as I believe, it can only be administered to a citizen, not to a civilly dead convict.

Although naïve sounding, the justice model is hardly foolish and might even have proved a boon to prison life in a different political context. In the 1970s, those on the political left had reason to believe that the law was an instrument of change and of good. Until this time, inmates had been virtual "slaves of the state" as courts practiced a "hands off" doctrine inside prisons. Prison litigation did much to improve basic standards of living within correctional facilities and to accord offenders religious and legal rights (DiIulio, 1990; Jacobs, 1983). What the justice model advocates did not anticipate, however, was that the expansion of constitutional protections to prisons would, when confronted by more conservative courts, stop far short of ensuring that inmates had a right to citizenship or a humane environment. Instead, the courts have taken a minimalist approach, protecting offenders from "cruel and unusual" prison conditions but not from much more than this (Palmer and Palmer, 1999).

One fundamental problem with the justice model, then, is that it is out of step with the times. In the early 1970s—in the midst of the Civil Rights Movement and in the shocking aftermath of the Attica riot and slaughter—it seemed reasonable to suggest that inmates were victims in need of rights. Today, however, policymakers and the public are likely to concur that inmates "have too many rights." Talk of "democratizing corrections" and turning "inmates into citizens" would prompt skepticism, if not the acerbic query of "who's running the joint now"? The justice model may have done some good, but it has now exhausted itself. It is incapable of fueling a new age of correctional reform in the twenty-first century.

The justice model and its legal prison also failed to provide a compelling answer to the "utilitarian" question of what role prisons would play in reducing crime. Advocates wished to suggest that through "voluntary rehabilitation" and the learning of "citizenship" offenders *might* lower their subsequent criminal participation. But having criticized rehabilitation as coercive and ineffective—the "noble lie" as Morris (1974, 20–22) put it—they were reluctant to say that offenders should change and that corrections *should* ultimately be about facilitating this outcome. As a result, they were wishy-washy on crime, failing to articulate how prisons could be employed to protect innocent citizens—whether through reha-bilitation or through tougher means, such as long-term incapacitation. Caught up with rectifying the injustices done to inmates, they largely forfeited the opportu-nity to show how their progressive-oriented reforms would make society safer. This mistake was not only intellectual but also political; for conservative com-mentators rushed into this void to tell policymakers and the public how to put an end to the lawlessness in the nation's streets.

THE PAINFUL PRISON

Clear (1994) characterizes American corrections over the past three decades as being in the throes of a "penal harm movement"—of a concerted effort to inflict increasing amounts of pain on offenders. The most visible sign of this campaign is the successful policy agenda to cram more and more lawbreakers behind bars for longer and longer periods of time. Although given less consideration, a col-lateral sign of the penal harm movement is the attempt to make inmates' stays in prison not only lengthier but also increasingly physically uncomfortable—what Sparks (1996) calls the policy of "penal austerity."

Given their progressive bent and their attraction to preaching that even the worst among us deserve humane treatment, criminologists have generally been disconcerted by these developments. Even so, while not brutish in their views, some criminologists have warmed to the idea that prisons should be painful rather than, say, therapeutic or contexts in which to practice citizenship.

Take, for example, Newman's (1983) "punishment manifesto" conveyed in his controversial *Just and Painful*. Embracing a retributivist position, Newman argues that imprisonment as a form of punishment should be used sparingly; instead, he favors corporal punishment, delivered most often through electric shocks and calibrated to the seriousness of the crime committed. When prison sentences are given, however, he contends that they should be reserved for those who have engaged in serious and/or repeated crimes. In these cases, the minimum penalty should be fifteen years of incarceration. Most noteworthy for our pur-poses, he envisions "prisons as purgatory" (p. 61); they should be harsh places so that inmates will suffer. Such punishments are justified, says Newman, because they are deserved and because they offer offenders the opportunity to truly atone for their evil acts and, in a sense, to save their souls.

Newman's proposals are provocative and tempting: would we be willing to take the current massive overuse of imprisonment and exchange it for the appli-cation of electric shocks to a great many offenders and lengthy sentences of extreme suffering by few offenders? But this deal will remain hypothetical because of Americans' cultural ambivalence about punishing the body of offend-ers and their embrace of imprisonment as a preferred sanction. The risk of New-man's proposal, then, is that it will be used in a piecemeal fashion. While it will not reduce the use of imprisonment, it potentially could add legitimacy to claims that prisons should be places in which *all* offenders, not a select few, suffer.

A milder version of the painful prison is set forth by Logan and Gaes (1993). These authors do not favor making prisons a purgatory or exposing inmates to gratuitous pain. They believe that prisons should meet constitutional standards of safety, decency, and amenities and should be governed firmly and fairly, not harshly and arbitrarily. Their "confinement model," however, embraces retribution or just desserts as its guiding principle and sees prison as a means of punishing. Unlike the more liberal advocates of just deserts, who looked to the justice model as a way of protecting inmates from the inherent coerciveness of imprisonment—and more like Newman (1983)—Logan and Gaes favor "punitive confinement" as a way of dramatizing the immorality of the offender's crime and of affirming the offender's "autonomy, responsibility, and dignity" (p. 255).

Logan and Gaes state clearly that they wish offenders to be sent to prison *as* punishment and not *for* punishment. Unless we misread between the lines of their essay, however, this caveat is meant to go only so far. They may not want prisons to be warehouses, but they seemingly do want them to be punitive and to involve no-frills living—to send, as they would say, a "cultural message" to the citizenry that crime is evil and will be judged harshly. Their view of rehabilitation is revealing. Treatment programs, they speculate, are paternalistic and convey the wrong message about crime and criminals to society; they deny offender responsibility and presumably increase the sales of Dershowitz's (1994) *The Abuse Excuse*. Rehabilitation is not to be fully excluded by their confinement model, but it is to be permitted only when it is "voluntary, is separated from punishment, and is not a privilege unavailable to those who are not in prison" (p. 257). Thus, participation in treatment is not to be tied to privileges of any sort; programs are to be delivered after imprisonment or inside prison by outside community social service agencies—and then only to foster institutional order, not to change offenders; and services given to offenders are to be governed by the principle of less eligibility.

Logan and Gaes's model of punitive confinement is principled, but it is not based on principles we wish to embrace. First, as with other retributivists, they must accept the legal fiction that crime is a free and autonomous choice. Even the economists—a discipline based on the assumption of rationality—understand that choice is bounded and is influenced by socially induced "tastes" or "preferences" (see also Boudon, 1998). Although we concur with their desire to hold offenders morally responsible, we believe that this is only half the moral equation: society, too, should be held accountable for its role in the criminal choices offenders make, and the correctional process should reflect this reality. Second, we are equally troubled by their rejection of the utility—the crime savings—that can be achieved through effective correctional intervention, especially with high-risk offenders (Andrews and Bonta, 1998). The easy sacrifice of this goal is tantamount to saying that prisons should play no role in *protecting future victims* from crime. Such a state interest is not only constitutionally permissible but, we believe, moral to pursue. Third, while this may be a case of "what's in the eye of the beholder," we reject their view that prison treatment programs send the cultural message that "crime's not the offender's fault." Rehabilitation can send other messages: that offenders have an obligation to change; that offenders are not a form of refuse but have the human dignity to be renewed; that offenders are worth investing in because they can change and contribute to society; and that we, as a society, are not only about "hating the sin" but, at least under some circumstances, about "loving the sinner."

Perhaps more important, we are troubled that like Newman, Logan and Gaes are seemingly untroubled by the prospect that their call for "punitive confinement" will not go as planned. We worry, however, that once the punitive genie is out of the bottle, it will not prove to be principled but more akin to Jafar—the evil Disney character in the *Aladdin* films who attempted to use his newfound, genie-like powers for self-interest and to harm others. We wonder, in particular, where the restraint will come from if we accept that prisons are an instrument for punishment—pure and simple. What will occur when even responsible scholars such as Logan and Gaes do not challenge the principle of less eligibility? What cultural message will politicians hear, and what can they be trusted to do?

The events from the penal harm movement give us considerable reason for concern. As Lacayo (1995, 31) observes, the "hottest development in criminal justice is a fast-spreading impulse to eliminate anything that might make it easier to endure a sentence behind bars." The roster of these austerity policies is now familiar: sending inmates out on chain gangs; eliminating Pell Grants and opportunities to participate in college programs; banning computers and televisions in cells; forbidding weightlifting; housing inmates in tents; eliminating steak from inmate diets; and so on. These policies are hardly part of a principled confinement model; rather they are intended to ensure that inmates are in prison *for punishment* and are undertaken with the utilitarian and criminologically ill-conceived notion that exposing offenders to rotten living conditions will deter their future wrongdoing. Worse still, these policies are trumpeted by politicians whose newfound campaign to immiserate inmates' lives seems rooted less in morality and more in a calculated desire to capture headlines and electoral capital. Such a vision for corrections should not go unchallenged—a task to which we now turn.

THE VIRTUOUS PRISON

Because nearly all correctional reforms historically have been misshapen when put into place and have failed to realize their ideals (Cullen and Gilbert, 1982; Rothman, 1990), we approach the task of outlining an alternative vision for the prison with much trepidation. It also is daunting to realize that a crafty critic could soon hone in on our proposal's vulnerabilities (e.g., the potential arrogance in claiming to be virtuous; its embrace of utility as a central correctional goal). Still, as argued previously, we are persuaded that progressives inadvertently have allowed agendas such as the "painful prison" to gain influence by paying insufficient attention to correctional policy as it pertains to life inside institutions. In a very real sense, there is a "culture war" under way over the fate of the nation's prisons. Without fresh ideas—others if not ours—progressives will remain on the defensive and do little to shape prison policies in the time ahead.

Restorative Rehabilitation

The mission of the virtuous prison is to use offenders' time of incarceration to cultivate moral awareness and the capacity to act virtuously. Although recognizing the deprivations inherent in total institutional life, the approach rejects the progressive view, held by many criminologists, that nothing productive can be accomplished in prison. This approach also rejects the notion of the painful or austere prison as having no utility—other than inflicting suffering—and as inhibiting the inculcation of virtue in offenders. The virtuous-prison approach rejects incapacitation because it is a utilitarian theory that, by not endorsing the goal of offender change, needlessly limits the crime savings—and thus the utility—that prisons can achieve. And this approach rejects retributivist ideas for their disinterest in crime control and for their belief, as Newman (1983, 142) writes, that "the most basic of all freedoms in a society" is "the freedom to break the law" and to be punished for it. The virtuous prison has a different vision—the idea that people, including inmates, have an *obligation* to obey the law, not to harm others, and that societal institutions, including the prison, should be organized to facilitate this goal.

Two principles form the foundation of the virtuous prison: *restorative justice* and the *rehabilitative ideal* (see Wilkinson, 1998). As alluded to earlier, restorative justice hinges on the premise that the harm from crime is morally wrong and that its effects need to be remedied. Offenders thus are called on to announce and publicly accept the blame for their wrongdoing. They are then expected to act virtuously by restoring victims they have harmed. Such restoration for victims might be emotional, such as when offenders apologize for their misdeeds, or might be material, such as when offenders provide restitution. Offenders also must recognize that breaches of the law damage the common welfare; therefore restoring the community through service activities is often mandated. The precise nature of this restorative justice remedy is reached at a conference where the offender, victim, family members, and concerned others meet to express their disappointment and hurt and to work out a way in which the offender can restore the harm he or she has caused. Ideally, and over time, the victim forgives and reconciles with the offender. The community is expected to do its part, too, by reintegrating, not rejecting, the repentant offender. In this whole process, the state is present but involved mainly as an arbiter, helping the parties to reach agreement.

Restorative justice is morally clear and it is unambiguous about requiring offenders to make amends. But this approach is sympathetic as well to the view that people, including lawbreakers, are capable of change. It also proposes that criminal sanctions should be used to rectify harm and to do good—not to heap more suffering on offenders in an aimless way or for purposes of mere retribution. It is backward-looking, shaming the conduct that has occurred; it is present-looking, applying a criminal sanction that does good; and it is future looking, trying to create victims who are restored and offenders capable of moral conduct (see, e.g., Braithwaite, 1998; Hahn, 1998; Van Ness and Strong, 1997).

Can restorative justice, however, be imported into the prison? To date, it has largely been conceptualized as a *community-based* approach; indeed, progressives have rushed to embrace it precisely because it is presented as an alternative to prison (for exceptions, see Hahn, 1998; Van Ness and Strong, 1997; see also, Lund, 1997; Wilkinson, 1998). In an otherwise thoughtful analysis of restorative justice, for example, Braithwaite (1998, 336) will "concede" only that "for a tiny fraction of people in our prisons, it may actually be necessary to protect the community from them by incarceration." This view not only is empirically problematic in its optimistic view of inmates (Logan and DiIulio, 1992), but also errs, we believe, in not seeing the role of restorative justice *within* prisons—a place, again, in which over 1.8 million people now reside in the United States. Regardless, prisons present two challenges to restorative justice: the removal of offenders from the community and a population of more serious, hardened offenders.

Although various scenarios could be devised to reconcile victims with prison-bound or prison-based offenders, the removal of the offender from the local community will make victim-offender conferences less likely to occur. Yet, even if specific agreements with specific victims are not reached, a virtuous prison could be organized around the principle that inmates should be engaged in activities that are restorative (e.g., contributing to a victim compensation fund; community service). In this way, what inmates do would be imbued with a clear moral and practical purpose: to restore harm to society that they and their fellow offenders have caused. In this approach, prisons thus would be an instrument for doing good for society. Although limited, it is noteworthy that prison programs based on restorative justice are beginning to emerge (see, e.g., Lund, 1997; Wilkinson, 1998).

Perhaps the more daunting challenge, however, is the depth of the criminality of the offenders who enter prison. A weakness of restorative justice is that the approach's understanding of offender behavioral change is speculative and based, at most, on only a slice of the criminological research about offenders (see Levrant, et al., 1998). The idea that the kind of high-risk offenders that frequently populate prisons will, with any regularity, be morally regenerated by a two-hour victim-offender reconciliation meeting or merely by furnishing restitution strains credulity. Such an understanding denies the pathology within many offenders that has been developing over a lifetime. It will take tough work and appropriate therapeutic techniques to change offenders—to prepare them to act morally outside the prison walls (see Wilkinson, 1998).

It is at this juncture, therefore, that the rehabilitative ideal should be merged with restorative justice—for two reasons. First, even more strongly than restorative justice, rehabilitation identifies the reform of the offender as a legitimate and important correctional goal—a goal whose attainment simultaneously benefits inmates and, by preventing crime, society. Second, there is now a growing body of empirically based knowledge specifying the correctional interventions that "work" to reduce recidivism, including among high-risk serious offenders (see, e.g., Andrews and Bonta, 1998; Andrews, Zinger, Hoge, Bonta, Gendreau, and Cullen, 1990; Gendreau, 1996; Gibbons 1999; Henggeler, 1997; Lipsey and Wilson, 1998; MacKenzie, 1998). This research suggests that certain "principles of effective intervention" should be followed in seeking to rehabilitate offenders. To a large extent, these principles are consistent with restorative justice because primary targets for change in this correctional approach are offenders' antisocial values and thinking (Gendreau, 1996). In any case, a restorative corrections approach will likely fail to impact recidivism if it is not informed by the extant research on rehabilitation. If one prefers, the principles of effective intervention can be seen as supplying the needed technology for offender restoration.

Prison Particulars

The goal of prison organization would be to create a "virtuous milieu." The task would be how to surround inmates with positive moral influences. Although our thoughts are still preliminary, we would propose seven general considerations.

First, inmate idleness would be eliminated. "Idle hands" may or may not be "the devil's workshop," but they are no friend to virtuous living. Wright (1994) contends that a "productive environment" reduces prisoner violence and disruption and also fosters hope—a sense of purpose—among inmates.

Second, the activities in which inmates engage would have a restorative purpose. Prison employment, for example, should not merely be to pass the time or to equip offenders with occupational skills but rather should have a larger purpose beyond the inmate's self-interest. Thus, inmate wages might be used to compensate victims, with offenders writing and sending the checks to victims. Or inmates might be engaged in jobs that produce products for the needy—toys for poor children or prefabricated houses for Habitat for Humanity. Similarly, community service would be encouraged—first inside the prison (e.g., writing to elderly shut-ins, training dogs for the seeing impaired, holding bake sales for "good causes") and then during the day outside the prison (e.g., fixing up a playground, making a house livable for a family) (Lund, 1997). When possible, moreover, inmates would be prompted to help restore one another, such as by tutoring someone who is less educated or leading self-help sessions. Which activities ultimately are implemented is less important than the fact that inmates are engaged in activities that have a *moral purpose*—that provide opportunities to be virtuous (see Van Ness and Strong, 1997, 108–109).

Third, contact with virtuous people would be encouraged. Although not unmindful of security risks, the virtuous prison would encourage as many upstanding community people as possible, including those religiously-inspired, to lead and/or participate in prison programs, to mentor inmates, and to visit and socialize with inmates. These volunteers should be seen not as a potential disruption but as a source of valuable human capital who will share their knowledge and values with inmates. Further, by coming into the prison—by devoting their time and effort to a worthy cause—such volunteers are modeling the very kind of pro-social, virtuous behavior that we wish inmates to learn.

Fourth, inmates would participate in rehabilitation programs that are based on criminological research and the principles of effective correctional intervention (again, see Andrews and Bonta,1998; Gendreau, 1996). An important principle of the virtuous prison would be that offenders have the *obligation* to seek restoration so as not to misbehave inside the institution or to recidivate in the community. The reciprocal obligation of the state is to provide quality treatment programs that have the greatest chance of facilitating this restoration. In this spirit, criminological knowledge would be welcomed and not dismissed. Programs shown not to work—such as boot camps—would be relegated to the therapeutic dustbin. Alternatively, programs shown to work—cognitive-behavioral interventions—would be implemented and evaluated. In the end, programs would be intended to give offenders the values, understanding of the world, and skills to live a productive life. This approach is much different, we should note, from punitive strategies that threaten offenders with punishment but provide no positive instruction on how to lead a life outside crime.

Fifth, the standard of inmate living would be as high as possible. A low standard of living—inflicting pain on offenders—serves no defensible moral or utilitarian purpose. It also is inconsistent with the very purpose of a virtuous prison, which takes seriously the maxim that "virtue begets virtue." Politically, the restorative orientation of the virtuous prison might make it less vulnerable to attempts to immiserate its population. Often, inmates are seen as part of the undeserving poor who no longer should receive social welfare "entitlements." In the virtuous prison, however, inmates will be engaged in activities in which they "give back to victims and the community"; in short, they may become more "deserving" in the eyes of policymakers and thus less attractive as targets for meanness.

Sixth, prison guards would be encouraged to function as "correctional" officers. In the virtuous prison, guards would be seen as professionals who deliver various types of human services (Johnson, 1996). Their tasks obviously would involve maintaining order, ensuring custody, and enforcing rules. But they also would be integral to the central institutional mission of fostering virtue in inmates. One cannot bifurcate staff into two neat divisions—"custodial" and "treatment"—because correctional officers are potentially too involved in inmates' daily lives and routines not to affect programmatic outcomes and the quality of the institution. Thus, while guards have their distinctive duties, they should, through participatory management, be brought into the planning of how best to achieve the virtuous prison's central mission. In particular, they should be relied on to advance, not stymie, the restoration or correction of the offenders in their charge. Research suggests that many correctional officers would welcome this enrichment of their occupational role (Cullen, Lutze, Link, and Wolfe, 1989; Johnson, 1996; Toch and Klofas, 1982).

Seventh, the virtuous prison would not be for all inmates. We would like to see the model of the virtuous prison spread far and wide, and we are confident that with enough experimentation and organizational development, this model could eventually be effective with a large proportion of the inmate population. Still, we are realistic enough to know that not every inmate could function effectively in this environment (e.g., the intractably recalcitrant, violent, or mentally disturbed inmate). At the very least, however, the virtuous prison would be appropriate for at least *some* inmates, with precisely how many remaining an empirical question to be discovered. If so, then there is reason to undertake an experiment with the prison we have proposed. The salient point is that success with even one model virtuous prison would be valuable because it would show that prisons can serve lofty goals and can be administered, within the limits of good sense, humanely. Some support for these views can be drawn from the current experimentation with "faith-based" prisons.

Faith-Based Prisons

In April of 1997, Prison Fellowship Ministries—the religiously based prison reform group begun by Charles Colson (of Watergate fame)—initiated the "Inner-Change Freedom Initiative" in a minimum-security prison (Jester II) located outside Houston and under the auspices of the Texas Department of Correction. Based on a model used to reform and administer prisons in Brazil (Leal, 1998), this initiative sought to develop a faith-based prison community. The inmate participants had diverse criminal histories and were required to be within twenty-one to twenty-four months of parole or release from prison. To ensure separation of church and state, Prison Fellowship Ministries funded the program's staff and operation (but not the correctional officers or inmate living costs) and accepted only inmates who volunteered. Other programs are being planned for prisons in Iowa and Kansas (Prison Fellowship Ministries 1999; Mattox, 1999; Niebuhr, 1998; see also, the Internet site of www.ifiprison.org).

The prison initiative is based on the belief that behavior is a reflection of values and worldview. For inmates, it is proposed that rehabilitation depends on a fundamental "inner change" that reconciles the person with Christ. This sacred relationship then allows the offender to reconcile human relationships and to embark on genuine, long-term behavioral change. The special focus on a religious transformation is a distinctive feature of the InnerChange Freedom Initiative. It also is what limits its widespread use, since the separation of church and state sets burdensome legal restrictions on the programmatic services a department of corrections can fund.

From our perspective, however, the InnerChange Freedom Initiative is instructive because the features incorporated into its prison community *besides religion* make it quite similar to the virtuous prison we have proposed. Thus, the Texas initiative largely embraces the dual principles of moral restoration and rehabilitation. It is extensively programmed and relies heavily on church-based volunteers to serve as chaplains, lead small groups, mentor inmates, provide educational and artistic tutoring, facilitate family support groups, and coordinate the community service project. It also has inmates participate in productive work so as to teach them to be "stewards of their time." The initiative is unabashed in expressing its desire not to inflict pain on inmates but to create a community of strong social bonds and love. Further, it is committed to using an aftercare program to reintegrate offenders, upon their release, into a supportive religious community.

To be sure, the appeal of the InnerChange Freedom Initiative stems in an important way from its faith-based orientation and because it was proposed by an influential religious ministry, Prison Fellowship. Still, the kind of prison community being created—a focus on moral restoration, concerted efforts to rehabilitate offenders, substantial support given to offenders during and after incarceration, a lack of mean-spirited rhetoric—did not render this project politically unfeasible. Indeed, by requiring inmates to strive in concrete ways toward change—to show that they were deserving of support—this program was the kind of "compassionate conservatism" that Texas Governor George W. Bush could embrace and use to bump up his ratings in the polls. This initiative thus shows that space exists to experiment with different models of imprisonment. It is relevant as well that, while the American public is punitive toward crime, repeated surveys reveal that there also is substantial support among citizens for the principles of restorative justice and of prison-based rehabilitation (see, e.g., Applegate, Cullen, and Fisher, 1997; Cullen, Fisher, and Applegate, forthcoming). In this context, the prospect of creating a virtuous prison does not seem farfetched.

CONCLUSION: DOING GOOD

As Binder and Geis (1984) show, criminologists have a tendency to feel happy when they can show that nothing the government does has any effect on crime. At times, there seems to be a special glee—a gotcha!—when scholars can reveal how people who hope to "do good" and express benevolent intentions end up putting reforms into place that have untoward unanticipated consequences. There is, of course, a need to puncture false claims and to save offenders from foolish, if not repressive, efforts to supposedly save them. Pushed too far, however, this professionally supported desire to delegitimate "state control" is smug and counterproductive. Nothing constructive—nothing that can work—is ever proposed.

Prisons, we believe, have suffered from criminologists' unwillingness to entertain the possibility that correctional institutions could be administered more humanely and more effectively. This risk of action is failure and, at times, messing things up. But the past three decades of penal harm should have taught us two lessons about corrections: First, doing good sometimes means that good is actually achieved. And second, doing good is almost always preferable to the alternative—neglect or, even worse, the conscious attempt to inflict pain. The challenge now is to devise those strategies that can, in fact, realize our benevolent sentiments in the difficult area of corrections. The virtuous prison is but one suggestion on how to "do good" in prison. Hopefully, it will soon be followed by many others.

REFERENCES

Allen, Francis A. 1981. *The Decline of the Rehabilitative Ideal: Penal Policy and Social Purpose.* New Haven: Yale University Press.

Andrews, D. A., and James Bonta. 1998. *The Psychology of Criminal Conduct*, 2nd ed. Cincinnati: Anderson.

Andrews, D. A., Ivan Zinger, R. D. Hoge, James Bonta, Paul Gendreau, and Francis T. Cullen. 1990. "Does Correctional Treatment Work? A Clinically-Relevant and Psychologically-Informed Meta-Analysis." *Criminology* 28:369–404.

Applegate, Brandon K., Francis T. Cullen, and Bonnie S. Fisher. 1997. "Public Support for Correctional Treatment: The Continuing Appeal of the Rehabilitative Ideal." *The Prison Journal* 77:237–58.

Bennett, William J., John J. DiIulio, Jr., and James P. Walters. 1996. *Body Count: Moral Poverty . . .and How to Win America's War Against Crime and Drugs.* New York: Simon & Shuster.

Binder, Arnold and Gilbert Geis. 1984. "*Ad Populum* Argumentation in Criminology: Juvenile Diversion as Rhetoric." *Crime and Delinquency* 30:624–47.

Boudon, Raymond. 1998. "Limitations of Rational Choice Theory." *American Journal of Sociology* 3:817–28.

Braithwaite, John. 1998. "Restorative Justice." Pp. 323–44 in *The Handbook of Crime and Punishment*, ed. M. Tonry. New York: Oxford University Press.

Brockway, Zebulon R. 1871. "The Ideal of a True Prison System for a State." Pp. 38–65 in *Transactions of the National Congress on Penitentiary and Reformatory Discipline*, ed. E. C. Wines. Albany, NY: Weed, Parsons.

Clear, Todd R. 1994. Harm in American Penology: Offenders, Victims, and Their Communities. Albany: State University of New York Press.

Conrad, John P. 1981. "Where There's Hope There's Life." Pp. 3–21 in *Justice as Fairness: Perspectives on the Justice Model*, ed. D. Fogel and J. Hudson. Cincinnati: Anderson.

Cullen, Francis T., Bonnie S. Fisher, and Brandon K. Applegate, Forthcoming. "Public Opinion About Punishment and Corrections." In *Crime and Justice: A Review of Research*, ed. M. Tonry. Chicago: University of Chicago Press.

Cullen, Francis T., and Karen E. Gilbert. 1982. *Reaffirming Rehabilitation*. Cincinnati: Anderson.

Cullen, Francis T., Faith E. Lutze, Bruce G. Link, and Nancy T. Wolfe. 1989. "The Correctional Orientation of Prison Guards: Do Officers Support Rehabilitation?" *Federal Probation* 53 (March):33–42.

Currie, Elliott 1998. *Crime and Punishment in America*. New York: Metropolitan Books.

Dershowitz, Alan M. 1994. *The Abuse Excuse—And Other Cop-Outs, Sob Stories, and Evasions of Responsibility*. Boston: Little, Brown.

DiIulio, Jr., John J. 1987. *Governing Prisons: A Comparative Study of Correctional Treatment*. New York: The Free Press.

_____, ed. 1990. *Courts, Corrections, and the Constitution: The Impact of Judicial Intervention on Prisons and Jails*. New York: Oxford University Press.

Fogel, David. 1979. "*. . .We Are the Living Proof. . .:*" *The Justice Model for Corrections*. 2nd ed. Cincinnati: Anderson.

_____. 1988. *On Doing Less Harm: Western European Alternatives to Incarceration*. Chicago: Office of the International Criminal Justice, University of Illinois at Chicago.

Fogel, David and Joe Hudson, eds. 1981. *Justice as Fairness: Perspectives on the Justice Model*. Cincinnati: Anderson.

Foucault, Michel. 1977. *Discipline and Punish: The Birth of the Prison*. New York: Pantheon.

Garland, David. 1990. *Punishment and Modern Society: A Study in Social Theory*. Chicago: University of Chicago Press.

_____. 1995. "Penal Modernism and Postmodernism." Pp. 181–209 in *Punishment and Social Control*, ed. T. G. Blomberg and S. Cohen. New York: Aldine de Gruyter.

Gaylin, Willard, Ira Glasser, Steven Marcus, and David J. Rothman. 1978. *Doing Good: The Limits of Benevolence*. New York: Pantheon.

Gendreau, Paul. 1996. "The Principles of Effective Intervention with Offenders." Pp. 117–30 in *Choosing Correctional Options That Work: Defining the Demand and Evaluating the Supply*, ed. A. T. Harland. Thousand Oaks, CA: Sage.

Gibbons, Don C. 1999. "Review Essay: Changing Lawbreakers—What Have We Learned Since the 1950s?" *Crime and Delinquency* 45:272–93.

Gilliard, Darrell K. 1998. *Prison and Jail Inmates at Midyear 1998*. Washington, DC: U.S. Department of Justice, Bureau of Justice Statistics.

Goffman, Erving. 1961. *Asylums: Essays on the Social Situation of Mental Patients and Other Inmates*. Garden City, NY: Anchor.

Gottfredson, Michael R. 1979. "Treatment Destruction Techniques." *Journal of Research in Crime and Delinquency* 16:39—54.

Hahn, P. H. 1998. *Emerging Criminal Justice: Three Pillars of a Proactive Justice System*. Thousand Oaks, CA: Sage.

Haney, Craig, W. Curtis Banks, and Philip G. Zimbardo. 1973. "Interpersonal Dynamics in a Simulated Prison." *International Journal of Criminology and Penology* 1:69–97.

Henggeler, Scott W. 1997. *Treating Serious Anti-Social Behavior in Youth: The MST Approach*. Washington, DC: OJJDP, U.S. Department of Justice.

Irwin, John and James Austin. 1994. *It's About Time: America's Imprisonment Binge*. Belmont, CA: Wadsworth.

Jacobs, James B., ed. 1983. *New Perspectives on Prisons and Imprisonment*. Ithaca, NY: Cornell University Press.

Johnson, Robert. 1996. *Hard Time: Understanding and Reforming the Prison*. 2nd ed. Belmont, CA: Wadsworth.

Lacayo, Richard. 1995. "The Real Hard Cell: Lawmakers Are Stripping Inmates of Their Perks." *Time*, September 4, pp. 31–32.

Langan, Patrick A., John V. Fundis, Lawrence A. Greenfeld, and Victoria W. Schneider. 1988. *Historical Statistics on Prisoners in State and Federal Institutions, Yearend 1925-86*. Washington, DC: U.S. Department of Justice, Bureau of Justice Statistics.

Leal, Cesar Barros. 1998. "The Association for the Protection and Assistance to the Convict: A Brazilian Experience." Paper presented at the annual meeting of the American Society of Criminology, November, Washington, DC.

Levrant, Sharon, Francis T. Cullen, Betsy Fulton, and John F. Wozniak. 1999. "Reconsidering Restorative Justice: The Corruption of Benevolence Revisited? *Crime and Delinquency* 45:3–27.

Lipsey, Mark W. and David B. Wilson. 1998. "Effective Intervention for Serious Juvenile Offenders: A Synthesis of Research." Pp. 313–45 in *Serious and Violent Juvenile Offenders: A Synthesis of Research*, ed. R. Loeber and D. P. Farrington. Thousand Oaks, CA: Sage.

Logan, Charles H. and John J. DiIulio, Jr. 1992. "Ten Deadly Myths About Crime and Punishment in the U.S." *Wisconsin Interest* 1 (No. 1):21–35.

Logan, Charles H. and Gerald G. Gaes. 1993. "Meta-Analysis and the Rehabilitation of Punishment." *Justice Quarterly* 10:245–63.

Lund, Laurie. 1997. "Restorative Justice from Prison." *ICCA Journal on Community Corrections* 8 (August):50–51, 55.

MacKenzie, Doris L. 1998. "Criminal Justice and Crime Prevention." Chapter 9 in *What Works, What Doesn't, What's Promising: A Report for the National Institute of Justice*, ed. L. W. Sherman, D. Gottfredson, D. Mackenzie, J. Eck, P. Reuter, and S. Bushway. Washington, DC: U.S. Department of Justice, National Institute of Justice.

Mattox, Jr., William R. 1999. "Prison Program Uses Faith to Transform Lives." *USA Today*, March 15, p. 17A.

Mauer, Marc. 1994. *Americans Behind Bars: The International Use of Incarceration*, 1992–1993. Washington, DC: The Sentencing Project.

Morris, Norval. 1974. *The Future of Imprisonment*. Chicago: University of Chicago Press.

Newman, Graeme. 1983. *Just and Painful: A Case for the Corporal Punishment of Criminals*. New York: Macmillan.

Niebuhr, Gustav. 1998. "Using Religion to Reform Criminals." *New York Times*, January 18, Section 1, p. 16.

Palmer John W. and Stephen E. Palmer. 1999. *Constitutional Rights of Prisoners*, 6th ed. Cincinnati, OH: Anderson.

Platt, Anthony M. 1969. *The Child Savers: The Invention of Delinquency*. Chicago: University of Chicago Press.

President's Commission on Law Enforcement and Administration of Justice. 1968. *The Challenge of Crime in a Free Society*. New York: Avon.

Prison Fellowship Ministries. 1999. *The InnerChange Freedom Initiative: Background, Fact Sheet, History, FAQs, and Legal Basis*. Washington, DC: Prison Fellowship Ministries.

Raine, Adrian. 1993. *The Psychopathology of Crime: Criminal Behavior as a Clinical Disorder*. San Diego: Academic Press.

Reynolds, Morgan O. 1997. *Crime and Punishment in America: 1997 Update*. Dallas, TX: National Center for Policy Analysis.

Rothman, David J. 1971. *The Discovery of the Asylum: Social Order and Disorder in the New Republic*. Boston: Little, Brown.

_____. 1980. *Conscience and Convenience: The Asylum and Its Alternatives in Progressive America*. Boston: Little, Brown.

Sparks, Richard.1996. "Penal 'Austerity': The Doctrine of Less Eligibility Reborn?" Pp. 74–93 in *Prisons 2000: An International Perspective on the Current State and Future of Imprisonment*, ed. R. Matthews and P. Francis. Hampshire, UK: MacMillan.

Toch, Hans.1997. *Corrections: A Humanistic Approach*. Guilderland, NY: Harrow and Heston.

Toch, Hans and John Klofas. 1982. "Alienation and Desire for Job Enrichment Among Correction Officers." *Federal Probation* 46 (March):35–44.

Travis III, Lawrence F. and Francis T. Cullen. 1984. "Radical Non-Intervention: The Myth of Doing No Harm." *Federal Probation* 48 (March):29–32.

Van Ness, Daniel W. and Karen H. Strong. 1997. *Restoring Justice*. Cincinnati: Anderson.

Webster's New Universal Unabridged Dictionary. 1979. 2nd ed. New York: Simon & Schuster.

Wilkinson, Reginald A. 1998. "The Impact of Community Service Work on Adult State Prisoners Using a Restorative Justice Framework." Ed.D. dissertation, Department of Educational Foundations, University of Cincinnati.

Wilson, James Q. 1975. *Thinking About Crime*. New York: Vintage.

Wright, Kevin N. 1994. *Effective Prison Leadership*. Binghamton, NY: William Neil.

Women in Policing:
A Tale of Cultural Conformity

Deborah Parsons
and
Paul Jesilow

❖

"There was a time, not many years ago, when a Police Department was No Woman's Land. As in other professions, police work was distinctly a man's job; the proper sphere for woman was the home. Today the idea of employing policewomen is an accepted one and their presence on the force does not seem more unusual than any other modern innovation."

Mary Hamilton, 1925[1]

Women have made enormous progress in their representation in the labor force, increasing nearly 200 percent since 1900.[2] While this statistic is impressive, women, in general, remain in less-powerful occupational positions. The majority of women remain in boring, subservient, low-paying jobs with no real prospect for promotion, and are concentrated in traditional occupations such as clerical, retail sales, and waitressing.[3]

Desire for higher pay, independence, and personal rewards have led many women to cross the occupational segregation line into jobs not traditionally held by women. They are seeking employment in both professional and blue-collar fields. Although motivations may differ, women are pursuing new and challenging opportunities, often entering what were once male-dominated occupations in greater numbers than in earlier years.[4] Additionally, more women are earning degrees in higher education, which translate into greater impact on public policy from a feminine perspective. Female physicians, for example, although relatively few in number only twenty years ago, now comprise more than 20 percent of all doctors[5] and are rapidly approaching 50 percent of students entering medical schools.[6] Public policy implications include more research into the effects of ailments and drug therapy on women. Large numbers of women are also attending law schools and seeking careers in the legal profession.

Women, however, have not made significant inroads in all occupations. Police patrol work is notable in this regard, with police departments continuing to be male-dominated. Eight decades after the first woman was given the title of policewoman, a large portion of society perceives a female officer as an oddity. Perhaps this is due, in part, to their few numbers or from the notion that police work should be a male occupation. Because of their sparse representation, a career as a police officer remains an uncharted frontier, and the women who enter policing are seen as pioneers.

Women, some argue, are more likely to possess the traits that are needed by today's officers. These researchers believe that women are more likely to use their intellectual, rather than physical, prowess to control others and, from that viewpoint, are a natural match for modern police work.[7] They argue that a larger female presence in policing would have a positive effect—that women will bring a nurturing, cooperative spirit into their police roles, which will mediate the aggressiveness underlying much volatile police behavior. Inherent in their position is a belief that the sexes are different—a position that has support. Carol Gilligan,[8] for example, argues that men and women have different moral orientations. Women see moral questions as problems of care involving empathy and compassion, while men see such problems as matters of rights. Other studies have found women to be supportive and men to be argumentative and competitive.[9]

The argument that the presence of women in policing will change the occupation is compelling on its face, but self-selection, police department screening, and officer socialization currently produce female cops that differ little from their male colleagues and, except in rare instances, do not utilize a different style.[10] Central to the argument is the notion that policing is perceived as predominately involving law enforcement activities and that fulfillment of this role requires characteristics usually attributed to men; for example, aggression, physical prowess, logic, and stability of emotions. Characteristics commonly considered feminine, such as compassion, empathy, nurturing, and strong emotions, are frequently perceived to be weaker, less appealing, less successful, and, especially in terms of policing, as possibly dangerous and life-threatening. It is the perpetuation of the law enforcement model that prevented women initially from entering policing and continues to keep their numbers low. The limited number of women who do enter policing either possess or assimilate the values already established in the system. In this piece we use material drawn from magazines contemporary to the periods to tell the tale of women's efforts to become cops and illustrate how cultural favoritism for law enforcement limited their integration.

POLICEWOMEN

Early policewomen held unique and comparably different positions than those held by their male counterparts. The advent of women in policing began as a cooperative effort, one in which men and women worked in separate spheres, although they held similar goals. Policewomen developed a distinctive place and gained some acceptance within, as well as outside, the law enforcement community. In early times, the special qualities of womanhood were celebrated as a valuable difference between men and women in police roles. One of the female pioneers in the occupation argued that "no woman can really be a good policewoman, unless she works as a woman and carries with her into a police department a woman's ideals."[11]

Women's entry into police work was part of a larger social reform movement that took place during the Progressive Era of the late nineteenth and the early twentieth centuries. Women were actively attempting to alter their place in society, as well as working toward the reformation of major social institutions.[12] They wanted women to have the right to vote, led the movement to ban alcohol, pushed for child worker laws, and urged the regulation of food and drugs.

Post Civil War industrialization in the United States created the economic conditions that galvanized the problems that policewomen[a] wanted to address. The same economic conditions also gave rise to the women who sought the position of policewoman. Industrialization created opportunities for individuals to leave farming communities and seek employment in the cities. The jobs also lured immigrants from Europe to the United States. The prosperity associated with the period created an expanded middle class, largely consisting of white, Anglo-Saxon Protestants. The women of this socioeconomic group viewed with displeasure the lives of the growing working class.

The laborers often were young and alone in the cities. Although most of their moments were spent working, by the end of the nineteenth century they did have some leisure time, and commercial efforts expanded to satisfy their desires for recreational activities. Professional baseball, for example, became a well-liked spectator endeavor for the workers. In addition, centers of amusement became popular, offering attendees a variety of entertainments. Arcades, featuring moving pictures and other newly created pastimes of the period, were particularly popular, as were dance halls.

The recreational centers attracted both male and female workers, who might attend the events alone or in groups with other laborers. The sight of women out on their own was a new situation and conflicted with the values of the American middle class. "Respectable" women of the period simply did not go to public places without a man.[13]

The motivation of women to seek a career in law enforcement began with reformation of conditions in jails and prisons. One matter was the new arrivals to the city, who often found life there less than what they had expected. The women, who had left rural areas seeking employment, were understandably poor and frequently without homes, a fact that brought them under police supervision. A chronicler of the history of policewomen noted that "police stations often also functioned as homeless shelters, and many of those who sought refuge were women and their children."[14] The upper middle-class women urged that females "should be available to assure that women seeking shelter, almost always poor and frequently intoxicated, were not vulnerable to advances by the men responsible for them."[15]

Another matter were suffragettes, who, as a result of their participation in demonstrations to win the right to vote, were sometimes arrested and jailed. They too sought reform of the penal institutions. Their middle-class sensibilities were stunned by the treatment they received when arrested and jailed for even a few hours. Middle- and upper-class "women were horrified to be touched by men, even when no violence, excessive force, or sexual assault threat was present."[16] Cultural norms dictated that only a spouse or immediate family member might be that intimate.

The reform-minded, upper-class Christian women, active in civic concerns, launched efforts to improve prisons and end the mistreatment of women and children. From their view, female officers were needed to handle the growing moral problems, and they urged the hiring of women into the occupation.[17] Law enforcement employment became an avenue for women to work as part of the "Child Saving Movement," designed to save wayward youth and women from the depravities of industrialism, alcoholism, and sexuality.[18] Members of the movement argued that degenerate women and children should fall under the jurisdiction of a social worker with police officer powers. They assumed that women were a natural for handling miscreant youth, since at home this was their domain.

Another issue for the reformers was the image of "white slavery"—the belief that virtuous women were being captured and sold into sexual slavery. Prostitutes of the day were seen as fallen women, but "the female reformers agitating for policewomen weren't really interested in these women. It was a class difference, with the reformers accepting male ideology that the hardened prostitute or alcoholic or homeless woman was indeed beyond redemption."[19] The religious leanings of the middle-class women played a part in how they viewed women "with a past." Protestants believed that God was not a forgiving sort; one did not sin, seek absolution, and then sin again. Rather, one trod a consistent religious path. People were predetermined to go to heaven or hell. The elect could be recognized by their stern religious performance, while the dammed, including delinquent women, were to be avoided.[20] The reformers were more interested in preventing good women from being led astray and sold into sexual bondage than they were in changing the ways of existing prostitutes.

The first American policewoman was Lola Baldwin, who was hired by the city of Portland in 1905 to protect women who were attending an Exposition,[21] but the most important early individual was Alice Stebbins Wells, appointed to the Los Angeles Police Department in 1910. Prior to Well's commission, she was a religious student and worker, who "became interested in the scientific study of crime."[22] For her, the handling of crime was "one of the greatest fields of applied Christianity." She posited that the "police department represents the strategic point at which virtue can meet vice, strength can meet weakness, and guide them into preventive and redemptive channels."[23] A few years after her appointment, she preached that:

> The battles of the future will be intellectual and moral battles, and a vast army of women have been studying and working to prepare themselves as no body of soldiers has ever done before to help wage victorious warfare against the forces that would destroy the race.[24]

In order to carry out her religious mission, Wells acquired "signatures to a petition asking for the necessary change in police regulations to admit a woman to the force," and she enlisted "the influence of various organizations of men and women to secure her appointment."[25] On the job, Wells did her best to maintain a separation from traditional, male policing. She wore no uniform, carried no weapon, and kept her badge in a handbag.[26] But, she must have been a strong-willed individual. Besides forcing the city fathers of Los Angeles to create her position, she established the parameters of the policewoman's job for decades to come.

Wells inspected the new palaces of leisure: "penny arcades, moving picture shows, skating rinks, dance halls, and other places of public amusement, including the parks on Sunday," and in these locales she saw sin and the potential for wayward youth to turn to crime. For her, the prevention of crime and immorality were the same activity. Most of the short films in the penny arcades, for example, she believed to be "suggestive of evil." To protect the young, she used her police powers to twist the arms of the amusement park owners to abide by her Victorian standards. Despite a lack of law to back her up, she was able to persist. A writer of the day noted, "Where there is no ordinance, she suggests the elimination of undesirable features and the introduction of protective measures, and since these places are dependent on the police commission for a license to continue in business, they hardly dare ignore her requests."[27]

During the coming decade, Wells gave talks around the country urging other cities to hire policewoman. In 1915, she helped form the International Association of Policewomen (IAP) which had as a primary objective the promoting of the concept of policewomen to police departments and communities.[28]

Following the appointment of Wells to the Los Angeles Police Department in 1910, news accounts describing policewomen grew steadily. Despite the press they received, the actual number of paid policewomen expanded very slowly. Seattle appointed five in 1912 and, during the same year, women were commissioned in Omaha and Denver. The next year Topeka, Kansas, and Rochester, New York appointed policewomen. By 1915, seventy women were earning police salaries in twenty-six different cities—a sizable percentage growth, but hardly a meaningful dent in the male-dominated occupation.[29] There was an increase in their number during World War I, when men were in shorter supply. The rise in England totaled thousands. But their growth in the United States "was on a limited scale."[30]

Most of the women had higher educations, many with advanced degrees in nursing, teaching, and social work, which they incorporated into law enforcement—all matters that improved the professional image of policing. The women recognized and promoted their unique differences in philosophy and ability from their male counterparts. They viewed themselves as social workers and not as "cops."[31] Illustrative are comments made at a national meeting of social workers in 1919:

> The police woman does not go out to arrest disorderly men, or to apprehend women who are soliciting on the streets for prostitution; from the very beginning, the chief duty of the police woman has been to protect and safeguard youth, and today her latest opportunity lies in the direction of protective work.[32]

New York City, in particular, took advantage of the women's missionary fervor. The city hired eighteen policewomen, but, according to written accounts from the period, also had a volunteer force numbering 5,000, which consisted of "prominent social welfare workers."[33] The women were organized into precincts and trained by paid officers. They were:

> to safeguard the morals of young women in the vicinity of cantonments and camps; to investigate crimes affecting women, such as compulsory prostitution, abortion cases and fortune-tellers. They also look after the wayward and missing girls, juvenile delinquents, and cases of improper guardianship. They secure employment for worthy girls and women, act the part of peacemakers in family difficulties, and, in fact, do general welfare work.[34]

Most of the women felt a strong calling to help humanity, to bring dignity back to women's lives, and to prevent crime by keeping a watchful eye on children. It was said that the "position of a woman in a police department is not unlike that of a mother in a home."[35]

During the early reform years, the average male officer believed that the concept and use of policewomen was a passing fad.[36] The success the women achieved was minimal. The social worker role, which the early female leaders wanted to fill, was not appreciated by male officers, who resented the new image being imposed on policing. The women recognized that to be accepted into the male-dominated world they had to have a function that differed from the men.[37] Their evaluation of the situation reflected an astute knowledge. One of their number wrote:

> The rules and regulations, customs and traditions of police departments, having developed completely under the regime of men, do not always function according to a woman's way of doing things. To attempt to accomplish everything one would like to do by disregarding the

system in operation, would be very unwise policy for policewomen to adopt. Effective service depends largely upon the extent to which the women cooperate with the men, for after all, policewomen have taken up policewomanship, not with the idea of replacing men in this work, but for the purpose of aiding and assisting them by seeking in a quiet, unassuming way to prevent crime.[38]

The women believed that male officers would accept females into the occupation as long as the women did not threaten male dominance and the role they sought fit within the traditional view of female activities. For these social activists, the "duties of the policeman and the policewoman must always be different."[39] Crime fighting and enforcement were male domains. Crime prevention, the women hoped, would become the female function. The measure of a policewomen's "success should not be the number of arrests made," they urged, "but rather the number of arrests prevented."[40] Policewomen were expected to accomplish their task by deterring or diminishing the determinants of vice, gambling, and lawlessness.[41]

Crime-prevention activities focused on youngsters because police believed "that the causes of crime were to be found in the effect of certain existing institutions upon the young people of the country, and that the attack on crime must be made among the young."[42] In general, it was felt that unsupervised juveniles would commit crimes; however, if they were watched more closely, crime would be prevented.[43]

Women were grudgingly accepted into police work, but almost exclusively because they handled situations disliked by the men, in particular, incidents involving women and children. Almost everywhere they existed, for example, policewomen were called upon to patrol theaters in search of truants and disruptive children. An inspection report for a 1925 department reported that its policewomen had visited "moving-picture houses" 2,446 times; removed 259 truants, 14 disorderly juveniles, and 37 children who were found asleep late at night. In addition, during their tours of the theaters, the female officers arrested thirteen men and one woman for indecent acts.[44] Male officers probably disliked monitoring the activities of theatergoers and willingly surrendered such assignments to the female constabulary.

Efforts by the women to define their mission as crime prevention, however, were often disregarded by police chiefs, who would occasionally send their female officers to assist in "discovering thieves and even murderers and to get evidence against criminals."[45] Not every department saw fit to use their female officers as quasisocial workers. In Chicago, for example, the superintendent of the police wrote in a letter that "the scope of the duties of police women in this city consists principally in ascertaining violations of the law" and that their "duties do not differ materially from those of police men."[46]

Across the United States, policewomen were required to perform many tasks that resembled standard police work, such as interview sexual assault victims, interrogate women felons, keep records, disseminate information to the public, take complaints, serve as decoys, and patrol areas of prostitution. Working undercover for the female officers was particularly "difficult because mingling with people after dark was just not a normal activity for respectable women."[47] One policewoman, who resigned because of the assignments, complained that she "had joined the force to help fallen women and wayward children." But instead, she "was forced to accompany men of the lowest type, professional stool pigeons, around town, to enter dives of the worst type and do work which could be done much better by men."[48]

The women who received praise within departments were those who fulfilled the law enforcement goal of policing. Illustrative was Josephine Roche, who was appointed to the Denver police in 1912. A year later, the Denver chief referred to her as "the best man" on his force.[49] Roche concentrated on enforcement and not social work activities, although she believed women had methods that differed from men. She wrote about her endeavors:

> [W]e no longer believe in the old theory that law must be enforced by the club or by the revolver. You cannot force people to do right. You cannot beat goodness into them. You have to show them why they should obey the law. Just because a woman is a woman and disassociated from the idea of force, she can frequently enforce the law with more ease than a man.[50]

The efforts of the female activists to create a crime prevention role for policewomen were only minimally successful and, by the 1930s, growth in their number came to a grinding halt. For one reason, the Depression reinforced traditional gender roles; women returned to the home and the diminished number of jobs went to men.[51] But, a change in the archetype of the police force had a more long-term effect.

During the 1930s, a new wave of police administrators infused departments with bureaucratization. The social worker–oriented policewoman had matched well the educated police professional urged by August Vollmer twenty years earlier. However, she had only a minimal role in the police order envisioned by O.W. Wilson and J. Edgar Hoover, who were actively pursuing law enforcement as the police goal.[52] Crime-prevention activities were relegated by the male leaders to minimal importance. Wilson, for example, "did not advocate expanded roles for policewomen. To the contrary, he believed that women were ill-equipped emotionally for leadership positions."[53] Hoover was much worse. While he was director of the Federal Bureau of Investigation (FBI), no women were hired as agents. He argued, "The Bureau's responsibilities were too taxing, too physically demanding, too complicated and serious for women, except insofar as they could help out in menial or subservient roles."[54] He wanted his agents to be "tough, fearless crime fighters." trained to use "the latest scientific crime fighting techniques."[55] He used the media to portray this image and to glorify himself and his agency. Women did not have much of a place in Hoover's world.

As a result of the police leaders' endeavors, the bureaucratic department of the 1930s emphasized crime fighting over the "order maintenance and service aspects of the police role," and officers on the street ridiculed such duties "as not being 'real' policework."[56] Women, who had the same law enforcement goals as their male colleagues, could survive within departments. By World War II, the major distinction between the work of male and female officers was not between law enforcement and prevention. Both groups of police officers probably emphasized crime-fighting activities. Rather, what differences there were between male and female activities stemmed from the belief that the police function required the use of authority and force and that women lacked the physical presence to fill the role.[57] Moreover, the specter of assault and possible death hung over the patrolmen's job and women, in general, were to be protected from such situations and not shoved, badge first, into them. These matters limited the opportunities for women's employment by law enforcement agencies. By 1938 there were slightly more than 500 policewomen nationwide; most probably worked a normal police officer's 48-hour, 6-day work week for which they received compensation comparable to male officers.[58]

Following World War II, there were few policewomen given the fanfare that had accompanied their introduction forty years earlier. A study conducted by the Woman's Bureau of the United States Department of Justice in 1949 concluded that policewomen were less than 1 percent of force personnel.[59] An estimated 1,000 were employed by about 140 cities with populations of more than 25,000; New York led the way with 174 followed by Chicago's crew of 79. Indicative of the crime-fighting role that many policewomen filled was the report that in forty cities the women were required to carry a firearm, while thirty-six cities made it optional. In a minority of the cities (forty-five), they did not carry arms.[60]

During the economic boom of the 1950s, the number of women hired into police work increased dramatically. By 1960, 5,617 female police officers and detectives were serving U.S. municipalities. Their number in New York City had grown to 253. There, and in other large departments, policewomen had the same powers as patrolmen, received the same salary, and had the opportunity to become detectives.[61] Most of the women were involved in law enforcement activities. Working in teams, the policewomen, in civilian clothes, patrolled locales where complaints indicated "the presence of degenerates, shoplifters and jostlers." The women, it was argued, were better suited for investigations involving "degenerates" because "the direct evidence necessary for a court conviction can best be obtained by a policewoman."[62] The women were also involved in surveillance, at times "tailing" suspects or finding employment in the suspect's social world so as to spy on him. And, of course, in rape cases, the women were used because they were "successful in obtaining information from women who may be reluctant to discuss delicate or sordid matters with male officers."[63]

Not all the new policewomen, however, were involved in the crime control arena. Some of the women had found employment because of expanding police responsibilities. The rapid postwar increase in automobiles, for example, quickly overburdened downtown parking capacities and police departments needed to expand the number of individuals assigned to traffic and parking duties. Female officers made handy "meter maids." A sergeant praised them, noting that they "are 'three times as rugged as men'—they don't complain so much about their feet and they hand out more tickets."[64] Some of the traffic officers were paid the same as their male counterparts, carried revolvers, and worked the same forty-eight-hour week. Those who were limited to checking for parking violations, however, received lower salaries.[65]

Women also entered police work during the 1950s because administrators found them useful support staff within the bureaucratic police world. One superintendent of communications, for example, noted that his staff of female dispatchers handled a call, on average, in nine seconds. "The girls seem to stand the pace much better than men," the reporter noted.[66]

By the middle of the 1960s, the President's Commission on Law Enforcement and the Administration of Justice, in the half page it devoted to them, urged an expanded role for women in policing:

> Police women can be an invaluable asset to modern law enforcement and their present role should be broadened. Qualified women should be utilized in such important staff service units as planning and research, training, intelligence, inspection, public information, community relations, and as legal advisors.
>
> Women could also serve in units such as computer programming and laboratory analyses and communications. Their value should not be considered as limited to staff functions or police work with juveniles; women should also serve regularly in patrol, vice, and investigative divisions. Finally, as more and more well-qualified women enter the service, they could assume administrative responsibilities.[67]

Nationally, however, potential positions for women remained limited, primarily because they were perceived as unable to handle the physical and emotional rigors of patrol, where most police jobs exist (and from where future administrators are chosen).

WOMEN ON PATROL

Revolutionary changes occurred in women's roles during the 1960s and 1970s, both in the larger society and in policing. Women sought equal access to employment opportunities, including jobs generally held by men, such as police patrol work. Rather than stressing their differences, these women pushed against what they correctly perceived to be artificial barriers, and sought occupational equality to men in patrol work. Of primary political importance, in 1972 Congress passed a number of pieces of legislation that have directly impacted women's opportunities for achievement. Title IX, because it opened athletics to women, is the most celebrated. But the same year, Congress enacted the Equal

Employment Opportunity (EEO) Act which unlocked the door that had kept women out of patrol. Municipalities were legally liable if they failed to hire and place on patrol worthy female applicants.[68]

In Indianapolis in 1968, and then with great fanfare in 1969 in Washington, D.C., policewomen were reassigned to patrol work. Some women who had entered policing to do social work were not happy with their new positions and objected.[69] But, increasingly from that moment, women entered policing as equals to men, to perform identical duties and receive identical rewards. The terms *policewoman* and *policeman* were dropped, and the more generic term *police officer* was adopted. The unique professional position of quasisocial worker, which the pioneer policewomen had worked so hard to create, vanished, leaving the crime control function of police unchallenged from the ranks of officers.

Since their integration into patrol, efforts to attract and hire women into law enforcement have been minimal and often required litigation to bring about change. However, such suits have failed to result in equality, in part because judicial decisions requiring police departments to hire minorities and females continue to underrepresent women. For example, a court order in 1979 required the San Francisco Police Department to reserve 20 percent of its recruit positions for women during the next decade. At the time of the judgment, the 1,670 member police department included about 60 women.[70]

Women wishing patrol assignment were not readily accepted into the bureaucratic police organization. For one thing, there existed a general belief among the men that women were incapable, or at least less capable, of police work. Basic to their belief was the notion that men and women are different and that police work requires some ability that only men possess. In general, those in society who hold this and similar views argue that behavior is, in part, biologically determined, and further assert that gender-based roles in society are rooted in biological makeup. Simply put, men, because they were hunters in earlier societies, are more aggressive and better fit for the conflict of modern life. Women, because they gave birth and had to nurse their offspring, are nurturing and better suited for domestic careers. Women who identified "with their traditional roles" were "commended for competency and ingenuity in problem solving."[71] But, women performing or desiring "male" occupations were considered abnormal. In order to do men's work, the position posited, they must deny their feminine nature. They must be tough, unemotional, and decisive; traits not stereotypically assigned to women.

In general, individuals who choose occupations not traditionally associated with their gender, such as female police officers, will feel great pressure from many in society to reconsider their decisions. Those who conform to societal expectations gain a feeling of solidarity by urging deviants to conform. Punishing deviants further reinforces this sense of solidarity or "group" and demonstrates the "evils" of nonconformity.[72] Male officers accomplished this function by ridiculing or excluding female officers from activities in the hope that they would quit.[73]

Women's entrance into patrol coincided with an expanded interest across the nation in law enforcement. Beginning with the presidential election of 1964, crime control became a high priority on the national agenda. The potential for violence had always been a core element of policework; the period that surrounded women's entrance into the male world of patrol was particularly so and probably further hindered their acceptance. Media presentations focused on law enforcement as the goal of policework and stressed the occupation's perils. Officers were portrayed as "ill-paid" and facing "danger and hardship"[74] in a world in which they had to deal with "criminals who would not stop at murder to carry out their purpose."[75] There was, according to some, "a war against the police" which involved "vicious attacks on officers, the murder and maiming of lawmen."[76] Citizens were instructed that the police "detect crime and apprehend criminals" and that "[i]t's not their job to be involved in private disputes such as landlord-tenant problems, or quarrels between neighbors, or in family disputes."[77]

Foremost among male verbal complaints about the entrance of women into patrol was that they would not perform well in potentially dangerous situations.[78] Some men maintained that women might cause violence.[b] Their diminutive size and strength, the argument went, were not conducive to physical confrontation.[c] Suspects might challenge the lady cop. For male officers, being tall and intimidating were important police tools.[79] The same philosophy had excluded shorter males from police acceptance. Priority was given to men, who were perceived as having "the brawn to deal with police problems."[80] A woman on patrol threatened the status quo of the cop culture, and in particular the officers' self-image as fierce individuals doing a job only tough men could accomplish.

Male cops insisted that they would hesitate to call the "weaker sex" to back them up in violent situations.[81] Moreover, the men feared that their fellow officers might abandon the chase of fleeing felons if the female officers got in trouble. The male instinct, they posited, would be to protect the women from harm.[82]

Antagonisms also developed between male officers and vocal feminists of the day who were demanding equal rights and equal pay. The demonstrators, along with criminals and civil rights activists, were perceived of as "enemies" by cops.[83]

ARE FEMALE COPS DIFFERENT?

Beginning in the 1970s, numerous studies were conducted on hypothesized differences between male and female cops utilizing measures of job performance—such as, arrest rates, self-initiated activities, dependability, observation skills, and stress control and composure.[84] Many of the investigators concluded that there was little difference between the way male cops did the job and the manner in which women accomplished it.[85] Some analysts, however, suggested that men and women do differ. Men made more arrests that did their female counterparts[86] and were overrepresented among officers who had been disciplined for brutality.[87] The lower rates of arrests and violence among female officers hint that they seek alternative ways to handle citizens' problems, which might indicate that women handle the situations better than male officers, if the latter caused incidents to escalate into confrontations, which resulted in unnecessary arrests.

Illustrative of the better studies was a pilot project conducted in New York City during 1975 and 1976.[88] Patrol performances of forty-one women officers were compared with a matched sample of forty-one male officers.[d] Police and civilian personnel observed the cops while they did their jobs. The authors of the research reported:

> In general, male and female officers performed similarly: they used the same techniques to gain and keep control and were equally unlikely to use force or to display a weapon. However, small differences in performance were observed. Female officers were judged by civilians to be more competent, pleasant, and respectful than their male counterparts, but were observed to be slightly less likely to engage in control-seeking behavior, and less apt to assert themselves in patrol-decision making. Compared to male officers, females were less often named as arresting officers, less likely to participate in strenuous physical activity, and took more sick time.[89]

The report noted that some of the differences may have been the result of the women "holding back," as they were new to the areas and riding with males who often wanted to take control of the situations. Although not mentioned in the report, many, if not most, of the male officers were former military men who viewed women as unable to lead and did not want to take orders from them. Historically, the exercise of authority and use of force were assigned to men. Women were rarely allowed to command and control others. Other matters likely also affected the situations. Male officers, for example, more often drove the patrol cars, chiefly because women drivers pulled the bench seat closer to the foot pedals, which cramped the long-legged males.[90]

The report explained that when female officers rode together, the women "were more active than when they rode with men."[91] These items and others led the researchers to note that the matter of yielding may be "a reflection of traditional male-female role behavior."[92] They determined that:

> The results of this study offer little support either to those who hold that women are unsuited to patrol or to those who argue that women do the job better than men. By and large, patrol performance of the women was more like that of the men than it was different.[93]

The results of the studies of police performance by gender were analogous to investigations done at about the same time of women's execution of other leadership roles. Where women were accepted, they performed their jobs as well as men.[94] For women entering police work (and other male-dominated occupations), the problem was not so much having the physical ability to do the job, but rather the lack of approval from male colleagues. To be appreciated the female recruits had to:

> accept the standards and the style of the male world. The male world, that is, will admit them if they can pass male tests and perform just as well as or better than men. They must become competitive, achievement-oriented, and reject the patterns characteristic of the woman's world.[95]

She must share the working personality of police work because "acceptance of the subcultures' principal norms and acceptance into the subcultures' informal social network are the keys to opportunity for mobility within the organization."[96] Rookies who do not conform to the group's norms are shunned or ridiculed by orthodox members of the cop culture.[97]

The occupational norms of policing are directly associated with the crime-control component of the job. Most important, for example, is "the requirement that an officer physically backup another officer or face rejection as a partner. . .and the belief that the means justifies the ends in the apprehension of a felon."[98] The female recruit, who wants to win the approval of her colleagues, must either bring with her to the job characteristics associated with the crime-control image or she must adopt them early in her career. One author, based on interviews of female patrol officers, concluded that a woman had to participate in a dangerous law enforcement situation to be accepted. Such an activity transformed her, in the eyes of other cops, from a woman into a police officer.[99]

DISCUSSION AND CONCLUSION

Women have a long history in police departments. Their introduction into the occupation was one of the earliest substantial alterations to policing. At the beginning of the twentieth century they fulfilled a unique position in many agencies. They were hired for their distinctive skills in mediating problems associated with women and children. As the century progressed, many proponents for female cops argued that women were better suited to the occupation than men. They noted that the many facets of police work require a wide range of personality traits. Some traits, such as the need for an officer to be patient and understanding, may stereotypically be associated with females, while aggression by police officers may likely cause trouble for other officers, their departments, and private citizens.

Pervasive negative beliefs concerning the abilities of women to perform the police role continue to exist, despite research findings that women perform equally as well as their male counterparts in the role of police officer. These attitudes appear resistant to change for a number of reasons. Some biological differences, for example, are unchangeable. Reproductive abilities—getting pregnant, carrying a baby, and giving birth—are biological realities that women must deal with. Prejudices against female officers may be reinforced by such biological facts.

Efforts to integrate women into police work have fallen short, in large part, because they have not altered the police value system, which supports certain attitudes and personality traits—some that police recruiters look for and some that are learned on the job and in the training process. Individuals who are attracted to law enforcement are selected by and soon socialized into a police subculture that rejects change and prizes loyalty to the system.

Of utmost importance in the police value system is the belief that their occupation is primarily law enforcement, emphasizing crime fighting over other services. Studies, however, reveal that their focus may be misplaced; only 10 percent of policing involves the law-enforcement component[100] and dangerous activities represent less than 1 percent of citizen-initiated complaints.[101] The police value system, with its emphasis on crime fighting, does not mesh well with what police work actually consists of—service activities and problem solving. This dilemma, we argue, has undermined most attempts to integrate women into the occupation. Individuals who end up as police officers prefer the law-enforcement component of their jobs. Subverted is the hope that female officers might differ from their male counterparts and elect the service role.

NOTES

a. Early writings on women in policing sometimes refer to *policewomen* and sometimes to *police women*. We will use the term *policewomen* unless we are quoting.

b. Illustrative of the view was the beating of Rodney King by officers of the Los Angeles Police Department following a freeway chase. Sgt. Stacey Koon initially took charge of the situation because he believed that Melanie Singer, the California Highway Patrol officer who was the first to confront King, might use the gun she had drawn. (Lou Cannon. 1977. *Official Negligence: How Rodney King and the Riots Changed Los Angeles and the LAPD*. New York: Times Books.

c. The men had tales of women that indicated lack of physical strength. One department in 1957 "had to send back twenty-one snub-nosed .38-caliber pistols it had ordered for its female officers after a trial shoot proved that none of the policewomen was strong enough to pull the trigger." (Steiner, P. (1957), "Policeman's Lot," *The New York Times Magazine*, Sept. 29:84).

REFERENCES

1. Hamilton, M. E. 1925. "Woman's Place in the Police Department." *The American City* 32: 194.

2. Foster, C., Siegel, M.A., and Jacobs, N. R., eds. 1990. "Women's Changing Role." *Information Plus* 18: 29–37.

3. Hammer-Higgins, P., and Atwood, V.A. 1989. "The Management Game: An Educational Intervention for Counseling Women with Nontraditional Career Goals." *The Career Development Quarterly* 38(1):6–23.

4. Foster, C., Siegel, M. A., and Jacobs, N. R., eds. 1990. "Women's Changing Role." *Information Plus* 18:29–37.

5. McGoldrick, K. 1988. "Gender and Economics." *Journal of the American Medical Women's Association* 43:103.

6. Allen, D. 1989. "Women in Medical Specialty Societies: An Update." *Journal of the American Medical Association* 262:3439–43.

7. Martin, S. 1980. *Breaking and Entering: Police Women on Patrol*. Berkeley: University of California Press.

8. Gilligan, C. 1982. *In A Different Voice*. Cambridge, MA: Harvard University Press.

9. Bernard, J. (1978) "Models for the Relationship Between the World of Women and the World of Men." In L. Kriesberg, ed., *Research in Social Movements, Conflicts and Change* (pp. 291–331). Greenwich, CT: J.A.I. Press; Betz, M., O'Connell, L. (1987) Gender and work: A look at sex differences among pharmacy students. *American Journal of Pharmaceutical Education* 51:39–43; Douvan, E., Adelson, J. (1966) *The Adolescent experience*. New York: John Wiley & Sons; Vinacke, W. E. (1959) Sex roles in three-person game. *Sociometry* 22:343–360.

10. Parsons, D.A. 1996. Police Officers' Perceptions: a Comparative Study by Gender and Organization. Ph.D. dissertation, University of California, Irvine.

11. Hamilton, M. E. 1924. *The Policewoman: Her Service and Ideals*. New York: F. A. Stokes.

12. Lord, L. K. 1986. A comparison of Male and Female Peace Officers: Stereotypic Perceptions of Women and Women Peace Officers. *Journal of Police Science and Administration* 14(2):83–97.

13. Segrave, K. 1995. *Policewomen: A History*. Jefferson, NC: McFarland.

14. Shultz, D. M. 1995. *From Social Worker to Crimefighters: Women in United States Municipal Policing*. Westport, CT: Praeger.

15. Shultz, D. M. 1995. *From Social Worker to Crimefighters: Women in United States Municipal Policing*. Westport, CT: Praeger.

16. Segrave, K. 1995. *Policewomen: A History*. Jefferson, NC: McFarland.

17. Odem, M. E. 1995. *Delinquent Daughters*. Chapel Hill, NC: The University of North Carolina Press.

18. Platt, A. 1977. *The Child Savers: The Invention of Delinquency*, ed. 2. Chicago, IL: University of Chicago Press.

19. Segrave, K. 1995. *Policewomen: A History*. Jefferson, NC: McFarland.

20. Weber, M. 1976. *The Protestant Ethic and the Spirit of Capitalism*, trans. Talcott Parsons. New York: Scribner.

21. Miner, M. 1919. "The Police Woman and the Girl Problem." In *Proceedings of the National Conference on Social Welfare*. Atlantic City, NJ: June 1–8, 134–142.

22. Smith, B. H. 1911. "The Policewoman." *Good Housekeeping*. 52(March):296–298.

23. Smith, B. H. 1911. "The Policewoman." *Good Housekeeping*. 52(March):296–298.

24. Wells, A. S. 1913. Women on the Police Force. *The American City*. 8(April):401.

25. Smith, B. H. 1911. "The Policewoman." *Good Housekeeping*. 52(March):296–298.

26. Smith, B. H. 1911. "The Policewoman." *Good Housekeeping*. 52(March):296–298.

27. Smith, B. H. 1911. "The Policewoman." *Good Housekeeping*. 52(March):296–298.

28. Horne, P. 1980. *Women in Law Enforcement* ed. 2. Springfield, IL: Charles C Thomas.

29. Miner, M. 1919. "The Police Woman and the Girl Problem." In *Proceedings of the National Conference on Social Welfare*. Atlantic City, NJ: June 1–8, 134–142.

30. Miner, M. 1919. "The Police Woman and the Girl Problem." In *Proceedings of the National Conference on Social Welfare*. Atlantic City, NJ: June 1–8, 134–142.

31. Feinman, C. 1980. *Women in the Criminal Justice System*. New York: Praeger.

32. Miner, M. 1919. "The Police Woman and the Girl Problem." In *Proceedings of the National Conference on Social Welfare*. Atlantic City, NJ: June 1–8, 134–142: 134.

33. O'Gary, E. A. 1919. "Policewomen and their Work." *The American City* January.

34. O'Gary, E. A. 1919. "Policewomen and their Work." *The American City* January.

35. Hamilton, M. E. 1924. *The Policewoman: Her Service and Ideals*. New York: F.A. Stokes.

36. Hutzel, E. L. 1933. *The Police Women's Handbook*. Colombia University Press: New York.

37. Walbrook, H. M. 1919. "Women police and their work." *Nineteenth Century and After* 85:377–382; Van Winkle, M. C. 1926. "The Policewoman a Socializing Agency." *The American City* 34:198–199; "The Police-Woman is Marching On (1914) *The American City* 9:403.

38. Hamilton, M. E. 1925. "Woman's Place in the Police Department." *The American City* 32:194.

39. Walbrook, H. M. 1919. "Women Police and their Work." *Nineteenth Century and After* 85:377–382.

40. Murray, V. M. 1921. Policewomen in Detroit. *The American City*, XXV(3):209–210.

41. Graper, E.D. 1921. *American Police Administration*. New York: Macmillan.

42. Brownlow, L. 1927. "Police and the Cause of Crime." *The American City* 36:797.

43. Moss, F. 1901. "National Danger from Police Corruption." *North American Review* 173:470–480; Hamilton, M. E. 1924. *The Policewoman: Her Service and Ideals*. New York: F. A. Stokes.

44. Pigeon, H. D. 1927. "Policewomen and public recreation." *The American City* October, 448–450.

45. Miner, M. 1919. "The Police Woman and the Girl Problem." *Proceedings of the National Conference on Social Welfare*. Atlantic City, NJ: June 1–8, 134–142.

46. Miner, M. 1919. "The Police Woman and the Girl Problem." In *Proceedings of the National Conference on Social Welfare*. Atlantic City, NJ: June 1–8, 134–142.

47. Hamilton, M. E. 1924. *The Policewoman: Her Service and Ideals*. New York: F. A. Stokes.

48. Hamilton, M. E. 1925. "Woman's Place in the Police Department." *The American City* 194.

49. Walbrook, H. M. 1919. "Women police and their work." *Nineteenth Century and After* 85:377–382.

50. Segrave, K. 1995. *Policewomen: A History*. Jefferson, NC: McFarland.

51. Shultz, D. M. 1995. *From Social Worker to Crimefighters: Women in United States Municipal Policing*. Westport, CT: Praeger.

52. Shultz, D. M. 1995. *From Social Worker to Crimefighters:Women in United States Municipal Policing*. Westport, CT: Praeger.

53. Shultz, D. M. 1995. *From Social Worker to Crimefighters: Women in United States Municipal Policing*. Westport, CT: Praeger.

54. Segrave, K. 1995. Policewomen: A History. Jefferson, NC: McFarland.

55. Walker, S. 1983. *The Police in America: An Introduction*. New York: McGraw-Hill.

56. Walker, S. 1983. *The Police in America: An Introduction*. New York: McGraw-Hill.

57. Martin, S. 1980. *Breaking and Entering: Police Women on Patrol*. Berkeley: University of California Press; More, H. W. 1991. *Special Topics in Policing*. Cincinnati: Anderson.

58. "Salaries and Working Conditions in Police Departments." 1941. *Monthly Labor Review* 52:817–826.

59. Boyd, M. M. 1953. "The Role of the Police Woman." In *Police Yearbook: Proceedings of the 59th Annual Conference of the International Association of Chiefs of Police.* Washington, DC: International Association of Chiefs of Police.

60. "More Cities Employ Policewomen." 1948. *The American City* (February).

61. President's Commission on Law Enforcement and Administration of Justice. 1968. *The Challenge of Crime in a Free Society.* New York: Avon Books.

62. Melchionne, T. M. 1960. "Where Policewomen are Better than Men." *American City* 75:161.

63. Melchionne, T. M. 1960. "Where Policewomen are Better than Men." *American City* 75:161.

64. Women are Tougher as Traffic Police. 1954. *The American City* 69(May):183.

65. Women are Tougher as Traffic Police. 1954. *The American City* 69(May):183.

66. "Girls Make Better Radio Dispatchers." 1953. *The American City* 68(November):149.

67. President's Commission on Law Enforcement and Administration of Justice. 1968. *The Challenge of Crime in a Free Society.* New York: Avon Books.

68. Warner, R. L., and Steel, D. S. 1989. "Affirmative Action in Times of Fiscal Stress and Changing Value Priorities: the Case of Women in Policing. *Public Personnel Management* 18(3): 291–309.

69. Segrave, K. 1995. *Policewomen: A History.* Jefferson, NC: McFarland; Abrecht, M. with Stern, B. L. 1976. *The Making of a Woman Cop.* New York: William Morrow.

70. Equal Opportunity Forum. 1979. *Affirmative Action Monthly* (February).

71. Wood, M. M. 1979. "Stress and the Corporate Woman." In Davis, R. H. ed. *Stress and the Organization.* Los Angeles: The University of Southern California Press.

72. Durkheim, E. 1984. The Division of Labor in Society, trans. W. D. Halls. New York: The Free Press.

73. Martin, S. 1980. *Breaking and Entering: Police Women on Patrol.* Berkeley: University of California Press; Segrave, K. 1995. *Policewomen: A History.* Jefferson, NC: McFarland; Drummond, D. S. 1988. "Law Enforcement: The Cultural Impact on an Occupation." Doctoral Project Presented to August Vollmer University; Fletcher, C. 1995. *Breaking and Entering: Women Cops talk about Life in the Ultimate Men's Club.* New York: Harper-Collins.

74. "The Policemen." 1965. *Saturday Evening Post* 238:100.

75. Murphy, E. F. 1966. "Men in Blue." *The New York Times Magazine* March 6, p. 52.

76. "The War Against the Police—Officers Tell their Story." 1970. *U.S. News & World Report,* October 26, pp. 82–86.

77. Brown, L. M. 1972. "When should you Call the Police?" *Better Homes and Garden* 50:78.

78. Alpert, G. P., and Dunham, R. G. 1992. Policing Urban America, ed. 2. Prospect Heights, IL: Waveland Press; Caiden, G. 1977. *Police Revitalization.* Lexington, MA: Lexington Books; "The Female Fuzz." 1972. *Newsweek* October 23, p. 172; Segrave, K. 1995. *Policewomen: A History.* Jefferson, NC: McFarland.

79. "The Female Fuzz." 1972. *Newsweek* October 23, p. 172.

80. More, H. W. 1991. *Special Topics in Policing.* Cincinnati: Anderson.

81. Caiden, G. 1977. *Police Revitalization.* Lexington, MA: Lexington Books.

82. Martin, S. 1980. *Breaking and Entering: Police Women on Patrol*. Berkeley: University of California Press.

83. More, H. W. 1991. *Special Topics in Policing*. Cincinnati: Anderson.

84. Bloch, P., and Anderson, D. 1974. *Policewomen on Patrol: Final Report*. Washington, DC: Police Foundation; Charles, M. T. 1981. "The Performance and Socialization of Female Recruits in the Michigan State Police Training Academy." *Journal of Police Science and Administration* 9:209–223; Jones, C. A. 1987. "Predicting the Effectiveness of Police Officers." Unpublished Master's Thesis, San Diego State University.

85. Charles, M. T. 1982. "Women in Policing: The Physical Aspect." *Journal of Police Science and Administration* 10(2):194–205; Gross, S. 1984. Women Becoming Cops: Developmental Issues and Solutions. *Police Chief* 51:32–35; Milton, C. H. 1972. *Women in Policing*. Washington, DC: Police Foundation; Sichel, J. L., Friedman, L. N., Quint, J. C., Smith, M. E. 1978. *Women on Patrol: A Pilot Study of Police Performance in New York City*. Washington, DC: U.S. Government Printing Office.

86. Koenig, Esther J. 1978. "An Overview of Attitudes Toward Women in Law Enforcement." *Public Administrative Review* 38:267–275; Sherman, L. W. 1975. "An Evaluation of Policewomen on Patrol in a Suburban Police Department." *Journal of Police Science and Administration* 3:434–438; Sichel, J. L., Friedman, L. N., Quint, J. C., Smith, M. E. 1978. *Women on Patrol: A Pilot Study of Police Performance in New York City*. Washington, DC: U.S. Government Printing Office.

87. "Report of the Independent Commission on the Los Angeles Police Department" 1991. Los Angeles, CA: Author.

88. Sichel, J. L., Friedman, L. N., Quint, J. C., and Smith, M. E. 1978. *Women on Patrol: A Pilot Study of Police Performance in New York City*. Washington, DC: U.S. Government Printing Office.

89. Sichel, J. L., Friedman, L. N., Quint, J. C., and Smith, M. E. 1978. *Women on Patrol: A Pilot Study of Police Performance in New York City*. Washington, DC: U.S. Government Printing Office.

90. Sichel, J. L., Friedman, L. N., Quint, J. C., and Smith, M. E. 1978. *Women on Patrol: A Pilot Study of Police Performance in New York City*. Washington, DC: U.S. Government Printing Office.

91. Sichel, J. L., Friedman, L. N., Quint, J. C., and Smith, M. E. 1978. *Women on Patrol: A Pilot Study of Police Performance in New York City*. Washington, DC: U.S. Government Printing Office.

92. Sichel, J. L., Friedman, L. N., Quint, J. C., and Smith, M. E. 1978. *Women on Patrol: A Pilot Study of Police Performance in New York City*. Washington, DC: U.S. Government Printing Office.

93. Sichel, J. L., Friedman, L. N., Quint, J. C., and Smith, M. E. 1978. *Women on Patrol: A Pilot Study of Police Performance in New York City*. Washington, DC: U.S. Government Printing Office.

94. Wood, M. M. 1979. "Stress and the Corporate Woman." In Davis, R. H., ed. 1979. *Stress and the Organization*. Los Angeles: The University of Southern California Press.

95. Bernard, J. 1978. "Models for the relationship between the world of women and the world of men." In Kriesberg, L., ed. *Research in Social Movements, Conflicts and Change*. Greenwich, CT: JAI Press.

96. Martin, S. 1980. *Breaking and Entering: Police Women on Patrol.* Berkeley: University of California Press.

97. Johnson, T. A., Misner, G. E., and Brown, L. P. 1981. *The Police and Society: An Environment for Collaboration and Confrontation.* Englewood Cliffs, NJ: Prentice-Hall; Martin, S. 1980. *Breaking and Entering: Police Women on Patrol.* Berkeley: University of California Press.

98. Martin, S. 1980. *Breaking and Entering: Police Women on Patrol.* Berkeley: University of California Press.

99. Heidensohn, F. 1992. *Women in Control? The Role of Women in Law Enforcement.* Oxford: Clarendon Press.

100. Reiss, A. J., Jr. 1971. *Police and the Public.* New Haven: Yale University Press; Kinnane, A. 1979. *Policing.* Chicago: Nelson-Hall; Martin, S. 1980. *Breaking and Entering, Policewomen on Patrol.* Berkeley: University of California Press.

101. Black, D. 1968. "Police Encounters and Social Organization." Doctoral dissertation, University of Michigan.

VI

INTERNATIONAL AND COMPARATIVE STUDIES

Cross-National Comparative Studies in Criminology

David P. Farrington

Cross-national comparative studies in criminology and criminal justice are important but relatively infrequent. In this chapter, I review my own cross-national comparisons of risk factors for delinquency, criminal career features, and rates of crime and punishment in different countries.

The main justification for cross-national comparisons is to establish the generalizability of theories and results and the boundary conditions under which they do or do not hold. It is also important to investigate how far interventions to prevent or reduce offending have similar effects in different times and places. It would be desirable to search for universal findings that can be replicated in different contexts. For example, Hirschi and Gottfredson[1] argued that the aggregate age-crime curve was invariant over different places, times, crime types, and so on. If cross-national differences are discovered, the challenge is to explain them by identifying the "active ingredients" (e.g. social, cultural, legal, or criminal justice processes in different countries) that cause them. It is important to search for theories and results that have a wide range of applicability.

Cross-national comparisons of criminal careers, crime rates, or offending are not easy to carry out, because of differences between countries in laws, legal processes, criminal justice systems, and other conditions. Comparative research may be carried out by the "safari" method or through collaboration. In the safari method, a researcher visits another country, reviews relevant literature and statistics, talks to key persons, and then goes home and compares his or her own country with the country visited. The collaborative method (which I use) involves cooperation between at least one knowledgeable researcher in each country.

The collaborative method is most satisfactory in overcoming language barriers and possible misunderstandings. As Klein[2] argued, "at this point we don't need more brief incursions into each other's territories as much as planned and shared, long-term collaborative cross-national journeys." There are many aspects of criminological data from any country that may be misunderstood by a researcher from outside that country. There are many pitfalls for the unwary, even in criminological data from one's own country, and it is important to know about these and to avoid mistakes of interpretation. The easiest cross-national comparison is between two countries, involving one researcher from each.

The International Crime Victims Survey (ICVS), carried out in 1989, 1992, and 1996, represents one of the most important cross-national comparative studies in criminology.[3] Using a telephone survey of about 1,500 to 2,000 adults in each country, this yields information over time about criminal victimization in more than ten Western industrialized countries. Painter and Farrington[4] compared victimization rates on a Caribbean island with victimization rates in the ICVS. The prevalence and incidence of some crimes on the island (e.g. robbery, vehicle theft) was relatively low, while for other crimes (e.g. burglary, assault, and sexual incidents) it was relatively high.

The other major cross-national comparative survey is the International Self-Reported Delinquency Survey (ISRD), carried out in 1992–93 in thirteen Western industrialized countries.[5] The same self-reported delinquency survey instrument was used to interview national and city samples of young people aged fourteen to twenty-five (typically). The success of these initiatives shows the feasibility of coordinated cross-national comparative studies.

RISK FACTORS FOR DELINQUENCY

The major risk factors for delinquency have been discovered in large-scale prospective longitudinal surveys and are well known. They include individual factors such as high impulsivity and low achievement, parental factors such as antisocial fathers and young mothers, socioeconomic factors such as low income and large families, and childrearing factors such as poor supervision and harsh discipline.[6] It is widely believed that these risk factors have similar effects in different times and places. However, there has previously been no systematic test of this hypothesis.

Systematic comparisons of results obtained in two longitudinal surveys are rare. Some researchers have compared their results with previously published data from other surveys. For example, Pulkkinen[7] analyzed her Finland longitudinal survey of males to see how comparable their criminal career features were to my London data. Direct, collaborative comparisons are less common. However, Pulkkinen and Tremblay[8] investigated similarities between two longitudinal studies of boys, in Jyvaskyla, Finland and Montreal, Canada. They cluster-analyzed five scales derived from teacher ratings (aggression, anxiety, inattention, hyperactivity, and prosocial behavior) and found that eight similar clusters of boys were obtained in each country. The multiple-problem boys were most likely to have later delinquent outcomes. This study has some similarities with the cross-sectional comparison of American and Dutch boys by Achenbach and his colleagues.[9] They factor-analyzed Child Behavior Checklists completed by parents in each country, and concluded that seven empirically derived behavioral syndromes were replicable.

The only previous systematic comparisons of risk factors for delinquency in two prospective longitudinal surveys in different countries were carried out by Farrington and his colleagues[10] and Moffitt and her colleagues[11]. Farrington and colleagues compared the relationship between personality factors and delinquency in London and Montreal. Moffitt and colleagues investigated the relationship between personality and intelligence measures and delinquency in the Dunedin (New Zealand) and Pittsburgh studies. They found that constraint (risk-taking as opposed to caution), negative emotionality (a low threshold for emotions such as anger and fear), and verbal intelligence were correlated with delinquency in both countries. The present comparison included a much wider range of risk factors and focused on their ability to predict later offending.

The transatlantic replicability of risk factors was investigated by comparing results obtained in the Cambridge Study in Delinquent Development[12] and in the Pittsburgh Youth Study.[13] The Cambridge Study is a prospective longitudinal survey of 411 London boys, originally aged eight to nine in 1961–62 and followed up to the present. The Pittsburgh Youth Study is a prospective longitudinal survey of three samples of Pittsburgh boys, originally aged seven, ten, and thirteen in 1987–88 and followed up to the present. For the closest comparability to the Cambridge Study, the middle sample of 508 boys, originally aged ten, was investigated.[14]

Both samples were of inner-city boys, but the Pittsburgh study was based on a wider geographical area. The London boys were almost all white (97 percent), but only 44 percent of the Pittsburgh boys were white. In London, 21 percent of the boys were convicted in court for delinquency (theft, burglary, violence, vandalism, fraud, or drug use) between ages ten and sixteen inclusive. In Pittsburgh, 28 percent of the boys were petitioned to the juvenile court between ages ten and sixteen for similar offenses. The interest was in investigating which risk factors in childhood (ages eight to ten) predicted delinquency in adolescence (ages ten to sixteen) in British and American samples of inner-city boys in different time periods (1963–70 in London and 1987–94 in Pittsburgh).

Some of the risk factors were only measured in one study (e.g., low IQ in London, bad neighborhood in Pittsburgh) and so cannot be compared. Table 1

TABLE 1   Comparable Predictors of Juvenile Court Delinquency

London	RR	Pittsburgh	RR
High impulsivity	1.19*	Hyperactive	1.5*
Poor concentration	1.9*	Attention deficit	1.5*
Low achievement	2.1*	Low achievement	1.7*
High nervousness	1.0	High anxiety	0.8
Shy/withdrawn	0.8	Shy/withdrawn	1.1
Few friends	0.6	Few friends	1.1
Church attender	0.7	High religiosity	1.0
Convicted parent	2.8*	Antisocial father	1.6*
Young mother	1.4	Young mother	1.5*
Nervous mother	1.4	Anxious parent	0.9
Large family	2.0*	Large family	1.7*
Low SES	1.4	Low SES	1.9*
Low income	2.1*	Family on welfare	2.3*
Poor housing	1.6*	Poor housing	1.2
Small home	0.9	Small home	1.3
Separated from parent	1.9*	Broken family	2.5*
Poor supervision	1.9*	Poor supervision	1.6*
Harsh discipline	2.4*	Physical punishment	1.1
Low reinforcement	1.3	Low reinforcement	1.3*
Leisure outside	1.8*	Boy not involved	1.3
Parental conflict	2.1*	Unhappy parents	1.9*

* Note: *p < .05 one-tailed. RR = Relative risk. SES = Socioeconomic status.

shows the results obtained with twenty-one dichotomous risk factors measured reasonably comparably in the two studies. Typically, a quarter of the boys were in the risk category. For ease of understanding, the *relative risk* (RR) of delinquency is shown. This is simply the probability of delinquency for the risk category divided by the probability of delinquency for the remainder. For example, 32 percent of the most impulsive boys in London (according to psychomotor tests) were delinquent, compared with 17 percent of the remainder (RR = 1.9, p = .001 on the chi-squared test). The RR indicates the strength of the relationship between each risk factor and delinquency.

Overall, the results in London and Pittsburgh were quite concordant. Twelve of the risk factors significantly predicted delinquency in London: high impulsivity, poor concentration (rated by teachers), low achievement, a convicted parent, a large family (four or more siblings), low family income, poor housing, separation from a parent (usually the father), poor parental supervision, harsh or erratic maternal discipline, the boy spending leisure time mainly outside the home, and parental disharmony. Family factors were based on interviews with mothers. In most cases, the presence of the risk factor doubled the risk of delinquency.

Nine of these twelve factors also significantly predicted delinquency in Pittsburgh: hyperactivity (rated by mothers and teachers), attention deficit, low achievement, behavior problems of the father, a large family (three or more siblings), low family income (dependence on welfare benefits), a broken family, poor parental supervision, and unhappy parents. Most of those factors were based on information from mothers. The RR in Pittsburgh tended to be slightly less than in London, because the prevalence of delinquency was slightly greater.

The three factors that did not predict in Pittsburgh were poor housing, physical punishment by the mother, and low involvement of the boy in family activities. Housing conditions were physically much better in Pittsburgh in the 1990s than in London in the 1960s, so it may be that only dilapidated slum housing predicts delinquency. The harsh maternal discipline measure in London logically included a cruel or neglecting attitude, but there was some suggestion in Pittsburgh that maternal physical punishment could sometimes be given in the context of a loving relationship and indicate that the mother cared about the boy. Regarding low involvement in family activities in Pittsburgh, some of these boys may have been shy or withdrawn, whereas spending leisure time outside the home in London usually meant hanging around the streets with other boys from the neighborhood, which is conducive to delinquency.

Nine of the factors did not predict delinquency in London: high nervousness of the boy, a shy/withdrawn boy, a boy with few friends, regular church attendance of the boy (viewed as a protective factor), a young mother (a teenager at the time of her first birth), a nervous mother, low socioeconomic status of the family, a small house (three or fewer rooms) and low parental reinforcement (praise).

Six of these nine factors also did not predict delinquency in Pittsburgh: high anxiety, a shy/withdrawn boy, few friends, high participation in religious services, an anxious parent, and small house (five or fewer rooms). Two others were only marginally significant in Pittsburgh: a young mother (age 17 or less at the time of her first birth), and low reinforcement (positive responses to the boy's behavior by the parents). Low socioeconomic status was a significant predictor in Pittsburgh but not in London. However, the measure in Pittsburgh included parental education as well as occupation, whereas in London it was based on occupational prestige only. Also, the range of variation in socioeconomic status (SES) was greater in Pittsburgh, because the sample was representative of the central city rather than being drawn from one small area (as in London).

The similarities between London and Pittsburgh in risk factors were quite surprising, in light of the many differences over time and place. In London in the 1960s, houses were smaller, housing conditions were worse, and families were larger. In Pittsburgh in the 1990s, mothers were younger, there were more broken families, and more families were dependent on welfare. For example, the risk category of young mothers in London were those age 19 or less (22 percent), whereas the comparable category in Pittsburgh were those age 17 or less (28 percent) at the time of their first birth. Changes in the prevalence of risk factors did not seem to affect the strength of their relationships with delinquency.

The conclusion is that several risk factors are replicable predictors of delinquency over time and place, especially impulsivity, poor concentration, low achievement, an antisocial parent, a large family, low family income, a broken family, poor parental supervision, and parental conflict. Where results were not replicated, this was attributed to differences in measurement or to differences over time and place. The major results are most compatible with delinquency theories that emphasize the importance of individual factors such as low self-control and impulsivity, the importance of childrearing methods practiced by parents in building up internal inhibitions against offending, and the importance of attachment to and separation from parents. More replication studies are needed to investigate the universality of the major risk factors for delinquency.

CRIMINAL CAREERS

A "criminal career" is defined as the longitudinal sequence of offenses committed by an individual offender, with no necessary suggestion that offenders use their criminal activity as an important means of earning a living. The criminal career approach is not a criminological theory but a framework within which theories can be proposed and tested.[15] A criminal career has a beginning (onset), an end (desistance) and a career length in between (duration). Only a certain proportion of the population (prevalence) has a criminal career and commits offenses. During their careers, offenders commit offenses at a certain rate (individual offending frequency). For those who commit several offenses, it is possible to investigate how far they specialize in certain types of offenses and how far the seriousness of their offending escalates over time.

The criminal career approach emphasizes the need to investigate such questions as why people start offending (onset), why they continue offending (persistence) and why people stop offending (desistance). The factors influencing onset may differ from those influencing other criminal career features such as persistence and desistance, if only because the different processes occur at different ages. Indeed, Farrington and Hawkins[16] in London found that there was no relationship between factors influencing prevalence (official offenders versus nonoffenders), those influencing early versus later onset, and those influencing desistance after age 21.

Farrington and Wikström[17] systematically compared criminal career features for the 411 London boys in the Cambridge Study and for 3,190 working-class Stockholm boys in Project Metropolitan.[18] This project is a longitudinal survey of all 15,117 children born in 1953 and living in Stockholm in 1963. The

London boys were also born in 1953 (mainly). Both cohorts were followed up in criminal records to age 25. The minimum age of criminal responsibility in England is ten. It is fifteen in Sweden, but information about recorded offending under age fifteen was obtained from the Child Welfare agency.

To some extent, the two projects have complementary strengths and weaknesses. The Stockholm project is based on a large representative sample but relies largely on data that could be collected from records. The London project is based on a small area sample, but it includes a wide variety of data from many different sources (the boys and their parents, teachers, and peers, as well as records). The definition of "working-class" was quite comparable, being based on skilled, semiskilled, or unskilled manual occupations of heads of households.

In the interests of achieving comparability of legal categories, the present analyses were restricted to theft (including burglary and receiving), violence (including robbery), vandalism (including arson), and drug and fraud offenses only. Other offenses (e.g. motoring, sex, possessing an offensive weapon, going equipped to steal) were excluded. The included offenses were quite comparable in London and Stockholm, except that violence in Stockholm was more comprehensive, because the English records excluded offenses of minor assault. The included offenses comprised 90 percent of all recorded London offenses and 75 percent of all recorded Stockholm offenses between ages ten and twenty-five. The difference is largely attributable to the proportion of recorded traffic offenses in Stockholm (17 percent of all recorded offenses).

Figure 1 shows that the cumulative prevalence of recorded offending was remarkably similar for the two cohorts. The Stockholm curve begins at age twelve because the child welfare records only specified offending up to that age. Up to age twenty-five, 33 percent of London males and 32 percent of Stockholm males were recorded offenders. Similarly, the cumulative prevalence of convictions up to age thirty-three was almost identical in the Cambridge Study of London boys born mainly in 1953 and in the Inner London study of boys born mainly in 1960.[19]

Other curves, however, were less similar. Figure 2 shows the individual offending frequency (the number of offenses per offender) at each age. There was a clear difference between London and Stockholm in this criminal career feature. Individual offending frequencies in London were tolerably constant with age, but in Stockholm they showed a peak at age fifteen.

This difference in frequency may be a function of the different data recorded in the two countries. The London data were of convictions, whereas the Stockholm data were of recorded offenses. In London, if a person was convicted for several different offenses committed on the same day, this was counted as only one conviction, whereas in Stockholm it would have been counted as several offenses. Consequently, there were on average ten offenses per offender in Stockholm but only four offenses per offender in London.

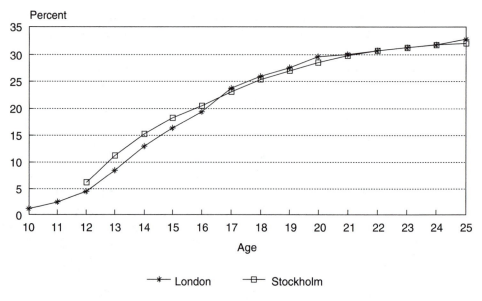

FIGURE 1

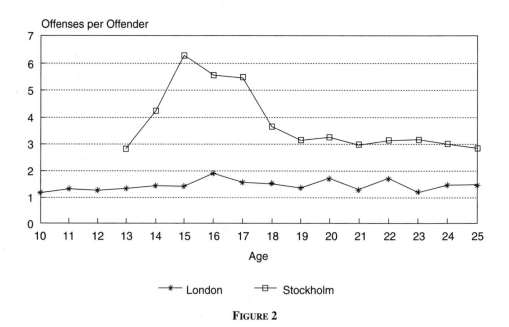

FIGURE 2

The aggregate age-crime curve (the number of offenses per one hundred males) was similar in London and Stockholm, peaking at about age seventeen. However, when this curve was disaggregated into prevalence and frequency, London and Stockholm were different. In London, the age-crime curve peaked at seventeen purely because the prevalence of offending (the number of different persons convicted at each age) peaked at seventeen; the frequency of offending did not vary with age. In Stockholm, the age-crime curve peaked at fifteen to seventeen mainly because frequency showed a clear peak in the teenage years.

The types of offenses committed in different age ranges were generally similar in both countries, although there were proportionally more violent offenses in London (despite the more wide-ranging definition of violence in Stockholm) and proportionally more drug offenses in Stockholm. Generally, ages of onset of offending were similar in London and Stockholm, as was the distribution of ages of presumed "desistance" (the age of the last recorded offense). Consequently, the distribution of criminal career lengths was similar in both countries. Also in both countries, an early age of onset of offending predicted a large number of offenses and a long criminal career.

After each successive offense, the probability of recidivism (committing a subsequent offense) increased similarly in both countries. In London, the probability of a first offense was .33, of a second offense after a first was .64, and of a third offense after a second was .72. The corresponding probabilities in Stockholm were .32, .62 and .76. After the third offense, these probabilities reached an asymptote of .80 to .90 in both countries.

In London, 6 percent of the cohort accounted for half of all offenses, and were termed the *chronic* offenders. In Stockholm, possibly because of the greater average frequency of recorded offending, only 2 percent of the cohort accounted for half of all the offenses. The London chronics each had a minimum of eight recorded offenses, whereas the Stockholm chronics each had a minimum of thirty-five recorded offenses. Interestingly, the mean age of onset (13.5), mean age of "desistance" (22.5), and mean career length (nine years) of chronics were almost identical in both countries.

The main conclusion of this cross-national comparison was that most criminal career features were similar in London and Stockholm. Where there were differences, this was mainly a function of the different data on which the analyses were based (convictions in London, recorded offenses in Stockholm). The peak in the aggregate age-crime curve largely reflected a peak in prevalence in London and a peak in the individual offending frequency in Stockholm. It is ironic that the relationship termed *invariant* by Hirschi and Gottfredson[20] was the source of the most important difference between the two cohorts.

Overall, the cross-cultural replicability of these criminal career results in London and Stockholm is quite impressive. However, this cross-national study is in many respects only a starting point. Further research is needed to establish the effects of different methods of measuring offending on criminal career features. Ideally, coordinated longitudinal studies of criminal careers in different countries are needed, including comparable self-report and official record measurements at different ages.[21] Such studies would help to determine the extent to which criminal career results were truly universal and replicable, and they would also help to locate the sources of any observed differences: in individual characteristics or in social, cultural, legal, or criminal justice processes.

CRIME AND JUSTICE

A criminal justice system involves a successive funnelling process. Out of all crimes committed, only some are reported to the police. Out of all crimes reported, only some are recorded by the police. Out of all recorded offenses, only some lead to a detected offender who is taken to court and convicted. Out of all offenders convicted in court, only some are sentenced to custody. These offenders receive different sentence lengths, and they only serve a proportion of their sentence in prison, thereby becoming the prison population.

While the system can easily be described in principle, it is quite difficult to describe in practice, specifying the exact numbers of offenders flowing through at each stage, and ultimately the exact times that offenders serve in prison. Such a specification would have great theoretical and practical relevance. For example, it could help to determine whether changes in prison populations were caused by changes in crime rates, reporting, recording, detection, findings of guilt, the probability of custody, lengths of sentences given, or lengths of time served. It is particularly difficult to estimate numbers in a national criminal justice system, because of the large numbers of crimes and offenders involved, and the diversity of the constituent areas.

Ideally, individual offenders should be tracked longitudinally through the different stages of a national criminal justice system using unique identifying numbers. Unfortunately, such identifying numbers do not exist in many countries, including England and the United States. However, it is possible to obtain aggregate national data on each of the stages separately (e.g. crimes committed, persons convicted, persons sentenced to custody). While these separate counts do not arise from tracking the same individuals across stages, when examined in relation to each other they permit reasonably accurate estimates of the flow of offenders from one stage to the next.

Farrington and Langan[22] presented the first offense-specific national estimates for the flow of offenders through the complete system described above. The figures were estimated for burglary, vehicle theft, robbery, serious assault, rape, and homicide. They provided this information not only for England (including Wales) and the United States but also for two time periods (1981 and 1986–87). Hence, they were able to compare not only variations between countries but also changes over time. These analyses were later extended to compare England, the United States, and Sweden between 1981 and 1991.[23]

The number of crimes committed and the probability of reporting to the police were obtained from national victim surveys. The probability of a reported crime being recorded was calculated by comparing the number of crimes reported with the number of comparable crimes recorded. The number of recorded crimes was obtained from national police statistics. The numbers of convictions and of persons sent to custody were obtained from national statistics in England and from surveys in the United States. The average sentence length and average time served were obtained from correctional data systems.

The most recent comparisons, between England and the United States in 1981-96, were published by Langan and Farrington.[24] Generally, during this time period, crime (according to national victim surveys) increased in England and stayed constant or decreased in the United States. Figure 3 shows the results for burglary. In 1981, the U.S. burglary rate was more than twice as high as the English burglary rate (106 burglaries per 1,000 households, compared with 41). By 1995, the picture was dramatically reversed: the English burglary rate was nearly twice as high as the U.S. burglary rate (83 burglaries per 1,000 households, compared with 48).

A very important statistic is the probability of an offense leading to a conviction. In estimating this, it is important to take account of co-offending. If two persons commit one offense together, this could lead to two convictions. For example, in England in 1995, there were 1,754,000 domestic burglaries according to the British Crime Survey, with an average of 1.8 offenders per offense (where this was known). If the criminal justice system had been 100 percent efficient, there could therefore have been 3,157,000 convictions for domestic burglary.

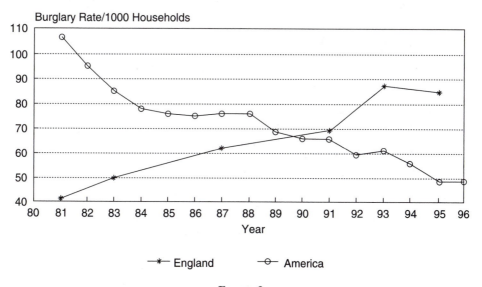

FIGURE 3

Since domestic burglaries accounted for almost exactly half (52 percent) of all burglaries in 1995, there were an estimated 6,080,000 burglary offenders (not *different* offenders; the same person could be counted more than once) who could in principle have been convicted. Since there were in fact 35,346 convictions for burglary in England in 1995, it followed that there were 172 offenders for every conviction, or alternatively that each offender could commit 172 burglaries on average for every one conviction. For ease of interpretation, this was expressed as 6 convictions per 1,000 offenders.

Figure 4 shows how the number of convictions per thousand offenders varied in England and the United States between 1981 and 1994-95. It can be seen that the risk of conviction decreased dramatically in England and increased somewhat in the United States. In 1981, the risk of conviction was nearly three times higher in England (27 convictions per 1,000 offenders, compared with 10). By 1994–95, the risk of conviction was more than twice as high in the United States (14 convictions per 1000 offenders, compared with 6).

Generally, the United States was far more punitive than England, in having a higher probability of custody and a much longer average time served. However, cross-national differences in these features did not change dramatically over this time period. The most startling contrasts between England and the United States concerned trends in crime rates and in the probability of conviction. This naturally raised the question of whether the risk of punishment had some causal effect on the likelihood of committing a crime.

Because of the many influences on crime rates that were not controlled in this research, causal conclusions could not be drawn with any degree of confidence. However, correlations between crime rates and the risk and severity of

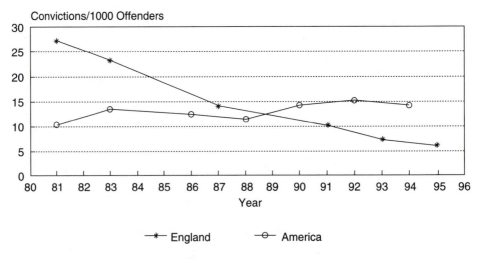

FIGURE 4

punishment over time were calculated in the two countries. In England (but not in the United States), there were consistent negative correlations between the risk of punishment and the crime rate. However, there were no consistent negative correlations between the severity of punishment and the crime rate in either country. The most consistent results concerned burglary: the crime rate (whether measured by the victim survey or by police statistics) was negatively correlated with the risk of punishment (whether measured by the conviction rate or the custody rate) in both countries. It is possible that crimes such as burglary are more rationally motivated than violent crimes such as assault, rape, or homicide.

These cross-national comparisons between indicators of crime and criminal justice are thought-provoking and need to be extended to more countries. Unfortunately, a great deal of effort is needed to obtain figures that are comparable both between countries and over time.

CONCLUSIONS

Cross-national comparative studies in criminology are important and should be carried out more frequently. The studies described here have advanced knowledge about risk factors for delinquency, criminal careers, crime rates, and criminal justice processes. The time is surely ripe to mount a coordinated program of cross-national comparative studies, which could lead to great advances in knowledge about criminal careers, risk factors, and effective crime prevention methods.

REFERENCES

1. Hirschi, T., and Gottfredson, M. 1983. "Age and the Explanation of Crime." *American Journal of Sociology* 89:552–584.

2. Klein, M. W. 1989. "Introduction." In M. W. Klein, ed. *Cross-national Research in Self-reported Crime and Delinquency*. Dordrecht, Netherlands: Kluwer.

3. Mayhew, P., and van Dijk, J. J. M. 1997. *Criminal Victimization in Eleven Industrialized Countries*. The Hague, Netherlands: Ministry of Justice.

4. Painter, K. A., and Farrington, D. P. 1998. "Criminal Victimization on a Caribbean Island." *International Review of Victimology* 6:1–16.

5. Junger-Tas, J., Terlouw, G-J., and Klein, M. W., eds. 1994. *Delinquent Behavior among Young People in the Western World*. Amsterdam, Netherlands: Kugler.

6. Farrington, D. P. 1999. "Conduct disorder and delinquency." In H-C. Steinhausen and F. C. Verhulst, eds. *Risks and Outcomes in Developmental Psychopathology*. Oxford: Oxford University Press. (In press.)

7. Pulkkinen, L. 1988. "Delinquent Development: Theoretical and Empirical Considerations." In M. Rutter, ed. *Studies of Psychosocial Risk*. Cambridge: Cambridge University Press.

8. Pulkkinen, L., and Tremblay, R. E. 1992. "Patterns of Boys' Social Adjustment in Two Cultures and at Different Ages: A Longitudinal Perspective." *International Journal of Behavioral Development* 15:527–553.

9. Achenbach, T. M., Verhulst, F. C., Baron, G. D., and Althaus, M. 1987. "A Comparison of Syndromes Derived from the Child Behavior Checklist for American and Dutch boys aged 6–11 and 12–16." *Journal of Child Psychology and Psychiatry* 28:437–453.

10. Farrington, D. P., Biron, L., and LeBlanc, M. 1982. "Personality and Delinquency in London and Montreal." In J. Gunn and D. P. Farrington, eds. *Abnormal Offenders, Delinquency, and the Criminal Justice System.* Chichester, England: Wiley.

11. Moffitt, T. E., Caspi, A., Silva, P. A., and Stouthamer-Loeber, M. 1995. "Individual Differences in Personality and Intelligence are Linked to Crime: Cross-context Evidence from Nations, Neighborhoods, Genders, Races, and Age-cohorts." In J. Hagan, ed. *Current perspectives on Aging and the Life Cycle.* vol. 4. *Delinquency and Disrepute in the Life Course.* Greenwich, CT: JAI Press.

12. Farrington, D. P. 1995. "The Development of Offending and Antisocial Behavior from Childhood: Key Findings from the Cambridge Study in Delinquent Development." *Journal of Child Psychology and Psychiatry* 36:929–964.

13. Loeber, R., Farrington, D. P., Stouthamer-Loeber, M., Moffitt, T. E., and Caspi, A. 1998. "The Development of Male Offending: Key Findings from the First Decade of the Pittsburgh Youth Study." *Studies on Crime and Crime Prevention* 7:141–171.

14. Farrington, D. P., and Loeber, R. 1999. "Transatlantic Replicability of Risk Factors in the Development of Delinquency." In P. Cohen, C. Slomkowski, and L. N. Robins, eds. *Historical and Geographical Influences on Psychopathology.* Mahwah, NJ: Lawrence Erlbaum.

15. Blumstein, A., Cohen, J., and Farrington D. P. 1988. "Criminal Career Research: Its Value for Criminology." *Criminology* 26:1–35.

16. Farrington, D. P., and Hawkins, J. D. 1991. "Predicting Participation, Early Onset, and Later Persistence in Officially Recorded Offending. *Criminal Behavior and Mental Health* 1:1–33.

17. Farrington, D. P., and Wikström, P-O. H. 1994. Criminal Careers in London and Stockholm: A Cross-national Comparative Study. In E. G. M. Weitekamp and H-J. Kerner, eds. *Cross-national Longitudinal Research on Human Development and Criminal Behavior.* Dordrecht, Netherlands: Kluwer. Reprinted in Pease, K., ed. 1999. *Uses of Crime Statistics.* Aldershot, England: Avebury. (In press.)

18. Janson, C-G. 1981. Project Metropolitan: A Longitudinal Study of a Stockholm Cohort (Sweden). In S. A. Mednick and A. E. Baert, eds. *Prospective Longitudinal Research.* Oxford: Oxford University Press.

19. Farrington, D. P., and Maughan, B. 1999. "Criminal Careers of Two London Cohorts." *Criminal Behavior and Mental Health* 9:91–106.

20. Hirschi & Gottfredson. 1983. op. cit., note 1.

21. Farrington, D. P. 1999. "A Criminological Research Agenda for the Next Millenium." *International Journal of Offender Therapy and Comparative Criminology* 43:154–167.

22. Farrington, D. P., and Langan, P. A. 1992. "Changes in Crime and Punishment in England and America in the 1980s." *Justice Quarterly* 9:5–46.

23. Farrington, D. P., Langan, P. A., and Wikström, P-O. H. 1994. "Changes in Crime and Punishment in America, England and Sweden between the 1980s and the 1990s." *Studies in Crime and Crime Prevention* 3:104–131. Reprinted in Lane, J., and Petersilia, J., eds. 1998. *Criminal Justice Policy.* Cheltenham, England: Edward Elgar.

24. Langan, P. A., and Farrington, D. P. 1998. *Crime and Justice in the United States and in England and Wales*, 1981–96. Washington, DC: Bureau of Justice Statistics.

The Role of Fraud
in the Japanese Financial Crisis:
A Comparative Study

Henry N. Pontell,
Stephen M. Rosoff,
and
Jason Lam

The Savings and Loan (S&L) debacle of the 1980s plundered America's financial resources and left behind a massive mountain of debt. With an estimated total cost to taxpayers, including interest payments, of approximately $500 billion, the crisis was an incredibly destructive financial disaster.[1] The causes of this debacle have been the subject of vigorous debate in various popular and scholarly outlets. On one side, a group consisting chiefly of thrift industry consultants and economists argue that fraud played only a minor role in creating this financial crisis. Instead, they point to various factors including, but not limited to, real estate collapses, incompetent management, and desperate gambles for success.[2] On the other side, law enforcement agencies, thrift regulators, and criminologists argue that various forms of white-collar crime were chiefly responsible for the fiasco.[3] Through the work of countless investigators, strong evidence of widespread fraud was uncovered and supported by testimonials of both regulators and S&L participants. The dispute between these two sides will, undoubtedly, continue on, but the purpose of this paper is not to continue that debate. Rather, it will document and explain the differing forms of material fraud and collusive practices that pervaded the S&L crisis, focusing on insider abuse, political collusion, and bribery, and draw comparisons between the role played by these white-collar crimes in America's S&L debacle and in Japan's current banking crisis.

In order to understand the S&L fiasco, a brief history is in order. Established after the Depression in the 1930s, the savings and loan program was intended to provide funds to both promote the creation of new homes and ensure support to financial institutions making loans for them (saving and loans, or "thrifts"). In addition, the Federal Home Loan Bank Board (FHLBB) was created by the Federal Home Loan Bank Act of 1932 to provide both additional reserve funds and oversight to the savings and loan programs. Finally, the National Housing Act of 1934 provided for the development of the Federal Savings and Loan Insurance Corporation (FSLIC) to insure S&L deposits.[4] In the 1970s, however, the inability of thrifts to offer adjustable rate mortgages, combined with an inflation level of 13.3 percent by 1979, resulted in severe losses and, eventually, industry insolvency by $150 million in 1982.[5] The establishment of the Reagan administration in 1980 began an era of a massive deregulation of the S&L industry. The passing of the Garn-St. Germain Depository Institutions Act in 1982 eradicated interest rate ceilings, authorized increases in consumer loans up to 30 percent of a thrift's assets, and allowed for 100 percent financing without requiring a down payment. In addition, in 1982 the FHLBB removed the 5 percent limit on brokered deposits as well as minimum stockholder requirements. Thus the deregulators believed that the stage was set for a profit-generating atmosphere that would supposedly provide the necessary economic incentives for the S&L industry to regain financial stability.

In comparison, Japan's powerful Ministry of Finance, which was founded in 1869, governs Japan's banking system. Japan's financial crisis (as well as those in other East Asian countries) shares a number of important characteristics with the S&L debacle. First, the "causes" of the crisis in Japan are as hotly debated now as were those of the S&L crisis earlier. Falling real estate prices and poor, but not illegal, loan management are blamed by members of the Diet (Japanese Parliament) and Ministry of Finance. On the other side of the debate, a group consisting of members of the media, government prosecutors, and academics argue that material fraud, insider abuse, and political collusion played a vital role in bringing about the crisis. In addition, the role played by organized crime in causing major losses to financial institutions has been highlighted in media reports.

Japan is the world's second-largest economy and single largest creditor nation.[6] Deemed Japan's oldest surviving power center, the Ministry of Finance controls all national taxing, spending, and defense.[7] It controls, under one government agency, the powers of the Department of the Treasury, the Federal Deposit Insurance Corporation, the Office of the Comptroller, and the Securities and Exchange Commission.[8] As such, it wields the power and influence to set fiscal policy and to control the banking system. In February of 1998, the government disclosed that the amount of bad loans against the country's banks was approximately $585 billion, nearly three times more than its previous estimate.[9] Only a few hours later, it released a new estimate of $610 billion.[10] The cost estimates of this crisis continue to grow as more and more evidence of poor loan management is uncovered. Reverberations of Japan's financial woes have proved troubling to the world's economy. Suicides, arrests, and resignations of high-ranking officials in Japan's Finance Ministry accompanied the drastic fall of Japan's benchmark Nikkei Stock Average.[11]

Calavita, Pontell, and Tillman analyzed the S&L debacle as the result of widespread insider fraud and political collusion.[12] They categorized "insiders" as directors, officers, and employees of the thrifts, whereas "outsiders" consisted of brokers, agents, and borrowers. Insider abuse consisted of three major forms: "hot deals," "looting," and "covering up." Though a number of forms of insider abuse occurred, almost all of them can be deemed variations of these three basic types. All of these forms of insider abuse are violations of federal bank fraud statutes, such as "knowingly or willfully falsifying or concealing material facts or making false statements,"[13] and "theft, embezzlement, or misapplication of funds."[14]

Evidence of insider abuse and politically collusive practices are present in Japan's banking crisis. Although the specific types of insider abuse may differ somewhat, they are all merely variations of the same forms of material fraud found in the S&L case. In addition, the political collusion that protected unscrupulous operators and provided for widespread cover-ups in the S&L crisis can be found in the Japanese banking debacle.

This paper will analyze forms of insider abuse in the S&L crisis and the Japanese banking debacle. It will then examine the role of political collusion in the genesis of these financial meltdowns, and the role played by organized crime in bringing down Japanese banks.

INSIDER ABUSE

Hot Deals

Hot deals were the most potent form of insider abuse in the S&L scandal, as they created both a significant source of funds and a tool for disguising the true nature of loans.[15] This category consisted of four central types of transactions: "land flips," "nominee loans," "reciprocal lending," and "linked financing."[16]

"Land flips" were a form of fraud in which two or more partners would sell a piece of property back and forth. At each trade, the price of the property was increased and refinanced. Finally, the last loan would be defaulted upon, and the trade-generated profit shared between the collaborators. As explained by Alt and Siglin:

> A sells a parcel of real estate to B for $1 million, its approximate market value. B finances the sale with a bank loan. B sells the property back to A for $2 million. A finances the sale with a bank loan, with the bank relying on a fraudulent appraisal. B repays his original loan and takes $1 million in 'profit' off the table, which he shares with A. A defaults on the loan, leaving the bank with a $1 million loss.[17]

"Nominee loans" consisted of the use of a "straw borrower," who could fraudulently borrow substantial funds from a financial institution for another individual or company who was limited by "loan-to-one-borrower" regulations or "insider borrowing" restrictions.[18] "Reciprocal lending" was another form of insider borrowing. Conspirators evaded capture by regulators by agreeing to make loans interdependent upon each other. "Linked financing" was almost identical to reciprocal lending. It involved the deposit of funds by an individual into a financial institution dependent upon an agreement that the institution would issue a loan (usually for a much greater amount) to the individual.

The prevalence of combinations and variations of the above-mentioned "hot deals" was evident during the investigation by regulators of insolvent thrifts. In fact, these forms of hot deals were pervasive in acquisition, development, and construction (ADC) loans at the heart of the crises in Texas.[19] The prevalence of this form of insider abuse was of great concern because of the severity of economic damage that it caused. The National Commission on Financial Institution Reform, Recovery and Enforcement (NCFIRRE) noted that, "In order to manufacture $14 of loan fees and interest, it was necessary to grant a $114 loan. If the loan proved to be worth only 50 percent of its face value, taxpayers were stuck with a $57 loss, even though the S&L operators only enriched themselves by $14."[20] Thus the economic damage caused by the unscrupulous acts of thrift managers is potentially ten times the amount gained by illegal activity.

Looting

Looting involves the direct removal of funds by insiders. During the S&L crisis, severe looting was committed not by lower-level employees but by owner/managers. The financial damage resulting from looting led the Commissioner of the California Department of Savings and Loans to state: "The best way to rob a bank is to own one."[21] Looting took on many forms, including, but not limited to, direct removal of funds and excessive forms of compensation for thrift executives.

The direct withdrawal of institutional funds was the simplest form of looting. In one celebrated case, John Molinaro and Donald Mangano utilized this method of looting when they stole more than $24 million from their Ramona Savings and Loan.[22] The drawback of this form of looting was that it was too obvious and thus too susceptible to capture and punishment.

A more common method of looting is found in excessive forms of compensation, such as inflated salaries, shopping sprees, and excessive bonuses. One extreme example of the improper use of thrift funds involved the case of David Paul of CenTrust Savings Bank in Miami. He spent over $40 million of the thrift's funds for a yacht, a Rubens painting, a sailboat, Limoges china, and Baccarat crystal.[23] In addition, he funded the creation of the CenTrust Tower with $170 million of the thrift's funds.[24] Another infamous example involves Ed McBirney of Sunbelt ("Gunbelt") Savings and Loan in Texas. He spent over $1 million of the thrift's funds on various parties, as well as treating various business partners and political allies to vacation resorts, bar tabs up to $1,000, and prostitutes.[25]

The looting scandals that plagued Japan differ only slightly from those in the S&L debacle. In Japan, unscrupulous individuals and organizations used one financial institution to loot another. One major example of this involves Nui Onoue, an Osaka restaurant owner.

State records show that Nui Onoue was born in 1930 in Nara-ken, a small village, in a family of modest means.[26] Like many of the young women of her time, as a teenager she moved to Minami, an entertainment center in Osaka, to work in a bar serving drinks to wealthy businessmen. At the age of 17 or 18, she was allegedly married to an unidentified businessman, but soon divorced after she was emotionally abused by her mother-in-law. According to interviews with her former co-workers, Nui was extremely attractive in her youth, as she closely resembled Kogiku Hanayagi, a popular prewar cinema actress who starred in Edo-era films. While she was in her early 20s, she worked at a large sukiyake restaurant in Minami and received a great deal of attention from her fellow workers and regulars at the restaurant for wearing a new kimono every day. In fact, she arranged to borrow so many outfits from a secondhand clothes dealer that she never wore the same kimono twice. After a number of sordid affairs with wealthy businessmen, she met a high-level executive of a construction company who provided her with substantial funds. By the age of 35, she built and owned her first restaurant, the "Egawa," and mah jong parlor, the "Daikokuya," in an entertainment sector of Sennichimae in Chuo-Ku, Osaka.[27] What happened next, however, is still unclear.

By her own accounts, Nui Onoue claimed to have attended and graduated from the state-run Nara Women's University, a well-respected school in Kansai. Her former co-workers, however, flatly deny that possibility, and attempts by Japanese newspapers have failed to uncover any record of her attendance at any college or university. The Japanese National Police investigated rumors that she was actively involved with members of the Yakuza, the Japanese-organized crime syndicate, who frequented her restaurant. What is known, however, is that she began to accumulate massive assets beginning in 1987.[28]

According to court documents, Nui Onoue held Yen (Y)77.2 billion in assets and Y62 billion in loans in 1987. In 1988, she held Y178.9 billion in assets and Y152.5 billion in loans. By 1990, she held the sum of Y264.9 billion ($1.99 billion) in assets and Y727.1 billion ($5.45 billion) in loans.[29] The origin of this massive wealth has never been sufficiently explained. According to Japan's National Police, Ms. Onoue's restaurant garnered approximately $7.4 million in 1990, but she never paid taxes because she claimed that her restaurant failed to show a profit.[30] Ironically, Nui Onoue was awarded her town's coveted prize for being the "Town's Most Honest Taxpayer," in 1991.[31]

In the late 1980s, Ms. Nui Onoue approached the prestigious Industrial Bank of Japan (IBJ) for an astounding loan of Y240 billion ($1.8 billion) using her IBJ debentures, a form of a certificate of deposit, worth an estimated Y290 billion. The purpose for acquiring this loan was never truly explained, but much of it was used for risky investments. According to Yo Kurosawa, president of IBJ, the bank had a stringent policy of evaluating the plans and financial stability of those with significant loans.[32] He could not explain why this strict policy was relaxed in this case with such an immense loan.[33]

The violation of such stringent bank policies is indeed curious given that the massive size of the loan itself should have required significant caution on the part of the institution. The funds from the IBJ loan were used to gamble, usually dangerously, in various stocks and bonds. It is important to note that even though she never had any experience working or investing in the financial markets, Onoue eventually became the "nation's single largest investor," and garnered the title of "bubble lady," after Japan's inflated, or "bubble," economy of the 1980s.[34] If any credence was to be given to her courtroom testimony, then it should have been abundantly clear to the loaning institutions that Ms. Onoue's investments in the financial markets were doomed to failure. In fact, she claimed that she thought that "warrant," was the name of a company, even as her investment portfolio showed that she often purchased bonds with warrants, or stock purchase rights.[35] In addition, she claimed to be ignorant of the term *gyakuzaya*, (when interest owed on loans surpasses the combined return on deposits and stock holdings) which was used, pervasively, by industry analysts.[36] While it would be a mistake to take her testimony completely at face value, it is likely that she was unaware of even the most basic processes involved in investments of stocks, bonds, and other financial instruments, since she was an uneducated restaurateur who never bothered to study the markets.

How was Nui Onoue able to invest and to lose so much money? The answer lies both with the greedy bankers and brokers who helped her, as well as her possible links to organized crime. As documented in the Japanese press, managers and veteran dealers of local securities firms were often seen entering Onoue's Daikokuya restaurant to compete for the privilege of investing her vast wealth. In addition, she was known to hold so much power that she was able to treat senior securities brokers with a significant lack of respect, often bordering on contempt. She often issued orders to these same brokers in a contemptuous fashion when she wanted information for massive stock purchases. An infamous example of this was brought to light when she banned the employees of a major Japanese securities firm in the autumn of 1989 from visiting her restaurant because they had sold her Tokyo Corporation stock at a slightly lower price than she had expected.[37] Firms that pleased her, however, were treated with respect, and allowed to oversee her restaurants when she was traveling. In fact, courts records show that a high-level director of the Kansai branch of an unidentified major securities company was interrogated by the Osaka Public Prosecutor's Offices because it was found that he spent almost all of his working hours in Onoue's office in the Daikokuya. Though the case record was sealed by the court, he was found guilty of serving as Onoue's behind-the-scenes advisor on stock investments.[38] This manager later testified that Onoue had no real knowledge of the stock market. Moreover, even though she had the ability to manipulate massive funds, she never attempted to speculate on specific stocks, a highly profitable venture, most probably because she didn't understand the process. By the end of 1990, she owned approximately $800 million worth of shares in over twenty different companies, and used those holdings to secure even more loans.[39] The beginning of 1991, however, saw a significant drop in stocks, and regulators now believe that she may have lost approximately $1 billion as a result.

After losing most of her loan money through questionable stock transactions and purchases of risky discount bonds, she convinced executives at the bank to allow her to withdraw her debentures. By doing this, the bank was, in essence, agreeing to provide Ms. Onoue with the tools necessary to defraud other banks by acquiring loans based on insufficient collateral. She colluded with managers at alternate banking institutions to create fraudulent bond certificates, which she used to replace the valid IBJ debentures that had been loaned to her. According to Yo Kurosawa of the IBJ, Ms. Onoue merely "took the bond certificates and returned with the fake ones."[40] According to officials at the IBJ, the bank placed their faith in the deposit certificates issued by other major banks, as well as Ms. Onoue's tax certificates. Only upon further review, however, did they find that both the certificates and the tax certificates were fake.

One significant partner-in-crime was Tomomi Mackawa, a Toyo Shinkin Branch Manager. He agreed to create Y340 billion worth of poorly forged Toyo Shinkin CDs to replace her IBJ funds.[41] According to official statements by the Toyo Shinkin Bank, the manager had issued a total of thirteen fraudulent certificates of deposit worth Y342 billion, or $2.48 billion.[42] Using these certificates, Onoue was able to defraud IBJ of $440 million.[43] She was also able to secure almost $2.6 billion in loans from almost a dozen other banks in Japan. Through the funds acquired by these other loans, she secured an additional $1.4 billion in loans from IBJ-affiliated financial firms.[44] In fact, IBJ officials may have played a significant role in persuading its affiliates to loan money to Ms. Onoue. During Onoue's criminal trial, the manager of Kogin Lease Company, an IBJ affiliate, claimed that he authorized a low-interest Y150 billion loan to Onoue at the specific request of IBJ officials.[45] In addition, the Tokai Bank affiliate Central Finance Company released a statement that it had Y30 billion, or $220 million, in outstanding loans to Ms. Onoue.[46] According to the company manager, Onoue owed the company approximately Y20 billion in May of 1989, but was approved, by the director in charge of funds of the Osaka bank, for an additional loan of Y130 billion set at only .3 to .5 percent higher than his firm's procurement rate.[47] More unsettling, however, was the fact that company officials secured Y85 billion in discount bonds for Onoue in return for stock certificates that were not only found to be invalid, but that never should have been used as collateral in the first place. This loan accounted for an astonishing 90 percent of all outstanding loans owed to the finance company.[48] In October of 1991, Onoue faced bankruptcy with estimated debts of more than Y400 billion.[49]

A number of stories have arisen that attempt to explain how Onoue received these loans. One story claims that the families of Ms. Onoue and Mr. Kisaburo Ikeura, the chairman of IBJ, come from the same part of Japan, and that Kisaburo personally authorized the loans. Another story, issued by the IBJ itself, claims that it was tricked and victimized by the unscrupulous intents of Ms. Onoue. Whatever the reason for the initial loan of Y240 billion, the combination of the release by IBJ of Ms. Onoue's debentures for the purpose of securing more loans from other banks, as well as the blatantly fraudulent Toyo Shinkin CDs, provide clear evidence of insider-assisted looting. Onoue's financial crime spree would have been impossible without collusion from those inside Japanese banks.

Ms. Onoue was convicted in 1998 of loan and financial fraud, and sentenced to 12 years in federal prison. The court determined that she had secured, and lost, Y1.2 trillion in loans for stock transactions and discount bond purchases. In a related trial, a former manager of Daishinpan (now Aplus Co.) was convicted of conspiring with Ms. Onoue to steal Y90.1 billion in discount investment bonds to be used as collateral for loans, and was sentenced to an undisclosed prison term.[50]

Covering Up

Covering up was the most common form of insider abuse in the S&L crisis. Its pervasiveness could be simply and rationally explained, for it was necessary to hide other forms of fraud. Covering up involves activities ranging from the doctoring of accounting books to the commission of fraudulent trades to the creation of false documents. One thrift examined by the GAO recorded $21 million in transactions during the last few days of 1985. These transactions were found to be fraudulent, but allowed the thrift to show a net worth of $9 million, rather than it's actual debt of $12 million.[51]

Charles Keating of Lincoln Savings and Loan was known to have forged numerous documents in an attempt to deceive regulators. In fact, his employees, upon his command, were so dedicated to the creation of fraudulent documents that, when caught by regulators shredding the original documents, they claimed to be merely "tidying up" in anticipation of an examination.[52]

The ability to successfully "cover-up" large financial losses and fraudulent activities requires, in many cases, not only intent by managers but also the cooperation of a host of others, including appraisers, lawyers, and, most importantly, accountants.[53] Appraisers were responsible for assessing property values and were necessary players in the real estate fraud game. Because their assessments were subjectively influenced, their professional futures were vulnerable to bankers and real estate developers who desired generous appraisals. In fact, in his testimony before Congress, William Crawford, the savings and loan commissioner in California, stated that, of the insolvent thrifts examined by his office, "nearly all 29 contained some form of. . .fraudulent appraisals."[54] Lawyers provided unscrupulous thrift operators with advice on loans that often violated federal regulations, and also provided legitimacy to these thrift schemes. Dependent upon referrals for continued success in their careers, accountants often chose to ignore evidence of wrongdoing. In fact, accountants from all Big Six accounting companies were successfully sued by the federal government for their participation in the S&L crisis.[55]

More than any other form of fraud, covering-up dominated the Japanese financial crisis. The importance of covering up is due not only to the financial damage it has wreaked in documented cases thus far, but because covering up is an essential part of the foundation of Japan's financial system. As such, the reporting of specific examples of covering-up by the popular media is nothing new to either the Japanese public or to the international audience. The severity, complexity, and disastrous nature of recent events, however, have caused public concern for the economic stability of financial institutions.

In October of 1995, the trial of bond trader Toshihide Iguchi exposed a massive and extensive pattern of cover-up at Daiwa Bank's New York Operations. Daiwa bank, the world's thirteenth largest, was charged with the cover-up of $1.1 billion in losses.[56] Mr. Iguchi, who gained a personal profit of more than $500,000 from his trading actions, was not merely a rogue trader who acted alone. Rather, he sent several letters to Akira Fujita, the president of Daiwa, "warning that his $1.1 billion loss might be detected if headquarters did not secretly cover his losses." If Daiwa colluded with him, he argued, "there is zero possibility that this case would be found out."[57] The severity of the loss, however, was too great to conceal, and Akira Fujita, Daiwa's president, met with Yoshimasa Nishimura, chief of the Japanese Ministry of Finance's banking bureau, to humbly acknowledge the existence of the problem.[58] Instead of ordering Mr. Fujita to alert U.S. banking authorities, however, Mr. Nishimura merely held onto the information. Only when U.S. officials were on the verge of discovering Daiwa's massive losses, a delay of almost six weeks, did the Ministry of Finance report the problem to the New York Federal board.[59] This massive cover-up by members of Daiwa bank and the Ministry of Finance infuriated American authorities and frightened European lending institutions. As a result, American officials revoked Daiwa's charter and filed twenty-four counts of criminal conspiracy and fraud against the bank. In addition, Masahiro Tsuda, general manager of Daiwa's New York office, was charged with deceiving federal regulators and creating false bank statements. Daiwa faced fines upward of $1 billion.[60] The bank agreed to settle with U.S. authorities in February of 1996, admitting to sixteen felony counts and penalties of $340 million.[61] More importantly, however, is the resulting fear of lending institutions worldwide, who question the integrity and well-being of the Ministry of Finance, the supervisory agent of Japan's banks. This has resulted in the "Japanese Premium" that Japanese banks must pay in order to borrow funds from foreign markets.

Other events have also revealed a pattern of covering up involving almost all of Japan's major banking institutions. In July of 1998, the Ministry of Finance admitted that bad loans, totaling nearly $600 billion, were burdening the nation's banks.[62] This admission of massive insolvency in the banking industry provides evidence of not only poor fiscal management but also of a complete lack of honest reporting to the public by the Ministry after both the Daiwa Bank and Yamiachi Securities scandals. The suicide of Yoichi Otsuki, a Ministry of Finance bureaucrat, who was being investigated for his role in covering up the most recent plethora of bad loans held by Japan's banks, provides additional evidence of a widespread cover-up reaching up to the Ministry of Finance.[63]

POLITICAL COLLUSION

The exact role played by political collusion in cases of white-collar crime is often difficult to ascertain, since the line dividing common political practices and corrupt acts is a fine one at best. Its presence as a central factor in the S&L crisis, however, has been widely documented. Former FHLBB Chairman Edwin Gray noted: "As bad as the financial crisis—that is to say, the 'thrift crisis' is. . .the real issues are far less 'financial' than they are 'political.' The thrift crisis is, and has been from the beginning, a political crisis."[64]

One troubling form of political collusion involves the use of both blatant and implicit bribes. A blatant bribe is one in which one party receives some form of economic goods or valuables in exchange for providing a service to the giver. In contrast, an implicit bribe is one in which no recognized agreement has been made regarding the exchange of goods or wealth for services. The difference between the two is a minor legal technicality, which presents very few problems, as "even a third-rate politico and a rather inexperienced lobbyist can and do find ways to observe the letter of the law."[65]

Implicit bribery played a central role in the development of the savings and loan scandal. Between 1983 and 1988, almost $4.5 million in political funding was provided to congressional members, with over $1 million presented to members of the banking committees by political action committees representing various savings and loans.[66] The use of implicit bribery has been shown to play a role during the deregulation of the industry, the political cover-up of the crisis, and the period of reregulation and criminal prosecution.[67]

The type and object of bribery differs significantly in American and Japanese cultures. Nevertheless, the presence of bribery was and is as pervasive, if not more so, in the Japanese financial crisis than in the S&L debacle. In fact, bribery is such an established aspect of the Japanese banking culture that banks created official posts and terms, such as "MOF-tan," whose responsibility was to gather intelligence on, and to influence the opinions of, Ministry officials.[68] Moreover, it was the responsibility of the "MOF-tan" to discover when the bank inspections were scheduled to occur, so that the institution would have time to hide information regarding bad loans and investments.[69] The most questionable and suspicious practice of Ministry officials, however, was the act of "amakudari," or "descent from heaven," in which retiring bureaucrats accepted cushy positions in companies they formerly regulated.[70]

In February of 1998, two key officials in the financial-control division of the Ministry's inspection department were accused of accepting bribes of $74,000 in lavish favors for turning a blind eye to damaging information in the banks they were regulating.[71] Their arrest marked the first time in fifty years that "sitting bureaucrats have been arrested."[72] As investigators made an unprecedented raid on Japan's most established and influential bureaucratic bulwark, Yoichi Otsuki, a Ministry of Finance official, committed suicide rather than face his impending arrest. He allegedly leaked information regarding government inspections and turned a blind eye to information regarding payoffs by Dai-Ichi Kangyo to members of organized crime. In exchange, he received discounts on his condominium and was treated to golfing trips and $300 dinners at restaurants in Tokyo's Shinjuku area that featured waitresses without underwear.[73]

The most serious example of bribery involved Yasuyuki Yoshizawa, a Ministry official who headed the division that determines short-term interest rates in Japan's money markets. His arrest came as the result of the first ever raid in Japan's central bank, the Bank of Japan. Mr. Yoshizawa had the authority to preview the Tankan, the Bank of Japan's widely observed economic indicator. In addition, he was extremely influential in determining interest rates that "influenced the cost of everything from government bonds to bank loans."[74] His information was invaluable for anyone who had a stake in the financial markets. For years, financial institutions and traders had been suspicious of a high-level leak because bond and currency prices often shifted before the Tankan was released. The arrest of Mr. Yoshizawa not only discredited the Japanese markets but also made foreign traders wary of any future investments. The incident led to the public resignations of both the Central Bank chief, Yasuo Matsushita, and the nation's finance minister, Hiroshi Mitsuzuka.[75]

Deregulation of the Savings and Loan Industry

One significant example of industry influence before deregulation of the S&L industry involves the case of Congressman Fernand St. Germain. As the Chair of the Housing Banking Committee, his ability to influence savings and loan policy was obvious. The Garn-St. Germain Depository Institutions Act of 1982 eradicated interest rate ceilings and expanded the powers of thrifts. Though he was, in the past, an ardent advocate for stronger regulations and control of the industry, he promoted a bill that effectively deregulated the industry. His change in position occurred at the same time that he began to develop a close relationship with the lobbyists at the U.S. League of Savings Institutions (The League).

His entertainment on the League's expense account was deemed "substantial evidence of serious and sustained misconduct," by the U.S. Department of Justice. However, no formal charges were brought, and he was voted out of office in 1988.[76]

A second example of implicit bribery can be found in the case of Richard Pratt, the FHLBB chair. His outspoken advocacy of industry deregulation was so well-known that the Garn-St. Germain bill was commonly referred to as the "Pratt Bill." The cause for his convictions, however, came into question when he left the FHLBB in 1983 and accepted a top-level position with Merrill Lynch, along with substantial benefits resulting from deregulation. In fact, he was placed in charge of Merrill Lynch's mortgage-backed securities department, which received substantial investments from the severely insolvent thrifts of Lincoln Savings of Irvine, Gibraltar Savings of Beverly Hills, and Imperial Savings of San Diego.[77]

Political Cover-up

The insolvency rate of the savings-and-loan industry had moved up to one-third by the fall of 1987, and many more were due to fall.[78] The pending national elections concerned members of both the Republican and Democratic parties, as both were intimately involved in the scandal. A massive campaign of political cover-up began, which ranged from politicians to appointed regulators. In fact, the newly appointed chief thrift regulator, Danny Wall, was chosen because he would both prevent the S&L crisis from becoming an issue during the 1988 presidential race and agree to "accentuate the positive."[79]

A financial plan was immediately proposed by Danny Wall to provide short-term solutions to the problems caused by the S&L crisis. His plan consisted of three general incentives: (1) the FSLIC assumption of a thrift's bad assets; (2) FSLIC IOUs; (and 3) tax deductions. The plan was outrageous by rational standards, as many of these incentives resulted in gifts to buyers who received $78 in assets and tax benefits for every $1 provided in capital.[80] It was obvious that this plan would greatly benefit the management of poorly regulated thrifts, at the cost of the financial health of the economy at large.

The responsibility of making fiscal decisions lies, in Japan, strictly in the hands of the powerful Ministry of Finance. Unlike it's American counterpart, Japan did not set up a political figurehead, such as Danny Wall, to initiate fiscal policies to solve its immediate financial woes. Instead, the Finance Ministry itself maintained tight fiscal control over the economy by controlling all financial markets, as well as maintaining a weak yen exchange rate that resulted in yearly government surpluses.[81] It maintained its control on the economy by exercising its power of selective enforcement of laws. Unlike America, Japan is ruled by a plethora of restrictive laws that govern everything from election funding to tax auditing. The enforcement of these laws, however, is selectively determined by the Ministry. In fact, the National Tax Agency of Japan is pervaded with career ministry officials, most of whom answer to, and will return to, the Ministry.

Political Protection

The May 1983 appointment of Edwin Gray as the new chair of the FHLBB was assumed, by corrupt legislators, to promote continued, cover-up policies. Gray, however, changed this perception after watching a homemade video of abandoned condominiums, funded by Empire Savings and Loan, along the I-20 corridor east of Dallas.[82] Convinced that the industry was headed toward an immense financial tragedy, he began to challenge lax regulations and unscrupulous operators.

By 1986, the GAO reported that the FSLIC would need an additional $20 billion to solve the current thrift crisis.[83] A recapitalization bill was proposed by the Reagan Administration and sent to Congress to provide the FSLIC with $15 billion. The League was adamantly opposed to such a bill, and expressed their concerns to their respective congressional representatives. This bill was used by various members of congress as a tool for protecting thrifts.

The most infamous example of political protection involved the case of Charles Keating, who made substantial contributions to numerous politicians. Five senators, known colloquially as the "Keating Five," received almost $2 million in political contributions. In fact, Alan Greenspan, Chairman of the Federal Reserve, as then-Chair of the Council of Economic Advisors, wrote letters on behalf of Keating's Lincoln Savings and Loan, attesting to its financial soundness. After a history of poor underwriting of loans and various investment irregularities, Lincoln Savings and Loan became the subject of an investigation by Edwin Gray and the FHLBB. On April 1987, four members of the Keating Five, Senators Dennis DeConcini, John McCain, John Glenn, and Alan Cranston, held a meeting with Edwin Gray, in which they intervened on behalf of Lincoln Savings and Loan and requested that he abandon his investigation.[84]

Political protectionism took a different form in Japan. The presence of favor from established members of the Ministry of Finance was often enough to assure banking officials of protection from regulatory or prosecutorial attacks. Disfavor, on the other hand, often resulted in punitive enforcement of tax and regulatory laws. A major example of this phenomenon can be found in the case of Nomura Securities.

In July of 1991, Nomura Securities, the largest securities firm in Japan, was consumed by allegations that it had compensated clients for their stockmarket losses and reported those payments as trading losses. Its president was asked by the ministry of finance to resign as a sign of "kejime," the point in the sand at which a line is drawn, through which a public sacrifice is offered. The president, Yoshihisa Tabuchi, however, declared that the Ministry was not only well aware of his actions, but had approved them beforehand. This act put Nomura in disfavor with the Ministry, which then retaliated by banning it from securities for an undisclosed period.[85] As a result, its stock dropped 65 percent.[86]

In a direct parallel to the Savings and Loan debacle, the Japanese Ministry of Finance attempted to thwart investigations into the financial stability of various institutions. Katsuhito Kumazaki, who led the raids on the Ministry in January of 1998, was in charge of investigating the collusive practices of finance officials and the institutions they regulated. The inability of the Ministry to control his activities resulted in his transfer to the Toyama prefecture, a remote area on Japan's northwest coast.[87] In addition, the creation of the semi-independent Securities and Financial Inspection Commission became an act of futility when the political influence of the Ministry was exercised. The purpose of the commission was to provide for independent oversight of Japan's financial markets. It became a weakened, and ineffective, however, when it fell under the jurisdiction of the Ministry itself. Thus, its ability to root out corruption was completely in the hands of the Ministry that it was supposed to help regulate.[88]

ORGANIZED CRIME

Organized crime has influenced Japan's culture and civilization for over three centuries. Historians of Japanese culture trace the origins of the Yakuza, Japan's organized crime syndicate, to feudal Japan in the early 1600s. In the Tokugawa era, better known as the shogunate, the end of massive civil wars in Japan facilitated the unification of the island by Ieyasu Tokugawa, the first shogun, in 1604.[89] The end of these civil wars also meant the sudden unemployment of over a half million samurai warriors. Although the majority of these samurai became members of the working merchant class, a significant number of them organized into criminal gangs called hatamoto-yakko, which attacked and plundered local towns and cities.[90] In defense of their towns, young townsmen formed machi-yakko—"servants of the town"—which developed the battle skills necessary to fend off the criminal gangs. Today's Yakuza claim links to, and identify with, the Robin Hood-esque bands of machi-yakko, for they claim to work for the good of the townspeople. The earliest existence of the true form of what is now known as the Yakuza can be found in seventeenth century Japan, where gamblers, ("bakuto") and street peddlers, ("tekiya") grew up, side-by-side, with the feudal towns.[91] Eventually, the Yakuza began to organize into hierarchical "families," led by a "grandfather/godfather." It differed from the Italian Mafia only in that it was organized around "father-son/mentor-mentee" relationships called "oyabun-kobun."[92] These relationships foster an undying sense of loyalty, while providing for the successful integration of new members.

Traditionally, the Yakuza enjoyed a friendly relationship with the Japanese police. Japan is famous throughout the world for its lack of violent street crime, and much of that is due to the role played by organized crime in Japanese society. In exchange for a "blind eye" to traditional Yakuza activities such as gambling, loan-sharking, and prostitution, the Yakuza aid the police by dealing severely with petty street criminals and violent offenders. The end of the bubble economy of the 1980s, however, has eliminated the Yakuza's traditional occupations, and has led many of them to turn to financial crimes.[93] In particular, the rise in the number of "Sokaiya" has terrified most financial institutions. Sokaiya are financial racketeers who profit by extorting money from image-conscious Japanese companies who may be trying to cover up their own scandals.[94] Though they often demand extortion money from a company to remain silent about embarrassing company information during a shareholder's meeting, they are also often paid by the company to maintain order and peace during those same meetings.[95] Unlike their western counterparts, whose yearly stockholder meetings often include critical questions by stockholders, Japanese companies take great pride in being able to end their meetings quickly—often within an hour—without any embarrassing questions being posed. One example of this occurred at the Mitsubishi Motor Corporation's 1996 stockholder meeting. Even though the firm was in a widely publicized scandal over sexual harassment incurred by workers in its United States plants, no questions about that scandal were raised during the meeting, and it ended within an hour amidst cheers of "bonzai" and extensive applause.[96] Even Japan's largest companies are not immune to this, as car-makers and financial goliaths such as Toyota and Nissan admitted making payments to Taihei, a company owned by corporate racketeers.[97]

One of the most famous Sokaiya was Ryuichi Koike, who garnered international attention for the havoc his actions wreaked upon Japan's various financial institutions. Between 1988 and 1996, he extorted over a quarter of a billion dollars in loans, at low interest, from Dai-Ichi Kangyo Bank, which he used to buy $15 million of stock in Nomura Securities, Japan's biggest brokerage.[98] He was able to extort such a massive amount in loans because he was originally hired by Nomura to maintain order at their meetings, but then threatened to expose the fact that they had hired him. He then used his status as a major stockholder to demand, and receive, $3.3 million to keep him quiet about embarrassing information he held about it's former chairman and president at various stockholder meetings.[99]

The Yakuza have also been shown to branch out to new forms of financial crime, such as "squatting." The fall in real estate prices has left many new housing developments insolvent. As such, developers are often forced into bankruptcy, and ownership of the newly developed property is reverted back to the lending financial institution.[100] The Yakuza, who utilize a huge network of financial advisors, then occupy the newly developed condominium, apartment, or office building and intimidate all bill collectors. The bank or finance company then has two (undesirable) choices. It must either initiate legal action, which can often take years, during which it will take a continuous loss on the property, or it can sell the property at a loss to the only buyers available, the Yakuza.[101]

In addition, it has been estimated by various financial regulators and banking institutions that bad debts occupied by the Yakuza could be as great as 10 percent of the nation's bad loans.[102] It has also become increasingly dangerous and difficult to collect from them. In fact, in September of 1994, a branch manager of the Nagoya branch of Sumitomo Bank was killed, execution style, because of his pressuring of members of the Yakuza to repay their loans.[103]

The role played by organized crime in financial fraud is extensive and often a difficult one to unravel. Although information in the popular media and in academic journals is often sketchy and contradictory, it is clear that organized crime played a significant role in the financial instability of various banks, financial institutions, and legitimate companies in Japan.

CONCLUSION

The damaged wreaked upon the American economy by the S&L crisis was, at that time, deemed the most severe financial crisis ever. Its destructive effects, however, pale in comparison to the economic and social costs suffered by all industrial nations as a result of the banking fiasco in Japan. Through a comparative analysis, this paper has attempted to show that examples of insider abuse, political collusion, and bribery were not merely isolated incidents of the proverbial bad apple. Rather, they are examples of the forms of material and financial fraud brought on by the very structure of the Japanese banking industry itself.

Even now, the extent of financial and social damage resulting from the S&L crisis have not yet been fully recognized. Though the debate as to its causes and effects continues, the S&L debacle's true value now is as a learning tool. Ineffective regulation in both the Japanese and American cases has led to major financial losses through widespread fraud.

Regarding Japan, pervasive material fraud, insider abuse, and political collusion have played a significant role in creating a fiscal crisis that has overshadowed the destructiveness of the S&L debacle. In addition, organized crime played a major role in creating financial instability in various banks, financial institutions, and legitimate companies, which led them to insolvency. As the world's second-largest economy, the fall of Japan would spell disaster not only for the economically troubled East Asian countries but for the world's economy as a whole.

In late 1997, President Clinton dismissed Asia's currency problems as "a few little glitches in the road."[104] From what is now known, the President was wrong on at least two counts. First, the economic problems in Asia turned out to be considerably larger than "glitches." Second, and more importantly, it is now clear that the financial problems in Japan and other Asian countries were not merely "currency crises," but instead, the result of major problems with financial institutions and their regulation. Banks and finance companies legally and illegally lent on overly risky projects, and this, combined with poor regulation from the start, has led to the loss of confidence in Asian economies of which their currency crises are but a symptom.[105]

As the world economy continues to grow and financial transactions increasingly occur across national boundaries, the potential for more severe financial crises has also grown exponentially. The future stability of the world economy depends on recognizing factors related to mistakes of the past, which include the role of white-collar crime in creating major financial debacles.

ENDNOTES

1. Calavita, Kitty, Robert Tillman, and Henry N. Pontell. 1997. "The Savings and Loan Debacle, Financial Crime, and the State." *Annual Review Sociology* 23:19–38.

2. Black, William K., Kitty Calavita, and Henry N. Pontell. 1995. "The Savings and Loan Debacle of the 1980s: White-Collar Crime or Risky Business?" *Law and Policy* 17(1):24–55.

3. Ibid.

4. 12 USC 1001 et. seq.
   12 USC 1724 et. seq.

5. Black, William K. "Substantive Positions of S&L Trade Associations, 1979–1989." *National Commission on Financial Institution Reform, Recovery and Enforcement* (Unpublished staff report No. 1), 1993.

6. Tashiro, Hiroko, and Sachiko Sakamaki. 1998. "End of an Era?" *Time International* 150(24): 14.

7. Fingleton, Eamonn. 1995. "Japan's Invisible Leviathan." *Foreign Affairs* 74,(2):69–86.

8. Ibid., p. 71.

9. Hiroko and Sakamaki, op. cit., p. 14.

10. Butler, Steven. 1998. "Good Life, Bad Loans: A Japanese Scandal." *U.S. News & World Report* 124(5)(9 February):47.

11. Ibid.

12. Calavita, Kitty, Henry N. Pontell, and Robert Tillman. 1997. *Big Money Crime: Fraud and Politics in the Savings and Loan Crisis.* Berkeley: University of California Press.

13. 18 USC 1001 et. seq.

14. 18 USC 656 et. seq.
    18 USC 961 et. seq.

15. Calavita, Tillman and Pontell, op. cit.

16. Alt, Conrad, and Kristen Siglin. Unpublished Memorandum on Bank and Thrift Fraud to Senate Banking Committee Members and Staff. (25 July 1990).

17. Ibid.

18. Calavita, Tillman and Pontell, op. cit.

19. United States. National Commission on Financial Institution Reform, Recovery and Enforcement. 1993. *Origins and Causes of the S&L Debacle: A Blueprint for Reform. A Report to the President and Congress of the United States.* Washington D. C.: Government Printing Office.

20. Ibid.

21. United States. House Committee on Government Operations. Combating Fraud, Abuse, and Misconduct in the Nation's Financial Institutions: Current Federal Efforts are Inadequate. Report by the Committee. 100th Congress, 2nd Session, 1988. H.Rept. 100–1088.

22. Pizzo, Stephen, Mary Fricker, and Paul Muolo. 1991. Inside Job: *The Looting of America's Savings and Loans*. New York: Harper-Collins.

23. Lowy, Martin. 1991. *High Rollers: Inside the Savings and Loan Debacle*. New York: Praeger.

24. Ibid., pp. 152–153.

25. Binsteing, Michael. 1989. "A Confederacy of Greed." *Regardies* July, p. 31.

26. "From Bullied Bride to Waitress to Billionaire. . .to Jail." *Daily Yomiuri* 21 August 1991, p. 3.

27. Helm, Leslie. "Ex-Hostess in Japan's Bank Scandal is Shadowy Figure." *Los Angeles Times* 16 September 1991, p. D2.

28. Ibid.

29. Oda, Minehiko. "Though Smashed Flat, 'Bubble Lady' Still Has Spunk." *Daily Yomiuri* 11 March 1998, p. 7.

30. Helm, op. cit.

31. Ibid.

32. "Bank Official in Japan Tells of Being Fooled Into Loans." *New York Times* (Late Edition-Final) 31 August 1991, p. 37.

33. Ibid.

34. Beech, Hanna. 1998. "Sentenced. Nui Onoue." *Time International* 150(29)(March 16):15.

35. Oda, op. cit.

36. Ibid.

37. "From Bullied Bride," op. cit.

38. Ibid.

39. Helm, op. cit.

40. "Bank Official in Japan Tells of Being Fooled Into Loans." op. cit.

41. Ibid.

42. Associated Press. "Big Japanese Bank Admits Ties to Key Figure in Scandal; Finance: Industrial Bank of Japan LTD. Said Nui Onoue, Who Allegedly Borrowed $2.48 Billion from A Credit Union Using False Documents As Collateral, Has Been One Of It's Clients For Four Years." *Reuters Byline*, 15 August 1991, Business, p. D2.

43. "Bank Official in Japan. . ." op. cit.

44. Associated Press, op. cit.

45. "Former Manager: 150 Billion Yen Loaned to Onoue; 90% of Kogin Lease's Outstanding Loans Were Owned by Osaka Restaurateur." *Daily Yomiuri* 19 May 1992, p. 2.

46. Associated Press, op. cit.

47. "Former Manager. . .", op. cit.

48. Ibid.

49. "Falling on Their Swords: Industrial Bank of Japan." 26 October 1991, p. 96.

50. "Onoue gets 12 Year Term for Fraud." *Daily Yomiuri* 3 March 1998, p. 2.

51. United States General Accounting Office. "Thrift Failures: Costly Failures Resulted From Regulatory Violations and Unsafe Practices." GAO/AFMD-89-62, Report to Congress 16 June 1989, pp. 41, 44–45.

52. Pizzo, et al., op. cit., p. 430.

53. Calavita, Pontell and Tillman, op. cit.

54. United States. House Committee on Government Operations, Subcommittee on Commerce, Consumer, and Monetary Affairs. "Fraud and Abuse by Insiders, Borrowers, and Appraisers in the California Thrift Industry. Hearings before the Subcommittee." 100th Congress, 1st Session, 13 June 1987, p. 26.

55. Ibid.

56. Chau-Eoan, Howard. 1995. "Lending a Hand to Godzilla." *Time* 146(18)(30 October):69–71.

57. Hirsh, Michael and Allen Sloan. 1995. "After the Deluge; the Scandal Surrounding Japan's Daiwa Bank gets Deeper by the Day." *Newsweek* 126(20)(13 Nov):56–58.

58. Hirsh, Michael. 1995. "Under Assault: the Ministry of Fear." *Newsweek* 126(17) (23 October):50.

59. Ibid.

60. Hirsh and Sloan, op. cit.

61. Donovan, Karen. 1996. "Was Culture a Player in Daiwa's Illegal Cover-up?" *National Law Journal* 18(28)(11 March):B1.

62. Tashiro and Sakamaki, op. cit.

63. Ibid.

64. Gray, Edwin J. 1990. "Warnings Ignored: The Politics of the Crisis." *Stanford Law and Policy Review* 2(Spring):139.

65. Etzioni, Amitai. "Keating Six?" (1990–1991) *The Responsive Community* 1:1.

66. Grundfest, Joseph A. 1990. "Son of S&L-The Sequel: The Conditions that Caused the Crisis Are Still With Us." *Washington Post* 3 June, p. D1.

67. Calavita, Pontell and Tillman, op. cit.

68. Tashiro and Sakamaki, op. cit.

69. Ibid.

70. Tashiro, Hiroko. 1998. "Ministries of Shame." *Time International* 150(3)(23 March):35.

71. Tashiro and Sakamaki, op. cit.

72. Ibid.

73. Ibid.

74. Tashiro, op. cit.

75. Ibid.

76. Calavita, Pontell and Tillman, op. cit.

77. Mayer, Martin. 1990. *The Greatest Ever Bank Robbery: The Collapse of the Savings and Loan Industry. New York*: Charles Scribner's Sons.

78. U.S. National Commission on Financial Institution Reform, Recovery and Enforcement, op. cit.

79. United States. Senate Committee on Banking, Housing, and Urban-Affairs. "Nomination of M. Danny Wall." Hearing before the Committee, 100th Congress, 1st Session (18 June 1987): p. 12.

80. Rosenblatt, Robert A. 1990. "Lawmaker says S&L Buyers got 78-to-1 Return." *Los Angeles Times* 29 August 1990, p. D2.

81. Fingleton, op. cit.

82. Black, William K. 1994. "Why (Some) Regulators Don't think Regulation Works." Paper prepared for the annual meeting of the Allied Social Science Association, Boston 3–5 January, p. 9.

83. United States General Accounting Office. "Thrift Industry Problems: Potential Demands on the FSLIC Insurance Fund." *GAO/GGD-86-48BR* 12 February 1986.

84. Calavita, Pontell and Tillman, op. cit.

85. "Mudslide: The effects of Japan's securities scandal are spreading; and there may well be more shocks to come." *Economist* 320(7714)(6 July 1991):77–79.

86. Desmond, Edward. 1998. "An ex-champ battles back." *Fortune* 137(11)(8 June):187–193.

87. Clark, Tanya. 1998. "Sayonara, reformer." *Forbes* 162(1)(6 July):46.

88. "Who watches the watchdog? Japanese financial regulation." *Economist* 320(7725)(21 September 1991):94–96.

89. Kapland, David E., and Alec Dubro. 1986. *Yakuza: the Explosive Account of Japan's Criminal Underworld.* New York: Addison-Wesley.

90. Ibid.

91. Ibid.

92. Ibid.

93. Efron, Sonni. "Japanese Gang up on the Mob; Growing Intolerance, a Recession and Anti-gangster Law have Many Yakuza Trying to Change their Ways." *Los Angeles Times* 22 March 1997, p. A1.

94. Ibid.

95. Ibid.

96. "Japan Steps Up the Fight Against a Tradition of Corporate Gangsters; Debt Before Dishonor." *South China Morning Post* 6 June 1997, p. 6.

97. "Japan's Car-makers Admit Paying out Extortion Cash." *Independent* (London) 19 August 1998, p. 13.

98. Fagler, Martin. 1997. "Japan: Banking on the Mob; the Old Ties between the Banks and the Yakuza may be coming to an End." *Independent* (London) 17 August, p. 3.

99. Ibid.

100. Baker, Gerald. 1996. "Mob Rule: Japan's Mafia: Troubled Times for Japan's Financial System mean a Lucrative line of Business for Gangsters." *Financial Times* (London) 16 March 1996, pp. 1–5.

101. Ibid.

102. Parry, Richard Lloyd. 1996. "Yakuza Settle Bad Debts with a Bullet as Japan Bubble Bursts." *Independent* (London) 4 February, p. 16.

103. Ibid.

104. "Why Did Asia Crash?" *Economist* 346(8050)(10 January 1998):66.

105. Ibid.

Transnational White-Collar Crime: Some Explorations of Victimization Impact

Michael Levi

The object of this article is *not* to examine how good or bad a job the investigation and prosecution agencies make of handling fraud (in the British sense, which includes elite as well as employee crime), but to discuss perceptions of the *importance* of the work done by them and what evidence is there of the incidence and prevalence of fraud internationally and transnationally. How serious is fraud, especially transnational fraud, and how serious is it seen to be by the various groupings that constitute "the public"? Is fraud really so harmful—and to whom? —as to justify all these efforts and expense, or is it a "victimless crime" that arguably should be treated as "not the law's business" (or at least as not the *criminal* law's business)? Finally, I explore some methodological issues that may be carried forward in the future.

The subject of crime seriousness is important because both the experience of crime and perceptions of it[1] tend to trigger:

1. Policing and prosecution powers
2. Investigative resources; and
3. Levels of punishment and disciplinary sanctions.

It is arguable that reactions to some crimes are "natural," reflecting biological programming about territoriality and security, and so on. However, reactions are also affected by our beliefs—accurate or not—about how *common* "the problem" is and about its likely effects. In this context, the media play a significant role, since they (along with discussions with family and with work and leisure companions) are the primary sources of information about crime. Indeed, the role of the media in publicizing (or not publicizing) white-collar crime is important both (a) at a symbolic level, of representing what "crime" and "criminals" constitute and (b) in terms of fraud prevention. Though there is an interaction between what the media publicize and what they believe will interest their readers and viewers, one may hypothesize that the less concern that the media show, the less serious fraud will be seen by offenders and by their reference groups (family, friends, and colleagues), and transnational fraudsters already see very little risk of penal or social stigma consequences compared with other forms of major crime (see Levi and Pithouse, forthcoming).

What difference does it make whether frauds are transnational and/or connected to "organized crime"? It makes a difference in our ability to control the behavior, to seek and obtain legal powers to investigate and to confiscate the proceeds of crime, and it may even be a way of attracting (or deterring) police attention to deal with offenders who are involved in other forms of serious crime. For although, in some respects, transnational frauds evoke the fear of "the stranger" that underpins many victimological concerns, at the same time, they create so many problems for the traditional territorially based reach of the nation-state in criminal and even regulatory matters that nonpursuit becomes the *de facto* default option. Insofar as the offenders are not locals who have set up artificial legal entities in secrecy jurisdictions (for which, see Blum et al., 1998), it may also be morally easier for them to rip off strangers. This is true especially where the victim is seen as remote and undeserving, like "government," national or collective, such as the European Union. (Though one should never underestimate the ability of people to define their own acts as morally acceptable, however evident their harmfulness is to others—see Benson, 1985, Friedrichs, 1996, and Levi, 1981.) But some frauds are very serious, even if they are domestic in origin and are not connected to drugs traffickers, money-launderers, or other "organized crime" types: a fraud can be very well organized in isolation from other crimes, and the harm that it causes to victims and/or to "the market" may be independent of the propensity of fraudsters—Godfather-style—to place horses' heads in the beds of their competitors!

THE IMPACT OF FRAUD

The first thing to emphasize is that "fraud" is not just one coherent sort of activity, and that its effects are extremely variable. Its impact can take the following forms (see further, Levi and Pithouse, forthcoming):

1. Direct effects on victims' health, sense of well-being, and life and financial opportunities, e.g. most obviously, "widows and orphans" frauds on investors and pensioners such as Barlow Clowes & Maxwell in the

United Kingdom, or some of the U.S. Savings & Loans frauds (Calavita and Pontell, 1994); but also, perhaps less obviously, unnecessary operations or operations charged for but not performed as part of medical practitioner fraud (Jesilow, et al., 1993). However, this also includes, less obviously, the suppliers of credit, whether these be financial institutions or industrial firms, who—unlike the victims of investment frauds by firms authorized under the U.K. Financial Services Act or its equivalents in other countries—receive no compensation at all when they are defrauded. In the case of frauds committed against persons or the state in developing countries, this can have an inhibiting effect on economic and social development (World Bank, 1997), not least through the theft of development funds by leaders.

2. Direct effects on the sense of security of members of the public or other business people, e.g. the Barings Bank collapse (Fay, 1996), which prompted the film *Rogue Trader*, and investments or pension frauds. Though corruption and fraud are only one source of economic devastation, we have only to look at developments during the mid and late 1990s in Russia, Albania, and, in a different way, Nigeria to see the way that both the experience and fear of fraud can harm widespread sections of society. Even in advanced industrial countries, with wider share ownership and increased need for private provision for old age and ill health, the *proportion* of the population who are affected, or who can imagine themselves as being affected, by fraud is much higher than it used to be. Large-scale fraud, in other words, is no longer just "rich people's business" and this fits—or ought to fit—into the political agenda of "Third Way" social democrats and conservative republicans alike, though the balance of who constitutes "blameless victims" may vary by political allegiance.

3. Loss of business in international capital markets as a result of (a) increased insecurity about compensation in the event of fraud, and (b) more intangible factors such as was stated by some Swiss bankers after revelations over insider insurance fraud at Lloyd's of London and the Maxwell collapse: "We don't want to do business in your country because you allow all these crooks to operate." Trust is an indispensable precondition of business (and "organized crime"), whether it is impersonal between strangers or personal between intimates or members of one's own ethnic group (Gambetta, 1988; Fukuyama, 1995, 1999).[2]

4. Loss of legitimacy in both political and criminal justice systems as a result of (a) a sense of betrayal that reasonable expectations of system integrity in "popular capitalism" have not been met, and (b) popular *perceptions* that there is "one law for the rich and another for the poor," and that those with friends in high places are untouchable for financial misconduct of a much wider scope than those who normally come to court.

This has had particularly obvious effects in Third World countries, but arguably, Italy and Japan have been badly hit by this delegitimization, and there are media and public cries for "tough justice'" for elite offenders in countries such as China. In 1997, almost 40 percent of the Chinese People's Congress voted to reject the Chief Procurator's annual report partly because of resentment that cases such as Chen Xi-Tong, ex-Mayor of Beijing, had not been prosecuted (personal communication). He was later tried and sentenced to a lengthy term of imprisonment. This is evidence of the importance of popular legitimization. Moreover, however spuriously, this alleged class bias is often used by "ordinary" offenders, from burglars to credit card fraudsters, to justify their own continued offending and to point up the "injustice" of their own treatment compared with the elite.

The Emotional Effects of Fraud

Another important dimension of the impact of fraud is the victim self-blame and shaming that often accompanies it. Some investors and depositors in securities scams and, to a lesser extent, BCCI (the Bank of Credit and Commerce International, which was closed down in 1991 largely because its fraud and money-laundering were considered unregulateable globally), were concerned that other people saw them as greedy speculators who "deserved what they got" because they were "going for rates that were higher than the market and there has to be a greater risk if you are getting a higher return." (Though BCCI's rates were only marginally higher than the rest of the market.) In other cases, where victims think that they are in particularly low-risk investments, the shock and the impact are especially great. Barlow Clowes investors repeatedly stated to me: "the newspaper adverts stated that the firm was 'safe as the Bank of England.'" And even though there was no objective basis for their feeling this way, many investors in a variety of schemes felt ashamed at having been duped and because others might regard them as "greedy:" this is one factor that also discourages reporting to the authorities. There are similarities there with the way that rape victims feel: many fraud and rape victims feel obliged to re-examine minutely whether they "should have seen it coming" and whether that somehow makes it *their* fault rather than that of the offender(s). (Alternatively, some just "put it down to experience" and try to forget what happened.)

An illustration of the enormous psychological impact on investment fraud victims may be found in the words of one quadriplegic I interviewed:

> "We were totally shattered. I just couldn't believe what had happened to us. [The broker], whom we had known for years, had come to our house and had sat on my bed and held my hand and explained to us about how this wonderful investment was 'safe as the Bank of England.' I had heard of bondwashing, you know, because I read the Financial Times you know, even though I am disabled, because I used to do accountancy work in my spare time

when I was fitter. And he had told us that there was nothing to worry about and that he had put a lot of his own money into it because it was so good. He said it was particularly suitable for us because it was so safe and he knew how much we needed the money so that I could be looked after. We have always been so careful and we have never been the victims of crime or taken any risks and there we were."

These effects can be very long term, even where investors are compensated. People new to investments may not absorb the financial warnings when they are buying what they regard as safe investments, or those investments may be completely fictitious: not only does fraud lead to "broken dreams;" it also closes off opportunities that, once passed, are irrecoverable. For older people, vulnerable anyway to loss of confidence in themselves, frauds can destroy happiness permanently, just as readily as any other crime, such as mugging or a more serious burglary. Indeed, more so, because victims know that they have supplied funds or goods voluntarily, and because the loss of their financial cushion makes meaningless all their lifelong savings and sacrifices. An example of "missed opportunities:"

"We were in the middle of negotiating to sell this house and my in-laws' houses and we were going to move up to the Lake District and buy a small hotel and all live there together. My mother, who was getting on, was going to move up with us and so were my children. Well, we just couldn't do it. Because all my spare money from my redundancy payments was put in Barlow Clowes, which I had been assured was a safe place with high interest till the deal was ready to be concluded. So we just had to abandon the whole move. Now we are still living here; my mother has died; my family have gone through all sorts of aggravations that we would not have done if we had been able to move then."

The sense of *personal betrayal*, of abused trust, was an almost universal theme among the individual victims that I have interviewed, and yet unlike many other victims, they are not treated as are most other crime victims: there is ambivalent sympathy for them. If they were denied the opportunity to pursue their grievances through the criminal justice system, this would contribute to their sense of alienation and self-blame.

Institutional victims are in a slightly different position. In some cases, were they to spend more money on fraud prevention, they could have avoided becoming victims (though whether that expenditure would have been *cost-effective* is another matter, and this argument could apply to the majority of crime victims). Yet if they have been conned, and if there are international teams of swindlers trotting around the globe trying to get loans and make other deals on the basis of billions of pounds worth of forged Certificates of Deposit and other documents—often at the expense of poor Third World or Eastern European countries—this can lower confidence in First World financial institutions, perhaps for decades, as well as damaging their own indigenous credit and capital markets. However unfair to honest individuals living there, the "actuarial risk" reputations of countries such as Nigeria powerfully affect their credit standing and rates of borrowing on international markets. Moreover, if no action other than civil reparation is taken against such swindlers, what will deter them from continuing indefinitely, and discourage others from moving into major financial crime?

OFFICIAL REACTIONS TO FRAUD

Cases handled by "serious fraud" or "anti-corruption" agencies are by no means the only frauds in which there is serious financial and psychological damage to individuals and institutions. Countries vary in how they organize their prosecution arrangements, but many major cases, especially those involving corruption, have been prosecuted by (in England) the Crown Prosecution Service or (in federal jurisdictions such as the United States, Germany, and Australia) state-level and local prosecutors. The U.K. Serious Fraud Office's (SFO) cases traditionally have been selected on the basis of (a) their impact on the economic system and national interest, as well as on individual people directly, and (b) the need for multidisciplinary investigation, especially transnational investigation, at a high level. But even in frauds prosecuted by high-status units, the *objective* impact of fraud varies enormously, and public ratings of their seriousness likewise. At one end of the spectrum, there are highly visible consequences for individuals—the collapse of an investment trust, for example—which are easily presented (to the media and public) as traditional evils, but where the *long-term impact* on victims is often underestimated. In all countries, these tend to be dealt with consistently as "serious crimes," making fulfilling the requirements for mutual legal assistance reasonably simple,[3] though prosecutors may often be satisfied with pleas of guilty on more modest or local charges only, without worrying about victims in other countries.[4]

At the other end, there are "market offenses" such as breaches of the law on covert purchases of one's own stocks or declarations of shareholding levels (as in the Guinness and Blue Arrow cases—see Levi, 1993), or even insider trading, which the current (1999) U.K. Serious Fraud Office Director has stated are more likely to be left to regulators in the future. These might well be prosecuted in the United States or Australia, but their effects are fairly abstract, being directed more at the principle of protecting the integrity of information supplied to the market than at harms to any particular individuals (especially to any "ordinary individuals"). This sometimes leads to complaints that what is being prosecuted is not (or ought not to be) criminal at all: it is simply adult commercial behavior (even if the other party was deceived about what it was consenting to)! In these sorts of offenses, though insider trading has been fairly well "internationalized" in law, there is usually little consistency of investigation and prosecution practices, and mutual assistance is harder to achieve. Whether this would be significantly different if there were greater media attention is open to question. However, currently, although almost all regulatory and criminal action is reported in the financial general and specialist media—and can affect share prices as well as, perhaps, stigma of persons and companies—the only time that "market offenses" are reported in popular newspapers is when either the corporate brand name or the individuals involved are famous and form part of celebrity-watching (Levi and Pithouse, forthcoming). This in turn has ramifications for resourcing and prosecution policy in populist-oriented police departments and governments.

The Socioeconomic Context of Reactions to Fraud

Why does all this matter? One reason it matters is because in most advanced economies, the manufacturing and primary sectors are in decline, and the service sector—including financial services—has become more important. Another is because savings media are strongly affected by what happens in the national and overseas financial markets. Despite 1998 cutbacks, the financial services sector employs roughly one in five of those Londoners who have jobs.[5]

Looking at financial data, by 1995, banking, financial and other business services accounted for about one fifth of U.K. Gross Domestic Product (compared with 13 percent in 1984). In the national accounts—the "Pink Book"—the net surplus of £9.8 billion on trade in financial services made it substantially the largest contributor to the 1998 U.K. balance of payments (British Invisibles, 1998). The net overseas earnings of U.K. financial institutions were £9.2 billion in 1984, and even between 1990 and 1997, rose from £11.9 billion to £25.2 billion: the rise was substantial in all areas except commodities and shipping, though except for blips in 1993 and 1995 (partly reflecting increased foreign ownership of merchant banks), by far the largest numerical increase was in banking (excluding bank dealing profits, which are classified as capital transactions in the national accounts). Net overseas earnings of "U.K." banks rose almost sixfold from £1,321 million in 1987 to £7,745 million in 1997. Whatever its causes and desirability or otherwise (from the perspective of increasing the depth of social exclusion for those who would have been manual workers), the reality is that this illustrates the dependence of the U.K. economy on financial and allied services. This context is important even though it is uncertain whether these developments are actually reflected in attitudes to or action against fraud: the relationship between material risk of harm, on the one hand, and perceptions of the probability and seriousness of crime, on the other, remains problematic in criminology.

From an international perspective, the United Kingdom appears to be more dependent than most countries on receipts from banking and insurance services, which in 1994 comprised 17.6 percent of UK GDP, compared with 14.8 percent for France, 8.7 percent for Italy, 7.4 percent Germany, 5 percent for United States and Canada, and 4.7 percent for Japan. Though only some of these receipts seem prone to global concern about the integrity of U.K. markets—arising as they do from the possession of assets overseas—and the United Kingdom's share of activity on international financial markets has not increased during the 1990s, the United Kingdom had the greatest share of international markets in foreign exchange, external bank lending, international bonds (both primary and second-ary markets), over-the-counter (but not exchange-traded) financial derivatives, and both marine and aviation insurance (net of reinsurance). However, the United States, Japan, and France (in descending order) had greater shares than the United Kingdom of world invisible export earnings. One consequence of these data—at least in the absence of a more interventionist industrial growth strategy—is that a loss of competitiveness and/or investor confidence in financial markets would have severe consequences for the United Kingdom balance of payments.

Another way of examining the material basis of psychological investment in commercial "law and order" is to review direct investment in "popular capital-ism." In 1979, less than 7 percent of the U.K. population owned shares, but by 1992, 22 percent did so: some 5.7 million people. Between the end of 1993 and the end of 1998, the percentage of males who owned shares rose from 26 to 30 percent, and the percentage of females rose from 19 to 24 percent. Nevertheless, reflecting the more indirect stake people hold by virtue of their pension and life assurance funds, the *proportion* of shares held by individuals fell over time, from 66 percent in 1957, falling to a record low of 16.5 percent in 1997. Meanwhile, over the period 1957–97, the percentage of U.K. equities (shares) owned by pen-sion funds rose from 3.4 to 22.1 percent; owned by insurance companies, rose from 8.8 to 23.5 percent; and, equally dramatically, owned by overseas holders, rose from 7 percent in 1963 to 24 percent in 1997. The latter particularly may be described as a globalization effect. So, although Thatcherite and Reaganite rhet-oric about the creation of a property-owning and share-owning democracy is overblown—not the least because of their greater disposable income, the propor-tion of equities and other investments owned by the wealthy is naturally far greater than that owned by the "lower" social classes—the data suggest, particu-larly when one takes into account disposable income and the affordability of losses, that there is ample scope for political as well as financial pain from actual and suspected securities fraud (as well as from lawful falls in share and house prices). This gives readers a rough indication of the proportion of the general population and particular subgroups who are *prima facie* likely to be affected by concern about losses due to fraud, though one should not overhomogenize that category: insider dealing risks, or the manipulation of stocks not widely marketed to the public, may rationally produce little impact.

In addition to any fall-out from the exposure of more people to securities fraud, other "scams" involving people's future expectations of post-retirement income are likely to have a severe effect on demands for policing and for redress (whether through criminal justice and/or civil compensation), as people can no longer rely on the state to provide for their welfare. OECD projections suggest that in all the G-7 advanced economies except Britain, the "dependency ratio" of elderly people to working people is expected to double by the year 2040, peaking at 60 to 70 percent in Japan, Germany, Italy and France, and at 40 to 50 percent in the United States, Canada, and the United Kingdom, with rising pension strains on government budgets, pension fraud (and simple inadequacy) issues are likely to become increasingly salient.

Currently, though there is harmonization within the European Union, there is substantial international variation in victim compensation levels for fraud. Investor compensation schemes and deposit protection schemes provide a limited safety net, but in the United Kingdom, especially since they have not been indexed for inflation, their coverage is rather modest in relation to people's perceived needs and expectations in old age: £30,000 in full and 90 percent of the next £20,000—i.e., a maximum of £48,000—for investments under the Financial Services Act 1986; 90 percent of a maximum £20,000 (i.e. £18,000) of savings held in a building society under the Building Societies Investor Protection Scheme; and—since it was raised following the Credit Institutions (Protection of Depositors) Regulations 1995, implementing the European Directive on Deposit Guarantee Schemes—90 percent of a maximum £20,000 (i.e. £18,000) per bank depositor under the Deposit Protection Fund. This hardly constitutes a satisfactory maximum repayment when this may cover only two years' expected annual income, and when £20,000 *per annum* is a modest sum in the late 1990s for private nursing home expenses. Partly for this reason, the European Directive on Investor Compensation contained no upper limit.

The position in the United States is slightly different. There, the payment of full compensation to bank depositors fully protects depositors (though it may have enabled Savings and Loans fraudsters to neutralize their behavior as "victimless" and may make for reckless investment behavior by law-abiding bankers). But the same insecurities about future income arise in the light of 1995 data from the Rand Corporation, which show that half of retired white families have savings of $90,000, while the bottom 10 percent having $800 or less. Among 51 to 61 year olds, the median white wealth is $17,300, while median black and Hispanic household wealth is $500 (*Financial Times*, 25 July 1995). Thus, for all except the very rich top 5 percent, there is serious vulnerability to losses from fraud (and from poor investment or unexpected falls in the stock market), especially when—aggravated by early "voluntary" retirement policies in many sectors, including financial services—few older people are able to recover their losses from future employment.

Compensation schemes vary considerably between countries, but the rise of private pension funds (whether or not under compulsory savings schemes) is an international phenomenon. In the United States, there are some 200 million members of 731,000 pension plans, whose asset values equal roughly $2.5 trillion (General Accounting Office, 1994), though an increasing proportion of company pension schemes are what are known as 401(k) accounts, which can be invested at employers' discretion in "employer-related real estate and securities," and are not underwritten by the Pension Benefit Guaranty Corporation: they can be misused to keep the business going when it is insolvent, leaving pension-holders penniless (*Wall St. Journal*, 12 June 1996). The benefits from these schemes are not guaranteed by the government but, despite the counter-vailing pressure on tax rates for the proportionately smaller working population, governments of whatever political color may fall under severe political pressure if and when regulators fail to ensure that the contributions are not either looted or invested unwisely, for example, by director-trustees into their own companies in the hope that the company will trade out of its losses. In my view, this is because of the basic voting logistics of what in the United States has been called the "Grey Panther" movement: the larger the proportion of the population who are past working age (as defined culturally) and can identify with an issue, the greater the political push to give in, whatever the cost or offense, to the princi-ple of private responsibility. Thus we note that profits are privatized and losses are socialized!

So, quite apart from the shift away from "the culture of contentment" toward a "culture of *job* insecurity," the *potential* climate of financial wealth insecurity is considerable, as was noted in the aftermath of the looting of some £400 million from company pension schemes by the late Robert Maxwell. Ironi-cally, a far more industry-wide scandal than the Maxwell losses, relating to the inappropriate advice to occupational pension scheme members to switch out of such schemes into mostly worse schemes, began to surface in 1992–93: but that was dealt with as a "regulatory" rather than "criminal" issue by the regulators, who ordered firms who sold pensions to investigate whether and to whom those schemes were improperly and unlawfully sold, which they did extremely slowly until the incoming Labour government turned up the heat in the latter half of 1997. Furthermore, the climate of fraud control can be affected by a moral back-lash against "unjust enrichment," noted also in support for Draconian provisions for confiscation of the proceeds of crime (Fisse, et al., 1992; European Journal, 1997) and in the resentment expressed from 1994 onward of the vast *noncrimi-nal* salary and share option/pension benefit hikes enjoyed by the senior "Fat Cat" officials of "executive agencies" and privatized industries, which led even the Confederation of British Industries and the Institute of Directors to call for con-trols. In a context such as this, the comments of (now Lord) Justice Henry in the first Guinness trial in 1989 that the profits made by the conspirators were "too big to be honest" strike a culturally concordant note.

ATTITUDES TO FRAUD

Many of the historic surveys of attitudes to white-collar crime require revision and greater sophistication. Survey findings are important indicators of the state of public sentiments and the degree of consensus that exists about the seriousness of different crimes. However, caution should be exercised in operationalizing their results into the criminal justice sphere. Comparisons of the human damage caused by white-collar and "common" crimes have tended to infer—usually implicitly—that all corporate harms will be held to be deliberate and therefore fall within the category of severely condemned acts. Yet questions of intentionality and culpability—individual and corporate—often bedevil criminal trials (Levi, 1993; Wells, 1993). Even in some instances where the media and "the public" have "anathematized" corporations, juries nevertheless have acquitted those charged with criminal violations. The classic example of this is the U.S. trial of Ford for manufacturing the exploding Pinto motor car: the fact that (partly because of technical exclusion of relevant evidence) Ford was acquitted by the jury—who, despite jury vetting for "highly prejudiced" people, may have reflected these serious judgments discovered in surveys—goes unmentioned in many accounts (e.g., Cullen et al., 1987).

"The fraudster" is not lodged in the public imagination as some familiar "folk demon." Hooligans, drug traffickers, child batterers, and terrorists are well established in our tabloid gallery of rogues and misfits. Yet "the fraudster" is generally absent among the usual targets of press and public opprobrium, appearing only occasionally in the role of the seedy confidence trickster. Here we find stories of the heartless conman preying on the vulnerable, such as elderly people parted from their savings, and the unemployed relieved of advance "fees" paid to put them in touch with nonexistent job opportunities abroad. The fraudulent use of a charitable status to appeal to the conscience and generosity of house occupiers so that they will buy overpriced, substandard goods is not uncommon. The fraudster who cruelly hoaxes his or, more rarely, her victim is more likely to attract the censorious headline than the more-sophisticated operator who robs larger sums but from less-vulnerable victims, especially if they are overseas. For example, swindling millions by not paying value-added tax, such as in the notorious "Krugerrand" frauds of the 1970s and early 1980s, did not invite public uproar or a vituperative press. Indeed, this large-scale and long-running fraud made fortunes and reputations for many in and on the fringes of the underworld. This type of fraudster is unlikely to become a public leper as is the common conman: indeed he or she is more likely to be lionized by peers in "the underworld" or in the less-salubrious parts of "the enterprise culture," and is unlikely to be shunned by a wider public who so far demonstrate little in the way of a deep resentment for this type of criminality. The (unqualified) internal accountant who stole some £5 million from the Metropolitan Police covert operations budget over several years before being prosecuted in 1995 was viewed as something of a hero and benefactor by the inhabitants of the remote Scottish village into which he plowed much of "his" wealth, whose barony he had purchased (all British national newspapers, 20 May 1995).

Many inhabitants of the Turkish Republic of North Cyprus likewise feel indebted to Asil Nadir, currently (1999) a refugee from the English justice system, for revitalizing their local economy, irrespective of whether or not he defrauded Polly Peck's U.K. shareholders and creditors. It was a commonplace attitude in Pakistan among those interviewed by this author that BCCI was brought down because a successful Islamic bank was too threatening to Western interests. (Similar points could be made about Latin American or even some U.S. "underclass" attitudes to some of their local major drugs traffickers: my point is not that these acts harm no one but that perceptions of harm may vary widely, depending on the "trickle-down" of benefits and perceptions of victims' desserts.)

All of this has to be protected by the regulatory and, where appropriate, the criminal justice regimes, against the wholesale fabrication of accounting records. Here, transnational frauds impose a severe burden, for if the fraudsters have obtained regulatory permission (in the European Union, North America, or Australia), then the industry or taxpayers picks up the bill, but if the "fraudsters" are not members of a regulatory body—and, for example, "cold call" prospective victims from remote jurisdictions, as happens in many telemarketing frauds—then the cost falls upon the victims and there is almost certainly no insurance. In short, "fraud" is no more homogeneous than "violence" in terms of dynamics of offender-victim interactions and social status, and one should distinguish between the effects of fraud on individuals (including individual corporations) and the effects on markets.

THE EXTENT OF INTERNATIONAL FRAUD

One aspect of financial white-collar crime that was relatively neglected by Sutherland (1983) and his (mainly North American) successors has been the multijurisdictional dimension, and its implications both for prevention and for the pursuit of criminal justice and civil restitution. Cross-border marketing—both licit and illicit—has expanded apace with global financial markets, and this means that questions of venue are becoming increasingly vexing, as there are numerous potential places where "offenders" can be sued or prosecuted. BCCI was perhaps the first truly global case in which these issues were manifested. One of the reasons that this is important is that it affects victim activation of the criminal justice system and the willingness of policing organizations to take on the cases (if the loss to investigative cost ratio is small or very negative, or even, at least in the United Kingdom, if the costs are significant to very tight police fraud squad budgets).

It is very difficult to measure fraud in different countries, as Deloitte and Touche (1997) discovered when preparing their report for the European Commission, and it is more difficult still to measure *transnational* fraud. There are conceptual difficulties, and data capture is also very poor, since neither companies nor the police typically keep records of the venues through which frauds operate: a fact that would improve strategic level antifraud measures if it were changed.

It is important to appreciate transnational effects within a model of criminal organization, including:

- Financing crime
- Organizing credibility
- Organizing the deprivation of money or goods from victims
- Laundering (perhaps in stages) the proceeds of crime
- Offender place of residence

Thus, transnational involvement can occur in any one of these phases.

The apparent absence of international research on the cost or even the extent of fraud reflects the level of political and organizational interest in this subject. The Deloitte and Touche study presents only the haziest of order-of-magnitude statements, since the time scale of the research and its costing did not enable them to do more original work. A study of the costs of crime in France in 1996 (Palle and Godefroy, 1998) estimated tax evasion at 50 to 100 billion francs; store theft at 13 to 18 billion; auto theft at 9,400 million; nonfraud computer crime at 7,850 million; counterfeit products at 25 billion; and the issue of bad checks—it is an offense in France to issue a check without having the funds to pay—3.9 billion francs, with bank card fraud less than 270 million francs. (Because of the effectiveness of the chip card combined with the requirement on cardholders to enter their personal identification number, there is almost no fraud on French plastic cards.) However, this tells us little about how much of this crime was *cross-border* (see further, Levi, 1998).

International Personal Crime Surveys Relating to Fraud and Corruption

Within Europe and North America, in 1996, the proportion of the surveyed population who stated that they had been victims of consumer fraud that year ranged from 4 percent (Northern Ireland) and 5 percent (England and Wales) through 7 percent in Canada and 10 percent in the United States—although the U.S. response rate was only 40 percent, to 15 percent in Finland. The U.K. countries had separately and collectively the highest rates of reporting such frauds to the police and non-police agencies, although the United States topped the reporting to the police, with 13 percent. But in every Third World country surveyed, consumer fraud was the form of criminal victimization experienced by the highest proportion of the population, with corruption typically being the second most common (except in Jakarta, Indonesia, where it was by far the most common, being experienced by over a third of the sample: see Mayhew et al., 1997). Again, however, the data on transnationality are absent, partly because victims may have little idea about where the crimes were financed and how the funds were laundered, but also because they were not asked detailed questions about how they became victims. Those who received the now-famous Nigerian letters offering corrupt funds in exchange for an advance fee will appreciate that these are (usually) transnational, but even where British-issued credit cards are used fraudulently in France or the United States, it may not be apparent from these "trans-national" data whether the victim was in the country where the cards were stolen and used (making it not really transnational) or whether the cards had been transported out of the United Kingdom to be used abroad (making it transnational). Where land borders exist, the process is simpler still.

In 1991, a U.S. national telephone survey examined twenty-one different types of fraud, including investment and consumer fraud. Fifty-eight percent had experienced one or more lifetime victimizations (including attempts); 31 percent within the previous 12 months, of which just under half (48 percent) were successful (Titus et. al., 1995). Thus fraud is a very common experience for U.S. citizens: more so than for most other crimes. Of those fraud attempts that were successful, nearly one in ten was over $2,000, and one in five was over $500. The likelihood of actually losing money through fraud has no significant association with any demographic variables such as age, education, ethnicity, area of residence, gender, and income. Frauds that occur most often and are most likely to be successful included appliances/car repairs, fraudulent prices for goods on sale, fraudulent subscriptions, and fake charities. Telemarketing has also reached serious growth levels, with an implausibly high guesstimated level of $40 billion in North America: there, much telemarketing fraud is transnational, not just between Canada and the United States but also from Europe, since telephone calls can be redirected from whichever country has the lowest call rates, without the victim being aware that the caller is not where his or here telephone number suggests s/he is. This is merely one method in which modern technology is enhancing the capacity for international fraud victimization, the other principal one being the Internet where, hitherto, convenience has overridden any concerns about security of personal and card identity transmission.

International Corporate Fraud Surveys

Data about levels of white-collar crime in different countries are extremely patchy, and it is hard to know which cases are truly transnational (see Levi and Pithouse, forthcoming). In Australia, business crime was estimated to cost organizations A$4 to $5 billion annually. Corporate crime surveys have been conducted internationally by some accountancy firms. A 1995 survey by KPMG found that in Australia, 43 percent of business respondents had experienced a fraud during the previous twelve months, compared with 77 percent in the United States and 61 percent in Canada. In Australia, the total cost of fraud to survey respondents was A$350 million.

A later survey by KPMG found that 52 percent of companies had experienced fraud in 1995: the percentages varied, but were 79 percent in what KPMG terms "Africa" (Botswana and Malawi), 66 percent in North America, and 41 percent in Australia. Of the half of respondents who did business internationally,

26 percent had experienced what they referred to as an international fraud. It is not easy to deduce any meaning from this, but total fraud reported by respondents was over US $1 billion.

In the smaller but more detailed international sampling by Ernst & Young (Levi and Sherwin,1996), three quarters of the respondents admitted to having suffered at least one fraud in the last five years, and 40 percent of respondents had experienced more than five frauds worldwide in the previous five years: many more in the United States, South Africa, and Ireland than in the other countries surveyed. A quarter of the victims—and over a third in the United States and France—had lost over US $1 million in total over that period. Executives were asked to give details of the largest fraud they had discovered in the previous twelve months: frauds (including attempts) totaled $780 million, of which $642 million was lost and only $70 million recovered (11 percent, including insurance recoveries). The average loss from these largest frauds was $1.9 million.

CONCLUDING COMMENTS ON MEASURING AND HANDLING TRANSNATIONAL FRAUD VICTIMIZATION

Estimation problems are universal in the white-collar, corporate crime, and money-laundering arenas, even excluding the social costs of crime. Current reporting *behavior* for white-collar crime is a complex function of company policies and expectations of action, and one can no more infer that present fraud-reporting decisions represent victims' ideals than one can assume this for victims of domestic violence.

Furthermore, there is a dilemma about how one should interpret the significance of cost-of-crime data: what would be most illuminating would be more risk-based than simply annual cost data. For large corporations (and, in many respects, for individuals also) the impact of fraud depends not so much on the absolute loss but on what it would take to replenish their profits or personal wealth. (The closest practice to this is auditors' judgments about "materiality" of fraud in deciding whether or not to include it in the annual accounts, which seldom happens.) In other words, in the case of businesses, losses from fraud (and bad debt/"non-performing loans," which can actually be unrecognized fraud) logically should be set against *profits*, not just sales volume or, in the case of individuals, should be set against their disposable income and wealth. One might take this "replenishability" approach (akin to a statistical z score) also with other forms of property crime, which gives a better notion of the real costs of crime in different social groups.

Fraud upon institutions is neither a necessary nor a sufficient condition for people losing their jobs—banks, for example, cut their staff to maximize profits anyway—but the dependence on trust in the financial world is paramount, and the public sometimes need to be educated that "fraud on financial institutions" (and upon the public revenue) affects them, too. Although there is room for argument about how harmful individual cases are, and what the prosecution priorities should be—and some forms of market misconduct might be dealt with more rapidly and thoughtfully by regulators rather than by criminal courts—institutional victims deserve some protection; first, in recognition of the central and community taxes that they pay, and second, because of the substantial proportion of the population that directly and indirectly are affected by their prosperity.

A casual attitude to creeping corruption (especially that in which elites are involved) can eventually require us to take the path that the Italian magistracy did in the *mani pulite* investigations, followed more recently by the French and Japanese prosecutors (Levi and Nelken, 1996). In an age where such concern is being expressed about the decline of public morality and about the ethos of the corporate culture also, it would be wholly inconsistent for prosecution agencies such as the U.K. Serious Fraud Office to stand back and declare open season for people to rip off with impunity any company or public sector activity that did not command complete public sympathy.

Transnational frauds are not always more serious than domestic ones: one may think, for example, of corrupt dictators who steal money from their own citizens, though if one incorporates my notion of "depth of field," one usually sees that at some stage—including money-laundering and corrupt fees for contracts—there is almost invariably a transnational component in their crimes. Such depth of field can only intermittently be captured by victimization survey methods; nor is there often the kind of in-house data so evocatively analyzed in Geis' (1967) classic study of price-fixing in the electricity industry to enable us to review the transnational component in financial white-collar crime outside of those fraud and money-laundering cases prosecuted. The study of civil suits of fraud and constructive trust can throw some major insights into the international component of such crimes, but whether or not we can properly classify these as 'crime' leads us back into precisely those terminological debates that have bedeviled the study of white-collar crime since Sutherland (1983) placed it on the criminological map.[6]

This is not merely a theoretical issue, however; it is also relevant to the determination of fitness and propriety to trade in financial services. The international securities regulators coordinating body, IOSCO, would like to see more effective communication of regulatory decisions to enable other countries to make more informed risk management decisions, thereby ensuring that people such as Nick Leeson (Fay, 1996), whose fictitious commodities profits bankrupted Barings Bank, who are refused licenses to deal in securities in the United Kingdom, would find it harder to obtain licenses elsewhere. One of the effects of globalization of financial services and communications is to create a need for a New World Order if we are to combat transnational fraud and corruption risks (Blum et al., 1998). Whatever one's view of the justifications for the parallel process of combating the international illegal drugs trade, this global interdependence has profound implications for conceptions of national sovereignty and for the rights of third-party "tax haven" and "banking secrecy" countries to regard corruption, insider trading, and tax evasion as "not their *national* law's business."

ENDNOTES

1. There is no space here to discuss this in depth, but the extent to which the relevant perceptions are those of governing elites or reflect mass opinions depends on the forms of democratic expression prevailing in any given society at any given time.

2. Fukuyama is far from explicit in (not) acknowledging the apparent contradiction between the socially integrating importance of trust and the vulnerability to which this gives rise when entrusting capital to strangers, or at least to those strangers who advertise in the media, on the Internet, and, more subtly, via personal contacts in local voluntary associations and religious networks. This is precisely why confidence tricksters insinuate their way into such networks. Sometimes, international agencies such as the IMF or World Bank may "invest" in a country despite a significant risk of default, for political reasons, but private-sector lending is based on tighter risk analysis, unless underwritten by governments in the form, for example, of export credit guarantees. This affects both domestic savings and international lending.

3. This is not as simple as it seems, however. Where the suspects or the victims are in countries that are unstable, chaotic or corrupt, for example Russia during the 1990s, the actual co-operation in providing evidence for overseas jurisdictions may be difficult, whether due to misconduct or simple administrative inefficiency.

4. This has been alleged by some interviewees in respect of U.S. prosecutors in some international telemarketing fraud cases.

5. Employment in British Bankers' Association members fell by about one fifth during the 1990s, accelerated by mergers and the Asian banking crisis as well as a focus on technology rather than personal service in retail banking. There has also been a shift from full-time, permanent jobs to part-time (and female) telephone sales staff.

6. For an early conceptual review of law-breaking statistics of white-collar crime, albeit one that does not address the transnational issues, see Reiss and Biderman (1980). For a process approach to the globalization of corporate crime, see Braithwaite (1984).

REFERENCES

Benson, M. 1985. "Denying the Guilty Mind: Accounting for Involvement in White-collar Crime." *Criminology* 23:583–607.

Blum, J., Levi, M., Naylor, T., and Williams, P. 1998. *Financial Havens, Banking Secrecy and Money-Laundering* Vienna: United Nations.

Braithwaite, J. 1984. *Corporate Crime in the Pharmaceutical Industry*. London: Routledge.

British Invisibles. 1998. *The 'City' Table 1998*. London: British Invisibles.

Calavita, K., and Pontell, H. 1994. "The State and White-collar Crime: Saving the Savings and Loans." *Law and Society Review* 28(2):297–324.

Cullen, F., Maakestad, W., and Cavender, G. 1987. *Corporate Crime under Attack*. Cincinnati: Anderson.

Deloitte and Touche. 1997. *Fraud without Frontiers*. Brussels: Secretariat-General, European Commission (Justice and Home Affairs, Judicial Co-operation Unit).

European Journal. 1997. "Special Issue on Proceeds of Crime Forfeiture." *European Journal of Crime, Criminal Law and Criminal Justice* 5(3).

Fay, S. 1996. *The Collapse of Barings*. London: Richard Cohen Books.

Fisse, B., Fraser, D., and Coss, G., eds. 1992. *The Money Trail*. Sydney: Law Book.

Friedrichs, D. 1996. *Trusted Criminals*. Belmont, CA: Wadsworth.

Fukuyama, F. 1995. *Trust*. London: Hamish Hamilton.

Fukuyama, F. 1999. *The Great Disruption: Human Nature and the Reconstitution of Social Order*. London: Profile.

Gambetta, D. 1988. *Trust: Making and Breaking Co-operative Relations*. Oxford: Blackwell.

Geis, G. 1967. "The Heavy Electrical Equipment Antitrust Cases of 1961." In M. Clinard and R. Quinney, eds. *Criminal Behavior Systems: A Typology*. New York: Holt, Rinehart & Winston.

Geis, G. 1992. "White-collar crime: what is it?" In K. Schlegel and D. Weisburd, eds. *White-Collar Crime Reconsidered*. Boston: Northeastern University Press.

General Accounting Office. 1994. *Pension Plans: Stronger Labor ERISA Enforcement Should Better Protect Plan Participants*. Report to Secretary of Labor, Washington, DC: Government Printing Office.

Jesilow, P., Pontell, H., and Geis, G. 1993. *Prescription for Profit: How Doctors Defraud Medicaid*. Berkeley: University of California Press.

Levi, M. 1981. *The Phantom Capitalists: the Organization and Control of Long-Firm Fraud*. London: Heinemann.

Levi, M. 1992. "White-collar Victimization." in K. Schlegel and D. Weisburd, eds. *White-Collar Crime Reconsidered*. Boston: Northeastern University Press.

Levi, M. 1993. *The Investigation, Prosecution and Trail of Serious Fraud*. Royal Commission on Criminal Justice Research Study No.14, London: HMSO.

Levi, M. 1998. "Offender Organization and Victim Responses: Credit Card Fraud in International Perspective." *Journal of Contemporary Criminal Justice* 14(4):368–383.

Levi, M., and Nelken, D. 1996. *The Corruption of Politics and the Politics of Corruption*. Oxford: Blackwell. (Also a Special Issue of the *Journal of Law and Society*.)

Levi, M., and Pithouse, A. forthcoming. *White-Collar Crime and its Victims: the Media and Social Construction of Business Fraud*. Oxford: Clarendon Press.

Levi, M., and Sherwin, D. 1996. *Fraud—the Unmanaged Risk: an International Survey of the Effects of Fraud on Business*. London: Ernst & Young.

Mayhew, P., and van Dijk, J. 1997. *Criminal Victimization in Eleven Industrialized Countries*. The Hague: WODC, Ministry of Justice.

Palle, C., and Godefroy, T. 1998. *Les Couts du Crime. Une estimation monetaire des delinquances en 1996*. Guyancourt, CESDIP, Etudes et Données Pénales, No. 79.

Reiss, A., and Biderman, A. 1980. *Data Sources on White-Collar Law-Breaking*. Washington, DC: National Institute of Justice.

Sutherland, E. 1983. *White-Collar Crime: the Uncut Version*. New Haven, CT: Yale University Press.

Titus, R., Heinzelmann, F., and Boyle, J. 1995. "Victimization of Persons by Fraud." *Crime & Delinquency* 41:54–72.

Wells, C. 1993. *Corporations and Criminal Liability*. Oxford: Clarendon Press.

World Bank. 1997. *Helping Countries Combat Corruption: the Role of the World Bank*. Washington, DC: World Bank.

Comparative Criminology: Purposes, Methods and Research Findings

Hans Joachim Schneider

ABSTRACT: During the last three decades, comparative criminology has changed from an empirical control method into an academic discipline of its own right. Many comparative studies were conducted in the eighties and nineties, showing that the various forms of crime are to a large extent determined by the different social, economic, and political structures of countries, regions, and cultures. In addition, it can be seen that there is a connection between socioeconomic progress and the spread of crime. This is of crucial importance, since many (and in particular Asian) countries are now transforming their social structures from agricultural into industrial ones. The following article discusses the aims and methods as well as the various theories of comparative criminology. Special emphasis is given to the "criminology of liberation" movement in Latin America.

Comparative criminology is an object of soaring interest, and chapters on comparative criminology have been added to many criminological textbooks (Adler, Mueller, and Laufer, 1998, chap. 15; Voigt, Thornton, Barrile, and Seaman, 1994, part 6; Beirne and Messerschmidt, 1995, chap. 16). Comments on its problems can be found in numerous influential books and essays by Brunon Holyst (1979) and Koichi Miyazawa (1981, 1063–1083; Kühne and Miyazawa, 1991). The importance of comparative criminology is likely to increase as European unification advances and as the nations of the world become more and more interlinked. In the recent past, a comparison between crime and its exploration and control in Japan and Germany turned out promising, for in both countries, the social conditions are very much alike (Schneider 1992a: 307–321): industrialization, urbanization, mobilization, lack of raw materials and similarities between the criminal laws, criminal justice systems, and the ways in which the police and penal institutions are organized belong to their marked characteristics. Admittedly, the social structures of the two countries are also dissimilar in many respects, which is why one finds unequal crime rates as well as different crime structures and control mechanisms.

CONCEPT AND PURPOSES

At first, the term *comparative criminology* designated a method of repeating empirical group comparisons between criminals and noncriminals on the basis of the same definitions and research procedures, yet in different societies. This method was intended to reveal crime causation factors independent of society (Glueck, 1964, 304–322). Comparative criminology today regards crime, the investigation into its causes, and its control as elements in a society, and compares both them and the different societies (Christie, 1970, 40–46; Ferracuti, 1980, 129–207; Szabo, 1981, 959–981; Clifford, 1981, 1084–1102). Crime and its examination and control are seen as phenomena that develop within social, economic, and political structures (Ferdinand, 1998). These phenomena are compared and interpreted on an international scale, under the different social, economic, and political conditions of other countries, in order to gain insight into the social, economic, and political causes that lead to a massive occurrence of crime. In addition, comparative criminology tries to make use of the diverse social control mechanisms for developing more effective crime control models.

METHODS

Comparative criminology employs the following two methods:

- It compares the extent, character, stage of development, and distribution of crime in a society (objective safety situation), the attitudes of the public toward crime (subjective safety situation), and the ways in which social control was exercised within different historical periods of the same society (historical criminology) (Brantingham, 1984, 93–210).
- The objective and subjective safety situation as well as the social control mechanisms of two distinct societies at present are compared with each other (Schneider, 1992b, 5–19).

Both methods require the objective and subjective safety situation as well as the mode of social control to be seen as elements in the overall stage of development of a social system (or several systems) only. Thus it is not enough to compare crime statistics. The respective economic and social structures, styles of behavior, motivations, and values of the peoples concerned must be taken into account. Furthermore, the position of the criminal justice system in a society should not be neglected.

RESEARCH FINDINGS

The Importance of the Social Structure and of Social Control

Comparative criminology has realized that crime rates and the occurrence of certain patterns of crime depend on the social structure and on the efficacy of social control exercised in a country, region, or city. The term *social structure* summarizes a complex network of social elements (styles of behavior, values, interrelations, and institutions), which interact with a relative continuity within a superordinate framework. These elements, however, may also conflict with each other (Smelser, 1988, 103–129). If considered from a sociostructural view, the economic success of a society is of appreciable, but not essential, criminological importance. There are, for example, economically underdeveloped countries, such as India (Shrivastava, 1992, 189–207), with a low crime rate, and rich welfare states, such as Sweden (Joutsen, 1992, 23–43), which have a high crime rate. The degree of social disintegration (Clinard, Abbott, 1973) and the extent to which subcultures (Brillon, 1980) are being formed are crucial factors for the development of crime and, consequently, for the lack of its control. A socially disintegrated area is marked by the falling apart of communities and by the destruction of interhuman relationships. A criminal subculture supports and tolerates criminal values and behavior patterns. The behavior of the individual, on the other hand, is determined by the values of society. A heterogeneous society with very distinct beliefs and behavior models (necessarily) generates a great number of conflicts, which are on the one hand capable of helping that society's advancement and adding to its cultural diversity, but which on the other hand also produce favorable conditions for high crime rates.

Comparative criminology differentiates between two kinds of social control, labelled formal and informal. Formal social control is characterized by formalization through criminal legislation and explicit norms of behavior. This implies sanctions provided by the criminal law, which are intended to support these norms of behavior, and the establishment of official control organs (authorities), which produce, interpret, and apply the norms laid down in the criminal law. Informal social control consists in a system of reactions, for example advice, mockery, critique or persuasion, by which society and its subgroups (family, neighborhood, etc.) induces its members to conform to generally accepted norms of behavior. Again, two kinds of informal social control can be distinguished. External social control is achieved through imitation of or reactions (admonition or restriction for instance) to a certain behavior in social groups, i.e., the family, groups of persons of the same age, etc. Internal social control (or self-control) describes the internalization of norms and expectations of behavior through inter-action and identification with others, for example, parents or individuals of the same age, in the process of socialization. Informal social control must have a strong influence for formal social control (the criminal justice system) to work effectively.

Crime Trends, Crime Structures and Crime Control in the World

Today, comparative criminology starts out from the assumption that in each social structure there is something unique to the way in which crime and its control mani-fests itself. Moreover, it is assumed that crime and crime control change as the social structure itself changes. In order to understand the character of crime and the various control mechanisms that can be found in a certain country, it is necessary to know the history, culture, and language of that country. Anyone who wants to assess a nation's crime problem needs to observe international crime trends, which is what the United Nations have done. The first of their four "World Crime Surveys" covers the period from 1970 to 1975, the second covers the years from 1975 to 1980, the third covers those from 1980 to 1986, and the fourth covers those from 1986 to 1990 (Adler, Mueller, and Laufer, 1998, 26). The headquarters of the United Nations based their collection of data largely on the official crime statistics of its member states, i.e., on reported and officially acknowledged crime. The first two surveys show that violent crime in the world has doubled between 1970 and 1980, while property crime has tre-bled in the same period (Voigt, Thornton, Barrile, and Seaman, 1994, 571–573).

Admittedly, crime and crime control in different countries cannot be com-pared with each other by referring to police crime reports alone (Vetere and New-man, 1977, 251–267). One also has to consider the different social structures, and in particular the diverse procedures of the criminal justice systems for the fol-lowing reasons: the norms incorporated in the various penal codes are by no means identical. Besides, they are applied differently by the courts and the police of the different states; public opinion about certain crimes and their severity dif-fers; the amount of crime thought endurable by the public and the inclination to report crimes varies from country to country; different times and places produce criminal justice systems unequal in reach and efficacy. Both factors affect the probability of crime detection. In addition, the methods of obtaining data and their efficacy differ. A state in which the public is sensitive to crime, with a high inclination to report offenses, a successful criminal justice system, and effective methods of data collection may yield high statistical crime rates. The objective safety situation in that country, however, might be better than that of another country, whose people are rather indifferent to crime and whose criminal justice system and methods of data recording are not so effective. In countries of the lat-ter type, the total amount of crime is made socially visible only to a small extent.

In this respect, modern international darkfield research, i.e., the questioning of representative groups of people in different countries on their criminal victimization, is a great progress, despite methodological shortcomings (small samples and low proportions of responses) and general results. In 1989, a random choice of people over sixteen in fourteen countries were asked if they had been victimized once or even more than once in 1988 (van Dijk and Mayhew, 1993, 1–85). They were interviewed via telephone, and the survey was backed by computer technology (computer-aided phone interviewing method) (van Dijk, Mayhew and Killias, 1989). The survey yielded the following results and was backed by more recent victimization surveys (van Dijk, Block, and Ollus, 1998; Mayhew and van Dijk, 1997; van Dijk and Mayhew, 1993):

- In 1988, the risk of car theft was highest in France, the United States, Australia, England, and Wales, and lowest in Finland, the Netherlands, the Federal Republic of Germany, and Switzerland. The total of all car thefts depends on the overall number of theft-prone vehicles (cars, motorbikes and bikes) in a country (opportunity theory).

- In the same year, burglaries were most frequent in Australia, the United States, and Canada. In Europe, France, the Netherlands, and Belgium also had a great number of burglaries. In most countries, those who had their flats watched by neighbors during absence took the smallest risk of burglary (significance of informal control).

- Robberies occurred most often in Spain and in the United States. Punishable sexual assaults (rape and attempt of rape) were most frequently reported by the women questioned in the United States, Canada, Australia, and the Federal Republic of Germany. Victims of sexual assaults had the strongest wish for special help and victim treatment.

- Considering the total number of offenses, the United States, Canada and Australia had the highest victimization risk. In Europe, victimization was highest in the Netherlands, followed by Spain and Germany. Countries with a high victimization risk are characterized by a high degree of urbanization.

Crime rate and crime structure are not the only factors that depend on the different social structures in each individual country. For the form of crime control in a certain country or region, the social structure is also of great significance (Ferdinand, 1998). In Austria, an empirical survey has shown that in the east of the country, convicts were sentenced to severer penalties than in the west of the country (Burgstaller, Császár, 1985a, 1–11, 43–47; 1985b, 417–427; Stangl, 1988, 141–143). Sentencing was most lenient and liberal in the court district of Innsbruck, especially with first-time offenders, and most strict and conservative in the court district of Vienna, where severe penalties were much more common. The total amount of punishment inflicted on convicts in the court district of Vienna is twice as high as that in the court district of Innsbruck. Graz and Linz are in the middle, but with a much greater distance to Vienna than to Innsbruck.

Criminologists try to explain the different sentencing habits at Austrian courts as follows: The differences are thought to be connected with different crime structures. It is supposed that in the court district of Vienna, serious crimes are perpetrated much more often. However, these circumstances explain the different sentencing habits only partly. The facts that regional legal cultures diverge and processes of socialization and tradition in different cultures of jurists and courts vary, are also held responsible for contrasting sentencing habits (Pilgram, 1988, 63; Hauptmann, 1989, 100). Of course, this explanation is still insufficient. Apart from the various crime structures, legal cultures, and court customs, the way in which crime is formally and informally reacted to is influenced by the entire social structure of a region. Economic and demographic circumstances, for example, also determine the attitudes and values of a certain region's inhabitants.

The character of formal control in a particular country can develop in a way markedly different from that of others. An example for this can be seen in the sentences of imprisonment (without probation) recently pronounced in Germany and the United States: the number of prisoners in Germany was rising between 1970 and 1984 (with ups and downs); from 1984 onward until the beginning of the nineties, however, it has been decreasing (Statistisches Bundesamt, 1998, 5). In contrast to this, the number of accused individuals sentenced to imprisonment without probation in the United States was constantly increasing between 1972 and 1995 (U.S. Department of Justice, 1997, 528). It must be asked what the causes for such a change in the sentencing habits are. Five major theories have been conceived in order to explain the temporary transformation of sentencing habits with respect to imprisonment. None of these theories, however, is universally valid, as empirical checks have proved (Zimring and Hawkins, 1991, 119–136):

- The number of prisoners grows or decreases according to the rise or decline of crime or serious offenses, e.g., violent offenses. But a sentence of imprisonment does not only depend on the frequency or seriousness of a crime.

- The inclination of courts to pronounce more or fewer sentences of imprisonment changes in the same way as the political climate in a society does, i.e., the number of prisoners decreases if politics become more liberal. If, on the other hand, conservatism gains ground, the number of prisoners rises. This theory could not be confirmed empirically, either. Neither is there a correlation of changing political attitudes with the inclination to send offenders to prison, nor do law-and-order campaigns, the overall amount of fear of crime, or the attitude of the public toward their criminal justice system have a direct influence on this.

- The demographic development influences the number of prisoners: if risk groups grow, i.e., groups whose members have proved to be prone to delinquency, for example, male adolescents and young male adults, then the number of offenses, and thus the prison population, will also grow.

This hypothesis could not be proved empirically until now. Changes in the demographic structure create no major impact on the number of prisoners.

- The economic conditions affect the way in which courts react to crime. There seems to be some sort of relationship between the extent of unemployment and upward or downward trends with regard to the number of prisoners in penal institutions. Unemployment, however, is only one factor in the economic development. The complexity of economic factors, which influence each other mutually, makes it extremely difficult to assess their impact on the reaction of judges to crime. Here, more empirical research is needed.

- The fifth and last theory puts changes in the prison population down to the extent of illicit drug use. In most cases, the use of such drugs is a criminal offense in itself. In addition, it involves a number of other crimes (drug-related crime). Illegal drug use, according to this theory, prolongs the times prisoners spend in prisons (longer confinement) and increases their inclination to relapse into crime. Although this theory could be confirmed in parts, definite empirical proof is still missing.

There is no generally accepted explanation for the fact that in the recent past the numbers of prisoners in the Federal Republic of Germany and the United States have developed differently. Important factors are probably the different influences of criminology on the criminal justice systems of the two countries and different attitudes of the public toward criminal policy. Although criminology in the United States is more advanced than in Germany, it has—compared with Germany—even less significance for the training of jurists. The impact of criminological research findings on political parties is also slighter in the United States than in Germany. As far as crime control is concerned, political parties and the public opinion in America believe even more strongly in repressive action and the exercise of force by the state than is the case in the Federal Republic.

Crime in Developing Countries

Comparative criminology has contrasted crime in the developing countries with crime in the industrial countries. Officially acknowledged crime is a lesser problem in developing countries (Birkbeck, 1992, 115; Oloruntimehin, 1992, 167; United Nations Asia and Far East Institute for the Prevention of Crime and Treatment of Offenders (UNAFEI) and Australian Institute of Criminology, 1990). However, modern darkfield research shows that the victimization rates of developing countries are quite high (Zvekic and del Frate, 1995). Some forms of crime, property crime, for example, grow extensively, and others, such as organized crime, arise newly. Four arguments account for the comparatively low officially acknowledged crime rates in developing countries:

- Their criminal justice systems are little developed and therefore not very effective. A great proportion of all crimes, especially in the country, is treated informally and in a traditional way by tribal courts. These crimes do not enter formal records (Brillon, 1980).

- Material goods are—if compared with the situation in industrial countries —not so easily obtainable, and thus, by contrast, easier to control (opportunity theory).

- In the developing countries, delinquent juvenile subcultures have evolved only to a small extent; the youth is well integrated into society (Hartjen, 1998; Hartjen and Kethineni, 1996; Hartjen and Priyadarsini, 1984).

- Conflict situations that arise within communities are settled by regulative mechanisms founded on custom and tradition (Villavicencio Terreros, 1989, 90–102).

The Development of Society and Crime

It can be observed in many developing countries that economic and social progress is accompanied by the spreading of crime (Brillon, 1986, 23–37; Clinard, 1983, 597–601; Schneider, 1990, 65–86). This is why the United Nations tried to elucidate this problem criminologically. At their 7th Congress on Crime Prevention and the Treatment of Offenders in Milan in 1985, the experts of the United Nations passed the "Milan-Plan of Action" (United Nations, 1986, 2, 3), which says: "Progress in itself does not cause crime. Unbalanced and inadequately planned progress, however, contributes to the development of crime." Comparative criminology tries to find out what "unbalanced and inadequately planned sociostructural development" means. Seven theories have been put forward in order to describe the emergence of crime and change of social control as a result of economic and social advancement.

A theory based on the critical observation of crime statistics suggests that crime grows only apparently while social and economic advances are being made. It is assumed that people's sensitivity to crime increases while the economy and society of a country are developing. The manner of social control changes. Informal social control by societal groups becomes more and more ineffective; the criminal justice system, on the other hand, becomes more important. Since the people's alertness to crime is heightened, they report more offenses to the police. It is further assumed that while the whole country is making progress, the criminal justice system is developing its abilities to work more effectively; it records more crimes and solves more cases. The people are becoming increasingly aware of their crime problem. According to this theory, it is not really the crime rate that is growing, but the darkfield of undetected and unreported crime that is diminishing. The importance of formal control, or the criminal justice system, is rising at the same time as economic and social progress is being made.

The economic theory has been worked out on the basis of empirical research done in Indonesia, Korea, Thailand and the Philippines (UNAFEI, 1988). In these countries, the social and economic changes are taking place so rapidly that it is impossible to build an adequate infrastructure. Moreover, accompanying education and social assistance programs are lacking; medical care is insufficient; city and family planning have not taken satisfactory effects. Since metropolitan centers grow much too fast due to unrestrained migration, overpopulated and socially disintegrated areas (slums, ghettos) emerge, in which an adequate infrastructure is wanting. There, deviant values and styles of behavior evolve from criminal subcultures. Simultaneously, rural areas become increasingly deserted for want of qualified agricultural workers. Their infrastructure is falling into decay because of underpopulation.

According to the opportunity theory (United Nations, 1988), the higher standard of living, resulting from economic and social progress, is responsible for a situation in which opportunities for committing crimes multiply. In the view of its supporters, property offenses are increasing strongly because material goods have become more easily obtainable and socially visible. Besides, it has become more difficult to safeguard these goods, since people in metropolitan centers lead more isolated lives. This makes it easier to commit crimes, whereas on the other hand, the criminal justice system has greater difficulties to find proof against offenders, thus having also greater problems to convict them. Moreover, the fact that material goods are easily available lowers their value in the minds of the people. Potential victims, therefore, do not take appropriate care of their belongings.

The demographic theory is linked to the juvenile subculture theory (Hartjen, 1986, 39–57; Friday, 1980, 100–129; Ferdinand, 1980, 279–296). While economic and social progress is being made, there is also a greater number of children being born. The number of young people in developing countries is disproportionally high. Offenders are relatively often found among youths, adolescents, and young adults. Scholars in favor of the demographic theory claim that this change in the age structure accounts at least partly for the growth of crime in times of economic and social advancement. Moreover, juvenile subcultures, with their characteristic lifestyles, value notions, and idols, are spreading in such times. In an agricultural society, the transition from youth to adulthood is relatively smooth. In an advancing society with an increasing industrial production, an expanding telecommunication network, and a growing service industry, however, youth is an independent period of life. It is entirely directed toward general and professional education, and toward the preparation for adult life. On the one hand, young people in this stage of life are in psychic and social respects still dependent on their elders, but in physical respect, on the other hand, they are already the equals of their elders. From this discrepancy follows a status-insecurity and a juvenile identity crisis. Young people alienate themselves from adult society; they cannot identify sufficiently with adults, for they follow youth idols in sports and popular music. Status-insecurity and juvenile identity crisis make young people prone to delinquency, and this proneness is supported by juvenile subcultures.

The theory of subjectively perceived disadvantage (deprivation theory) (Shelley, 1981) ascribes rising crime in times of economic and social development to the "revolution of raising expectations": While economic and social changes are taking place, the social structure is changing, too. People at the top and at the bottom of society are subjected to this change. There are winners and losers. In the course of advancing development, the general conditions of life are improving. However, people's expectations with regard to their standard of living become so tremendously high that they cannot be actually fulfilled. Thus winners and losers alike see themselves at a disadvantage. The losers feel disadvantaged because they have experienced a positive setback; the winners feel disadvantaged because they think they have not risen high enough. The subjective feeling of being at a disadvantage causes frustration, which, according to the deprivation theory, results in a greater inclination to commit crimes.

The theory of subjectively perceived disadvantage is closely linked with modernization theory. According to this theory, the modernization of societies in developing countries is responsible for increasing crime and changing crime structures in these countries (Shelley, 1986, 7–27). The modernization process, so the theory suggests, originates from economic and technological progress. It exists in a more elaborate social structure, i.e., the norms of social organization are getting more complex. This development is thought to result in a growing social tension, more social conflicts, and a decline in social harmony. Supporters of the modernization theory claim that the spreading of crime can only be kept within certain limits if the society in question succeeds in amalgamating traditional values and styles of behavior with modernizing tendencies (Buendia, 1989).

Finally, the theory of anomie and synnomie tries to explain the growth of crime and juvenile delinquency in the course of social change (Adler, 1983). It is based on the assumption that a changing economic and social structure produces a change in the lifestyle and in the value and behavior system of a society. Industrialization, urbanization, and mobilization (including motorization) are thought capable of causing anomie, i.e., the collapse of value systems, disorientation, social disintegration, and the falling apart of communities. The theory further suggests that the coexistence of traditional and progressive lifestyles and norms of behavior in a changing society necessarily contributes to a growing number of conflicts that can be neither subdued nor solved by force. Thus society and its social groups have to learn to settle such conflicts peacefully. If, according to the theory, these conflicts destroy social groups or individual personalities because they have been internalized, but not socially digested, then anomie or a decline of values will be the consequence. If, on the other hand, a peaceful psychic and social digestion of these conflicts succeeds, a renewed psychic and social cohesion or agreement on values (synnomie) might be achieved.

All seven theories offer insights into various aspects of crime development in context with economic and social progress. The approach based on crime statistics and the anomie and synnomie theory are best suited for describing the influence of economic and social advancement on crime development and crime control.

Developed Industrial Countries with Low Crime Rates

Comparative criminology has investigated which developed industrial countries have low crime rates and for what reasons. Switzerland and Japan can be taken as examples. Switzerland has a relatively low crime rate (Clinard, 1978; Adler, 1983, 15–23; critical of this: Balvig, 1988). Nonetheless, alcohol abuse, suicide, and white-collar crime are widespread in Switzerland. The reasons for the low crime rate are seen in the following sociostructural conditions: Thanks to water and energy resources, which are available almost everywhere, the Swiss industry is evenly distributed over the whole country. Conurbations with socially disintegrated areas have not developed. The Swiss have retained their autonomy and their community spirit, despite industrialization and urbanization (they have not become dependent on state administration as in Sweden). Thus in Switzerland, crime is kept at a low level by means of a vigorous (voluntary) informal control. The Swiss youth is well integrated into society.

In contrast with comparable industrial countries, Japan has a low crime rate, in spite of her organized crime (Shikita and Tsuchinya, 1992). The reasons for this are to be found in some peculiarities of Japan's social structure (Katoh, 1992, 79–80; Kühne and Miyazawa, 1991; Westermann and Burfeind, 1991, 25–48; Adler, 1983, 95–105): The Japanese society is very homogeneous; its value notions and styles of behavior are extraordinarily similar and uniform. The individual is group-oriented. He or she is ashamed if he or she has brought disgrace over his/her group, family, school, or team. The group feels responsible for the behavior of its members. Moreover, socially disintegrated areas have scarcely emerged; the staff communities of the companies have rather substituted the village communities in industrialized and urbanized areas. The Japanese criminal justice system is deeply respected and very popular with the people. The community as a whole supports *its* police; the police seeks closeness to *its* community. The people participate in *their* criminal justice system (Schneider, 1992a, 1987, 261–268).

Criminology of Liberation in Latin America

The term *criminology of liberation*, which is related to the philosophy of liberation and the theology of liberation, stands for a critical criminological movement. It has developed in some Latin-American countries during the seventies and opposes the traditional established clinical criminology. While the latter confirms the existing social order and tends to react repressively to conflicts (only the individual or the law-breaker is guilty), the critical criminology of liberation challenges the social order. It shows sympathy for deviant fringe groups and doubts the existence of a moral basis for punishment by demanding punishment through the state to be restricted (society is guilty) (Garcia-Pablos de Molina, 1988, 134). This critically oriented movement of criminology starts out from the assumption that traditional criminology is unable to give an adequate theoretical explanation for the phenomenon of crime and that the solutions suggested by traditional criminology are of little use in law enforcement. The critical criminologists are seeking a method that does not put the individual in the center of criminological scrutiny, but which facilitates research into society and its power structures, thereby transforming microcriminology into macrocriminology. Since traditional control systems are thought to have failed, critical criminology's basic concept aims at restructuring society rather than at a renewed adaptation of offenders to society (Manzanera, 1997, 448, 451).

Among the various books that formulate a theory of criminology of liberation, Lola Aniyar de Castro's is the most comprehensive one (1987). According to her theory, the new critical movement deliberately wants to separate itself from traditional criminology, which is seen as a mere instrument intended to maintain existing class and power structures in Latin America. It is their declared aim to uncover and condemn these power structures, which are protected by a highly repressive social control system. Moreover, critical criminologists want to draw attention to the legitimizing function of traditional criminology and aim at conceiving a new critical theory of social control for Latin America, a theory for the benefit of the masses of the Latin-American people, who by its help shall be freed from exploitation and suppression, from the influence of the powerful on education, religion, the arts, and justice and criminology. Criminology of liberation supports the following two main theses:

- Crime evolves in Latin America because of the impoverishment of the people, resulting from the exploitation of raw materials by the international monopolistic capital (Bergalli, 1982). Criminal justice systems serve the supremacy of propertied and privileged minorities, who co-operate with the international monopolistic capital (del Olmo, 1984). These groups push the lower classes of the people to the brink of society (they are marginalized and criminalized) (Manzanera, 1997, 439–454; Birkbeck, 1986/87, 9–38). It is necessary, therefore, to restrict the use of the penal code as an instrument of power (Zaffaroni, 1989).

- The mass media and schools and universities, being tools of the privileged minorities, fulfill a legitimizing function in order to maintain existing class and power structures. Only the children of the powerful receive a good education from the school system, which thus stabilizes the existing class system and power structures for the future. Crime prevention programs and imprisonment of offenders are ideological instruments that serve the purpose of suppressing the lower classes (Aniyar de Castro 1987).

The deliberate rejection of traditional criminology, which developed in Europe, and which was taken over by Latin American countries, is, together with the wish to create a new, specifically Latin-American criminology, a manifestation of the constant effort to become independent from the Old World and to develop autonomously. Admittedly, one has to remark critically that marxism, on which the criminology of liberation is founded, also comes from Europe. The demand for a liberating criminology can be put down to the social structures of many Latin-American countries, which are determined by undemocratic political structures, and which put great parts of the population at an economic disadvantage.

Comparative criminology and the criminology of liberation agree in so far as both see the causes of crime not only in the offender's personality but also in social structures and power structures. Moreover, both draw attention to crimes committed by persons who are in powerful positions, i.e., to economic, environmental, and political crime.

The criminology of liberation differs from comparative criminology in that it is specifically geared to Latin American social and economic conditions and cannot be transferred to North America or Europe. Even for Latin America, the criminology of liberation describes only a partial truth, which is one-sided and ideologically simplified.

One has to be critical of the criminology of liberation, for its advocates rely too much on mere speculation and undertake too little empirical research (Garcia-Pablos de Molina, 1992, 204–206). Their moralizing, utopical, and philosophically abstract criminal policy demands a complete socialist restructuring of Latin-American society, which must be regarded with great doubt after the failures of socialist experiments in Eastern Europe and Russia.

What can be learned from the criminology of liberation is that not only do the character and proliferation of crime or the shape of social control depend on a country's social structure, but that the social structure also influences criminological theory and research to a large extent.

Characteristics of Social Structures in Countries with Low Crime Rates

By means of comparative criminology, it was found out that social structures of societies with low crime rates are mainly marked by three traits:

- Informal social control by social groups, i.e., the family, the neighborhood, schools, work, and leisure groups, plays a major role. Crime prevention and crime control is not solely left to the criminal justice system and to the institutions of formal control. Instead, people have developed a sense of responsibility for themselves. The burden of crime control does not rest on an almighty state alone, keeping its citizens dependent and unable to further their self-reliance; what can rather be met with is social commitment, founded on one's own initiative. The state makes only little use of its monopoly of power, for during the process of civilization, the people have also become increasingly sensitive to institutionalized power (van Dijk 1989, 191–204).

• Public spirit is of crucial importance in countries whose social structure is characterized by low crime rates. Communities could either maintain themselves or develop newly, as the commercial and industrial communities in Japan exemplify. There are almost no socially disintegrated areas or ghettos in big cities or industrial centers. These disintegrated areas with high crime and delinquency rates are characterized by communities falling apart, disrupted interhuman relationships, and inhabitants who tolerate crime and, in particular, juvenile delinquency. Children and youths in these areas learn delinquent behavior in playgroups or juvenile groups without supervision, from the time of their earliest infancy onward. Such juvenile subcultures, with their specifically youth-related behavior patterns, models, and value notions have, on the contrary, not developed in areas whose social structures are marked by little crime and delinquency. There, youths and adults have not become alienated from each other. The young are fairly well integrated into adult society.

• Criminal justice systems are highly respected in social structures with low crime rates. The police are seeking close contact with the community. Citizens do honorary work in order to support the police, courts, or prisons. Prison subcultures with their own criminal value notions could not evolve because offenders are—if possible—supervised and treated within the community. Sentences of imprisonment are rarely pronounced. Offenders who nonetheless have to serve an appropriate time are kept in small or medium-size prisons, where they are supervised and employed by well-trained staff that is also sufficient in number. For that reason, a "professional" class of criminals committing the greater part of all crimes and, in particular, the very serious crimes, could not develop. Criminals who serve a long time in big prisons, and who are not adequately supervised and employed due to small and badly trained prison personnel, learn even more criminal techniques, attitudes and value notions from their fellow prisoners. Long stays in such prisons cause the prisoner to develop a criminal identity.

CONCLUSION

Humans are individuals, but at the same time also social beings. Thus initiative of one's own and social commitment have to be related meaningfully. Crime originates from individual and social processes. The German sociologist Ferdinand Tönnies has compared the two terms *Gemeinschaft* (community) and

Gesellschaft (society) (1887, repr. 1979), a distinction that might point the way ahead in this respect. The community is characterized by intimate and emotional human relations. Loose, rational, and pragmatic relations between humans are, on the other hand, typical for society. The community has low crime rates. Society, in contrast, brings about many offenses, since in society far more interhuman conflicts arise. These conflicts are on the one hand necessary for society's advancement, but can on the other hand also cause its destruction if they no longer can be controlled socially. The individual does not perish within a community. The social ties rather enable the individual to develop fully. Being a member of a community and being at the same time responsible for oneself do not exclude, but rather presuppose, one another. The destruction of social ties and the growing isolation of individuals in an amorphous mass make people susceptible to crime and victimization. Anomie, the collapse of value systems or the absence of norms, makes it easier for crime to grow. Synnomie, the cohesion of and agreement on values, inhibits the development of crime (Adler, 1983, 157). In destroyed communities, children and youths learn delinquency, for delinquent and crime-friendly styles of behavior, attitudes, and value notions predominate in socially disintegrated areas. Behavior is shaped not only through the reaction patterns of reward and punishment (learning by trial and error) but also by the ability to learn symbolically, i.e., by imaginatively taking somebody else's place, thereby sharing this person's experience. Humans also adopt roles, attitudes, and value notions that have been set as examples in the course of social processes. They can be motivated by an imaginative anticipation of future consequences (intensified expectation). In self-regulating processes, humans select those stimuli that influence them. These stimuli are then arranged and transformed. They even influence their own behavior by individually produced stimuli and imagined consequences. In processes of self-approval or self-disapproval, they reward or punish themselves. Through their actions, humans create the external circumstances that in later course again react upon their actions. They learn by mere habituation (and thus without rewarding mechanisms) and by having become convinced that a certain behavior is right or necessary. Delinquent and criminal behavior is learned if such behavior is more strongly supported than socially conforming behavior, or if it is defined as being desirable in a social group, or if it is at least justified and thus made acceptable. Of course, delinquency and crime also develop if the socialization of children and youths (the learning of socially conforming behavior) has been unsuccessful.

BIBLIOGRAPHY

Adler, F. 1983. *Nations not Obsessed with Crime.* Littleton, CO: Fred B. Rothman.

Adler, F., Mueller, G.O.W., and Laufer, W.S. 1998. *Criminology*, 3rd ed. New York:McGraw-Hill.

Aniyar de Castro, L. 1987. *Criminología de la Liberación.* Maracaibo: Universidad del Zulia.

Balvig, F. 1988. *"The Snow-White Image. The Hidden Reality of Crime in Switzerland."* Oxford: Norwegian University Press.

Beirne, P., and Messerschmidt, J. 1995. *Criminology*, 2nd ed. San Diego: Harcourt Brace.

Bergalli, R. 1982. *Crítica a la Criminología*. Bogotá: Temis Libreria.

Birkbeck, C.H. 1992. Crime and Control in Venezuela. In H.-G. Heiland, L.I. Shelley, H. Katoh, eds. *Crime and Control in Comparative Perspectives*. New York: Walter de Gruyter.

Birkbeck, C.H. 1986/87. "Clase Social y Criminalizacion Diferencial: Un Estudio Empirico Referido al Area Metropolitana de Merida." *Revista Cenipec* 10:9–38.

Brantingham, P.J., and P. Brantingham. 1984. *Patterns in Crime*. New York: Macmillan.

Brillon, Yves. 1986. "Les Incidences du Développment sur la Criminalité Africaine." *Annales Internationales de Criminologie* 24:23–37.

Brillon, Yves. 1980. *Ethnocriminologie de l'Afrique Noire*. Paris: Vrin/Presses de l'Université de Montreal.

Buendia, H.G., ed. 1989. *Urban Crime: Global Trends and Policies*. Hong Kong: United Nations University.

Burgstaller, M., and Császár, F. 1985a. "Zur regionalen Strafenpraxis in Österreich." *Österreichische Juristen-Zeitung* 40:1–11, 43–47.

Burgstaller, M., and Császár, F. 1985b. Ergänzungsuntersuchungen zur regionalen Strafenpraxis. *Österreichische Juristen-Zeitung* 40:417–427.

Christie, N. 1970. "Comparative Criminology." *Canadian Journal of Corrections* 12:40–46.

Clifford, W. 1981. "Vergleichende Kriminologie: Afrika, Asien und Australien." In H.J. Schneider, ed. *Die Psychologie des 20. Jahrhunderts*. vol. XIV. Auswirkungen auf die Kriminologie. Zurich: Kindler.

Clinard, M.B. 1983. Crime in Developing Countries. Pp. 597–601 in S.H. Kadish, ed. *Encyclopedia of Crime and Justice*. vol. 2. New York: Free Press.

Clinard, M.B. 1978. *Cities with Little Crime. The Case of Switzerland*. New York: Cambridge University Press.

Clinard, M.B., and Abbott, D.J. 1973. *Crime in Developing Countries*. New York: John Wiley.

van Dijk, J.J.M. 1989. "Penal Sanctions and the Process of Civilization." *International Annals of Criminology*. 27:191–204.

van Dijk, J.J.M., Block, C. Ollus, N. 1998. "The Crime Situation in Europe and North America." In K. Kangaspunta, M. Joutsen, and N. Ollus, eds. *Crime and Criminal Justice in Europe and North America 1990—1994*. Helsinki: HEUNI.

van Dijk, J.J.M., and Mayhew, P. 1993. "Criminal Victimization in the Industrialized World: Key Findings of the 1989 and 1992 International Crime Surveys." In A.A. del Frate, U. Zvekic, and J.J.M. van Dijk, eds. *Understanding Crime: Experiences of Crime and Crime Control*. Rome: UNICRI.

van Dijk, J.J.M., Mayhew, P., and Killias, M. 1990. *Experiences of Crime across the World. Key Findings from the 1989 International Crime Survey*. Deventer, Boston: Kluwer.

Ferdinand, T.N. 1998. "Comparative Criminology Done Well." Pp. 469–481 in H.D. Schwind, E. Kube, H.H. Kühne, eds. *Essays in Honor of Hans Joachim Schneider*. New York: Walter de Gruyter.

Ferdinand, T.N. 1980. "Delinquency in Developing and Developed Societies." In D. Shichor and D.H. Kelly, eds. *Critical Issues in Juvenile Delinquency*. Lexington, MA: D.C. Heath.

Ferracuti, F. 1980. "Possibilities and Limits of Comparative Research in Criminology." Pp. 129–207 in: H.H. Jescheck and G. Kaiser, eds. *Vergleichung als Methode der Strafrechtswissenschaft und der Kriminologie*. Berlin: Dunker and Humblot.

Friday, P. 1980. "International Review of Youth Crime and Delinquency." In G.R. Newman, ed. *Crime and Deviance*. Beverly Hills: Sage Publications.

García-Pablos de Molina, A. 1992. *Criminologia*. Valencia: Tirant Lo Blanch.

García-Pablos de Molina, A. 1988. *Manual de Criminología: Introducción y Teorias de Criminalidad*. Madrid: Espasa Calpe.

Glueck, S. 1964. Wanted: A Comparative Criminology. In S. and E. Glueck, eds. *Ventures in Criminology*. London: Tavistock.

Hartjen, C.A. 1998. "Investigating Youth-Crime and Justice Around the World. Pp. 523–538 in H.D. Schwind, E. Kube, and H.H. Kühne, eds. *Essays in Honor of Hans Joachim Schneider*. New York: Walter de Gruyter.

Hartjen, C.A. 1986. "Crime and Development: Some Observations on Women and Children in India." *International Annals of Criminology* 24:39–57.

Hartjen, C.A., and Kethineni, S. 1996. *Comparative Delinquency: India and the United States*. New York: Garland.

Hartjen, C.A., and Priyadarsini, S. 1984. *Delinquency in India*. New Brunswick, NJ: Rutgers University Press.

Hauptmann, W. 1989. *Psychologie für Juristen—Kriminologie für Psychologen*. Munich: R. Oldenbourg.

Holyst, B. 1979. *Comparative Criminology*. Lexington, MA: D.C. Heath.

Joutsen, M. 1992. "Developments in Delinquency and Criminal Justice: A Nordic Perspective." Pp. 23–43 in H.G. Heiland, L.I. Shelley, and H. Katoh, eds. *Crime and Control in Comparative Perspectives*. New York: Walter de Gruyter.

Katoh, H. 1992. "The Development of Delinquency and Criminal Justice in Japan." Pp. 69–81 in H.G. Heiland, L.I. Shelley, and H. Katoh, eds. *Crime and Control in Comparative Perspectives*. New York: Walter de Gruyter.

Kühne, H.H., and Miyazawa, K. 1991. *Kriminalität und Kriminalitätsbekämpfung in Japan*. 2nd ed. Wiesbaden: Bundeskriminalamt.

Manzanera, L.R. 1997. *Criminología*. 12th ed. Mexico: Editorial Porrúa.

Mayhew, P., and van Dijk, J.J.M. 1997. *Criminal Victimization in Eleven Industrialized Countries*. London: Documentatiecentrum/Home Office.

Miyazawa, K. 1981. "Vergleichende Kriminologie: Japan." Pp. 1063–1083 in H.J. Schneider, ed. *Die Psychologie des 20. Jahrhunderts*. Vol. XIV. Auswirkungen auf die Kriminologie. Zurich: Kindler.

Olmo, R. del. 1984. *America Latina y su Criminología*. 2nd ed. Mexico: Siglo.

Oloruntimehin, O. 1992. "Crime and Control in Nigeria." Pp. 163–188 in H.G. Heiland, L.I. Shelley, and H. Katoh, eds. *Crime and Control in Comparative Perspectives*. New York: Walter de Gruyter.

Pilgram, A. 1988. "Entwicklungen der Kriminologie in Österreich seit dem Wiener Weltkongreß 1983." Pp. 57–81 in G. Kaiser, H. Kury, and H.J. Albrecht, eds. *Kriminologische Forschung in den 80er Jahren*. Freiburg i.Br.: Max Planck Institut.

Schneider, H.J. 1992a. "Crime and its Control in Japan and in the Federal Republic of Germany." *International Journal of Offender Therapy and Comparative Criminology* 36:307–321.

Schneider, H.J. 1992b. "Life in a Societal No-Man's Land: Aboriginal Crime in Central Australia." *International Journal of Offender Therapy and Comparative Criminology* 36:5–19.

Schneider, H.J. 1990. "The Impact of Economic and Societal Development on Crime Causation and Control." In United Nations Asia and Far East Institute for the Prevention of Crime and Treatment of Offenders (UNAFEI) (ed.), Report for 1989 and Resource Material Series No. 37. Tokyo: UNAFEI.

Schneider, H.J. 1987. *Kriminologie*. New York: Walter de Gruyter.

Shelley, L.I. 1986. "Crime and Modernization Reexamined." *International Annals of Criminology* 24:7–27.

Shelley, L.I. 1981. *Crime and Modernization*. Carbondale, IL: Southern Illinois University Press.

Shikita, M., and Tsuchinya, S. 1992. Crime and Criminal Policy in Japan. New York: Springer.

Shrivastava, R.S. 1992. "Crime and Control in Comparative Perspectives. The Case of India." Pp. 189–207 in H.G. Heiland, L.I. Shelley, and H. Katoh, eds. *Crime and Control in Comparative Perspectives*. Berlin, New York: Walter de Gruyter.

Smelser, N.J. 1988. "Social Structure." In N.J. Smelser, ed. *Handbook of Sociology*. Newbury Park: Sage Publications.

Stangl, W. 1988. *Wege in eine gefängnislose Gesellschaft*. Vienna: Österreichische Staatsdruckerei.

Statistisches Bundesamt, ed. 1998. *Strafvollzug—Anstalten, Bestand und Bewegung der Gefangenen 1997*. Stuttgart: Metzler/Poeschel.

Szabo, D. 1981. "Vergleichende Kriminologie: Grundlagen." Pp. 959–981 in H.J. Schneider, ed. *Die Psychologie des 20. Jahrhunderts*. Vol. XIV: Auswirkungen auf die Kriminologie. Zurich: Kindler.

Tönnies, F. 1979. *Gemeinschaft und Gesellschaft* (1887). Darmstadt: Wissenschaftlliche Buchgesellschaft.

U.S. Department of Justice, ed. 1997. *Sourcebook of Criminal Justice Statistics 1996*. Washington DC: Government Printing Office.

United Nations, ed. 1988. Report on the Interregional Preparatory Meeting for the Eighth United Nations Congress on the Prevention of Crime and the Treatment of Offenders on Topic I: "Crime Prevention and Criminal Justice in the Context of Development: Realities and Perspectives of International Co-Operation." Vienna: United Nations.

United Nations, ed. 1986. Seventh United Nations Congress on the Prevention of Crime and the Treatment of Offenders. New York: United Nations.

United Nations Asia and Far East Institute for the Prevention of Crime and the Treatment of Offenders (UNAFEI), ed. 1988. The Empirical Study on Development and Crime Prevention. Tokyo: UNAFEI.

United Nations Asia and Far East Institute for the Prevention of Crime and the Treatment of Offenders (UNAFEI), Australian Institute of Criminology, eds. 1990. Crime and Justice in Asia and the Pacific. Tokyo: UNAFEI/Australian Institute.

Vetere, E., and Newman, G. 1977. "International Crime Statistics: An Overview from a Comparative Perspective." In *Abstracts on Criminology and Penology* 17:251–267.

Villavicencio Terreros, F.A. 1989. Mecanismos Naturales de Regulación Social en Comunidades Andinas y Amazonicas Peruanas. *Criminalia* 55:90–102.

Voigt, L., Thornton, W.E., Barrile, L., and Seaman, J.M. 1994. *Criminology and Justice*. New York: McGraw-Hill.

Westermann, T.D., and Burfeind, J.W. 1991. Crime and Justice in Two Societies: Japan and the United States. Pacific Grove, CA: Brooks/Cole.

Zaffaroni, R.E. 1989. *En Busca de las Penas Perdidas*. Buenos Aires: Ediar.

Zimring, F.E., and Hawkins, G. 1991. *The Scale of Imprisonment*. Chicago: University of Chicago Press.

Zvekic, U., and Frate, A.A. del. 1995. *Criminal Victimization in the Developing World*. Rome: UNICRI.

VARIOUS FORMS OF CRIME

When a Crime is not a Crime: Economic Transformations and the Evolution in Bankruptcy Law

Susan Will
and
Kitty Calavita

It has been more than fifty years since Tappan[1] warned that criminologists had been distracted by a new "fashion," according to which subjective criteria were replacing legal definitions of crime as a basis for research. Arguing against this trend in "white-collar criminology," he insisted that criminologists must confine their study to those who have been convicted of a particular offense. Otherwise, "[t]he emancipated criminologist reasons himself into a cul-de-sac," where the absence of objective yardsticks "invites individual systems of private values to run riot. . ."[2] Tappan had set up a dichotomy. Either we rely on the criminal justice system to determine who is criminal, or we resort to hopelessly subjective value judgments of social injury.

Sutherland[3] responded by pointing out that if we ground our studies on the biases of the criminal justice system, we perpetuate those biases and lose all claims to science. As Geis[4] put it, "Sutherland got much the better of th[e] debate by arguing that it was what the person actually had done in terms of the mandate of the. . .law, not. . .how the criminal justice system responded to what they had done, that was essential to whether they should be regarded as criminal offenders." It was one of Sutherland's major contributions to underline the folly of relying on criminal convictions to define the population of offenders, given the differential ability of higher-status individuals to evade the criminal justice system. Indeed, Sutherland's insight launched several decades of research into the class biases of the criminal justice system and the differential treatment of white-collar criminals, not only confirming the theoretical merit of his proposals but putting to rest the notion that white-collar crime research was a "fashion."

But, less attention has been given to another one of Sutherland's core postulates. As he explained in *White Collar Crime*, the preferential treatment of corporate offenders is derived from at least three factors. First, judges and other high-status legal personnel identify with white-collar offenders, whose social standing is similar to their own and who are hence reluctant to view them as criminal. Second, these offenders have substantial resources with which to mount formidable legal defenses. Finally, and most important here, *laws themselves are formulated in such a way as to exclude much white-collar behavior from the category of crime*. This last factor has been largely neglected by most white-collar crime scholars, who have chosen to focus on the class bias of detection and prosecution rather than on the ability of corporate actors to influence the law itself, probably in an effort to avoid the danger that Tappan had pointed out so long ago. That is, by confining their analyses to behavior that the law has categorized as criminal, and focusing on the class bias of *implementation*, white-collar criminologists avoid altogether the potentially subjective question of how "socially injurious" behavior is classified in the first place. But, this strategy leaves relatively unexplored one of Sutherland's central insights.

This chapter draws on the white-collar crime tradition originated by Sutherland and so prolifically and charismatically recharged by Geis,[5] and indirectly takes up the challenge posed by Tappan. Rather than attempting to answer the question of whose values should define what we call "criminal" (a question that itself leads into an intellectual "cul de sac"), we instead provide an illustration of the process to which Sutherland referred: shifting legal definitions of criminality in response to corporate power. Specifically, we show how bankruptcy—once considered a criminal offense punishable by death—has been decriminalized and destigmatized *in tandem* with its use by corporate actors and its central place in the new "casino economy" of finance capitalism.[6] In so doing, we provide confirmation for Sutherland's proposition that white-collar crime is less frequent than street crime in part because of the class bias of the laws themselves. And, by focusing on the ways in which historical definitions of criminality vary—rather than engaging in a normative debate about which behaviors are more socially injurious—we expose the limitations of the dichotomy constructed by Tappan and neutralize concerns about the injection of "private values" into the analysis.

HISTORICAL OVERVIEW OF BANKRUPTCY LAW

Falliti sunt deceptores et fraudores

(Bankrupts are deceivers and frauds)[7]

Under Roman law, the approach to bankruptcy was straightforward. When debtors were unable to pay their debts, their goods were sold and failure to pay off the remainder of the debt meant that a person could be sold into slavery, put in prison, or even executed.[8] The Code of Hammurabi prescribed that insolvent debtors and often also their kinsmen be sold into slavery to pay off their obligations;[9] the Twelve Tables of Rome decreed that debtors who failed to reimburse their creditors be cut in pieces or sold beyond the Tiber.[10]

Bankruptcy law in Medieval Europe was directed at the pursuit and punishment of those who committed what was considered an intentional criminal act.[11] It was during this period that the term bankruptcy, derived from the "custom of breaking the bench (*banca rupta*) of a banker or a tradesman who had absconded with the money or goods of his creditors," originated in the northern Italian city-states.[12] The first English bankruptcy statute, passed in 1543, was a criminal law directed at preventing fraud against creditors and was punishable by imprisonment or worse. The law was unambiguous: The bankrupt's failure to pay for goods and services received constituted theft, and was dealt with accordingly.[13]

By the eighteenth century in England, the emphasis on punishment slowly began to wane, as the burgeoning international trade that brought unprecedented wealth to England and its merchants was subject to extensive losses from piracy and shipwrecks. The resulting increase in business failures, combined with creditors' realization that punishing debtors did nothing to improve their own financial positions and in fact decreased the likelihood of repayment, paved the way for a reconsideration of the focus on punishment.[14] In addition, the state, prizing its share of the wealth from these ventures, was more interested in devising ways to encourage risk and generate capital than in penalizing failure. As a result, the goal of English bankruptcy law was gradually, and at first tentatively, transformed from punishment to a rational distribution of assets and payment of debts.[15] Despite an increasing leniency for bankrupt merchants and entrepreneurs during this period, small debtors and individual consumers remained subject to harsh criminal penalties for insolvency.[16]

Bankruptcy law in the United States in the earliest years consisted of a hodge-podge of laws borrowed from England, fragmented across the various states, and with an uneven focus on punishment and restitution. Creditors generally had the exclusive power to force debtors into bankruptcy, a fate that often brought with it the shame and hardship of debtors' prison. By the end of the nineteenth century, it had become clear that a national bankruptcy policy was critical.[17] The experience of the distressed railroads was illustrative. By the late nineteenth century, victims of a changing economy, increased competition, heavy debt, and new technology, many of the nation's railroads were on the brink of failure, and the absence of a federal bankruptcy law made them susceptible to seizure by individual creditors—a fate that neither the railroad barons nor the federal government welcomed.

In response to such financial dilemmas, a young lawyer from Saint Louis, John Torrey, drafted bankruptcy legislation in 1890 that was finally signed into law in 1898.[18] Besides explicitly linking creditors' interests and their debtors' ability to reorganize, this law for the first time in the United States defined bankruptcy primarily as a financial condition, or an economic "state of affairs."[19] The focus of the law was not on penalties but on providing business with mechanisms with which to secure relief from debt and to survive their insolvency.

The Chandler Act of 1938 formally endorsed such restructuring and vastly simplified it. A Depression-era scholar[20] explained:

> . . .the chief interest of the Nation lies in the continuance of a man's business and the conservation of his property for the benefit of creditors and himself, and not in the sale and distribution of his assets among his creditors. . .Forced stoppage of a business. . .constitutes loss to the Nation at large, as well as to individual debtors and creditors.

Under the Chandler Act, the goal of bankruptcy reorganization was to limit disruption to the nation's economic life by allowing firms to continue to operate despite their paper insolvency. Partial employment, partial salaries, and partial payment on debts were all viewed as preferable to dismantling a firm altogether, particularly during this period of devastating depression.

FROM FRAUD TO MANAGEMENT TOOL: THE BANKRUPTCY REFORM ACT OF 1978

Between World War II and the mid-1970s, despite an expanding economy, bankruptcy filings increased by more than one thousand annually. While the majority of these were individual consumer bankrupcies, some, like that of Penn Central Railroad in 1970, were headline news.[21] Dimancescu[22] argues that Congress used a few celebrated large cases—for example, Penn Central, and the financial difficulties facing Chrysler and New York City—to change bankruptcy law as it applied to corporations. The very size of these cases caused alarm, and the number of creditors, suppliers, and employees potentially impacted by their failure was staggering. In response to the perception that Chapter 10 of the Chandler Act, providing for business reorganizations, was cumbersome and expensive, Congress passed the Bankruptcy Reform Act of 1978. The reform made a number of changes in the jurisdictions and authority of bankruptcy judges and the procedures employed in filing. More important, however, were its radical substantive changes. Specifically, the Act revised the chapters governing business reorganizations and introduced the revolutionary concept of "equity insolvency."

Arguing that Chapter 10 was invoked too late in a business insolvency to provide a real opportunity to restructure and survive, the new Chapter 11 permitted corporate debtors to declare bankruptcy *before* they were actually insolvent, based on projections that their *future* liabilities might exceed their assets. This concept of equity insolvency not only was the final step in de-criminalizing and de-stigmatizing bankruptcy (at least as it applied to corporations), but it changed the very definition of bankruptcy.[23] If the Chandler Act in 1938 had established bankruptcy as a simple economic condition or "state of affairs"—insolvency—the Reform Act of 1978 went one step further, decoupling bankruptcy from the condition of insolvency altogether. Now, bankruptcy was not only destigmatized and not criminal, but it was actually a desirable legal status for some businesses.

As Delaney documents in his award-winning book, *Strategic Bankruptcy*, Chapter 11 came to be used by corporations to free themselves from bothersome labor contracts, liability suits, and unprofitable divisions that negatively impacted, or were projected to in the future, their balance sheets. Examples of such strategic bankruptcies include Eastern and Continental Airlines, which were the result of labor-management struggles; Public Services of New Hampshire, which was building the Seabrooks nuclear power plant at the time of the Chernobyl accident; and Johns Manville, the target of huge tort liabilities related to their asbestos production.[24]

An explosion in the number of business bankruptcies followed the passage of the Bankruptcy Reform Act.[25] By 1981, the rate of business filings was four times the annual rate in each of the preceding twenty-five years,[26] and by 1982 the rate equalled that reached in 1933, in the midst of the Great Depression. And, use of Chapter 11 continued to escalate, as well as the size of the firms declaring bankruptcy. Between 1988 and 1992, thirty-five firms with assets of at least a billion dollars each sought bankruptcy protection.[27] In the last year for which complete data are available, 1997, there were 54,993 bankruptcy filings by businesses—over 10,000 more than in 1980.

One of the earliest and most famous cases involving equity insolvency was the bankruptcy of Johns Manville Corporation. Manville, along with several other companies, manufactured or used products that contained asbestos. Hailed for its lifesaving fire-retardant quality, asbestos had an insidious side, as its tiny fibers were found to cause chronic lung disease and cancer. Tens of thousands of people—many of them workers for Manville—were exposed to the potentially fatal asbestos fibers, and began filing and winning lawsuits against Manville in 1971. In 1976, there were 159 such liability suits, and by 1982 they were being filed at a rate of 6,000 a year.[28] When Manville's liability insurance refused to cover the expenses, it filed for bankruptcy protection against future claims—in spite of reported earnings of almost $2 billion a year.[29]

Prior to filing, corporate officials and bankruptcy attorneys met to determine their strategy. In the spring of 1981, corporate managers restructured the company to distance the bulk of the corporation from the asbestos problem.[30] Central to their strategy was to form a new parent corporation—the Manville Corporation—that conducted no business other than to own stock in five subsidiary companies. The Johns-Manville Corporation—one of the five subsidiaries—became the repository for all the corporation's asbestos-mining and manufacturing operations, and a separate trust was set up to handle all future claims.[31] The purpose behind this restructuring was clear; Manville's management intended to insulate the rest of the corporation from the financial impact of asbestos litigation.

The primary legal problems that Manville and its lawyers faced were not only how to deal with present claims, but more importantly how to handle claims that were expected to arise in the future. Without the ability to "put a fence around" the problem of future asbestos claims, bankruptcy would provide only temporary relief, not a solution to Manville's long-term problems. Establishing a trust and channeling future claimants to it, Manville attorneys were able simultaneously to reorganize through bankruptcy and to protect long-term viability by ensuring that future tort payments be limited and, at least as important, handled in a routine and predictable manner. The Manville restructuring accomplished several things. It reinforced the notion that a business does not have to be insolvent to file for bankruptcy; it provided a mechanism with which to protect a company from its liabilities; and, it *increased* corporate value. In short, it helped turn bankruptcy into a strategic management tool. Bankruptcy was now an *alternative* to insolvency, not a response to it. It was not long before other corporations followed suit. In fact, many of the attorneys who were involved in the Manville bankruptcy went on to represent other corporate clients in bankruptcy court in the mid-1980s, expanding on the groundwork laid by Manville. "Bankruptcy protection" had now fully lived up to its nomenclature, as bankruptcy served to shield businesses from their liabilities and protect their assets. As each new bankruptcy progressed, it became clear to other businesses and their lawyers that this was a valuable way to circumvent a host of knotty problems.

BUYOUTS AND BUST-OUTS:
BANKRUPTCY IN THE CASINO ECONOMY

Among those problems was the question of how to avoid insolvency and ruin as a consequence of unsuccessful speculation with the increasing range of new financial instruments and devices that proliferated in the late twentieth century economy. While Johns Manville's bankruptcy had hinged on tort liabilities derived from its *manufacturing* activity, a plethora of new bankruptcies were used as a hedge against risk in speculative enterprises.

Although speculation and finance had always played an important role in capitalist economies, until the second half of the twentieth century profits had come primarily from the manufacture and distribution of tangible goods such as clothing, food, iron, machinery, etc. By the second half of the twentieth century, as profit margins declined in manufacturing, the U.S. economy moved from industrial capitalism to a postindustrialist finance capitalism where profits were derived from ever-more-complex speculation and investment schemes. Even corporations that were previously engaged in manufacturing increasingly replaced production with speculative activities as the primary source of profit.[32] French economist and Nobel Prize winner, Maurice Allais, highlights the magnitude of this shift from an economy based on the circulation of goods to one circulating money itself, pointing out that "more than $400 billion is exchanged every day on the foreign exchange markets, while the flow of commercial transactions is only about $12 billion."[33]

With greater profits now derived from "fiddling with money"[34] than from production, or even services, investors have turned in greater and greater numbers to paper entrepreneurism.[35] In this "casino," they gamble in the commodities, stock, and real estate markets, and use magical devices such as junk bonds to finance leveraged buyouts (LBOs) and derivatives to reap huge returns on their investments. Excessive speculation is financed by *ex nihilo* credit, and debt-financing has become a way of life.[36]

By using leverage—debt—profits can increase dramatically. If one can realize a $30 profit from a $100 investment, a profit of $300 on a $1000 investment is that much better, even if it means borrowing $900 at ten percent interest. The down side is that not all bets pay off, and many of the most dramatic failures of the 1980s and 1990s—including the savings and loan debacle, the Orange County insolvency, and the Long-Term Capital Management hedge fund collapse—have been the result of debt-leveraged speculation gone awry. The epidemic of leveraged buyouts (LBOs) beginning in the 1980s provides an excellent illustration of the logic of debt-financed investment and the role of bankruptcy in cushioning investors from the negative impacts of their risk. Indeed, as we will see, in the context of LBOs, bankruptcy itself was turned into a tool for profit.

The ideal target of an LBO, or takeover, is an undervalued, publicly traded company with a large cash reserve. In this case, an acquirer can buy all the equity in the target company at a price that is significantly higher than its market price, using borrowed funds and the target company's own assets for collateral. Thus the target company assumes substantial responsibility for repayment of the debt incurred to purchase the company's stock. The company in effect buys itself, but the title is in the acquirer's name. Assuming an ideal target company with plentiful assets and an undervalued stock, acquirers can make large profits, as can the stockholders and creditors. Between 1981 and 1988, bank loans to finance leveraged buyouts increased twenty-fold from about $1.5 billion to $34.1 billion.[37]

As ideal targets for takeovers became increasingly difficult to find, greater risks were taken and less care given to the financial well-being of the target company, and soon investors—with little at risk personally—were over-leveraging their purchases. Once the assets of the target company had been depleted, it could file for bankruptcy protection or, as was often the case in the heyday of the 1980s buyout craze, other speculative acquirers could be found to purchase the gutted company, in what was essentially a pyramid scheme. Stockholders made a hefty profit at the expense of the bought-out company and its unsecured creditors. The arrangement bears an uncanny resemblance to what in other contexts would be called a "fraudulent conveyance."[38] The Wieboldt Stores Inc. buyouts provide a dramatic illustration of this logic.

Wieboldt was a 12-store chain in the Chicago area with over 4,000 employees in the early 1980s.[39] In 1982, it was experiencing financial problems when the Trump brothers (no relation to Donald Trump) purchased 30 percent of its stock for $5 per share. The company, even though already heavily in debt and on the verge of bankruptcy, was effectively purchased using its own (already heavily encumbered) assets as collateral. Windfall profits were made, as shareholders reaped the benefits of turning a would-be bankruptcy into a lucrative sale. When the heavily debt-burdened company continued to falter, it was taken off the Trumps' hands three years later by the WSI Acquisition Corporation, which paid them $13.5 million a share. In three years, the Trumps and other shareholders had made a hefty $8.50 per share profit for this company, which was losing money by the day and heavily in debt.[40] When the Wieboldt Company eventually had to file for bankruptcy protection in 1986, the bankruptcy trustee, on behalf of its creditors and the Wieboldt estate, argued that the Trumps and 118 others had engaged in a "pre-bankruptcy transfer" that effectively constituted a fraudulent conveyance. In effect, they contended that the Trumps and the other shareholders withheld payment to Wieboldt's unsecured creditors and avoided shouldering the burden of bankruptcy by signing over the assets of the company as collateral for its repurchase. As one observer put it, "They [Wieboldt's controlling shareholders] were bailing themselves out in advance of Wieboldt's fall, because they knew they'd lose money" if it went into bankruptcy.[41] Lawyers for the Trumps countered that their clients were protected under the "good faith transfer for value" clause in Section 550 of the Bankruptcy Code.[42] With the legal issues at a stalemate, a settlement was eventually negotiated that allowed the Trumps to emerge with an unscathed reputation and left the legal issues in limbo.

Several points are important here. First, speculators in the 1980s and 1990s were able to turn insolvency itself into a profit making device in the form of LBOs. Finding a company on the verge of bankruptcy and financing its purchase with its own assets, then reselling it to others with the same intention, was a pyramid scheme that worked remarkably well for a while and for some investors.[43] In essence, it meant that insolvency did not necessarily lead to bankruptcy as long as there were others with the same speculative mentality who were willing to buy you out for a profit.[44] Only the last in line had to actually declare the long-pending bankruptcy, and this could be relatively painless under Chapter 11 reorganization protections. In some cases, there were even signs that partnerships and agreements among the parties allowed for the spreading around of profits and risks in the event of bankruptcy.[45]

Second, the destigmatization of bankruptcy is thus complete. Not only is bankruptcy no longer criminal, nor is it used only as a shield against *losses*, as in the strategic bankruptcies discussed by Delaney[46] and described above. In the case of LBOs and other such speculative devices, what is effectively a bankruptcy—or at least insolvency—can actually be used to turn a *profit*. Indicative of the prevailing corporate culture, a cottage industry of lectures, books, and seminars teaching eager executives and their attorneys how to "profit from bankruptcy" emerged in the 1980s.[47]

Finally, these LBOs and the bankruptcy-for-profit formula they utilize are strikingly similar to what are called bust-outs by organized crime, and what has been dubbed elsewhere "collective embezzlement."[48] Bust-outs by organized criminals involve the buying of a legitimate business and looting it of its assets. Similarly, collective embezzlement, a term coined by Calavita, et al. to describe the activities of some savings and loan operators in the 1980s, refers to the systematic siphoning off of assets by management from their own company for personal gain, usually leaving the company in ruin. Using Wheeler and Rothman's terminology, the corporation subjected to collective embezzlement is thus both weapon *and* victim.[49] Despite their apparent similarity to bust-outs and fraudulent conveyances, BYOs of insolvent companies, financed with collateral from those companies, are not in themselves illegal even if they result in an entirely predictable bankruptcy, and courts have rarely exacted penalties even in the most egregious cases.

ECONOMIC ELITES, LAW, AND THE DEFINITION OF CRIME

It is beyond the scope of this essay to determine the precise mechanisms through which bankruptcy has been transformed from a crime punishable by death to a "state of affairs" to, finally, a way for astute management and high-rolling investors to enhance profits. What is apparent is that these shifts follow closely transformations in the economic structure and the ventures of economic elites that correspond to those transformations. As mercantile and early capitalist activities in seventeenth-century England enhanced the Crown's wealth, bankruptcy laws were increasingly drawn so as not to penalize risk taking or discourage entrepreneurship. By the early twentieth century in the United States, the concept of corporate reorganization was introduced, and as the casino economy of late capitalism opens wide its doors, bankruptcy—at least as applied to corporations and large investors—not only has lost its stigma but is applauded as smart business.

A few contemporary scholars have studied specific historical periods that are considered economic watersheds to examine how emerging economic elites forge alliances with lawyers and political leaders to transform the legal system. Michael Tigar and Madeleine Levy,[50] for example, trace the shift from feudalism to capitalism in England and France from the eleventh through the nineteenth centuries. Documenting the active role of the emerging bourgeoisie in shaping the form and content of the law to accommodate their commercial needs and facilitate their enterprises, Tigar and Levy coined the term *jurisprudence of insurgency* to refer to the process whereby the existing legal system is transformed altogether over time through relatively incremental changes.[51] Substantive changes discussed by Tigar and Levy include the introduction of the legal concepts of free contract and private property, and a variety of civil and criminal rights.

Similarly, Sklar[52] and Horwitz[53] link economic, political, and legal transformations in the United States from the revolutionary period through the 1960s. While Sklar concentrates on the formation of monopoly capitalism and the rise of corporate culture from 1890 to World War I, Horwitz's two volumes emphasize the role of lawyers and courts in the *de facto* lawmaking process. Despite their differences, each of these authors uses close historical analysis to reveal the multiple connections between the needs of shifting economic elites over time and transformations in the legal system to embrace those needs.

Others have focused their analytical lens on specific laws and their relationship to the interests of economic elites. For example, William J. Chambliss, in his classic work on the invention of the concept of vagrancy in fourteenth-century England, documents the connection between this legal invention and the tight labor market and rising wages following the bubonic plague, which had decimated 50 percent of the labor force.[54] Jerome Hall similarly traces the broadening of the concept of theft in fifteenth-century Europe to the development of mercantilism, and its further expansion in the eighteenth century as trade and early capitalist endeavors flourished (at the same time that bankruptcy law began to soften):

> Growth [in the concept of theft] in the eighteenth century is so accelerated that it protrudes conspicuously from the pattern of the whole course of the criminal law. . .It is in this century that one comes upon the law of receiving stolen property, larceny by trick, obtaining goods by false pretenses, and embezzlement.[55]

This analysis of the transformation of bankruptcy from a criminal act to an investor's device and management tool, as feudalism and mercantilism give way to industrial capitalism and, finally, paper entrepreneurism, follows in this socoiolegal tradition. It is interesting to point out that while much of the literature cited above focuses on the criminalization of activities considered detrimental to the interests of economic elites (such as theft and vagrancy), bankruptcy provides an illustration of the reverse process—the de-criminalization of a condition endemic to an economic system based on capital investment and speculation. As one bankruptcy lawyer told the first author, "If you are going to have an entrepreneurial capitalist economy, you got to have a release valve. You can't encourage people to try and then throw them into jail for failing."[56]

That the transformation of bankruptcy law reflects shifts in the economic structure and corresponding elite interests is corroborated by two additional points. First, and perhaps most tellingly, is the *selective* nature of the decriminalization of bankruptcy. In eighteenth-century England when bankruptcy law first began to shift its focus from punishment to restitution, small debtors continued to receive harsh criminal penalties.[57] Today, consumer debtors and small businesses are still penalized for their failures, even as corporations are lauded for their inventive reorganizations to escape financial obligations. A few contemporary studies reveal sharp distinctions in the ways bankruptcy law responds to debtors.

For example, Seron[58] concludes that bankruptcy court works to the benefit of wealthier debtors and large companies who bring "business type" cases. She contends that consumer bankruptcies are managed in a routinized, boilerplate manner, while complex corporate bankruptcies are given great time and care. Others have similarly pointed out that representation of bankrupts tends to be routine and unimaginative except in the largest and most lucrative cases.[59]

The Bankruptcy Code itself makes distinctions between the liquidation that most individual and small business bankruptcies entail (Chapter 7) and the reorganization procedures with strict repayment plans for individuals on one hand (Chapter 13), and the generous restructuring allowed large investors and corporations in Chapter 11, on the other. The bankruptcy reform bills now before Congress would dramatically increase these distinctions. Largely in response to powerful credit card interests, Congress is considering making it more difficult for individuals to obtain bankruptcy protection and establishing a rigid and uniform means test for repayment of individual debts, while the generous corporate restructuring provisions in the law would remain unaffected.[60] Contesting the flagrant inequalities in the reforms that seem destined to pass this year, bankruptcy expert Douglas Baird[61] was to the point: "A new bankruptcy law that provides a fresh start to our businessmen but denies it to our widow is indecent."

The second clue that the shift in legal definitions of bankruptcy reflects corporate interests, rather than any intrinsic or objective shifts in the nature of bankruptcy itself, has to do with the fact that the decriminalization of bankruptcy—and its current status as a celebrated management tool—is occurring *in tandem* with what appears to be increasing similarities between the corporate use of bankruptcy and behaviors that in other contexts are defined as criminal. As discussed earlier, bankruptcy is now used intentionally by corporations such as Johns Manville to protect their assets from those who might have a claim to them, a transparently deliberate act of "withholding" that in earlier periods would have been considered the most egregious of offenses. Similarly, LBOs and other techniques of avoiding the transfer of assets to creditors bear a close resemblance to fraudulent conveyance, as some creditors' attorneys and bankruptcy trustees have taken pains to point out.[62] The point here is that there is nothing inherent in contemporary bankruptcy behavior that renders it less morally repugnant than in the past; if anything, the corporate use of bankruptcy has come ever closer to the margins of what in other contexts are considered intentional acts of fraud.

DISCUSSION

Geis, Meier, and Salinger[63] summarize one of Sutherland's main postulates: "White-collar crime indicates the distribution of power in our society. An examination of the statute books shows what kinds of corporate and occupational acts have come to be included within the criminal code and regulatory laws and what kind go unproscribed." The dangers inherent in questioning why certain apparently injurious behaviors are not proscribed by the criminal code, while less harmful behavior is proscribed, have been highlighted by Tappan and others.[64] Most importantly, how does one determine what is more or less injurious without resorting to subjective value systems and undermining the scientific rigor of one's analysis? In part probably because of such troublesome questions, white-collar crime scholars have focused almost exclusively on the differential enforcement of street crime and suite crime, rather than the prior question of differential influences in the lawmaking process.

This chapter takes up this latter question, with a specific focus on bankruptcy law. Avoiding the normative issue of whether or not bankruptcy *should* be penalized, we demonstrate that historically it *has been*, and that shifts in the definition of bankruptcy as a criminal act correspond to transformations in the economic system and concomitant needs of the economic elite. Bankruptcy is a valuable forum in which to examine this question, since it is an arena in which economic realignments tend to be exposed. Although many economic innovations may be conceived elsewhere, bankruptcy court is where legally sanctioned reconstruction or death occurs. It is a site where changes in the law facilitate (or inhibit) economic and social changes, and shifts in the economic and social environment recursively mirror modifications in the law.

While we have shown that bankruptcy has been decriminalized over time, this is not to say that certain behaviors surrounding bankruptcy are not defined as fraudulent. A range of activities associated with bankruptcy still constitute crimes, for example, the formation of bankruptcy rings that milk and churn assets from debtors' estates. Even here, however, the ability to shape the law to one's own interests through the use of innovative lawyers can transform what is ostensibly a criminal act into a smart business strategy. In McBarnet's study of tax evasion, she asked rhetorically, "If law was a 'material to be worked on,' was it possible to manipulate law and legal institutions to achieve the same goals as crime—escaping legal prohibitions or requirements—without risking penalties or stigma?"[65] As she reveals, aggressive and motivated lawyers can shield their corporate clients from the impact of any "disadvantageous law" through "careful manipulation of activities to fall just outside the law's ambit."[66]

We hope that this essay may contribute to our understanding of the influence of white-collar and corporate actors in the lawmaking process, and thus advance a neglected area of white-collar crime research. At the same time, our essay clearly highlights the commonalities between the fields of white-collar criminology and the sociology of law, traditions that have long shared some underlying premises and paradigms but have, for whatever reason, rarely intersected.

Among the questions that remain unanswered here, and that may be the focus of future research, are issues that relate to *intra-class* differences in the ability to influence law. In many of the cases discussed above, both the debtors *and* the creditors were powerful white-collar and corporate actors. If harsh penalties were inflicted in the fifteenth century for bankruptcy, this was no doubt in part because of the lower status of most bankrupts—who by definition were destitute—relative to their creditors. In the contemporary period, however, corporate entities who file for bankruptcy protection or who trade insolvency for profit in an LBO, may leave a number of powerful institutional creditors in their wake. Preliminary evidence suggests that the largest creditors, such as banks and other lending institutions, are generally able to minimize their losses in bankruptcy court.[67] Nonetheless, the dramatically improved position over time of institutional debtors *vis-a-vis* their creditors, as reflected in transformations in bankruptcy law, might be a productive avenue for further research. Such work might further enrich our knowledge of the precise mechanisms through which law reflects prevailing economic interests, and advance what remains a relatively undeveloped aspect of Sutherland's theory of white-collar crime.

ENDNOTES

1. Paul W. Tappan, "Who Is the Criminal?" *American Sociological Review* 12 (1947): 96–102.

2. Ibid., 97, 100.

3. Edwin Sutherland, *White Collar Crime* (New York: Dryden, 1949). See also Edwin Sutherland, "Is 'White Collar Crime' Crime?" *American Sociological Review* 10 (1945):132–39.

4. Gil Geis, "White-Collar Crime: What Is It?" in *White-Collar Crime Reconsidered*, edited by K. Schlegel and D. Weisburd (Boston: Northeastern University Press, 1992), 36.

5. Gil Geis, "The Heavy Electrical Equipment Antitrust Cases of 1961," in *Criminal Behavior Systems*, edited by M.B. Clinard and R. Quinney (New York: Holt, Rinehart and Winston, 1967), 139–50; Gil Geis, *White-Collar Criminal: The Offender in Business and the Professions* (New York: Atherton, 1968); Gil Geis, "Criminal Penalties for Corporate Criminals," *Criminal Law Bulletin* 8 (1972): 277–92; Gil Geis, *On White-Collar Crime* (Lexington, MA: Lexington Books, 1982); Gil Geis, "White-Collar and Corporate Crime," in *Major Forms of Crime*, edited by R. Meier (Beverly Hills: Sage, 1984); Gil Geis, "White-Collar Crime: What Is It?"; Gil Geis and Joseph Dimento, "Should We Prosecute Corporations and/or Individuals?" in *Corporate Crime: Contemporary Debates*, edited by F. Pearce and L. Snider (Toronto: University of Toronto Press, 1995), 72–86.

6. Anthony Bianco, "The Casino Society," *Business Week*, 16 September 1985, 78–90.

7. Quoted in Israel Treiman, "A History of the English Law of Bankruptcy," Doctoral Dissertation, Faculty of Law, Oxford University (1927), 5.

8. Kevin Delaney, *Strategic Bankruptcy: How Corporations and Creditors Use Chapter 11 to their Advantage* (Berkeley: University of California Press, 1992).

9. Louis Edward Levinthal, "The Early History of Bankruptcy Law," *University of Pennsylvania Law Review* 66 (1918):230.

10. Doug Henwood, "Behind the Bankruptcy Boom: Failures in the System," *Nation* 255, 5 October 1992:345+.

11. Israel Treiman, "Acts of Bankruptcy: A Medieval Concept in Modern Bankruptcy Law," *Harvard Law Review* 52 (1938):194.

12. Ibid., 189.

13. Harvey R. Miller and Erica M. Ryland, *The Development of Bankruptcy and Reorganization Law in the Courts of the Second Circuit of the United States* (New York: Matthew Bender, 1995), 192–193.

14. Lawrence M. Friedman and Thadeus F. Niemira, "The Concept of the 'Trader' in Early Bankruptcy Law," *St. Louis University Law Journal* 5 (1958):233.

15. Delaney, *Strategic Bankruptcy*, 17.

16. Miller and Ryland, *The Development of Bankruptcy and Reorganization Law*, 196.

17. Three earlier attempts to secure federal bankruptcy laws—1800, 1841, and 1867, had been repealed soon after their enactment.

18. Dan Dimancescu, *Deferred Future: Corporate and World Debt and Bankruptcy* (Cambridge, MA: Ballinger, 1983), 24.

19. Charles Warren, *Bankruptcy in United States History* (New York: Da Capo Press, 1935).

20. Ibid., 144.

21. Chairman of the Commission on Bankruptcy Laws of the United States, Harold March, claimed that although Penn Central's collapse directed attention to the inadequacies of the Chandler Act and that the Commission was established thirty-three days later, the two events were largely independent of each other (United States Senate, Hearing before the Subcommittee on Improvements in the Judicial Machinery, "The Bankruptcy Reform Act," 94th Congress, 1st Session, 1975).

22. Dimancescu, *Deferred Future*, xiv-xv.

23. Ibid., 43.

24. The provision also made it possible for some individuals to extricate themselves from binding contracts. For example, recording stars and other artists whose career has taken off subsequent to a big hit may use the reorganization provision in bankruptcy law to nullify contracts entered into before their rise to fame. This application of the law is being re-considered under the bankruptcy reform initiatives currently under discussion in Congress (Justin Pritchard, "Hatch, Union in Harmony on Bankruptcy Reform Bill, *"Los Angeles Times*, 23 June 1999, C1).

25. Donald L. Bartlett and James B. Steele, *America: What Went Wrong?* (Kansas City, MO: Andrews and McMeel, 1992), 68; Delaney, *Strategic Bankruptcy*, 27; Laurence H. Kallen, *Corporate Welfare: The Megabankruptcies of the 80s and 90s* (Seacaucus, NJ: A Lyle Stuart Book, Carol Publishing, 1991).

26. Dimancescu, *Deferred Future*, 10.

27. Edward I. Altman, *Corporate Financial Distress and Bankruptcy: A Complete Guide to Predicting and Avoiding Distress and Profiting from Bankruptcy*. 2nd ed. New York: John Wiley & Sons, 1993), vii. While some corporations that have filed mega-Chapter 11's have failed—such as Braniff, Pan Am, and Eastern Airlines—many more are considered successes. Continental is still flying, as are America West and TWA, and Johns Manville and Texaco are still in business.

28. Paul Brodeur, "The Annals of Law: The Asbestos Industry on Trial, III—Judgement," *New Yorker*. 24 June 1985:37

29. Delaney, *Strategic Bankruptcy*.

30. Kallen, *Corporate Welfare*, 232.

31. Brodeur, "The Annals of Law," 41.

32. Rudolf Hilferding, *Finance Capital: A Study of the Last Phase of Capital Development*, translated by Morris Watnick and Sam Gordon (London: Routledge & Kegan Paul, 1981).

33. Quoted in James Bates, "Columbia S&L Puts Its Loss at $226.3 Million," *Los Angeles Times*, 26 October 1989, D1.

34. Calvin Trillin, "Zsa Zsa's Crowd Knows Why the Rich and Famous Deserve the Capital-Gains Cut," *Los Angeles Times*, 4 October 1989, B7.

35. Robert B. Reich, *The Next American Frontier* (New York: Times Books, 1983); David Harvey, *The Condition of Postmodernity: An Enquiry into the Origins of Cultural Change* (Cambridge, MA: Blackwell, 1990), 163; Anthony Bianco, "The Casino Society," *Business Week*, 16 September 1985, 81.

36. Bennett Harrison and Barry Bluestone, *The Great U-Turn: Corporate Restructuring and the Polarizing of America* (New York: Basic Books, 1988), 25; Kallen, *Corporate Welfare*, 39; Harvey, *The Condition of Postmodernity*; Dimancescu, *Deferred Future*, 7.

37. George Anders, *Merchants of Debt: KKR and the Mortgaging of American Business* (New York: Basic Books, 1992), 61.

38. Fraudulence conveyance laws have been in use since 1570 in England to curtail the hiding of assets by debtors. The law was designed to protect creditors from dishonest debtors who signed over their assets for a nominal sum to a friendly third party, until after the creditor had given up trying to collect on the debt.

39. Brian Bremner, "Fees Gut Bankrupt Wieboldt," *Crain's Chicago Business*, 28 March 1988, 1.

40. Of course not all such deals pan out for their investors, which is why the shares that are sold to help purchase these takeovers are called "junk bonds." They are essentially underwriting the purchase of "junk." As those enticed by Michael Milken's sales pitch and hard-ball tactics in the 1980s discovered, not all junk is gold. See Stephen Pizzo, Mary Fricker, and Paul Muolo, *Inside Job: The Looting of America's Savings and Loans* (New York: Harper Collins, 1991) for the role of junk bonds in the savings and loan debacle.

41. Quoted in Janet Key, "Wieboldt's Sues to Reverse Buyout," *Chicago Tribune*, 19 September 1987, C7.

42. Alyssa A. Lappen, "Seller Beware," *Forbes*, 22 January 1990, 43. See David G. Epstein, *Bankruptcy and Other Debtor-Creditor Laws* (St Paul, MN: West, 1995).

43. Many also benefitted from the tax breaks associated with their purchase of an insolvent company.

44. Thus, insolvency and bankruptcy have been definitively decoupled: Just as in strategic bankruptcy, the declaration of bankruptcy does not mean a company is insolvent—or even close—so it is in the case of leveraged buyouts that instead of spelling bankruptcy, insolvency may lead to windfall profits.

45. See Pizzo et. al., *Inside Job*, 385–408.

46. Delaney, *Strategic Bankruptcy*.

47. Altman, *Corporate Financial Distress and Bankruptcy*.

48. Kitty Calavita, Henry N. Pontell, and Robert H. Tillman, *Big Money Crime: Fraud and Politics in the Savings and Loan Crisis* (Berkeley: University of California Press, 1997).

49. Stanton Wheeler and Mitchell Lewis Rothman, "The Organization as Weapon in White Collar Crime," *Michigan Law Review* 80 (1982): 1403–1426.

50. Michael E. Tigar and Madeleine R. Levy, *Law and the Rise of Capitalism* (New York: Monthly Review Press, 1977).

51. Borrowing Tigar and Levy's turn of phrase, the case under consideration might be called the "jurisprudence of insolvency."

52. Martin Sklar, *The Corporate Reconstruction of American Capitalism, 1890–1916: The Market, the Law, and Politics* (Cambridge: Cambridge University Press, 1988).

53. Morton Horwitz, *The Transformation of American Law, 1780–1860* (Cambridge, MA: Harvard University Press, 1977) and *The Transformation of American Law, 1870–1960: The Crisis of Legal Orthodoxy* (New York: Oxford University Press, 1992).

54. William J. Chambliss, "A Sociological Analysis of the Law of Vagrancy," *Social Problems* 12 (1964):67–77.

55. Jerome Hall, *Theft, Law, and Society*, 2nd ed. (Indianapolis: Bobbs-Merrill, 1952):34–35.

56. Interview, October 1996.

57. Miller and Ryland, *The Development of Bankruptcy and Reorganization Law. . .*, 196.

58. Carroll Seron, *Judicial Reorganization* (Lexington, MA: D.C. Heath, 1978), 117.

59. David T. Stanley and Marjorie Girth, *Bankruptcy: Problems, Process, Reform* (Washington, DC: The Brookings Institute, 1971), 3.

60. Lisa Hill Fenning, "Bankruptcy Reform Bills Would Make Things Worse," *Los Angeles Times*, 21 June 1999, B5.

61. Quoted in Robert Scheer, "Congress Is on Wrong Track on Bankruptcy," *Los Angeles Times*, 29 June 1999, B7.

62. Allan H. Ickowitz and Geoffrey D. Genz, "Lender Fraud: Courts Sift through LBO Suits," *National Law Journal*, 30 November 1992, A27+; Andrew Blum, "Lawyers Sued in Bankruptcy," *National Law Journal*, 26 June 1995, A6.

63. Gilbert Geis, Robert F. Meier and Lawrence M. Salinger, *White-Collar Crime: Classic and Contemporary Views*. 3rd ed. (New York: Free Press, 1995).

64. Tappan, "Who is the Criminal?" Ernest Burgess, "Comment," *American Journal of Sociology* 56 (1950):32–33; Robert G. Caldwell, "A Re-Examination of the Concept of White-Collar Crime," *Federal Probation* 22 (1958):30–36; Leonard Orland, "Reflections on Corporate Crime: Law in Search of Theory and Scholarship," *American Criminal Law Review* 17 (1980): 501–20.

65. Doreen McBarnet, "Tax Evasion, Tax-Avoidance, and the Boundaries of Legality," *The Journal of Human Justice* 3 (1992):58.

66. Doreen McBarnet, "Law and Capital: The Role of Legal Form and Legal Actors," *International Journal of the Sociology of Law* 12 (1984):232.

67. Susan Will, *Economic Transformation, Legal Innovation, and Social Change: A Case Study of Bankruptcy Lawyers*, Doctoral Dissertation, University of California, Irvine.

Youth Gangs, Crime, and Public Policy

C. Ronald Huff

Many communities throughout the nation have been attempting to address the emergence of gangs and their related criminal behavior since the mid-1980s, when the number of youth gangs and gang members began to grow dramatically.[1] A significant number of young people report that there are gangs (and weapons) in their schools and in their neighborhoods. Newspaper headlines, television stories, and "gang movies" showing at local theaters often focus on the more dramatic and violent behavior of gangs and their members or on inner-city minority gang members selling crack cocaine. But such information is often sensationalized and is not based on careful research. Some of the most important questions left unanswered by the media coverage are:

- What is the real nature and extent of criminal behavior committed by current youth gangs?
- To what extent are gang members involved in drug sales?
- How well armed are gang members and how lethal are their weapons?
- Can young people safely resist joining gangs if approached?
- Does the criminal behavior of gang members vary by gender?

To address these important issues, two research projects were carried out for the National Institute of Justice and the Ohio Office of Criminal Justice Services. Samples of gang members were developed in four U.S. communities (Denver and Aurora, Colorado; Broward County, Florida; and Cleveland, Ohio). In developing these samples, it was important not to rely significantly on official police records of gang members. Although a number of research studies have used law enforcement databases, such samples include considerable bias, from a scientific standpoint, since they include only those who have been arrested or have had contact with the police. Left out of such samples are those who have been able to avoid police involvement, and they may or may not be comparable with those with official police records or contact.

Our samples of gang members were based on knowledge gained from expert informants concerning (1) existing gangs in each of the four sites and (2) who is, or has recently been, active in those gangs. Sources of information included a large number of individuals who interact with gangs and gang members on a daily basis, including social service and community outreach workers (especially those with current "street knowledge" of gang members), school personnel, gang prevention experts, and law enforcement experts. In each of the four sites, the proposed sample included 50 gang members, yielding a total of 200 gang members. The actual (final) sample size for valid, useable interviews was 187.

Interviewers at each site were selected and trained, using an interview instrument developed for this study. Scheduling was established so that the safety of all human subjects would be protected. For example, members of rival gangs were never scheduled for sequential interviews so as to avoid their arriving at the same site at the same time. All gang members who were interviewed were paid for their time with either movie coupons purchased from a local theater chain or McDonald's coupons. Given the neighborhood "turf rivalries" that exist among gangs in different neighborhoods, a substantial amount of time was required to identify theater chains whose outlets were located in all of the different "gang areas" so that our interviewees could actually use their movie coupons without fear of being attacked by "intruding" into "enemy territory" to go to the movies. Otherwise, we could hardly call these movie coupons a "reward" for their cooperation. (This was not a problem for the McDonald's coupons, since the large number of McDonald's restaurants permits easy access.) In addition to these coupons, those individuals who had been ordered by the courts to complete community service requirements were given the opportunity to request that the principal investigator contact the appropriate courts in their behalf to ask that their cooperation in the study be counted toward the community service requirement.

SUMMARY OF MAJOR FINDINGS

For the Colorado and Florida sites, the gang members in our samples averaged eighteen years of age and had completed the tenth grade. In Cleveland, gang members' average age was sixteen, and they had completed the ninth grade. Nearly nine in ten were male in all four locations. African-Americans comprised 50 percent of the overall sample; 25.3 percent were European-Americans (white); 16.1 percent were Hispanic-Americans; 1.1 percent were Asian-Americans; and 7.5 percent were of mixed racial heritage. Only four in ten gang members lived in a two-parent family, and most of the others had little or no contact with their missing parent.

The median total number of arrests for gang members was four, and the median age at first arrest was fourteen. Since gang members told us that they began hanging out with gangs (the "wannabe" stage when they want to be a gang member) at age thirteen and joined at age fourteen, it is important to note that their age at first arrest is identical to the average age at which they joined a gang. This finding provides additional evidence that gangs are highly "criminogenic." More importantly, longitudinal studies that followed young people over time have shown that those who join gangs are more involved in crime during the time they are in a gang than they were before they joined the gang or after they left the gang.[2]

Hoops and Drivebys: Gang Member Criminal Behavior

What kinds of crimes do gang members really commit? To address this issue, a large number of interview questions sought to determine the involvement of our respondents in such criminal behavior. Table 1 presents the findings with respect to our individual gang member respondents. Certain types of crime (such as shoplifting) are engaged in frequently by many youths, whether or not they are gang-involved, while other crimes (such as kidnapping) are engaged in very infrequently by youths, and again this does not depend on gang membership. But for a large number of crimes, especially violent offenses and major property crimes, both criminological theory and our field experience over the years suggest that gang members are likely to exhibit greater involvement in these illegal behaviors. Theoretically, adolescents' attempts to deal with the problems associated with "coming of age" (biological, social, and economic challenges) often result in their parent(s) or other significant adult caregivers being drawn into conflict with the independence-seeking youth. The strain that ensues can help push the adolescent even more toward social groups outside his/her family in a search for gratification, acceptance, and reassurance. Both classic learning theory and more contemporary social control theory suggest that when the youth makes a commitment to a primary social group (the gang) whose values and social reward system favor certain types of criminal behavior, that youth is more likely to engage in such criminal behavior. For the youth gang, criminal behavior occurs as part of the group dynamics, along with other ("normal") adolescent social activities such as "hanging out" with friends, listening to music and going to rock concerts, and "cruising the malls"—behaviors that typify noncriminal adolescent groups and reflect their focal concerns with peer acceptance.

As the data in Table 1 show, gangs are significantly involved in criminal behavior, including the most serious crimes of violence and major property crimes. The rates for gang member involvement in serious crimes such as homicide,

TABLE 1 Criminal Behavior by Gang Members (% of Respondents)
(n = 187)

	Aurora	Broward Co.	Cleveland	Denver
Shoplifting	57.1	62.0	30.4	45.0
Check forgery	4.1	18.0	2.1	4.8
Credit card theft	12.2	46.0	6.4	9.5
Auto theft	44.9	67.3	44.7	61.9
Theft—other	59.2	80.0	51.1	52.4
Sell stolen goods	44.9	70.0	29.8	52.4
Assault rivals	81.6	94.0	72.3	71.4
Assault own members	31.3	40.0	30.4	26.2
Assault police	28.6	22.0	10.6	31.0
Assault teachers	26.5	16.3	14.9	26.8
Assault students	58.3	66.0	51.1	53.7
Mug people	26.5	52.0	10.6	33.3
Assault in streets	42.9	56.0	29.8	52.4
Bribe police	12.2	10.0	10.6	11.9
Burglary (unoccupied)	26.5	64.0	8.5	42.9
Burglary (occupied)	8.3	34.0	2.1	14.6
Guns in school	53.1	46.0	40.4	46.3
Knives in school	50.0	58.3	38.3	37.5
Concealed weapons	87.8	84.0	78.7	88.1
Drug use	49.0	76.0	27.7	51.2
Drug sales (school)	26.5	34.0	19.1	38.1
Drug sales (other)	75.0	58.0	61.7	64.3
Drug theft	31.9	44.9	21.3	23.1
Arson	12.2	12.0	8.5	14.3
Kidnapping	6.1	4.0	4.3	9.5
Sexual assault/molest	4.1	4.0	2.1	0.0
Rape	2.0	4.0	2.1	0.0
Robbery	14.3	30.0	17.0	26.2
Intimidate/assault victims/witnesses	39.6	46.0	34.0	47.6
Intimidate/assault shoppers	31.3	42.0	23.4	40.5
Driveby shooting	51.0	68.0	40.4	50.0
Homicide	12.2	20.0	15.2	19.5

driveby shootings, carrying concealed weapons, taking guns and/or knives to school, and auto theft are especially alarming. What is even more alarming is the casual acceptance by many gang members of serious, violent criminal behavior as a normal part of their lives. For example, one gang member, when asked about an affiliation between his gang and another gang, replied, "We shoot hoops together; we do drivebys together; we do crime together. You know, we're just kickin'." Mentioning basketball, crime, and driveby shootings in the same sentence reveals the extent to which crime and violence can become routinized in the lives of many gang members.

As indicated in Table 1, the least common criminal behaviors committed by our respondents are rape,[3] sexual assault/molestation, kidnapping, check forgery, bribing police, and arson. The base expectancy rate of these offenses is generally low to very low for adolescents whether they are gang-involved or not, so this finding is not surprising.

Peddling Dope: Gang Member Involvement in Drug Sales

Another major purpose of this study was to examine the extent to which gang members engage in drug sales and the nature of their drug sales. Table 2 reflects the self-reported involvement of our gang members in drug sales in each of the four sites represented in our study.

One of the major debates in recent years has been whether gangs and drug trafficking are nearly "synonymous," and whether gangs "control" drug trafficking markets. For our sample of gang members, the following findings are clear:

- Although they seldom join gangs initially to sell drugs (they are most likely to join in search of a sense of family and belonging to something), individual gang members are significantly involved in the sales of crack cocaine, powder cocaine, and marijuana, with much less involvement in the sale of PCP, LSD/mushrooms, heroin, and crystal methamphetamine ("ice").[4]

- Many gang members in our sample who sell drugs even do so on a daily basis.

- Gang members who sell drugs report that they make, on the average, between $750 to $1,000 per week, with about 25 to 30 customers per week.

- Less than 5 percent of gang members reported that they use any of their drug profits to buy drugs for their own use.[5]

TABLE 2 Gang Member Drug Sales (% of Respondents)
(n = 187)

	Aurora	Broward Co.	Cleveland	Denver
Crack cocaine	57.1	38.7	65.9	63.4
Powder cocaine	24.5	51.0	26.1	41.5
Marijuana	57.1	73.5	48.9	62.5
PCP	6.3	14.3	4.3	12.2
LSD/mushrooms	18.4	38.8	2.1	25.0
Heroin	6.3	17.0	4.3	14.6
Crystal methamphetamine	10.2	14.6	4.3	9.7

- When asked how much money, in legitimate wages per hour, it would take to induce them and their peers to stop selling drugs, gang members thought it would take about $20 per hour. It should be noted, however, that although this median figure is the most representative response, this means that 50 percent of the overall sample believed that a lower wage would be an acceptable inducement to stop selling drugs. Some respondents' answers to this question suggest that there are individuals who may be willing to stop selling drugs in return for legitimate wages that are not much higher than are currently being paid by fast-food restaurants.[6] However, gang members are often unable to obtain a sufficient number of *hours* of work per week at legitimate wages to offset their *total* earnings from illegal drug sales. While this is often an accurate statement, it may also serve to reinforce the gang member's own convenient neutralization (rationalization) of his/her criminal behavior.

- Finally, gang members do not believe that gangs control drug markets. About 70 percent to 80 percent believe that other organizations control drugs. It is especially noteworthy that gang members, who are much more likely to be involved in drug sales and therefore more likely to have better knowledge of the dynamics of drug markets, are also more likely to believe that other organizations (such as foreign groups and organized crime) control drug markets.

Guns, Gangs, and "Wannabes"

Another question of interest is the extent to which gang members possess guns and what types of guns they possess. Our findings suggest that guns are quite prevalent among gangs. About three fourths of our gang sample indicated that most or nearly all of their fellow gang members own guns. The lethality of these weapons is even more sobering. Unlike gangs and youth groups of previous decades, who fought with fists, clubs, "zip guns" made from broken radio antennas, and similar weapons, contemporary gangs and other youth are all-too-likely to have access to powerful and highly lethal weaponry. Nearly nine out of ten (89%) of the gang respondents report that members of their gangs possess weapons that are more powerful than small-caliber handguns. A close examination of our data reveals that most of these groups have members with weapons more powerful and more lethal than the standard weapons issued to law enforcement officers (often a 9 mm or comparable handgun).

The data collected in our survey also permit us to examine the progression from (1) "hanging out" with the gang (commonly known as the gang "wannabe" or associate stage) to (2) joining the gang to (3) getting arrested. As shown in Table 3, our gang member respondents reported that they first began associating

TABLE 3   Age At First Association With Gang To Age At First Arrest
         (n = 187)

	Aurora	Broward Co.	Cleveland	Denver
First association	13.1	13.3	12.9	12.4
Joined gang	14.2	14.3	13.4	13.5
First arrest	14.0	14.0	14.0	14.0

with the gang at twelve and a half to thirteen years of age. They joined, on the average, from six months to a year later. They were then arrested for the first time at age fourteen, about one year after beginning to associate with the gang and about the same time that they joined.

Just Say "No" (Politely!)

Table 4 presents important data concerning gang resistance and its consequences. We asked gang members whether they knew someone who had been approached to join a gang but had refused. About two thirds of the gang members in our sample knew someone who had resisted the gang's "invitation" to join. Many different techniques were mentioned, but the most prominent single technique was "said no" (respectfully declined), followed by "stopped associating." Other techniques mentioned included changing one's dress, activities, etc.[7] Interestingly, of those cases *for which our respondents had knowledge of what happened to those individuals who refused*, the ratio of "nothing" (no harm) to physical harm was nearly 3:1 overall (better than 5:1 in Cleveland, 6:1 in Aurora). This means that an individual who resists gang involvement is significantly more likely to avoid physical reprisals than he is to endure some physical harm. This finding takes on even more meaning when one considers that most of our gang members reported that the most common type of gang initiation ritual involves fighting, usually getting "beaten in" (physically beaten) by gang members. Thus, if one joins a gang, he/she is quite likely to be severely assaulted physically just to become a member, while resistance is far less likely to result

TABLE 4   Gang Resistance and Consequences (%)
         (n = 187)

	Aurora	Broward Co.	Cleveland	Denver
Know someone who refused to join	59.2	72.0	71.7	65.9
Consequences: physical harm	6.1	16.0	12.1	17.5
Consequences: nothing	36.7	34.0	66.7	30.0

in physical harm, and, when it does, the physical harm is usually less severe than being "beaten in" to the gang.

Girls and Gangs

Another important question that our study addressed is whether the criminal behavior of gang members differs by gender. Contemporary discussions of this issue range all the way from the traditional view that girls' delinquency is minor in nature and focuses on either running away from home or their sexuality to the radical, alarmist view that we are suddenly witnessing a surge in autonomous, violent female gangs.[8] For the most part (with notable exceptions), females have either been auxiliary members of male gangs or they have had their own gangs, which were auxiliaries to male gangs. They were often expected to assist the males by concealing their weapons or drugs whenever a law enforcement officer approached, for example, since it was thought less likely that the female would be suspected or searched. Consider the following excerpt from one of our interviews with a female gang member:

Q: *Why do you believe you were able to get away with these things without being arrested?*
A: *Because I'm a female.*

Q: *Really? Why do you think that makes a difference?*
A: *Because the cops will look at me and won't want to arrest me because I'm a female and I don't dress like a gang member, so they don't suspect anything.*

Q :   *Do you own a gun?*
A: *Yeah, a 22.*

Q :   *How many members of your gang own guns?*
A: *All of 'em.*

Q :   *What types of guns do they own?*
A: *Uzis, auto shotguns, Tech 9s, any kind of gun.*

Clearly, this girl recognizes that stereotypes exist concerning who is or is not likely to be a gang member and/or possess a weapon, and she feels largely immune from suspicion even though she herself is a gang member and owns a gun. But what about the actual criminal behavior of such girls? Table 5 compares the criminal behavior of male and female gang members in our sample.

With notable exceptions (such as homicide, selling drugs at school, kidnapping, rape, and sexual assault), our female gang members generally reported that they were involved in the same kinds of criminal behavior as our male gang members, though often to a lesser extent. The data raise new questions as well, such as why the female gang members in our sample apparently do not sell drugs at school and how to explain the fact that although nearly one-half of our female gang members admitted participating in driveby shootings, none of them

TABLE 5   Gang Member Criminal Behavior by Gender
            (n = 187, Males = 87%, Females = 13%)
            (p = level of statistical significance; N.S. = not significant)

Offense Category	Males (%)	Females (%)	Statistical Significance
Put up graffiti	64.2	50.0	N.S.
Cross out graffiti	62.7	62.5	N.S.
Shoplifting	46.9	62.5	N.S.
Check forgery	8.0	4.2	N.S.
Credit card theft	21.5	4.2	$p = < .05$
Auto theft	58.6	29.2	$p = < .01$
Theft—other	63.8	41.7	$p = < .05$
Sell stolen goods	52.8	25.0	$p = < .05$
Assault rivals	84.0	54.2	$p = < .001$
Assault own members	34.0	21.7	N.S.
Assault police	22.1	29.2	N.S.
Assault teachers	19.8	33.3	N.S.
Assault students	58.4	50.0	N.S.
Mug people	33.7	12.5	$p = < .05$
Bribe police	9.9	16.7	N.S.
Burglary (unoccupied)	37.4	16.7	$p = < .05$
Burglary (occupied)	15.3	4.3	N.S.
Guns in school	50.0	20.8	$p = < .05$
Knives in school	44.9	62.5	N.S.
Concealed weapons	85.9	75.0	N.S.
Drug use	52.1	45.8	N.S.
Drug sales (school)	32.7	0.0	$p = < .001$
Drug sales (other)	67.3	45.8	$p = < .05$
Drug theft	34.8	0.0	$p = < .001$
Arson	12.3	4.2	N.S.
Kidnapping	6.1	0.0	N.S.
Sexual assault/molestation	3.1	0.0	N.S.
Rape	2.5	0.0	N.S.
Robbery	22.7	16.7	N.S.
Intimidation/assault victims/witnesses	42.6	37.5	N.S.
Intimidation/assault shoppers	34.2	33.3	N.S.
Driveby shooting	53.7	45.8	N.S.
Homicide	19.3	0.0	$p = < .05$
Own a gun	42.6	17.4	$P = < .05$
Sell crack cocaine	57.1	45.8	N.S.
Sell powder cocaine	38.5	16.7	N.S.
Sell marijuana	63.4	54.2	N.S.
Sell PCP	10.0	4.2	N.S.
Sell LSD/mushrooms	24.4	8.3	N.S.
Sell heroin	11.5	0.0	N.S.
Sell crystal methamphetamine ("ice")	12.4	0.0	N.S.
Sell drugs daily	36.1	25.0	N.S.

acknowledged killing anyone. One possible explanation for the latter apparent discrepancy is that the female gang members want to take part in driveby shootings to demonstrate their loyalty, but they manage not to kill anyone in the process. (This explanation would be consistent with the fact that many gang members, when first confronted with the violence of the gang, find that they are "in over their heads" and become quite frightened and "want out.") It seems likely that neither the traditional view of female delinquency as consisting of only minor offenses (often involving either running away from home or their sexuality) or the more radical vision of a surge in young female killers accurately describes reality. Instead, female gang members are often more than just "groupies" or auxiliaries to male gangs and are committing a wide variety of crimes but are not as involved in lethal violence as are male gang members.

CONCLUSIONS AND PUBLIC POLICY RECOMMENDATIONS

Those who join gangs tend to begin their association with gangs at about age thirteen, join about a year later, and get arrested about the same time that they join the gang (age fourteen, on average). This underscores the highly criminogenic nature of gangs and the vital importance of gang resistance education programs and other primary and secondary prevention initiatives directed at preteens. These initiatives are especially important for those young people who have significant exposure to multiple risk factors for delinquent and violent behavior.[9] Such risk factors (all of which impact upon the samples used in this study) include economic deprivation;[10] neighborhood disorganization;[11] dysfunctional family structure and/or parenting;[12] poor health and inadequate health care;[13] school failure and inadequate schools;[14] and the availability of weapons,[15] among others.

Our data also demonstrate that, contrary to much of the common wisdom and folklore that surround the issue of gang resistance, young people can refuse to join gangs without incurring a substantial risk of physical harm. Furthermore, based on probability, they are far better off to resist joining gangs than to expose themselves to the beating they are likely to take upon initiation and to the increased risk of arrest, incarceration, injury, and death known to be associated with gang membership. It should also be noted that a recent study by Decker and Lauritsen[16] provides empirical evidence that the process of gang *desistance* (leaving the gang) has also been surrounded by a great deal of misinformation and folklore. Their study demonstrates that the process of leaving the gang may be more common than previously thought and that many gang members may be more amenable to intervention efforts at a time when they are experiencing negative reactions to the violence associated with gang life.[17]

Since primary prevention and early intervention efforts will not deter all young people from associating with gangs, we must also address the brief "window of intervention" that opens in that year between first association with the gang (the "wannabe" stage) and first arrest. It is imperative that we fund, develop, evaluate, improve, and sustain intervention programs that target this group of "wannabe" gang associates and successfully divert them from the gang into meaningful and effective programs during that one year window of opportunity.[18]

Certain types of crimes are especially likely to involve gang members, and a sudden increase in those crimes may be viewed as a potential "distant early warning signal" that crime in the community may be increasingly gang-related. Crimes that may be especially worth monitoring closely are assaults involving rival groups; auto theft and credit card theft; carrying concealed weapons; taking weapons to school; assault/intimidation of victims, witnesses, and shoppers; drug trafficking; driveby shootings;[19] and homicide, all of which frequently involve gang members and may serve as reasonably accurate "gang markers" in some communities at some points in time.

Data from this study suggest that gang members are often involved in the sale of drugs and many even sell drugs on a daily basis. This underscores the need for prevention and early intervention programs that are designed to divert "wannabes" before they have an opportunity to get "hooked" on the illegal earnings that are possible through activities such as drug sales.

Although many gang members indicate that it would require a legitimate wage of around $20 per hour to induce them or their peers to stop selling drugs, a significant number of youth are likely to be amenable to far-lower legitimate wages, especially if they can obtain a large number of hours of work per week in order to increase their total income. However, this is difficult because many employers will offer only part-time jobs, partly to avoid paying the fringe benefits associated with full-time employment. We must, as a nation, develop more effective policies and programs that address the school-to-work transition problem, both in terms of vocational education and training and in terms of national employment and training priorities for youth.[20] The United States will not be able to compete economically on a global scale if it does not have an educated, skilled work force. That work force will eventually consist entirely of today's youth, and it will include increasing numbers of minorities. For example, it was predicted that about 45 percent of all net additions to the U.S. labor force in the 1990s would be nonwhite.[21]

Gangs are likely to possess powerful and highly lethal weapons, despite the fact that many gang members are not yet old enough to drive a car legally. Efforts to reduce the number of illegal weapons possessed by youth and adults (such as the recent Kansas City experiment) should be emphasized and could have substantial impact in reducing gun-related crimes.[22]

Finally, gangs should be viewed not as *the* problem, but rather as a symptom of more complex and pervasive problems in our society. Addressing these problems will require, first, that we begin to develop integrated, coordinated, and carefully developed *youth policy*. The fact is that our youth are our nation's most valuable resource, yet we do not have carefully coordinated youth policy in our nation, our states, or our communities. The development of such policy, along with the establishment of *healthy communities*[23] in which youth can develop into responsible and productive citizens, should be at the top of our public policy agenda. We must address these problems in the broader context of reconstructing our communities[24] and providing community-based interventions and services.[25] Otherwise, the problems represented by gangs and drugs are likely to remain severe and our states and our nation are likely to decline in economic competitiveness because of our failure to cultivate an educated, skilled, and productive citizenry by ensuring that our legitimate economic opportunities are more available and more compelling than those illegitimate opportunities that are available to our youth. The Achilles heel of a free, democratic society is the inability to produce responsible and productive citizens. Gangs, and the problems associated with gangs, reflect this problem and underscore the importance of developing a coordinated public policy response that emphasizes the importance of healthy, functional communities.

ENDNOTES

1. To illustrate the extent to which the perceived "gang problem" has been growing, it is interesting to note that prior to 1961, only fifty-four cities reported having gangs. By 1970, ninety-four cities acknowledged the existence of gangs, a figure which grew to 172 by 1980. However, the real explosion in the growth of gangs appeared to occur between 1980 and 1992, by which time 766 cities reported that they had gangs (M. W. Klein, *The American Street Gang.* New York: Oxford University Press, 1995, p. 91.

2. Longitudinal studies in Denver; Rochester, New York; and Seattle have provided extensive data that demonstrate the relationship between criminal behavior and gang membership. Youths are more involved in delinquent and criminal behavior, while active in gangs than either before they join or after they leave gangs. See Esbensen, F.-A., and D. Huizinga, "Gangs, Drugs, and Delinquency in a Survey of Urban Youth," *Criminology* 31 (1993): 565-589; Thornberry, T. P. et. al., "The Role of Juvenile Gangs in Facilitating Delinquent Behavior," *Journal of Research in Crime and Delinquency* 30 (1993): 55-87; and Battin, S. R. et. al., "The Contribution of Gang Membership to Delinquency Beyond Delinquent Friends," *Criminology* 36 (1998): 93-115.

3. In interpreting gang members' self-reported data for rape, one must note that these rates may be underreported, since gang members tend not to define as rape "consensual" (from their perspective) sexual intercourse with female gang members during or subsequent to gang initiation rituals. However, this researcher believes that in many of these incidents, sufficient coercion/intimidation exists to support a rape charge and that the male gang members tend to engage in neutralization (denial) when discussing the degree to which these incidents were truly consensual.

4. Although the media often portray gangs as highly organized drug distribution networks, empirical research demonstrates that this is seldom the case. Most often, individual gang members or cliques of gang members sell drugs without overall gang coordination or involvement. The media also frequently refer to certain groups who do have highly organized drug distribution networks (such as the Jamaicans posses) as gangs, when our own definitions would classify them as organized crime groups.

5. The only gang members who reported using some of their drug profits to buy drugs for their own use were located in Broward County, Florida. None of the gang members in Ohio or Colorado reported using drug money for their own drug use. In fact, gangs and drug suppliers typically do not trust someone to sell drugs if they are "hooked" on drugs themselves, since they are viewed as unreliable (unstable, not to be trusted with money, and easily pressured into becoming witnesses for law enforcement).

6. A number of gang members, tired of living a life of fear, told us that they would give up selling drugs if they could earn as little as $1,000 per month. Although this figure is not much higher than one could earn at a fast-food restaurant ($5 per hour x 40 hours per week = $800 per month), it is very difficult to find forty hours of employment at such restaurants, which typically offer part-time work and few if any benefits. Although one can point out to gang members that selling drugs also does not offer benefits (and neither the health nor the retirement plans are good!), many young gang members are fatalistic about their futures and are oriented toward immediate gratification.

7. One strategy that I have developed for gang resistance is based on gang interviews over the past twelve years and is anchored in cognitive dissonance theory in the field of psychology. That theory holds that it is difficult to accept two competing ideas at the same time in one's cognitive system. Since gang members generally express great affection for their mothers and often recognize that they have disappointed them by their criminal behavior, youth who are attempting to resist gang involvement might tell their peers that they respect them and might *like* to join the gang, but their mother does not want them to join a gang and they do not want to disrespect their own mother. This could facilitate gang resistance, since gang members overwhelmingly told us that they would not join the gang if they had a chance to make that decision again and they do not want their siblings to join gangs. They may recognize that the youth, in respecting his mother's wishes, is doing what they themselves *wish* they had done, in retrospect.

8. For a useful overview of female delinquency, see M. Chesney-Lind and R. G. Shelden, *Girls, Delinquency, and Juvenile Justice.* Pacific Grove, CA: Brooks/Cole, 1992.

9. J.D. Hawkins, D.M. Lishner, J.M. Jenson, and R.F. Catalano, Jr., "Delinquents and Drugs: What the Evidence Suggests About Prevention and Treatment Programming." Pp. 81–131 in B.S. Brown and A.R. Mills (eds.), *Youth at High Risk for Substance Abuse.* Rockville, MD: U.S. Department of Health and Human Services, 1987.

10. D. Farrington, "Childhood Aggression and Adult Violence." Pp. 5–29 in *The Development and Treatment of Childhood Aggression.* Hillsdale, NJ: Lawrence Erlbaum, 1991; National Research Council, *Losing Generations: Adolescents in High-Risk Settings.* Washington, DC: National Academy Press, 1993.

11. National Research Council, 1993 (op. cit.); R.J. Sampson, "Community-Level Factors in the Development of Violent Behavior: Implications for Social Policy" (unpublished paper, 1994).

12. National Research Council, 1993 (op. cit.).

13. National Research Council, 1993 (op. cit.).

14. National Research Council, 1993 (op. cit.).

15. A.J. Reiss, Jr., and J.A. Roth (eds.), *Understanding and Preventing Violence.* Washington, DC: National Academy Press, 1993.

16. S.H. Decker and J.L. Lauritsen, "Breaking the Bonds of Membership: Leaving the Gang." Pp. 103–122 in C.R. Huff (ed.), *Gangs in America* (2nd ed.). Thousand Oaks, CA: Sage Publications, 1996.

17. An experienced probation officer in Columbus, Ohio, told this researcher that whenever he is assigned to supervise a gang member who has been placed on probation, he instructs the gang member to request a "leave of absence" from his gang while he is under probation supervision "because my probation officer will not allow me to associate with the gang while I am under his supervision." The probation officer then uses this "leave of absence" period to intervene with the gang member and attempt to divert him from the gang permanently.

18. See, for example, A.P. Goldstein and C.R. Huff, *The Gang Intervention Handbook*. Champaign, IL: Research Press, 1993; J.C. Howell, B. Krisberg, J.D. Hawkins, and J.J. Wilson (eds.), *Serious, Violent, & Chronic Juvenile Offenders: A Sourcebook*. Thousand Oaks, CA: Sage Publications, 1995.

19. Also see M.W. Klein, 1995 (op cit.), pp. 117-118.

20. Note that the United States alone, among Western democracies, failed to develop extensive apprenticeship and job training programs for youth at the conclusion of World War II. Time series data for unemployment since that time suggest that U.S. job markets are highly segmented and that the youth unemployment problem has been one of the most persistent public policy challenges facing the United States.

21. H.N. Fullerton, "Labor Force Projections: 1986-2000," *Monthly Labor Review*, September 1987, pp. 16-29; W. Johnston, "Global Work Force 2000: The New World Labor Market," *Harvard Business Review*, 69 (March–April, 1991), pp. 115–127.

22. See P.J. Cook and M.H. Moore, "Gun Control." Pp. 267-294 in J.Q. Wilson and J. Petersilia (eds.), *Crime*. San Francisco: ICS Press, 1995.

23. See J.D. Hawkins and R.F. Catalano, Jr., *Communities That Care*. San Francisco: Jossey-Bass, 1992.

24. See E. Currie, *Reckoning: Drugs, the Cities, and the American Future*. New York: Hill and Wang, 1993.

25. National Research Council, 1993 (op. cit.), pp. 193–234.

VII

Searching a Dwelling: Deterrence and the Undeterred Residential Burglar

Richard Wright

In most jurisdictions, a residential burglary has been completed in the eyes of the law the moment an offender enters a dwelling without permission, intending to commit a crime therein. But seen through the eyes of the burglars themselves, a break-in is far from complete at this point. Indeed, the offense has just begun. They must still transform their illicit intentions into action—which, in practice, almost invariably involves searching for goods and stealing them—and escape from the scene without getting caught, injured, or killed. But in doing this offenders are on the horns of a dilemma. On the one hand, the more time they spend searching a residence, the better chance they stand of realizing a large financial reward. On the other hand, the longer they remain inside a target, the greater risk they run of being discovered. Having entered a dwelling, then, offenders must strike a deceptively complex, subjective balance that maximizes reward within the limits of acceptable risk. How is such a balance actually struck? Criminologists interested in the decision-making of residential burglars have devoted almost no attention to this process, despite the fact that such offenders obviously continue to make decisions throughout the commission of their break-ins. An examination of this matter is crucial to the development of a fuller understanding of the decision-making calculus of property offenders.

Adapted from Chapter 5 of *Burglars on the Job: Streetlife and Residential Break-ins* by Richard T. Wright and Scott H. Decker (Northeastern University Press, 1994). Used with permission from the publisher.

In an attempt to learn more about the tactics used by offenders to search dwellings, a colleague, Scott Decker, and I located and interviewed 105 currently active residential burglars in St. Louis, Missouri. The residential burglars were recruited through the efforts of a field-based informant—an ex-offender with a solid reputation for integrity and trustworthiness in the criminal underworld. Working through chains of street referrals, the field recruiter contacted active residential burglars, convinced them to take part in the project, and sat in on interviews that lasted two hours or more. In the pages that follow, I report just a small portion of what the offenders said during those interviews, focusing on how they search dwellings once they have broken into them.

Once inside a target, the first concern of most offenders is to reassure themselves that no one is at home. They do this in a variety of ways. Some run through the dwelling and take a quick glance into every room. Others remain still and silent, listening for any sound of movement. Still others call out something along the lines of "Is anybody home?" More than anything, such actions probably represent an attempt by offenders to put worries about being attacked by an occupant behind them so that they can devote their attention to searching for cash and goods.

> When you first get inside, you go through all the rooms to make sure no one's home. Once [you see] there's no one home, that's when you start gettin' busy, doin' your job.

Thus having reassured themselves, offenders often experience a sudden realization that everything inside the residence is theirs for the taking. One female offender said this realization made her feel as if she was in Disneyland— calling to mind a magical world in which fantasy had become reality. Another offender likened the feeling he got inside an unoccupied dwelling to being in a fashionable shopping mall, "except you don't have to pay for stuff; just take it." Such comments suggest that, during this phase of the burglary process, offenders perceive themselves to be operating in a world that is qualitatively different from the one they inhabit day-to-day. Jack Katz refers to this world as "an enchanted land," the phenomenological creation of a mind bent on crime.[1]

Inside dwellings, shielded from public view, many offenders also experience a marked reduction in anxiety. They already have broken in, there is no turning back, and it makes little sense to agonize over the potentially negative consequences of their actions. Recognizing this, offenders have a tendency to settle down and turn their attention to searching the residence. This is not to suggest that the burglars stop worrying about the risks altogether. Most of them continue to be somewhat fearful, with the length of time they are willing to spend inside targets providing a rough indication of the gravity of their concern.

THE BRIEF SEARCH

The outside world does not stand still while burglars are searching dwellings and, as noted above, their vulnerability to discovery increases the longer they remain inside them. Occupants may return unexpectedly. Neighbors may become suspicious and call the police. Patrolling officers may spot a broken window and stop to investigate. Burglars are well aware of these risks, and the vast majority of them try to limit the time they spend in places.

> When you first get in [to a dwelling], do whatever you gon do; do it quick and get on out of there!
>   When you doin' [a burglary], you work fast. You go straight to what you want to get and then you come out of there.
>   I know three minutes don't seem like a long time, but in a house that's long! You just go straight and do what you got to do; [three minutes is] a long time.

The ability of the burglars to locate goods without undue delay is facilitated by strict adherence to a cognitive script that guides their actions almost automatically as they move through dwellings; this script allows them to flow through the search process without periodically having to stop to calculate their next step. Virtually all of the burglars reported having a tried-and-true method of searching residences which, they believe, produces the maximum yield in cash and goods per unit of time invested. The search pattern varies somewhat from offender to offender, largely as a function of the time an individual is prepared to remain inside a given target. With few exceptions, however, the burglars agree that, upon entering a dwelling, one should make a beeline for the master bedroom; this is where cash, jewelry, and guns are most likely to be found. These items are highly prized because they are light, easy to conceal, and represent excellent pound-for-pound value.

> I'm hittin' that bedroom first. I'd rather hit that bedroom than the living room cause it's more valuables in the bedroom than it is in the living room—jewelry, guns and money. So everything is in the back [of the dwelling] somewhere; most likely in the bedroom.
>   The first thing you always do when you get to a house is you always go to the bedroom. That's your first move. . .[b]ecause that's where the majority of people keep they stuff like jewelry or cash. You know it's gon be a jewelry box in the bedroom; you know you ain't gon find it in the living room. Guns, you ain't gon find that too much in the living room.

The burglars believed that searching the master bedroom first also enhances their personal safety, especially when this room is located on the second floor. They feel particularly vulnerable upstairs because their only escape route—the stairway—can easily be cut off should an occupant return unexpectedly. As a result, most of them want to begin their search on the second floor and get downstairs as quickly as possible.

The burglars reported searching four main places within the master bedroom. The first stop for most of them is the dresser, where they quickly go through each drawer—often dumping the contents onto the floor or bed—looking primarily for cash and jewelry.

> [Y]ou got to look around, you got to ransack a little. You got to realize too that you don't have very much time to ransack neither. . .You always start in the bedrooms, in the drawers; that's where they keep the money and the jewelry.

They typically turn next to the bedside table, hoping to find a handgun and, perhaps, some cash and jewelry. From there, many of them search the bed itself because some people, especially those who are elderly or poor, continue to keep their savings under the mattress. Lastly, the burglars usually will rummage through the bedroom closet, looking mainly for cash and pistols hidden in a shoebox or similar container.

If the search of the main bedroom has been moderately successful, some of the burglars will not bother to look through the remaining rooms, preferring simply to make good their escape. They know full well that a more exhaustive search of the premises could net them a larger financial return, but are unwilling to assume the increased risk entailed in spending longer inside the target. As one burglar who typically searches only the master bedroom explained: "You miss a lot, but it's all gravy if you get away." A majority of the burglars, however, conduct at least a cursory search of the rest of the dwelling before departing. A number of them said they usually have a quick look around the kitchen. Surprisingly, most of these burglars are not searching for silverware or kitchen appliances so much as for cash and jewelry; they claimed that such items sometimes can be found hidden in a cookie jar or in the refrigerator/freezer.

> [The valuables are located in] either the freezer, the icebox, in they bedroom. . .in the dresser drawer or under the mattress. . .People put money in plastic bags behind the meat in they freezer.

Some of the burglars also search the bathroom, concentrating on the medicine cabinet where they hope to find not only psychoactive prescription drugs (e.g. valium), but perhaps hidden money and valuables.

> Like a lot of times I've [gone through] the medicine cabinets, quite a few people leave money in the medicine cabinet. I don't know if you've ever heard of that, but I. . .found about forty dollars in there once and the second time I found about twenty-five dollars.

Few burglars, however, bother to rummage about in bedrooms occupied by young children because, in their view, such rooms are unlikely to contain anything worth stealing.

> I ain't gon even worry about the kids' bedrooms. Mom and Dad have all the jewelry and stuff in they room. I know the little kids ain't got nothing in they room.
>
> Little kids' rooms, I don't usually go in there because they don't usually have much. I don't have any kids so ain't no sense me goin' in there unless one of my little nieces or nephews might want something and I might keep an eye out for them.

Most of the burglars usually search the living room just prior to leaving the target because the items kept there tend to be heavy or bulky (e.g., television sets, videocassette recorders, stereo units); hence they best are left to the last minute. Indeed, some offenders do not bother to search the living room because carrying out the cumbersome goods located therein is likely to draw the attention of neighbors. As one offender explained: "I don't carry no T.V.s. . .because that's an easy bust." And another added: "You never take nothing big. You look for [something small]; something won't nobody see you bringin' out."

By employing such strategies to search dwellings, the burglars usually can locate enough cash and other valuables to meet their immediate needs in a matter of minutes. As one said: "You'd be surprised how fast a man can go through your house." Occasionally, however, the predetermined search strategies used by offenders fail to yield the expected results. This may cause some of them to depart from their normal modus operandi, remaining in the residence for longer than they feel is safe in order to find something of value.

> [I] go straight to the main spots where I think the main stuff is in. Never mess around with, well, at least try not to, stay out the petty spots. Bathrooms, you know, what you goin' in there for? I may go in there if the house ain't no good, you know, [isn't] what I thought it was; then I start gettin' desperate and stuff and lookin' everywhere. Gotta get somethin'. Let me see if they got a gold toothbrush, you know, just anything.

In breaking into the dwelling, these offenders already have assumed considerable risk and they are determined to locate something worth stealing, if only to justify having taken that risk in the first place. Add to this the fact that most of them are under pressure to obtain money quickly, and their decision to carry on searching despite the increasing risk of being discovered seems more sensible still; to abandon the offense would require quickly finding and breaking into an alternative target, with all of the attendant hazards.

On other occasions, offenders are tempted to linger in residences when they discover something that convinces them that an especially desirable item must be hidden elsewhere in the building. Put differently, they are enticed into accepting a higher level of risk, believing that the extra time devoted to searching is justified by the potential reward.

> Then when I'm goin' through the dresser drawer or somethin', I might find shell boxes; they got a gun! Definitely! And I'm gon find it.

It is at this point that we can begin to glimpse the danger of allowing oneself to be seduced by the possibility of realizing a large financial gain. As noted above, the burglars are operating in a world that is qualitatively different from the one they inhabit day-to-day; a world in which they can take whatever catches their fancy. It is easy to see how they could get carried away by the project at hand, trying to take everything and disregarding the risks altogether. Generally speaking, the burglars are aware of this threat and try their best to avoid becoming so wrapped up in the offense as to throw caution to the wind. They do this by focusing on the items they originally intended to steal, resolving not to get greedy.

> [M]ost of the time you want to get in and get out as quick as possible. See, that's how a lot of people get caught; they get greedy. You go in and get what you first made up your mind to get. When you take the time to ramble for other things, and look through this and look through that, you taking a chance.
>
> I put my mind on one thing. That's what I'm a get. I ain't gon be ransackin' all through there. . .See, I don't get greedy once I go in and do a burglary.

From the perspective of these burglars, it makes little sense to steal more than necessary to meet their immediate needs because doing so involves additional risk. Besides, most of them could not transport more than they already had. As one put it: "I don't want to be in [the dwelling] that long. I ain't gon be able to carry all that stuff anyway."

Not surprisingly, some offenders did report getting carried away during particular offenses, being seduced by the allure of the available goods such that they forgot all about the risks of lingering in the target.

> The stuff that was in there, it just had this attraction to your eyes. It made you feel like, 'God, I need that!', you know. So that's what, so we just kept on. . .everything just attracted our eyes.
>
> I was downstairs just lookin' around cause I was real choicy; I was real choicy this last job I had. [My partner] came downstairs and said, 'Man, you better get what you gon get and come on!' 'Man, what time is it?' I said, 'I got about fifteen minutes.' He said, 'Man, you better hurry up!' You know, he was rushin' me then cause usually I be rushin' them. 'Alright then, I'm a take this V.C.R., this T.V., let's go.'

Cases such as these, though, are the exception rather than the rule; almost all of the burglars usually adhere to a well-rehearsed cognitive script in searching targets. Admittedly, not all of them enter dwellings intending to steal specific items, preferring instead to allow themselves to be seduced by whatever catches their eye. But even these offenders typically stick to a set pattern in moving through residences.

> When you go in [to a target], the first thing you do is go straight to the back. As you go to the back, you already lookin'. While you lookin', you pick certain things out that you gon take with you that you know you can get. You can pick them out just by lookin' as you walkin'. Then, when you turn around to come out of there, you already know what you gon get. . .It depends on what I spot and if I think it's of value; not no particular things.

Many residential burglars, of course, commit their offenses acting in concert with others. As Neal Shover has observed, co-offending appeals to many burglars because "it facilitates management of the diverse practical demands of stealing".[2] Foremost among these demands is avoiding detection. Working with others allows offenders to locate and transport goods more quickly, thereby reducing the risk of being caught in the act.

> [I have searched dwellings more extensively], but that was only when I do it with friends. Cause I have more time; while I'm downstairs, he's upstairs. It's all timing. Fast as you do it and then get out of there.
>
> I guess [I work with others] because it would take so much time for me to have to look for everything all by myself. If it's two or three of us it will be that much quicker.
>
> A lot of times the places that I normally pick, it's quite a few items there. . .But then I use someone else so we can get the job done and move on out; get away as soon as possible instead of making a lot of trips to get everything [out of the dwelling].
>
> [I commit burglaries with a partner] just in case they have lots of stuff in there I want. We can hurry up an' get it out.

A number of the burglars also reported that working with one or more accomplices is safer than operating alone because it permits them to post a look-out.

> It's always good to go in a house with at least three dudes. You know, two of you'll get the stuff together. The other one look out the window; he be the watch.
>
> [I]t's almost always a little safer to have someone else with you. . .Because if you got someone outside, they can always give a little signal and let you know when someone's coming or whatever. If you're alone, you can't hear these things.

These offenders believe that using a look-out not only is objectively safer, it also carries the subjective benefit of eliminating concerns about being caught by surprise and thus enhances their ability to concentrate on searching for goods to steal. As one of them noted: "By yourself, you never know who behind you."

Several offenders pointed out that accomplices represent ready assistance should they encounter unanticipated resistance.

> Sometime you want somebody with you. . .Sometimes I like to do [residential burglaries] with someone because I like to have protection in case something do happen.
>
> [I work with someone else] because we spent five and a half years together and we can handle ourselves real well. I can trust him; if I get in a tough situation, he would kick ass for me. If a guy with a big baseball bat is going to come kill me, he'll come to the rescue type of thing.

A few offenders chose to work with others in the belief that, should the police arrive unexpectedly, this increases the odds of at least one of them getting away.

> [Working with others decreases the risk] because if it's more than one [offender] and the police do come, then somebody is bound to get away. I guess if you get caught, you know, [the police] gonna catch one of yas, to put it that way, if you're gonna get caught, they're gonna catch one of ya, one of yas always gotta chance of getting away.

The logic underlying this belief is that two or more offenders can split up, running in different directions so that officers have to decide who to chase and who to allow to escape. The delusional aspect of this position is self-evident; why should the police elect not to pursue these offenders in favor of catching their accomplices? Here we are confronting a force that transcends rationality. The burglars acknowledge the risk of apprehension but believe that, because luck is on their side, they personally will avoid such a fate. That said, it remains true that by working with others, offenders may well reduce their individual risk of being caught during a police chase. One subject referred specifically to this fact: "I work with some partners because it's a better chance of gettin' away. They might get caught and I might get away." Along the same lines, another burglar said that he liked working with others because witnesses have a tendency to confuse the features of multiple offenders, making it difficult for them to provide the police with a good description of individual suspects.

Quite a few of the burglars who commit their break-ins with others reported doing so just in case they do get caught. Most of them simply want the reassurance of knowing that, should they be arrested, their co-offenders will be there to share the guilt and shame.[3]

> [I work with others] cause I feel if I get caught, I want them to get caught with me. I mean, I don't want to get caught by myself. . .They gon get caught with me. . .I feel I won't be so guilty if I have somebody with me. Then I won't feel so guilty, I'll feel kind of safe.

Two experienced female offenders, however, do not want to share the blame with accomplices, but rather hope to shift it entirely onto their associates. Both of these offenders work exclusively with men, believing that the police will show leniency toward a woman who claims that she was coerced into an offense by her male partner.

> I think down in my mind, when I first started doing burglary I saw a show and in it the woman claimed mental incompetent; that she'd been brainwashed. And I guess I feel like if we ever got caught that I could blame it on him. That's a pretty shit attitude, but. . .I don't know, I kind of feel like I'm smarter than [the male burglars] are.

There may be a grain of truth in this belief.[4] Be that as it may, the important point for our purposes is that these women are convinced this is the case, and thus are able to mentally discount the threat of arrest and punishment. This allows them to get on with the business of searching dwellings, unimpeded by concerns about getting caught.

In short, the burglars who choose to work with others in committing their residential break-ins do so not only for practical reasons, but for psychological ones as well; the company of co-offenders dampens their fear of apprehension and bolsters their confidence.

> Like I told you, I know it sounds strange, but I be scared when I do [a residential burglary]. Then if I have somebody with me and they say, 'Ah, you can do it,' they boost me up and I go on and do it.
>
> [I work with someone else] when I don't really know about that place, you know, I'm kind of nervous about it. So I feel like I wouldn't be as nervous by me havin' somebody with me on a place that I don't know too much about.

While co-offending has a number of potential advantages, working with other criminals inevitably entails certain risks. In the best of circumstances, such individuals are of dubious reliability, and the pressures inherent in offending can undermine their trustworthiness still further. Several of the burglars said they are becoming increasingly reluctant to work with others, having been let down in the past by co-offenders who failed to carry their weight during offenses.

> See, you can't depend on no one else. That's why I'm goin' to court now. . .I had this so-called buddy of mine supposed to be watchin' this house for me [while I was inside]. And I told him to stand across the street so when I come out I can look across the street and see him. When I came out, he was gone and I had merchandise up under my arm. So I said, 'Let me get on out of here.' I don't know what happened, he might have just left me. So I was gettin' nervous and I just went on and left. And there the police was! Walked right into they arms!

Even those who continue to work with others typically believe that, should something go wrong, their crime partners might well let them down. Many expressed doubts about the ability of accomplices to withstand police interrogation without naming them as co-participants.

> You never know, it just ain't no sure thing. I just say, 'Do unto others what's done unto you'. So I'm not banking on [my partner's ability to remain silent]; if he get caught, then maybe that's damn near my ass is probably caught too. Cause I know if the police say, 'Was somebody with you?' he'll probably say, 'Yeah, yeah, oh yes.' Police talk to you, you know; [partners] start spillin' they guts. They scared and then all they thinkin' about is themselves. So to be truthful with you, yeah, I never bank on [silence].

Most of these offenders appeared to accept the potential for duplicity among their colleagues with equanimity. As they see it, the police put pressure on arrestees to inform on their partners, and it is naïve to expect them to remain silent. One put it this way "[My co-offenders] would probably tell on me, but, to be honest, I'd probably tell on them too."

Perhaps the aspect of co-offending that the burglars find most irksome involves what they perceive as a tendency for accomplices to "cuff" (that is, neglect to tell them about) some of the loot found during the search of a target. In their eyes, it is bad enough having to split the proceeds of their crimes, without having to deal with the possibility that their co-workers will try to cheat them. Some offenders attempt to reduce the risk of being cheated by working only with those they know well. For a few, this strategy seems to pay off.

> Well, like they say, 'There's no honor among thieves.' That's what they say, [but] I believe that they really are wrong about that because this here is really loyal. We done did one house, man, where this guy had [a pistol he found during the search] in his pocket already and we didn't know. But he came out and told us when we was splittin' everything up. He took it out and he put it with the rest of the shit to be split up. I wouldn't a did it; I would've kept that.

But most of them continue to believe that even close acquaintances might try to deceive them by cuffing booty.

> That's why I work with the same people, you know what I mean? He don't know what I got from downstairs. I might have found a ten thousand dollar diamond ring. Of course, you got to trust these damn fools, you know? It's easy to do man; it's easy for somebody to rip you off.

One offender reported that he and his usual burglary partner have an agreement whereby they always search the master bedroom together. The logic behind their agreement is that the most easily concealed valuables tend to be found in this room; going through it together represents a means of "keeping each other honest."

Despite the risks of co-offending, the fact remains that a majority of the burglars continue to work with others. As much as anything, their decision to do so undoubtedly reflects the powerful influence of routine. The burglars are used to co-offending. Many of them work with regular partners, and have developed cognitive scripts that incorporate roles for their accomplices. These roles are well understood by their co-offenders and therefore break-ins can be carried out efficiently, with a minimum of confusion or conflict.

> I work with him because when you get a [regular] partner, it's like two pieces of a machine; two gears clicking together and that's the way me and him work.
>   Everybody has they routine. I check upstairs and then they stay downstairs and get the VCRs and everything. That's the routine we been doing for years.

When the pressures that give rise to burglaries intensify, then, it makes little sense for offenders to deviate from their typical modus operandi and set off alone. These pressures often arise in the context of partying—a group activity—where a shared desire to obtain fast cash for more alcohol or drugs precipitates a decision among those present to commit an offense.[5] As one burglar explained: "We be gettin' high together anyway, I might as well go [with] them. I come back by myself, they gon get high with me anyway."

THE LEISURELY SEARCH

On any given residential burglary, the safest course of action for offenders is to search the target quickly and then leave without delay. Adopting this approach, however, means that they seldom will come away from offenses having stolen more than is necessary to meet their immediate financial needs; there is unlikely to be anything left over to help them deal with their next monetary crisis. The price of reducing the risks in the short term, therefore, may well be a foreshortening of the time between break-ins and a consequent increase in the frequency with which those risks must be taken. Some burglars, albeit a small minority, are unwilling to pay this price, preferring instead to remain in targets long enough to make certain they have found everything of value.

> [I take] the whole day going through the whole house, sitting down and eating and things of that nature. . .On a burglary, you get all that you can. Some people will just go get certain items, [but] I can just take everything cause everything has a value.

These burglars claim to understand the schedules kept by occupants of their targets and to have a clear idea about how long residents will be out. Thus they can proceed unimpeded by concerns about being discovered in the act of searching places.

> When I do a burglary, I don't go in there and come back out. I go in there and stay! I go in there and stay for a couple of hours. I know these people won't be back home until about five in the evening if they leave at seven in the morning. I be done ransacked the house by then.

Even offenders who do not routinely linger in targets occasionally succumb to the temptation to stay longer when they know that the occupants will be away for some time. Their reasons for doing so, however, often seem to transcend the desire for greater financial rewards. Indeed, many devote this extra time almost wholly to relaxation and entertainment.

> I usually go straight to the bedroom and then I walk around to the living room. I have set at people's house and cooked me some food, watched T.V. and played the stereo. . .I knew they wouldn't be there. But I usually go straight to the bedroom.

The offenders recognize that these offenses are special, being largely free of the temporal constraints that circumscribe most of their break-ins. They respond by taking full advantage of the situation and making themselves at home. In effect, they are acting out the widely held adolescent fantasy of having the run of a place without the obligation to answer to anyone. Some of them, of course, are adolescents. But even among those who are older, few have any experience of being in full control of their living space; the majority still stay with their mothers or have no fixed address. It is easy to appreciate why they enjoy having someplace to themselves. The irony is that they seldom do anything very outrageous. Like teenagers left alone for the weekend by their parents, most simply help themselves to whatever alcohol and food is available and take pleasure in not having to clean up afterward. One, for instance, reported: "Sometimes I cook me some breakfast, but I never wash the dishes."

A number of the burglars said that they sometimes urinate or defecate inside their targets. They attributed their need to do so to the emotional pressures involved in offending. Contrary to popular media accounts, however, they generally do not use the carpet for this purpose; most of them reported using the toilet, sometimes not flushing it afterwards because the resulting noise can drown out the warning sounds of approaching danger. A couple of the burglars did admit to sometimes relieving themselves in rooms other than the bathroom, but they explained this action in terms of safety—they do not want to get cornered, literally with their pants down, in a small space with just one exit—rather than attributing it to any special contempt for the residents.[6] At the same time, these burglars seemed untroubled about the distress this might cause their victims; their sole concern is for their own well-being.

SUMMARY

The vast majority of residential burglars want to search dwellings as quickly as possible in the belief that the longer they remain inside, the more chance they stand of being discovered. They do this by adhering to a cognitive script developed through trial and error to assist them in locating the maximum amount of cash and goods per unit of time invested. Using this script, burglars can proceed almost automatically, without having to make complicated decisions at each stage of the search process. Although the script varies from one offender to the next, it usually calls for them to search the master bedroom first; this is where money, jewelry, and guns are most likely to be found. The living room typically is searched last because the items kept there tend to be difficult to carry and hence are best left until the last minute. Many burglars work with others to expedite the search process; co-offenders can explore one part of the residence while they look through another. By employing a consistent, well-rehearsed modus operandi in searching dwellings, burglars often can locate enough valuables to meet their immediate needs in a matter of minutes. Having successfully done so, most leave without delay.

By the time offenders have entered a target with the intention to steal, a burglary has been committed; the offense can no longer be deterred or prevented. It is at this point that criminologists and crime prevention experts show a marked tendency to lose interest, ceding the field to victimologists and police investigators. This is unfortunate because the activities of offenders during break-ins also may have implications both for decision-making theory, especially in regard to deterrence, and for crime prevention policy. To be sure, the burglars have not been deterred by the threat of sanctions, but that threat nevertheless seems to have a pronounced effect on their actions as they search targets. Most are unwilling to remain inside for long, foregoing the possibility of greater rewards in favor of reducing the risk of being discovered. In fact, for actual offenders this may be where deterrence operates most effectively. And while it is too late to prevent the burglaries, there is still an opportunity to limit the loss of cash and goods if we can understand the cognitive scripts used by burglars to search dwellings well enough to be able to disrupt those scripts.

ENDNOTES

1. Jack Katz. 1988. *Seductions of Crime: Moral and Sensual Attractions in Doing Evil.* New York: Basic Books.

2. Neal Shover. 1991. "Burglary." In Michael Tonry *Crime and Justice: An Annual Review of Research.* Chicago: University of Chicago Press.

3. Ibid.

4. Rita Simon. 1975. *Women and Crime.* Lexington, MA: D.C. Heath.

5. Richard Wright and Scott Decker. 1994. *Burglars on the Job: Streetlife and Residential Break-ins,* Boston: Northeastern University Press.

6. Dermot Walsh. 1980. "Why Do Burglars Crap on the Carpet?" *New Society* 54:10–1.